IN THIS NEW INTERPRETATION of the historical development of economic thought, Mark Perlman and Charles R. McCann Jr. illuminate the foundations of economic inquiry during the past three hundred years. Writing from the standpoint of the impact of cultural pluralism on economic thinking, their purpose is to show how modern economic thinking is shaped by a small number of cultural legacies that explain not only how economic questions are asked but also how they are formulated. *The Pillars of Economic Understanding* is thus distinguished by the attention that it gives to the philosophical ideas that are the cultural legacies upon which the structure of economics is built.

What are some of these cultural legacies? The authors consider the principal writings of British, French, German, Austrian, and American economists, mainly from the seventeenth century onward. Underlying these writings are questions posed by Hobbes, Francis Bacon, Descartes, Bentham, Cournot, Walras, Pareto, and such Americans as Bates Clark, Wesley Mitchell, and Commons. An example of the authors' attention to philosophical issues is their discussion of the way much of early economics was written in opposition to Hobbes's belief in the primacy of force. Locke's belief in the God-Man relationship seen in unalienable rights and the right of private property are only two of the answers. Other questions relate to the faith in the primacy of Cartesian logic and the need to establish a just society with some controls over the unequal division of the product.

This is a major contribution to the history of economic thought and an important source for all with an interest in the deep issues posed by the study and modeling of the economy.

Mark Perlman is Professor of Economics, Emeritus, University of Pittsburgh.

Charles R. McCann Jr. is an independent scholar.

The Pillars of Economic Understanding

Ideas and Traditions

The Pillars of Economic Understanding

Ideas and Traditions

Mark Perlman and
Charles R. McCann Jr.

Ann Arbor

THE UNIVERSITY OF MICHIGAN PRESS

Copyright © by the University of Michigan 1998
All rights reserved
Published in the United States of America by
The University of Michigan Press
Manufactured in the United States of America
⊚ Printed on acid-free paper

2001   2000   1999   1998   4   3   2   1

A CIP catalog record for this book is available from the British Library

Library of Congress Cataloging-in-Publication Data

Perlman, Mark.
      The pillars of economic understanding : ideas and traditions /
   Mark Perlman and Charles R. McCann Jr.
         p.   cm.
   Includes bibliographical references and index.
      ISBN 0-472-10907-3
      1. Economics—History.   I. McCann, Charles R. (Charles Robert),
   56–   II. Title.
   HB75 .P453   1998
   330'.09—dc21   98-8953
                                                          CIP

While this volume could be dedicated to many, we have chosen to dedicate it to two whose imaginations are legendary

ANTOINE AUGUSTIN COURNOT
In a delayed celebration of his highly original seminal work in abstraction, and how he proposed to use it in the formulation of French public policy.

GEORGE LENNOX SHARMAN SHACKLE
In recollection of his charisma, his understanding of the key role of epistemics, the warmth of his character, and the felicity of his style.

Acknowledgments

We have many to thank.

This and the companion volume were "in embryo" for decades. During those years Perlman lectured on the history of economic thought and enjoyed not only the support of his own university (Pittsburgh) but appointments at the University of Melbourne (1968), the University of Cambridge (1976–77), the Technische Universität, Vienna (1982), the University of Augsburg (1994), and the University of Chemnitz (1996).

We have also to thank Professor Roger Backhouse (University of Birmingham, U.K.), who has read and commented carefully on two complete drafts. Professors Phyllis Deane (University of Cambridge, U.K.), Sonya Gold (Claremont Graduate School, California), and a brace of anonymous critics have also read and commented on an earlier version of the lengthy manuscript.

And we must mention Dr. Colin Day, Director of the University of Michigan Press, who has kept an avuncular eye on the project from its inception. He shares our fascination with the problems of rhetoric in putting the pieces together.

Several institutions have supported the research efforts. These include the Institute for Advanced Study (1981–82), the Rockefeller Foundation's Villa Serbelloni at Bellagio (1983), and the Earhart Foundation (1996–97).

While we acknowledge our debt to them, we cannot, of course, ask them to share any responsibility for what emerged in the course of our writing and revising.

We have also benefited from the generosity of the Office of Special Collections at Johns Hopkins University's Eisenhower Library and from the willingness of Professor Dieter Grüske to share the legacy of his teacher (and our friend), Professor Horst-Claus Recktenwald in the matter of the pictures. The Hopkins Collection contains the testimonial photographs offered to Professor Carl Menger on the occasion of his seventieth birthday.

We also thank Mrs. Naomi Perlman and Mr. Morgan Marietta for their help in editing.

M.P.
C.R.M.
Pittsburgh, 1998

 Contents

 Preface

> Another damned, thick, square book! Always scribble,
> scribble, scribble! Eh! Mr. Gibbon?
> WILLIAM HENRY, DUKE OF GLOUCESTER

> Of making many books there is no end, and much study is
> wearisome to the flesh.   ECCLESIASTES 12:12

If you are of a mind initially to dismiss this effort as but another excursion into the literature on the history of economic theory and thinking, be assured, we are up to something different. In spite of the apparent physical bulk, this book is not an attempt to replace Schumpeter's encyclopedic *History of Economic Analysis*. We do not pretend to a comprehensive treatment of the history and evolution of the economics discipline. We are not aspiring here to trace the genesis of truth as it applies to matters economic or as it emerges from ignorance or falsehood. Neither are we offering a textbook treatment for specialists in the history of economic thought or even doctoral candidates who are sometimes required to know the famous names, the important dates, and the titles of the leading books (and more recently the articles) associated with the discipline. Instead, we set out to develop a conceptual framework from which to organize the principal parts of the literature of economics, offering a broad-spectrum interpretation of the disparities among the various foundations of modern economic thought.

Anything as old and as complex as the professional discipline of economics requires not only information but also insights into the contradictions in its background. Such a treatise should (1) identify the work's many objectives, and also (2) offer from a scholarly standpoint what the authors believe to be the principal fruits of their harvest. To the second of these points we return at the book's end, but here let us take up the first.

We have in this study four principal objectives.

First, to offer a more general (but not necessarily more complete) interpretation of the evolution of economic thinking than is currently available. The three standard magisterial interpretations to which we shall make reference throughout are those of Karl Pribram, Wesley Clair Mitchell, and Joseph Alois Schumpeter, each a work of profound influence and significance. These works set the standard, and each is important not merely for the topics discussed or the scope of the coverage, but equally for the form of presentation. These authors were, and we ourselves are, interested in the role played by the *method of expression* of economic doctrines, an emphasis at least as important as the *substance* of those arguments. In other words, rhetoric plays a major (some may say critical) role in the construction and ultimate acceptance of modes of thought and analysis. The basic questions to be answered here include, What ideas in economics developed over the centuries? and What has served to persuade members of the professional economics fraternity to accept and hold to their intellectual positions?

Second, to attempt to separate the questions economists have decided were and are within the purview of their specialties from the grand ideas and central themes or paradigms of economics which have been more or less ignored. Handling these paradigms requires grasping the confining social and philosophical assumptions, often unarticulated, which all "bookish" people employ. Economists, as members of a disciplinary fraternity, usually unconsciously define for themselves those characteristics of the social milieu that are to serve as the data upon which their theories rely. In so doing, they tend to neglect broader, underlying issues. They tend to employ an aberration of Occam's Razor and oversimplify, framing their questions in relation to their own limited apprehensions of the constituency of the subject, while ignoring wherever possible the larger questions. But these larger questions are themselves of signal importance, if only because an understanding and appreciation of them serves to demonstrate what economists and others perceive as irrelevant or inconsequential. Thus we must ask, What are these more general and essential questions? Why are they of such importance to the specialists? Are they questions to which an answer is even readily forthcoming?

Third, and in response to the second point, to cast our approach in the light of a small variety of basic questions relating to the underlying nature of most modern "western" social organizations. To proceed from the grand to the specific: What is the contribution of the economics discipline to an understanding of the purposes and problems of the modern "western" state? What have been the roles of British Utilitarianism, Austrian subjectivism, German historicism, French (mathematical) formalism, and American Institutionalism in the development of the discipline? What rhetorical devices have been employed by the representatives of each of these schools in the furtherance of their agendas? These questions concern such extraeconomic issues as Natural Law and natural rights, property rights, the design of social structures, and even philosophical questions regarding the basic elements of human nature. Based on the answers, we then can turn our attention in the companion volume (entitled *Factors and Markets*) to the modern era, with its emphasis on the professionalization of the study of factor markets (labor, capital,

resources, and entrepreneurship) as well as the purposes and the characteristics of economic markets themselves. There we turn to the question
of the scientific nature of economics. In this volume, the "basic questions" frame the paradigm and so structure the debate; the "modern era"
must proceed within the basic structure of this frame.

Finally, we summarize the current conflict between economists
who fancy themselves practitioners of "pure science"—those of the
Platonic/Cartesian variety who emphasize deductive reasoning and logical analysis—and those of a more Aristotelian nature—who rely on a
blend of inductive and deductive reasoning in their arguments, and who
differentiate between the "hard sciences" (for example, physics and
chemistry), and the "soft sciences" (social disciplines best treated as
culture and time-and-place situated subjects). We further attempt to
place this conflict into a series of frameworks we will term *patristic
legacies.* Patristic legacies, we suggest, are but other ways of perceiving
the evolution of economics, and in this perception we offer a raison
d'être for studying systematically our intellectual past in order to understand who we, ourselves, are.

While there is a basic chronology to the present approach, the chronology itself is dampened by our interest in offering a balanced treatment
of various topics, or intellectual Gestalten, and the "problem environments" in which they developed. As modern economics is a hybrid
science—the product of the combined thought of moral philosophers,
social commentators and pamphleteers, natural scientists, psychologists,
sociologists, political scientists, et al.—and as the treatment of any single
economic problem is best understood not within a chronological framework but rather within a topical one, the presentation must proceed along
these lines.

Thus the task here is to present in moderate but necessary detail an
interpretation of the history of economic thinking. This interpretation
rests on an understanding of numerous specific cultural contributions to
the subject (that is, cultural or patristic legacies). As each person's understanding relates to his own cultural heritage, we do not maintain that
this interpretation will be acceptable to all. Yet it should be of general
interest.

It is considered wise to appreciate the audience for whom one writes. We
target as our potential audience the serious, college-trained (or otherwise
well-read, for the two are not necessarily the same) person who seeks to
make sense of the current divisions in what had once been a loosely
unified fraternity. What are the bases for the traditional view of political
economy as a study of the way in which people go about earning a
livelihood? Why has the traditional political economy approach been
largely abandoned by those who think principally in terms of abstract
models?

The reader, as we perceive him, seeks a reasonable presentation of the ideas that have been promoted by and debated among economists and others (including historians, legal scholars, philosophers, and other assorted pundits) whom modern-day historians of economic thought have generally taken to be within and at times outside the economics fraternity. He is concerned with uncovering the ways in which these grand themes have manifested themselves in policy debates and general societal questions of ethics and social welfare. He is, further, not content with presentations loaded down with jargon, incomprehensible to all but those within the fraternity, nor is he willing to accept the pseudo-intellectual clamorings of those with a political agenda who mask their cause in economic terms in an effort to lend it an air of respectability. The serious-minded reader wishes to know and understand (1) the rationale behind this endless clamor; (2) what an exploration of the subject will reveal about the cycle of discussion, the sense of optimism and then of failure regarding socioeconomic reform; and (3) how all this relates to the topic of general human knowledge. In short, the reader seeks to comprehend the contribution of economics to the overall social conversation. He strives to comprehend the connections between the current debate and its historical antecedents. He seeks to discover from whom economics has borrowed and why. Finally, he desires to understand what imaginative thinkers have and will make of it all as they contemplate the future.

The questions which comprise these categories are questions that have been largely ignored in presentations of the history of economic thought, but which are nonetheless extremely important in classifying and so increasing our understanding of the evolution of economic doctrine. If nothing else, they provide for historians of thought and economics theorists as well an expansion of the existing "data base." Our aspiration, of course, is that in reading this book one will acquire not only an expanded data base (read, spectrum of knowledge of facts and frameworks), but also an improved understanding of the manner in which generations of economists have come to explain themselves and their mode of thinking.

Toward the end of his *Meditations,* Marcus Aurelius maintained that the quality of an actor's performance is measured not by whether his part survives to the final curtain, but rather by how well he has played it. What is true of actors is not at all true of authors or teachers! At the end of this endeavor we shall attempt to assess the clamor, for, unlike the performance of a successful actor in a stage play, the proof of a successful argument is its endurance.

CHAPTER I

The Patristic Traditions in Economics
The Foundations of Our Study

> We fully acknowledge the old authorities' greatness and our own insignificance; but like pygmies riding on giants' shoulders, we see farther than the giants, when we use their knowledge and experience.
> Z. ANAV, *SHIBBOLÉ HALEKET* (THIRTEENTH CENTURY)

> To say that authority, whether secular or religious, supplies no ground for morality is not to deny the obvious fact that it supplies a sanction.
> ALFRED AYER, *THE MEANING OF LIFE AND OTHER ESSAYS* (1990)

> Haven't the words of the wise been compared to nails? The nails are fixed, while the generations suspend from them ... their thoughts and aspirations. ... Thus, the burden of the heritage grows in extent and profundity. But while the generations come and go, the nails remain.
> J. B. AGUS, *JEWISH FRONTIER* (JULY 1952)

Our Patristic Traditions and What Their Study Teaches Us

Introduction

This volume aims at giving structure to the historical evolution of economic thought. Specifically, we seek to frame the arguments so as to allow the reader an appreciation of the maturing of the various economic schools and modes of thought. Not separate from that change is the adaptation of the rhetoric employed (that is, the methods of persuasion) when the composition of the audience shifted (who was to be persuaded, how, and why).

In their quest to evaluate the evolution of thought in their specialized fields, historians of a discipline need to specify their starting point. Ideally, it could be a historical event, a person, or the appearance of a new idea, one who or which may be legitimately taken as the source of our current knowledge or belief. The dilemma of course becomes just how far into the past it is necessary to travel. When can we be (reasonably) certain that we have adequately identified the questions posed, and attributed the answers offered, to their true progenitors? In other words, how far must

we as intellectual historians—historians of economic *thought*—explore
to discover the First Cause of events or the Adam behind the doctrine or
even the science? Indeed, is it really necessary to begin at the beginning,
or is it sufficient to do no more than stipulate that we will begin from
point A, or even point Q, and that this will serve as the commencement of
our tradition? To use George J. Stigler's (1955) terminology, is it worth
the effort to try to distinguish at great cost the innovators from the
'technical' originators? However we decide about the starting point, we
must be clear as to the reasons for this choice.

Our preferred points of departure reflect the emergence of several
different patristic traditions—traditions providing us with nodes from
which all of the ideas within the confines of the discipline radiate. These
single persons, definitive published works, or even derived interpretations
of seminal thoughts often define the manner in which we proceed with
our disciplinary analytics. Defining the question is only one thing; equally
important is how the discussions then evolve. To see the implication of all
this for economics in particular, and for other disciplines as well, we must
explore the nature of the patristic approach as a general method of historical appraisal.

1.2   The Patristic Approach Defined

The general line of argument is that, as social scientists, we study the past
to learn about man, and in this particular effort about his economic
thinking. Studies of the past involve conjecture and theory-building, and
historians bring to the task individual cultural predilections, to say nothing of formal and informal intellectual training as well as experiences and
a host of other intangibles that frame their perceptions of the subject
matter. As expositors of the historical "record," we have strived to select
the best available evidence for the portrayal of our subjects. We are much
like portraitists, for whom painting is not merely a matter of color and
process, but also of background and often symbols incorporated into the
work. To extend the metaphor, historians of economic thought can be
likened to art historians. We study the historical traditions of economics
to see not only how different schools of thought shift technique but also
how they change the reference symbols found in the picture—classical
allusions as against cognitive impressions.

With the foregoing in mind, let our attention now return to our
approach, something quite apart from the traditional historical approaches to the economics discipline. This "something" is a deeper appreciation of the influence of patristic thinking—that is, thinking along some
paradigmatic lines determined by the cultural crucible in which the stuff
of our minds is initially mixed.

The obvious question to be asked is simply enough posed: What is
meant by a patristic approach? *Patristic* refers to *father*, and like it or not,

"father," the paternal presence and influence, has been and continues to be interpreted generally as an authority figure.[1] The contrast with the "mother" figure is particularly interesting and indeed striking. Theologians have observed that "mother" is a generosity figure: "Mother Earth," to take but one example, gives us the good things of life. The "Sky Father," to quote from one usual self-assertion, is, by contrast, "a Man of War," (Exod. 15:3; Isa. 63) or "a jealous God" (Exod. 34:14). Mother is a caring and nursing being; father is a controlling, dominant one. Patristic approaches can be understood in terms of this distinction. They are basically the approaches (including but by no means limited to the theological realm) recognizing an appeal to authority, to those figures accepted as fulfilling a paternalistic role. "By what line of thinking do you hold or believe or act or claim?" is the usual reference to the patristic approach.

Having defined the term, the next obvious question concerns the rationale for even bothering with patristic approaches. Many modern scholars claim that they do not so bother. The patristic approach, an appeal to the wisdom of the past, affords for these scholars no more appeal or validity than any current vogue. Modern commentators are, after all, according to this view, at least as authoritative as the ancients; their apparent (but not real) weakness is in their youth, the fact that they are of the wrong century. Given enough time, they too will take on the mantle of the wise Father. This claim notwithstanding, a case can be made to the effect that we do have patristic elements almost indelibly etched upon our minds.

The foregoing is conceptual. We must add that few of those educated in the modern world are the products of a single patristic influence. On the contrary, most have been exposed to numerous such legacies. Consequently, our minds respond to a plethora of stimuli: our ethical beliefs, our social and political understandings, and even our approaches to academic study all derive from these influences; indeed, the mind-set which serves as the foundation for action may seem a hodgepodge of remnant spirits of the past, interpreting our thoughts and observations in the present.

Understanding the problems dealt with by economists (as with so many others) begins with a grasp of the patristic legacies underlying their mind-sets. This interpretation is not without its critics—particularly those who feel that concern with the past is a waste of time and effort,

---

1. No small number of those with whom we have discussed this work have felt uncomfortable with the choice of the word *patristic*, some holding that it raised hackles because it suggests an appeal to the Roman Catholic Church Fathers. Upon reflection, this may be little more than a reaction to unwanted and unappreciated authority. "Patristic legacies," as we employ the term, are not always appreciated; indeed, in many instances choices are a negative reaction to a particular patristic legacy. The authority issue need not presume obedience; it only presumes a guiding factor.

that we should be forward-looking, not nostalgic. C. P. Snow, in his famous 1959 essay "Two Cultures and the Scientific Revolution," argued in favor of the forward-looking view. Sir Isaiah Berlin,[2] on the other hand, offered the view that the hand of the past is neither dead nor of little influence; this is the view expressed here. One difference between the two is that Snow felt that not only was he a spectator at the scene of the development of new paradigms in modern science, especially physics, but he was offended by the arrogance of those academics who defined intellectualism in terms of traditional topics. Berlin, himself the product of perhaps five cultures (Jewish, Russian, German, French, and English), sought to demonstrate to critics that from the mixture of different legacies one could discern explainable differences in emphasis, ends, and certainly means.

To return to an earlier point, perhaps the most important reason to be cognizant of patristic legacies is that the mixture of patristic approaches does much to define the rhetoric employed in argumentation. The complex of patristic heritages sets the stage for our civilization, in the sense that it establishes a tradition that serves to guide us intellectually, socially, morally, and spiritually, in all aspects of life. In the present context, the appropriate mixture is the European intellectual tradition, which is not only the dominant *cultural* influence in the world, despite protestations to the contrary, but also the dominant *intellectual strain* in the historical development of economic thought. We cannot readily escape the tradition and history of our forebears. We can neither deny the legacies they have left, nor can we escape from what we are and from whence we came.

1.3 The Source of Authority

The patristic approach is one based on and around authority. As such, it exerts a powerful influence on our rhetoric and our beliefs. But what is the source of authority, and why is it authoritative? Religious revelation is one obvious source, wherein the authority is ordained and so accepted by an appeal to faith. Religious commandments are held to be the true word of the Deity or prophet of the religious order and shape and guide behavior as they serve as codes of ethics and moral conduct.

But there are other sources of authority as well. Cultural norms, the test of compatibility with religious or political or aesthetic or sexual or linguistic heritages (and others too numerous to mention), can also serve as authorities. Our intellectual environment (later we call it our intellectual baggage) in this view is the source of our ethos and belief structure. "Custom," wrote David Hume in his *Enquiry Concerning Human Understanding*, "is the great guide of human life" (Hume 1777 § v, 28). It can

---

2. See especially John Gray (1996).

as well serve as an authority. Oliver Wendell Holmes Jr. in his seminal book on the English Common Law was somewhat more specific. He held that the tradition of the Common Law, based on the judicial use of stare decisis (precedent), reflected the life and the will of the people. To the extent that life and will have binding elements, they are authoritative; as they were handed down by our forefathers—the founders of our culture and belief system—they are also patristic. If there is a moral to all this, it may well be summed up in the admonition "Do not reject authoritarianism too quickly." It may have a wicked surface, but beneath, there is a solid foundation.

The importance (not to mention the ubiquity) of the patristic approach is easily shown. All civilizations have at their heart sets of categorical imperatives (authorities or law codes, if you prefer) derived from appeals to preexisting patristic beliefs. These codifications of acceptable behavior define the boundaries within which individuals in a civilized society must function if the civilization is to endure. Civilization in the abstract may be defined with respect to a general set of influences; specific civilizations may then be studied by analyzing the culture-specific patristic influences adopted. The categorical imperatives function themselves as a codification of a basic patristic system.[3] Certainly interpretations of these codes evolve; no society can function without an evolutionary legal, moral, ethical, and social structure. Nowhere is this evolution more evident than in the rhetoric that is employed as a tool for the promulgation and continuation of these structural norms. It is the pattern of this evolution which is most fundamental, for it goes to the very heart of the process of social dynamics.

Having identified this very important constituent of our heritage, we now consider some of its manifestations.

The Classical Greek Patristic Legacy 2

Introduction 2.1

Much that passes for the history of economic thought begins with discussions of the philosophers of ancient Greece. Pythagoras (582–507 B.C.), Heraclitus (535–475 B.C.), Democritus (460–370 B.C.), Epicurus

---

3. Here are but two important propositions from which have evolved various social structures:

(1) The evolution inherent in the traditional basic Jewish question of "By what authority can matters involving ethics and ritual be determined?" and

(2) The parameters and implications of the Christian question "How can God simultaneously condemn man for his sins when an omnipotent and an omniscient God controls man?"

(342–270 B.C.), and of course Plato (427–347 B.C.) and Aristotle (384–322 B.C.) are typically cited as the true patristic sources of moral and political philosophy. Joseph Schumpeter (1954) and Henry Spiegel (1991) both began their histories of economic thought with discussions of the contributions of these truly seminal writers and thinkers. Classical economic tracts and philosophical treatises, which have been accepted as precursors to analytical economics, all derived in some form or other their inspiration if not their actual content from these early Greek philosophers.

The reason typically advanced for commencing the study of economics by reference to early classical Greek contributions is that they were here first. This is accurate at least in the development of the European culture that produced modern economics (as the subject is generally known). The very word *economics* derives from the Greek *oikonomia*; as defined by S. Todd Lowry, the term means "a formal, administrative art directed toward the minimization of costs and the maximization of returns," having "as its prime aim the efficient management of resources for the achievement of desired objectives" (Lowry 1987, 12). Thus the chief reason for commencing the study of economic thought with the Greeks is that they in fact defined the area of study and in effect gave it its cachet.

While this alone is a good enough reason for beginning with the Greek contributions, a second may also be advanced: the seminal, if at times troublesome, answers they offered to certain economic (and social) questions. The Greek responses to economic problems seem to possess some attractive primordial qualities and seem, by and large, to center on the belief that one must at the outset assert simple truths to serve as cornerstones. One can then get on with the application of these truths to the more empirical (social, political, economic) matters. The questions given central place in early Greek thought are the legitimacy, reasons for being, and the role to be played by government, the role of education in promoting socialization and ease of governance, the appropriate unit for social control (individual, family, or collective), the appropriate individual and social ethos, and even the more readily acknowledgeable economic questions of the division of labor, the taking of interest, and the role within the society of wealth and property.

Unfortunately, the Greek answers are (currently) not fully satisfying; they leave unanswered many of the ethical and moral questions which confront a society. Even so, this is no reason to forget or ignore them. Indeed, the Greek answers sometimes present a paradox, revealing some not-very-simple qualities of most of our own self-perceptions. The initial paradox involves the differences between the neatness of what we, using our reason, would like to believe, and that which we actually observe. One Greek tradition (perhaps not a very good one) is the general hunger for authority as a simplifying device for getting through life. Life would be easy if only there were someone to dictate what should be done, how it should be done, when it should be done, and by whom it should be done. But this simplistic solution raises more questions and dilemmas than it answers, for it begs the question of authority. In other words, the answers provided by the classical Greeks are bothersome rather than satisfying. They were better with their questions than with their answers.

Plato   2.2

Generally the Greek tradition has been advanced by studying the role of key philosophers and philosophical schools. We are asked, for instance, to consider the contributions of the Cynics, the Stoics, the Epicureans, the Pythagoreans, and others, as representatives of particular *schools* of Greek thought. A truly self-conscious *economics,* however, may be said to have begun with the work of Plato, especially as it is presented in the *Republic* (here an expression of youthful exuberance, but diluted somewhat in the *Laws* as age, wisdom, and experience prevailed). While not an economic tract or treatise, but rather a philosophical treatment on the form of an ideal republic, it is (or should be considered to be) nevertheless a truly patristic work for economists. Many of the ideas presented can readily be seen to have been at the center of some of the great debates throughout the history of economics. Even so, Plato's contribution lay not so much in applications to what is today understood as economics as it did in his approach to the problems he chose to confront; his rhetoric is oftentimes more important than his message.

Plato sought to understand not simply the empirical manifestations of reality, but the underlying essential nature of objects. He argued that "true knowledge" requires us to have complete apprehension and understanding of the general nature of things, knowledge of the entire class of which an object is but a single member. In other words, true knowledge is apprehension of the "essence" of a thing. In our everyday experience, however, we apprehend only particulars, objects brought to our attention via our sensory organs. This is knowledge of a *member* of a larger reference class, not of the *nature* of the class itself. Knowledge of the particular cannot be true knowledge, since it cannot be extrapolated from the individual member to the broader class. It is better thought of as opinion that is neither true nor false.

To achieve true knowledge beyond the particular, beyond mere *opinion,* we need to rely on *reason,* not sensory experiences. We cannot restrict knowledge to that which we see, feel, hear, smell, or taste; knowledge requires that we develop an *idea* of the general class. We must gain an insight into the essential nature of the ideal form. These ideal forms or concepts are *universals.* It is the universals, not the particulars, which are the objects of knowledge. Knowledge is attained when we achieve an understanding that what we perceive is not necessarily the *object* of our knowledge; it is the discernment of the universal *qualities* of the objects (or the concepts underlying them) that matters, something which is independent of any individual, imperfect manifestation. The ideal form is for Plato the only reality; all manifestations (that is, all empirically observed objects) are but illusory.

Plato's analysis is supposedly based entirely on the a priori approach, his avowed emphasis on the process of pure reasoning. Yet this did not entirely exclude an appreciation for the concrete. He addressed questions of operational efficiency within the city-state even while maintaining an equity base (the meaning of justice between the natural divisions of society, predicated on natural inequalities between types of men). He sipped from the institutional bottle (whenever he addressed particular problems or selected his examples, he was forced to something more cognitively observable), but his reputation was built on his preference for abstraction—for what today we would call theoretical modeling.

2.3 Aristotle

Plato may be said to have created the environment in which a mind such as that of Aristotle could flourish. As with Plato's *Republic,* Aristotle's *Politics* is one of the seminal political and economic texts of all time, especially in regard to the economic debates that have been stimulated (whether acknowledged or not) by its pronouncements. In fact, much that passed for economic commentary from the time of the Scholastics through Marx and even the Austrian economists of the late nineteenth and early twentieth centuries was little more than an explicit commentary on Aristotle's philosophy and economics.

Aristotle's approach has been described by Bertrand Russell as "Plato diluted by common sense" (1945, 162). While for Plato the apprehension of the universal was the attainment of true knowledge, for Aristotle universals are not substantial. They are instead broad reference classes that cannot exist outside of their constituent members. Thus Aristotle's philosophy was based as much or more on the observation of particulars, of things, as it was on abstract reasoning behind the existence of universals.

Aristotle believed in the necessity of First Principles upon which could be based rational argument. These principles, to which he made repeated reference in his writings, are analytic, self-evident truths; as such, they do not require proof of their validity. But these truths are not based on intuition or derived by an appeal to reason. Rather they are descriptions of the essence or identity of an object (its properties) derived from our observations. We begin with a comprehensive series of data or "facts," the substances of a thing. These "facts," taken as a collective, present to us principles which can be perceived, and which generate facts themselves. Induction allows us to discern from these facts the First Principles, which can then be employed syllogistically to reason about specifics.

Only knowledge derived in this manner is true and certain; principles derived from reason may be true or false or contingently true, but can never be certain, since we can never be sure that our reason is not clouded by opinion and mistaken belief. This leads Aristotle to place great faith in the power of "tradition." Tradition is the accumulated wisdom of the ages, which has been refined and reconstituted over time by the admixture of the experiences of a multitude of different individuals. This is the patristic influence.

The Ideal Society of Plato   2.4

As a practical demonstration of the approaches of Plato and Aristotle, one directly related to the general topics of this work, we will examine their views of the structure of an ideal society, especially their respective views of the form of the state, the role of education, and the role to be played, if any, by the institution of private property.

Plato held to a very strict view of specialization of activities within a society: each citizen must perform the task for which he is best suited, or most "naturally fitted," forsaking all others. Essential to this view is that individuals are inherently unequal in regard to skills, knowledge, and the capacity for learning; we are not "all created equal." Despite this obvious fact, each of us is endowed with the ability to perform at *some* level. As each individual performs the task for which he is comparatively best suited, society as a whole will be most efficiently organized. The farmer produces agricultural commodities, merchants handle the export trade, craftsmen (blacksmiths, shoemakers, toolmakers, weavers, et al.) ply their trades, and there is even provision for a class to arrange market transactions, much on the order of present-day wholesalers and retailers.[4] In addition to these specialized trades, the society needs manual laborers, wage earners who "market their strength and call the return they get for it their wages" (*Republic* 371e).

As the society progresses from the spartan "base state," wherein are produced and consumed only the barest necessities, the number and complexity of occupations increase and so require an expansion in the types and composition of professions neither required nor even imagined in the base state. The society is now capable of producing and consuming luxury items, so that positions become defined for painters, poets, sculptors, and others of the newly emerged artisan class, and also for servants and cooks, and newly demanded professionals such as doctors and even lawyers!

But this expansion of the state necessitated by the expansion of population and the integration of the populace to a social consciousness also creates a demand for the services of a protector class, as the territory

---

4. For Plato, this class consists "of those who are least fit physically, and unsuitable for other work. For their job ties them to the market place, where they buy goods from those who want to sell and sell goods to those who want to buy" (*Republic* 371c–d).

of the state must inevitably expand. Other, neighboring, states also feel the pressure for expansion. The situation quickly develops into a conflict between groups previously remote from one another for more and better land with which the demands of a growing citizenry can be met. Thus a class willing and able to defend and if necessary initiate offensive operations for the greater benefit of the republic must come into being. As with the specialization in the economic and social spheres, the new guardian class is an armed force staffed by professional soldiers whose duties are confined to the military service of the state (*Republic* 374a–b).

It soon becomes evident, however, that the mere acceptance of such a strict degree of specialization in each and every phase of social life requires a class structure, albeit one predicated on status, not wealth. It is the acceptance of this stratified system that defines for Plato the concept of justice and the formation of a legal structure. The origin of law is therefore to reduce if not eliminate the effects of an injustice. A "social contract" is necessary to provide a means by which injustices may be corrected.

> . . . it is according to nature a good thing to inflict wrong or injury, and a bad thing to suffer it, but that the disadvantages of suffering it exceed the advantages of inflicting it; after a taste of both, therefore, men decide that, as they can't evade the one and achieve the other, it will pay to make a compact with each other by which they forego both. They accordingly proceed to make laws and mutual agreements, and what the law lays down they call lawful and right. This is the origin and nature of justice. It lies between what is most desirable, to do wrong and avoid punishment, and what is most undesirable, to suffer wrong without being able to get redress; justice lies between these two and is accepted not as being good in itself, but as having a relative value due to our inability to do wrong. (*Republic* 358e–359b)

Justice requires no imposition of a restrictive superstructure; justice is simply "minding your own business and not interfering with other people" (433b).

In the area of property rights and ownership, an important topic even in much of the early economic literature, Plato believed that communal ownership among the ruling elites was the most just and efficient form of organization for the creation and maintenance of a unified state.[5] As all is commonly held, the antisocial elements associated with family and individual cohesion, such as placing individual and familial interests above those of the state, and of placing the needs of one's own children above the interest which the state may have in their upbringing, are

---

5. Communal ownership of property is not synonymous with communism. The latter is a nineteenth-century construct, which required the rise of an industrial society. It is a concept dealing with ownership of the means of production, not of property.

eliminated. To this end he had to reject the integrity of the familial unit as the principal structure in society. Women and children would be common property, the responsibility of the state. Sex would be a regulated activity, relegated to mating rituals in breeding colonies.[6] As Plato rejected the family as the basic unit of society, at least for the ruling and protector classes, only under a social structure with resources held in common, including women and children, could everyone (that is, every male of the upper classes) share in the output of the community.[7]

Plato desired the institution of the perfect, Ideal society. To this end he was obliged to dissect and scrutinize the forms of what he took to be "imperfect societies," actual manifestations of social arrangements rather than theoretical social or political constructs. He defined these political and social forms as the *timocratic,* the *oligarchic,* the *democratic,* and the *despotic.* We proceed here to review the features of each in turn, since Plato's apprehension of these systems, whether they actually ever existed in the form in which he describes them, has served to color the apprehensions of others who built on Plato's model, whether knowingly or unknowingly.

The timocratic society Plato suggested was represented by Sparta. The Spartan society he viewed as feudal, one with a military aristocracy ruling over a peasant underclass. To retain power, the ruling elite felt compelled to hold to a rigid code of conduct regulating every aspect of their lives. Education was undertaken in a formal, communitarian setting, boys sent for highly disciplined military training, girls prepared for their roles as breeders of children for the state. Every aspect of the lives of the elites was to be directed to the betterment of the state and the preservation of the ruling stratum. As every aspect of individualism was removed, devotion being entirely to the state, property had to be commonly held, so that wealth acquisition was unheard of.

The oligarchic society emerges from the collapse of the timocratic. In contrast to timocracy, oligarchy is defined as a society based on the accumulation of wealth as the measure of social and personal prestige. Political control in this social setting rests entirely in the hands of a wealthy elite, who invariably exploit the poor to the furtherance of their own selfish ends (*Republic* 550d). The acquisitive nature of man, an inclination repressed for a time out of feelings of devotion to the state, surfaces as he matures, leading ultimately to the destruction in the old elite of feelings of community and devotion to the greater interests of the collective.

This accumulation of wealth, however, excites all the baser instincts of man, such as jealousy, avarice, suspicion, and finally moral degradation. The new elites value money and possessions over goodness, morality,

---

6. See especially the *Republic* 459, on the desire to breed a super race and the need for breeding colonies.

7. It is not clear that Plato desired the communitarian model of property and social relations for the lower classes in his republic.

ethics, and a spirit of community (*Republic* 550e). There follows ultimately a disparity between the wealthy elites and the political elites, some of whom were held over from the timocratic regimes. From this economic and political disparity arises a desire for political power. The problem of course is that the very abilities that lead to the creation of wealth do not necessarily lead to competence in the political sphere, so that the system becomes unmeritocratic: positions are advanced on the basis of wealth, not competence and ability.

Democracy is the next societal form Plato asks us to consider. A democratic society evolves from the oligarchic, as the poor revolt against the elites and "kill or exile their opponents, and give the rest equal civil rights and opportunities of office, appointment to office being as a rule by lot" (*Republic* 557a). The *individual* is the center of the democratic state, and "every individual is free to do as he likes" (557b). But while democracy has some clearly attractive qualities to Plato, these very attributes are also its weaknesses. Plato required in his Ideal society that man be indoctrinated with a sound moral sense, good mental habits promoted and encouraged through the very environment in which he lives. Democracy as Plato envisioned it, however, "sweeps all this away" (558b) by encouraging an atmosphere wherein all inhabitants are treated as of equal worth, "whether they are equal or not" (558c).

Finally, the democratic society dissolves into tyranny. The excessive desire for and pursuit of *wealth* under the oligarchy leads to a reaction whereby *liberty* becomes the new object of obsession (*Republic* 562b). The citizens demand and the leaders acquiesce in granting as few restrictions on behavior as possible. Rulers cannot effectively rule for fear of being labeled antidemocratic or dictatorial; teachers cannot teach for fear of being perceived as imposing themselves and their beliefs or morality on the youth. This excessive, zealous attachment to the pursuit of unrestricted freedom leads to a situation whereby "the least vestige of restraint is resented as intolerable, till finally . . . in their determination to have no master they disregard all laws, written or unwritten" (563d). Eventually the "drones" and the "masses" conspire against the rich, who still exist as a vestige of the previous social structures,[8] and install a single leader whom they feel compelled to endow with "greatness." As he is popular and commands respect and allegiance, he also is easily changed into a tyrant, leading the masses against the remnants of the rich in an effort to consolidate his own power and realize his own ambitions.

Thus it was from his empirical analysis of actual (?) social arrangements that Plato proceeded to his own structure for society. From the

---

8. Plato's democracy had three groups: the rich, those successful in manipulation and wealth generation; the masses, who work hard but otherwise take no interest in public affairs, and whose leaders "rob the rich, keep as much of the proceeds as they can for themselves, and distribute the rest to the people" (*Republic* 565a); and the drones, a class of "thriftless idlers" (564b).

faults discovered in these imperfect societies, Plato arrived at his Ideal type. Plato's "preferred system" was a society organized and controlled by philosophers. These "philosopher kings" were enlightened autocrats, more committed to social efficiency than to personal probity. As mentioned above, the socialization of property and of education applied in strict fashion only to the Philosophers and the Guardians. To instill the requisite ethic required that property, and even women and children, be commonly held. The dominant class, in being removed from the temptations which are manifest in a society that recognizes private property and the utility of personal social relations, is, under the condition of communal ownership and use, relieved of any potentially socially harmful extraneous influences that may compromise their ability to rule and to be "good." For lesser types, the need to appeal to their baser instincts might make personal property rights the appropriate kind of incentive or opiate; ownership is not a right, simply a means necessary for men who were not properly educated.

The process of education must first concentrate on shaping the "mind and character" of the individuals in the society (or rather of those on whom the duty of governance and the protection of the state is to fall, namely the Guardians and the Philosophers). Plato's educator must attempt to shape the *morals* and *ethics* of the new man above all else. To achieve the degree of education demanded in the new republic, the state must be the sole provider. But Plato wished more than state provision; he demanded state control, effectively making the educational system a propaganda organ for the promotion of the principles of the state and none other. In fulfilling this role, it is perfectly legitimate for the state to design curricula and strictly control the opinions expressed in the academies. It is not important to supply the facts or to answer all questions; it is more important that the correct moral story be presented (*Republic* 379a). Facts are secondary to the task of perfecting the mind.[9] Plato's approach was then not developmental; it was static. It stressed above all else the efficient coordination and planning of the use of resources, the mind being the most precious of all.

The Ideal Society of Aristotle   2.5

In Plato's Ideal state the family unit had no role to play as the central unifying structure in the ruling classes. For Aristotle, the family unit was essential in ultimately defining the structure and the purposes of the state, as well as the limits to its power. Consider the structure of the household, as the smallest economic unit, and the emergence of the state, as the largest. Aristotle held there to be two natural and fundamental

---

9. ". . . we must reject the conception of education professed by those who say that they can put into the mind knowledge that was not there before—rather as if they could put sight into blind eyes" (*Republic* 518c).

relationships preceding social development: (1) the relationship between man and woman (the procreational relation), and (2) the relationship between ruler and ruled (the political relation). These two relationships are "natural" in that nature itself engages in specialization and allows that differential needs and endowments will be satisfied through mutual association: "she makes each thing for a single use, and every instrument is best made when intended for one and not for many uses" (*Politics* 1252b3–4). From these relations arise first the *family*—"the association established by nature for the supply of men's everyday wants" (1252b12–13). In the family group we see the emergence of the male/female role, and the ruler/ruled role. (The latter comes from the observation that the family group will include slaves, either human or animal—oxen, for example, being "the poor man's slave" [1252b12].)

In an evolutionary chain, the association of groups of families forms the social unit of the *village* or *colony*, developed to provide "something more than the supply of daily needs" (*Politics* 1252b17). While the family provides sustenance, the village provides necessary social interactions and allows for specialization across family units. Villages in turn form *communities* or *states*, associations "originating in the bare needs of life, and continuing in existence for the sake of a good life" (1252b30–31). Thus the highest form of association extends the nature of the collectivity from mere procreational needs to the maintenance of the very "soul" of the collective. Although the state antedates the family, Aristotle nonetheless held the family to be the most natural unit upon which to base a social structure.[10] The reason is simple, and more empirical than rational: we have a natural affinity for our own, but can neither care for nor especially sympathize with that which is held in common.

This was likewise the rationale for the existence of private property. The state is an entity composed of individual *households*, not simply *individuals*, and the task of household management includes the acquisition of property:

> Property is a part of the household, and the art of acquiring property is a part of the art of managing the household; for no man can live well, or indeed live at all, unless he is provided with necessaries. And as in the arts which have a definite sphere the workers must have their own proper instruments for the accomplishment of their work, so it is in the management of a household. (*Politics* 1253b23–28)

Only under conditions of private ownership could the members of the society have any stake in its preservation and maintenance. But Aristotle's concept of private property is not that which we usually consider

---

10. "The proof that the state is a creation of nature and prior to the individual is that the individual, when isolated, is not self-sufficing; and therefore he is like a part in relation to the whole. . . . A social instinct is implanted in all men by nature, and yet he who first founded the state was the greatest of benefactors" (*Politics* 1253a25–31).

in modern-day definitions. It placed restrictions on ownership that redefined the purely private aspects. Specifically, Aristotle favored private *ownership,* but common *use.* Even more important, the communal use of private property should be encouraged as a legislative priority, for it promotes a spirit of social unity and fosters an ethos which serves as a fundamental requirement for the consolidation of a civil polity. While all property is held in common, there is no feeling of compassion or community or sympathy, since a community depends upon feelings of generosity and reciprocity and benevolence. Common ownership by definition cannot provide the impetus to such sympathies.

> Property should be in a certain sense common, but, as a general rule, private; for, when everyone has a distinct interest, men will not complain of one another, and they will make more progress, because everyone will be attending to his own business. . . . It is clearly better that property should be private, but the use of it common; and the special business of the legislator is to create in men this benevolent disposition. (*Politics* 1263a25–41)

To hold property privately, while parceling out its use to others in the community, Aristotle held to be a vital source of moral education. The act breeds an atmosphere of generosity and moral virtue, constituents of a healthy social ethic, in opposition to the hostility and general indifference engendered when everything is held in common and no personal sacrifices are required.

Other Contributions   2.6

While there were other Greek contributors to what we have defined herein as the patristic tradition—for example, Xenophon and the foundation of the labor theory of value and specialization—the need for brevity forces an end to discussion at this point.[11] But to go on is not to abandon

---

11. Todd Lowry (1979, 1987) surveyed the literature and gave an efficient overview of the Greek contributions. A contrary view was presented by Moses Finley (1973), who argued that what economics really amounts to, an "analytical method," was missing in Greek thought. He maintained that ancient Greek thought did not provide any economic rationale for division of labor or returns to scale, nor did the Greeks perceive the market process as distinct from the political process. Given that division of labor and returns to scale are relatively modern "realizations," the importance of which is not universally accepted, and that—as anyone cognizant of world affairs can readily ascertain—market process and political process often go hand in hand, perhaps the Greeks were not so wrong after all. Finally, Scott Meikle (1995) maintained that Aristotle did indeed present elements of a coherent "theory" of value, wealth, property, money, and exchange, but did so within the confines of a theory of ethics, not of economics. As shall be made clear throughout the present effort, economics has developed along the lines of an ethical theory, and it is simply not possible to make other than arbitrary distinctions between the two. Even John Maynard Keynes was eventually to conclude that economics was but a branch of ethics (as we shall maintain in chapter 8).

our interest in what the classical Greeks gave us, for these contributions reappear throughout the history of economic thought. Among other things, they stressed that the basic economic questions relate to the allocation of scarce resources. The Greeks identified the indivisibility of economics and ethics, as well as outlined the connections between economics and politics. They identified various arrangements in the area of property rights and social organizational structures which have molded opinions, and in some cases become doctrine, up to our own time. However, what they failed to give us was any clear solution to the problems they identified; in many instances we must derive these from other legacies.

3 The Judeo-Christian Legacies

Among the other legacies from which we derive our patristic heritage, the Judeo-Christian is perhaps the strongest in terms of its influence and its proximity to our own times.[12] Here, having mentioned that strange term, *Judeo-Christian legacy,* we must pause and ask just how its two constituent parts are related. In part the relation is chronological, the Christian legacy being said to have grown (in whole or in part) out of the Jewish; much like the English and the Americans, they are united and divided by a common language. In a second part, the relationship focuses on monotheism and a single cosmic plan.

While the Jewish and the Christian heritages share a common history, their interpretations of that history differ markedly. The differences lay in the form of the *basic* question. In the Jewish tradition, the question was "By what authority?" while for the Christian it centered on the accommodation of the City of Man to the rules of the City of God. The names associated with the interpretations seem to be less important than the subtlety of the differences themselves. For the Jewish tradition one need only follow the reasoning of Moses Maimonides (1135–1204), a practicing physician as well as a Jewish Aristotelian, and for the Christian tradition the reasoning of St. Thomas Aquinas (1225–74), a Dominican theologian, professor at the University of Paris, Aristotelian, and later principal (Roman Catholic) Church Father. The problems about which they wrote were primarily of a theological and philosophical nature, including questions of right and wrong, morality, and ethics. Fortunately

---

12. Barry Gordon (1989) identified both Greek and Hebraic elements in modern Christian patristic approaches to the "economic problem" (scarcity of means in a world of multiple ends). The Pharisaic observation of law and ritual, the Prophetic stress on the mediation of the current with the Ideal, and the later emphasis on skepticism and ultimate punishment for the unjust are just three of the Hebraic elements. Personal admission to the Kingdom of God, the model of Apostolic poverty, including dependence, a desire for communalism of the spirit and the environment, and a query about the meaning of social responsibility toward those who rejected the Christian salvation and to whom charity might be extended were some of the themes that derived from the Greek tradition.

for us as economists, one of the issues they handled was the more mundane problem of the nature and origin of economic concerns. We shall begin to approach this difficult question by asking what is the point of the shared Book of Genesis concerning the inadequacy of Man.[13]

Apparently, whatever were His expectations, God became disappointed with Man. Man (and *particularly* Woman, perhaps since men wrote up the history and so could not accept sole responsibility for actions contributing to the Fall) did not live up to His idealizations, His grand design. (What that says about His omniscience and even His omnipotence may be another matter.) Suffice it to say that the pristine state of nature into which man was placed did not, and probably could not, endure. Events, it may be argued, took an inevitable course. It is equally arguable that man chose his fate from among an (exhaustive) list of potential options. In any event, mankind was informed that it had "fallen" from Grace and consequently has been made to suffer ever since. To explore further this line of inquiry involves delving into the consequences of the actions leading to the Fall from Grace, and how they relate to the basic questions of economics. Let us begin with two of the most basic and important questions: (1) What was the sin? and (2) What was the punishment?

The sin seems to have been something combining (1) inability to leave well-enough alone; (2) greed, involving things (something forbidden) and time (instant gratification); (3) excessive curiosity; (4) inability to follow precise directions; and (5) a willingness to be tempted, particularly when one could assert that "one was only doing what everyone else [*sic*] was doing."[14] In short, the sin comprised the basic elements of the essential nature of man.

---

13. An even earlier major point is that everything is said to have had a prior cause, with the Prime Cause being God.

14. Cf. Gen. 3: 9–12, 16, 17.

[9] But the Lord God called to the man and said to him, "Where are you?" [10] He replied,"I heard the sound as you were walking the garden, and I was afraid because I was naked, and I hid myself." [11] God answered, "Who told you that you were naked? Have you eaten from the tree which I forbade you?" [12] The man said, "The woman you gave me for a companion, she gave me fruit from the tree and I ate." [Note: the story as recalled suggests that Adam was dependent upon Eve (for what?), and the price of that dependency was to be agreeable to Eve ("it was really all her fault—I only did what You [God] had laid out for me").]

[16] To the woman he said:
    I will increase your labor and your groaning,
    and in labor you shall bear children.
    You shall feel an urge for your husband,
    and he shall be your master.

[17] And to the man he said:
    Because you have listened to your wife
    and have eaten from the tree which I forbade you,

The punishment is less easily defined, but purportedly a distinction can be made between that which happened to Man and that which happened to Woman (considering differing sexual roles, with Woman the homebody and Man the outside worker). One clear answer to the question of punishment, particularly as seen by Thomas Aquinas (and by most economists ever since), was that man and woman after the Fall were made to live in a world of scarcity, in which they would henceforth be responsible for their own physical survival. It would only be by the "sweat of the brow" and the labor of the back that life could be maintained, and even then it was of limited duration. Hence, the economic problem, the absence of plenty of goods and services, is fundamentally God's curse on mankind. Man, by labor and by ingenuity, must strive (albeit for the most part unsuccessfully) to overcome scarcity; he must attempt to achieve a fruitful existence in the face of insurmountable obstacles placed in his path (in the guise of resource constraints) that serve to thwart him at every turn. The study of the economics of the production of goods and services, it follows, is the result of this original sin. Since Eve was the proximate cause of the Fall, and Eve represents sexual attraction or desire, some (particularly St. Paul, whose opinion of womankind was problematic) have considered that sexual attraction was in some way even more responsible for the Fall than anything else.[15]

Another point needs to be considered. This concerns the possibility that scarcity may not have been the greatest punishment that could have been inflicted. Where scarcity simply means that one has to allocate between one's preferences, man could always use his reason to allocate time and resources and priorities, thereby overcoming the greater disasters of scarcity. This may lead one to conclude that the punishment was more on the order of forcing man to rely on his own ingenuity instead of having him continue to rely on an omnipotent, omniscient provider. While man was left to fend for himself in a hostile environment, he was also endowed with the means for his survival, and even eventual domination, over hardship.

Yet there was a greater punishment, one even more basic to life. In Maimonides' view, God's real punishment was to push man beyond the limits of his reason. Reason could take man only so far; beyond that point, a realization of fallibility set in. This point leads to the view that until the Fall, man *knew;* knowledge was certain and unfailing and complete for his

---

accursed shall be the ground on your account
With labor you shall win your food from it
all the days of your life.
It will grow thorns and thistles for you,
none but wild plants for you to eat.
You shall gain your bread by the sweat of your brow
until you return to the ground;
for from it you were taken.
Dust you are, to dust you shall return.

15. Put crudely, even if economics is not a sexy subject, its origins were sexual.

needs. After the Fall, he had only *opinions;*[16] he was forced to hypothesize, to guess, to take chances on the unknown. This is God's punishment. The certainty with which decisions had been made yielded to probability and contingency and a sense of dread of the unknown; it led, if you will, from the infallibility induced by perfect knowledge to a reliance on faith and hope and imagination. The key to the solution of the scarcity problem is reason; the key to the solution of the uncertainty problem is imagination. Requisite to omnipotence is omniscience, and what man lost was the claim to that which he might have had. He might have been master, dominant over all he surveyed; he had to settle instead for an existence that put him into constant conflict with his environment. In other words, what truly underlies the misery of scarcity is neither hunger nor thirst, but the lack of knowledge of what one's preference schedule will do to one's happiness. For if one had complete knowledge (including foreknowledge) one could compensate accordingly. Lacking such knowledge, chance and caprice rule.

If one pursues Maimonides' line of inquiry, it seems that uncertainty (which is based on not only ignorance of information that can be known, but also on ignorance of the unknowable) is the real punishment of man. Unable to achieve complete knowledge (or even apprehension) of his world, man was relegated to forming conjectures that in turn shaped his focus. In other words, man was reduced from a position of ontological certitude toward the world to one of intrinsic uncertainty. The concept of uncertainty can thus be seen, under most circumstances, to be not only an essential part of our patristic thinking, but also a fundamental concern of the economics discipline.

The Patristic Tradition through the Middle Ages   4

The Development of Medieval Thinking   4.1

Let us turn now to the Christian patristic tradition as most of us have encountered it.[17] We are, of course, for the most part products of western

---

16. This point is to be found through an expansion of the thinking of Maimonides (*Guide of the Perplexed;* see especially chap. 2), whose principal question relates to the state of man's knowledge before and after the Fall. The line of his argument is that man did not have any worries before the Fall, because everything was taken care of. The Fall, coming about only because God had told man to avoid just one thing which man then did not avoid, led to man no longer being taken care of, and man, having become mortal, having to spend his days worrying about the unknown. Where once man could count on a certain future, now man had to worry about the unknown, about which he could only have limited expectations. Maimonides, a native of Cordoba (Spain), spent the greatest part of his career in Cairo, where he was the court physician. Maimonides is one of the great Aristotelians, and although much of his theology was considered questionable by Thomas Aquinas, Aquinas appears to have had little trouble with Maimonides' Aristotelianism.

17. See Jacob Viner (1978a) for a more thorough discussion of the economic doctrines of the Christian Fathers.

civilization and are consequently shaped significantly by the great institutions of that civilization. For better or worse, the Roman Catholic Church has in terms of historical hegemony been the leading institution in the molding and shaping of this tradition, and although there is much to persuade us that it derived its underlying values from religions preceding it, its synthesis still dominates our thought.[18] Our "filter" has been the interpretations of the works of the scholastics, as developed from the thirteenth to the fifteenth centuries.[19]

There are two ways to perceive of the development of economic thinking during the period of medieval Roman Catholic theological hegemony. One stresses the use of categorical imperatives—certain things are allowed, others are forbidden. It then employs the rules of ratiocinative reasoning from premises laid out by theology or (more usual in practice) by canonical law. This approach appeared mainly in writings, either as applications of theology to the mundane practices of economic life or as efforts to lay out broad theological and derivative philosophical principles.

The second approach has fostered explanations as to how certain Natural Law solutions could be harmonized with what we today refer to as economic scarcity premises. It comes down to the question, "In this imperfect world, what would a good Christian man do?" These practices (or rationalizations) evolved into two separate bodies of literature. One was a "cookbook" or "how-to-do-it" manual. The other advocated an ordered relationship, designed to explain why doing something one way was either the least of all evils or an acceptable alternative (not necessarily the same thing).

Perhaps the Christian patristic tradition should then be seen as having two sides. On the one hand, it was authoritative, since it can be said to have arisen from a compromise between that which should transpire in the City of God and that to which good citizens of the City of Man should aspire. On the other hand, it had a pragmatic, rhetorical appeal, in that it represented an effort at explaining, in rational terms, acceptable Christian practice (truly acceptable to God as well as to man) as exemplified in effective norms.

To many observers, there seems to be a contradiction between these two approaches, since the second appears to maintain sophistries designed to circumvent the first. For example, no economic idea is more patristic than the prohibition against usury, which may be defined

18. Monotheism and the ethics derived therefrom may have come principally from Pharisaical (more properly legalistic or rabbinic) Judaism (of which general movement Jesus of Nazareth was part, albeit a dissident part). The perception of individual salvation seems to have derived not from Judaism, but from one of the Greek mystery sects, which promised the perfect afterlife for the faithful. The dualistic perception of the God/Devil relationship seems to have derived from Zoroastrianism, a Persian religion.

19. On this background see Pribram 1983, chapters 1 and 2, and Rothbard 1995, vol. I.

broadly for our purposes as any injustice in trade. Yet church authorities managed to evade any such proscriptions by very inventive means. The authorities circumvented the prohibition on interest, specifically, by creating and then implementing four principles said to be in line with conventional Biblical teaching: *dammum emergens, lucrum cessans, poena conventianalis,* and *periculum sortis.*[20] While pragmatically perhaps a wise and indeed liberal rendering of the prevailing morality, the contradiction in such a position is nonetheless clear: the Christians' taking of interest seems to be just one of those things disallowed under God's law (since it apparently represented the exploitation of the poor by the rich) while still being practiced by those who viewed themselves as pious believers.[21]

Medieval society was hierarchical, but the social situation was generally fluid (albeit viscous). Feudalism had its own internal critics; indeed, between the persuasiveness of these ideological critics and the bellicosity within the nobility, possessions seemed continually to be changing hands. Many groups, particularly the merchants, knew how to be *tertius gaudens*—the third party beneficiary—when it came to church–state conflicts. By the eleventh and twelfth centuries, slavery (particularly peonage in the cities) had largely disappeared—although youth and women were still considered chattels in many important ways. In the countryside, there were developing certain forms of legal redress of grievances—at worst the fear of peasant rebellion kept many lords of the manor from acting capriciously.

Both the religious tradition and the secular needs of the nobility and clergy exalted the virtues of labor. No one should be idle; even the nobility were expected to participate generously and responsibly in the social process (hence the doctrine of *noblesse oblige*). While it was true that this world was meant as a place of preparation, there were, nonetheless, cathedrals to be erected to the immediate and proximate greater glory of God.

---

20. *Dammum emergens* held that no lender should have to suffer an actual loss from lending, but would instead need to be compensated. *Lucrum cessans* held that the lender should be compensated for the loss brought about by the forgone gains from missed opportunities. *Poena conventianalis* held that the lender should be compensated for the late repayment of a loan. *Periculum sortis* held that the lender should be compensated for the risk incurred in granting the loan.

21. While interest taking was supposed to be forbidden to everyone, it is clear that it was particularly forbidden to the clergy (including the monastic and holy orders). It is part of the mythology of the Renaissance that only Jews were moneylenders; some thus credit modern capitalism with all of its emphasis on productive efficiency and the expansion of consumption-goods distribution to the Jews, while others tar the Jews with the brush of excessive materialism. The real point is that, while the Jews may have been moneylenders, so were the Germans (the Fuggars) and the Italians (the Medici). In fact, after the Jews were expelled from London, moneylending increased markedly.

Moreover, Aristotle (whose views, when not in conflict with those of the Church, seemed to embody the best of man's reasoning) held that money was not fertile—unlike the product of the sweat and toil of manual labor—and so was not productive.

While Scholastic doctrine is indeed identifiable by modern historians of economic thought as a form of economic reasoning—as distinct from the theological ruminations of the pre-Scholastics—there is in these early writings much that should be viewed from our vantage point as patristic. It has been suggested (for example, Barry Gordon 1987) that the first major patristic figure in this respect was Justin Martyr (110–65), but we will begin here with the "last," St. Augustine of Hippo (354–430).[22] A Doctor of the Catholic Church and an extremely influential figure in the development of Catholic thinking, Augustine relied heavily in his theological writings on Platonic reasoning. In his *City of God,* he commended Plato for his vigorous defense of rationalism over empiricism; in his *Confessions,* he noted similarities between Platonist philosophy and Christian thinking. Yet he denied, for practical as well as idealistic reasons, certain worldly aspects of Plato's philosophy. For example, while the patristic Fathers of the Church had advocated a form of primitive communism, Augustine denied the validity of holding property as a communal good, cleaving instead to a distinction between divine and material rights.[23] In light of his tremendous influence on the structure of Christian thought and doctrine, one must regard Augustine's legacy as truly patristic in terms even beyond its influence on Catholic doctrine, representing a doctrinal guide (one stressing imperatives) rather than a practical guide to everyday life.

Albert, Count of Bollstadt, a Dominican theologian known also as Albertus Magnus (1193?–1280), is really the first of the medieval figures to whom we can turn. Albertus was not only an Aristotelian, relying on observation for his studies in botany as well as in the relationships between men, but was also fascinated with economic concepts, such as the relation between cost and price and the concept of the "just price."[24] The just price as it developed in this period may best be understood as a constructed price for a good, stipulated to cover only raw materials and labor expended in production. In essence it was a measure of the cost of production, which was then to serve as a fair value. The just price thus derived from the normative constructions of the medieval period: the price of a good in the market *should* reflect the cost to the seller of its production and thus *should not* reflect the nature of demand. This consideration may suggest that the seller seeks to take undue advantage of a

---

22. We should also mention in respect of the patristic figures of this period the names of Clement of Alexandria (150–215), Tertullian (155–222), Lactantius (260–340), and St. Jerome (342–420).

23. As Pribram (1983) noted, "Communist tenets were rejected by the church as heretic as early as the fifth century . . ." (10).

24. The foundation of the concept of the "just price" Schumpeter (1954) attributed to Aristotle. Other interesting interpretations can be found in Raymond de Roover (1958) and George Wilson (1975).

buyer who has a profound need.[25] Albertus Magnus held strongly to the belief that price should reflect labor input, and that thus one is entitled to all the fruits of one's labor as a matter of justice.

Aquinas as the Model for a Moral Economics   4.2

It was Albertus' pupil, St. Thomas Aquinas, *Doctor Communis* of the Catholic Church, whose synthesis of Catholic thinking came to be considered as more or less basic.[26] Aquinas held that revelation and knowledge are not separate, but are component parts of a single, unified truth. The Thomistic line is an integrated system, a set of rules that explain what *must* be known. The truth of a proposition can be known because of its self-evident nature, or because it can be derived through an appeal to known truths. Aquinas thus could not accept Aristotle's position that only empirically demonstrable principles are meaningful, but rather held that truth is a unity since it originates with God. (He did not, for instance, accept that one could *prove* the existence of God by an appeal to empirical evidence.) In this way, the first principles are revealed as undisputed, necessary truth. Textual instruction becomes on this view very important, but even more so is the admonition against deviating from this tradition. The essence of Aquinas' thought is found in his massive *Summa Theologiæ,* a wide-ranging treatise covering virtually every aspect of Christian Scholastic law, philosophy, and ethics, including such economics topics as property and value.

Beginning with the question of property, Aquinas accepted the Aristotelian idea of decoupling rights of use from rights of ownership. He began his disquisition on the subject by accepting the proposition that the private possession of goods was not a "natural" state of affairs; "man has no power over external things, since he cannot change their nature" (*Summa,* 2, 2, ques. 66, art. 1, 65).[27] But Aquinas then defined "external things" in two ways, in respect of their "nature" and in respect of "use

---

25. But as Pribram (1983, 14–15) observed, this is not to concede that the "just price" implied a labor theory of value, since utility entered also into the calculation.

26. Aquinas was less authoritative in his own time than later. Aquinas was canonized in 1323, but it was not until 1879 that Pope Leo XIII made his philosophy official church doctrine. In 1914 his views were condensed, by a group working in the Vatican, into 24 propositions. In his own lifetime he was forever engaged in controversy, and after he died his work was repudiated by the Archbishop of Paris (which repudiation was later withdrawn). In recent years, those who consider him as *the* Catholic authority in matters philosophical, specifically in matters of an epistemological nature, are less prominent than was true even a half-century ago.

27. The *Summa Theologiæ* is separated into four parts: Prima Pars, Prima Secundæ, Secunda Secundæ, and Tertia Pars, usually abbreviated as (1, 1), (1, 2), (2, 2), and (3). The "questions" are numbered consecutively, from 1 to 90. Page numbers are from the 1975 edition, which includes Latin text and English translation.

and management." In the first instance, all things belong only to God and so are commonly held by man in his corporeal form on earth. In the second, it can reasonably be argued that "man has a natural dominion over external things, for he has a mind and a will with which to turn them to his own account" (65). Thus the earth is provided for all to hold in common, while at the same time man is endowed with an *ability* to amass private holdings.

But the argument extends only so far. In article 2, Aquinas argued that it is *not* legitimate for a man to possess anything as his own, since Natural Law dictates that everything is to be held in common. Thus, appropriation of common property by any individual is illegitimate. The apparent conflict engendered in allowing dominion and stewardship but denying private holdings Aquinas handled by reaffirming the Aristotelian principles of ownership. Man has been granted stewardship over the common resources of the earth, and in so undertaking this trust he has a "two-fold competence": (1) "to care for and distribute the earth's resources" and (2) "to use and manage" them. In support of the first, care and distribution, and by implication support of a form of private property right, Aquinas offered three compelling rationales, following directly in the Aristotelian line:[28]

> First, because each person takes more trouble to care for something that is his sole responsibility than what is held in common or by many—for in such a case each individual shirks the work and leaves the responsibility to somebody else, which is what happens when too many officials are involved. Second, because human affairs are more efficiently organized if each person has his own responsibility to discharge; there would be chaos if everybody cared for everything. Third, because men live together in greater peace where everyone is content with his task. We do, in fact, notice that quarrels often break out amongst men who hold things in common without distinction. (*Summa*, 2, 2, ques. 66, art. 2, 67–69)

In support of the second "competence," the use and management of resources is to be undertaken "in the interests of all" with a duty "to share them with others in case of necessity" (*Summa*, 2, 2, ques. 66, art. 2, 69). The "two competences" taken together suggest that, while private ownership is the most effective way to encourage responsible management, such management is not to be confined solely to the interest of the single individual but rather to the interests of society.

Of particular note here is the role played by Natural Law. As

---

28. In a footnote to the translation, the editor, Marcus Lefébure, noted that the three arguments presented by Aquinas were "taken almost *verbatim* from Aristotle: *Politics* II, 5, 1262b38." It is interesting to note that these "takings" occur in Question 66: Theft and Robbery with Violence, and precede article 3: "Does the surreptitious taking of another's property constitute theft?"

Aquinas understood it, Natural Law would seem to hold that nothing is to be granted to individual possession, yet (as we have seen) just such a form of distribution must exist. Aquinas circumvented the problem by maintaining that such questions as distribution are pragmatic ones, to be decided by human agreement, and so are outside the bounds of Natural Law. Thus society devises rules of possession and distribution *commensurate with* Natural Law but not dictated in substance by it. Possession and distribution are not themselves derivatives of Natural Law, but are rather defined instrumentally as "what rational beings conclude as an *addition to* the Natural Law" (*Summa*, 2, 2, ques. 66, art. 2, 69; emphasis added). Natural Law could thus speak neither one way nor the other on the question of the institution of private property. Private property arrangements derive from *positive* law; private ownership exists solely because it *works* in promoting social order. In Aquinas' world, the end is the achievement of God's Grace; the uses of wealth and property are but means to that end.[29]

We turn now to Aquinas' views on value. Aquinas regarded value as being derived through the utility provided.[30] Thus his view of the "just price" was that it derived from some notion of *utility*, rather than from the cost of production. Specifically, Aquinas refined the concept to account for "considerations" on the part of the seller to engage in trade in the first place. In question 77, Aquinas considered two views of a "contract of sale." In the first, the transaction benefits the parties to the agreement in the same measure. In this instance, since "what is equally useful to both should not involve more of a burden for one than for the other," it is evident "that the balance of justice is upset if either the price exceeds the value of the good in question or the thing exceeds the price. To sell for more or to buy for less than a thing is worth is, therefore, unjust and illicit in itself" (*Summa*, 2, 2, ques. 77, art. 1, 215).

The second view holds that one party benefits at the expense of another; in other words, there is for one party to the transaction a greater need for the item. Here demand considerations are allowed to enter the price calculation, and so "the estimation of the just price will have to take into account not merely the commodity to be sold but also the loss which the seller incurs in selling it. The commodity can here be sold for more than it is worth in itself though not for more than it is worth to the possessor" (*Summa*, 2, 2, ques. 77, art. 1, 215). Thus the just price could fluctuate within an acceptable range, but the "just" element suggested that the range could not be too great. So while demand can serve as a justification to increase price over the cost of production, it cannot be used as a rationale for the seller to appropriate any and all surplus value.

It was in this ability to recognize the realities of commerce—

29. On Aquinas' view of property and justice, see Viner 1978b.

30. This is discussed at some length by Pribram (1983, 12–14). See also David Friedman (1980).

specifically in accepting that commerce per se was not an illicit or immoral undertaking—that Aquinas should be seen as an important contributor to economic theory. He began the evolution of perspective on economic problems from a moral to a full-cost basis, where cost was not to be confined simply to the value of labor input, but could include increases in value for a host of other reasons. For example, a seller may ask a price for a good exceeding his purchase price "either because he has improved the thing in some fashion, or because prices have gone up in response to local changes or the lapse of time, or because he has incurred risks in transporting it about or in having it delivered" (*Summa*, 2, 2, ques. 77, art. 4, 229–31). But he is enjoined from gain resulting from hedging, monopoly, or arbitrage.

As a foil to Aquinas we need only offer the Franciscan John Duns Scotus (1265–1308), a Scottish philosopher who studied at both Cambridge and Oxford. As an "economist," Duns Scotus has some claim to fame: Schumpeter credited him "with having discovered the condition of competitive equilibrium which came to be known in the nineteenth century as the Law of Cost" (Schumpeter 1954, 93).[31] As a Platonist, as well as an "Oxford Franciscan," he was at odds with Aquinas (the Aristotelian Dominican), especially over the issues of the property right and the just price (although he seems to have been sympathetic to Augustine). Duns Scotus—the Subtle Doctor—held that the Fall of Man effectively obliterated the Natural-Law foundation of communal property, while the just price restrictions could be circumvented through mutual agreement. (Russell [1945, 467–68] argued that Duns Scotus' interpretation of the "principle of individuation"—the principle underlying the distinctness of things—was based on *form*, not *matter*; Aquinas held the opposite view. This may explain the different interpretations given.)

4.3 Summary

One may view the Christian patristic tradition as it developed from the medieval period through the writings of the Scholastics as the source of many interesting points. It reinvigorated the conflict between Platonic idealism and the Aristotelian method. It reflected, in other words, the combined effects of "transcendental idealism" (the Platonic approach) and "practical idealism," the practical element being something more secular than the transcendental. It offered precious little economic theorizing, although it offered fine examples of extended chains of syllogistic

---

31. "This is not imputing too much: for if we identify the just price of a good with its competitive common value, as Duns Scotus certainly did, and if we further equate that just price to the cost of the good (taking account of risk, as he did not fail to observe), then we have ipso facto, at least by implication, stated the law of cost not only as a normative but also as an analytic proposition" (Schumpeter 1954, 93). On this point Pribram (1983) disagreed.

logic. Most of all, it attempted a working-out of a unified approach to life as it is with life as we wish it to be.

Magisterial Interpretations of Economics 5

The Setting 5.1

Having set forth a brief introduction to the development of patristic thinking as it has affected economic thought and discourse, we come now to the historical development of economics itself as a discipline and what we perceive to be modern patristic interpretations of that discipline. By *discipline* we mean nothing beyond a shared perception of a body of knowledge. Its sets of questions, data, and analytical methods, are common to those who are identified or identify themselves as members of that profession. In other words, we seek to determine the emergence of the field of economics as viewed as a doctrine of intellectual import by those who identify themselves as working within the parameters of the field. In this regard there can be identified three modern magisterial treatments of the history of economic thought, magisterial because they have created frameworks that serve to link together interpretations over time and across other boundaries as well, and because modern historians of thought may well identify these treatments as encompassing and uniquely interpretive.

Pribram: Philosophical Tensions 5.2

The first of these magisterial approaches is one associated with Karl Pribram (1877–1973), a University of Vienna–trained scholar who later in life became a civil servant.[32] In his massive history of economic thought, *A History of Economic Reasoning* (1983), he stressed the continual tensions in the philosophical approaches taken to the subject. The principal dissonance is between those advocating pure reason as the means to knowledge, and those opting for a compromise between reason and sensory cognition. This tension—in essence a methodological contradiction—is most pronounced in the clash between the advocates of Platonic idealism and those favoring Aristotelian methods, the latter emphasizing observation and designed to flesh out the Platonic transcendental realities. In this argument, Platonist deductivism—as manifested in the Scholastic philosophy of Duns Scotus and the Franciscans—was set into conflict with

---

32. Pribram was a student of Friedrich von Wieser, one of the founders of the Austrian school of economics. As evidence of the practical motive of his economics, Pribram was highly instrumental in establishing the Austrian social security system and was even consulted for his expertise in this area by the U.S. government when the decision was made to institute the U.S. social security system.

Aristotelian inductivism—a "hypothetical" (empirical) form of reasoning associated with the philosophical stance of Aquinas and the Dominicans. There is, in other words, a contrast between the focus on *individual* phenomena and the reality solely of *universals*.

This conflict—between observation and reason—resurfaces from time to time in philosophical discourse. The Aristotelian Pierre Abelard (1079–1142) and the Franciscan scholar-monk Roger Bacon (1214–94)[33] attempted to alleviate this tension with the idea that there existed within individuals "innate" thought processes which allowed one to analyze nature through the use of scientific procedure. We could gain insight into universals (and, by extension, the mind of God) by studying individual objects or phenomena with scientific precision. In the seventeenth and eighteenth centuries, Francis Bacon (1561–1626), Thomas Hobbes (1588–1679), John Locke (1632–1704), and David Hume (1711–76) firmly established the Abelard–Roger Bacon line as the basis of the British scientific method.[34] On the Continent, at about the same time, the scholastic line regained supremacy with the appearance of René Descartes (1596–1650)[35] in France, and Gottfried Leibniz (1646–1716) and Immanuel Kant (1724–1804) in the Germanic states. Cartesian rationalism, with its emphasis on the search for certainty through systematic doubt, and the belief that such certainty was indeed attainable, became the basis of the epistemological positions of many within the French tradition. Within economics itself, as it was later to be constituted, the argument emerged in the clash between the pronouncements of the mercantilists (seen by Pribram to be of the Aristotelian-Francis Bacon mold—Pribram in fact labeled this development the era of "Baconian Mercantilism") and the physiocrats (holding to the Platonist-Cartesian line).

Pribram argued that the late eighteenth- and early nineteenth-century conflict between Kant and Georg Hegel (1770–1831) was another example of this basic division. The political debate in the twentieth century over communism and fascism was juxtaposed in much the same way. In

---

33. The Oxford-educated Bacon is regarded as a true pioneer of modern science, recognizing the importance of the experimental method. Despite (or perhaps because of) his advocacy of scientific education—in the areas of mathematics, optics, and alchemy—and his unique abilities at foreseeing future scientific advances—such as "flying machines" (well before Leonardo da Vinci), the telescope, and even horseless carriages—he was branded a heretic by the Franciscans, his reputation redeemed only well after his death.

34. We will discuss each of these figures in the following chapters.

35. Descartes will be of great importance in the discussion to follow, especially in chapters 4 and 10, and so some biographical information should be presented. Educated in the Jesuit tradition in the philosophy of Aristotle, he is often referred to as the founder of modern philosophy. A towering figure in the history of mathematics—his efforts at creating a unified mathematics led to what we call today the system of Cartesian coordinates—he attempted to provide a philosophical structure to Copernican physics and even tried to explain the workings of the human body through reference to mechanical laws. In the area of epistemology, he is regarded as one of the leading figures in the development of rationalism.

economics again, the debate between American free-tradism (emphasizing theoretical free-market solutions) and the Keynesian view of macro-economics (emphasizing short-term problem solving) was likewise a manifestation of this old antagonism.

In short, Pribram's approach to the study of economics stresses the continuation of the essential tensions dating from the time of the early Greeks. It asserts that the development of the economics discipline, through its many manifestations and incarnations, is essentially tied to an ages-old Greek philosophical preoccupation with the question of the basis of our knowledge of the world. By confronting this and a host of other related questions of an epistemological and ontological[36] nature, questions of perhaps greater import than those accepted as being of traditional disciplinary interest, Pribram sought to extend the intellectual concerns and frameworks of the past to the concerns of the present and the future. These early questions serve as the basis for the patristic tradition of the field, for surely one views the intellectual future as an adaptation of the historical, intellectual past.

Pribram's work is manifestly a subjective study of the formation of *sets of ideas* (our patristic legacies), not confined to schools tied to periods or individuals or even to the unfolding of historical events. The attempt to place the emergence of economic doctrines within the framework of the clash of philosophical ideals, coupled with Pribram's own preference for a rationalism of the Platonic-Cartesian variety, has some appeal, although it cannot pretend to handle many of the nuances that affect the course of the evolution of economic thought.

Mitchell: Synthetic Theory   5.3

A second magisterial approach to the history of economic thought is associated with the work of the American institutional economist Wesley Clair Mitchell (1874–1948). Mitchell came to believe that modern economics was essentially a set of ideas reflecting certain conflicts engendered by the industrialization of western society and the social reorganization (for example, urbanization) that followed. He certainly did not believe that economics as such came into being only after the Industrial Revolution, although he began his approach to the historical evolution of the subject with the systematic analysis of Adam Smith. Rather, he argued that the elements of interest to modern society, and to economists in particular in their attempts to study that society—those things considered relevant in the pursuit of the discipline—tended to be of a more modern vintage, and that the historical background served as unnecessary clutter.

Throughout his writings, Mitchell stressed the primacy of observation; economic theories develop as a means of explaining the events of the

---

36. Epistemology refers to a theory of knowledge; ontology refers to a theory of existence or being.

time.[37] When and if one chose to connect and explain observations by means of a theoretical construct, that construct appeared more often than not to be idiosyncratic in nature, reflective of the prevailing social, economic, and political environments. Specifically, Mitchell became convinced that there were no immutable laws of economics, no natural laws upon which the system was founded. He rather felt that economic laws were valid only within the institutional framework existing at the time and the place of their elucidation. His method was one of *particularism,* an understanding of the here and now. Modern economic theory then was for Mitchell nothing more than an effort to explain the significance of these phenomena and describe the linkages among them; economic theory is highly synthetic and completely idiosyncratic, a venture he dismissed as "excogitation."[38] Thus the development of economic thought did not proceed and could not be understood as a progression along a temporal dimension; economic thought could only be understood as the rationalizations of particular individuals to a given set of historical episodes and events. Economic "truths" likewise are not objective deductions from established premises, but are subjective judgments based on personal values.

This subjective form of theorizing did not, however, prevent Mitchell from employing technical apparatus in his analysis of economic data. As with Aristotle, he was interested first and foremost in observation; unlike Aristotle, however, Mitchell was not particularly interested in the commodity of ideas. While cognizant of the formative development of the discipline, and taking a sympathetic attitude toward the rhetorical basis upon which it rested, he nonetheless in his own work employed a quite different and more rigorous methodology, one he felt was better suited to the problems at hand. Above all else, he deplored casual abstraction and a lack of a suitable method behind the collection of statistical data. But this was not out of line with his view of the historical development of economics. On the contrary, his conviction drew him to employ as a rule the techniques of quantitative analysis in many of his studies, if not throughout most of his work.[39]

37. Mitchell was not a professional historian. However, his views of the necessity of recording (and, if possible, measuring) the full spectrum of socioeconomic phenomena would likely have put him in consonance with the *Annales* school of historical research.

38. George J. Stigler noted that Mitchell's theory of the development of economic thought, wherein environmental conditions serve to drive theoretical advances, failed to explain the advances after 1870 and the development of abstract theoretical economics (see Stigler 1983). See also the approach of Robert V. Eagly (1974), wherein classical economics is structured around the concept of capital.

39. Yet despite this reliance on quantitative methods, Mitchell cannot be said to have had unlimited faith in numerical quantification. One of his major critics, Tjalling Koopmans, claimed that Mitchell only collected data, but could not arrange it in any meaningful way. While Mitchell's skills and his perceptions were clearly temporally and spatially bound, today we must merely observe that what Koopmans attributed to Mitchell should be judged in terms of what was new and true: the parts of Koopmans's criticisms which were true were not new, and the parts which were new were not true.

Schumpeter: The Definition of a "Science" of Economics   *5.4*

A third approach to the history of economic thought is identified with the work of Joseph Alois Schumpeter (1883–1950). Early in his career, Schumpeter drew heavily (although without acknowledgment) in his theoretical work on the writings of an Italian scholar, Luigi Cossa, of whom mention must be made if only to ensure he not be relegated to the ranks of the completely forgotten. In this early work, Schumpeter was fascinated with the distinction between what he termed "scientific economics" and the "art of political economy" or "sociological economics" (or even "ideological economics"). To the extent it is a "science," economics pretends to rigor and may lead to the discovery of universally valid, analytical truths. To the extent it is an "art," economics must deal with a philosophical legacy and so must develop bodies of ideas which describe (and so explain) the intellectual sources behind the interactions of the passions, particularly those passions involved in the production and distribution of goods and services.

In his unfinished *History of Economic Analysis* (1954), Schumpeter divided the evolution of economic thought into four distinct phases. The first, or Hellenistic, phase extended from the philosophies of the ancient Greeks to the publication of Adam Smith's *Wealth of Nations,* or from the "golden men" to the "wooden Scottish philosopher." The second, or classical, phase began with the works of Jeremy Bentham and the early utilitarians and lasted until around 1870 with the advent of the "marginal revolution." The third phase covered the development of a disparate group of "schools," including the German and American Historical movements, marginal utility economics, and Marxian, Marshallian, and Walrasian economics. The fourth and final phase was taken as the present and future development of the discipline and included not merely an extension of the formalism inherited from the previous phase, but also historical and sociological dimensions hitherto neglected.

Schumpeter argued that, in every phase of its development, economics had become influenced by its intellectual environment, and even proposed a label, "the filiation of economic ideas"—"the process by which men's efforts to understand economic phenomena produce, improve, and pull down analytic structures in an unending sequence" (Schumpeter 1954, 6). As societies and perceptions change, so do the approaches to the solutions of the problems of interest to economists. Schumpeter subsequently sought to discover not only the form of those changes, but from whence those changes sprang. In addressing this latter question, he suggested that in part the changes were the result of the emergence of a new data base (the very thing Mitchell would have thought of as "basic"). In part, however, these changes infiltrated economics from other intellectual traditions—Newton's calculus placed emphasis on physical and then economic equilibrium; new philosophical schools (such as logical positivism) offered new approaches to economic thinking; different approaches to historical interpretation offered not only new data bases, but also new analytical frameworks. Certainly the discovery of new statistical and computational methods has played an important role in the interpretation of uncertainty and the manner of its incorporation into economic models.

Perhaps more to the point, Schumpeter contended that economics could only be labeled a "science" if by science one meant "any kind of knowledge that has been the object of conscious efforts to improve it. Such efforts produce habits of mind—methods or 'techniques'—and a command of facts unearthed by these techniques which are beyond the range of the mental habits and the factual knowledge of everyday life" (7). Science for Schumpeter was thus a modification of the (Francis) Baconian scientific method. To this end he counseled economists to study law, sociology, history, and even literature, so as to broaden the scope and method of economic discourse. The sources for an understanding of the changes in economic analysis Schumpeter clearly believed derived from the wealth of methods which these other disciplines offered, and also from their usually overlooked assumptions, which served to tie their methods to their findings.

5.5 Summary

Magisterial treatments are no more than intellectual mappings, or intellectual handles useful to grasp massive amounts of material. The reason we chose to illustrate what we mean by "patristic legacies" even before we turn to the three magisterial treatments of the history of economic thought is that we believe an appreciation of these legacies can offer yet another approach to grasping the subject.

If we wish to understand our discipline in its own terms, we can profit from all of the maps or handles provided by philosopher-economist-historians. In other disciplines a magisterial grasp has grown from a theoretical framework, but in general magisterial interpretations are illustrative rather than analytical.[40]

Magisterial handles or interpretations should be seen for what they

40. Isaac Newton was a great mathematician largely because he was trying to explain the phenomena of physical mechanics—his magisterial interpretation explained the workings of the solar system but not the universe. Economists' unquestioning emulation of Newton and his successors has led them to look everywhere for planetary-type equilibria. The reason John von Neumann developed the mini-max principle is probably unknown (perhaps he may have been trying to explain how his father, an investment banker, combined concerns about profit maximization with concerns about risk minimization), but it has become a handle for explaining a great deal in economic theory. However, more than a few economists have been led by their unquestioning emulation of von Neumann and his successors to confuse risk management with uncertainty. Game theory is better suited to the first than to the second.

are. It is said that Franz Liszt and Arthur Rubinstein, both celebrated concert pianists, occasionally missed some of the notes. Nonetheless, their interpretations were magisterial, even if not perfect. To be magisterial is to give a strong interpretation; it is not to be authoritative.

In what follows in this volume we refer regularly to other magisterial treatments, particularly Pribram and Schumpeter's. We do not seek to choose between them. Yet we dare to offer our own interpretation, which at best supplements their work and Mitchell's. The proof of the utility of magisterial treatments is like pudding—in the useful consumption. But also of interpretations as of puddings, *De gustibus non est disputandum.* We hope that our confection pleases you.

With all this in mind—examples of what we mean by patristic legacies and the uses to which we put magisterial interpretations—we can now survey the history of economic thought and the patristic legacies illuminated therein.

CHAPTER 2

The British Patristic Legacy
Understanding the Hobbes Challenge

Pray for the welfare of the government, since but for the fear
thereof men would swallow each other alive.
PIRKE AVOTH ([SAYINGS OF THE FATHERS], CHAP. 3)

Misrule is better than no rule, and an ill Government, a bad
Government, is better than none at all.
OLIVER CROMWELL, SPEECH TO PARLIAMENT
(JANUARY 25, 1658)

Nothing turns out to be so oppressive and unjust as a feeble
government.
EDMUND BURKE, REFLECTIONS ON THE FRENCH
REVOLUTION (1790)

Introduction   1

It is a commonplace that modern economics commenced with Adam
Smith's 1776 treatise, *An Inquiry into the Nature and Causes of the
Wealth of Nations*. Indeed, such was the judgment of Wesley Clair Mitchell (1967, 1969), who held modern economic theory to be little more than
an effort to explain the workings of the industrial system.[1] The specification of a point of reference is important. One can realistically identify the
year 1776 with the "discovery" of the essential cooling jacket for steam
engines, and with the framing of the American (Lockean) Declaration of
Independence. The year can then, beyond serving as the point of departure of modern economics, serve also as the starting point of what we
typically refer to as the Industrial Revolution, and the birth date of the
prototypical divided check-and-balance form of government. In identifying 1776 with the genesis of the Industrial Revolution and the modern
democratic republic, historians seek a definite point of departure for
modern events; they desire to in effect identify a zero point from which
they can create a scale to measure the impact of what followed. Likewise

1. The second chapter of his history of economic thought is entitled, "Adam Smith
and How Political Economy Came to be Systematized in England."

with Mitchell, he defined 1776 as the year of the genesis of modern economic thought, not because he believed one could or even should ignore that which went before. Surely he was more of a historian than that. The point he wished to impress upon his audience was that the historical record had relevance for modern thought only so far as it cast light on what had transpired since the departure point. Historians of economic thought, declared Mitchell, thus begin with Smith in an effort to anchor modern thought; Smith is important as a starting point "because his formulation was the earliest which exercised a potent influence upon the work of later times. In large measure Adam Smith summed up and presented in superior form the contributions of his predecessors . . ." Mitchell 1967, vol. I, 48–49).

The line of argument of this chapter does not deal with the watershed of manufacturing technology, notwithstanding its great import to economics, as it led directly to a restructuring of economic relationships and resulted in a transformation of political and social arrangements as well. Instead, the argument here examines the watershed of British political theory and its rationales during the seventeenth and eighteenth centuries. Thomas Hobbes initiated the tradition by posing the problem and attempting an answer. John Locke accepted the basic problem, but took a different approach to a solution. These two approaches are fundamental in setting the debate on economic paradigms, as they serve to orient the conversation.

Smith's importance is in having provided the first critical hinge in thinking, as economists turned from the original question posed by Hobbes and the solutions posed by his critics, toward questions of their own making. Smith's own advocacies occupy one side of the hinge; the other side is comprised of those advocates of the philosophy of individualism, a philosophical stance occasionally, though erroneously, attributed to Smith. Thus we must consider that Smith's role in the drama was not confined to questions regarded today as uniquely "economic," but rather went deeper, tackling the more essential, if broad, questions of the time. In short, while the ostensible concern of Smith in *The Wealth of Nations* was with economic growth in the advancement of national wealth, Smith was even more interested in how one could show persuasively just what were the bases of successful social organization: the best organizational structure is the one that promotes the greatest expansion of national wealth. While it is indeed true that in *The Wealth of Nations* he treated of the bases of economic efficiency, that was not his primary interest, as will become evident in what follows. The emphasis here is on Smith's philosophical beliefs, which are central to his economic understandings.

While we will in due course take up Smith's *economic* contributions (in the companion volume *Factors and Markets*), he first must be placed in historical and intellectual perspective. To achieve this purpose we will begin, even prior to a discussion of the philosophical underpinnings of his economics, by attending to the great watershed in political thinking that took place at the time in which he wrote.

The Nature and Significance of Hobbes's Challenge   2

The Intellectual Environment   2.1

In many ways the peculiar development of economic thought, particularly as it is perceived virtually universally today, reflects English experience with the tensions between religious and secular thought. The conflict within the Church of England did not follow basic theological lines so much as it did the establishment of rival clergies. The Church of England clergy, often very High Church (meaning ritual- or rites-minded), eschewed much of the individualism that characterized Protestant developments on the Continent during this same period and the Low Church (chapel) movement of the eighteenth and nineteenth centuries in England, Wales, and Scotland. In other words, the fight was not always but more frequently than not between clergymen, pitting the High Church types in continuing conflict with Low Church partisans. What leavened the conflict was the insinuation into the debate of essentially semi–Low Church non-clergy (or ex-clergy) such as the Unitarian Isaac Newton and a host of Scottish philosophers who embraced what may be referred to as "Common Sense" thinking. As shall be seen, much of their effort went into arguing the old question of whether cognition was built on faith or vice versa.

No small part of the intellectual battle was fought out on the plane of Parliament versus the Crown, but the contestants also included judges. Two are particularly interesting: Francis (Lord) Bacon (1561–1626)[2]— King James's advocate, who headed the Equity Court System, serving as Chief Justice of the King's Bench—and Edward Coke (1552–1634)[3]— the Parliament's "advocate," who headed the Common Law Court System as Chief Justice of the High Court. Bacon's legal specialty derived

---

2. Francis Bacon, Baron Verulum, Viscount St. Albans, was an amazing figure, at once a lawyer, philosopher, scientist, essayist, and even statesman. At age 12 he entered Trinity College, Cambridge; at 23 he was elected to Parliament. His official positions under James I included Solicitor-General (1609), Attorney-General (1613), Lord Keeper of the Great Seal (1617), and Lord Chancellor (1618). His major works include *The Advancement of Learning* (1605) and *Novum Organum* (1620).

3. Coke was educated at Trinity College, Cambridge, served as solicitor general and speaker of the House of Commons, then was appointed attorney general by Elizabeth I (1594). James I appointed him chief justice of the Court of Common Pleas (1606), but in this capacity he became a vocal opponent of the Court of High Commission, favoring the Common Law over the prerogatives of the Crown. This stance led to his appointment (on the advice of Bacon) to a lesser court, and to his eventual dismissal in 1616. In 1620 he returned to Parliament.

from judgments wherein the law, lacking specificity, required attention to procedure; if followed, this path gave authority to the judges to render opinions which were "right" (many requests to appeal to this court open with the words, "that right may be done"). This is essentially the Natural Law tradition: there was at work an unseen but nonetheless prevailing mechanism that served to drive the system to the provision of the good.[4] Coke's specialty, by way of contrast, was to employ previously accepted court decisions to give flesh to the bones of legislative enactment and royal decrees; that is, he invoked the inviolability of precedent.[5] Actions are not to be restrained by appeal to moral or ethical strictures which antedate social incorporation, but are instead regulated by an appeal to governmental prescription, namely, legal codes. This debate was to continue in the Hobbes–Locke and Mandeville–Smith arguments and is alive and well in the present day.

Aside from the developments within theology and law, there was a concurrent development in English political theory.[6] The challenger in this intellectual crusade was Thomas Hobbes (1588–1679),[7] a graduate of Magdalen College, Oxford, and a physician by training, whose career included having been a literary secretary (really something of an apprentice-amanuensis) to Francis Bacon. It was Bacon who in a sense forged Hobbes's view of science and method. After Bacon's death, Hobbes, having rejected the Scholastic method as a result of Bacon's influence, embraced the approach of Euclid and Galileo. This was the "resolutive-compositive method," by which one first asserted that a

---

4. As Overton H. Taylor stated the principle: "In the eighteenth century . . . this idea [of mechanistic determinism] was still combined with the theological idea of an harmonious 'Order of Nature,' in which every thing or being has a definite, ideal function to fulfill in the wisely planned economy of the cosmos. The world-machine was admired as a wise contrivance of the Deity for causing every part of the whole to fulfill its function. Hence the 'laws of nature,' tho conceived as laws of mechanical causation, were also and at the same time conceived as 'canons of conduct' providentially imposed upon things" (Taylor 1929, 8).

5. The consensus is that the Coke position in the end came to dominate, although Karl Polyani (1944) argued that the position succeeded primarily because the royal opposition slowed the process to the point where it could be assimilated without an upheaval. This was something akin to the French revolutionary turmoil which destroyed so much and which was in the end itself resolved in an antirevolutionary but unstable victory.

6. Such changes had also occurred in France and Italy. Cf. such French writers as Jean Bodin (1576), Montaigne (1595), and Montesquieu (1721, 1734, and most important of all 1748), and the Italian Niccolò Machiavelli (1532).

7. At Oxford, Hobbes specialized in mathematics and physics. After Oxford, he served for a time as tutor to the children of the son of William Cavendish, Lord Hardwick, and later as secretary to Cavendish (the second Earl of Devonshire). He remained a family retainer and returned as tutor on more than one occasion. He also traveled extensively and became a corresponding friend with men of the likes of Galileo Galilei. At one point he was tutor to the crown prince (later Charles II) while in exile. Hobbes, whose views were anything but those of the house of Stuart, returned to England during the Cromwellian Commonwealth. He was wont to keep a low profile, but nonetheless was received at court by the restored Charles II.

complex (observable) event or phenomenon was actually the result of simpler, but unobservable, factors, and then "imagined" the correct set of factors that could produce the observed phenomenon.[8] Hobbes sought to extend this scientific method to the social and political realms. In effect he attempted to create a "science" of politics and social order, and in so doing produced in 1651 one of the great seminal treatises of Western civilization, *Leviathan*.

Leviathan: *The Crucible*   2.2

In *Leviathan: Or the Matter, Forme and Power of a Commonwealth Ecclesiasticall and Civil,* Hobbes sought to explain "historically" (although in point of fact he proceeded logically) the bases for the organization of society and of government, specifically as they affect the monarchy. He sought, in short, to identify both the essential nature of man and the underlying motivations behind his actions. Once these explanations for behavior were accepted, the form of social organization best suited to this behavior could be exposed and such a society created.[9]

Hobbes's view of being allows him at times to draw authoritative conclusions from his "empirical," sometimes even anecdotal, observations.[10] But this should not be taken as evidence that he was a strict empiricist,[11] for he held to a fundamental belief in the primacy of ratiocination (including *histoire raisonnée*).[12] He believed, following on the scientific methodology of Euclid and Galileo, that the resolutive-compositive method could be applied to social and political concerns, especially the direction of the monarchical state. More importantly, as Pribram (1983, 62) has suggested, the idea of security as the basis for the Hobbesian social contract emerged as a *utilitarian*—"useful is as useful does"—objective, replacing the Scholastic philosophers' *moral* objective of the pursuit of the greatest good.

According to Hobbes, that which we perceive is not merely a simple,

---

8. On this view of Hobbes's method, and the influence on his thought of Galileo, see the introduction to *Leviathan* by C. B. Macpherson.

9. Macpherson (1962) held that Hobbes's "observations" were of his contemporary England and the relations engendered by the rise of commercialism. Isaiah Berlin (1962) disagreed, and, in an extended review of Macpherson's book, concluded that Macpherson had viewed Hobbes through the lens of Marx and so had infused Hobbes's timeless savage with the attributes of the seventeenth-century merchant.

10. As Bertrand Russell summed up Hobbes's methodology: "He is impatient of subtleties, and too much inclined to cut the Gordian knot. His solutions of problems are logical, but are attained by omitting awkward facts. He is vigorous, but crude; he wields the battle-axe better than the rapier" (Russell 1945, 546).

11. Steven Shapin and Simon Schaffer (1985) noted that, in his feud with Robert Boyle, Hobbes demonstrated his ability to reject the experimental method in favor of reason.

12. This is sometimes translated as conjectural history. In use it amounts to the position that, "if the facts do not bear out this point, they should."

atomic "fact"; it is rather a composite, a complex whole, composed of simpler, unobservable but not imponderable constituent parts. These constituents, while hidden from sensory perception, are nonetheless not beyond imagination, and so they are readily made known to any insightful intellect which takes the time to ponder their existence and to accept their self-evident nature. This is a reason for considering Hobbes as a "rational materialist." As this method is valuable in the sciences, it can be extended to politics; the motions (motives) of man can be fathomed in the same course as the motions of physical bodies. But the difference is that in politics one must constantly reaffirm one's eductions through introspection. As Hobbes insisted,

> . . . *Wisedome* is acquired, not by reading of *Books,* but of *Men.* . . . But there is another saying not of late understood, by which they might learn truly to read one another, if they would take the pains; and that is, *Nosce teipsum, Read thy self.* . . . [F]or the similitude of the thoughts, and Passions of one man, to the thoughts, and Passions of another, whosoever looketh into himself, and considereth what he doth, when he does *think, opine, hope, feare, &c,* and upon what grounds; he shall thereby read and know, what are the thoughts, and *Passions* of all other men, upon the like occasions. . . . And though by mens actions wee do discover their designe sometimes; yet to do it without comparing them with our own, and distinguishing all circumstances, by which the case may come to be altered, is to decypher without a key, and be for the most part deceived, by too much trust, or by too much diffidence. . . .
> . . . He that is to govern a whole Nation, must read in himself, not this, or that particular man; but Man-kind. . . . [W]hen I shall have set down my own reading orderly, and perspicuously, the pains left another, will be onely to consider, if he also find not the same in himself. For this kind of Doctrine, admitteth no other Demonstration. (Hobbes 1651, Introduction, 82–83; emphasis in original)

Each of the composite parts of the representative human actor—his senses, imagination, thought processes, reasonings, impulses, and so on—is capable of examination and explanation. Once so dissected and understood, these constituents can be reassembled to give an understanding of the actor himself and the method of his apprehension of the environment, including his methods of reasoning and reacting. The whole is for Hobbes precisely the sum of its parts; the human actor is after all no more complex than is the mechanism of a watch.[13] A simple application of the principles of Newton's physics or Euclid's geometry is sufficient to

---

13. "For what is the *Heart,* but a *Spring;* and the *Nerves,* but so many *Strings;* and the *Joynts,* but so many *Wheeles,* giving motion to the whole Body, such as was intended by the Artificer?" (Hobbes 1651, Introduction, 81; emphasis in original).

understand the functioning of an individual and the social and political system of which he is a part.[14]

Further, the system as an organic whole—the state—is no more complicated than the representative human agent, and so the society is ponderable as a complete and viable organism. Consequently, the state (or Leviathan) "is but an Artificiall Man" (1651, Introduction, 82). We may therefore "know" the state in precisely the same manner in which we "know" ourselves and other men. The state is a body whose constitution is perceived as a single unity, but which is nonetheless divisible and understandable as the sum of its constituent parts, much as is the human body by the anatomist. The "Body Politique" is an organism[15]

> ... in which, the *Soveraignty* is an Artificiall *Soul,* as giving life and motion to the whole body; The *Magistrates,* and other *Officers* of Judicature and Execution, artificiall *Joynts; Reward* and *Punishment* (by which fastned to the seate of the Soveraignty, every joynt and member is moved to performe his duty) are the *Nerves,* that do the same in the Body Naturall; The *Wealth* and *Riches* of all the particular members, are the *Strength; Salus Populi* (the *peoples safety*) its *Businesse; Counsellors,* by whom all things needfull for it to know, are suggested unto it, are the *Memory; Equity* and *Lawes,* an artificiall *Reason* and *Will; Concord, Health; Sedition, Sicknesse;* and *Civill war, Death.* Lastly, the *Pacts* and *Covenants,* by which the parts of this Body Politique were at first made, set together, and united, resemble that *Fiat,* or the *Let us make man,* pronounced by God in the Creation. (1651, Introduction, 81–2; emphasis in original)

For Hobbes, all men are created equal "in the faculties of body, and mind" and are viewed by others as such in a crude state of nature (1651, chap. 13, 183).[16] But man is continually confronted by two countervailing forces: the desire for self-preservation and the desire for conquest. These sometimes conflicting, sometimes concerted forces create tensions which must ultimately drive the ungoverned masses, in their constant competition for limited resources, to conflict. These forces impinging on the

---

14. Paul P. Christensen esteemed Hobbes to have contributed to economic method in providing the basis for "a physiologically based psychology and a physiological economics," in contrast to the mechanistic (Newtonian) economics usually attributed to him (Christensen 1989, 690).

15. See the previous note.

16. Note Hobbes: "[A]s that though there bee found one man sometimes manifestly stronger in body, or of quicker mind then another; yet when all is reckoned together, the difference between man, and man, is not so considerable, as that one man can thereupon claim to himselfe any benefit, to which another may not pretend, as well as he. For as to the strength of body, the weakest has strength enough to kill the strongest, either by secret machination, or by confederacy with others, that are in the same danger with himselfe" (Hobbes 1651, chap. 13, 183).

individual give rise to "laws of nature." Such laws represent Hobbes's perception of a reasonable man's psychology.[17] He avers that he derived them empirically from personal scrutiny; they are neither definitions nor intellectual constructs, although Hobbes asserts that once they are elucidated, their existence is self-evident.[18] The state of nature is therefore tantamount to a perpetual state of war.

> Whatsoever therefore is consequent to a time of Warre, where every man is Enemy to every man; the same is consequent to the time, wherein men live without other security, than what their own strength, and their own invention shall furnish them withall. In such condition, there is no place for Industry; because the fruit thereof is uncertain: and consequently no Culture of the Earth; no Navigation, nor use of the commodities that may be imported by Sea; no commodious Building; no Instruments of moving; and removing such things as require much force; no Knowledge of the face of the Earth; no account of Time; no Arts; no Letters; no Society; and which is worst of all, continuall feare, and danger of violent death; And the life of man, solitary, poore, nasty, brutish, and short. (1651, part I, chap. 13, 186)

One premise is that life is a struggle and so only those suited to the struggle will survive. Hobbes's "empirical" findings and the premise itself become, by virtue of Hobbes's intellectual standing, authoritative if only as rhetoric. The point fundamental to our interpretation is that these "findings" have been treated throughout the centuries as patristic.

In all, one of Hobbes's fundamental points was to demonstrate the existence of two types of human agreement: the social and the governmental. But what exactly did Hobbes mean by agreement? Two classes may be distinguished, the contract and the covenant. A contract is an agreement between equals (one man with another) requiring mutuality of concerns, while a covenant is an agreement between unequals which is, strictly speaking, not enforceable by the weaker against the stronger. The initial agreement whereby the Leviathan is constituted is a contract, since man is initially in a state of equality. As contracts, these agreements are

17. Hobbes's first and underlying law of nature is "That every man, ought to endeavour Peace, as farre as he has hope of obtaining it; and when he cannot obtain it, that he may seek, and use, all helps, and advantages of Warre." This thought decomposes to "seek Peace, and follow it," and "By all means we can, to defend our selves" (Hobbes 1651, pt. 1, chap. 14, 190).

His second law of nature is "That a man be willing, when others are so too, as farreforth, as for Peace, and defence of himselfe he shall think it necessary, to lay down this right to all things; and be contented with so much liberty against other men, as he would allow other men against himselfe" (190).

18. Hobbes was, after all, a nominalist. See Russell (1945, 549). But Martin Hollis and Edward Nell (1975, 178) regarded his definition of man as real, but perceived as an abstraction.

entered into voluntarily and are legally and morally binding on the parties concerned. The agreements afterward between the state and the populace are covenants, the state being the all-powerful entity to which all are subordinate. Thus the distinction between contract and covenant can be further elaborated as to the role played by fear and the ability to guarantee enforcement of an agreement to which all parties are not of equal stature. Hobbes specified that the original contract if constituted by fear is void, since under such a condition there is no mutuality. On the other hand, a covenant engaged in under the threat of fear is legitimate (or at least not illegitimate), since this is (arguably) the basis for its enactment. While a contract provides an escape for either party, an individual is free from a covenant only by performance or by forgiveness.

So while Hobbes's political and social framework began with the notion of the primacy of the individual, his idealized social order very soon evolved into a prototype of a collectivist, statist society. In effect he accepted the rationalist's need for structure—in this instance the structure afforded by the English monarchy—while basing his arguments on observations. The importance of this conceptualization to economics will become evident throughout the remainder of this work.

Put simply, given the nature of man as Hobbes understood it, the form of social organization and the form of governance was preordained and self-evident. For Hobbes, society had to be "structured" to restrict the base nature of man; he did not trust that man was capable of either organizing or living in a democratic society in which social contracts were arrived at and maintained through peaceful agreement. Democracy could not even be considered as an alternative form of social organization, for the essential nature of man required that his passions be restrained by the coercive force exerted by a strict authority.

The goal of any form of governance is to preserve peaceful coexistence among the citizenry in an arena in which unrestrained desires led naturally to conflict.[19] The most efficient state structure for the attainment of this goal must be, from the Hobbesian perspective, an absolute monarchy, brought about by a sort of social covenant. Under this covenant, all concerned agree that they are better served if they are less free in the pursuit of their individual goals; man is best served if his instinct to natural competitiveness is restrained.[20] While rejecting the suggestion that a society predicated upon a strong centralized authority has to take the form of a hereditary monarchy *divinely* ordained, Hobbes did argue that the ruling authority, in Hobbes's case the monarch, had to possess *absolute* power. The legitimacy and power of the government was predicated

---

19. The determinism, indeed fatalism, of Hobbes is apparent from this statement.

20. Schumpeter argued that this conclusion of Hobbes did not derive from his stated premises: "the thesis of governmental omnipotence has no analytic standing. . . . Hobbes simply deduced it from the imaginary covenant by arbitrarily interpreting it in such a way as to imply unconditional surrender of the citizen" (Schumpeter 1954, 119–20).

on its capacity to use overwhelming force, when necessary, as a means of controlling the populace and the internal political climate. Since a strong case could be made for peaceful compliance, force need not necessarily be employed. When the provision of law and order become threatened, however, force must be used, lest the monarch be accused of losing his purpose and his mandate to govern. This would risk his replacement by one whose willingness to keep the internal order was not so compromised.

2.3 Challenges to Hobbes

Hobbes's ideas as to the problem of reconciling individual motives and desires with social and political order brought forth not one but several storms of protest. These served as the bases for later intellectual developments, some of which will be dealt with here. The first challenge centered on Hobbes's epistemology. His materialism—the insistence that knowledge begins with cognition—seemed at odds with the Christian assertion that one not only can but must begin with pure faith.[21] Hobbes's views, when considered seriously, flew straight in the face of what seemed the most basic Christian doctrine, namely the importance of salvation and everything else Godly (cf. the doctrine of transubstantiation).[22] Hence the Hobbesian system could not escape being labeled as heretical.

A second challenge centered on Hobbes's view of the relations between men and nations. His perception that force underlay virtually all social systems and social relationships suggested that for man there was no immutable right and wrong, no moral imperatives, but only naked, brute compulsion. The right was that which served to secure for each man the most power. Good could be defined accordingly. Thus was laid an intellectual foundation for the economic theories of Malthus and Steuart, and even for a rudimentary form of natural selection.

A third challenge centered on the argument that consensus could be (and generally was) achieved by force. One gained consensus when the relevant enemies (the opposition) were no longer in a position to oppose or thwart one's wishes. If the strong ensure that their will is manifest, this dictum seemed to strip leadership of its preeminent claim to having, per se, any moral authority or dignity.

Leviathan precipitated several lines of critical thinking. Of these, five are truly worth noting. Four of these shall be discussed later in more detail.

- The first was the ecclesiastical answer proposed by the Christian clerics Bishop Butler and Bishop Berkeley, as well as Lord Shaftesbury.

---

21. That is to say, Platonic ideas.

22. Transubstantiation is the Roman Catholic doctrine of the essential transformation of the bread (wafer) and wine of communion into the body and blood, respectively, of Christ.

- The second was the politicoeconomic answer advanced by John Locke. This answer is exceptionally important, because it not only brought forth what Americans take to be the theory of limited representative government, but also offered a rationale for the establishment of the property right, that is, the right of estate.[23]

- The third answer was the proposal of Bernard de Mandeville in his *Fable of the Bees*. This is the argument of the empiricists. It is also important as the facilitator of much discussion as to the role of selfishness in the smooth and efficient functioning of an economic system. For this reason alone Mandeville's commentary itself precipitated several lines of rebuttal.

- The fourth answer was Adam Smith's dual position that (1) Hobbes's observation about the individualistic and brutal nature of man derived from a partly erroneous observation about men's instincts, and (2) that the love of plenty could be enough to encourage individuals to cooperate with one another (to the point of generating a spirit of mutual dependence). Each man need only be assured that the cooperation was essentially his own voluntary decision, that is, that no outcome was imposed. Smith's answers also served as a rebuttal to Mandeville and so set the stage for consideration of motives behind human economizing.

- The fifth was the development of a theory of individualism and utilitarianism (the topic of a later chapter) which, while at the center of Hobbes's philosophy, had been for him subsumed by the interests of the collective.

Confronting the Hobbes Challenge: The Ecclesiastical Answer   3

The Nature of the Challenges   3.1

As Hobbes was writing about the nature of man, the nature of social organization, and the relationship between man and truth (God's truth, if you will), the obvious reactions to the crushing burden of these views were left to those who dealt with these metaphysical topics. The nature of man is one of the points of entry of Christian doctrine (Original Sin). It is not surprising then that the ecclesiastics got into the act early and stayed late.

The ecclesiastical answers to Hobbes were immediately forthcoming. At the time Hobbes wrote, he was a political conservative, although his religious views were not broadcast. While he took care to give no

---

23. Cf. M. Perlman (1996).

explicit offense either to the Catholics or to the Cromwellian reformers and Puritans, his method clearly suggested that the source of authority was not God, but power. Power relationships were the most important because they were readily seen as the most effective, as offering empirical evidence of a correlation with success and achievement and the ways of the world. Such a position should have been, and indeed was, an offense to anyone who reckoned God as the Benign Author of the system.

The Hobbes position generated great reaction from these quarters. Among these were a variety of truly self-consciously Christian responses.

3.2 Joseph Bishop Butler

One Christian argument held that reason, along with revelation—together God's great gifts to mankind—underlay the English equivalent of St. Augustine's City of God. Joseph Bishop Butler (1692–1752)[24] argued that he could construct a rational defense of the Christian godly system, one eschewing force and embracing love, in contrast to the system of Hobbes. Butler's point was that if one obeyed the Beatitudes and the injunctions deriving therefrom, Christ would reappear and we would enjoy "heaven on earth." The Butler argument was based on a brand of "corporatism"— simply, if everyone would do the Christian (read "proper") thing, the system would fuse, leading sin and pain to disappear. To paraphrase Browning, 'God's in His heaven—All's right with the world!' Butler posed his system as an alternative to the one of crude force advanced by Hobbes, but the result was not dissimilar: the individual was subordinated to the interests of the greater whole. The difference emerges in the *form* of the collective, and this difference is important. Hobbes's collective was secular, Butler's religious. To put it bluntly, reason led, according to Butler, to Christian cooperation, the emergence of a Christian state, and eventually the Second Coming. Thus we arrive at quite a different outcome from the one envisioned by Hobbes.

3.3 George Bishop Berkeley

Another Christian argument dealt with revelation (i.e., faith) and whether it was truly separate from reason. The Hobbesian system was not completely without faith, but its role was surely downplayed—particularly when it came to the sources of informed knowledge. For Hobbes, material reality was the only existence; spirituality and belief (i.e., belief in an otherworldly existence beyond the material) must be denied. For him, any explanation of existence must be made in materialistic, Newtonian me-

---

24. Butler is well-known for his 1726 *Fifteen Sermons* and his 1736 *The Analogy of Religion, Natural and Revealed, to the Constitution and Course of Nature.* An anti-Deist, he favored the Trinitarian Christian approach.

chanical terms. George Bishop Berkeley (1685–1753)[25] argued that faith was at the bottom of every system, including that of Hobbes. He differed from Hobbes in believing that Christian faith was benign and led ultimately to the realization of the Augustinian City of God, while he noted that Hobbes required the services of God only in the act of Creation. For those who questioned the rational basis of faith, Berkeley replied that one had faith about the existence of natural phenomena that were outside of our immediate perceptions, irrespective of what else was said. One "solves" the dilemmas of induction and empiricism by positing an Omniscient Being who sees all. We require a metaphysic in order to justify assertions about things of which we are not completely and constantly aware. In this way we make logical sense of the workings of nature.[26]

Thus, whereas Butler held that the Christian faith alone would suffice, Berkeley advanced the thought that faith and reason were not merely opposite sides of the same coin. True reason, he suggested, was not the result simply of processed empirical observation or of Platonic essences; it could be a combination of the two.

Anthony Ashley Cooper, Lord Shaftesbury   3.4

One of the more interesting ecclesiastical answers to Hobbes was enunciated by Anthony Ashley Cooper (1671–1713), the third Earl of Shaftesbury.[27] Tutored by Locke, Cooper was undoubtedly influenced by the fact

---

25. Berkeley was an able man given to causes, one of which was an ill-fated college in Bermuda established to train native Americans. To prepare himself he lived three years in Rhode Island but chose to return to Britain when the project's financing fouled. An articulate writer against atheism, he was a thorough believer in subjective idealism, differing from Locke who believed that although some topics were entirely subjective, others, even if subjectively perceived, were objective. Berkeley traced the divine influence as present through God's regular penetration of each person's subjective consciousness, and everything became a matter of belief in God. God manipulates us through our minds, and therefore through our faith. Everything is a God-derived sense of quality; things as such are derivative.

Berkeley wrote prolifically. In 1709 he published *Essay Towards a New Theory of Vision*, in 1710 *A Treatise Concerning the Principles of Human Knowledge*, and in 1713 *Three Dialogues Between Hylas and Philonous*, to list but three.

26. "As a balance therefore to this weight of prejudice, let us throw into the scale the great advantages that arise from the belief of immaterialism, both in regard to religion and human learning. The being of a God, and incorruptibility of the soul, those great articles of religion, are they not proved with the clearest and most immediate evidence? When I say the being of a *God,* I do not mean an obscure general cause of things, whereof we have no conception, but *God,* in the strict and proper sense of the word. . . . Then with relation to human sciences; in natural philosophy, what intricacies, what obscurities, what contradictions, has the belief of matter led men into!" (Berkeley 1713, 202–3).

27. The third Earl of Shaftesbury, Baron Cooper of Pawlett, Baron Ashley of Wimborne St. Giles, attended Winchester College. In 1695 he entered Parliament, becoming a member of the House of Lords with his succession as the third Earl in 1699. He is most noted for his collection, *Characteristics of Men, Manners, Opinions, and Times* (1711).

that Locke was politically and socially allied with his grandfather, the first Earl (about whom more later). Locke's influence aside, the dominant influence on Cooper's thinking seems to have been the Cambridge Platonists, a group of philosophers who attempted to blend the ethics of Christianity with the logic of rational humanism. The philosopher John Austin is also said to have been a strong influence on his thinking.

Cooper was interested primarily in the origins of right and wrong. Essentially antirationalist, he held that morality was a balanced sense between the extremes of egoism and altruism. The test of the balance was the recognition of an actual personal happiness simultaneous with the development of a general social well-being. Granted that the author of right was God, his question centered on the degree to which the individual has instilled in him a feeling for right (and thereby wrong). His answer was that just as every human being is born with the usual five cognitive senses (seeing, smelling, feeling, hearing, and tasting), he is also born with an ethical sense of right and wrong. This "sixth sense" is a sense of morality, or to use a characteristic adjectival inflection, a "moral sense." In other words, in every "normal" person, normal in birth and in development, there is, to use the phrase from the Book of Kings, a "still, small voice." Cooper held that when individuals are taught to listen for and to the voice, they know what is right.[28]

3.5 Dissatisfaction with the Ecclesiastical Answers

It is neither particularly difficult nor all that easy to understand why these answers to Hobbes satisfied some just as they failed to persuade others. If one had religious faith, these answers, built as they were on that faith, made rational sense. Yet, if one lacked Christian faith and a belief in the Divine mysteries, there was nothing to build upon. A somewhat more rationally challenging answer to the Hobbes question can be found in the extensive and equally provocative writings of John Locke (1632–1704).[29]

28. As Pribram noted, "the belief in the general validity of ethical judgments was based on the view that feelings for fellow human beings are bound to develop in those who live habitually in society, and that such feelings are likely to prevail over the exercise of pure self-interest" (Pribram 1983, 121). Pribram associated Shaftesbury's philosophy with (Millian) Utilitarianism; the connection with Smith will become evident in the discussion of the *Theory of Moral Sentiments*.

29. Locke was born into a family of wealthy clothiers, who had elevated themselves to the minor gentry; his father was a notary who had acquired land holdings, and who supported Parliament in the English Civil War. Educated at the Westminster School (where he was named King's Scholar), Locke won a scholarship to Christ Church, Oxford (1652), where he studied in the classics, rhetoric, languages, moral philosophy, natural philosophy, logic, and metaphysics (B.A., 1656; M.A., 1659). At about the time he received his M.A., he was elected a student of Christ Church (the equivalent of a fellow).

Following brief stints as Lecturer in Greek (1660) and Lecturer in Rhetoric (1662), he was elected Censor of Moral Philosophy (1663), in which capacity he lectured on the "Law of Nature." In 1665 he was named secretary to a diplomatic mission to Brandenburg,

Confronting the Hobbes Challenge: Locke's Political   4
Answer and Its Economic Implications

Locke's Entrance   4.1

Although the ecclesiastical responses to Hobbes's challenge initiated the seventeenth-century debate concerning the nature of man and the appropriate form of governance, it was John Locke's answer to Hobbes's question, phrased in terms of "the rights of government," which from the start commanded virtually universal attention. The reason seems to be obvious. Hobbes and Locke, writing in a time and place when most things were affected by (or even devoted to) civil turmoil, mirrored in their writing and thinking the discussions that both caused that turmoil and were its result. Locke viewed the process from the perspective of an eyewitness to events: he had been for much of his adult life part of the household of Anthony Ashley Cooper, first Earl of Shaftesbury (1621–83),[30] serving

Prussia. Upon his return he reentered Oxford. At Oxford, the senior studentships were largely reserved for those who had taken holy orders: of the sixty positions, only five—two in law, two in medicine, and one in moral philosophy—were open to those who did not take the orders. Locke decided to study medicine to circumvent the requirement, as he had been fascinated with the subject at least since his arrival at Oxford. (His medical training included work with the experimental scientist and renowned chemist Robert Boyle and the physician Thomas Sydenham.) By 1666 Locke had completed enough of the requirements to be considered a competent physician (although he never received his doctorate in the subject). With the weight of a personal letter written on his behalf by Charles II to the Dean of the Chapters of Christ Church, Locke was relieved of the necessity of taking holy orders and was granted a position at the college, free of any obligation to teach.

His acquaintance with Cooper, the first Earl of Shaftesbury (from 1666, at which time Cooper was Lord Ashley) furthered his political fortunes (of which more below). In 1674, as Shaftesbury's political fortunes were on the decline, Locke returned to Oxford and received the degree of Bachelor of Medicine. Unsatisfied with Oxford, and suffering from asthma, he left for France, where he spent the next four years (1675–79), after which he returned to Oxford. With the exile of Lord Shaftesbury—following the discovery of his role in the Monmouth Rebellion—Locke fled to Holland (he had been placed on the Duke of York's 'enemies list'), where he continued work on his *Essay Concerning Human Understanding* (published 1690); he remained there from 1683 to 1689. In 1689 he returned to England (at the ascension of William of Orange), where he became renowned for his political and economic insights.

Locke was elected a fellow of the Royal Society in 1668.

30. The first Earl of Shaftesbury, Baron Cooper of Pawlett, Baron Ashley of Wimborne St. Giles was also, from the age of ten, Sir Anthony Ashley Cooper, 2d Baronet. He entered the Short Parliament (1640) for Tewkesbury, but did not continue in the Long. Through his marriage to Lady Cecil, sister of the Earl of Exeter, he secured membership on a committee for legal reform. From this platform, he was selected for the Barebone's Parliament (1653), where he was active in authorizing powers for Cromwell. With the return of Charles II, he was named Privy Councillor (1660) and Baron Ashley (1661). In 1672, the year he became Lord High Chancellor of England (and was named first Earl of Shaftesbury), he also formed and headed the Privy Council Committee for Trade and the Plantations. In 1681 Cooper was arrested and imprisoned in the Tower of London on a charge of treason for his part in the Monmouth Rebellion.

in the capacity of resident physician. It was through his relationship with Lord Shaftesbury that Locke turned his attention from the pursuit of medicine to problems of a more political and philosophical nature.[31]

The Cooper (Shaftesbury) family, as one of the leading Whig families of the period, was attempting at this time to create a governmental system that could provide stability without what the Whigs thought would be royal tyranny. The first Earl, Lord Shaftesbury had been deeply involved in the political machinations of the period. During the English Civil War, he first took the side of the monarch, then less than a year later (1644) sided with the Parliament. Instrumental as a member of the Barebones Parliament in bringing Oliver Cromwell to power, he served under Cromwell in the Council of State (1654), but eventually became concerned with the Lord Protector's authoritarianism. Having withdrawn from politics for several years, in 1660 he was appointed to the commission to persuade Charles II to accept the crown. For his efforts he was named Lord High Chancellor (1672), but was later removed from all political office for among other things conspiring to deny the crown to Charles's brother, the (Roman Catholic) James, Duke of York. Upon his rehabilitation and emergence as a major Whig parliamentarian, he again incurred the wrath of Charles by crusading against the succession to the throne by the Duke of York, which efforts included an attempt to replace the successor with Charles's illegitimate son, the Duke of Monmouth. These incidents undoubtedly influenced the political and social philosophy of Locke, who was in the midst of these actions an adviser to Lord Shaftesbury. In addition, his medical training secured in him a belief in the efficacy of argument by analogy and induction.[32] Thus Locke came on his philosophy of government as he had his philosophy of medicine:

---

31. When Shaftesbury asked Locke whether a bill to lower the usury rate should be enacted, Locke wrote what William Letwin (1963) asserted was the first "scientific" (meaning abstract) economic tract. Locke argued that lowering the interest rate ceiling would give the merchants greater profits, that greater profits would lead them to buy more land, that buying more land would drive up the price of land, and that the landholding aristocracy would benefit.

Americans owe much to Locke. He drafted (for Lord Shaftesbury) the Constitution of the Colony of South Carolina. Locke's phraseology was even adopted in the original draft of the American Declaration of Independence: "We hold these truths to be self-evident— that all men are endowed by their Creator with the inalienable rights of life, liberty, and property." In the second draft Jefferson, Adams, and Franklin (the framers), each a wealthy man, chose to substitute the phrase, "the pursuit of happiness," for "property" or "estate." But the framers of the American Constitution some eleven years later were not so squeamish; the term property appears in the Due Process Clause of the Fifth Amendment.

32. Locke served for a time as amanuensis to Thomas Sydenham (1624–89) in the preparation of the latter's *De Arte Medica;* the draft text, in fact, appears in Locke's hand, a point which has contributed to its being attributed to him (even to the present, as Patrick Romanell [1984] recently made the attribution). See William O. Coleman (1995) for a discussion of Locke's medical views within the confines of the rationalist–antirationalist "debates" over medicine.

he viewed both through the lens of empiricism (or, as William Coleman preferred, antirationalism);[33] certainly, in this context at least, Locke was decidedly much more the pure pragmatist than was Hobbes.[34]

The Emergence of the Social Contract

Locke's answer to the Hobbes challenge was presented in his 1690 *Second Treatise of Government*. The answer was complex, but two parts seem especially relevant to the current discussion. The first part sets forth the basis for the design of the social contract; the second establishes the conditions for the existence and maintenance of a right of property. However, before discussing these components of Locke's philosophy, we must begin, as we did with Hobbes, with a discussion of Locke's view of man and society.

As did Hobbes, Locke believed that man's original state was the base state of nature. Thus both accepted the primacy of the individual in the initial scheme of things. The difference lies in the behavior of each man in the society toward every other man, that is, the motivating force behind social interaction. This results in a different political and social structure within which the individual must function. Whereas in Hobbes's primitive state men are in a continual struggle, a constant state of war with one another, Locke's state is guided by divinely inspired Natural Law. In contrast to the order depicted by Hobbes, Locke allows a place for the working of free will.[35] As with Hobbes's man, Locke's man exists initially in a state of equality with all other men; unlike Hobbes's man, Locke's accepts a peaceful coexistence with others, even though he is continually under pressure to act in favor of his own best interests, perhaps to the detriment of the social order. But Locke's man is restrained by the dictates of a strong sense of moral obligation; in other words, Locke invokes Natural Law as a behavioral code.

> To understand political power right, and derive it from its original, we must consider, what state all men are naturally in, and that is, a

33. Coleman defined rationalism as a set of doctrines maintaining that "the world is a structure, not an anarchy. It is a system, not a chaos. This structure is commonly supposed . . . to be a *structure of hierarchy*." Antirationalists hold, by contrast, that the "world is not a structure; it is a heap. The variety we observe is a reality, not a phantom; it is fundamental, not superficial. Specific realities can be explained only by reference to other specific realities, not by fewer and fewer general laws" (W. O. Coleman 1995, 2–3).

34. Russell (1945, 609) even regarded Locke as the founder of empiricism.

35. Free will is the belief that God forwent His Omniscience to man to allow him to fashion his own designs. It may then be seen that Hobbes demands a deterministic universe in all spheres, the mechanical and the moral (political), while Locke accepts that in the moral sphere Natural Laws serve as points toward which we must, willingly because of God's beneficence, inevitably and inexorably gravitate. This is more in the realm of habit and custom, serving as guideposts for behavior divorced from any mechanistic analogy. On this see O. Taylor 1929, 12–14.

state of perfect freedom to order their actions, and dispose of their possessions and persons, as they think fit, within the bounds of the law of nature, without asking leave, or depending upon the will of any other man. (Locke 1690, chap. II, sec. 4, 8; emphasis in original)

The state of nature, characterized by "Men living together according to reason, without a common superior on earth" (chap. III, sec. 19, 15), is seen as opposite to a state of war. But the state of nature cannot last. The society requires a formal apparatus for the protection of individual rights, especially the right of property. While Hobbes's solution relied on the subjugation of the individual to the sovereign, Locke demanded a solution which sought to protect and nurture the individual. To satisfy this need, the individual members of this base state institute a social contract.

In rejecting Hobbes's assertion that power underlay social organization, Locke asserted instead that social power must have limits. He denied that absolute monarchy was a legitimate form of government, since there did not appear to exist under this structure any means to restrict the (potentially) coercive powers of the sovereign. The same applies to all autocratic regimes and all nonconstitutional systems of governance.[36] The limits on Locke's government are the underlying ("Constitutional")[37] authorizations—somewhat reminiscent of the "by what authority" theme of the Biblical patristic tradition. The "authority" here was most probably a Protestant perception of the direct relationship (outside the hierarchical clerical system) between individual man and his God.

Whatever the origin, Locke's position is diametrically opposed to that of Hobbes. Locke's man is under obligation by his Creator to maintain a moral society. Civil society is only possible when "any number of men are so united into one society, as to quit every one his executive power of the law of nature, and to resign it to the public" (1690, chap.

---

36. ". . . he who attempts to get another man into his absolute power, does thereby *put himself into a state of war* with him. . . ." (Locke 1690, chap. III, sec. 17, 14; emphasis in original).

37. Constitutions may be said to exist, even if they do not appear as formal documents. Indeed, the American Constitution is unique not only because it has been in force so long, but because it was written out all at once, albeit formally amended more than 20 times. The French are now into their sixth constitution, and that does not count the number of times they have reverted to monarchy or various other forms of plenary power systems since 1789. The British, on the other hand, do not have a written constitution, as such, but do consider a number of parliamentary acts as basic; all other legislation has to be framed and interpreted within those acts. The French pattern has been to repudiate one constitution and to enact another, an act which permits unlimited discussion. The British constitution can be amended by any Parliament, but parliamentary self-restraint has been necessary to keep too many modifications from diluting the original acts. The American system depends in no small degree on a process inhibiting easy enactment of amendments. In a significant sense, however, the American system, particularly, also relies on judicial reinterpretation of the meaning of the words in the 1787 document and particularly the Bill of Rights (the first ten) and the Fourteenth Amendment.

VII, sec. 89, 47). This is not, however, to suggest that liberty is absolute or that Locke held it to be so. Liberty does not imply the right to move up in the social or economic order; it was simply untenable for Locke to attempt to enumerate ad nauseam a series of rights qua social contrivances predicated on a suspect social or economic or political theory. Changes of this last type (social and economic status, for instance) were beyond Locke's immediate consideration.[38]

> But though this be a *state of liberty,* yet *it is not a state of licence:* though man in that state have an uncontroulable liberty to dispose of his person or possessions, yet he has not liberty to destroy himself, or so much as any creature in his possession, but where some nobler use than its bare preservation calls for it. The *state of nature* has a law of nature to govern it, which obliges every one: and reason, which is that law, teaches all mankind, who will but consult it, that being all *equal and independent,* no one ought to harm another in his life, health, liberty, or possessions. . . . (1690, chap. II, sec. 6, 9; emphasis in original)

The Right of Property   4.3

Locke's perception of the right of property ("estate," as expressed in Locke 1690, sec. 87) is even more complex than it at first seems.[39] For Hobbes, the property right never enters the picture; in the crude state of nature it does not exist. Following the organization of a central (autocratic) governing authority possessing absolute power, any right to property is decided entirely by the government. Locke, to the contrary, held that every individual had the God-given right to life, liberty, and property.[40] His perception of liberty went so far as to include, among other things, the freedom of travel and settlement, that is, the right to flee a place in which one was unhappy. Denial of liberty (equivalent to slavery) meant no more and no less than a restriction on this freedom to flee a tyrannical authority. In the Lockean system, the right to liberty (to move away) meant nothing if one lacked the means to support that move. Hence, to have liberty one may well need (usually did need) property in the form of money, chattel, or land. To deny a property right was tantamount to denying first liberty and then, by extension, life.

---

38. Pribram concluded that "Locke had failed to give a conclusive answer to the dilemma of how to reconcile undesirable human traits, such as greed, avarice, and the like, with the interests of the community" (1983, 120).

39. Mitchell declared that Locke's presentation defined the "modern concept of property" (Mitchell 1969, vol. II, 722). William Coleman declared Locke's notion of property to have been "entirely *a priori*" but still steeped in antirationalism (Coleman 1995, 20–21).

40. "God, who hath given the world to men in common, hath also given them reason to make use of it to the best advantage of life, and convenience. The earth, and all that is therein, is given to men for the support and comfort of their being" (Locke 1690, chap. V, sec. 26, 18).

But property played an even more important role in Locke's system. It was the foundation of his theory of economic relationships between men. The property right in this regard is the right to one's own labor. But the right of property is not an unlimited one; again Natural Law restricts the landholdings to which any single person may lay claim. Locke insisted, for instance, that in agricultural pursuits, a man could own no more land than he could cultivate by his own labor (although he amended this provision by admitting that one could hire another to perform the cultivation, thereby trading labor for remuneration).[41] It was the individual's combining his personal labor with natural resources (or other factors) which expressed the rationale for ownership. Thus ownership (the exercising of the property right) derived from previous labor. Labor was the means by which man asserted his rights of property, and property was the means by which he generally exercised the right to liberty. Thus Locke provided a rationale for a true labor theory of value, a theory not fully exploited until the nineteenth century, and then by the "scientific" economics of Ricardo and Marx.[42]

4.4 Justification of Limited Government

From these arguments Locke fashioned a justification of systems of limited government. The individual retains the primacy attributed to him in the base state, contrary to the position of Hobbes. Governments are to be limited in nature and can only justify their existence in terms of the original and continual consent of the governed (the American case) or through their capacity to permit an orderly transition. American constitutional development is the Lockean argument writ modern. Governments cannot be imposed upon the social structure; they are not simply organizational modes independent of time and place, but are the natural outcomes of social interactions, of the basic human desire for security and support. Locke's thinking is mentioned here for two reasons: one is to indicate that it was a major answer to the Hobbesian gestalt; the other is to indicate how labor-input became perceived as *the* source of market value.

5 A Literary Response: Mandeville's *Fable*[43]

Bernard de Mandeville (1670–1733) responded to the Hobbes question in the form of an allegorical poem, *The Grumbling Hive, Or Knaves*

---

41. ". . . men have agreed to a disproportionate and unequal *possession of the earth*, they having, by a tacit and voluntary consent, found out a way how a man may fairly possess more land than he himself can use the product of, by receiving in exchange for the overplus gold and silver . . ." (Locke 1690, chap. V, sec. 50, 29; emphasis in original).

42. Cf. Karen Vaughn (1980, 87).

43. This section is derived from Mark Perlman (1996).

Turn'd Honest (1705).[44] In its earliest form, Mandeville's poem concerns the activity of a mythical beehive, very much fashioned after the England of his day.[45] In this hive, everyone practices fraud and deceit, while all the time articulating a commitment to piety. The bees, in realizing their own individual desires without respect to social consequences, are all individually corrupt. They are also hypocrites; each pursues naked self-interest, while incidentally asserting his belief in the Christian virtues. The merchants cheat; the soldiers are cowardly and run from their duty to protect the hive; the lawyers litigate without respect to morality, ethics, or legality; the clergy seek to live an easy life instead of caring for the spiritual needs of the community, and so forth. No one regards societal consequences, since one's own aggrandizement must always be preferable to the unknown desires and needs of others. All the while, however, they assert their acceptance of the Christian life with its emphasis on the spirit of benevolence and caring. In spite of the immorality and hypocrisy of it all, the beehive flourishes and prospers as no other hive has ever prospered. In fact, its prosperity is the envy of all the other hives. Mandeville's generalization was that personal immorality had led to social welfare.

Jove, listening to all this pious cant, decides to remove the hypocrisy of the hive; he grants them their wishes to be pious citizens, and in so doing reforms the personalities of the bees. Lo, all the wickedness disappears! Moral virtue and ethical behavior replace rampant vice and corruption. Every member of the hive suddenly begins to live a life structured upon Christian precepts. Merchants give honest weight, soldiers perform their duties with honor, lawyers behave ethically and with reverence to justice, the clergy devotes itself to the spiritual needs of the community and the interests of the poor, and so on. Actions are taken with an eye to propriety and not simply as an avenue for the attainment of social praise. Individual wickedness and unrestrained nihilistic self-interest are eradicated. However, along with the wickedness disappears the prosperity of the hive; chaos reigns while social welfare declines.

The paradox of the fable is that the proliferation of personal vices (private immorality) leads to social virtue and economic prosperity (social good), while personal virtue leads to community disaster and economic depression. Individual cant and dishonesty leads to public happiness;

---

44. In 1714 Mandeville reissued the poem as a book, *The Fable of the Bees*. In 1723 he reissued the earlier edition, including two additional essays. This edition was condemned by the Grand Jury of Middlesex County. In 1724 Mandeville brought out yet another edition and appended the indictment, a letter attacking the book, and his reply. See M. Perlman (1996) for a detailed description of the poem and its subsequent set of remarks, and Hayek (1966) for additional commentary on Mandeville.

45. According to Pribram, Mandeville's poem was predicated on "traditional mercantilist propositions that the ultimate goal of economic policy consisted in achieving the greatest possible national power and that the balance of trade provided the yardstick for measuring economic progress" (1983, 120). The mercantilist interpretation is but one of several possible interpretations, but not the one considered here. See also notes 48 and 49.

individual piety leads to public disharmony. In effect, the social order is maintained not by human design, but by the unintentional interactions of personal egos; in the complexity of human society, the pursuit by individuals of personal ends (irrespective of motive) leads to unanticipated socially beneficial results, in a way that no rational imposition of order could possibly have maintained.[46]

Thus there appears to be a contradiction between morality as practiced individually and the economic and political viability of the society. Private immorality, while destructive of the basic principles of political and social order, is nonetheless essential to its furtherance. But the meaning of Mandeville's morality play is unclear. Did he mean to suggest that the social end, in this case the economic prosperity of the collective, could not be promoted through a morally virtuous citizenry? Or did he mean to suggest that individual virtuosity and morality were fundamentally incompatible with social harmony and thus should be abandoned? Or was he simply stating a paradoxical situation for which no answer could be forthcoming?[47]

Withal, Mandeville sought to address the question of social order in the face of individual (sometimes conflicting) self-interests and the social desirability of the pursuit of naked self-aggrandizement. In demonstrating his position, he found himself in direct conflict with Hobbes, for whom the road to social order lay in the imposition of order designed

---

46. On this see Hayek 1966, 129.

47. In the 1714 reissue of the *Fable*, Mandeville expanded the points he had wished to assert in the first edition. For example, he presented the scenario beginning with a highwayman robbing an honest traveler. Clearly this act is a sin as well as a crime. The highwayman then uses his ill-gotten gains to contract the services of a prostitute, thus committing another sin. However, the prostitute uses the money to purchase bread for herself, which transaction is not sinful. The baker of the bread uses the proceeds of the sale to pay his worker, a transaction which is clearly good morally. The worker then uses the wages to pay a butcher, a transaction that has changed the nature of the money involved from being morally tainted to being something akin to godly. The money has attained a patina of goodness. For Mandeville the entire process is quite confusing; he can only conclude that money is nothing more nor less than a medium of exchange and so is of itself amoral. Through a series of transactions, what began as an immoral act has ended as something altogether different; wickedness has become virtue.

Another point made by Mandeville was that the poor seem to be made happy by work, but miserable by idleness; if they live at the subsistence level, they find satisfaction in the very struggle for survival, but if they are paid too well, their aspirations quickly outstrip any possible means they may be likely to attain for their satisfaction. To keep the poor happy, it is best to attempt to lure foreign capital, so as to provide employment in the production of goods for export. This has the dual result of keeping the domestic poor employed, while entertaining the wealthy entrepreneurs from abroad. The wealthy, both at home and abroad, should be encouraged to adopt a hedonistic lifestyle, so that they too would be compelled to work even harder and more diligently to keep their personal resources at a level commensurate with such high living. The nation would on this account prosper, although the rich should be encouraged to forget about considerations of apostolic poverty to their own situations.

explicitly to restrict conflict.[48] In short, under the conditions recounted by Mandeville, the economic system works even if predicated on Hobbesian ruthless competitiveness and self-aggrandizing individualism. An "invisible hand" acts as a guiding influence to channel the most base instincts of man to the preservation of the overall good. This is the Natural Law element at work, wherein the motivations behind actions are quite irrelevant to an explanation of the end result. The system will be driven ultimately toward the realization of a goal consistent with the preservation, if not the redemption, of society. Thus Mandeville set forth a reasonable description of the workings of a Christian society—in which it is better to live under proscriptive rather than prescriptive limitations, so that the citizenry can do pretty much as it pleases within the bounds stipulated—while most of the Christian theology of the time was in Mandeville's estimation based on little more than pious cant.

The gist of Mandeville's approach is that it is not important to accept categorical imperatives blindly so long as the individual is free to pursue his own ends. Social institutions promoting the public wealth (the common weal) will emerge spontaneously. Thus, the immediate need of the leadership of any society is to keep its members governable. As the citizens are self-willed and full of selfish passions, all sorts of artifices will be employed by the rulers to counter the natural centrifugal forces as unleashed by the citizens' imperfect natures. Mandeville viewed the act of governing itself as encouraging, indeed requiring, the construction of a comprehensive (non-Christian) pseudomorality.[49]

Mandeville's *Fable* reasserted the Hobbesian methodological framework, in that he relied at first on imagination to identify certain basic characteristics of human nature. A physician by profession—Hayek (1966) suggested he even practiced an early form of psychiatry—Mandeville sought to describe things *as they are* rather than *as they ought to be,* a position which gave him much in common, at least methodologically, with Hobbes. Mandeville had learned to suspend any visible professional commitment to the enforcement of the accepted norms of behavior.[50] He effectively made the case for individual liberty in matters of right and wrong. What emerges socially as a result of individual interactions is really not the concern of the individual: absent a fear of unpopularity or conviction for a criminal act (as society defined it), life is as he makes it.

48. As Hayek suggested, Mandeville's "individual strivings" could be "channeled" to the service of the whole of society by the mere presence of "institutions, practices, and rules," which had emerged spontaneously through a sort of natural selection process. See Hayek 1966, 129.

49. This is one explanation of Mandeville's theme. There are four others: The essay represented (1) an extension of the Hobbesian method, with Hobbesian conclusions following; (2) an exercise in seventeenth-century mercantilism; (3) a truly "modern" Christian tract (God in his mysterious ways brings order from the chaos); or (4) a cornerstone of the emerging British utilitarian tradition. See especially M. Perlman 1996.

50. William Coleman (1995) held that Mandeville was, like Locke, an antirationalist.

While Locke and Hobbes stressed variety and hence confusion (in the absence of any organizational or contractual arrangement), Mandeville believed that the system was regular and naturally ordered. Mandeville's theme—that individually we make our own decisions in as reasonable (rational?) a manner as possible, and society shapes these decisions into a workable structure—is in essence a statement of the position later advanced by Smith in his own version of the doctrine of the "invisible hand."[51]

6 Adam Smith's Two Answers: The One to Hobbes's Theory of the Brutish Nature of Man, and the Other to Hobbes's Incomplete Understanding of the Roles of Greed and Self-Determination

6.1 Smith's First Response: The Theory of Moral Sentiments

Adam Smith (1723–90)—Oxford-educated, product of an important Scottish family, Professor of Moral Philosophy at Glasgow[52]—came to the problem of social organization in his 1759 philosophical masterwork, *The Theory of Moral Sentiments*. The importance of this work cannot be

---

51. See Marina Bianchi (1993) for an assessment of Mandeville's position using the tools of game theory to demonstrate the spontaneous emergence of institutional arrangements (in the sense of Hayek) on the basis of self-interest.

52. Smith was born in Kirkcaldy, Scotland, the only child of a lawyer. (His father, also named Adam Smith, died before the child was born.) At age fourteen, he entered the University of Glasgow—at the time something of an intellectual magnet. He remained there until 1740, during which year he won a Snell Scholarship to Balliol College, Oxford, where he stayed until 1746.

After leaving Oxford, Smith returned to Scotland. From 1748 to 1751, he delivered a series of public lectures in Edinburgh on the topics of belles lettres and jurisprudence. These lectures drew the critical attention of notable figures, which attention helped secure for him a position in the faculty of logic at Glasgow. He later (1752) became Professor of Moral Philosophy.

Smith resigned his professorship in 1764 and left for France, where he served as tutor to the Duke of Buccleuch. By 1766 he had returned to Kirkcaldy (where he lived with his mother, who died in 1784) to work on *The Wealth of Nations*, a task which occupied him for the next ten years.

In 1777, he was appointed Commissioner of Customs and Commissioner of Salt Duties for Scotland; in 1783, he was instrumental in the founding of the Royal Society of Edinburgh. He ended his career as Rector of Glasgow University.

In a paper presented at the 1994 meeting of the History of Economics Society, Paul A. Heise painted a vivid portrait of Smith, in stark contrast to the view of him as confused and befuddled. Smith came from a very influential family—his father had served in the capacities of Private Secretary to the earl of London, Clerk of the Courts Martial, and Keeper of the Signet—and so had cultivated many important political connections. "Our" Adam Smith may have used this influence to gain the Snell scholarship and almost certainly did so in his application to the Chair of Logic at Glasgow, for he seems to have been the only applicant! (See Heise 1994 for details.)

overestimated, for the philosophical beliefs presented served as the ethical foundations to the economic superstructure that later emerged in *The Wealth of Nations*.

In his first line of attack on Hobbes, Smith asserted that his own observations on the nature of man were quite different from his predecessor's. Understanding the constitution of Smith's man and Hobbes's man is essential to understanding the type of society each deemed desirable and achievable; these differences determine the manner in which man is to be governed, and the rationale behind the appropriateness and necessity of this choice. Both held that the nature of man defines the nature of the system best suited to his governance. Hobbes's conception of man, according to Smith, is as a simple, fearful animal, who enters into social arrangements, social contracts, out of a sense of impending doom—a pathological fear of the motives and actions of his fellow men—and not from any desire for the company of others.

> According to Mr. Hobbes . . . man is driven to take refuge in society, not by any natural love which he bears to his own kind, but because without the assistance of others he is incapable of subsisting with ease or safety. Society, upon this account, becomes necessary to him, and whatever tends to its support and welfare, he considers as having a remote tendency to his own interest; and, on the contrary, whatever is likely to disturb or destroy it, he regards as in some measure hurtful or pernicious to himself. Virtue is the great support, and vice the great disturber of human society. (Smith 1790, part VII, sec. iii, chap. 1, 315)

Man enters into a social contract because he is compelled to do so, not because he has any sympathetic feeling for his fellow men, or any felt desire for or spirit of community.

Smith's man is, on the other hand, of a completely different mold. Smith's man "has a natural love for society, and desires that the union of mankind should be preserved for its own sake, and though he himself was to derive no benefit from it" (1790, part II, sec. ii, chap. III, 88). While Smith is aware that there exists in man what may be termed a selfish nature—that man undertakes actions primarily for what are perceived as solipsistic[53] motives—this is not in fact the whole of his underlying motivations. While it is true that man often engages in activities that have the outward appearance of being motivated by selfish concerns, these actions are only superficially so; there is a more complex rationale behind man's actions—his sense of morality and idea of community.[54] Order and community are of paramount importance. For Smith's man, "[t]he orderly

---

53. Solipsism is the theory that the self is the only thing that can be known and verified; it is the only reality.

54. William Coleman (1995) held that Smith maintained a posture of "instrumental rationality," blurring the rationalist–antirationalist distinction.

and flourishing state of society is agreeable to him, and he takes delight in contemplating it. Its disorder and confusion, on the contrary, is the object of his aversion, and he is chagrined at whatever tends to produce it" (88). In fact, Smith began the *Theory of Moral Sentiments* with a note of optimism about the nature of man:

> How selfish soever man may be supposed, there are evidently some principles in his nature, which interest him in the fortune of others, and render their happiness necessary to him, though he derives nothing from it except the pleasure of seeing it. (Part I, sec. i, chap. 1, 9)

This feeling that man has a sense of the requirements and needs of his fellow man is what Smith terms "sympathy," where the term "denote[s] our fellow-feeling with any passion whatever" (10). This is in essence Smith's rephrasing of Cooper's sentimental morality.[55] Sympathy does not here mean a feeling of shared sorrow, but rather is something more. Sympathy as Smith employed the term is an important part of the basic moral sense, one which guides us away from the bestiality ascribed to Hobbes's man and toward a more Christian attitude. Schumpeter identified sympathy as understood and presented by Smith as an ethical principle, allowing us to judge our own individual actions by reference to the principles we employ in judging the actions of others (Schumpeter 1954, 129–30). But sympathy alone is not *sufficient* to *action*, although it may be sufficient to *motivation* or *judgment*; to initiate the drive to action, the *sympathetic* feeling must be tempered by a feeling of *self-love*, a feeling akin to, but different in all fundamentals from, the baser instinct of *selfishness*.

> Sympathy, however, cannot, in any sense, be regarded as a selfish principle. When I sympathize with your sorrow or your indignation, it may be pretended, indeed, that my emotion is founded in self-love, because it arises from bringing your case home to myself, from putting myself in your situation, and thence conceiving what I should feel in the like circumstances. . . . It is not, therefore, in the least selfish. How can that be regarded as a selfish passion, which does not arise even from the imagination of any thing that has befallen, or that relates to myself, in my own proper person and character, but which is entirely occupied about what relates to you? . . . That whole account of human nature, however, which deduces all sentiments and affections from self-love, which has made so much noise in the world, but which, so far as I know, has never yet been fully and distinctly explained, seems to me to have arisen from some confused misapprehension of the system of sympathy. (Smith 1790, part VII, sec. iii, chap. 1, 317)

---

55. *The Theory of Moral Sentiments* developed from Smith's lectures on moral philosophy presented at the University of Glasgow.

Thus Smith's man is equipped with a very great moral sense, as well as a spirit of benevolence and even utility.[56] Smith's man is a caring and a reasoning (calculating? canny?) being, not a solitary but rather a gregarious type. He understands in a detached (sympathetic) way the needs and desires of others, and, even more interestingly, his own choices. He is truly community-oriented, a social being. He needs to engage with others in the type of interactions engendered in a civil society, not out of a feeling of trepidation, but rather out of feelings of community and belonging.

> All the members of human society stand in need of each others [sic] assistance, and are likewise exposed to mutual injuries. Where the necessary assistance is reciprocally afforded from love, from gratitude, from friendship, and esteem, the society flourishes and is happy. All the different members of it are bound together by the agreeable bands of love and affection, and are, as it were, drawn to one common centre of mutual good offices. (Part II, sec. ii, chap. 3, 85)

Hobbes's man, by contrast, forms social bonds out of fear, that is, out of a desire to maximize his welfare by increasing his degree of safety. He cannot perceive commonality because he is blinded by an apprehension of chaos, anarchy, and the manifest inevitability of a return to the law of the jungle, to a society dominated by the strong and governed by the survival of the fittest. Smith's man desires and requires pattern and regularity, and also understands the price one pays in terms of consequences for unadulterated selfishness (hence his requirement that the ever-present and basic human tenet of self-love be tempered by a degree of sympathy, and vice versa). Hobbes's man (and Mandeville's, for, according to Smith, Mandeville is but a Hobbes disciple)[57] is not bonded by emotional or sympathetic ties to the rest of humanity, but looks solely to his own selfish interest (in contrast to self-love). Smith's man struggles to suppress (discipline) his emotional reactions, while being cognizant of the sympathies of others. In short, Smith's man is much like Smith. More important to Smith's man than his sense of selfish purpose is his desire to control his own decisions through the instrument of his own reason.[58] David Hume's (1740) man also held sympathy and sentimentality to be of great import. But unlike Hume's man, for whom reason is "the slave of the passions," Smith's fights his passions in the making up of his mind;

---

56. Thus the opinion of Henry Spiegel (1991, 229) that "Smith rejects moral sense, benevolence, or utility as the basis of ethics" seems rather an unfounded conclusion, for sympathy and self-love encompass all three.

57. See *The Theory of Moral Sentiments*, part VII, sec. iii, chap. 1, 315n. Smith considered that Mandeville in his Fable "seems to take away altogether the distinction between vice and virtue. . . ." (sec. ii, chap. 4, 308).

58. It is thus difficult to accept Pribram's assertion that "Smith's great success was largely due to the fact that he established the pursuance of self-interest as the rational principle of all economic activities" (1983, 132–33).

Smith's man is sympathetic but rational, and it is reason which must in the end triumph.[59]

Even though he is a man of reason, Smith's man is not, as he believed Mandeville's (and by extension Hobbes's) man to be, a duplicitous soul; in fact, Smith's man is rather limited in the degree of his cunningness. As he expressed his position with respect to Mandeville:

> Dr. Mandeville is not satisfied with representing the frivolous motive of vanity, as the source of all those actions which are commonly accounted virtuous. He endeavours to point out the imperfection of human virtue in many other respects. In every case, he pretends, it falls short of that complete self-denial which it pretends to, and, instead of a conquest, is commonly no more than a concealed indulgence of our passions. . . . Every thing, according to him, is luxury which exceeds what is absolutely necessary for the support of human nature, so that there is vice even in the use of a clean shirt, or of a convenient habitation. (Smith 1790, part VII, sec. ii, chap. 4, 311–12)

Thus Smith accuses Mandeville of equating vice with vanity and virtue with altruism. But Smith then turned his impression of Mandeville's argument against Mandeville, arguing that if ostentation be an indulgence of the passions, then this indulgence is not selfish nor vain or vicious, but is rather a public benefit: "since without the qualities upon which he thinks proper to bestow such opprobrious names, the arts of refinement could never find encouragement, and must languish for want of employment" (313). So the employment of selfish motives could indeed be to the benefit of society, keeping in mind that this is an illusion, a deception necessary, in fact designed, to keep society in a continual state of motion (part IV, chap. i, 183).

Hobbes's view on the nature of man was not the only troubling aspect of his philosophy. Hobbes's alleged atheism also proved to be anathema to Smith; it was this atheism that Smith felt had led Hobbes to his erroneous conclusions as to the character and temperament of man, and dictated in a fashion the subsequent solution he proposed. In response to Hobbes's dissertation on the nature of man, Smith wrote:

> It was the avowed intention of Mr Hobbes . . . to subject the consciences of men immediately to the civil, and not to the ecclesiastical powers. . . . His doctrine . . . was peculiarly offensive to the theologians. . . . It was likewise offensive to all sound moralists, as it supposed that there was no natural distinction between right and wrong, that these were mutable and changeable, and depended upon the mere arbitrary will of the civil magistrate. . . .
>   In order to confute so odious a doctrine, it was necessary to

59. This is the position of A. L. Macfie (1959).

prove, that antecedent to all law or positive institution, the mind was naturally endowed with a faculty, by which it distinguished in certain actions and affections, the qualities of right, laudable, and virtuous, and in others those of wrong, blamable, and vicious. (Part VII, sec. iii, chap. 2, 318)

It is vital to recall in this regard that Smith was an eighteenth-century gentleman, neither a businessman nor a party politico. He enjoyed leisure and trusted judgments produced by leisure. He disliked pressure and was fearful of abrupt changes. Smith's prototypical man was, as was Smith, a Deist, who saw the personally beneficial as well as the consequential results of trying to understand the Single System.

Smith accepted many of the Stoic virtues as principles of his moral system. Societal rules of conduct, morals, ethics, and legal strictures and obligations cannot be disentangled. The origin of these codes of behavior is Natural Law, or, as Smith phrased it, "natural jurisprudence" (part VI, sec. ii, intro., 218). Positive laws and enumerative rights are nothing but attempts at approaching the ideal of a Natural Law ethic, but these attempts are doomed to failure as they must invariably be fashioned on the ethical precepts of the lawmaker. Thus the idea that man as a social being requires subjugation to the rule of the sovereign was simply untenable to Smith. As he believed that Natural Law was a necessary antecedent to any institutional framework invented by man, he could not accept the Hobbesian perception that, absent any man-made civil institutional structure, including a strong centralized authoritarian regime that demanded obedience to its fiats, man was doomed to an anarchic existence.[60] He was more inclined to accept the view that Natural Law precepts worked in concert with free will, and so did not view societal development as having a determinism we must accept fatalistically.[61]

Smith's answer to the Hobbes challenge in *The Theory of Moral Sentiments* was to absorb the Hobbesian emphasis on empirical information, but to extend it to an examination of human behavior. While Hobbes saw man as inherently antagonistic, constantly engaged in a

---

60. "To preserve society, therefore, according to him [Hobbes], was to support civil government, and to destroy civil government was the same thing as to put an end to society. But the existence of civil government depends upon the obedience that is paid to the supreme magistrate. The moment he loses his authority, all government is at an end" (Smith, *Theory of Moral Sentiments*, 1790, 318).

61. As Taylor (1929) expressed the philosophy of the classical economists of the eighteenth century: ". . . the classical economists never held that 'economic laws' describe a 'natural course of things' in the economic world which human efforts cannot alter. They believed in natural tendencies, processes of adjustment or equilibration, which are in some cases socially beneficent, and in some cases not; which can be engineered, manipulated, or controlled, given sufficient knowledge and the right methods; but which cannot be abolished or thwarted by simple decree, cannot be ignored in devising sound legislation, and should not be tampered or interfered with in cases where we are not in a position to control them properly and in a way that is really in the common interest" (25).

quest for power and advantage, Smith saw man as fundamentally moral and at times altruistic. Hobbes's secular-humanistic system allowed no place for moral imperatives; Smith's Natural Law system demanded them. Yet Smith suggested that individuals do not possess an innate moral *sense*. On the contrary, they seem to possess an innate need to seek out human company and so form moral codes. Man is not a solitary being whose sole motivation is to strive for self-aggrandizement; he is instead a communal creature, one whose nature is to cultivate relationships with others of his kind. Men are for Smith more akin to horses and sheep than they are to goats.

Without any *innate* moral sense, the "sense" by which we arrive at judgments of right and wrong or good and evil was for Smith a constructed sense, a synthetic moral code. It is formed inductively over time, but eventually achieves a formal status to which is applied the term *rule of morality*. It is our sense of reason, the basis of the code, that we term Natural Law. Rather than a strictly determinate path, it is more a tendency toward which society gravitates, and so exists in concert with free will. Once established and codified, these ethical principles govern behavior.

> That virtue consists in conformity to reason, is true in some respects. . . . It is by reason that we discover those general rules of justice by which we ought to regulate our actions. . . . The general maxims of morality are formed, like all other general maxims, from experience and induction. . . . But induction is always regarded as one of the operations of reason.
>
> But though reason is undoubtedly the source of the general rules of morality, and of all the moral judgments which we form by means of them; it is altogether absurd and unintelligible to suppose that the first perceptions of right and wrong can be derived from reason. . . . It is by finding in a vast variety of instances that one tenor of conduct constantly pleases in a certain manner, and that another as constantly displeases the mind, that we form the general rules of morality. (Part VII, sec. iii, chap. 2, 319, 320)

As a Scot, Smith held the traditional Scottish sociopolitical view toward personal endowment—environment was far more important than heredity. This view was in no small part the Scottish rationalization as to why and how the English amassed the social and economic spoils. It was the English hold on the British social system that *through personal prejudice* kept able Scots from realizing their potential. Smith's enthusiasm for the relatively open social system of the Americans reflects this "prejudice." The habits of governing cliques to restrain social efficiency in order to preserve their historic status (at the cost of forgone efficiency) extended in the Smithian view well beyond the landholders. Any form of monopoly power having access to the government (which held the monopoly on force) must be reduced: hence, the principle of *laissez-faire, laissez-passer* and his bugaboo, the mercantilists. It is clear that he held this belief intellectually and, insofar as he was capable, emotionally, but on the other hand the world was the world.[62]

Smith's Second Response: The Wealth of Nations   6.2

Smith's second response to the Hobbes challenge was presented in his 1776 classic on the fundamental nature of the workings of the economic system. Just why Smith came to write his *Inquiry into the Nature and Causes of the Wealth of Nations* is not all that clear. Wesley Clair Mitchell wrote that this work derived from the fourth part of Smith's course on moral philosophy, dealing with the topic of "expediency" (Mitchell 1967, vol. I, 137).[63] In any event, in *The Wealth of Nations*, Smith continued the program he had initiated in *The Theory of Moral Sentiments*. Perhaps this explains his failure in *The Wealth of Nations* to elaborate a deontological and epistemological position that could serve as the foundation of his economic and political theories: he had already provided such a foundation in the earlier work.

The basis for the legitimacy of the sovereign Smith held to be Natural Law, while the basis for human conduct is sympathy and self-love. Natural Law and the human emotions of sympathy and self-love act so as to make unnecessary in most areas of social activities the autocratic rule of the sovereign. Sympathy and self-love act to restrict the actions of the individual to those that will, in the end, despite his apparent selfishness, benefit the society as a whole. So long as the individual conforms to the dictates of the society, so long as he accepts his role within the larger social framework, he can do pretty much as he wishes, being limited by his moral sense and the social constraints that apply to all those accepting of the social contract. The sovereign can do nothing to interfere with the individual in the everyday pursuance of his affairs.

In *The Wealth of Nations*, Smith presented his views on this subject more clearly than in *The Theory of Moral Sentiments*, although the two works treat of essentially the same topics, albeit in different realms. While *The Theory of Moral Sentiments* treats the basis of morals and legislation, *The Wealth of Nations* extends the argument to the political and economic spheres, that is, into the domain of the "moral sciences." In *The Wealth of Nations*, specifically, Smith sought to question the justification for and the legitimacy of the sovereign in the commonwealth, so as to delimit his powers and duties; he sought also to promote the notion

---

62. Apparently, in spite of his convictions, Smith had no trouble accepting the income of Collector of Customs of Scotland, and his *amour propre* forced him to do a conscientious job.

63. The other three parts of the course were natural theology, ethics (from which emerged *The Theory of Moral Sentiments*), and justice.

that the individual should be the true center of decision making, as he alone is in the best position to judge his own interests.[64] The actions of the sovereign are confined to but a few very limited areas, all beyond the ability of the individual citizen to handle given his meager abilities.

> Every man, as long as he does not violate the laws of justice, is left perfectly free to pursue his own interest his own way, and to bring both his industry and capital into competition with those of any other man, or order of men. The sovereign is completely discharged from a duty, in the attempting to perform which he must always be exposed to innumerable delusions, and for the proper performance of which no human wisdom or knowledge could ever be sufficient; the duty of superintending the industry of private people, and of directing it towards the employments most suitable to the interest of the society. According to the system of natural liberty, the sovereign has only three duties to attend to; three duties of great importance, indeed, but plain and intelligible to common understandings: first, the duty of protecting the society from the violence and invasion of other independent societies; secondly, the duty of protecting, as far as possible, every member of the society from the injustice or oppression of every other member of it, or the duty of establishing an exact administration of justice; and, thirdly, the duty of erecting and maintaining certain public works and certain public institutions, which it can never be for the interest of any individual, or small number of individuals, to erect and maintain; because the profit could never repay the expence to any individual or small number of individuals, though it may frequently do much more than repay it to a great society. (*The Wealth of Nations*, 1789, book IV, chap. IX, 651)

The appeal to Natural Law and natural rights combines with sympathy and self-love to guarantee that the Smithian man would behave in a manner wholly inconsistent with the Hobbesian man, and the Mandevillian man as well. Natural Law and natural rights limit the areas to which the sovereign's power applies to protection of the nation and the individual citizen from domestic violence and foreign invasion, the provision of a court system and a codification of laws, and the funding of projects which are beyond the means of the individual to provide.[65]

Smith asserted that one of the principal purposes of government, in fact the most important of its three functions, is to act as a guarantor and protector of the property right. Smith thought that different levels of

---

64. Frank Petrella noted that this was the "principal mechanism for socioeconomic control in the *Wealth of Nations*" (Petrella 1970, 153).

65. As Macfie (1959, 215) opined: "The way in which sympathy acts to create social opportunities, duties, and institutions works through its social reflection in public opinion. Thus, through its reasoning side, it establishes a proper code of social behavior."

civilization could and did coexist at the same time.[66] In the early stages of social organization, that is, in the premodern forms of society that still could be found in many places around the world, wherein the idea of private property holdings was virtually nonexistent, Smith considered that acts of violence committed by one man against another were of such a personal nature as to require no remedial governmental action. No property was involved in the encounters; thus he held that the government was powerless to act, since there had been no attempt at appropriating by means of force the rightful property of another. "Where there is no property, or at least none that exceeds the value of two or three days labour, civil government is not so necessary" (book V, chap. I, part II, 670). It is the institution of private property, in its engendering of "great inequality," which makes imperative the provision of an authority structure to ensure its preservation:

> The affluence of the rich excites the indignation of the poor, who are often both driven by want, and prompted by envy, to invade his possessions. It is only under the shelter of the civil magistrate that the owner of that valuable property, which is acquired by the labour of many years, or perhaps of many successive generations, can sleep a single night in security. He is at all times surrounded by unknown enemies, whom, though he never provoked, he can never appease, and from whose injustice he can be protected only by the powerful arm of the civil magistrate continually held up to chastise it. The acquisition of valuable and extensive property, therefore, necessarily requires the establishment of civil government. (670)

Smith's perception of social evolution differed from that of Hobbes, which Smith may have thought was little more than an example of *post hoc, ergo propter hoc* theorizing. The American Indian system, for instance, based on hunting and fishing, served as an example of a first-level society. This form of social arrangement allowed a great deal of individual independence, but the advantages it offered were purchased at a high economic price (including the use of a great deal of labor input for little material output). The Tartar/Arab system, as an example of the next level in Smith's hierarchy, invoked the concept of personal property (cattle). However, this configuration resulted in diminished personal independence by causing to be established rudimentary governments to protect not only the principle of the property right, but also the poor from the rich. Yet undoubtedly the property right enhanced the efficiency of production, making "labor" prices lower. In the later substages of the second level, the property concept was broadened to include land titles as well as ultimately the ownership of (material and movable) chattels. Governments tended to be local (feudal) with a mixture of interdependence

---

66. See especially the discussion in book V, chapter I, part I, pages 653–57.

involving rights and responsibilities. The problem with feudalism was that the sovereign had in many instances been simply too weak to curb local tyrannies. In time, however, the sovereigns allied themselves with the urban "republicks" to gain national political control, as well as to lower further the labor-time costs of goods—many of which arose by trade rather than by production. As the cities grew, the demand for food increased and those holding farmlands turned to more efficient ways of production to capture food rents. The townspeople, however, rejecting the political power of the landholders, rephrased the rights and responsibilities of the national governments. These new responsibilities were increasingly narrowed to the assurance of trade routes and the protection of the public from outside influences. Thus, a desire for more material output (per labor input) led Smith to argue that what was involved was a thorough social reorganization—a new kind of governmental priority underlying a quest for productive efficiency.

From a similar rhetorical standpoint, Smith proposed an economic system wherein prices hovered about the traditional ("natural") level. The system therefore had the quality of a Newtonian or Boylian self-equilibrating mechanism: at too high a price, competition led to increased output, raising input costs; at too low a price, competition led to decreased output, and a lowering of input costs. Yet at the same time the system appears to have been structured on a rational albeit "invisible" order. This equilibration has a divine ring about it—the "invisible hand" of Smith. This is the same term he employed in *The Theory of Moral Sentiments* to maintain the paradox that the rich advance the general interests of the society even while in the (apparent) selfish pursuance of their own ends.[67]

> They [the rich] are led by an invisible hand to make nearly the same distribution of the necessaries of life, which would have been made, had the earth been divided into equal portions among all its inhabitants, and thus without intending it, without knowing it, advance the interest of the society, and afford means to the multiplication of the species. (Smith 1790, Part IV, chap. I, 184–85)

In *The Wealth of Nations,* the instrument of the "invisible hand" takes only a slightly different form, but in essentials is unchanged:

> By preferring the support of domestic to that of foreign industry, he [the businessman or entrepreneur] intends only his own security; and by directing that industry in such a manner as its produce may be of the greatest value, he intends only his own gain, and he is in this, as in many other cases, led by an invisible hand to promote an end which was no part of his intention. (Smith 1789, Book IV, chap. II, 423)

---

67. As noted by Basil Willey (1953) and Joseph J. Spengler (1984), the term "invisible hand" was first used by Joseph Glanville in his 1661 *The Variety of Dogmatizing.*

Of particular interest here—as the reader may have noted—is the similarity between Smith's view of the basis of order and the view of Mandeville. In both, order was seen as the result of accident, not design. The main difference lay in the moral character of individuals: crass egoism versus altruistic sympathy. Thus Smith's denigration of Mandeville's position was at best halfhearted for, while he may have objected to the basis of the underlying order—substituting virtue for Mandeville's vice, sympathy for self-interest—he nonetheless arrived at the Mandevillian conclusions.

But there are other implications as well for the action of a hidden, systematic, omnipresent agent shaping and guiding men's destinies, and these are the observable economic realities. Land rents would be associated with the size of the population and the prevailing wage rates. If land rents were too low, food prices would be low, populations would thrive, the increased demand for food would lead to more land usage, and that would lead to higher rents. Higher rents would lead to higher food prices, and populations would do less well. Smith, himself a "friend" of the landholding aristocracy, saw the landholders as both the political leaders and the potential monopoly-rent recipients. He perceived businessmen (the capitalists and the entrepreneurs) as the most able of men, a group whose inherent ability gave them an edge in intergroup conflict with the landholders. At the bottom of the system was the wage laborer, for whom Smith had by far the greatest expressed sympathy, even though he was quick to point out that sympathy was not enough. In the end the worthy worker got the short end of every deal.

Whatever Smith wrote about the advantages of "less" government, his ideal government had very important roles to perform. Government should act to provide for the common defense, protect internal order, facilitate commerce by setting standards, educate children and to some degree consumers, and even play a role in public health. Smith did not share what later in the United States came to be known as the Jeffersonian view, that government was so inherently corrupt that it ought regularly to be overthrown. Smith did not even consider the dissolution of the government, since its existence lay in the idea of a Lockean social contract; he did not believe the arrangement would be in danger of being violated, as both the governors and the governed held the same moral sense with its central core of sympathy and self-love (self-interest) driving them toward actions to the benefit of the community. In Smith, Mandeville's natural order thus met Locke's and Hobbes's inherent chaos, with the social contract being a sufficient (but not necessary) means to the continuation of that order. Order would prevail nonetheless, but the contract provided insurance. In perhaps the most oft-quoted phrase in *The Wealth of Nations*, Smith stated:

> It is not from the benevolence of the butcher, the brewer, or the baker, that we expect our dinner, but from their regard to their own

interest. We address ourselves, not to their humanity but to their self-love, and never talk to them of our own necessities but of their advantages. (Book I, chap. II, 14)

The impact of *The Wealth of Nations* was immediate, great, and long lasting. It was quoted in Parliament. Alexander Hamilton knew its contents well and clearly had it in mind when he spoke and politicked at the American Constitutional Convention. It was David Ricardo's reading of the work which led him to economics, as it did Jean-Baptiste Say, and through Ricardo and Say modern "scientific" economic analysis was formed.

6.3 An Appraisal of Smith

There is a tendency among practicing economists, even historians of economic thought, to appraise Adam Smith as the father of modern economic analysis. This view has served to make the economics profession believe that *The Wealth of Nations* was Smith's great book. But the estimation of Smith's importance would be greatly enhanced if his writings in moral philosophy were examined as closely as his writings in economics once were (although even the knowledge of the latter today derives almost exclusively from secondary sources). In Smith's own estimation, and in terms of contemporary insights, the *Theory of Moral Sentiments* is the more profound work.[68]

7 Conclusion

The "Hobbes question" and its various proposed solutions offer a taxonomic device by which to classify the essential rhetorical structures of economic theories. Hobbes's own "solution" begins with the individual and ends with the collective; state action is defined as the necessary outgrowth of social interactions. The philosophies of Locke and Smith begin with the Deity and the individual and end with the individual and other individuals. The property right identified is for most intents and purposes, subject to appropriate restrictions, inviolate. A two-strand approach is thus developed that continues to resurface throughout the history of economic thought. This approach appears in different guises (only some of which have been touched upon in the above treatment), but the fundament appears the same: collectivism vs. individualism; positivism vs. normativism; determinism based on assumptions of stability and nor-

---

68. Schumpeter (1954) esteemed Smith as the last of the great economic philosophers, albeit one whose stature had been diminished somewhat by virtue of his being compared with the likes of Plato and Aristotle. It is in this sense that Schumpeter's phrase "wooden Scottish philosopher" can best be understood.

mality vs. indeterminism based on assumptions of individual nonrationality and the use of imagination and belief; the certainty engendered by mathematical convergence theorems vs. the uncertainty engendered by the inherent unknowability of the consequences of human activity. These tensions will be seen more clearly in later chapters.

At this point we are prepared to study the evolution of a literature on state and economy-building. We turn now to Mercantilism and Cameralism.

CHAPTER 3

Mercantilism and the Rise of the Nation-State

Tyre, the crowning city, whose merchants are princes.
ISAIAH 23:8

Trade is the natural enemy of all violent passions. Trade loves
moderation, delights in compromise, and is most careful to avoid
anger. It is patient, supple, and insinuating, only resorting to
extreme measures in cases of absolute necessity. Trade makes
men independent of one another and gives them a high idea of
their own personal importance; it leads them to want to manage
their own affairs and teaches them to succeed therein. Hence it
makes them inclined to liberty, but disinclined to revolution.
ALEXIS DE TOCQUEVILLE, *DEMOCRACY IN AMERICA* (1840)

Business? it's quite simple; it's other people's money.
ALEXANDER DUMAS (GIRAUD, IN *LA QUESTION D'ARGENT*)

The Rise of the Nation-State   1

Reculer pour mieux sauter. Before proceeding to discuss the evolution of
a literature on the nation-state (both its government and its economy) it is
worthwhile to pause for a moment to summarize our approach. In the
first chapter we discussed different approaches to the topic, noting three
magisterial treatments. We suggested another interpretation based on
identifying the historical and cultural foundations of modern economic
thinking, namely patristic legacies. The purpose of the second chapter
was to introduce two of the dominant elements in modern western social
thought—the relation of the individual to the community, and his relation to the community's governmental process.

Given an appreciation of these two prior objectives we now turn to
the record found in the actual economic writings. Our investigation begins with the rise of the nation-state. The very nature of this radical
departure from previous forms of collective arrangements led to the emergence of an entirely new set of fundamental questions. The answers to
these questions prescribed the rise of the philosophical schools that
served as precursors to modern economic rhetoric.

1.1 *The Question of Legitimacy*

The emergence of the state as an agent of revolutionary change is an old subject, one going back to and beyond Plato and Aristotle. Hobbes and Locke, whose contributions are particularly vital to our exposition, were but two of the countless social and political philosophers who have written on the theme of the requisites for cohesive social, political, and economic unions.[1] For the purposes of historical perspective, it is useful to mention that by the eleventh century national political and economic institutional arrangements had been established in England under the reign of William the Conqueror: power and control were centralized, a national system of taxation was implemented, and the shifting of influence from the feudal barons to the monarch had begun. The founding of a parliament in London in the thirteenth century and the establishment of a unified system of law and justice were certainly effective institutional forces in concentrating power at the national level. But in terms of an identifiable *intellectual* concept, the notion of a unified national political *and economic* entity seems to have originated during the mid-fifteenth century.

By late in the sixteenth century the discussion seems to have shifted from the political realm to the economic. Schumpeter held that the advent of the nation-state was largely accidental; the development may have coincided with the decline of feudalism and the emergence of capitalism as a coordinating mechanism, but it is very likely that national political and economic units would have emerged in the same guise under other conditions (Schumpeter 1954, 144). The class structure that had been dominant in the feudal period continued to dominate politically, culturally, and economically even after the bourgeoisie came into its own; the nascent precapitalist merchant class, the creators of new forms of wealth, could be (and indeed were) exploited in the interests of an increasingly anachronistic political power structure which had little understanding of the true potential behind the wealth-generating mechanism that was developing. The state as a national political and economic force did not, then, evolve to its present form as a result of the triumph of the merchant class over the traditional elites, but rather did so because of pressures placed on these elites to conform to the new realities. The feudal structures from which the political power of the traditional elites had initially derived had collapsed, requiring them to seek out new sources of support. This support they found in an uneasy alliance with the new centers of economic power and expansion, the merchants.

What we see as important in this discussion is not the question of the manner in which a state is *founded,* or for whom and from whence

---

1. For an interesting discussion of the rise of the nation-state from a politico-mercantilist perspective, see Paul Kennedy (1987).

this *legitimacy* arises (as was the concern of, among others, Plato and Hobbes); rather the concern here is with the manner in which certain interest groups sought the *cover of legitimacy* in their efforts at taking control of the state as both a political and economic instrument. The legitimation of the state as a force for the pursuit of goals put forth by recognizable political and social and economic entities is an important but overlooked historical episode. This transformation has led to the emergence of the doctrines subsumed under the banner of economics or "political economy," creating as it were a rubric instead of a subject.

Just when the European nation-state emerged as an idea is less important than the fact that during the transition from the fifteenth to the sixteenth century it seems to have begun to change its character from one the legitimacy of which was predicated on a theological base into something with a more purely secular design and purpose. Previously, social and political cohesion was achieved by force, by a consolidation under the control of a dominant governing authority or doctrine. The Roman Empire (and others that had preceded it) achieved cohesion by demanding compliance by those within its conquered territories to overall control, including control of certain basic belief systems, by a central authority. The dissolution of the Roman Empire saw the cohesiveness that had been achieved by military conquest replaced by a new cohesiveness achieved by religious authority, that of the Catholic Church centered in Rome. While indeed it is true that for a time the two "empires"—the ecclesiastical and the civil—had coexisted in a tenuous union, the Church eventually became dominant, meaning its role became viewed as authoritative. But this dominion soon declined, as the position of the Roman Church authorities came to be called into question.[2] What emerged was a radical altering of the traditional concept of territoriality and the means by which cohesion could legitimately be pursued. The emergence of new and competing modes of thought as to the most appropriate form of social reorganization, and the dominance of no one particular view, led to this reappraisal.

Emphasis began to shift from a concern with the role of the state as a political unifier to the role of the state as a coordinator, as an entity providing a sort of organizational framework for *economic activity*. In Western Europe generally, and England specifically, those who wrote as advocates of the assimilative role of the state focused more on the role of social organization in the process and less on theological legitimacy. The process occurred over many centuries in Europe as the post-Charlemagne Holy Roman Empire disintegrated first into smaller kingdoms, later into

---

2. Schumpeter (1954) held this to be the third of the three events that led to the emergence of the nation-state (the first we have already mentioned above, the second being the discovery of precious metals reserves in South America). In his view, the victory of the Church was Pyrrhic; the popes lost authority as a consequence. But there was nothing inevitable about the collapse of the civil feudal authority.

feudal realms, and finally into sociopolitical national units, reflecting many changes in the prevailing economic, political, and social structures and interrelationships. What emerged after almost a millennium of ecclesiastical dominance was the rise to prominence of secular authorities intent upon the consolidation of civil society. The bourgeoisie, hardly new on the scene, began to insinuate itself into political and economic debates, as it aspired to an overall social leadership that would equal (or, rather, consolidate) its economic role. Such leadership clearly had its political side; indeed, political leadership appeared as the principal goal of this newly emergent group.[3]

With the emergence of this new economically inspired leadership, the foundations of the new nation-state shifted, moving from being exclusively political (including the theocracy as part of the political system) to being something significantly more socially integrating, encompassing political, moral, social, and economic interests. No longer could the traditional political elites impose political solutions on an impotent economic class; the system itself had to change in order to deal with the competition for power and control mounted by the emerging merchant classes, cliques not content with an outside, sometimes secondary, role. To facilitate the dramatic shift in authority, an additional element integrated the economic, political, and social groupings, which had to that time been viewed as having separate institutional structures, and even as being separate classes. This additional element involved more than the restructuring of economic relationships within the existing socioeconomic framework. It demanded as well the incorporation of a specialized perception of economic relations, integrating a growing national, and often private, wealth into the political realm.

While there are many different schools of thought that seek to provide a rationale for this shift in the structure of the nation-state as a single unifying political entity, it is sufficient to note that these changes came about for a great many reasons. A few of the more important factors to be considered are: (1) technological (primarily military technology) improvements and innovations, such as the invention of the English longbow and the importation of gun powder, which tilted the odds with respect to warfare from defense to offense; (2) the widespread and devastating influence of diseases and pestilence, specifically the repeated appearance of the Plague, creating labor shortages previously little known; (3) seemingly interminable feudal civil warfare, which took its toll on the hereditary leadership; (4) xenophobic (especially anti-Italian) sentiments, coupled with the politics of the Roman Catholic Church, which made for a particularly bloodthirsty climate and straitjacketed the structure of alliances; and (5) the spread of literacy as the introduction of the printing

---

3. The goal of political leadership was obvious to the old leaders, the military types. Because the societies were essentially military in nature, the military leaders were also the political leaders.

press made the written word more readily accessible, effectively destroying the quasi-monopoly held by the ecclesiastical authorities on the educational and record-keeping processes. Further, the "Age of Discovery" served not merely to open exploration to the Far East and the New World of the Americas, but also to open pathways to new, different, and challenging opportunities in other fields. All of these developments combined to accelerate change, change of a revolutionary nature that had been neither planned nor at the time particularly welcomed. These changes took the form of shifts in social power, which had defined the traditional relationships, a refocus on the relative significance of the material here-and-now as distinguished from the Platonic plane, and perhaps most trenchant of all, a major alteration in individual material expectations.

It is intellectual canon to refer to this period as the era of the rise of the nation-state. Intellectual canon serves its purpose: generally it identifies important elements in terms of a school and serves as a shorthand rhetorical device. But we wish to go beyond this to observe that the rise of the nation-state involved more than a consolidation of lesser political units into social groupings. What it involved in the European case were a myriad of conceptual questions, including: What were the historical (objective or material) reasons for social organization? What was (or should be) the basic social unit? What were the contesting roles of anointment, force, rational voluntary cooperation, and even serendipity, in first explaining and then justifying (declaring *legitimate*) political events? Indeed, what was meant by the interests of the state? Was it the interest of the monarch, his family, and his allies or the interest of some particular nonmonarchical party such as the ecclesiastical leaders or the merchant guilds? Or was it to promote what now seems to have been a particularly abstract concept such as the Common Will or the Common People or Cultural Destiny?

Whose State and Whose Economy?   1.2

The foregoing explanation is not intended merely to elucidate the conceptual foundations of sixteenth- and seventeenth- (and even eighteenth- and nineteenth-) century Mercantilism. It is rather, and far more importantly, to introduce the concept of the national organization of economies—what today we call macroeconomics. While many historians of economic thought regard macroeconomics as having achieved its formal significance with the work of John Maynard Keynes (although the term originated with the econometrician Ragnar Frisch), the concern with macroeconomic problems has been manifest since the advent of the nation-state. The problems that have become evident of late with macroeconomic analysis as a formal discipline center around the question of whether the concept still has any validity in the increasingly interdependent framework of national and supernational concentrations that has developed since the mid–nineteenth century. What is likely the intellectual battle of our time concerns this fundamental evolutionary change in the character of the state as unit of analysis, that is, whether the national macroeconomic unit is becoming a fossil. Is there life left in it, or is it going the way of provincial and town economies?

The manner in which one approaches this topic is of some interest. One suggestion is to begin with grand ideas, worked out in the area of political theory, and to apply those concepts to the study of national economies. Central to that position is a view of national political and economic units as power-political blocs, engaged in a zero-sum struggle for international advantage. Another suggestion is to begin with the economic groups themselves. This approach illuminates how they established rules of thumb designed to "solve" such conundrums as the "correct" method of pricing input factors to secure a favorable trade balance, of tilting currency exchange ratios to encourage sales and bullionized profits, and of attracting foreign capital to pay for what domestic capital would otherwise have to undertake.

The approach taken here entails consideration not so much of the evolution of Mercantilism or Physiocracy or any of a number of competing schools of economic thought which materialized and flourished over this period, as it does a consideration of the basis for social (including political, moral, and economic) control. It is remarkable how we typically assume that somehow all societies have the same political or sociopolitical institutional needs, so that when societies do differ, we assume that the differences relate primarily to intellectual distinctions, for example, individualism vs. communitarianism, oligarchy vs. democracy, material progress vs. psychic refinement. Such is not necessarily so. What evolves as the modern domestic dilemma is a different question entirely, taking into account the role of the household and the question of who is to be the majordomo. So it was in the sixteenth century in regard to national political and economic development. Who was to take on the role as the chief among the staff?

1.3 The Shaping of the Argument

The problems inherent in the creation of a unified theory of national economies are, as maintained previously, ages old. Our interest at present focuses mainly on the handling of these questions since the latter part of the sixteenth century.[4] The choice of period is indeed somewhat arbitrary,

---

4. Karl Pribram (1983) began his study of the topic with the fifteenth century, a time when Scholastic doctrine was in decline and the Italian Renaissance was ushering in an era of artistic, intellectual, and commercial achievement. For Pribram, the defining elements of this epoch can be identified through a study of emerging philosophical movements—refined Aristotelianism, neo-Platonism, and humanism—that competed for intellectual dominance throughout the period.

but the sixteenth century seems a good historical watershed, if only because prior to that time what underlay most strife was the conflict between the dynastic ambitions of royal and ducal houses and the ambitious designs of religious prelates for achieving their own versions of a
temporal Augustinian City of God. The movement toward the creation of
a theory of national economies had previously been largely confined to
the intellectual plane; power consolidation had been tenuous at best. By
1550 the dynastic authorities had become established as the dominant
forces in Italy, France, Spain, and England, and the modern age of secular
authority, always of course (with the exception of England) claiming a
preference for existence under the Roman Catholic aegis, had begun.

The question of public or private "market control" has become the
ideological litmus test of the present decade. "For whom is the state
run?"—whether for the greatest good of the greatest number, or for the
promotion of the goals of special-interest groups[5]—is the oft-repeated
phrase of political candidates and social reformers. That measuring the
"greatest good for the greatest number" is of course impossible even
conceptually (despite the fact that attempts have been and continue to be
made to achieve some such valuation), or that one man's consensus is
another's special-interest group, does not seem to have affected this dispute, and so the debate continues unabated.

The Background of Mercantilism   2

Definition   2.1

Mercantilism is most often defined as a doctrine whereby the private
commercial interests and activities of individual entrepreneurs, while still
remaining ostensibly in private hands, are subordinated to the purposes
of the state. Gustav von Schmoller, founder of the German Historical
School of Economics, found the essence of Mercantilism "in the total
transformation of society and its organisation, as well as of the state and
its institutions, in the replacing of a local and territorial economic policy
by that of the national state" (Schmoller 1884, 51). More broadly, it may
be seen as the doctrine of the promotion of *merchant-inspired* governmental interference in the economic affairs of the nation. Indeed, Adam
Smith, in *The Wealth of Nations,* was one of the first to argue that there

---

5. In the Tenth Federalist Paper, James Madison noted wryly that putting down the
special interest group may make the cure worse than the disease. His remedy was to attempt
to break the group into several subgroups and even encourage the creation of counter–
special-interest groups. Consensus was not Madison's goal; indeed, he feared the origins of
consensus. What he favored was the compromise found in the legislative product. In the
case of consensus "I strive for what I desire"; in the case of the legislative product, "I settle
for what I can get."

had developed a school of economic thought predicated on the self-interest of the merchant class, a "school" in the very loosest sense of the term; he coined the expression "mercantilist," following the lead of the Marquis de Mirabeau, who had earlier identified in European trade a system of state-sponsored protectionism.[6] These self-interested promoters advocated policies designed not for the good of the *citizenry* of a state, but for the good of the state in the *abstract,* as it appeared as an extension of their own politicoeconomic concerns. That most industrialized societies have long experience with governments affecting economic activity is not in dispute, nor was it a particularly perplexing issue with Smith. In fact, insinuation of various groups into economic affairs for the advancement of their own interests seems to be a defining characteristic of government. What concerns us here, however, are two specific questions: (1) How did the nation-state come to reflect a variety of pressures, some clearly economic and some not? and (2) In making choices between different organizations of government, what were the factors that seem to have been dominant in the sought-for frameworks?

2.2 The Beginnings of Mercantilist Doctrine

The study of Mercantilism generally commences with the observation of an early attempt by an outside group—the merchants or the bourgeois class—to gain and exploit political power. While their efforts have often been taken as being directed partly against the *traditional dynastic rulers* (the Crown or the ducal family, holdovers from the feudal past), more often than not it seems as if these efforts were directed against the established *landed feudal aristocracy,* a group that had made tremendous *economic,* but relatively little *political,* gain from the feudal organization of society. It was not that the merchants had ideological ties to either group, but rather that the Crown often was driven to alliances with the merchants because the merchants' wealth was essential for maintaining the Crown's armies, and because the Crown's "natural" domestic enemies were typically the landed feudal aristocracy. This shift in importance took place within the confines of a larger structural shift, from the Christian legacy of the nobility to the bourgeois legacy of economic efficiency and rational markets. The literature explaining these changes in the structure of society represents the literature on Mercantilism. It also forms the foundation of this section of the present work.

European Mercantilism, an economic system so denoted only after its eclipse by the Classical school of political economy, and then in a deprecating sense, seems to have emerged during the Renaissance (about 1500) and to have lasted until about 1800. The historian William Cun-

---

6. This point was made by Pribram (1983, 36). Of course, one can also suggest that Mercantilism has been defined with respect to the *outcomes* it engendered and so deny it had any real *purpose* at all.

ningham, in *The Growth of English Industry and Commerce during the Early and Middle Ages* (1910), held that it actually had its beginnings in the mid–fourteenth century with the efforts of the London Fishmongers, the Vintners, and the Drapers in forcing policies favoring trade discrimination and politicking in support of trading privileges (Cunningham 1910, 378, 382).[7] Parliament, during the reign of Richard II (1377–99), adopted programs aimed at fostering domestic industry, restricting foreign entry to markets, introducing a shipping fleet, and increasing bullion reserves—all policies advanced as part of the later mercantilist agenda (470). While these measures were largely discarded during the reign of Edward VI (1547–53), they nonetheless never lost their appeal and in fact reemerged during the sixteenth century for much the same reasons they had been initially proposed. Whichever date one chooses to accept, the important thing to understand is that this was a time when the modern nation-state was coming into being, and the emerging nonnoble patrician bourgeoisie was attempting to lay claim to a substantial political power base. It was also a period during which a class of commercial entrepreneurs surfaced who exploited and were in turn exploited by those advocating strong national economies and political institutional structures. The remnants of a feudal era continued to control the political machinery and, in their attempts at consolidation of influence and power, employed any and all means at their disposal. It is this aspect of the period—the degree to which one class exploited the other in a quest for dominance—that appears to be another defining element of Mercantilism, albeit one which is very difficult to identify causally. Was it the case that the entrepreneurial merchant class exploited the political class as a means of consolidating its position, or was it the political elites who attempted to consolidate their power by exploiting the emerging mercantile class? Or was it a combination of the two?

Mercantilism and Political-Economic Power   2.3

Power relations are a continuing theme running throughout the early mercantilist literature. This is not surprising given the circumstances that preceded and nurtured its development; the economic argument simply mirrored the political reality. Countervailing concentrations of wealth and power were seen as a natural outgrowth of a form of Hobbesian selection; exploitation in the ultimate pursuit of advantage, of the governors by the merchants and vice versa, was *the* rule of the game. The writers of the mercantilist period were not individualists, as were the

---

7. Shepard Clough and Charles Cole maintained that the first organized economic interest groups actually preceded by several centuries these trading collectives. They noted in particular the weavers of Mainz (1099), fishers of Worms (1106), shoemakers of Wurzburg (1128), blanket weavers of Cologne (1149), and bakers of Pontoise (1162). See Clough and Cole 1952, 29.

political economists of the Classical tradition (e.g., Adam Smith), a tradition that in many ways supplanted Mercantilism. On the contrary, they
were collectivists and statists in their orientation toward political and
economic relationships. They advocated a state role in economic affairs,
including the concentration of competing sources of power and institu-
tionalization of competition among large blocs, blending with and har-
nessing business and political interests to the service of the overall objectives of the state. This is not to say that they boldly advocated state
control over all social, political, and economic activity, but rather that
they advocated state-corporate *coordination* such that the corporate unit
(collectives of entrepreneurs) would be granted state monopolies in trade
and commerce with an eye to the enlargement of state power. The rhetoric was usually crafted to appeal to the power appetites of those in a
position to affect policy decisions. The state was ostensibly the ultimate
economic unit; nationalism in turn became the mercantilist rallying cry.[8]

Eli F. Heckscher, considered one of the leading authorities on the
subject of Mercantilism, held that the doctrine was "primarily an *agent of
unification*," its objective being "to make the state's purposes decisive in
a uniform economic sphere and to make all economic activity subservient
to considerations corresponding to the requirements of the state and to
the state's domain regarded as uniform in nature" (Heckscher 1935, vol.
1, 22; emphasis in original). Heckscher noted that Mercantilism at heart

---

8. Ephraim Lipson, in his study of English economic history, made the point well:

> [Mercantilism's] underlying idea was to establish the power or strength of a State
> by making it independent of other States in the economic sphere. . . . it tended
> inevitably to assume the appearance of an aggressive economic nationalism. The
> development of the national resources was intended to promote national security,
> and "consideration of power" took precedence over "consideration of plenty."
> (1931, 1–2)

This same point was reiterated by John Maynard Keynes, who went even further than
Lipson and noted the militaristic element present in mercantilist thought:

> The mercantilists were under no illusions as to the nationalistic character of their
> policies and their tendency to promote war. It was *national* advantage and *relative*
> strength at which they were admittedly aiming. (1936, 348; emphasis in original)

Viner, who understood the basis of mercantilist doctrine to be primarily economic, conceded
that one identifiable objective was the increase of national power, economic and political.

> It would be difficult to find convincing evidence that any of the prominent mercan-
> tilists regarded power and prosperity as generally conflicting and inharmonious
> objectives of national policy. On the contrary, it was a matter of general agreement
> among them that for England the only certain path to national power and glory
> was through promotion of trade and increase of wealth. (Viner 1937, 112)

Schumpeter also held that the "militarist" element of the newly emerged nation-state was
part of their constitution: "The new sovereign powers were warlike by virtue of their social
structures" (1954, 146). Schumpeter (1954, 336n.4) acknowledged his indebtedness to
Viner's study of Mercantilism.

was but a component of a broader political doctrine, a doctrine he termed Colbertism after policies advocated by Jean-Baptiste Colbert (1619–83), the French finance minister under Louis XIV (from 1661 to 1683).[9] Mercantilism, Heckscher concluded, was a "system for forcing economic policy into the service of power as an end in itself" (Heckscher 1935, vol. II, 17). Heckscher interpreted Colbert as having employed in his trade and manufacturing policy such a means–end framework: "The end was war, and essential to its purpose was a healthy state of finance, which in turn presupposed an active and vital economic system" (vol. II, 17). The rationale employed by Colbert was simple: To everything there is a political motive, especially foreign trade; whosoever controls trade controls the world. The result of this view was the development of the state as "both the subject and the object of mercantilist economic policy" (vol. I, 21).

Craft Guilds as the Foundation of Mercantilist Practice   2.4

Despite the power-political rhetoric that was ultimately to dominate the dialogue of the mercantilist writers, the genesis of mercantilist doctrine may be found in a different domain entirely. The craft guilds emerged during the Middle Ages as order-preserving collectives. They developed out of (1) a need for a "voluntary association for mutual benefit among craftsmen engaged in the same line of work" and (2) the need "of the governing authorities to encourage association among the craftsmen for purposes of regulation, control, and taxation" (Clough and Cole 1952, 27). As the early contributors to the historical debate on the advent of British Mercantilism, notably William Ashley (1914) and George Unwin (1966), have noted, the guilds promoted a collectivization which worked to the advantage of the members, they became in effect countervailing centers of economic power. It had by the sixteenth century become dogma that individuals simply could not hope to achieve material gain in an environment of open competition; as the selling groups began to collectivize and so achieve a degree of power over their product, it became evident that agglomerations could provide the means for improved bargaining positions on a larger scale. Thus did the guild materialize as a force by which craftsmen could ensure themselves a voice in the economic affairs which directly affected their trade. The emergence of craft guilds "was the gradual and almost unconscious result of the coalescence of two

9. Pribram defined Colbertism as a political doctrine advocating "a network of economic and social measures dominated by the objective of ambitious national power politics" (Pribram 1983, 50). Pribram also noted a major difference between Mercantilism as an English phenomenon and Colbertism: English Mercantilism emerged as an *intellectual* movement, its proponents desirous of providing a rigorous statement of first principles; Colbertism by contrast was fundamentally *practical politics*, its French proponents "not animated by the search for a promising methodology" (50).

groups of forces—forces from below, tending towards association and union, and forces from above, especially the pressure of municipal government, tending towards corporate responsibility" (Ashley 1914, 29).[10]

The historian William Cunningham held that the guilds were, in modern parlance, much in the manner of a police system. As monolithic organizations with a single purpose, they served to channel the actions of the membership to the pursuit of the overall interests and objectives of the group. The guilds had tremendous power to enforce their laws and so could guarantee stability and order and of course, by so doing, also generate financial opportunities for the members. The enforcement mechanism is particularly relevant to the present discussion. For the second of the two forces that served to generate the collective relationships, that is, the need for order-preserving institutions (as agents of "regulation, control, and taxation"), the guild structure was ideally suited. Guilds were incorporated so as to inhibit inappropriate activity; they

> served the purpose of bringing home the responsibility for every mischief and scandal to some one or other. The city authorities looked to the wardens of each craft to keep the men under their charge in order; and thus for every public scandal, or underhand attempt to cheat, some one was responsible, and the responsibility could generally speaking be brought home to the right person. (Cunningham 1910, 466)

What proved successful for the guild could prove successful for the state. If the individual commercial interests could be aggregated to create a powerful *commercial* union, the same principle could work to the advantage of the *nation* in designing an organized, efficient center of concentrated power. As one aspect of this extension of power lay in the encouragement of foreign trade, regulated so as to achieve maximum effect, the government granted status to private conglomerates, Companies of Merchant Adventurers. These groups led the way in the expansion of Britain's overseas commercial relations. Domestically, similar arrangements resulted from the granting of licenses to traders in industries thought advantageous in the promotion of state interests. It is but a small step to extend to the nation-state what guided the fortunes and enhanced the power and prestige of the private companies, as a means of achieving

---

10. Unwin stated the argument in terms very similar to those of Ashley, recognizing that, despite the exclusivity inherent in the very idea of a consolidated interest group, the guilds had their beginnings as noble efforts to advance the economic interests of the membership and by extension the whole of mankind:

> The deliberate policy of the gild . . . was of a restrictive and negative character. . . . But, in its earlier and more elastic form, when it was continually receiving new members and lifting them out of more rigid and backward forms of association, the gild must be conceived of as a creator of economic values and a beneficent agent of human progress. (Unwin 1966, 34)

the same goals on a larger scale. This success was to be emulated for the good of the state, not only as a vehicle for the enhancement and extension of state power and national prestige, but also as a revenue-enhancement scheme.[11] Mercantilist proposals and programs were designed to promote just such autarky and enhance state power, albeit with the expressed goal of social betterment through responsible agglomerations.

Stability—political, social, and economic—was a critical component in the rationale for governmental control over economic activity in general and trade in particular. The view of Cunningham was that the position of the nation-state as a domestic order–preserving force was the most fundamental concept to emerge from the period of the Reformation (1910, 467). The example of the stability and power gained through an organizational structure such as that of the guild proved tempting as a model for the national state. This suggests that, from the standpoint of the promotion of stability, national policy required restrictions to be placed on activities that had the potential for harm. As Cunningham phrased the argument:[12]

> Naval power was affected by the use of foreign shipping, and native vessels were preferred; so too, the export of bullion was prohibited as it led to the impoverishment of the realm. Any importation which interfered with the employment of the people, the woolgrowing and clothmaking which threatened the food supply, and the unthrifty games which interfered with their military training, were all authoritatively checked . . . (1910, 467)

This quest for power became the overriding objective of the state, becoming more desirable as its effectiveness became evident. With increased effectiveness came the ability to mold the power principle to positive ends. "under its guidance commercial enterprises and industrial skill were stimulated, while they were combined into a great national economic system" (1910, 468).

Smith held that the mercantilists saw individual rights and privileges as subordinate to the survival of the state. Again the influence of Hobbes is evident in the mercantilist argument, at least as Smith understood it. Not accepting Natural Law as a force leading to the equilibration of social and economic forces, the mercantilists opted for a more explicit and more worldly mechanism of temporal government. The importance of stability

---

11. Unwin's thesis was that the expansion of *society*, not the power of the *state*, led to the expansion of the British empire. "Society expanded to escape from the pressure of the State; and when the State . . . attempted to follow up the expanding society and to reestablish its pressure, a federation of new States arose to resist the realization of an Empire which had so far existed merely for the purposes of rhetoric" (Unwin 1966, 341).

12. For Cunningham, power depends on the accumulation of treasure, the promotion of shipping (including the maintenance of a strong national naval presence for the protection of trade), and the regulation of the population (Cunningham 1910, 481).

cannot be overstated; it may be the most important consideration for the state, since the power of the state can only be effectively employed if the state is internally secure.[13]

The English government, in an effort to solidify its position vis-à-vis the other major European economic and military powers, quickly established a policy to channel trade to its benefit. Whereas prior to this time England had been somewhat backward in the area of manufacturing enterprise, this was to change dramatically; the government would henceforth take the initiative in the promotion of trade and production. Always the paternalistic motive was advanced in explaining the concentration of economic activity, and this explanation invariably centered around the best interests of the state. Wool sales, for example, were to go through a fixed marketplace, a center dedicated solely to the trade, "so that it might with facility be both protected and taxed" (Ashley 1914, 75). As with the guilds, this concentration resulted from two forces: merchant interest in combination and state interest in regulation.[14]

Likewise, agricultural reform became synonymous with increased collectivization, again in the interests of state power. Large-scale farms replaced small plots, as it became evident (at least to those engaged in the creation of the huge agricultural tracts) that this was the most efficient form for agricultural production. The small plots were, after all, producing haphazardly and inefficiently, each proprietor taking the initiative in the production and distribution of his own output. This form of production gave the individual as proprietor a great deal of control over his own production decisions, but had the potential for weakening centralized control over supplies. Aggregation offered a more efficient model, as decisions could be made on a large scale (even a national scale) with each individual farmer gaining as a result of the more efficient production, distribution, and promotion of agricultural produce. The creation of an agricultural cartel, with the blessing and encouragement of the state, could, under this reorientation of control, aid the farmers and the state at the same time. While this seemed intuitively obvious to some, it soon became dogma as it gained the necessary theoretical foundation: "as soon as the economists made their appearance in the first half of the nineteenth

---

13. As Ashley stated the point:

> The government was not inclined to look on passively [at the cyclical nature of the export business enterprises]; both because its whole social policy rested on the assumption that the willing workman could always get paid employment, and also because weavers out of work were apt to be turbulent and a danger to the public peace. (Ashley 1914, 115)

14. Ashley described the two forces as "the impulse towards fellowship spontaneously felt by men engaged in the same business, men having the same interests and running the same risks, and the need of regulation and control felt by the government, partly for fiscal reasons, but partly, also, from an honest desire to safeguard national interests" (75).

century, the agricultural writers had the supposed authority of political economy on their side" (Ashley 1914, 138).

The Eclipse of Mercantilist Thought   2.5

With the advent of the Industrial Revolution in England in the mid–eighteenth century, attitudes had reversed from the Hobbesian to a more Lockean design; the government should limit its intervention in the social, political, and economic spheres to the provision of law and order and the maintenance of the individual's freedom of contract.[15] No longer were the interests of the state to be elevated to supremacy over the rights and liberties of the individual. On the contrary, the individual would be elevated to a position of supremacy as the center of economic activity and as a basis for political power, a position he would continue to enjoy in the later philosophical tracts of the British utilitarians. But the idea of the state as the center of power, and the coalescence of power centers as economic entities—as atomic units—remained the hallmark of Mercantilism. As Viner identified the distinction between the mercantilists and the Classical political economists:

> . . . the classical economists argued that men in pursuing their selfish interests were at the same time, by a providential harmony of interests, either rendering the best service of which they were capable to the common good or at least rendering better service than if their activities were closely regulated by government, whereas the mercantilists deplored the selfishness of the merchant and insisted that to prevent it from ruining the nation it was necessary to subject it to rigorous control. (Viner 1937, 93)

Of course, mercantilist doctrine differed between eras and among countries. Not only did the structures of each of the nation-states differ, but mercantilist thinking varied with regard to both the objectives and the policies of the writers and practitioners in all of the major countries in which it was practiced (England, France, Spain, Austria, the Low Countries). There also were distinct differences in thought patterns within each of these countries. To a consideration of these differences we now turn.

Interpretations of Mercantilist Doctrine   3

Delineation of a "Mercantilist Period"   3.1

Some historians have claimed that there was no such historical episode as the "mercantilist period," that such a denomination is but a crude concept into which the data of the time period have been forced by "theory-minded

---

15. On this, see especially Ashley 1914, 161.

economists."[16] They contend that it is simplistic to argue that the writers characterized as mercantilists had any recognizable theoretical or policy-oriented doctrines to which could be applied the label of a "school." But, if we look today at the political currents and note the number of groups seeking to resolve their own national economic problems by concentrating on the use of domestic controls and various types of bargaining restrictions on trade with other countries, it is not at all difficult to absorb the original concept of Mercantilism. Some, such as Nicholas Kaldor, argued that the mercantilist approach is the "natural" one in the formation of national economic policy, and that arguing for free trade is merely an aberration, a special case, wherein certain production factors favor a particular nation.

For most economists and historians of economic thought, the standard authorities on Mercantilism are Heckscher (1933 and 1935) and Viner (1937).[17] These authorities commence their analyses with the assumption *cum* judgment that such a thing as a mercantilist school *could be said* to have existed, but not as coherent economic theory. Mercantilism was a loose classification of policies which combined a peculiarly new view (political economy) toward statecraft and economic policy. Heckscher in particular maintained that Mercantilism was designed from a set of policy instruments dedicated to the pursuance of power-political ends and was not, strictly speaking, a doctrine for the promotion of protectionism and state control over commercial activity; it is "only an instrumental concept which, if aptly chosen, should enable us to understand a particular historical period more clearly than we otherwise might" (1935, vol. I, 19). On this interpretation it is no more and no less than "a phase in the history of economic policy" (19).[18]

---

16. Mitchell viewed Mercantilism as "a paper system. No efficient administrative services to enforce it" (Mitchell 1967, 41).

17. Others who have written extensively on the subject and are particularly valuable references are E. A. J. Johnson (1937), William Letwin (1964), D. C. Coleman (1957, 1969), and Terence Hutchison (1988).

18. A more modern critic, William R. Allen, concurred, summing up the argument very succinctly:

> To be sure, one can now discern in (or construct from) the writings of the seventeenth and early eighteenth centuries something of an orientation and a perspective, a range of general policy priorities and grand communal objectives, a more or less common set of topics to discuss and problems to be resolved, a schematic but variable body of biases, some recurring themes which a generalizing hindsight may now codify and even label "theory." But all this hardly constitutes a mode or engine of analysis, a developed toolbox of analytic techniques, constructs, and procedures, a generally recognized and accepted body of mutually consistent, rigorously derived, and empirically testable hypotheses. The mercantilist writers may have provided an inelegantly formulated philosophy of sorts—"essentially a folk doctrine," Viner calls it. But in neither the large nor the small, in neither the abstract nor the concrete did they provide an explanation of economic order and system—a vital omission not merely illustrated

Writers on Mercantilism as a reform-minded doctrine, such as Viner and, to a lesser extent, Heckscher, viewed underlying social reform as the basis of the mercantilist movement, but still with a concern for the welfare of the state. Economic and social doctrines focusing on international trade were seen by these interpreters as being the most important determinants of a nation's well-being. The center of power and influence had by the time period in which mercantilist writers fashioned their theories of the state shifted from the hereditary heads of state and government to the newly established landed and trading classes, and this transition appears to have been orderly and nearly complete. The interests of the nation or the duchy no longer implied the importance of the Crown or the ducal family; rather it could mean principally the desires and demands of the rich bourgeoisie (particularly notable in Holland) or the landed nobility. Even so, it is evident that no one writing from the mercantilist position during the period we are discussing (from the sixteenth century through 1776) really acted as though the interests of the nation could imply universal suffrage.

Some writers on the subject, notably Eric Roll (1974), have perceived Mercantilism as representing a unidirectional causality, from economic structure to political institutional change. On this view, power politics did not *precede,* but was the *result of,* shifts in trading regimes. These shifts were themselves brought about by the rapid decline of the feudal economies and their attendant institutions, and their replacement with competitive trading blocs. Capitalism as a force for the molding of social, political, and economic conditions was the chief culprit in the transition. Feudal relations, it is alleged, did not persist until forced by counterinfluences, brought about by an emerging merchant class, to relinquish control. On the contrary, capitalism even in its embryonic form was directly responsible for the destruction of the old order. From this starting point the mercantilist doctrines developed. The growing role of the state in the pursuit of economic growth as a tool for the furtherance of international political objectives was predicated not on a desire to increase state power, but rather on purely egoistic grounds of the expansion of commercial trading interests. The principles of Mercantilism offered on this view nothing more than an apology for radical revolutionary social change. The similarity of this view with the Marxian view of the stages of economic growth is probably not coincidental.[19]

Pribram (1983) went so far as to suggest that Mercantilism was something more encompassing than a single doctrine based on a narrow set of interests. He identified three strains of mercantilist thought, each dependent on a particular epistemological position. These three positions were bullionism, Baconian Mercantilism, and refined Mercantilism. The

---

by, but largely consisting in, their failure to provide an adequate "price" theory. (1970, 382–83)

19. It was against this interpretation that Schumpeter commented (1954).

first of these, bullionism, developed in the sixteenth century as the merchants came into conflict with the traditional ethical and moral teachings of the Scholastics. The conflict centered around the definitions of wealth and ownership, and the role of precious metals as a measure of a nation's wealth. The second strain, Baconian Mercantilism, originated in the mid–seventeenth century as philosophers began to write of the "scientific" underpinnings of society. The idea of a Natural-Law basis to economic activity, which of course precluded governmental intervention in the workings of the system, was particularly appealing to the merchants. The empirical method advanced by Francis Bacon was applied to the traditionally moral concerns about which the Church authorities had written. These new methods adjudged the profit motive, for example, as morally and ethically neutral. The third strain, refined Mercantilism, appeared in the early eighteenth century. The defining characteristic of this form of Mercantilism is the attempt to identify in a formal way an "economic system" and to recognize and systematize the role of government within this system.

Yet, there are others who have held that, from a historian's evidentiary standpoint, not only did there never exist a mercantilist school of economics—at most it was a group of partisans writing on the same topic—but to so denote such a disconnected body of work is to misperceive the true scope and purpose of these writings. D. C. Coleman (1957, 1969) concluded that while there may have been writers who had agreed with respect to an underlying *theoretical structure,* in practice the *policies* advanced did not easily coalesce around any core principles. While those branded as "mercantilists" may have advanced policy positions that had the same or similar ends in view, the means to those ends were so different as to be categorizable into many different belief structures.[20] The status granted to Mercantilism as a coherent doctrine—even if that doctrine is an instrumental one—is thus the result of nothing more than the historian of economics being obsessed with cataloging. Coleman's view held that Mercantilism came to be elevated to the status of an economic "school" because economists were (and are) too prone to see the interrelatedness of ideas; he held that ideas-in-action are what count, and if one chooses one's political issues carefully, one inevitably finds "coalescence."

More recently, some economists, for example, Robert Ekelund and Robert Tollison (1981), have suggested that the mercantilist view was nothing more or less than so much mainstream economics, so that one can forgo the interdisciplinary discussions found in the presentations of Heckscher, Viner, Coleman, and so on. They held that the mercantilists,

20. As Coleman expressed the position, the catchphrase of Mercantilism "seems to give a false unity to disparate events, to conceal the close up reality of particular times and circumstances, to blot out the vital intermixture of ideas and preconceptions, of interests and influences, political and economic, and of the personalities of men" (Coleman 1957, 25).

as such, did indeed maintain a coherent economic theory that could be translated easily into a consistent economic policy; the theory was the maximization of the merchant group's monopoly profits. Based on this belief, they then focused attention on the cartel arrangements evident in so many of the mercantilist policy prescriptions. For Ekelund and Tollison (and others who accept this interpretation), mercantilist policy was little more than the act of simple profit maximization by certain of the trading groups. The actors were merely behaving rationally, as these economists define the term. On this orientation, the variations among nations in the practical application of the mercantilist doctrine may be seen to have been caused by differences in national constitution. Take, for example, the cases of France and Britain. The "mainstream" economic interpretation of the policies pursued by these governments would highlight the manner in which the monopolization process vis-à-vis both the Crown and the legislative institutions could be most efficiently pursued. In Britain, where Parliament and the Crown were constantly feuding, the merchants found that they had to concentrate for political reasons on exploiting the foreign markets, since both "big players" (Parliament and Crown) attempted to checkmate them as they were checkmating one another. In France, by way of contrast, the Crown and the merchants could squeeze their rents out of the locals, largely because the French Parlement did not have the powers comparable to that of the British Parliament.[21]

This is the opinion of the (prototypical) mainstream neoclassical economist cum historian of economic doctrines. The problem with such an approach is the mechanical apparatus required; their matrix is so fixed that it eschews the definition of profits, the time period over which the said maximization is to take place, and the social costs, if any, involved. If we can agree to what is meant by each of these points, then perhaps we can answer the questions posed. But this has been achieved in the past by deciding what the answer involves and then attributing that set of meanings to the original question.

Still others have seen the mercantilist movement as representing the efficient use of scarce resources (usually identified as capital) employed in the furtherance of the public interest. This is taken to be true whether the interest is held to be in the name of the Crown, in the name of the bourgeoisie, or in the name of some combination of the two. George Unwin, once the preeminent historian of the English Tudor period, held

---

21. During the reign of the *ancien régime* the function of the French Parlement was to "engross" legislation (i.e., make decrees official) rather than to initiate legislation. By and large the Parlement flexed its muscle only when it had the opportunity to amend a royal last will and testament. With the former monarch dead and the new monarch not fully entrenched in power, the Parlement could make its opinion felt. On virtually all other occasions, the monarch was simply too powerful to brook more than the occasional delay in engrossment of his decrees.

that the success of the Tudors was tied to their realization that the delega-tion of social control to certain bourgeois economic interests made tax collection less necessary and thereby made social control all the easier. Schumpeter seems to have taken a similar position. He stated that the mercantilist writers advanced policy positions that "were not only under-standable in the sense in which everything is, crime and folly included, but also in the much more significant sense that, taking account of the circumstances and opportunities of the time, they constituted adequate means for securing what with the same proviso were rationally defensible ends" (Schumpeter 1954, 337).

By way of contrast, William Ashley, a leading historian of the En-glish Stuart period, concluded that the rapaciousness of the Whig Parlia-mentary party was so great that such little social stability as England enjoyed came from the repeated efforts of the Stuarts to police the bour-geoisie, a costly effort in terms of two of the monarchs' reigns. Finally, Douglas Irwin (1991) has examined the conflicts between the British and the Dutch East India Companies and asserted that the way to understand the policies is not to tie them to anything so fundamental as the general pursuit of economic or political monopoly powers as the temporal and spatial rivalry over specific markets by tacticians.[22]

3.2 The Historical Setting in Britain

It is probably necessary, in order to understand the mercantilist theory as it developed in any country, to have a fair degree of familiarity with the political history of that country. To gain an appreciation of Mercantilism as an economic program, we will at this point examine the growth of mercantilist doctrine as a British phenomenon.[23] As defined herein, Mer-cantilism is an economic theory dedicated to the advancement of national power through the encouragement of collective antagonisms, or counter-vailing power centers. As an example of this perception, let us take the case of the emergence of the English nation-state.[24] We have already noted that the Parliament of Richard II passed legislative acts devoted to mercantilist prescriptions; these had been rejected by the Parliament of Edward VI on the ground that the kingdom simply could not afford so restrictive an

---

22. In this he appears to have been in agreement with Viner, who opined:

> The laws and proclamations were not all, as some modern admirers of the virtues of mercantilism would have us believe, the outcome of a noble zeal for a strong and glorious nation, directed against the selfishness of the profit-seeking mer-chant, but were the product of conflicting interests of varying degrees of respect-ability. (1937, 58)

23. We will come to French Mercantilism in the next chapter. For a review of Swedish Mercantilism, see Lars Magnusson (1987).

24. There are several good general works on this subject, including Cunningham (1907, 1910), and Langer (1940).

economic and trade policy. The reappearance, in not so different form, of these same measures then requires an investigation of the historical background that led to their resurrection. The actual chronology appears as Appendix I, but several generalizations are worth pointing out here. For the English case, the chronology includes the following developments in respect to the political need to direct the functions of the economy:

(1) In the mid–fourteenth century, in an effort to expand the state coffers, Edward III granted to a group of merchants a monopoly on wool exports, ostensibly because the group could more efficiently collect the tax receipts. The organization soon went bankrupt. Edward then extended monopoly privileges to the Merchants of the Staple, a larger group of several hundred merchants. Under this agreement, wool bound for export would pass through a central staging point, from which it would be shipped to another central point on the Continent. This arrangement allowed the merchants to keep wholesale prices down and export receipts high, leading to greater tax receipts for the Crown. In 1486 the Fellowship of Merchants Adventurers of London was incorporated and granted the exclusive right to export wool. By 1497, *any* exporter of wool was required by statute to join the Merchant Adventurers, at a very high price of admission.

(2) Politically, the traditional government of England was virtually destroyed by a civil war between two factions of the royal family (the War of the Roses). What emerged from the carnage was a money-short monarchy whose hold on power was tenuous at best because of questionable legitimacy. The old nobility had been exhausted by the long and bitter fight and, of course, much of it was distrusted by the new monarch and his successors. Henry VII (around 1485) began the quest to rebuild a more centralized monarchy, an effort which continued under the succeeding Tudor monarchs (the Tudors reigned from 1485 to 1603). In an effort to buttress its powers, the House of Tudor (under Henry VII and Henry VIII) introduced new legal enactments and resurrected old ones, with the aim of promoting domestic production (including where necessary the importation of raw materials), halting the exportation of bullion, and rebuilding the military and naval forces. As part of his program, Henry VIII implemented a policy of confiscation of the monasteries and convents, even undertaking negotiations with the Commons (whose leaders included rich merchants) to achieve the desired ends.

In an effort to establish its legitimacy abroad, the Tudors also sought major military and commercial alliances against England's traditional enemy, France. The principal alliance in this regard was to be with Spain, also a newly emerged monarchy. The alliance failed.[25]

---

25. Among the reasons for this failure was (1) the death of the English crown prince and (2) the desire on the part of Henry VIII to divorce his wife, the Spanish princess, which led to his excommunication and the establishment of the Church of England.

(3) During the reign of Queen Elizabeth I (1558–1603), the grants of monopoly privilege to merchant companies took on extravagant dimensions. In an effort to consolidate control, the Merchant Adventurers were constituted and more strictly controlled as a state bureaucracy. The restrictions on wool exports had the unintended consequence of expanding the English domestic woolens industry, and so creating an alternative outlet to the monopoly traders. However, the monopolists soon rebelled, appealing to the Crown for restrictions designed to maintain their monopoly status.

In 1555 Parliament passed the Weaver's Act as a protection for the cloth manufacturers. This act, among other things, placed a strict limit on the number of looms allowed per manufacturer.[26] In 1563 Elizabeth initiated the Statute of Artificers, designed to augment the Weaver's Act by training workers to produce higher-quality cloth and by placing all producers within the authority of the guilds.[27] Under Elizabeth, monopolies were granted for the production of such items as soap, salt, and window glass; imports that competed with domestic goods were restricted; wool and leather exports were forbidden; even the wearing of felt hats was made unlawful so as to favor the wool industry (except of course for those persons holding the rank of knight or above, for whom velvet hats were permitted) (Clough and Cole 1952, 226).

(4) Elizabeth was succeeded by the Stuart King James I (previously James VI, King of Scotland). Taking the (now joint) throne in 1603, the Stuart monarchs reigned (except for the Commonwealth period of 1649–60) until 1714. Forever short of funds, and desiring to further the consolidation and control of the economy, James instituted even more regulations. In 1605 he arranged for all English wool products to be under the inspection of a "royal aulnager" (one who certifies quality); in 1606 restrictions were placed on silk dyeing. The second Stuart monarch, Charles I, went so far as to incorporate the small number of silk producers into a guild. Throughout the Stuart reign, the list of organized guilds grew dramatically.[28] But events were to alter the political situation and

26. The act "provided that no clothier (cloth merchant) outside a corporate town was to control more than one loom, or rent looms, or rent houses with looms in them; that no weaver outside a town was to have or control more than two looms, nor to have more than two apprentices, nor to have a fulling mill or to act as fuller or dyer; that no fullers or dyers were to have looms; that no new clothiers were to have weaving done for them outside of a city or town; and that no one was to be a weaver without an apprenticeship of seven years" (Clough and Cole 1952, 224).

27. "The statute listed thirty-two crafts . . . which were to be taught only in corporate towns and only to sons of freeholders, and twenty-one other crafts . . . which could be taught anywhere to anyone" (Clough and Cole 1952, 224–25).

28. Included were "feltmakers, musicians, turners, fruiterers, gardeners, pinmakers, shipwrights, woodmongers, butchers, curriers, plumbers, founders, apothecaries, scriveners, bowyers, starchmakers, upholsterers, playing card makers, silk throwers, spectaclemakers, clockmakers, silkmen, combmakers, beaver makers, distillers, glaziers, glovers, gunmakers, hatband makers, horners, soapmakers, and coachmen" (Clough and Cole 1952, 228).

therefore the turn toward centralization and regulation of the economy. As a result of his efforts to raise taxes Charles so managed to antagonize the Parliament that it revolted. Twice the parliamentary forces conquered the king's armies, and, reluctantly, the leader of the parliamentary forces, Oliver Cromwell, directed the execution of Charles I. After about a decade of Cromwellian rule, the English army recalled the crown prince, who ruled as Charles II. Apparently having learned the lessons of his father, Charles II halted further regulation of the economy and did not seek from Parliament any demand for large taxes. Instead, he lived off the largesse of England's traditional enemy, Louis XIV of France.

The Source of Political Legitimacy   3.3

One of the critical questions that the study of Mercantilism seeks to answer concerns the source of political legitimacy. Under the political protection of the Tudors, the power of the merchant class in England grew steadily. Courting favor with the emerging economic and political class was seen by the monarchy as a way to break the hold of the traditional power centers, the noble landholders, as well as a way to provide badly needed financial backing for various military and commercial endeavors. The monarchs realized the promise of such an alliance and attempted to direct the growth of the economy in favor of the merchant class and against the power of the landed aristocracy (the nobles). They were in this regard generally successful. Under the Stuarts, however, the pattern of alliances ultimately changed, and the bourgeoisie (including the merchants) allied themselves with the landed aristocracy against the monarchs.

As the conflicts often were argued out on the intellectual plane, pamphleteers ("pens for hire") and philosophers, intent upon providing a substitute for the traditional "everything belongs to the sovereign" theme, created a body of literature dedicated to the subject of the legitimacy of governance. Who has the right or obligation to rule? How is this rule to be legitimized? What is the role in this process of those who are to be governed? These were just a few of the questions they asked and attempted to answer. For the most part, this literature was the *result* of differing political interests, not the *cause* of it. But exceptions surfaced, and in some instances the literature became more fundamental and truly creative, thanks to such writers as Hobbes, Locke, Butler, Berkeley, Cooper, Mandeville, and Smith.

Elements of a Prototypical Mercantilist Theory   3.4

While there are many ways to perceive Mercantilism, there are certain elements which constitute a prototypical mercantilist theory. Some factors that seem common to all of the many interpretations are:

1. An emphasis on the subordination of traditional religious matters to the interest of political, economic, and other secular concerns, including the secularization of political control.

2. A belief that international independence (meaning self-sufficiency) and economic wealth provide the basis of political power (the source as well as index). The political and economic spheres are seen to be inextricably intertwined, so much so that the doctrine has become synonymous with nationalism. In the German form, Cameralism, the political and economic functions merge into a single entity. (For Mercantilism, bullion initially played the role of wealth, but there were some who saw beyond this fallacy and understood the role of alternative time horizons.)[29]

3. Promotion of state control of the economic process such that leadership came from the bourgeoisie (the merchant class) as much as or more than from the landed aristocracy. All aspects of economic life could be placed within the province of the state. The desired instruments of control varied among writers, but always included efforts at fiscal regulation, establishing monetary exchange controls, regulating interest rates, and policing entry into product markets (sometimes locally but always internationally).[30]

4. A belief in an economic hierarchy of occupations, with agriculture at the bottom of the ladder, manufactures occupying a somewhat higher rung, and merchandise trade at the top.

5. A belief that trade should be manipulated for the benefit of the state and would be optimized the more that exports exceeded imports, again in the pursuit of self-sufficiency. The Corn Laws and the Navigation Acts were but two of the measures designed to this end. After 1620 no English mercantilist really believed that each deal had to promote an export surplus, so long as such a surplus accrued in the aggregate.

6. A belief that work was man's duty, but with the understanding that both low and medium paid workers as a rule should not be rewarded well enough to encourage them to consume what would otherwise be exported (shades of Mandeville). That which made men work harder was better; generally, but not always, this point was expressed in the argument that wages be kept very low.[31]

---

29. As Viner noted, " 'the bullionist' regulations were either repealed or had become obsolete long before 1620, or persisted and even were strengthened long after 1620" (Viner 1937, 4).

30. "Freedom for themselves, restrictions for others, such was the essence of the usual program of legislation of the mercantilist tracts of merchant authorship" (Viner 1937, 59).

31. As Viner stated, "The mercantilists . . . were led by their obsession with the balance of trade . . . to deal with questions affecting labor as if laborers were a set of somewhat troublesome tools rather than human beings whose own comfort and happiness were a proper and primary object of concern for statesmen" (Viner 1937, 56). On the labor theories of the English mercantilists, see Edgar S. Furniss (1918).

That these features common in mercantilist tracts exist in different degrees and with different emphasis is one reason for the divergence of opinion as to just what a mercantilist program entailed.

Mercantilist Writers: General Statements of Mercantilism   4

Overview   4.1

The various writers on the general subject of Mercantilism may be classified into two categories: those advancing a general statement, replete with a secure philosophical motivation for their views on the appropriate role of a trade-based national economy, and those writing on specific issues, whose work is classified as "mercantilist" because of an advocacy of policies respecting commercial and political cooperation.

The advocates of a "general" statement of the mercantilist position presented the clearest analytical program for the promotion of mercantilist beliefs. Here are included three representative writers, Antoyne de Montchrétien (France), Thomas Mun (England), and Phillip von Hornigk (Austria), each working at different times in the seventeenth century and in different social and political milieus. Each is selected not because his specific contribution is taken as authoritative, but rather to express the flavor of the main elements of Mercantilism as it developed in different sociopolitical and economic environments.

Antoyne de Montchrétien (1576–1621)   4.2

One of the earliest mentions of the phrase "political economy" (according to Schumpeter 1954) is to be found in Antoyne de Montchrétien's[32] 1615 *Traité de l'oeconomie politique,* a tract devoted to a chauvinistic view of the state. As in the later work of Hobbes, Montchrétien recommended policies dedicated to the advancement of the interests of the state, above and beyond all other parochial interests. The *Traité,* written in response to the failure of the Valois kings to centralize control of the nation (a concern we take up in the next chapter in the context of Physiocracy), is divided into four parts. Each concerns aspects of the wealth of the state: manufactures, commerce, navigation, and the role of the Crown.[33] Of these, the

---

32. Montchrétien, noted as a poet and playwright, was born in Falaise, Normandy. Educated in Caen, his artistic period led him to publish the classic French plays *Hector* and *L'Écossaise.* Following his participation in a duel, Montchrétien moved to England, but returned to Normandy in 1610 to marry a wealthy widow who established him in business as a knife producer.

33. As Cole noted, however, the division should perhaps be geographic location, the supply of resources, population, and the ability to coordinate and regulate the three (Cole 1931, 115–16).

efficient regulation of all the resources at the disposal of the state is the most important. Lacking a regulatory apparatus, the maximum efficiency afforded by coordination will never be attained.[34]

As the state interest was paramount, the monarch (in this case Louis XIII, "assisted" by Marie de Medici, the Queen Mother and Regent)[35] should direct his concerns to the preservation of order. The individual in his many guises was deemed irrelevant in the advancement of a grander scheme; individual interests, be they of the person or the company or the guild or the locality, were all of secondary importance, as were supernational (bloc) interests, if for no other reason than that they competed and conflicted with a strong national entity. Specifically, Montchrétien suggested that a national, not a regional, economic and political interest must dominate in all the affairs of the state, since, after all, the uniqueness of a national culture is what makes for a dominant, cohesive force. France, the country of and for which he wrote, can and should strive for economic self-sufficiency, not only as a necessary (positive) condition, but as a desirable (normative) one. The individual did, however, have a role to play in the progress of the state. This role was to work and to produce. The nature of man is not to be idle, but to be in constant toil. Idleness promotes sin; work promotes happiness.

Following on this premise, and his belief that France should be self-sufficient in production, Montchrétien declared that the government is duty-bound to protect the country's workers from competing with those of other nations. Indeed, labor is a source of the political stability of a nation (especially France at the time he wrote), and so protecting labor from the vicissitudes of international market forces could only have beneficial effects on the country as a whole. Goods produced domestically favored

---

34. Your Majesties possess a great state, agreeable in geographic situation, abounding in wealth, flourishing in peoples, powerful in good and strong cities, invincible in arms, triumphant in glory. The extent of its land is sufficient for the infinite number of its inhabitants, its fertility for their support, its wealth of domestic animals for their clothing; for the maintenance of their health and happiness they have gentle skies, balmy air, sweet waters. For their defence and housing there are materials suitable and fit for building houses and fortifications. . . . France alone can do without everything that she gets from neighboring lands, while they can not dispense with her. She has infinite wealth, known, and yet to be discovered. . . . In every one of her provinces are sites where all sorts of beautiful and useful trades can be established. By herself she can be a whole world. The least of the provinces of France furnishes your Majesties with its grains, its wines, its salt, its linens, its woolens, its iron, its oil, its dye, making France richer than all the Perus in the world. . . . But of these great riches the greatest is the inexhaustible abundance of its men, who know how to husband its wealth; because they are noble in mind, active and possessed of a flame-like intelligence restrained by a clever and cultured nature capable of thought and deed. (Montchrétien 1615, 23–24; quoted in Cole 1931, 116–17)

35. *Traité de l'oeconomie politique* was actually dedicated to Louis XIII and Marie de Medici.

domestic workers, keeping unemployment low and the wealth of the nation intact; goods produced elsewhere reflected the corrupting influence of foreign competition and served as a disincentive to domestic employment in industries dedicated to their production. Likewise, foreign-owned companies producing domestically should be restricted since the profits accrued not to France but to the foreign governments. Montchrétien did not deny that trade could be favorable; he simply argued that foreign trade should be pursued only if advantages to France could be clearly shown. The function of the state is, after all, the accumulation of wealth. Trade is but a tool for the achievement of this purpose. If trade were not advantageous, produce at home. Thus emerged an early argument for the policy of import substitution.

Of particular interest was Montchrétien's nonmercantilist position in regard to agriculture. In his *Traité* he went so far as to treat agriculture as the "first industry." It is agriculture that is responsible for the initial production of wealth, all other industry being dependent on its product. In terms of advancing the political interests of France in relation to potential adversaries, Montchrétien held a rather interesting position, one which can only be described as "strategic trade." Prior to the initiation of hostile actions against a foe, France should undertake to sell the adversary expensive furs "so as to draw thence gold and silver and other advantages and, after he has been thus enfeebled, to be able to conquer him more easily and to become his master" (quoted in Heckscher 1935, vol. II, 43–44).

Thomas Mun (1571–1641)   4.3

Thomas Mun[36] came from an established merchant family with political connections. His 1621 pamphlet *A Discourse of Trade from England unto the East-Indies; answering to diverse Objections which are usually made against the same* was published as a defense of the East India Company. He became a director of the company in 1615 and served in that capacity until his death. To Mun, the success of the company advanced the English economy and the status of Britain. His line of reasoning employed the concept of opportunity costs and competitive advantage.

The argument as Mun presented it is straightforward. The East India Company, in acquiring spices and other "exotic" commodities directly for the British market, saved the Crown and the British consumer from paying too high a price for the same goods imported through brokers and third parties. Prior to the involvement of the East India Company and the exploitation of its ocean route to England, spices and other treasures imported from the Indies had been transported to intermediate

---

36. Mun was the son of a mercer, and the grandson of the provost of moneyers at the Royal Mint. His stepfather was a director of the East India Company.

points along an overland trade route, most notably through Turkey. At each step in the journey, the middlemen exacted a profit from the transportation of the goods. The all-water route of the company was thus a great improvement, making goods markedly less expensive than those imported via the previous system. This benefited the economy by ensuring a favorable trade balance, since the reexport of the goods resulted in a total value of goods which exceeded the outflow of bullion.

Mun's greatest work, *England's Treasure by Forraign Trade, or the Ballance of our Forraign Trade Is the Rule of Our Treasure,* published posthumously in 1664 (but written in 1630),[37] became for more than a century the authoritative, definitive work on the subject of trade from a mercantilist perspective. Adam Smith in fact commented in *The Wealth of Nations* that the title alone had become "a fundamental maxim in the political oeconomy, not of England only, but of all other commercial countries" (1789, 403).[38] In this tract, Mun preached against "unnecessary" government intervention in trade channels, where the issue was the protection of the domestic money supply (stocks of bullion) and given exchange rates. The merchant as entrepreneur is given the central position in a theory of economic growth and development. The most important determinant of the wealth of a nation was taken to be its trade balance, not the amount of gold and silver accumulated; in fact Mun held this to be a rule: "to sell more to strangers yearly than wee consume of theirs in value" (Mun 1664, 5). Considering that the financial matters of a nation are similar in constitution to those of an individual, Mun believed that, just as a man may prosper only if he spends but a portion of his income while not consuming from his wealth, so a nation will become wealthy only if it exports more than it imports. Specie flow, he held, was the result of an excess of either imports or exports. Further, Mun stressed that it was not imports, but their consumption, which was the cause of the troubles.

The worst policy a nation could adopt was one of trade restrictions. Mun believed that restraints on trade such as the Statute of Employment violated the Law of Commerce: "that whatsoever (in this kind) we shall impose upon strangers here, will presently be made a Law for us in their Countreys . . ." (1664, 35). Trade demanded refinements to account for the peculiarities of situation and need. There is no single, universal trade regime:

> For as the use of forraign trade is alike unto all Nations, so may we easily perceive what will be done therein by strangers, when we do

---

37. Alexander Gray noted that Mun wrote this book "for the better upbringing and instruction of his son" (Gray 1931, 73).

38. Johnson (1937, 77) declared that Smith had "unconsciously patterned" his *Wealth of Nations* on the model of *England's Treasure.* Schumpeter (1954, 196n.4), however, declared Mun to be "overrated."

but observe our own proceedings in this waighty business, by which we do not only seek with the vent of our own commodities to supply our wants of forraign wares, but also to enrich our selves with treasure: all which is done by a different manner of trading according to our own occasions and the nature of the places whereunto we do trade; as namely in some Countrys we sell our commodities and bring away their wares, or part in mony; in other Countreys we sell our goods and take their mony, because they have little or no wares that fits our turns: again in some places we have need of their commodities, but they have little use of ours; so they take our mony which we get in other Countreys: And thus by a course of traffick (which changeth according to the accurrents of time) the particular members do accommodate each other, and all accomplish the whole body of the trade, which will ever languish if the harmony of her health be distempered by the diseases of excess at home, violence abroad, charges and restrictions at home or abroad. . . . (1664, 34–35)

In *England's Treasure by Forraign Trade*, Mun also identified quite clearly the differing interests of the merchants and the Commonwealth, the former being interested in increased profits, the latter in the general welfare. But the merchant has a distinct role to play as a facilitator of commerce, albeit ultimately his function is to undertake trade and commerce for the good of the state. His role consists not merely of his being a transporter of goods, but also requires him to be an employer and a source of revenue for the state.

While stressing the centrality of the merchant, Mun also stressed the point that the Crown might very well enrich itself at the *expense* of the merchants, that is, that the Crown may prosper while the merchants sink into debt. The merchant is important precisely because he facilitates trade in an efficient and expeditious manner. He buys at the lowest price possible, from the source, along the way paying insurance premiums and freight costs, wages and salaries, customs duties, and so on. These payments benefit the state in a way in which a more direct importation, for example, of a commodity purchased from a European middleman and hence not dependent on British merchant shipping, could not. Mun allowed that in fact there were three types of "gain," each of which were predicated on the notion of a zero-sum outcome: (1) the gain of the state at the expense of the merchant, (2) the gain of the merchant at the expense of the state, and (3) the gain of the sovereign at the expense of both the merchant *and* the state (1664, 25). While such a policy could ultimately be self-destructive and so betray the differing interests of the commercial classes and the state, this division of interests was not, however, to be seen as indicative of a trade balance problem; what counted in the end was not what each party gained, but rather the national aggregate.

Mun's policies were, despite the focus on the merchant as the essential cog in the machine, directed to the enhancement of state power. The world economy consisted of a fixed pie, so that trading could be viewed as a zero-sum game. The positive result of the trading regime of the East India Company was not in the provision of goods at a lower cost than was possible with the overland route; it was rather the effect this trading had on the expansion of British power and sovereignty over those states which had previously profited from the overland trade. In addition, the trade balance was the preferred mechanism because specie-flow and foreign-exchange controls were beyond the control of any single nation. One policy advocated by Mun was price discrimination based on the relative availability of goods in foreign markets. If England had a monopoly in the production of a good, it should charge more than if there were several sellers. In similar fashion Mun also advanced an early argument in favor of "dumping" as a national policy, an argument again predicated on a zero-sum outcome and power-political considerations (that is, based on the desire to advance the objectives of the state in commercial dealings).[39]

In short, among the policies Mun advocated were restraint in the consumption of imports and freedom for the merchants to exploit trade opportunities. Policy recommendations included restraining consumption of foreign luxury goods (domestic wares were as good as the foreign products, and their purchase by the aristocracy and the bourgeois classes served a patriotic function), restricting fishing rights in British waters (since fish are a national resource, their harvest employing British seamen), reestablishing the cartelized selling of British wool intended for export (the Staple), and shipping exclusively in British bottoms (this to profit the merchants, and to make for the state and private insurers a profit on insurance and shipping charges).

Of special importance for Mun was the desirability of establishing trade relations with far-distant countries. In direct merchant trade with the more remote lands, the profit margins purportedly will be larger than if these same goods were purchased from neighboring states which had traded for them from the source. Since British merchant shipping can acquire these goods directly, without having to pass through a middleman, "the wares also sent thither and receiv'd from thence are far more profitable unto the kingdom than by our trades neer at hand" (1664, 10).

---

39. But the superfluity of our commodities which strangers use, and may also have the same from other Nations, or may abate their vent by the use of some such like wares from other places, and with little inconvenience; we must in this case strive to sell as cheap as possible we can, rather than to lose the utterance of such wares. For we have found of late years by good experience, that being able to sell our Cloth cheap in Turkey, we have greatly encreased the vent thereof, and the *Venetians* have lost as much in the utterance of theirs in those Countreys, because it is dearer. (1664, 8; emphasis in original)

While the nation as a whole will pay the same price for the commodities whether they are imported from near or far, the fact that a merchant fleet ships from the source makes a huge difference for the overall aggrandizement of the state. Merchants must in preparation for these voyages purchase ships, pay wages to crews, remit taxes and customs duties (as noted above), all of which provide employment and revenue to the state which would be lacking if the goods were purchased from middlemen. Such trade also results in the creation of an export trade sector, wherein the commodities imported from the source (in this case the Indies) can be reexported to other European countries. Should the imports be raw materials, so much the better; domestic labor could then be applied for finishing and processing, yielding value to these goods for reexport.[40]

Philipp Wilhelm von Hornigk (1638–1712)   4.4

Philipp Wilhelm von Hornigk was a lawyer and civil servant in Austria, not a merchant or philosopher as were many of the other mercantilist writers. This background may help to explain the overly terse, bland construction of his writings, as the rhetoric employed is geared more toward the policy recommendations of a civil servant than toward an exercise in public persuasion. As Schumpeter (1954) opined, he wrote from the standpoint of one who lived in a country under the constant threat of Turkish invasion.

Hornigk was truly an economic nationalist and in many ways a pure mercantilist; his policy prescriptions generally eschewed international trade relations in favor of an Austria-first stance. At the time, of course, Austria was poor in resources and lacked any significant manufacturing base. Hornigk's policy recommendations, therefore, took the form of suggestions for the expansion of state power through the promotion of economic development, specifically through policies which would in a much later period be labeled import substitution and infant industry protection. His 1684 Österreich über Alles wan es nur will (roughly translated as "Austria Can Be Victorious, If Only It Has the Will"),[41] a

---

40. Among his other recommendations:

(1) Cultivation of waste ground, particularly with exportable crops, such as hemp and tobacco

(2) Employing the poor (those without estate); if possible get foreigners to do so, since that will bring in foreign capital

(3) Exporting money, but only as a last resort and then in as niggardly a manner as possible; money is, after all, a commodity

(4) Remitting taxes on luxuries (presumably very profitable) when exported. (Mun 1664, 7–13)

41. The complete title is: Österreich über alles, wann es nur will. Das ist: Wohlmeinender Fürschlag, Wie Mittelst einer Wohlbestellten Landes-Öconomie, die Kayserl. Erb-Lande in kurtzen über alle andern Staaten von Europa zu erheben, und mehr als einiger derselben, von denen andern independent zu machen.

truly definitive statement of economic nationalism and the application of the mercantilist credo, is itself a set of policy recommendations addressed to administrators of a self-sufficient corporate state. As evidence of his interest in the promotion of such a strong centralized state, we need only point to Hornigk's belief that, while a particular enterprise may be unprofitable from the standpoint of the individual, this same undertaking could be run by the state at a profit; businessmen look to income and outflow, profit and loss, while the state is more concerned with total output and the income of the economy in the aggregate.

The policies for economic development that Hornigk formulated were dedicated to the maintenance of an isolated, self-sufficient economy. He saw them as necessary conditions for the creation and expansion of an autonomous, prosperous, and militarily and economically strong nation-state. The nine rules of Hornigk are:

(1) Exploit the land to the greatest degree possible. This includes not only agricultural production, which requires the cultivation of the more adaptable and profitable foodstuffs, and even experimentation with new and better varieties, but also includes mining, especially for gold and silver.

(2) Use natural resources within the country; do not export raw materials, but finished goods only.

(3) Increase the population to as large a number as can be supported. Focus on education and technical instruction in the trades, so as to enable the population to be fully employed and their skills to be exploited more completely.

(4) Precious metals are to be neither exported nor hoarded.

(5) To encourage domestic production the people should do without, as far as possible, imported goods.

(6) If imports are necessary, do not purchase them with gold or silver, but trade for them.

(7) Import goods in raw or unfinished form, so as to provide employment to the domestic industries.

(8) Seek out markets throughout the globe. The focus of the effort should be selling goods in their final form, in exchange for precious metals.

(9) Do not import anything which you yourself can produce at home, no matter how cheap in price the import may be. (See Monroe 1924, 223–25; and Gray 1931, 80–81.)

Finally, we should note that Hornigk's policy prescriptions were far from limited in application. In fact, as we shall see below, they later resurfaced in the policies of the cameralists. In addition, as derived from the work in economic development of the German economist Friedrich List, such policies became part of a larger approach to the fostering of economic growth in newly developing economies, serving as the basis for the "economic miracles" of the Asian economies in the mid- to late twentieth century.

Mercantilist Solutions to the Issues of the Day 5

The Setting 5.1

In addition to those noted above who advanced general statements of a mercantilist position, there were those who advanced specific policy objectives that were consistent with the general themes. Indeed, as we noted previously, many historians of economic thought—such as D. C. Coleman, Barry Supple, Charles Wilson, and R. W. K. Hinton—have held Mercantilism to have been a mere response to certain events and issues of the day, not a coherent set of policies dictated by reference to a central theoretical and philosophical core. These historians have held that Mercantilism is simply a categorical box into which economists, sympathetic to the simplicity afforded by the classification of economic "schools," have placed disparate sets of ideas. They point to the variations in the contents of those ideas as proof that a "school" of mercantilist thought did not exist; they argue that the policy recommendations just happen to be consistent with certain overarching themes. But the fact that these treatments are of the same subject may make them alternatives as well as complements. What follows is a set of controversies on specific issues. The reader will note that, despite the differences in the focus of the debates on the three issues, there remains the common thread of the preservation and enhancement of the power and security of the state.

Issue I: Exchange Rate Parities and the Export of Bullion 5.2

The first of the great debates with which we shall deal centered on the question of the impact of trade on the outflow of bullion. The three major protagonists in this debate were Gerard de Malynes, Edward Misselden, and Thomas Mun (again). While they differed on specifics, all were agreed that the outflow of bullion, in that it led directly to a liquidity crunch, was the cause of the depression of 1620.

Gerard de Malynes (ca. 1586–1641),[42] a British immigrant born in Antwerp, Belgium, worked variously as a merchant and as a civil servant. In two tracts published in 1601—*Saint George for England Allegorically*

---

42. Malynes was born into the Flemish van Mechelen family. In the 1580s he emigrated to London, where he served as assay master at the Royal Mint and advised the Privy Council on commercial policy during the reigns of Elizabeth I and James I. Well versed in mathematics, literature, and philosophy, he served on a Royal Commission set up to study problems of the British economy. For his involvement in a fraudulent business scheme, he was sentenced for a time to debtors' prison.

Described and *A Treatise on the Canker of England's Commonwealth*[43]— Malynes presented an early form of the quantity theory of money.[44]

An advocate of direct governmental control of the exchanges— going so far as to insist on the reinstitution of the office of Royal Exchanger, an office dating from the Middle Ages up to the time of Charles I—Malynes substantiated his position by maintaining that the market for foreign exchange was not self-equilibrating; it was in fact negatively reinforcing. Malynes held that it was exchange-rate fluctuations which influenced and in turn were influenced by the trade balance. A fall in the value of the pound, brought about initially by an adverse trade balance, would not lead to commensurate corrective changes in the trade balance (increasing exports and reducing imports), but would rather exacerbate the trade imbalances (by increasing import costs and reducing the value of exports even further). The result would be to precipitate an even greater outflow of bullion (as foreign currencies would become too expensive in terms of the pound). But this was only part of the story. The "disease" afflicting England was the reduction in national wealth brought about by three major factors: the exportation of bullion, the exportation of domestically produced goods at too low a price, and the importation of foreign goods at too high a price. In other words, a balance of trade deficit led inexorably to an outflow of specie.[45] As a remedy, he suggested fixed exchange rates, higher customs duties, and a prohibition of the export of bullion.

The fault lay partly in the conspiratorial activities of the bankers and exchange dealers, buying and selling foreign currencies. These early tracts betrayed a strikingly antibanker posture. Malynes argued that the bankers were in fact monopolists, indifferent if not in fact hostile to the national interest. Their monopoly position meant that they could determine the exchange rate, and that they could control this rate for their own ends, which were more often than not to the detriment of the nation. It was this institutionalized monopoly control which led, according to Malynes, to the outflow of specie experienced in the England of the time. In this Malynes seems to have been sympathetic to the Scholastic position

---

43. The complete title is: *A Treatise on the Canker of England's Commonwealth, divided into three parts; wherein the author, imitating the rule of good phisitions, first, declareth the disease; secondarily, sheweth the efficient cause thereof; lastly, a remedy for the same.*

44. In the *Treatise on the Canker*, Malynes showed an awareness that increased money flows resulted in higher prices, and he employed similar reasoning to explain price increases in terms of goods flows: ". . . plenty of money maketh generally things dear, and scarcity of money maketh likewise generally things good cheap. Whereas things particularly are also dear or good cheap according to plenty or scarcity of the things themselves, or the use of them" (Malynes 1601b, 387; quoted in Viner 1937, 41).

45. Heckscher held that Malynes's argument was "water-tight" but at the same time "altogether unreal," since "he supposed the situation to be permanent" (Heckscher 1935, vol. II, 246–47).

against usury, but extended the argument from domestic interest rates to the international trading sphere.[46]

Malynes is perhaps best known for his *Consuetudo, vel, Lex Mercatoria: Or the Ancient Law-Merchant* (1622a), a general treatise on mercantile law and the development of the customs of merchants.[47] In this work, he divided trade into three component parts, or "Simples": the body (commodities), the soul (money), and the spirit (the exchanges).[48] Barter (trade in commodities) was the original form of trade, and it "upheld the World" until replaced by coin. Coin, in like fashion, "did infuse life to Traffick, by the meanes of Equality and Equity, preventing advantage between Buyers and Sellers." Finally, development of the exchanges "corroborateth the vital Spirit of Traffick, directing and controlling, by just proportions, the Prices and Values of Commodities and Moneys" (Malynes 1622a, Preface and 44). The importance of the exchanges cannot be overemphasized: while money (coin) could be seen as the "publick measure between men and men," the exchanges represented the far more important "publick measure between nations" in the facilitation of commerce.

These three "Simples," the "Essential parts of Traffick," lend themselves to a tripartite exchange arrangement, so that one must consider trade in "Commodities for Commodities; Commodities for Money, and Commodities for Exchange of Money by Bills of Exchange" (1622a, 44). It is in this "Tripartite Exchange" that Malynes perceived the problem in regard to the state. The three different possibilities for exchange could be exploited by the merchant for his own gain, over the best interests of the state, leading invariably to a decline in the national wealth.[49] The causes of

46. Johnson maintained that Malynes's mistake was in attempting "to apply scholastic reasoning to a new field, to an area where that type of reasoning was really vulnerable" (Johnson 1937, 54).

47. The full title is: *Consuetudo, vel, Lex Mercatoria: Or the Ancient Law-Merchant. Divided into Three Parts, according to the Essential Parts of Traffick. Necessary for All Statesmen, Judges, Magistrates, Temporal and Civil Lawyers, Mint-Men, Merchants, Mariners, and all Others Negotiating in all Places of the World.*

48. "All the Traffick and Commerce between Nation and Nation, or man and man, is performed under three Simples which are properly the Essential parts of Traffick: Namely, *Commodities, Money,* and *Exchange for Money by Bills of Exchanges:* Which is effected by Number, Weight, and Measure . . ." (Malynes 1622a, 44).

49. For some Merchants do negotiate all for Commodities, others all for Money, or Exchanges, or for all three or any of them which yeeldeth them most benefit and gain: And herein is their particular profit, or *Privatum Commodum,* more respected than the generall good of the Common Wealth, whereby corruptable and unnecessary Commodities are given for Staple wares and durable Commodities, to the impoverishing of Kingdomes and Common-weals. And not only is this Commutation or Exchange abused in kind, but also in the price, paying too dear for the one, and selling the other too good cheape: Whereby cometh an over-ballancing of Commodities in price, and quality, and not in quantity; whereby in effect, Monies are given to boot, and as it were over and above the reasonable estimation of things; and herein is the course of Exchanges by Bills predominant, and over-ruling both the course of Commodities, and Money . . . (1622a, 44).

the national decline in wealth were thus three: selling too cheap, buying too dear, and transporting money in specie "when the Exchange of Moneys doth not answer the true value of it, by Bills of Exchanges" (1622a, 45). The solution to the problem was to avoid the "over-balancing of Commodities in price and quality" (45). To ensure this outcome, the "prince" had to take care that the national expenditures did not exceed revenues, meaning that there be maintained at all times "a certain Equality in the Traffick between his Kingdom and foreign Nations" (45).

The foil to Malynes was Edward Misselden (fl. 1608–54).[50] Misselden was, as was Malynes, a merchant, but unlike Malynes he had gained some diplomatic experiences in the Low Countries, where he represented the London Company of Merchant Adventurers. In his 1622 *Free Trade, or the Meanes to Make Trade Florish*,[51] Misselden propounded his own views of trade as the means to augment the power of the English state. His general views on trade serve as an important prologue to his views on the export of bullion.

According to Misselden, the primary reason for the English to engage in trade was to bolster the economic and political positions of the English state with respect to other nations. Once a thriving trade was established, the effects would redound to the domestic economy.[52] Measures to remedy the decay of trade must thus become part of the explicit policy objectives of the state (1622, 6).

Trade Misselden held to be of two forms: the natural and the artificial. The natural form of trade is merchandise—"which *Merchants* from the end of *Trade* have stiled *Commodities*"—while the artificial form is money—"which hath obtained the title of *Sinews* of *Warre* and of *State*" (1622, 7; emphasis in original). As to the artificial form of trade, there are two general reasons for the holding of money: the immediate, and the mediate or remote. The immediate reason for holding money is the value of the coin; it is "occasioned by the *Under-valuation* of *his* Majesties *Coyne*, to that of our Neighbour *Countries*," and serves to "*Hinder* the *Importation*; or . . . *Cause* the *Exportation* thereof" (7–8; emphasis in original).

The most general mediate domestic[53] reason for wanting money is the unfavorable trade balance, itself a result of "the *great Excesse* of this *Kingdome*, in consuming the *Commodities* of *Forrein Countries*, which

---

50. Misselden served as Deputy Governor of the Merchant Adventurer's Company in Delft (1623–33), later associating himself with the British East India Company.

51. The full title is: *Free Trade, or the Meanes to Make Trade Florish. Wherein, the Causes of the Decay of Trade in this Kingdome are Discovered: And the Remedies also to remoove the Same, are represented.*

52. "For when *Trade flourisheth, the Kings revenue is augmented, Lands and Rents improoved, Navigation is encreased, the poore employed,* But if *Trade* decay, *All these* decline with it" (Misselden 1622, 4; emphasis in original).

53. The foreign causes "are either in respect of the *Warres in Christendome,* or the *Trades out of Christendome*" (Misselden 1622, 17; emphasis in original).

prove to us *Discommodities,* in hindering us of so much *Treasure,* which otherwise would bee brought in, in lieu of those *Toyes* [luxury goods]" (1622, 11; emphasis in original). It was in respect of the special remote (domestic) cause of the want of money that the East India Company stock was in such demand at home. This Misselden felt to be of great concern, since it "causeth the *Body* of this *Common-wealth* to bee wounded sore, through the sides of many particular members thereof" (13; emphasis in original). Thus one of the principal reasons for the English depression was the increasing demand by foreign nations for English coin.

The solutions favored by Misselden were in direct opposition to Malynes's interest in fixed exchange rates. Misselden claimed that such regulations slowed the devaluation process necessary to encourage the usual trade balance mechanism to equilibrate. His own remedies involved measures to increase the flow of money into the kingdom, and to keep it from flowing out. To increase the flow of money to England he suggested (1) raising the value of English coin and (2) keeping it on a par with foreign currencies. To prevent the outflow he suggested (1) a reinvigoration of the Statute of Employments, which required foreign merchants to pay for purchases of English goods in bullion and (2) negotiation with foreign powers "to keepe a more constant course in the values of their Coines" (1622, 103–4). (But note that Misselden must have assumed these measures would have had no impact on the balance of trade, since otherwise the increase in the value of coin would *reduce* exports, not *increase* the inflow of bullion or coin.)

The natural form of trade was merchandise trade, "that naturall matter of *Commerce,* whereby men busie themselves in buying and selling, chopping and changing, to the encrease of *Artes,* and enriching of *Common-wealths.*" These commercial activities between nations Misselden held to have been at the invitation of God himself, "so that which is wanting to the *One,* might be supplied by the other, that all might have sufficient" (1622, 25). The decay of trade is thus the result of *deficient* or *efficient* causes impinging on its pursuit. The deficient causes are the want of money and East India Company stock, the former being the lifeblood of trade (here Misselden employed the biological analogy), the latter being responsible for the destruction of much of England's industrial and artistic vitality. The efficient causes are usury and "Unnecessary Suits in Law," the former being a form of extortion, the latter being a system abused to the point where "Suites of Law doe seeme immortall: time doth encrease them . . ." (29–33). Having to account for these causes is wasteful, since "time and meanes [are] spent in *Law,* which should be employed in *Trade* . . . (34; emphasis in original).

In all, for Misselden, the ideal state is likened to a family, the head of which is obliged to keep revenues ahead of expenditures. Only through the maintenance of a surplus could wealth be accumulated.[54] In terms of international trade, in general Misselden advocated free trade over any form of monopoly, again in terms applicable to the advancement of state power. But he did so with a proviso: while free trade is certainly to the advantage of the state, the state has an obligation to the common weal to control the flow and direction of trade, that is, to restrain "unskilfull and disorderly trade" (1622, 54). Free trade is not of itself a desirable state of affairs, as it promotes an unfettered environment in which the nation stands to lose in the end. Unrestrained trade is as undesirable as monopoly, since both result in a diminution of total wealth. The only recourse is to institute some form of order in the market. The argument Misselden gave in support of his conjecture is a simple and utilitarian one. The granting of a special license by Elizabeth I to the Merchant Adventurers, while establishing in essence a monopolistic trading company, had the effect of increasing the national wealth, because "the *Utilitie* that hereby arose to the *Common-wealth*, did farre exceede the restraint of the *Publique Libertie*" (63; emphasis in original). This increase of total societal utility was enough to make the case. Thus it was clear to Misselden that not "all subjects should bee alike free to bee Merchants in all Trades," if for no other reason that it is contrary to "the *Publique Utility*" that there be so many merchants involved in the same trade (65–66). In particular, he felt that England would gain in the long run by promoting an expansion of exports, while at the same time placing restrictions on imported goods. This would have the effect of expanding the export sector of the British economy and expanding the sectors that had suffered from forced competition from cheaper imported goods, the production costs of which were higher in England than elsewhere. In effect, Misselden argued for a "managed trade" regime, in which England would aggressively promote exports, while protecting the domestic infant industries from international competitive pressures.

Despite his stance on the granting of restrictive trading licenses, Misselden was very anti–East India Company, primarily because the company held a license to export bullion along with goods, and because it was a competitor (of sorts) of his own company (although he did eventually join the East India Company). A bullionist, Misselden argued (as did Malynes) that any trade that resulted in an outflow of bullion was contrary to the interests of the English state; the East India Company (the leading trading company) merely traded precious metals for consumables, so the state gained nothing in the process. By contrast, his own

---

54. "Even so a *Common-wealth* that excessively spendeth the *Forreigne* Commodities deere, and uttereth the *Native* fewer and cheaper, shall enrich other *Common-wealths*, but begger it selfe. When on the contrary, if it vented fewer of the *Forreigne,* and more of the *Native* the residue must needes return in treasure" (1622, 12).

company sold English-produced consumer goods for other European goods, a practice he held to be more enlightened since it showed a greater national devotion in international trade.

Malynes replied to Misselden in *The Maintenance of Free Trade* (1622b),[55] repeating his earlier arguments and reprising his statements from the *Ancient Law-Merchant*. Malynes accused Misselden directly of not having considered the critical role played in trade by the exchanges.[56] Considering again the "three Simples" regarding international trade, namely, commodities, money, and the mechanism for the exchange of money, but this time employing the example of the mechanism of a clock, Malynes observed that money "became the first wheele which stirreth the wheele of *Commodities* and inforceth the *Action*" (1622b, 6; emphasis in original). The exchanges were thus the "active" device in control of the "passive" money and commodities.

In offering a rebuttal to Malynes, Misselden then published a wild attack, *The circle of commerce or the balance of trade* (1623),[57] charging Malynes with plagiarism, in that he had in the *Ancient Law-Merchant* copied the work of Thomas Gresham.[58] (Of course, upon analysis, one can see that Misselden as well had borrowed copiously without crediting others.) In this tract, Misselden advanced the thesis that the exchange rate was no different from any other price: it was determined in a competitive market. He rejected the view of Malynes that exchange-rate differentials were responsible for specie flows, maintaining that the totality of foreign trade dictated by demand-supply conditions was the dominant controlling factor. This led Misselden to argue in favor of policies encouraging

55. The full title is: *The Maintenance of Free Trade, According to the Three Essentiall Parts of Traffique; Namely, Commodities, Moneys and Exchange of Moneys, by Bills of Exchange for other Countries. Or, An answer to a Treatise of Free Trade, or the meanes to make Trade Flourish, lately Published.*

56. In the Dedicatory, Malynes proclaimed: "Where upon having lately perused a *Treatise* intituled *Free Trade, or, The meanes to make Trade flourish;* wherein the Author, either ignorantly or wilfully, hath omitted to handle *The Predominant Part of Trade,* namely, *the Mystery of Exchange:* which is the *Publike measure* betweene us and other Nations, according to which, all our Commodities are bought and sold in forraine parts: his only *Scope* being, to have the Moneys of the Kingdome inhaunced in price, and the forraine Coynes made Currant within the Realm at high Rates . . ." (Malynes 1662b).

57. The full title is: *The Circle of Commerce. Or the Ballance of Trade, in defence of free Trade: Opposed to Malynes Little Fish and his great Whale, and poized against them in the Scale. Wherein also, Exchanges in generall are considered: and therein the Whole Trade of the Kingdome with forraine Countries, is digested into a Ballance of Trade, for the benefite of the Publique. Necessary for the present and future times.*

58. Thomas Gresham (ca. 1519–79) was something of an economic genius who managed to advise three British monarchs, Elizabeth I, Mary, and James I. Gresham was by trade a mercer, but entered the Goldsmith's Company and became a major banker. He was personally somewhat less than deferential, and his continued success should be attributed to a repeated royal recognition of the value of his advice. Gresham is best known for "Gresham's Law," which holds that "bad money doth drive out good."

exports and discouraging imports, which would result in a greater inflow of treasure.[59]

Finally, Thomas Mun, whose general views were mentioned above, advanced opinions on this issue which were anti-Malynes and pro-Misselden in the sense that he had doubts as to how well exchange-rate controls could work. Exchange differentials were not the problem; that is, the undervaluation of the British pound was not the reason for the flow of money out of the kingdom. The reason was the trade imbalance: "it is not the undervaluing of our money in exchange, but the over-ballancing of our trade that carrieth away our treasure" (Mun 1664, 41). Malynes's mistake, according to Mun, had been in failing to see the trade imbalance as the true cause of an outflow of money. Malynes confused a "secondary means" with "the Principle Efficient," that is, he confused exchange-rate differentials with trade imbalances, thus arriving at a pro-posed remedy that did not address the problem.

For Mun, specie served merely as a facilitative medium; its sole purpose was to promote ease of transaction. He could then decouple the mere outflow of specie from any effects on the prosperity of the nation; what mattered was the trade balance. It simply did not matter how many pounds the English spent for imports, so long as exports remained at a greater level. In fact, Mun advocated trade in money as well as goods, since the trade in money could be very lucrative, especially in those instances in which the country with which trade was to take place did not need the physical goods produced for export. "It would be very beneficial to export money as well as wares, being done in trade only, it would encrease our Treasure" (1664, 11). Eventually, this money so exported will return in any event:

> if we have such a quantity of wares as doth fully provide us of all things needful from beyond the seas: why should we then doubt that our monys sent out in trade, must not necessarily come back again in treasure. . . .
>
> For if we only behold the actions of the husbandman in the seed-time when he casteth away much good corn into the ground, we will rather accompt him a mad man than a husbandman: but when we consider his labours in the harvest which is the end of his endeavours, we find the worth and plentiful encrease of his actions. (1664, 19)

Although he accepted that the East India Company had the author-ity to export bullion in exchange for goods, he could discount this part of the trade on the grounds that the overall drain of bullion was negligible. As Mun was an East India Company director, and an antibullionist, he

---

59. Incidentally, Misselden also in the tract abandoned his earlier position regarding the East India Company. Johnson noted that the *Circle of Commerce* "was published in the same year that he [Misselden] was chosen by the India Company to negotiate a private treaty with the Dutch" (Johnson 1937, 61).

sided in the debate with the company. Thus emerges an interesting compromise: "Rome" (the East India Company) came to embrace "Luther" (Misselden). But what the contribution of Mun also shows is that the functional (pragmatic) test was involved in no small way. Mun desired to keep the value of coin stable, since "mony is not only the true measure of all our other means in the Kingdom, but also of our forraign commerce with strangers, which therefore ought to be kept just and constant to avoid those confusions which ever accompany such alterations" (1664, 28).

Issue II: Establishing Artificially Low Interest Rates (Measures against Usury)

5.3

A second problem facing the mercantilists was the question of the role of the state in the establishment of low (nonusurious) interest rates. Sir Josiah Child (1630–99),[60] a principal in this debate, was, as were many mercantilists, an unusually successful merchant and later a Director (1673) and then (1681) Governor of the British East India Company (as well as an adviser to Oliver Cromwell, and to the later Stuart monarchs). He was also a member of the Council of Trade, the membership of which included Lord Shaftesbury.[61]

In his 1668 Brief observations concerning trade and interest of money, Child argued for the English to emulate the Dutch in trading practices, so as to secure a similar growth in domestic and foreign trade. At the time, the English were involved in a war with the Dutch over trade. It was becoming clear that England was in danger of losing its position in world commerce: the sale of English cloth to foreigners was stagnant, the Newfoundland fish catch was declining, English cattle producers faced competition from the Irish, and the Dutch were becoming masters of commercial shipping. Child's "remedy" took the form of fifteen specific policy recommendations,[62] but the one held (by Child himself) to have

---

60. Little is known of Child's early years. In 1653 he was an agent for the Admiralty Commissioners and in 1655 became Deputy of the Navy Treasurer at Portsmouth. Also in that year he became burgess, and in 1658 he was selected mayor of Portsmouth. After 1665 (he had been removed from his posts by Charles II and banned from any dealings with the Royal Navy in 1662, but had reestablished his connections three years later), he purchased a brewery in Southwark and supplied the Navy with beer (he also secured a commission as Brewer to the King). In 1671 he proceeded to purchase stock in the East India Company, eventually becoming the largest stockholder, and so was named a director. In 1673 he was elected to Parliament, and in 1678 he was named a Baronet. On Child see particularly Letwin 1964, chapter 1.

61. Child's membership angered the Duke of York (later Charles II), who saw it as too pro-Parliament.

62. (1) Introduce into the government the merchants, whose experiences in trade gave them practical knowledge of the situation, and heed their counsel; (2) reform the laws of estate to allow an equal share to be granted to each child; (3) demand quality in the production of domestically produced commodities (especially those destined for export) so

been the most significant was restriction of the rate of interest. Child held that the maximum allowable rate of interest was in fact the "*causa causans*" of the wealth of the Dutch. Specifically, he argued that if the English lowered *slightly* the allowable interest rate—from the prevailing rate of six percent to around four percent—the economy would expand and "it would in a short time render us as Rich and Considerable in Trade as they [the Dutch] are now, and consequently be of greater dammage to them, and advantage to us, then can happen by the Issue of this present War . . ." (1668, 7). He believed, against the opinions of many, that the rate of interest directly affected the level of wealth, not vice versa. The historical record made this clear, demonstrating that lower interest rates did indeed encourage merchants to expand their activities, allowing them to gain ever larger aggregates *and profits.*

The entire nation would gain, Child reasoned, in the following ways, and in opposition to the dire consequences suggested by his critics. First, the lowering of the maximum allowable rate of interest would have little effect on Dutch money in English banks and Dutch investment in English firms, since the Dutch interest rate was even lower than that advocated. Should in fact the Dutch money flee, this would be to England's favor, since it would no longer be at the mercy of Dutch funding.[63] In addition, should Parliament enact Child's law respecting debt transfer, the effect of any Dutch action would be negligible.

Secondly, to the charge that a lowering of the allowable rate of interest would increase rents and the prices of commodities, Child held this to be nothing if not evidence of an increase in the general level of prosperity: "*wherever Provisions are for continuance of years dear in any Country, the People are rich; and where they are most cheap throughout the World, for the most part the People are very poor*" (1668, 11, emphasis in original). The impact on the poor would be overall positive, as the

---

as to gain a reputation for excellence in manufacturing; (4) grant patent and copyright protections to encourage invention; (5) build a more efficient and competitive commercial shipping fleet; (6) encourage savings; (7) expand the educational system to provide for universal training (including girls), especially in arithmetic and accounting; (8) lower the customs taxes while increasing the excise taxes; (9) employ the poor (do not leave them to the care of the parishes); (10) establish commercial banks; (11) tolerate divergent religious opinions; (12) establish a system of law-merchants to facilitate the handling of disputes between merchants and tradesmen; (13) institute a discount market for the transference of debt, so as to free the merchants from the need to collect from a sale before commencing again in trade; (14) establish a system of public records to record transactions of real estate; and (15) restrict the rate of interest allowed (Child 1668, 3–6).

63. As Child stated (emphatically): "HE THAT USETH A STOCK THAT IS NONE OF HIS OWN, BEING FORCED FOR THE UPHOLDING HIS REPUTATION TO LIVE TO THE FULL, IF NOT ABOVE THE PROPORTION OF WHAT HE DOTH SO USE, WHILE THE LENDER POSSESSING MUCH, AND USING LITTLE OR NONE, LIVES ONELY AT THE CHARGE OF WHAT HE USETH, AND NOT OF WHAT HE HATH" (Child 1668, 11; uppercase emphasis in original).

dearness of goods would force them to work harder for the provision of their daily needs.[64]

Thirdly, the reductions would not cause the wealthy to recall their loans, since (as with the Dutch) they cannot receive a higher return anywhere else. Fourthly, the ability of the sovereign to secure funds in time of emergency would be strengthened, since, as he previously paid a premium above the legal maximum to secure needed funding, his rate would also be reduced, with the result being a substantial savings to the Crown.

Finally, to those on a fixed pension, the reduction would be also favorable, since the executors would then be in a position to invest the estates in trade or land, and so amass a greater return. In sum, Child's argument eventually won out, as Parliament in 1669 passed the bill reducing the maximum allowable rate of interest.

Child went on to extend his views slightly in his anonymously published *Discourse about Trade* (1690), arguing that the policy of a low interest rate was more effective than restrictions on bullion. This work, a revised edition of his *Brief Observations,* took up once again the argument of the power position of the state. The East India Company, as an authorized trading monopoly, was lauded as performing a public service. In defense of the Navigation Acts, he argued that "trade was really a form of war" and that, in the quest for victory, one needed good soldiers able to fight the battles, irrespective of their religion (thus he favored Jews having access to economic life in London). It was Child who may be said to have best enunciated the mercantilist position in catchphrase form: "Foreign trade produces riches, riches power, power preserves our trade and religion" (quoted in Viner 1937, 112).

Not all mercantilist writers, however, agreed entirely with Child's prescriptions. Having disposed of the problem of the general pattern of trade, Malynes then considered usury, a problem at the fore of his trade theory. He defined usury as "any thing taken above the Principal" (1622a, 225), and after presenting a lengthy excursion into the early positions on the subject, concluded that "in regard of Traffick and Trade," usury was "a necessary evil" (227). Thus he was led to accept a less strict definition: "the matter of Conscience consisteth in the not getting of your debtor, and not in the taking of much or little Interest" (228), implying that the taking of interest was acceptable provided the borrower would not be adversely affected by the transaction.

Apart from the moral questions involved, usury presented a problem in the operation of trade, for it is "according to the rate of Usury [that] men do measure all their actions by trade and traffick, or purchase,

---

64. Heckscher noted that Child even suggested increasing wages, since the Dutch had done so and in the process had been able to attract a better-skilled work force. High wages were thus proof of a strong national economy: "Where ever wages are high universally throughout the whole World, it is an infallible evidence of the Riches of that Country" (Heckscher 1935, vol. II, 169).

build, plant and bargain in all things accordingly" (1622a, 230). Malynes indeed saw a direct link between the increase in usury and the decay of trade, "as pasturage doth increase with the decrease of tilling" (230). The remedy is

> to have plenty of Mony really *in specie* within the Realm, together with the means used in other Countries in the lieu of Monies. . . . For plenty of Money will not only prevent, but also effect the benefits intended . . . , making Usury to decrease in price . . . : Then will the Kings Customs increase, and Commerce flourish, Noblemens and Gentlemens lands be improved, Merchants and Artificers be incouraged, young Beginners be inabled, Labourers find quick imployment, and Usurers may have land for their Monies. (232)

The entire economy thus will gain, even the usurers, from the simple expedient of maintaining a greater supply of money within the nation.

It was not simply the search for a nonusurious rate of interest that intrigued the mercantilists; the search for stability was also of paramount importance. In the present century, John Maynard Keynes attempted to rehabilitate a mercantilist position concerning the role of the state in the maintenance of a stable rate of interest. The doctrine, which for Keynes "deserves rehabilitation and honor," held "that the rate of interest is not self-adjusting at a level best suited to the social advantage but constantly tends to rise too high, so that a wise Government is concerned to curb it by statute and custom and even by invoking the sanctions of the moral law" (Keynes 1936, 351).

5.4 Issue III: Should the Extrinsic Value of Coin Approximate Its Intrinsic Worth?

The final issue with which we shall deal is whether the value of money (coin) should be tied to its value in terms of bullion. One problem with which the British mercantilists dealt was the basic shortage of coin.[65] By the late seventeenth century it had become evident that the English people had lost confidence in the value of the silver coins circulating as legal tender. Merchants went so far as to weigh coins offered for payment and accept only the value of the "true" weight, which was not necessarily the monetary face value of the coin. No small part of the problem was the physical incidental and deliberate debasement of the coin (a problem known as "clipping"), as well as the uncertainty of political stability (which made the legitimacy of the government and hence fiat money questionable), the hunger of each business faction for

---

65. See J. Keith Horsefield (1960) and William Letwin (1964) for fine discussions of the background to the recoinage issue. A particularly good reference is Ming Hsun Li (1969).

pecuniary gain, and the competitiveness within and among the various social groups.

The Great Recoinage of 1696 was an effort to reestablish confidence in English coins. By 1663 it became technically possible to mint uniform coins that foiled the clippers and, incidentally, minimized wear. As the new coins were thicker than the old, they tended to be hoarded and so removed from circulation. It soon became obvious that the government, in an effort to reestablish confidence in the monetary system, had to take steps to demonetize the old coins, leaving the new, uniform coins as the only unit of exchange.

The first figure in this episode is Nicholas Barbon (1637?–98).[66] A physician by training, Barbon entered early into the fray. In his *Discourse of Trade* (1690)[67] he argued that the value of money, as with any other measure, is arbitrary, this value being set by the state; "Mony is a Value made by a Law," not a derivative from the metal content of the coin (Barbon 1690, 16). Barbon reasoned as follows: there does not exist any "natural" system of measurement or weight; every such system is invented for the benefit of uniformity in trade, and its integrity is protected by the power of the state. Thus all intrinsic values are abstractions and thus meaningless unless made instrumental by legal statute. As Barbon phrased it:

> Nothing in itself hath a certain Value; One thing is as much worth as another: And it is time, and place, that give a difference to the Value of all things. (1690, 18)

As for goods, so for money. As money serves as (1) a measure of value, and (2) a means of exchange, "the Value of Mony must be made certain by Law, or else it could not be made a certain Measure, nor an Exchange for the Value of all things" (1690, 16). Should the intrinsic value of the metal used as coin be taken as a measure of the value of the coin, it is clear that, as the value of the metal itself fluctuates, so would the value of the commodity money. In fact, Barbon denied that metals such as gold and silver had any "Intrinsick Vertue or Quality" at all, and he maintained that scarcity alone was the chief agent responsible for their value (18). For Barbon, as the value of money is determined solely by law,

---

66. Educated at Leyden and Utrecht (M.D., 1661), Barbon was elected Honorary Fellow of the College of Physicians in London in 1664. He also played a major role in the [mal]construction of St. Paul's Cathedral and set up one of the first fire insurance companies as well as a land bank (using land titles as an asset for security). Generally Barbon was believed to be interested only in self-advancement.

For those interested in historical oddities, Barbon's father had been christened Unless-Jesus-Christ-Had-Died-for-Thee-Thou-Hadst-Been-Damned Barbon; he came to be known as Praisegod Barbon.

67. The *Discourse of Trade* also contained his views on the basis of trade, in which he expressed his disagreement with Mun, and his views on the interest controversy, in which he concurred with Child.

it follows that, so long as the state is politically and economically stable, the material content of the coin should not present itself as an issue.[68]

In technical parlance, Barbon maintained a fiduciary theory of money, one which would provide the basis for the later use of paper currency. As the paper itself has no intrinsic value, the value of the printed note derives from government fiat and maintains because of the continued faith of the people in the stability of the government.[69] The precious metals could thus leave the country, as they may in any event through their use as plate or ornamentation, and the state need not have occasion for concern.[70]

A second leading figure in the debate on the Great Recoinage was none other than John Locke, an adviser to the Warden (later Master) of the Mint, Sir Isaac Newton.[71] Locke argued persuasively in his 1691 *Some Considerations of the Consequences of the Lowering of Interest, and Raising the Value of Money* that the value of the coin must be reestablished at its previous value. The basis of the coin—in this instance silver—had an intrinsic value, one which cannot be altered simply by fiat or enactment.

Locke began by noting, as did Barbon, that money serves two functions: as a medium of exchange and as a measure of value, or as "counter" and "pledge."[72] For Locke, money has "no other value, but as

---

68. Mony hath the same Value, and performs the same Uses, if it be made of Brass, Copper, Tin, or any thing else. The Brass Mony of *Spain,* the copper Mony of *Sweeden,* and Tin Farthings of *England,* have the same Value in Exchange, according to the Rate they are set at and perform the same Uses, to Cast up the Value of things, as the Gold and Silver Mony does; . . . : Therefore, all Foreign Coins go by Weight, and are of no certain Value, but rise and fall with the Price of the Metal. (1690, 16–17)

In addition, Barbon noted the important role of *credit,* which served also as a form of money: "Credit is a Value raised by Opinion, it buys Goods as Mony doe's; and in all Trading Citys, there's more Wares sold upon Credit, then for present Mony" (Barbon 1690, 18–19).

69. Yet despite his contention that money acquired value only a result of fiat, Barbon held there to be a very compelling reason for the state to require the use of the precious metals as the basis of coin, this being to prevent counterfeiting:

for Silver and Gold, being Metals of great Value, those who design Profit by Counterfeiting the Coin, must Counterfeit the Metals, as well as the Stamp, which is more difficult than the Stamp. (1690, 17)

70. Barbon's position was also quite distinct from that of many of the other mercantilist writers, for he denied the proposition that the state was the simple extension of the individual. While the individual may be constrained by resource considerations, a nation need not be so hampered in its operations. The macroeconomy is not to be viewed as the simple aggregation of households.

71. Newton (1642–1727) is said to have been uncompromising on the issue of counterfeiting, sending a number of counterfeiters to the gallows.

72. Money is necessary . . . as serving both for Counters and for Pledges, and so carrying with it even Reckoning, and Security, that he, that receives it, shall have the same Value for it again, of other things that he wants, whenever he pleases. The one of these it does by its Stamp and Denomination; the other by its intrinsick Value, which is its *Quantity.* (1691, 31)

Pledges to procure, what one wants or desires" (1691, 31). Money, he granted, has an "imaginary" value determined by the state, through the agreement of the citizenry. Following on this "consent" to value, the citizens of the state agree to a set ratio of exchange, "to receive equally valuable things to those they parted with for any *quantity* of these Metals" (31; emphasis in original). But this value must be a "true" or natural value. In essence, intrinsic values exchange for intrinsic values.

Further, the use of money as a "counter," which is the sole import of the state's stamp or denomination, is not in fact particularly significant; it is the intrinsic value—money as a pledge—which is significant for trade, both domestic and international. The reason is obvious enough, comprising elements of the social contract (mutual consent) and trust in the ability of the state to guarantee the value of its own currency.[73]

In essence, Locke maintained that money, to be accepted, must first pass a test of usefulness: it must be of a "known" value, one "better fixed by Name, Number, and Weight, to enable us, to reckon, what the Proportion of Scarcity and Vent of one Commodity is to another" (1691, 52). It is the common and accepted measure which is important: for Locke, should silver and lead exchange in fixed proportions for a given measure of wheat, it would not be valid to suggest that the lead will *purchase* that quantity of wheat. While we use silver as a basis of exchange, we are not accustomed to so using lead—lead "is not generally used to this sort of Reckoning," while silver and other precious metals "are measures whose ideas by constant use are settled in every English Man's mind" (53).

Continuing along in his definition, Locke held that money "is really a standing measure of the falling and rising value of other Things in reference to one another: and the alteration of price is truly in them only" (1691, 70). Thus while all other commodities are created to be sold ("vented"), money is fundamentally different: the desire is to keep as much of this commodity as possible. Thus it must be the case that

> nothing can *raise* or *fall the value* of your Money, but the proportion of its Plenty, or Scarcity, in proportion to the Plenty, Scarcity, or Vent of any other Commodity, with which you compare it, or for which you would exchange it. And thus Silver, which makes the

---

73. Since the Bill, Bond, or other Note of Debt, I receive from one Man will not be accepted as Security by another, he not knowing that the Bill or Bond is true or legal, or that the Man bound to me is honest or responsible; and so is not valuable enough to become a current Pledge, nor can by publick Authority be well made so, as in the Case of Assigning of Bills. Because a Law cannot give to Bills that intrinsick Value, which the universal Consent of Mankind has annexed to Silver and Gold. And hence Foreigners can never be brought to take your Bills, or Writings for any part of Payment, though perhaps they might pass as valuable Considerations among your own People, did not this very much hinder, *viz.* That they are liable to unavoidable Doubt, Dispute, and Counterfeiting, and require other Proofs; to assure us that they are true and good Security, than our Eyes or a Touchstone. (Locke 1691, 32)

Intrinsick Value of Money, compar'd with it self, under any Stamp or Denomination of the same or different Countries, cannot be *raised*. For an Ounce of Silver, whether in *Pence, Groats,* or *Crown* Pieces, *Stivers* or *Ducatoons,* or in Bullion, is and always eternally will be of equal Value to any other Ounce of Silver, under what Stamp or Denomination soever; unless it can be shewn that any Stamp can add any new and better qualities to one parcel of Silver, which another parcel of Silver wants.

Silver therefore being always of equal Value to *Silver,* the *value of Coin,* compar'd with Coin, is greater, less, or equal, only as it has more, less or equal *Silver* in it: And in this respect, you can by no manner of way raise or fall your Money. (135; emphasis in original)

The best one can hope to achieve in this regard is "to *alter the Denomination,* and call that a Crown now, which before by the Law was but a part of a Crown" (1691, 136; emphasis in original). This may be done in one of two ways, either by (1) increasing the value of one species of money, or (2) increasing the value of all at once. To the first, Locke held it to be nothing more than a legal "clipping" of the money, with the consequence being a reduction in public compliance, an "unavoidable inconvenience" to the domestic public, and a boon to foreigners. To the second, the consequences will also be dire, since the change will affect creditors adversely and lead to a general rise in prices (139). In the end, money is valued by its silver content alone (145).

In his *Further Consideration Concerning Raising the Value of Money* (1695), Locke reiterated his position from that in the 1691 tract, that the state was compelled to maintain a standard of monetary value. For the government to maintain a value for the monetary instrument that diverged from the intrinsic value of the commodity metal would be self-defeating, for the public would not accept the standard as a basis for exchange or of value. Thus Locke's position, unlike Barbon's, did not require the continued faith of the public in the legitimacy and stability of the government for the currency to retain value; even if the public were to express grave doubt in the legitimacy of the state, this would in no sense affect trade, since the value of the monetary medium is independently determined, not established through government fiat.[74]

6 Cameralism: Unity of State and Economy

6.1 Cameralism Defined

Thus far we have portrayed Mercantilism as primarily a British phenomenon, allowing for French and Austrian influences. (We shall revisit the

---

74. In the *Discourse Concerning Coining the New Lighter Money* (1696) Barbon responded to Locke, continuing in the direction of his earlier pamphlet.

French mercantilists in the next chapter.) But a quite different form of state control of the economy developed in the German states in the seventeenth century—the doctrine of Cameralism.

Cameralism was a uniquely German (specifically Prussian) concept—the German form of the word, *Kameralwissenschaft,* means literally the science of economic administration.[75] The sociologist Albion Small defined it thus:

> Exaggerating almost to paradox, we may say that cameralism was not a theory and practice of economics but of politics. Cameralism was a technique and a theory of administering a peculiar type of state in a society constructed out of peculiar types of purposes. To be sure, economic conditions and purposes formed their share of the circumstances to which cameralism was an adaptation. . . . Cameralism raised, directly and deliberately, no fundamental questions of pure economics. It was primarily a theory and a technique of government. Solution of problems of the nature and laws of wealth is *logically* antecedent to governmental institutions, to be sure, but until the last quarter of the eighteenth century the principle had been generally ignored. Governmental theory dealt with economic problems of course. Instead of formulating these separately as economic problems, however, it recognized no economic problems of the degree of generality familiar since Adam Smith's time. It dealt with economic relations as merely incidental to the application of governmental principles, and the latter, as proclaimed at the time, were in many respects narrowly provincial. (Small 1909, 3; emphasis in original)

Small did not believe that Cameralism was a version of Mercantilism (or vice versa); Mercantilism "as political economy, in the sense at present associated with that term, in contrast with political policy, did not exist among the cameralists" (1909, 14). To the cameralists, the central concern was with the welfare of the state; for the mercantilists, the policy was international competition, akin to war. Heckscher, however, did equate Cameralism with Mercantilism, the similarity being in the desire of each for the furtherance of the political power of the state. As Heckscher put it, "the task of the cameralists consisted in filling the 'chamber' of the prince, in other words, they were to ensure that the sources of his income did not run dry" (Heckscher 1935, vol. II, 20).

Despite the similarity, it may be said that Cameralism differs from Mercantilism in that the latter is a characterization of efforts by governments to *direct* their economies through legislation, while the former is a doctrine wherein the state and the economy are so *intertwined* as to be

---

75. Keith Tribe (1988) noted that the term derived from the Latin and Greek root *camera.* The German *Kammer* referred to the apartment of the prince.

indistinguishable. Small held that conditions in the Germanic states of the seventeenth and eighteenth centuries were particularly conducive to the development of a doctrine of state supremacy. Relevant factors included natural endowments, the constitution of the old Holy Roman Empire, the state of contemporary science, philosophy, and technology, and the inherited (Roman and Teuton) legal tradition (Small 1909, 3–4).[76] State interests became paramount, and the cameralists, as dutiful servants of the state, held that by identifying the state interest, all other interests would be determined by extension. "Cameralism was the system elaborated by the chief agents of the rulers, partly as mere classification of practices which the rulers had already adopted; partly as ways and means of accomplishing more of the purposes which the state proposed" (4). Its most important facet is the Hobbesian belief in *"the paramount value of the collective interests, or in other words the subordination of the interests of the individual to the interests of the community"* (16; emphasis in original).

In his study of the evolution of German economic rhetoric from 1750 to 1840, Keith Tribe noted distinct changes in Prussian attitudes toward government that led to the development of Cameralism. Tribe maintained that Cameralism began in the Prussian universities as a means of creating a more efficient system for the administration of the Prussian bureaucracy.[77] This coincided with a fundamental change in attitude toward the role of the state in governance—a change from *Staatskunst* or "the art of governing," to *Staatswissenschaft,* "the science of governing" (Tribe 1988, 8).[78]

---

76. Small suggested that "the German territorial sovereignties in the period of the Reformation were essentially more like a typical Virginia plantation, in the most flourishing days of the Old Dominion, than like any political unit with which modern Americans are familiar" (Small 1909, 4).

77. Tribe noted that Friedrich Wilhelm I, on July 24, 1727, appointed Simon Peter Gasser (1676–1745)—former Extraordinary Professor of Law at the University of Halle, and known as a fine administrator—to a chair in "Oeconomie, Policey und Cammersachen" at Halle. The purpose of the chair was to provide the students there with " 'a good grounding in the aforementioned sciences in good time and before they are employed in service' " (Tribe 1988, 42). Gasser's lectures were presented in the Faculty of Law and were "chiefly concerned with details of domain administration—buildings, cattle, fields, milling, duties and taxation, forestry, and hunting" (43).

78. Tribe interpreted the evolution thus:

> The wise monarch had to balance his need for revenue against the general welfare of his subjects—money was needed for the army which protected the ruler, but there was no future in impoverishing the ruler's subjects, since this would simply destroy his financial base. In these circumstances, governing was an art, the true nature of which was proposed by tracts addressed to the ruler but which could be read with profit by state officials. In the early eighteenth century, however, *Staatskunst* was replaced by *Staatswissenschaft.* . . . The teachings of Natural Law soon modified this [purely descriptive approach] towards the inherent regularities in society and economy, and it was here that Cameralism, as the science of governing with respect to economic processes, played an important part. In so far as the reform of administrative practice represents

The role of Natural Law in this connection is important. While Locke's view of Natural Law centered on the primacy of the individual, for the cameralists the individual is considered only so far as he is part of the larger social polity. In contrast to Locke, with his atomistic view of society, the cameralists held that society was more along the lines of an organic whole, implying that order must be imposed (as in Hobbes) for the benefit of the entire organism, a position consistent with the philosophy of the German philosopher Gottfried Leibniz.[79] Individual concerns then become secondary to social order, to the health of the entire organism: "the rationale appears to be based on the assumption that social order is owed uniquely to governing activity and not to any human qualities, whether selfish or selfless" (Tribe 1988, 29).

The Founders of the Movement   6.2

According to Small, the notion of *Kameralwissenschaft* can be traced to the establishment by Emperor Maximilian I of several *Reichskammer* in about 1495. In terms of intellectual development of the theory of Cameralism, Melchior von Osse (1506–57) in his *Testament* of 1555 did much to set the parameters of the study. In terms of formal structure, Small referred to Veit Ludwig von Seckendorff (1626–92) as the "Adam Smith of cameralism" (Small 1909, 69); Pribram esteemed him as "probably the first German author to propound a coordinated program of public administration" (Pribram 1983, 91). Seckendorff's 1655 *Der Teutsche Fürsten Staat* is a guide to the establishment of an administrative state. Here he described the governing activity of the typical German state as follows:

> . . . the princely government in the German principalities and lands, as in almost every rightly and wisely ordered *Policey,* is nothing else than the supreme and highest dominion of the properly ruling territorial prince or lord, which is enforced and exercised by him over the estates and subjects of the principality, also over the land itself

---

an attempt to establish an effective symbiotic relationship between these economic processes and the activity of governing, the "Cameralistic sciences" play a strategic role in the constitution of Prussian bureaucratic rule and, by extension, in the modern bureaucratic state. (1988, 8)

79. In correspondence, Leibniz expressed his admiration for Hobbes's theory of the state. Specifically, in Letters 189 and 195 in *The Correspondence of Thomas Hobbes,* Leibniz commented thus:

> I am not in the habit of flattering, but everyone who has been able to understand your writings on political theory agrees with me that nothing can possibly be added to the clarity of their arguments, which is so admirable when they are expressed so concisely. (Letter 189, 716–17)

> I can see clearly enough that your demonstrations [of the basis of human society], like those of geometry, are universal and abstracted from the matter which they deal with . . . (Letter 195, 734–35)

and its appurtenances, for the maintenance and promotion of the common profit and welfare, and for the administration of justice. (Quoted in Small 1909, 74)

While Seckendorff maintained that the rulers were attuned to the "common profit and welfare," and were thus not autocrats—for to be such would imply that the ruler "regards himself as the highest, and . . . , with or without right, uses the greatest power upon all the others for his profit and advantage, according to his will and caprice alone" (1909, 74)—Small did note that the "profit and welfare" promoted was often that of the *ruler*, not the *ruled*. Thus Cameralism even in its earliest phases represented a legitimation of autocratic rule: it "was the technique and the philosophy of states in which this situation was taken for granted" (1909, 75).[80]

In all, Seckendorff presented the fundamentals of a system which "posited the dignity and power of the government as the foremost consideration" (Small 1909, 82). To attempt to understand the principles of Cameralism without reference to this central concern is, as Small maintained, to "radically" misconstrue the entire focus of the school.

While Seckendorff certainly set the stage in the development of a cameralist view of economy and society, it was Johann Heinrich Gottlob von Justi (1717–68)[81] who produced the most dramatic statement of the principles of the movement. Small went so far as to cast him as "the John Stuart Mill of the movement," and so it is on his contributions that we shall here focus.[82] A man of varied interests and great intellect, he wrote on numerous subjects, including philosophy, the natural sciences, history, and law. (Small actually devoted five entire chapters to a discussion of various aspects of Justi's economics and his cameralist theories.)

Justi's recommendations were set forth in his 1760 *Natur und Wesen der Staaten als die Grundwissenschaft der Staatskunst, der Polizei und aller Regierungswissenschaften,* basically a treatise on the appropriate form for the study of scientific state administration. In order to provide a justification for the prescriptions recommended, Justi maintained

---

80. To the end of providing for the general "profit and welfare," Seckendorff enumerated four categories of prerogatives of the German prince: (1) to assert his power so as to promote the efficiency of the government; (2) to establish a fair and equitable system of laws, designed first and foremost to promote the power of the prince; (3) to adjudicate as the supreme authority in a fair manner, with due enforcement; and (4) to construct the institutional infrastructure for the administration of the above (Small 1909, 76).

81. Justi—described by Tribe as "a self-ennobled adventurer" (Tribe 1988, 55)—held the chair of cameral science at the Theresianum in Vienna (1750). The date of birth is from Small. Tribe gave the birth date as 1720; Pribram stated it as 1705. Schumpeter (1954) gave the date of death as 1771.

82. We should also mention here the work of Johann Joachim Becher (1635–82), especially *Politische Discurs von den eigentlichen Ursachen des Auff- und Abnehmens der Städt Länder und Republicken* (1668), and Wilhelm Freiherr von Schröder, especially *Disquisito Politica vom absoluten Fürstenrecht.* It should be mentioned that Becher was Hornigk's brother-in-law.

that both *Staatskunst* (the art of state administration, or statecraft) and *Policeywissenschaft* (the science of policy formation) as elements of the "cameral sciences" actually had roots in antiquity:

> People have always been obliged to observe appropriate rules in exploiting their estates, and rulers of republics have found themselves constrained to adopt expedient measures both for organizing the state and for thrift and order in the same. (Quoted in Small 1909, 295)

The purpose of the "art" of administration, or statecraft, "is to assure complete security for the community, both against external and internal dangers." The policy aspect, on the other hand, "is concerned chiefly with the conduct and sustenance of the subjects, and its great purpose is to put both in such equilibrium and correlation that the subjects of the republic will be useful, and in a position easily to support themselves" (328).

Withal, it was the very "scientific" nature of Cameralism, as a science of administration, that gave it import. The cameralist, trained in the science of administration, will have been (on Justi's account) indoctrinated with a set of principles that have universal applicability, thus giving him a degree of understanding he cannot obtain by merely studying particular forms of governance. One who seeks to learn by merely observing or by engaging in a specific area of administration can never become a "universal" cameralist, for, not being trained in the scientific principles of governance, he will invariably come to question whether his prescriptions have some unforeseen consequence to those under his administration.[83] The chief function of the university system thus became to educate a class of state administrators by providing training in economics and the cameral sciences;[84] in fact such training could only be regarded as being in the highest interests of the state.[85]

---

83. From lack of coherent basic principles he will never walk with secure steps. At every unusual occurrence he will waver and seize upon questionable decisions. If he thinks he has introduced important improvements in this part of the administrative organization, he will at last come to the perception that he has thereby caused disproportionate injury in another part of the great housekeeping of the state, because he did not sufficiently understand the correlation of this great system and the influence which all circumstances of the entire system have upon one another. (Small 1909, 301)

84. There are very few positions of responsibility in the state in which expertness in the economic and the cameral sciences would not be the chief matter, if the duties of the position were fulfilled and good service to the state performed. (Small 1909, 299)

85. Justi even suggested preparing young school children in the "art" of state administration, especially "in the very meanest schools, in which the children of the lowest rabble are instructed. . . ." This would instill in them "the duties which they at some time, as citizens and inhabitants of the state, and as fathers of families, will have to observe" (quoted in Small 1909, 302).

Turning now to the substance of Justi's cameralist science, we can see that he began his efforts with a Hobbesian description of the state:

> A republic or state is a unification of a multitude of people under a supreme power, for the ultimate purpose of their happiness; or we may say, a republic consists of a multitude of people who are combined with each other by means of a general interdependence and certain fixed institutions, in order, with their united energies, and under a superimposed supreme power, to promote their common happiness. (Small 1909, 317–18)

Note the specification that the governed subject themselves to "a supreme power." This Justi took to be definitive in granting legitimacy to the state. From this understanding of the social contract derived his "first and universal principle" of scientific state administration: "All the administrative transactions of a state must be so ordered that by means of them the happiness of the same (i.e., of the state) shall be promoted," a principle he held to follow from his assertion that the ultimate *purpose* of such administration is "the common happiness" (Small 1909, 319).

As with Seckendorff, Justi held the ruler to be "the supreme head of the state, or of the republic, who possesses the highest power in order that by means of it he may take care of all the affairs of the community and may apply efficient means for promoting the common happiness" (Small 1909, 324). In the same manner as Seckendorff, the "common happiness" is not to be taken as meaning the general interest of the governed. Although Justi qualified his delineation of the duties of the ruler by maintaining that his prime commitment was "in guardianship of the happiness of the subjects," he immediately qualified this again, granting the ruler a place above the process and granting to him the position of protector of the interests of the state.[86]

As the "supreme power" is taken to be "the use of the total means and powers of the state in order thereby to attain the ultimate end of the same" (Small 1909, 325), it is not to be limited in its scope, but must be understood as extending to the whole of the state. Thus the supreme power must encompass all the resources, including the talents of the people, marshaled to the benefit of the ruler and, by extension, the benefit of the state.[87] There followed from these comments on the inseparability

---

86. We should form a very erroneous idea of the monarch if we thought of him as an administrator or superintendent of the supreme power and of the affairs of the community. In this way we should make of the monarch merely the servant of the state, and place the republic over him, so that he could not be distinguished from a *Staathalter*. This is the false notion held by the *Monarchomachi*, from which so many harmful and dangerous conclusions follow. (Small 1909, 324)

87. We should limit the supreme power much too narrowly if we should make it consist merely in laws, ordinances, penalties, etc. To the means and powers of the state belong not only all sorts of goods, both fixed and movable, within the

of the state, the ruler, and the society, Justi's definition of a cameralist science, and the relation of the science of government to the science of the economy:

> We call the sciences dedicated to the government of a state the economic as well as the cameralistic sciences, or the economic and cameralistic sciences. Economics or *Haushaltungskunst* has for its aim to teach how the means of private persons . . . are to be preserved, increased, and reasonably applied. What economics attempts to do in connection with the goods of private persons, the governmental sciences aim to do in the case of the total means of the state. Hence they properly bear the name, the economic sciences.
>
> It is our business to set in order the principles of these governmental sciences, which the nature of things, truth, and sound reason demand. These principles must be derived from the ultimate purpose of the state. (Small 1909, 316–17)

In addition to his work on the science of efficient governance, Justi also wrote on the topic of *Wohlfahrsstaat*—the "welfare state." In his 1760–61 *Die Grundfeste zu der Macht und Glückseeligkeit der Staaten oder ausführliche Vorstellung der desmaten Polizeywissenschaft* (The groundwork of the power and welfare of states, or the comprehensive presentation of the science of public policy), he extended his analysis of the scientific basis of efficient organization to include religion, science, public safety, insurance, morality, and virtue, and even social and individual decorum. The theme of this work is that government has an important and undeniable role to play in every aspect of the life of its citizens. But this should be tempered with the understanding that government cannot and should not control by fiat. What he proposed was a nearly complete *regulation* of society, but with the proviso that, within the restrictive guidelines, there was room for freedom of activity.

Cameralism and Hobbes   6.3

Cameralism—the science of state administration—developed in a sense as a logical extension of Mercantilism. It is but a small step from the political use of the economy in the interests of the power position of the state, to the control of the economy as a fundamental element of state authority.

More important for our purpose was the belief that the axiom, "the interest of the State and the sovereign are one and the same, inseparable from the 'common happiness,' " became a guiding principle in state

---

boundaries of the country, but also all the talents and abilities of the persons who reside in the country. The reasonable use of all these things, then, and the prerogative of such use, is therefore the supreme power. (Small 1909, 326)

administration. In this sense the German cameralists—the inventors of the German administrative sciences—seem to have been in tune with the precepts of Hobbes in his portrayal of the statist Ideal. While the influence may have been indirect—the influence on the German cameralists being Leibniz, not Hobbes—the problems with which Hobbes dealt and the answer he offered, while perhaps ill-suited to the English model for which it was proposed, was nonetheless in perfect harmony with the German experience. Thus, perhaps even more than Mercantilism, Cameralism appears to have been the extension of the Hobbesian political Ideal and in a way came to manifest its demise.

7 The (British) Cameralism of Sir James Steuart

7.1 The Weltanschauung of Mercantilism

While we have thus far dealt with certain seventeenth-century mercantilist writers and some of the topics upon which they wrote, we have seen that the outstanding feature of this group as a school is its *Weltanschauung*, more so than any of the details of the programs or policies suggested or the reasoning employed. The position of the mercantilists was that there were no Natural Law constraints acting to produce an equilibrating harmony between competing forces; indeed there was a constant need for vigilance so that the system did not collapse. This is in marked contrast to the position of the cameralists, who held that Natural Law itself led to a (Hobbesian) centralized governmental order, irrespective of the base nature of man, and to the (later) physiocrats, who maintained that efforts at socioeconomic control were doomed to failure since the natural (Lockean) state of affairs leads to stability, to a unique equilibrium solution.

On the mercantilist view, a key assumption of many (but by no means all) of the writers connected with that program was that there existed selfless, good men who, when in positions of power, used that power for what could be demonstrably and objectively defined as the common good. Certainly unforeseen circumstances could act to thwart ambitions; but, in the hands of these selfless individuals, what they could not foresee, they could at least handle in the least pernicious manner.[88] Likewise with the cameralists, who extended the scope of activities to the *entire* realm of administrative—social, political, economic—interest (albeit selflessness played no role). To see how Mercantilism ultimately unfolded, and how in a sense Cameralism came to be anglicized, we proceed now to a review of the beliefs of one of the most far-reaching British writers of the eighteenth century, Sir James Steuart.

88. At the root of the debate between advocates and foes of Natural Law is the question of patristic assumptions. Does one address a question on the basis of a rational solution, or along the lines of intrinsic uncertainty?

Principles of Political Œconomy   7.2

The principal contribution of Sir James Steuart (later Steuart-Denham) (1712–80)[89] to the elucidation of policies identified within the confines of Cameralism (in a uniquely British variant) was his magnum opus, *Principles of Political Œconomy*, published in 1767;[90] Johnson held this work to be "the best summation of pre-Smithian British economic theory" (1937, 234).[91] "Economy," by which he meant political economy, Steuart interpreted as "the art of providing for all the wants of a family, with prudence and frugality" (book I, Introduction, vol. I, 1). Economy has as its chief object the most basic prerequisite of "want":

> If any thing necessary or useful be found wanting, if any thing
> provided be lost or misapplied, if any servant, any animal, be

89. Steuart descended from an old Scottish Protestant political family. His great-grandfather, Sir James Stewart of Kirkfield and Coltness (1608–81), was Lord Provost of Edinburgh (1648–49, 1658–59), Member of Parliament for Edinburgh, and Accountant-General for the Scottish Army; his grandfather, Sir James Steuart of Goodtrees (1635–1713) was Lord Advocate of Scotland (1692–1708, 1711–13); his father, Sir James Steuart of Goodtrees and Coltness (1681–1727), served as Solicitor-General of Scotland and a Scottish Member of Parliament for Edinburgh, and his mother, Anne Dalrymple, was the daughter of the Lord President of the Court of Session at Edinburgh, Sir Hugh Dalrymple.

James attended the University of Edinburgh (at age 11), studying philosophy and languages, and later reading in the law; just prior to his fourteenth birthday, his father died and so James inherited the title. As an adult, he became involved with the Stuart Pretender and was a leading advocate of the Jacobite Restoration: he negotiated for the Pretender in Paris during the 1745 Rebellion and was, for his troubles, effectively exiled until 1763. George III, persuaded by Lord Bute, pardoned him in 1771. During the interval, he lived in Europe, where he learned a great deal about various continental economies. Upon his return to England he became a principal adviser to the British East India Company, for which he wrote in 1772 a comprehensive tract, *The Principles of Money, Applied to the Present State of the Coin of Bengal,* concerning the operation of its monetary policy. In 1773 Steuart was offered a rich inheritance, provided he would change his name; hence he is listed in the (British) *Dictionary of National Biography* as Denham, Sir James Steuart. But, as that was after the appearance of his major economics works, he is almost always identified by economists with the name appearing on the title pages of his two major works, James Steuart, Bart. An excellent biographical summary is W. L. Taylor (1957).

90. The full title of this brilliant, but dull, work is *An Inquiry into the Principles of Political Oeconomy: being an Essay on the Science of Domestic Policy in Free Nations. In which are particularly considered Population, Agriculture, Trade, Industry, Money, Coin, Interest, Circulation, Banks, Exchange, Public Credit, and Taxes.* The edition used here is part of the six-volume collection, *The Works Political, Metaphysical and Chronological of Sir James Steuart,* edited by his son, General Sir James Steuart, and published in 1805.

91. Johnson further noted that Smith ignored the book, which "undoubtedly contributed to the rapid eclipse of his countryman's treatise and, except for a single note of muffled criticism, no one of his contemporaries arose to defend the repatriated baronet" (Johnson 1937, 209).

Tribe referred to the work as having been the "most widely cited British text of the 1780's and early 1790's" in German economic tracts and suggested that its cameralist overtones probably resulted from Steuart's having resided in Tübingen while drafting books I and II (Tribe 1988, 136–37).

supernumerary or useless, if any one sick or infirm be neglected, we immediately perceive a want of oeconomy. (1)

The basis of economy—the "economic problem" as we term it today—is principally the satisfaction of wants.

Having defined the problem, the question then arises as to the unit of analysis. For Steuart, perhaps taking his cue from Hobbes and Aristotle, the unit of importance is ultimately the state. But in terms of his rhetoric, he was compelled (as was Aristotle) to begin by defining economic activity in terms of the "private family." The ends for which the private family strives are "to provide for the nourishment, the other wants, and the employment of every individual" within its dominion (1767, book I, Introduction, vol. I, 1). The head of the family coordinates the familial enterprise in an effort to satisfy these needs, the children and servants of the family being the objects of his concern; each group thus has a role to play in the functioning of the household. Again, we see the influence of Aristotle in the designating of "natural" roles. Continuing with his example, Steuart maintained that the head of this familial economy has two competing functions which fall to him alone: (1) to establish the laws by which the unit can function (the role of lord), and (2) to execute these laws (the role of steward). Functioning as lord, he commands; functioning as steward, he must ensure right conduct and also obey his own laws.[92]

The extension of this exemplar economy to the state is straightforward, with two modifications: (1) there are no servants of the state, only children; and (2) national economies are not formed, but are given, having been the result of an evolutionary process of development. Further, this system is not static but is constantly changing to fit the spirit of the times. This suggests that political economy is faced with a daunting task: on the one hand, to "adapt the different operations of it to the spirit, manners, habits, and customs of the people; and afterwards to model these circumstances so as to be able to introduce a set of new and more useful institutions" (1767, book I, Introduction, vol. I, 3). Thus while we must adapt to the vagaries of the economy, we are also in a position to alter it to conform to our developing needs.

Returning to the analogy of the family, the object of the state is to provide for the wants and needs of its "children." The function of political economy is to provide the wherewithal to ensure this provision.[93] For

92. Cf. this statement to Small's interpretation of German Cameralism: "The people were accordingly held to be dedicated by dispensation of Providence and the laws of nature to the condition of wardship, and to be fit for action only under authority" (Small 1909, 5).

93. The principal object of this science is to secure a certain fund of subsistence for all the inhabitants, to obviate every circumstance which may render it precarious; to provide every thing necessary for supplying the wants of the society, and to employ the inhabitants (supposing them to be freemen) in such a manner as naturally to create reciprocal relations and dependencies between them, so as to

Steuart, man is a social creature desirous and demanding of dependence; dependence is the socializing tool, which man creates and from which he benefits. Each man agrees, despite individual differences, to voluntarily subordinate his individualism to the promotion of the social good (chap. I, 8). In essence the state is but a single organism comprised of individual cells but understandable only as the organic whole, a position derived from the epistemology of Leibniz and extended to the administration of state activity by the cameralists.

This belief in social organicism explains to a great extent Steuart's insistence on the *state* as the principal unit, and not the *individual*. For the individual to be at the center of the universe, self-interest would surely be granted priority as the primary instrument of motivation; with the state given central status, self-interest can be removed from consideration in favor of a greater interest, the welfare of the "family" or the entire social organism. "It is the business of a statesman to judge of the expediency of different schemes of oeconomy, and by degrees to model the minds of his subjects so as to induce them, from the allurement of private interest, to concur in the execution of his plan" (1767, Intro., 4). The reason for this emphasis on social welfare as opposed to individual interest is actually very simple. The paramount end of the state is the promotion of justice and virtue; for the state as the unit of control, this implies "no more than a tender affection for the whole society, and an exact and impartial regard for the interest of every class" (chap. I, 8). To the extent that the statesman can exploit the need for dependency and the desire for justice and virtue, he can channel the will of the people to the ends of a strong, robust, and powerful central state.[94] Concerns with egoistic individualism could have nothing but dire consequences for the health and prosperity (to say nothing of the power position) of the state. Steuart was all too well aware of the power of the status quo and of "insider," or vested, interests. For him, hope rested in the disinterested public servant—precisely the point at which Smith perceived the initiation of despair.[95]

---

make their several interests lead them to supply one another with their recipro-cal wants. (Steuart 1767, book I, Introduction, vol. I, 3)

94. "In turning and working upon the spirit of a people, nothing is impossible to an able statesman. When a people can be engaged to murder their wives and children, and to burn themselves, rather than submit to a foreign enemy; when they can be brought to give their most precious effects, their ornaments of gold and silver, for the support of a common cause; when women are brought to give their hair to make ropes, and the most decrepit old men to mount the walls of a town for its defence; I think I may say, that by properly conducting and managing the spirit of a people, nothing is impossible to be accomplished. But when I say, nothing is impossible, I must be understood to mean, that nothing essen-tially necessary for the good of the people is impossible; and this is all that is required in government" (Steuart 1767, bk. I, chap. II, 15).

95. Skinner (1966) argued that Steuart's exile prevented his knowing just how selfish the Whigs and Tories really were. He confused England with some petty duchy where the duke perceived himself truly to be (and was so perceived as) the father of those under his control.

Thus we see that Steuart's system was essentially organized around the problems of an organic nation-state, while he was also intimately concerned with questions of social morality and social responsibility as well as technical efficiency. Steuart's system seems to rely on the presumption of a moral (religious) right and wrong, so that the task of the public administrator is to see that right is done; selflessness is not a prerequisite (as it was for the mercantilists) since order is the sole purpose of governance.[96] Further, the administrator knows what is right—what benefits the nation-state in the long run; underlying this conviction is a confidence that the "right thing" is likely to be divined according to correct moral and religious values. Steuart's interest in and understanding of the production process was hardly trivial, but he was not primarily concerned with the *efficiency* of the economy. Rather, he was concerned with that equity and efficiency combination that yielded growth and led most effectively to the administration of the functions of the nation-state, a concern that reflected the priorities of cameralist doctrine.

Steuart thus perceived the aggregated national economy as the basic planning unit, and he clearly anticipated all of the beneficial (but apparently none of the negative) aspects of the modern welfare state. For example, perhaps as a result of his statist orientation, he held that taxes in general were not a burden to society nor to the individuals who were compelled to pay them—if one derived from the payment of taxes a sense of national achievement and social responsibility, the effect on the individual could not and should not be an issue. In some senses the underlying platform upon which his *Weltanschauung* was built was the faith in technique that we find in mid-twentieth-century socialist economic theory[97] and a faith in social authority which seems to have had a religious (patristic) quality.

Steuart's rhetorical method involved the elaboration of and reliance on institutional mechanisms (often presented within a historical context) rather than the assertion of universals or abstractions. An example is the handling of money. Steuart devoted much attention to the ways in which money achieved an institutional importance as it serves as an indispensable and unique commodity, without which trade is impossible. It adds to his stature that he realized that the institutional rules governing credit, for example, could be more complex than the institutional rules governing money.

Putting his work in context, one could say that Steuart was over-

---

96. The great art of governing is to divest oneself of prejudices and attachments to particular opinions, particular classes, and above all to particular persons; to consult the spirit of the people, to give way to it in appearance, and in so doing to give it a turn capable of inspiring those sentiments which may induce them to relish the change, which an alteration of circumstances has rendered necessary. (Chap. II, 16)

97. See, e.g., A. P. Lerner (1944).

whelmingly committed to national economic development through planning by the Crown's advisers (Schumpeterian Consultant-Administrators). The fulfillment of state potential required a coordinated effort, conducted under the auspices of a committed body. Only a centralized authority, comprised of dedicated bureaucrats, could be trusted to channel resources to the achievement of national goals. All other aspirations, such as the Lockean goals of personal liberty and individual creativity, served only to reduce the resources available to the achievement of the ultimate aim of the betterment of the state. Once again, as with so many others of similar political attitude, Hobbesian statism is the dominant philosophical influence, perhaps admitting (grudgingly) the Hanover force over the Stuart legitimacy.

Conclusion 8

Just as this lengthy chapter began with reference to the questions raised by Hobbes, so we return to it here. The Hobbes Patristic Legacy, seen both in the negative and positive senses, is almost without parallel as an influence in the development of economic thought in the English-speaking world. On the negative side it stimulated a variety of antitheses, from which modern constitutional government as well as modern economics have derived their justifications; and on the positive side, it incarnated the foundations of scientific empiricism.

A reason for pausing over Mercantilism is simply to tie what we term the Hobbesian Patristic Legacy to the earliest economic literature. Despite protestations to the contrary by many historians on the subject, the mercantilists very clearly held to a Hobbesian view of the duties of the individual in relation to the good of the state.[98] Cameralism sought to extend the Hobbesian legitimacy and supremacy of the state even further by denying any other motivation but efficient state administration. This submission was not a direct one, however, but rather required the expansion of state power through a partnership with corporate-collectivist entrepreneurs—not entrepreneurs in the traditional sense of the term, as individual risk-takers, but entrepreneurs as businesspeople engaged in a pooling of risk so as to reduce variability.

The emergence of a strong central state was not a climactic moment, however, but rather the genesis of a new movement. This move-

---

98. This was also suggested by the political scientist Philip W. Buck: "The close-knit logic of Hobbes's *Leviathan*, with its insistence upon the importance of stability and order in government, resembled the mercantilists' regard for domestic peace as a necessary prerequisite to commercial prosperity. Their horror of disorder was fully as great as his—the state of nature was no environment for the development of industry and trade. The arguments Hobbes advanced for the monarchical form of government were all of a nature to appeal to these economic writers" (Buck 1942, 169).

ment involved the use of the power and resources of the state not in concert with business, as advocated by the mercantilists, but as a means of controlling and coordinating economic activity without the seeming necessity for the Invisible Hand. Before we give space to this discussion, however, it gives modern body to the subject if we turn our attention to the linchpin of this revolution, the movement toward an accounting framework and the evolution of a doctrine of national accounting. For these we now turn to the technical legacies of William Petty and François Quesnay.

Appendix: Chronology of Certain Events in Britain

1485	Henry VII (the Tudor) was confirmed as King and established the Star Chamber
1502	Henry VII's oldest daughter married James IV of Scotland
1509	Henry VIII ascended to the throne and almost immediately married his older brother's widow, Catherine of Aragon
1521–27	Henry (and Thomas More) write a tract against Luther for which the Pope gave Henry the still-used title "Defender of the Faith"
1533	Henry tried to and then did divorce Catherine of Aragon
1534	Act of Supremacy set up the test of loyalty
1536	Thomas Cromwell suppressed smaller monasteries
1539	Thomas Cromwell suppressed larger monasteries
1547	Edward VI ascended to the throne (he was 10 years old)
1553	Edward VI died and first Lady Jane Grey and then Mary Tudor ascended the throne; Mary married the Spanish heir, Philip; Effort made to reestablish the Church of Rome
1558	Mary died and her sister, Elizabeth I, ascended the throne
1563	39 Articles of Church of England Faith were adopted as well as the Statute of Artificers (organizing control of town labor)
1577	Alliance with the Low Countries (the Netherlands)
1587	Open war with Spain
1588	Unexpected defeat of the Spanish Armada
1600	First charter of the East India Company (though other companies were chartered earlier and later)
1601	Elizabethan Poor Laws enacted, placing responsibility on the parishes for the unlanded
1603	Elizabeth I died and was succeeded by James VI of Scotland (who became James I of England)
1610	James I dissolved Parliament convened in 1604
1614	The Addled Parliament
1621	Third Parliament, which authorized supply (finance) for a war in the Palatinate; Francis Bacon impeached
1622	James I dissolved Parliament and destroyed the page asserting that self-government is part of the English birthright
1624	Fourth Parliament convened
1625	Charles I ascended to the throne; his first Parliament convened and dissolved
1626	Charles I convened his second Parliament, adjourned and then dissolved it
1628	Charles I convened his third Parliament, which passed the Petition of Right: (1) Prohibition of benevolences and taxation without parliamentary consent, (2) No billeting of soldiers in private homes, (3) No martial law in peacetime, (4) Writ of habeas corpus Parliament prorogued
1629	Parliament reassembled and then dissolved
1640	Charles convened his fourth Parliament, the Long Parliament

1641   The Star Chamber and High Commission abolished
1642   Simmering conflict between Parliament and Charles I turned into
            Civil War
1644   Charles I summoned a Loyalist Parliament at Oxford
1645   Charles I surrendered himself to the Scots, and they turned him
            over to Parliament (1647); thus the First Civil War ended
1648   Charles I rejected the Four Bills:
                (1) Parliament to control the Army for 20 years,
                (2) All moves against Parliament to be recalled,
                (3) Peers created recently not to be seated,
                (4) The two Houses could adjourn at their own pleasure
            Second Civil War breaks out, and decision made to try Charles I for
            High Treason
1649   Charles I found guilty of High Treason and executed; Common-
            wealth established
1653   Oliver Cromwell became Lord Protector
1658   Oliver Cromwell died and his son, Richard, succeeded him
1660   General Monk brought back Charles II, who then continued to live
            on French subsidies
1672   War with Holland (ended in 1674)
1679   *Habeas Corpus* act
1685   Charles II died and James II ascended the throne; Monmouth (the
            natural son of Charles II) rebelled, was captured, and was executed
1687   James II issued the first Declaration of [the Pro-Catholic] Liberty of
            Conscience
1688   James's wife had a son, and fear grew that the Stuart Catholic royal-
            ist branch would continue; James II ordered second Declaration of
            Liberty of Conscience to be read in the Churches, and the Arch-
            bishop of Canterbury and six other bishops were imprisoned for
            refusing to comply; they were tried and acquitted by the Lords;
            Seven eminent persons invited William of Orange (son-in-law of
            James II) to take throne; James II captured, but escaped to France
1689   Parliament offered crown to Mary and the regency to William; Not
            good enough; Parliament then offered the crown to both
1694   Mary II died
1701   Act of Settlement; Parliament directs succession to Sophia of Hano-
            ver (granddaughter of James I) and her successors, providing they
            were Protestant
1702   William III died and succeeded by sister-in-law (daughter of James
            II), Anne I
1707   Act of Union between England and Scotland; Second Parliament of
            Anne and last royal veto
1708   Anne's third Parliament, Whig majority
1710   Anne's fourth Parliament, Tory majority
1714   Anne died (none of her 17 children survived her), succeeded by So-
            phia's successor, George I
1727   George II ascended to throne
1752   Gregorian calendar adopted: 11 days between Sept. 2 and 14 were
            omitted
1760   George III ascended to throne

CHAPTER 4

The Measurement of Economic Magnitudes

All depends on the measure.   *MISHNA: BAB METZIA*

I know of no pursuit in which more real and important services can be rendered to any country than by improving its agriculture, its breed of useful animals, and other branches of a husbandman's cares.   GEORGE WASHINGTON (JULY 20, 1794)

With the introduction of agriculture mankind entered upon a long period of meanness, misery, and madness, from which they are only now being freed by the beneficent operation of the machine.
BERTRAND RUSSELL,
THE CONQUEST OF HAPPINESS (1930)

Introduction   1

The locus of thinking now turns to how three groups of brilliant writers sought to give system to the economic aspect of national state formation. We have chosen to combine in this chapter three generally dissimilar approaches not only because they revolve about the same issue, but more particularly because one can make comparisons in terms of the priorities they assign to different patristic legacies.

First, what was their common problem? Sixteenth-, seventeenth-, and eighteenth-century Mercantilism as a Zeitgeist involved not only secularization of thinking, but also the reorientation of social leadership to the objective of state building. By marrying the interests of the old feudal elites with the newly constituted commercial class, Mercantilism as a political and economic philosophy gave legitimacy to policies designed for the collectivization of the economy and the enhancement of state authority and control, especially in economic matters; it involved, in short, the subjugation of the interests of the individual to the more pressing interests of the stabilization and enhancement of the power and international prestige of the state. Mercantilism also, by virtue of its emphasis on collectivization and national planning, ushered in an era characterized by reliance on data collection and statistical analysis.

By virtue of its advocacy of strong nationalism and the superiority of the homeland, Mercantilism highlighted the need for a comprehensive and centralized census of wealth. Mercantilist doctrines then may be said to have made national income accounting—which developed formally only in the early twentieth century—an inevitability. Mercantilist policies simply could not have succeeded (to the extent they did) absent a solid empirical (statistical) basis upon which to gauge the direction of trade, the extent of the disparities that policies were advanced to alleviate, and the magnitudes of the power positions of the states vis-à-vis the rest of the world. An accounting framework also made it easier to "sell" the mercantilist policy prescriptions to the nobility and the clergy, who had been, after all, the centers of power at the time. Data helped frame a more persuasive argument.

While mercantilist and premercantilist writers created the framework for the analysis, the real impetus, however, to the development of a national accounting *network* may be said to have been the doctrines of the French physiocrats. While perhaps not immediately apparent in their policy pronouncements, the statements of economic nationalism put forth by these French writers were tailored to numerical presentation. This form of rhetoric allowed a place for economic planning and for the employment of sophisticated accounting techniques.

The physiocratic analytic framework welcomed, in fact demanded, the application of the accounting matrix developed by John Graunt, William Petty, et al., which we will examine below. The very philosophy is unworkable absent such a rigorous analytical structure. While accounting as such had been practiced since at least the thirteenth century,[1] it had not been thought of much consequence in terms of serving as a tool for the promotion of national interests, its use being restricted to more practical, business matters. The theoretical reorientation of the French economists provided the impetus for the use of mathematically oriented methods that could serve to channel resources to nationally responsible ends. The doctrine of Physiocracy advocated reliance and the focus of resources on the agricultural sector of the economy, engendering a belief in national self-sufficiency. From the sixteenth to the eighteenth centuries, its promulgators advanced theories of production and distribution that required for their application a detailed atlas of commercial activities. In this they also demanded a coordinated accounting network to handle the interrelationships about which they wrote.

To facilitate the use of an accounting matrix, Physiocracy provided the framework of the circular flow. This theoretical advance made pos-

---

1. Spiegel (1991) credited Leonardo of Pisa with its invention in 1202. Schumpeter (1954) cited Fra Luca Paccioli (1494), *Summa de arithmetica, geometria, proportioni e proportionalita*.

sible the state's exploitation of what had been up to that time disorganized and localized production data. It provided a method of aggregation which was to be of great importance to planners of a national economy, whose ambition was the advancement of national goals. What was lacking, however, was a means of operationalizing these primarily diagrammatic presentations.

We pause for a moment to tie these writers to their patristic legacies. The British started from observation, thus exemplifying Francis Bacon's perception of a science as initially cognitive, leading to statistical comparisons and generalizations. The French, by way of contrast, started from a Cartesian preference for initial logical connection. The British political arithmeticians are an exemplar of one type of legacy; the physiocrats are of another.

While the principal purpose of this chapter is to explore the movement toward an integrated national accounting framework, we have chosen to go into some detail not only because the story is worth telling, but because it reveals to us why the two approaches are so dissimilar. Beginning with a look at the early efforts of John Graunt at the collection of statistical data to describe social phenomena, we then proceed to the efforts of the political arithmeticians who sought to tailor their (primarily mercantilist) theories to the stories told by the data. This is seen to be the beginning of what has come to be known as "social accounting." We then turn to the work of the physiocrats (including the circular flow diagram), whose theories of the national economy established the frameworks upon which the later empirical studies would build. These theoretical models are readily seen to be linked to the more empirically grounded national accounting framework; in fact they rely on something akin to a system of national accounts.

Two other points should be noted. We think that the link between the British writers of the late seventeenth century and the French writers of the second half of the eighteenth century was Richard Cantillon—a fascinating and brilliant (if not always forthright) Irishman whose major work was done in France. From the standpoint of personal identification, Cantillon had a foot in both camps. The second point refers to an American politician, Alexander Hamilton, whose economic knowledge was for his profession simply precocious and who in developing his political agenda clearly grasped what the British camp as well as the French camp had produced.

John Graunt and Descriptive Statistics   2

For many centuries the governing classes of the countries of Europe, especially Britain and Germany, have, with almost a manic obsession, collected social and economic data. The famous "Domesday Book" prepared in 1086 under the auspices of William the Conqueror was one such collection, a register of the lands under William's control. The purpose of this catalog was to allow a more efficient means for assessing taxes and collecting revenue.[2] In 1268, Étienne Boileau prepared a statistical register of trade regulations in Paris.[3] The London Bills of Mortality, probably initially undertaken under the orders of Henry VIII, date to at least 1517, although the purpose of their collection is not clear. Apart from these endeavors, however, statistical data were often accumulated with no apparent rationale as to how they could and should be used, beyond the readily apparent one of facilitating tax collection. It is now, of course, abundantly clear to us how this data can and should be exploited, but during this formative period, the practical demand for such figures was limited. The numbers had been available for consultation, but no one cared to take any notice of the statistical regularities or correlations among different attributes, which may have been able to tell a story about the workings of the system. What was lacking was any framework within which this voluminous data could be analyzed. Without an accepted methodology, statistics are of little practical utility, and so their collection serves no practical function.

One of the earliest attempts at rectifying this problem was that of John Graunt (1620–74).[4] In his 1662 *Observations upon the Bills of Mortality*,[5] Graunt—lacking any formal training in mathematics—attempted to comment upon the nature of Britain by analyzing the tables of mortality which had been constructed since the late sixteenth century, but had to that time been treated as a mere curiosity. The tables were highly detailed listings of deaths, categorized by cause, gender, age, and geographical area of residence but otherwise presented without commentary as to what the figures were meant to show or the manner in which they should be employed. Graunt desired to see what the data had to say. He sought any regularities that might present themselves based on the large amount of data available (regionally and temporally); in other words, he engaged in what is today referred to as descriptive statistical analysis. In the Dedica-

2. The "Domesday" book also had a consolidating feature, as the surveyors demanded from the landowners a pledge of loyalty to William.

3. See Schumpeter 1954, 162.

4. Little is known of Graunt, other than he had served in the British Army, was a draper by profession (at the time an important organization, protected by a powerful guild), and was something of an art collector. Upon the publication of the *Observations*, he was made a member of the newly founded Royal Society.

5. The full title of this work is *Natural and Political Observations Mentioned in a following Index, and made upon the Bills of Mortality. With reference to the Government, Religion, Trade, Growth, Air, Diseases, and several Changes of the said City*. This pamphlet has been identified at times as having been the work of William Petty, and in fact appears in the Hull edition of his collected economic writings, but Graunt's authorship is now (more or less firmly) established, at least within the community of philosophers and probability theorists. On the issue of the disputed authorship, see Hull's introduction to Petty's works, especially pages xxxix–liv. See also D. V. Glass (1963) and Peter Groenewegen (1967).

tory to the Lord Privy Seal, the Right Honourable John (Lord) Roberts, Graunt declared his intention as being (rather modestly) "to have reduced several great confused *Volumes* into a few perspicuous *Tables,* and abridged such *Observations* as naturally flowed from them, into a few succinct *Paragraphs,* without any long Series of *multiloquious Deductions* . . ." (1662, 320; emphasis in original). Graunt's task was in fact simple and straightforward: he desired to establish the healthfulness, or lack of the same, of London by examining the statistics on mortality. As he phrased the purpose of his investigations:

> In the foregoing Observations we ventured to make a Standard of the healthfulness of the *Air* from the proportion of *acute* and *Epidemical* Diseases, and of the wholsomness of the food, from that of the *Chronical.* (1662, 351–52; emphasis in original)

From these individual statistics, Graunt determined that various of the series he constructed, such as those showing mortality from several diseases and from accidental and self-inflicted causes, remained in a near-constant proportion to the total number of burials in the city.[6] In other, more modern, parlance, many homogeneous series of statistical data on various maladies affecting the population of London (derived from the Bills of Mortality) showed an almost lawlike regularity.

Graunt's conclusion, however, went beyond the mere cataloging of disease and pestilence plaguing London and England generally. His raison d'être was more pronounced, as his interest lay not in the mere enumeration of instances, but rather in the application of the conclusions derived from the statistical data to questions of national welfare. He was not above using his figures as justification in pronouncing warnings on social and moral problems, even when the figures themselves could not sustain such conclusions. The purpose of the exercise was, after all, to promote state regulation of trade and the economy. "Objective" numerical data (which Graunt professed to have presented) provided the authorities with incontrovertible evidence—in contrast to testamentary evidence, which is necessarily suspect as it is subject to multiple interpretations that can easily mislead. As Graunt characterized it:

> I conclude, That a clear knowledge of all these particulars, and many more, whereat I have shot but at rovers, is necessary, in order to good, certain, and easie Government, and even to balance Parties and Factions both in *Church* and *State.* (1662, 397; emphasis in original)

In this belief Graunt was clearly at one with the work of William Petty and others of the political arithmeticians to be discussed later—

---

6. A. M. Endres (1985) held Graunt's "constructs" to be "one step below that of *indicators.*"

hence the misapprehension as to the true authorship of Graunt's only published work. The difference between Graunt and the political arithmeticians is in their understanding of the underlying purpose of their examinations of the data. This bears directly on the question of the appropriate methodology for analysis: is the purpose of analysis to disentangle from the data the "true" reality which it purports to represent, or is it to employ the data as another tool to prove a point or assert a conclusion we already believe to be true? Graunt opted for the former, the political arithmeticians the latter. It is for this reason that Graunt's work is clearly superior to that of his intellectual descendants. It is to these descendants that we now turn.

3 The Method of Political Arithmetic

One of the most interesting approaches to the problem of employing social statistics as a tool for national and regional economic and social analysis was worked out by a group of empirical-minded enumerators collectively termed the political arithmeticians.[7] A crude but nonetheless identifiable forerunner of econometrics, Political Arithmetic developed as a reaction to the internal and external forces which threatened English power and social stability. Domestically, the English Civil Wars (1642–46; 1648); the ascendancy of the Lord Protector, Oliver Cromwell (whose reign of power oversaw the suppression of rebellions in Ireland and Scotland); the eventual restoration of the monarchy (Charles II in 1660); and the triumph of William of Orange (1689) were events which, in their breadth and scope, betrayed the problems inherent in the lack of any consistent census of the lands and wealth of the kingdom. Internationally, the two wars with the Netherlands (1652–54; 1665–67) and a war with Spain (1656–59) highlighted the need for a census of lands and people, an accurate index of the productive potential of the realm, and a means of gauging military preparedness. In short, the chaotic situations demanded a precision not possible relying on the rhetoric of the day. These presentations were for the most part mere descriptive pictures of the economy and its ability to meet the needs of the people and the state. Precision could only be had through a rhetoric based on analysis predicated on numerical statistics.

In an effort to remove from political discourse the metaphysical pronouncements of their ancestors and contemporaries, the newly formed art of Political Arithmetic sought to recast the arguments in a secular (positive) rhetoric, one which would illuminate more clearly the problems at hand. They proceeded methodically in true "scientific" manner: (1)

7. For a general treatment of the political arithmeticians, see the article by Phyllis Deane in the *New Palgrave* (1987b). See also Paul Studenski (1958, 26–40) and A. M. Endres (1985).

develop a set of procedures for the collection of numerical data (in some instances preceded by stipulating a "desirable" hypothesis), (2) collect the data according to the procedural rules, (3) using the data, identify patterns or consistencies, and (4) using these patterns, develop a series of statistical indicators that themselves may be employed as shorthand devices to guide policy.[8] Support for policymakers and specific policy proposals was always the goal behind the collection and use of these data and the constructed statistics. The political arithmeticians must thus be viewed as having undertaken their investigations in support of the national cause.

The importance of this group is the way in which it bridged the gap between the philosophical discussions of the physiocrats and the more practical interests of those involved in the (much later) derivation of national income accounts.

Petty: Political Arithmetic as a Means of Consolidating Power

4

Introduction

4.1

Sir William Petty (1623–87)[9] was one of those rare individuals whose genius is such as to overturn completely what preceded him, and whose new proposals force acknowledgment of this genius. A supremely talented and exceedingly gifted man—Schumpeter (1954, 210n2) listed his credits as "physician, surgeon, mathematician, theoretical engineer, member of parliament, public servant, and businessman"—Petty was above all a practicing empiricist, having been trained by Hobbes (while in Paris) in medicine and anatomy. He was also an explicit quoter (with

---

8. This list is with slight alterations given also by Endres (1985, 258–59).

9. Petty, the son of a clothier, was sent to sea at the age of thirteen. Stranded in France with a broken leg, he decided to stay on, and later enrolled at the Jesuit College at Caen, where he acquired a knowledge of Latin, Greek, French, astronomy, and mathematics. Studies at Utrecht and Amsterdam followed, and he eventually finished his formal studies on the Continent as a medical student at Leyden. Returning to Paris—with a letter of introduction from John Pell, Professor of Mathematics at Amsterdam—he met Hobbes, serving for a time as his secretary. He also made the acquaintance of Father Mersenne, the gifted mathematician, whose circle included Descartes, Fermat, and Pascal. Returning to England, Petty wrote a tract in which he outlined the structure of what would later become the Royal Society. He then entered Oxford, was granted a Doctor of Physic degree in 1649, and became Professor of Anatomy in 1651. In 1652, he was appointed physician-general to the British Army in Ireland under Cromwell, a position he turned to his own pecuniary advantage. He sat for the Irish Parliament from Enniscorthy, in which position he was invited back into English society by Charles II after the Restoration. He was knighted by Charles II in 1662, at the incorporation of the Royal Society.

Particulars of Petty's life may be found in the introduction to his collected economic writings, prepared by Hull (1899), especially pages xiii–xxxiii. Another superb source is the citation on Petty in the *Dictionary of National Biography*.

approval) of Bacon's scientific method. From Hobbes he appropriated ideas respecting the political structure of society, especially in regard to the role of the sovereign. According to the editor of Petty's collected economic writings, Charles Hull, the influence of Hobbes "appears most strikingly in the assumption that the government is justified in doing anything by which the national wealth can be increased. Again and again Petty advocated sweeping public measures that took no account whatever of the rights and sensibilities of the citizenry. He was quite ready to suggest, for example, that the majority of the Irish and Scotch be transplanted to England "whether they consent or not" (Hull 1899, lxii). As for Bacon, his influence on Petty was more profound, for it resided in the *method* of investigation that Petty was to apply throughout his work. This is the empirical method, the method of scientific experimentation.

Despite his acceptance of Baconian experimentation and his belief in Hobbesian-Baconian induction, Petty was not interested in the simple enumeration of instances; his interest in statistics was not limited to the collection of crude numerical indicators. On the contrary, Petty's statistical work complemented his theoretical advances: he collected his statistics in order to enable his theoretical work to be grounded on a sound empirical foundation.[10] By the same token, he was not a deductivist of the Platonic or Cartesian variety; his focus was on measurement, not purely theoretical pursuits. This is probably fortunate for economists, since it is Petty's work on measurement, first of the Irish and then the English national accounts, that shows the hallmark of true genius.

4.2 Verbum Sapienti

Petty's 1664 *Verbum Sapienti,* written just after the publication of Graunt's *Observations* but published posthumously in 1691 (and then as an addendum to *Political Anatomy of Ireland*), ranks as one of the earliest attempts at producing national income accounts.[11] As no such accounts or accounting procedures of this type existed at the time, nor was

---

10. Schumpeter labeled Petty "first and last a theorist. But he was one of those theorists for whom science is indeed measurement; who forge analytical tools that will work with numerical facts and heartily despise any others; whose generalizations are the joint products of figures and reasoning that are never allowed to part company" (Schumpeter 1954, 211). Schumpeter was not charitable to Petty, considering him not an original thinker, but more of an integrator of existing views.

Pribram was more kind in his assessment. He commented that "Petty's studies marked the beginning of a new period in the development of economic reasoning. They initiated the formulation of economic problems in terms of relations among measurable magnitudes" (Pribram 1983, 65).

11. Studenski (1958, 26) gave Petty credit for being the first to estimate national income.

there any expression of a methodological basis for their calculation, this work should be esteemed as one of the most important in the area of empirical macroeconomics. The techniques pursued in this endeavor while perhaps ridiculed today as simplistic and highly subjective, demonstrate a great deal of inventiveness and initiative, ranking Petty as an innovator of national income accounting, if not an originator in the Stiglerian sense.[12]

An essay of ten chapters, *Verbum Sapienti* deals with methods of computing the wealth of the kingdom of Britain so as to allow a more equitable levying of the tax burden and a more efficient means of collection.[13] One of the methods involved the employment of a sampling technique, which Petty developed specifically for the purpose of the study. To simplify his approach, Petty studied carefully the hearth tax reports for each district. Obtaining an average (a simple arithmetic mean) of tax receipts, he multiplied these by an estimate of the number of hearths in a district, then, summing over all the districts, arrived at a national average.

In attempting his computations of the British national income, Petty began with an accounting of the British population, accepting a figure of six million inhabitants for England and Wales. Using this figure, and assuming an average expenditure per person per year (of £6, 13s, 4d), he could calculate total national (kingdom-wide) expenditures on "necessities" as being £40 million per year. Since Petty implicitly accepted that expenditures and income were equal (if not equivalent), this figure also served as an estimate of national income.

Petty then calculated, based on the accepted figure of 24 million acres of land in the kingdom, the total value and annual rental receipts of land; further, based on the number of houses "within the Liberties" of London (taken to be 28,000), and their rental values (£15 per year), and assuming twelve years' purchase, he could then calculate the total value of housing within London proper as £5,040,000. By extrapolation to the rural parts of England and Wales, Petty arrived at a total valuation of £30 million for housing in the entire kingdom.[14]

In like manner Petty estimated the value of shipping (500,000 tons @ 6d per ton), the value of livestock (one-quarter of the value of the land at sale), the value of coin, and of miscellaneous wares and merchandise (these last three values being stipulated, not calculated). He thus arrived at a total value of the product of England and Wales:

---

12. This refers to George J. Stigler's (1955) distinction between innovators and originators.

13. Johnson referred to Petty's "point of orientation" as that of "the tax-gatherer's bursary" (Johnson 1937, 97).

14. " 'Tis probable, that the Housing of all the Cities and Market-Towns, are double in number to those of all *London,* though of no more worth.

" 'Tis also probable, that the housing without the Cities and Towns, are more in number than those within (*London* excepted) but of no more value" (Petty 1899, 106; emphasis in original).

Value (in millions):

land value:	£ 144
real estate (house) value:	30
shipping:	3
livestock:	36
coin:	6
wares, merchandise, etc.:	31
total	£ 250

Eschewing any conceptual apparatus that would serve to frame the collection and interpretation of data, Petty nevertheless was able to construct a workable estimate of the value of wealth in England and Wales, which was, after all, his intended purpose. Thus was promulgated one of the earliest attempts to estimate the total wealth of a nation.

On the expenditure side, Petty surmised that the total annual expenditures of the kingdom (as mentioned above) were £40 million, but noted that he could only account for £15 million pounds from the "Annual proceed of the Stock, or Wealth of the Nation" (the national income); this £15 million he held was responsible for yielding the £250 million value noted in the table. The remainder had to arise from "the labour of the people" (Petty 1899, 108). Treating this remainder, the figure being £25 million, as an annual flow, Petty estimated the value or "worth" of the population (the value of "human capital") as £416 2/3 million, from which he could derive a value per capita. With this value, Petty (ingeniously) estimated the loss to England in monetary terms from the Great Plague. Here we see one of the earliest examples of the science of demography.[15]

Continuing in his estimations, Petty derived values not only for the expenses and revenues of the kingdom, but also suggested a method for apportioning taxes, estimated the expenses of the military and sought to determine the amount of money needed to serve the "circulation" of trade (this Petty determined as being dependent on the frequency of payment). He ended the essay with an interesting comment on the need to employ labor for the benefit of the state. England should not be satisfied that it had achieved its national goals with respect to the production of exportable commodities until "we have certainly more Money than any of our Neighbour States" (1899, 119). Thus Petty was not entirely free of the influence of the British mercantilistic past, although his concern was for monetary wealth, and not the amassing of bullion supplies.

---

15. Anthony Brewer credited Graunt with having "virtually founded modern demography" (Brewer 1992, 714).

The Political Anatomy of Ireland 4.3

Petty's personal history suggests a long and interesting fascination with Ireland,[16] a relationship that led to his *Political Anatomy of Ireland* (1672, but published posthumously in 1691),[17] a comprehensive account of the Irish economy. The purpose of the work was ostensibly to advance the cause of economic development for Ireland, work he began in 1652 when, under Cromwell, he was granted a contract to undertake the Down Survey of Irish land, designed to make taxation of the island more efficient; he completed the survey during a six-year period when he also served as Physician-General.[18] In the *Political Anatomy*, Petty outlined a program of national development along similar lines, for submission to the king and the Privy Council. However, it is equally clear that the *Political Anatomy* was undertaken in an effort to discern better the ability of the British government to handle the "Irish problem."

The very title of this work, *Political Anatomy*, suggests the profound influence on Petty of the experimental methods of Hobbes and Bacon. It intimates an application of the principles of anatomical research (which at the time was primarily empirical and descriptive) to the problem of economic development. Much contemporary medical research consisted of experimentation, in which samples were analyzed under what were purported to be controlled circumstances. Since such direct experimentation is not possible in the social realm, Petty had to be content with observation, and he directed the task of analyzing the Irish economy not so much toward prescription as description. He looked upon the Irish economy, in fact, as a form of experimental social laboratory, a country so constituted as to allow him to observe, much as an experimenter observes his subjects in the medical scientific laboratory. The Irish people were perfect specimens in this regard, and the Irish economy the perfect laboratory, having the attributes of a controllable experimental research environment. As Petty noted in the Preface to his *Political Anatomy:*

---

16. Tony Aspromourgos (1988) suggested this had to do with Petty's "lifelong antagonism" to universities, and "a contempt for orthodox learning," combined with a commitment to the Baconian scientific (experimental) legacy.

17. Little of Petty's intellectual output, never written in any event for a general audience, was published during his lifetime. Johnson noted that "so many of his writings were merely outline records, they lacked organization, continuity and completeness, but they did contain a host of ideas" (Johnson 1937, 96).

18. At the time, Ireland had been divided, with half the land allotted to the army, and half to a group of London "adventurers." Upon completion of the survey, Petty was appointed to the commission established to carry out the designated distribution. In the process, Petty arranged to buy the best of the Irish lands and became wealthy. For the rest of his life he was principally concerned with the management of his estates. On this see Hull (1899, xvi) and Johnson (1937, 94).

Sir Francis Bacon, *in his* Advancement of Learning, *hath made a judicious* Parallel *in many particulars, between the* Body Natural, *and* Body Politick, *and between the Arts of preserving both in Health and Strength: And it is as reasonable, that as* Anatomy *is the best foundation of one, so also of the other; and that to practice upon the Politick, without knowing the* Symmetry, Fabrick, *and* Proportion *of it, is as* casual *as the practice of Old-women and* Empyricks.

Now, because Anatomy *is not only necessary in Physicians, but laudable in every Philosophical person whatsoever; I therefore, who profess no Politicks, have, for my curiosity, at large attempted* the first Essay of Political Anatomy.

Furthermore, as Students in Medicine, practice their inquiries upon cheap and common Animals, and such whose actions they are best acquainted with, and where there is the least confusion and perplexure of Parts; I have chosen Ireland *as such a* Political Animal, *who is scarce Twenty years old; where the* Intrigue *of* State *is not very complicate, and with which I have been conversant from an* Embrion; *and in which, if I have done amiss, the fault may be easily amended by another.* (Petty 1899, 129; emphasis in original)

Thus could Petty dissect and analyze Ireland as a pathologist would dissect and analyze a cadaver, knowing that the repercussions from a badly performed operation would be inconsequential, at least in regard to himself. If mistakes were made, then someone else at some later time could always be counted on to correct them, with no harm done.

Although presented as a forum for the elaboration of new ideas in the area of measurement and analysis, the *Political Anatomy* had also a more important justification. While providing a more efficient method of survey than had previously existed, it also served to redefine and simplify the *procedure* for valuation comparisons among essentially incommensurable factors. This has come to be known (by some) as the "problem of the par," that is, ascertaining a single, consistent unit of measure or value with which all values could be equivalently measured and compared. Petty viewed the "problem of the par" as being "the most important Consideration in Political Oeconomies, *viz.* how to make a *Par* and *Equation* between Lands and Labour, so as to express the Value of any thing by either alone" (1899, 181; emphasis in original). Being a proponent of a labor theory of value, labor became perhaps naturally Petty's preferred unit of value and also the basis for comparison, with the value of the land input being converted to labor units. Thus the following on the appropriate means of valuing a cabin: "I valued an *Irish* Cabbin at the number of days food, which the Maker spent in building of it" (182). So it seems as though Petty could reduce value to labor input not as represented by days or hours worked per laborer, but rather by the caloric intake required for the completion of the task. Whether this was an appropriate use of the par is a question that would later confront Cantillon.

Political Arithmetick   4.4

Petty's primary ambition for the *Political Arithmetick*[19] (written around 1676, published in 1690)—a work Johnson referred to as "one of the best illustrations of Petty's efforts to apply the methods of experimental science to economic problems" (Johnson 1937, 111–12)—seems to have been to advance a thesis that the disparity in size (of both land and population) between Britain and continental European powers was actually to Britain's advantage. While Britain was smaller in area and less populous than most of the continental military powers, its people were more productive and its international trade potentially much more lucrative. Petty arrived at this conclusion by extrapolation, examining the position of Holland in relation to that of France. At the time Petty wrote, the Dutch, with a fraction of the total land area and population of France, dominated merchant shipping. The size differential and the geographic advantages of Holland as compared to France—Holland having been built up from the sea, France having lengthy, exposed borders which needed constant attention—left Holland in a position that it could and did exploit to the fullest. The implication here was that Britain, in many respects not unlike Holland, could also reap the benefits from its geographic situation, both from a military and a politicoeconomic standpoint. In entering into commercial warfare with, for example, France, England thus had a natural advantage because of its position as a small but easily defensible island nation with a powerful merchant and military fleet, and because of its small but industrious population. Any impediments to greatness, military and economic, Petty viewed as contingent and removable; the natural advantages remained to be exploited. This work continued Petty's program of grounding intellectual arguments on an empirical basis. It also mirrored the Hobbesian program of providing an empirical basis for the further empowerment of the sovereign or the state in general.

A second ambition of Petty's best known work was to provide an incontrovertible measure of national welfare. Taxation may be employed as a device to increase national income if the levy shifts resources from profligate spending to investment (Petty 1899, 268–69). To *know* whether

---

19. The full title of this work is, *Political Arithmetick, or a Discourse Concerning, The Extent and Value of Lands, People, Buildings; Husbandry, Manufacture, Commerce, Fishery, Artizans, Seamen, Soldiers; Publick Revenues, Interest, Taxes, Superlucration, Registries, Banks; Valuation of Men, Increasing of Seamen, of Militia's, Harbours, Situation, Shipping, Power at Sea, &c. As the same relates to every Country in general, but more particularly to the Territories of His Majesty of Great Britain, and his Neighbours of Holland, Zealand, and France.*

taxation would have a positive or negative effect on national income and national welfare, however, demands an accurate assessment of the "State of the People, and their employments" (270). One must be clear as to not only the population of the nation, but also their ability "to perform the work of the Nation in its present State and Measure" (270). In a peculiar twist of logic, employing *post hoc, ergo propter hoc* reasoning, Petty argued that taxation had actually resulted in greater wealth-producing capability throughout the British Isles: "since the Year 1636, the Taxes and Publick Levies made in *England, Scotland,* and *Ireland,* have been prodigiously greater than at any time heretofore; and yet the said Kingdoms have increased in their Wealth and Strength for these last Forty Years" (271).

But Petty did not desire to extract more from the citizenry than they were able to pay. With this in mind, he arrived at an interesting solution to the problem of imports: institute a tax on the three kingdoms at a similar rate (2 s) to be paid in terms of their comparative advantages. The Irish will pay in flax, the English in linen, and the Scots in herring (1899, 272–74, 277). He also proposed a series of agricultural reforms, actually support programs, whereby the government would appropriate surpluses of corn and grains.[20] His general conclusion in the essay was that the people of Britain were undertaxed relative to the citizens of France and Holland. This he thought detrimental to the ultimate interest of the nation.

It was, though, the *method* employed by Petty in the *Political Arithmetick* more than the conclusions of the essay that served to make it an important contribution to the literature of quantitative economic analysis. In concert with the conclusions and policy recommendations Petty sought to advance, which he may have had in mind before any analysis ever took place, was the need to provide precise numerical measurements of the variables of interest to policymakers. Petty recognized that the rhetoric of the time was changing, that it demanded precision from those who desired to address questions of policy. He responded in such a manner that his conclusions could not be ignored: How indeed could one ignore the numbers that Petty placed at the disposal of anyone examining the problems upon which he wrote? Are not objective numerical data superior to mere testamentary evidence (as Graunt had also maintained) since the data do not admit of imprecision of narrative or style? In the Preface to this essay, Petty explained his method:

> The Method I take to do this, is not yet very usual; for instead of using only comparative and superlative Words, and intellectual Arguments, I have taken the course (as a Specimen of the Political Arithmetick I have long aimed at) to express my self in Terms of

---

20. Petty was apparently the first to note the positive correlation between cheap food and high-wage labor. See the comment by Hull in a footnote to this essay in the collected writings.

Number, Weight, or *Measure;* to use only Arguments of Sense, and to consider only such Causes, as have visible Foundations in Nature; leaving those that depend upon the mutable Minds, Opinions, Appetites, and Passions of particular Men, to the Consideration of others. (1899, 244; emphasis in original)

Although he was committed to precision in his work—hence the need to reduce phenomena to *"Number, Weight,* or *Measure"*—Petty would nonetheless not let such a trivial thing as the falsity of a conclusion based on observation stand in the way of his determination to advance a particular position. He considered that observations and subsequent hypotheses and policy proposals "are either true, or not apparently false, and which if they are not already true, certain, and evident, yet may be made so by the Sovereign Power, *Nam id certum est quod certum reddi potest,* and if they are false, not so false as to destroy the Argument they are brought for; but at worst are sufficient as Suppositions to shew the way to that Knowledge I aim at" (1899, 245; emphasis in original). Thus Mitchell was led to conclude that Petty "produced a high score of speculative discussions on problems which were not 'bottomed' on number and measure" (1967, vol. I, 149).

Expositors of the Faith: King and Davenant   5

Gregory King   5.1

Among those who were influenced by Petty were Gregory King (1648–1712)[21] and Charles Davenant (1656–1714). King, who was somewhat of a scholarly minded type, and Davenant, a Tory politico and later pamphleteer, undertook the measurement of British, French, and then Dutch national income as part of the social policy question regarding war objectives in the Anglo-Dutch alliance against Louis XIV. These writers improved greatly the accounting framework developed by Graunt and Petty, providing a foundation which eventually led to the elaboration of an economic venue for which national income accounting was the appropriate analytical tool. In so doing they also served to bring into its own the new discipline of statistics.

King's major work on the subject of national income accounting was *Natural and Politicall Observations and Conclusions Upon the State*

---

21. King was born at Litchfield, Staffordshire, his father a mathematician and surveyor. In the *Dictionary of National Biography,* King is identified as having been a "herald, genealogist, engraver, and statistician. . . ." Interestingly, as a herald one of his tasks would have been to travel about the kingdom to ensure that no one called himself a gentleman unless so entitled. Given the responsibilities of that duty, it is likely that he observed the conditions in the economy beyond London.

and Condition of England (1696).[22] Apparently King wrote this essay in an effort to provide the English monarch an account of the economic constitution of the nation. As he proclaimed in the Preface:

> If to be well apprized of the true State and Condition of a Nation, Especially in the Two maine Articles of it's People, and Wealth, be a Piece of Politicall Knowledge, of all others, and at all times, the most usefull, and Necessary; Than surely at a Time when a long and very Expensive Warr against a Potent Monarch . . . Seems to be at it's [sic] Crisis, Such a Knowledge of our own Nation must be of the Highest concern: But since the attaining thereof (how necessary and disireable soever) is next to impossible, We must Content our selves with such near approaches to it as the Grounds We have to go upon will enable us to make.
>
> However if haveing better Foundations than heretofore for Calculations of this kind, We have been Enabled to come very near the Truth; Then doubtlesse the following observations & conclusions will be acceptable to those who have not entirely given up themselves to an Implicit Beleif of Popular Falcehoods. But the Vanity of People in overvaluing their own Strength is so natural to all nations as well as ours; That as it has influenc'd all former Calculations of this Kind both at Home and Abroad, So if these, even these Papers may be allowed not to have erred on that hand, I am of opinion they will not be found to have Erred on the other. (King 1696, 13)

By analyzing the available data, extrapolating and interpolating to similar situations and periods where necessary, he could arrive at reasonable estimates of the population, its composition (by age, sex, and occupation), its density (and comparisons with France and Holland), the national income, national expenditures, the value of output, tax revenue, and the general state of the kingdom.

But there was another area of investigation which for economic theory was even more significant. This dealt with an empirical generalization concerning the efficacy of increased taxation, and particularly selective taxation. Contrary to the position of Petty that increasing taxes would lead to the expansion of a nation's wealth, King derived empirically a "proof" of the proposition that increasing taxes on a consumable good decreased consumption of that good, thus reducing revenues. More to the point, the tax increase shifted consumption to goods or to activities not subjected to the tax. Comparing the consumption of malt and ale in 1688 and 1695, King noticed that the increase in the excise tax between the two years corresponded to a decrease in the total consumption of

22. Schumpeter (1954) referred to this work as "a pioneer of quantitative economics and one of the best examples of what Political Arithmetick stood for" (212n4). It was not, however, published until 1801, although the book's ideas had been disseminated prior to this time, as parts had been incorporated into the works of Davenant.

malt (used to produce the ale) and the amount of ale brewed for public consumption (which were subjected to the tax), while the proportion of ale brewed privately, not subject to the tax, increased in both production and consumption over the same period (1696, 40–41). The tax had evidently shifted production to the more lucrative private-use ale, the price of which was unaffected by the tax change.

Unlike Petty's work, which could not escape the Hobbesian influence emphasizing empirical data over theoretical structure, King's work began with the elaboration of a theory of economics. One begins any scientific endeavor with a conceptual framework of "boxes," into which are fitted, to the greatest extent possible, the statistical data available. This allows the framework to be extended beyond the available data. As statistical data collection becomes more advanced and refined, the new data can be readily incorporated into the framework, without the framework having to be restructured. The framework itself becomes an analytical tool, one which is data-insensitive. It may also explain the deliberateness that King showed in his analysis, his unwillingness to make conclusions beyond what the data would allow.

Charles Davenant   5.2

It is through the work of Davenant that we know of the work of King.[23] Davenant's own contribution to the field of national income accounting appears to be his clarification of concepts and definitions. Indeed, much of his work is given to elaboration of central concepts instead of statistical collection and interpretation. His 1698 *Discourses on the Publick Revenues and on the Trade of England* provided a foundation for the expansion of Political Arithmetic to areas not entirely economic but nonetheless desirable for the expansion of state power. He defined the method of Political Arithmetic thus:

> A great statesman, by consulting all sort of men, and by contemplating the universal posture of the nation, its power, strength, trade, wealth and revenues, in any counsel he is to offer, by summing up the difficulties on either side, and by computing upon the whole, shall be able to form a sound judgment, and to give a right advice:

---

23. Davenant was the son of the poet William D'Avenant. The *Dictionary of National Biography* lists him as Charles Davenant, LL.D., but notes that the degree was probably obtained by "favour and money," since his name appears nowhere in a roster of graduates at the British universities. Throughout his writings he expressed policy positions that tended to further his own interests and those of the Tories. From 1678 to 1689 he held the post of commissioner of excise, being removed upon the assumption to the throne of William III. He served in Parliament from Cornwall in the reign of James II, and in the same capacity from Great Bedwin in the reign of William. With the assumption to the throne of Anne, Davenant was appointed inspector-general of exports and imports.

and this is what we mean by Political Arithmetic. (Davenant 1698, vol. I, 135)

Political Arithmetic, according to Davenant, had the potential to become a very powerful instrument in the state control of economic activity. It could be employed to estimate not only domestic income and product, but also the product of one's rivals (economically and politically), just as easily as it could aid the state in identifying sources of tax revenue, the original purpose behind its invention.[24] It could also aid military planners in the mobilization of men and materiel in the event of a war or other national emergency.[25] In effect, its usefulness seemed to be limited only by the imagination, and the availability of statistical data relevant to the subject.

5.3 An Assessment

To conclude this section, we will take note of two "appreciations" of the work of the political arithmeticians by those writing in their aftermath. Adam Smith, in commenting on the corn trade, and using data in support of his conclusions on the matter, nonetheless declared he had "no great faith in political arithmetic" (1789, bk. II, chap. V, 501). The computations presented, he argued, were too liable to imprecision to allow anything more than the offering of qualitative conclusions.

Smith's beliefs aside, a more important appreciation came in the form of a satirical piece written in 1729 by Jonathan Swift (1667–1745),[26] better known as the author of *Gulliver's Travels*. Entitled *A Modest Proposal, for Preventing the Children of Poor People in Ireland, from being a Burden to their Parents or Country; and for Making them Beneficial to the Publick,* it struck at the heart of the English attitude toward the Irish people and at the same time pointed to the inadequacies of basing policies regarding the wealth and welfare of the nation on efficiency criteria alone, without considering the consequences of those policies for the people affected.

Swift essentially turned the argument of Petty on its head. Petty had noted that Ireland was greatly underpopulated, so a reversal of this situa-

---

24. In the eighteenth century this effort to estimate British national income was expanded upon by Arthur Young.

25. During World War II, the work of statisticians such as Simon Kuznets and Robert Nathan allowed the United States to mobilize rapidly in preparation for the war. Likewise in Britain, the work of Richard Stone and James Meade was instrumental in calculating the level of sustainable (noninflationary) demand.

26. Swift was educated at Trinity College, Dublin, the city of his birth. In 1689 he served in London as secretary to Sir William Temple, but returned to Ireland where he took holy orders. By 1696 he had returned to London in the employ of Temple, remaining until 1699.

Politically a Whig, he eventually turned to support the Tories. In 1713 he became Dean of Saint Patrick's Cathedral in Dublin (and so is known as Dean Swift).

tion could only be to the overall benefit of England and Britain as a whole. Swift's position was just the opposite: Ireland was overpopulated, and he could demonstrate just as easily as the political arithmeticians a method for the alleviation of the problem, one which would at the same time benefit the material needs of England. The problem centered on the inability of the society to care for the children whose parents could not support them. So important did Swift think a solution, that he proclaimed: "whosoever could find out a fair, cheap, and easy Method of making these Children sound and useful Members of the Commonwealth; would deserve so well of the Publick, as to have his Statue set up for a Preserver of the Nation" (1729, 143).

In proposing his solution, Swift began, as did Petty, with an estimate of the population of Britain, which he took to be about 1.5 million. From this number "I calculate there may be about Two Hundred Thousand Couple whose Wives are Breeders." From this figure, "subtract thirty thousand Couples, who are able to maintain their own Children," and a further "Fifty Thousand, for those Women who miscarry, or whose Children die by Accident, or Disease, within the year." This leaves a figure of "an Hundred and Twenty Thousand Children of poor Parents, annually born" (1729, 144).

Now, based on the opinions of merchants, Swift was assured that a child under the age of twelve "will not yield above Three Pounds, or Three Pounds and half a Crown at most, on the Exchange," a value much below the cost of care. The "proposal"—one Swift hoped would "not be liable to the least Objection"—thus was to use the children of the poor as "a most delicious, nourishing, and wholesome Food" (1729, 145). Of the 120,000 born annually, 20,000 would be held back for the purposes of "Breeding" (and only one-fourth of these need to be males), the remainder to "be offered in Sale to the Persons of Quality and Fortune, through the Kingdom" (145).

The entire population would gain in the enterprise. Given an average annual cost of two shillings for nursing a "Beggar's Child," a price per child of ten shillings would gain the mother a profit of eight shillings, to be used to tide her over until she can again give birth; she will then also no longer be a burden to the public welfare. As to the nation as a whole, because the cost of maintenance of 100,000 children over the age of two is ten shillings per child per annum, "the Nation's Stock will be thereby increased Fifty Thousand Pounds per Annum," this being in addition to "the Profit of a new Dish, introduced to the Tables of all Gentlemen of Fortune in the Kingdom, who have any Refinement in Taste" (1729, 148). In addition to these national benefits, the policy had other national advantages—a reduction in the number of Catholics in Britain (since Swift had it on good authority that Catholics, in great number among the Irish, were born in disproportionate numbers nine months after Lent); an increase in the trade of taverns and inns, which would become houses catering to the needs of the upper classes in providing so delectable a dish; and an inducement to marriage, since the profit motive is overwhelming. Thus as far as Swift could determine, based solely on the desire to increase the national welfare and stimulate the economy, the policy had only positive benefits and no negative aspects. What more could one ask from Political Arithmetic?

In a more serious vein, and lest it be thought we have in some sense overestimated the importance and significance of the contributions of Graunt, Petty, King, and Davenant to the foundations of econometrics, we offer in support of the political arithmeticians the opinion of Richard Stone.

> They [Petty, King, and Davenant] were convinced that by combining numbers and economic theory one could produce analyses useful for the policy-maker, and they acted on their conviction. It is true that their data were sparse and imperfect, their economic theory rudimentary and statistical theory virtually unthought of. But they were inventive, energetic and determined and between them they managed to put together a corpus of economic estimates which is remarkable for its range and consistency and gives us a pretty good picture of the English economy in the second half of that century. (Stone 1988, 19)

6 Cantillon as the Critical Hinge

6.1 *The* Essai

Richard Cantillon (1680?–1734?),[27] typically taken as being a French economist[28] but actually of Irish descent, occupies a unique position in the

---

27. Cantillon's exact date of birth is questionable, some placing his birth as late as 1697, but the usual statement (as expressed in the biographical review by Henry Higgs) is that he was born in Ballyheigue, County Kerry, Ireland between 1680 and 1690. Higgs quoted from an affidavit sworn by Cantillon in 1724, to the effect that he had been born in Great Britain, but worked as a banker in Paris until 1719, after which time he engaged in various business ventures apparently involving the use of what we today refer to as venture capital. Accused of usurious banking practices, he apparently, at some time, again fled to England, presumably because of his involvement in John Law's "Mississippi Bubble" scheme (from which he had reportedly profited handsomely), but returned to Paris in 1729 where he was arrested for his banking irregularities (although immediately released).

There is some question also about the date and the circumstances surrounding his death. Supposedly, while asleep at his London home on the night of May 13, 1734, he was murdered by a discharged cook, who also allegedly burned his house. However, there is also the very real possibility that Cantillon burned the house himself, fleeing to Guiana, where he died peacefully after many years of self-imposed exile. See Antoin Murphy (1986) for a more comprehensive account of the life and work of Cantillon.

28. Schumpeter, for instance, classified him as French because his influence was more closely felt there than it was in either England or Ireland (Schumpeter 1954, 217n.4).

emergence of national income accounting, being (according to Schumpeter) a descendant of Petty and an ancestor to the physiocrats. Schumpeter (1954) went so far as to proclaim that "few sequences in the history of economic analysis are so important for us to see, to understand, and to fix in our minds, as is the sequence: Petty–Cantillon–Quesnay" (218).[29] Cantillon's method comprised elements of both, in that he arrived at the conclusions advanced by Petty while predicating his analysis on the rationalism and Natural-Law foundations later accepted by the French writers.

Cantillon's principal economic work was his 1730 *Essai sur la nature du commerce en général* (*Essay on the Nature of Trade,* published posthumously in 1755). It was called by William Stanley Jevons "*the first treatise on economics*" and "The Cradle of Political Economy" (Jevons 1881, 67–68; emphasis in original) and esteemed by Schumpeter as having been the accomplishment of Petty's ideas (Schumpeter 1954, 218).[30] This work, lost to the English speaking world for a century after its completion, continued the program begun by Petty and greatly influenced the subsequent work of Quesnay and Turgot.[31]

Cantillon's *Essai* was an exercise in pure economic analysis; as such it differed from earlier dissertations on subjects economic in that it did not attempt to structure the argument in a moral or political rhetoric, but relied instead on what can today be identified as a uniquely *economic* rhetoric.

At the outset of this work, Cantillon proposed a definition of wealth, identifying labor and land as combining in its production. Unlike previous writers on the subject, Cantillon did not assert that there was a single *source* for wealth creation, but rather that land and labor *together* enter into the enterprise.

> The Land is the Source or Matter from whence all Wealth is produced. The Labour of man is the Form which produces it: and Wealth in itself is nothing but the Maintenance, Conveniencies, and Superfluities of Life. (1755, 3)

This association of land and labor with wealth then led directly to a theory of value. Cantillon began by making a clear distinction between

---

29. Studenski (1958) does not even mention Cantillon as a player in this area.

30. Brewer referred to the *Essai* as "the first coherent analysis of an economy as a single interdependent whole" (Brewer 1988, 447). He also characterized Cantillon as having advanced "clearly mercantilist" policies, "in the rather loose sense of the term current in discussion of the history of economics," by which he meant "a rather inchoate body of literature advocating nationalist economic policies and centering on the control of trade" (447 and n.3).

31. The book itself has a rather interesting history. The title page of the 1755 French edition states that it was translated from the English, but no one has has yet come upon this edition. The book was "discovered" by William Stanley Jevons (presumably at one of the used-book stalls that line the banks of the Seine near the Sorbonne), who arranged for the book to be (re?)translated.

value and price. The *value* of goods is directly related to the produce of the land and the quality of the labor involved in production (1755, 27). One good attains a value greater than another by virtue of the labor input involved in its production; agricultural goods, however, are valued according to the productive powers of the land (29). But in general, "the intrinsic value of any thing may be measured by the quantity of Land used in its production and the quantity of Labour which enters into it" (41). It was in this context that Cantillon took issue with Petty, although the difference centered more on the rhetoric employed than the conclusions drawn.[32] As we have discussed above, Petty in the *Political Anatomy of Ireland* had shown a similar relation between land and labor in the creation of intrinsic value. There Petty advanced the notion of the "par"—an index of sorts by which one of the two principal factors ("natural Denominations," as Petty classed them) could be reduced to the other—but his presentation of the idea seemed confused, as he employed it in support of a labor-value theory. It was Cantillon who actually employed the idea to recover a labor-cost equivalent to land, in support of a consistent land theory of value.[33] Cantillon ridiculed Petty's use of the concept, and held that Petty's *method* of arriving at his conclusions was "fanciful and remote from natural laws, because he has attached himself not to causes and principles but only to effects" (43), obviously an allusion to Petty's inductivist stance. Cantillon felt his own derivations—from obvious, self-evident propositions—to be the more scientific (although he did make frequent reference to a statistical "supplement" to the *Essai*, long since lost, which he alleged provided numerical support to his generalizations).

Thus Cantillon deduced *value* by the combination of the original inputs of labor and land. We are still left to determine the *market price*, which is fundamentally different from *value*. Price is for the most part determined not by the value of the labor and land input to its production, but rather by "the Humours and Fancies of men and on their consumption" (1755, 29); in other words, it is a subjectively determined quantity which is demand-driven. Price is ultimately determined by what someone agrees to offer, and so it will in the main differ from the "intrinsic" value instilled in it by the productive factors. While the cost of production is an important determinant of value, a good will have no "price" unless someone is willing to offer a sum for its procurement. The main difference, however, between value and price is that value is unchanging, while price cannot be held constant.

> There is never a variation in intrinsic values, but the impossibility of proportioning the production of merchandise and produce in a

---

32. On the similarities and differences between Petty and Cantillon, see Brewer (1992). Brewer held Petty to have been something of a glorified accountant, while Cantillon was esteemed as more the pure theorist.

33. On this see Brewer 1992, 720–22.

State to their consumption causes a daily variation, and a perpetual
ebb and flow in Market Prices. (1755, 31)

The exception to this "rule" occurs when the consumption of the good is
relatively constant. In this instance, value and price will tend to be more
closely related and so exhibit constancy.

Cantillon was in the main an advocate of laissez-faire, holding the
economy to be but a system composed of interrelated parts, coordinated
through a natural order; the whole is self-equilibrating. But this order is
not perfect. As to the issue of the ownership of resources, for example,
Cantillon held to a fatalism that led him to conclude that there was little
that could be done to prevent an uneven distribution: "Which way soever
a Society of Men is formed the ownership of the Land they inhabit will
necessarily belong to a small number among them" (1755, 3). Should it
be the case that land is distributed equally to all the inhabitants of a
society, it will become consolidated again within a very short time,
whether through sale or generational transfer or death intestate, into the
hands of a few. It is simply not possible, nor even conceivable, that any
equal distribution of resources will remain so indefinitely; the evolutionary dynamic generates inequality. In any event, even should some equalization scheme be advanced that would account for generational changes
in the allocation of resources, it was not clear to Cantillon just how a
society could be structured in the absence of some form of settled legal
(meaning private) ownership of land (7). Aristotle still held sway over
Plato.

While ownership was one thing, the *use* of land was another question altogether, and here one sees the touch of Aristotle and Aquinas.
Cantillon held that land, first and foremost, should be used for the production of the necessities of life, meaning for the maintenance of those
who work and till the land. The owners of the land are of course entitled
to a portion of the output, but first the needs of those engaged directly in
cultivation must be met. Only then could the land be exploited to "the
Humour and Fashion of Living of the Prince, the Lords, and the Owner"
(1755, 7). The owner thus has in a sense a moral obligation, as part of his
right of control, to provide for the maintenance of his own tenants, for
only in this way can the society be served.

Cantillon's Influence   6.2

The connection of Cantillon's thought to that of Petty is evident in the
manner in which Cantillon painstakingly detailed the flows of wealth
from origination in the land and labor input to the remuneration of the
landlord and the profit of the manufacturer. He commenced with a
simple "fact" of allocation, that the proprietor receives one-third of the
value of the produce of his land (presumably for maintenance), while

the cultivator (the farmer) receives two-thirds, of which half is paid to direct costs of production and half is profit (1755, 43). On these distributional ratios Cantillon based the remuneration schedule to ownership and to factor inputs.

While consistent with Petty in his attempt to ground his findings on a numerical basis, Cantillon disagreed with Petty on a number of his statistical pronouncements. For example, Cantillon took issue with Petty's statistics of population for the various countries of Europe, considering that they had been grounded on too little appreciation for the actual patterns of events. Petty's estimates, while seemingly convincing and certainly plausible, simply did not match the reality of the situation; they were, in other words, not coupled with any appreciation of the underlying economics of supply and demand and the attendant effects of agricultural production on population.

> Sir Wm Petty, and after him Mr Davenant, . . . seem to depart from nature when they try to estimate the propagation of the race by progressive generations from Adam, the first Father. Their calculations seem to be purely imaginary and drawn up at hazard. (1755, 83)

Much of Cantillon's argument also shows a great affinity with the later views of the physiocratic writers. For instance, his belief that land is the first and most important factor of production, and provides when combined with labor the only true and meaningful measure of wealth, is certainly a proposition with which any physiocrat would be sympathetic. Likewise his advocacy of agricultural production in the interest of the power relations of the state is music to the ears of any good physiocratic philosopher. Consider but two of Cantillon's pronouncements:

> The natural and constant way of increasing Population in a State is to find employment for the People there, and to make the Land serve for the production of their Means of Support.

> . . . when the Nobility and Proprietors of Land draw from Foreign Manufactures their Cloths, Silks, Laces, etc. and pay for them by sending to the Foreigner their native produce they diminish extraordinarily the food of the People and increase that of Foreigners who often become Enemies of the State. (1755, 85, 75)

In addition, it should be noted that Schumpeter (1954) gave Cantillon the credit for making the first explicit mention of the concept of the circular flow and enunciating a form of the *tableau économique*, although to be sure his presentation differed in form from Quesnay's. As Cantillon proclaimed in his effort to tie the contributions of one group of participants in the economic system to other groups who may be viewed for very parochial reasons as mere customers, "all the Inhabitants of a

State are dependent" (1755, 55). Thus Cantillon represents for us one of the most interesting figures in the history of the science of national economies; he is truly a member of a small, select group of "innovative" economic thinkers.[34]

But Cantillon's *Essai* also contained aspects of mercantilist doctrine, insofar as he advocated the control of trade and the promotion of manufacturing for the benefit of state power.[35] Consider but the following statements:

> It is by examining the results of each branch of commerce singly that Foreign trade can be usefully regulated. It cannot be distinctly apprehended by abstract reasons. It will always be found by examining particular cases that the exportation of all Manufactured articles is advantageous to the State, because in this case the Foreigner always pays and supports Workmen useful to the State: that the best returns or payments imported are specie, and in default of specie the produce of Foreign land into which there enters the least labour. By these methods of trading States which have very little raw produce are often seen to support inhabitants in great numbers at the expense of Foreigners, and large States maintain their inhabitants in greater ease and abundance.

> I will conclude then by observing that the trade most essential to a State for the increase or decrease of its power is foreign trade, that the home trade is not of equally great importance politically, that foreign trade is only half supported when no care is taken to increase and maintain large merchants who are natives of the country, ships, sailors, workmen and manufactures, and above all that care must always be taken to maintain the balance against the foreigner. (1755, 233, 243)

According to Cantillon, the state should purchase raw materials from abroad and export manufactured goods. The result would be not only an increase in national wealth, but also an increase in employment and population (as it would no longer be constrained by domestic agricultural production). He also advocated, in line with mercantilist dogma, (1) that the state should endeavor to expand its stocks of bullion and (2) that the state should maintain sufficient stocks of money in the event of war.[36]

---

34. Pribram (1983) regarded Cantillon as "[t]he only economist prior to the middle of the eighteenth century who appears to have grasped the conception of an economic system of a more or less mechanical type" (79).

35. Brewer (1988) made this point particularly well.

36. "It is clear that every State which has more money in circulation than its neighbours has an advantage over them so long as it maintains this abundance of money. . . . This gives the State, in case of war or dispute, the means to gain all sorts of advantages over its adversaries with whom money is scarce" (Cantillon 1755, 189).

The only "special interest" in Cantillon's version of the mercantilist doctrine was the interest of the state.

As significant as his contributions to economic thought were, of equal importance was the manner of his presentation. Cantillon's rhetoric relied upon abstraction; his technical competence and mastery of the subject is tremendous. Despite their complexity, the central principles of his system are very quickly and easily comprehended. He is generally regarded as being either the discoverer or the anticipator of much that appears under the names of others, such as Walras, Marshall, and Knight. His obscurity is probably due to his desire not to publish his works and his general reluctance to discuss his ideas (in this he is akin to Petty, whose works were published only after his death).

7 The Physiocrats

7.1 Definition

With the development by the political arithmeticians of a technical apparatus, an intellectual vacuum of sorts had been created: a divergence appeared between the sophistication of the tools of analysis and the analytical structure behind them. In other words, practical advancements had surpassed the ability of the theoretical base to exploit their potential most effectively: measurement was moving ahead of theory. What was required was an analytical schema that would accept this new apparatus, and use it to its fullest advantage. This theoretical advance was to come in the guise of the French doctrine of Physiocracy.

Physiocracy as the first truly consistent school of economic thought developed in the wake of Cantillon's *Essai*. Formally known as *les économistes,* the group adhered to a socio-political-economic doctrine predicated on the rule of Natural Law—the word *Physiocracy* in fact means "natural rule." In its simplest form, physiocratic doctrine had as its chief elements the removal of internal tariff barriers and the overall reinvigoration of the agricultural sector. According to the usual presentation of this doctrine, manufacturing is sterile; industry produces no net additions to national income and wealth. Only agriculture—the truly productive sector of the economy—is capable of producing real net additions to national wealth. Value begins and ends with the land and the produce therefrom.

For the purposes of the present work we must understand the historical prelude to the emergence of this "radical" doctrine, the chain of events leading to the formation of a physiocratic "school." As the school was a distinctly French movement, a review of political events in France, particularly from the time of Louis XIV, is particularly helpful. The discussion that follows concerns French history from about 1515 to 1787, a period during which weak kings were followed by strong ones and which ended, ultimately, with the excesses of the French Revolution.

Pre-Physiocratic French Political Economy: 7.2
The French Mercantilist Tradition

Physiocracy did not develop in a sociopolitical vacuum, but rather emerged as a reaction to events and failed policies and doctrines. One of the most important of the policy-oriented approaches was that of French Mercantilism, which began, as with its English counterpart, in about the late Middle Ages. Louis XI (reigned 1461–83) attempted in 1462 to prevent the outflow of bullion by expanding the fairs of Lyon, and in 1471 he took steps to expand the mining industry. As with the Stuart kings of England, the French monarchs extended the government's role in the economy by regulating, among other things, the wearing of jewelry and cloth made of gold or silver; they also introduced restrictions on the use of imported cloth as a measure to favor home-produced wool goods. Wool production was further regulated in 1571 by laws that established size and quality standards. In 1581 a law was enacted to foster a guild system in virtually all commercial activities.

It was during this period that Jean Bodin (1530–96)—philosopher, statesman, jurist, and an official in the French government—published *Les Six Livres de la République* (1576), a work dedicated to the rationalization of the French economy, especially the tax system.[37] For Bodin, before the French economy could be restructured and strengthened, it was necessary to undertake a complete census of the economic wealth of the nation. Such a census would facilitate tax collection and serve to create a more equitable tax system, one that (in Bodin's estimation) did not favor the landed aristocracy over the merchants. As an advocate of monarchical absolutist rule tempered by justice, Bodin offered policies that stressed the mercantilist goal of securing the power of the state. He advocated customs taxes as a means to generate revenue while at the same time promote (and protect) French producers, higher import taxes on foreign goods to promote import substitution, lower taxes on the importation of raw materials to benefit domestic industry, and higher export taxes on "necessaries." In all, Bodin stressed rational management of the tax system to the benefit of the state.

Under Henry IV (1589–1610), in consultation with his adviser Barthélemy de Laffemas (1545–1611), the mercantilist policies of France expanded. Laffemas, a tailor and valet to Henry (while he was still Henry of Navarre), had acquired a sizable fortune in the cloth trade. He came to believe that the fault behind the economic ills of France lay in its dependence on foreign goods. So influential was Laffemas that when Henry in

---

37. A discussion of Bodin can be found in Cynthia Taft Morris (1957).

1601 established a commission on trade—soon after to become the Council of Commerce—Laffemas was given a leading role in its dealings.[38] He was appointed Controller-General of Commerce in 1602, and in 1604 submitted to Henry a plan for the industrialization of France.

Under Laffemas the Commission of Commerce—technically the *Commission consultative sur le faict du commerce général et de l'établissement des manufacturers*—embarked on a wide variety of economic ventures, including the promotion of horse breeding, linen manufacture, glass works, and silk production (going so far as to introduce mulberry trees into France). It also encouraged invention (including processes to bleach flour and to produce white lead), advocated restrictions on exports, pressured foreign manufacturers operating in France to offer apprenticeships to French youth, and encouraged monopolies for the production and trade of certain designated goods (Clough and Cole 1952, 217–18). Laffemas himself advocated the augmenting of French supplies of bullion—he held the shortage to have been at the root of the problems of French agriculture—but did not advocate hoarding. He encouraged the regulation of all commerce, insisting that the "free fairs" had destroyed the ability of the French to manufacture quality merchandise and so had led to an outflow of specie, to the detriment of the French economy. He sought to rebuild and regulate manufacturing so as to replace imported goods with domestically produced ones; this policy of import substitution involved revitalizing the guild system and preventing the export of raw materials and unfinished, intermediate goods (Cole 1939, vol. I, ch. II). For his part, Henry desired to expand French trading internationally by founding a French East India Company and a Company of the Arctic Pole to compete directly with the trading companies of the Dutch.

The succession to power of Louis XIII, following the assassination of Henry IV, placed the authority of the Crown in the hands of two very able Catholic cardinals: Armand Jean du Plessis, Cardinal, Duc de Richelieu (1585–1642)[39] and Jules Cardinal Mazarin (1602–61).[40] Richelieu, a product of the "lesser" nobility and chief adviser to Marie de Medici, Queen-Mother and Regent (during the period of exile), was a major political force in Europe. During the Thirty Years' War (1618–48), Richelieu gained a tremendous degree of power; his position as cardinal and prime minister (from 1624 until his death) gave him the mantle of author-

---

38. C. W. Cole (1939, vol. I) held that the commission was important primarily as a vehicle to implement the policies of Laffemas.

39. Cardinal, Duc de Richelieu was born in Poitou, France, of a French noble but impoverished family. Installed as bishop of Luçon by Henry IV (1606), he became the chief adviser to Marie de Medici. In 1622 he was elevated to cardinal. In 1624, he became prime minister, holding the position until his death. His major works include *Memoirs on the Reign of Louis XIII* and *Political Testament*.

40. Mazarin was born in Sicily and educated in Rome by the Jesuits, where he took a doctorate in law. Eventually he became a diplomat in the service of the pope.

ity in the consolidation of the anti-Hapsburg coalition. He held to a very nationalistic political position, believing that France could be strengthened as a world power by invoking mercantilist policies designed to promote economic self-sufficiency, especially in commerce. To this end he founded an order of knights (the order of the Holy Trinity) that would engage in colonial ventures. He also established trading companies, such as the Company of Morbihan (1626) and the Company of St. Peter's Boat with Lilies (1627), both of which failed; the Company of New France (1627) to exploit the Canadian fur trade; the Company of the Islands of America (1635), which succeeded (for a short period) in expanding the trade in tobacco, indigo, and sugar; and the Company of the East (1641) to encourage trade in spices (Clough and Cole 1952, 220–21).

Mazarin, a Sicilian and papal diplomat who had befriended Richelieu while papal nuncio to France, had, as Richelieu, become a cardinal (1641) and, at Richelieu's death, prime minister of France, a position he also held until his death. Mazarin reconstituted the Commission of Commerce under the superintendent of finances, Nicolas Fouquet, and even took an active role in the promotion of policies for the relief of the poor. Mazarin's influence was so great that at the death of Louis XIII in 1642 he became, during the regency of Anne of Austria, the de facto ruler of France.[41]

The roles of Richelieu and Mazarin were thus by no means marginal, nor are they mentioned here as historical curiosities. Both were important in directing French national policy along the mercantilist road, in an effort to strengthen and revitalize France. Their wiliness and considerable political skills managed to preserve the fortunes of the Crown (and themselves) through several decades of boy-kings and a politically unpopular Italian (Medici) Queen-Mother Regent. Still, and despite the obvious *political* skills of the regents and surrogates, the period of the regency (1642–60) marked a decline in French agriculture. Taxation was at oppressive levels, as Mazarin had increased the *taille* (the tax on agriculture), the *gabelle* (the tax on salt), and the *aides* (the tax on wine). This took a toll on output, as did the policies in support of nationalist ventures. It was into this climate that Louis XIV came to power.

France was quite clearly in this epoch the dominant force on the Continent, culturally and militarily. Louis XIV, who had the great fortune to be in power at this precise epoch of French glory, exploited the situation to the fullest. Under the guidance of his finance minister, Jean-Baptiste Colbert, who served from 1663 to 1683, Louis's political ambitions were given voice. Colbert—comptroller-general of finance—was a man of great integrity and talent, and was concerned only in fostering the

---

41. In 1643, Louis XIV (then age five) ascended the throne, although France at this time was still actually ruled by Cardinal Mazarin. Louis took control of the throne at age 23 at Mazarin's death.

best interests of France. While he realized the necessity to reform the system instituted by Mazarin and others, like his predecessors his chief interest lay in the enrichment of France. He maintained that, in order to strengthen French *political* power, Louis had to first ensure French *economic* power, meaning the command over resources. In general terms, Louis (and Colbert) insisted on the accomplishment of three important and mutually reinforcing objectives: (1) to aggrandize France, (2) to expand his own political power, and (3) to enhance the power and influence of the Church. To fulfill these objectives, Colbert recommended shifting the focus of the economy toward rapid industrialization, a program designed to promote a centralized (state) bureaucratic apparatus and a corporatist enterprise structure. Critical to this end was the appropriation by the state of administrative control over the direction of the economy, including the creation of monopolies, the elimination of internal barriers to trade (to facilitate state control), the tightening of international trade restrictions (amounting to a declaration of economic war), and the imposition of additional revenue-enhancement measures (including taxes on agriculture and land).[42] Trade was, after all, merely a means to an end, a form of warfare.

In aggrandizing France and Louis, Colbert demanded the exploitation of *all* sectors of the economy and the society, including the cultural and the artistic. This was to prove financially disastrous, as Louis's quest for greater national and personal power took its toll. His lavish spending on personal projects, such as the magnificent palace at Versailles, as well as his foreign military adventures, such as the War of the Spanish Succession, reduced severely the ability of the economy to continue with industrialization efforts. The constant necessity to discover additional sources of revenue to pay for these projects led to the enactment of schemes such as a prohibitive land tax, the effect of which was virtually to destroy the agricultural sector of the economy.

Even before Louis's death, France's glory had waned, and the deleterious effects of policies designed to promote power and international prestige were being felt. By 1715, France was producing one-third less in the way of agriculture, the birth rate had fallen while mortality rates had risen, and worst of all over half of what was collected in taxes went into the process of the collecting. Perhaps most important in this regard, France had succeeded in ridding itself of the Huguenots (among whom were the country's largest group of entrepreneurs), a change which was most probably the underlying reason for the emergence of Physiocracy. Adam Smith summed up the situation very nicely, laying much of the blame for the devastation of French agriculture at the hands of Colbert,

---

42. Revenues were badly needed to pay for military adventures under Louis XIV, which included constant wars on the Continent and magnificent efforts in India and the New World.

whose policy recommendations leaned heavily on mercantilist programs (including, but not limited to, the prohibition of agricultural exports):

> The industry and commerce of a great country he endeavoured to regulate upon the same model as the departments of a public office; and instead of allowing every man to pursue his own interest his own way, upon the liberal plan of equality, liberty and justice, he bestowed upon certain branches of industry extraordinary privileges, while he laid others under as extraordinary restraints. He was not only disposed, like other European ministers, to encourage more the industry of the towns than that of the country; but, in order to support the industry of the towns, he was willing even to depress and keep down that of the country. In order to render provisions cheap to the inhabitants of the towns, and thereby to encourage manufactures and foreign commerce, he prohibited altogether the exportation of corn, and thus excluded the inhabitants of the country from every foreign market for by far the most important part of the produce of their industry. This prohibition, joined to the restraints imposed by the ancient provincial laws of France upon the transportation of corn from one province to another, and to the arbitrary and degrading taxes which are levied upon the cultivators in almost all the provinces, discouraged and kept down the agriculture of that country very much below the state to which it would naturally have risen in so very fertile a soil and so very happy a climate. This state of discouragement and depression was felt more or less in every different part of the country, and many different inquiries were set on foot concerning the causes of it. One of those causes appeared to be the preference given, by the institutions of Mr. Colbert, to the industry of the towns above that of the country. (1789, book IV, chap. IX, 627–28)

There can be no doubt that the disastrous situation with respect to French agriculture was evident for some time before Louis's death, the level of disaster having become generally apparent by about 1700. By that time there was much interest in trying to improve the calamitous state of the French economy. Enter at this point in the drama the reaction to French Mercantilism.[43] Maréchal Sébastien le Prestre, Seigneur de Vauban (1633–1707),[44] for one, presented a radical proposal of reform in 1707 in his *Projet d'une dixme royale* (Project for a royal tithe), an

---

43. C. W. Cole (1943) has written a particularly good presentation of this subject.

44. Vauban's full name and title were Sébastien le Prestre, Seigneur de Vauban, Bazoches, Pierre-Perthuis, Pouilly, La Chaume, Épiry et autres lieux, Maréchal de France. Born in Burgundy, he had a quite impressive military career, which consisted primarily in his designing fortifications for many of the cities and towns throughout France and devising means for their defense. Upon his retirement from the military (named Marshall of France in 1703), he spent the remaining years of his life writing on social concerns. The material presented here on Vauban is primarily from Studenski (1958, 54–60) and Cole (1943, 231–35). See also Nannerl Keohane (1980).

essay on taxation and the French national income.[45] Not an economist, but rather an engineer of military background and training, he nonetheless made important contributions in economics and finance. In matters concerning France, he was a chauvinist of the first order. This is especially noticeable in his position on foreign trade:

> Foreign commerce should scarcely be permitted save for goods necessary to life, dress, medicine, and certain industries, for which the materials are not found at home, unless one does as the Dutch, who go to seek useless things abroad only to resell them elsewhere. It should be forbidden when, for goods which have to do only with luxury and fashion, it causes more money to go out of the kingdom than it brings in; but that which can bring us new money cannot be sought after too zealously. (Quoted in Cole 1943, 234–35)

Vauban firmly and devoutly supported the monarchy, his work in the area of taxation and creation of a framework of national accounts seemingly undertaken with an eye to the expansion of the wealth of the nation and hence the stability of the monarchy. He argued, for example, that the French tax system as it existed at the time was too confiscatory toward one small sector of the economy, this being smallholder agriculture. His solution called for the abolition of the tax structure in its then-current form, to be replaced with a multitiered, proportional one. This new system was basically the tithe, a flat-rate income tax levied on *all* income. The tax system would be composed of four "Funds." The first would be derived from in-kind levies on agricultural production; the second from income[46] taxes; the third from taxes on salt; the fourth from duties, fees, and charges on luxury goods and spirits. For Vauban, national income was nothing more than a source of tax revenue.

But for his exertions, Vauban lost his influence with Louis XIV; his book was condemned and the publisher prosecuted. Yet Vauban had an important supporter,[47] Pierre le Pesant, Sieur de Boisguillebert (1646–

---

45. Of this book Schumpeter proclaimed: "This is one of the outstanding performances in the field of public finance, unsurpassed, before or after, in the neatness and cogency of the argument" (Schumpeter 1954, 203–4). Studenski was less charitable in his assessment: "Vauban . . . was neither a good economic theorist nor a good statistician. But, being an engineer by training, he brought to the task the same respect for precision that characterized his military work" (Studenski 1958, 54–55).

Pribram, in a rather charitable assessment, remarked: "His contributions to the problems of taxation have been regarded as a remarkable achievement, since he fully realized the influence exercised by methods of taxation on different elements of the economy, and, in addition, endeavored to use facts and figures to substantiate and justify his recommendations" (Pribram 1983, 97).

46. As Studenski noted, this would include "incomes from the rent of houses, profits of businesses and grain mills, the operation of public properties, money wages, pensions, and fees of government offices" (1958, 55–56).

47. Another supporter of Vauban was Charles Irénée Castel, Abbé de Saint-Pierre (1658–1743). A social reformer and advocate of the "theory of indefinite progress," he is

1714).[48] His 1697 book *Le Détail de la France* (A detailed account of France)[49] took up a theme similar to that advanced by Vauban—Hazel v. Dyke Roberts even suggested that Vauban "borrowed" much from *Le Détail* for his own tract (Roberts 1935, 35). Boisguillebert's work, however, proved to be politically more palatable, as it was published only after the death of Louis XIV.[50]

Boisguillebert, in many ways a precursor of the physiocrats, actually expressed views of both a pro- and antimercantilist variety. He suggested that the French sovereign focus attention on the augmentation of the agricultural sector in order to expand the French economy, as agriculture served as the basis of manufacturing and commerce. Contemporary practice had virtually destroyed agriculture in an ill-fated effort to subsidize urban expansion. The economic policies of Henry IV and his advisers, of Mazarin, and of Colbert under Louis XIV had decimated the French

---

best known for his *Observations on the Continuous Progress of Universal Reason* (1737). His reforms reached into virtually every aspect of society—including education, government, and the economy—and he is said to have actually introduced the word *bienfaisance* into the French language. He accepted that government had an important role in shaping society, and that it could, if in the control of the right people, actually result in greater human happiness. Yet he did not favor state intervention in commercial affairs, except in such necessary areas as the postal service. Among other things, he favored tax reform and poor relief. A Cartesian and Deist, his publications include *Discourse Against Mohammedanism* and *Physical Explanation of an Apparition*. The most extensive treatment of St. Pierre's work is in J. B. Bury (1932).

48. Boisguillebert was born in Rouen in Normandy, part of the civil-service gentry. His father, Nicholas le Pesant, had been councillor to the king; his grandfather served as secretary. Educated by the Jesuits at Rouen, he was sent to Paris to continue his studies, first at Port Royal then at the École de Driot. His Jesuit educational background suggests he held a deep interest in the classics of Greek literature, even publishing translations of Xenophilus and Herodotus; he also studied in the law, becoming an *avocat*. In 1678 Boisguillebert became Vicomte de Montivilliers in Normandy (until 1689). In 1689 he purchased the offices of président and lieutenant-général of the bailliage and présidial of Rouen. Details of Boisguillebert's life and his economics are from Hazel van Dyke Roberts (1935), Schumpeter (1954, 215–16n.1), Studenski (1958, 52–54), and Cole (1965, 231–32).

49. This book, according to Schumpeter, had such classy subtitles as *La France ruinée sous le règne de Louis XIV* (France ruined, under the reign of Louis XIV) and *Moyens très-facile de faire reçevoir au Roy 300 millions par-dessus la capitation, practicable par deux heures de travail des Messieurs les Ministres* (A quick recipe to give the King 300 million livres through capitation, feasible with only two-hours of work by his ministers). Studenski (1958, 58) suggested that Vauban read this work in manuscript form, agreeing with most of the policy prescriptions.

50. The work of Boisguillebert and that of Vauban were connected through the desire of each to promote the best interests of France, irrespective of who would gain the credit. Vauban and Boisguillebert "had differed over the means to be taken, but they had fought for the same end: to save France from greed, self-interest, and incompetence. He [Boisguillebert] had never regarded Vauban as the real author of the proposal for a dime royale. He thought the proposal unworthy of the marshal whose special knowledge lay in another field. It was as if he would share his own life's work as a monument worthy of the aims of the other. A single memorial it would be for the two who had labored and suffered for the same cause: the cause of the people of France" (Roberts 1935, 92).

economy through the levying of exorbitant taxes on agriculture without respect to the negative effects of such taxes on income and productivity. These mercantilist policies had led to the destruction of the agricultural sector by prohibiting the export of agricultural products, especially grains, and had impoverished the largest productive component of the French economy, the farmers who actually cultivated the soil.[51] Agriculture for Boisguillebert was simply the most important sector of the French economy, both in terms of its role in support of manufacturing and in its role as the primary source of income, wealth, and employment.

Boisguillebert was keenly aware of the economy as an ordered system of relations; Joseph Spengler went so far as to suggest that he "was among the first, if not the first, to conceive, albeit imperfectly, of the system of relations that underlies the economic order" (Spengler 1984, 73). His importance, however, lay not in the discovery of an organic unity in these relations, or even in the application to economic relationships of a physical analogue. The interesting twist Boisguillebert provided was in suggesting that the economic order could be understood apart from the political order, as a partition of the society with a separate set of relationships subject to specific laws of action.

Yet despite its autonomous character, the fact remained that circumstances in the political order could have a great impact on the economic, and vice versa. This can be demonstrated by examining Boisguillebert's analysis of wealth. The means to promote national wealth were not for Boisguillebert measured by the inflow of bullion; national wealth was determined and fostered by the production and export of agricultural commodities. Government policies favoring manufacturing interfered with the pricing mechanism (he believed in the notion of the optimal price) and led to price depression in agriculture. The government, in desiring to expand manufacturing, had instead succeeded in weakening agriculture and, as a consequence of the interdependencies between sectors, in weakening manufacturing as well.

Boisguillebert favored market solutions to the problems of allocation. The social collective is, after all, nothing but an aggregation of individuals who agree to social arrangements in an effort to advance their own self-interests. This competition results in beneficial outcomes, namely, wealth production and economic prosperity for all; as Spengler noted, the environment envisioned by Boisguillebert was a nonzero-sum game, wherein everyone could gain as the total pie expanded (Spengler 1984, 75). In the absence of state interferences with individual initiatives, the result would be a smoothly functioning economic and social system.

51. Cole arrived at the opposite conclusion, alleging that Colbert had actually made a success of his mercantilist policies. Of Boisguillebert he proclaimed, "His statistics on prices and other matters were faulty, to put it mildly, his knowledge of economic history even of the period of his own youth was scant. But intuitively he *knew* whom to blame" (Cole 1943, 240; emphasis in original).

Always in his work was the concern with greater freedom and less intervention. As a proponent of Natural Law and the attendant theory of the equilibration of economic forces, he had to conclude that the most appropriate measures for the state to introduce were those that augmented the natural tendencies inherent in the system; Natural-Law forces would inevitably bring the various competing interests into harmony. Where these forces are thwarted—as when the state interferes with private contracts or otherwise restricts competition—the result is a reduced level of social and economic efficiency, as the interests now conflict instead of harmonize.

To rectify the state of affairs in the France of his time, Boisguillebert suggested policy measures designed to promote social, political, and economic harmony and reduce strife. The tax system, for example, should be overhauled, the income tax retained but made proportional and applicable to all incomes, and a poll tax enacted. As with Gregory King in the British example, Boisguillebert believed that these revisions to the tax code, while being less confiscatory, would be more efficient and so result in a greater revenue flow to the government.[52] The central point was that governmental measures designed for one purpose (such as revenue enhancement) often had negative consequences (such as the redoubling of efforts to evade payment), consequences which had been ignored to the detriment of the kingdom. Fiscal policy should thus be implemented with the understanding that the policy itself may have a negative impact on the workings of the market. Secondly, the government should halt the implicit subsidization of urban dwellers, which served only to depress agriculture and rural incomes, thereby stifling rural (and hence French national) development. Third, as agriculture held the key to the expansion of French national wealth, the government should abandon regulation that hampered the functioning of the free market in agricultural produce and undertake instead proactive measures to support and encourage agriculture, even at the expense of manufacturing. Within this sphere, free trade—he advanced an early notion of *laissez faire* (*le systèm naturel*) a half-century before Smith[53]—should be encouraged to stimulate further production and expand income.

---

52. Boisguillebert wrote other works on agriculture and the shortage of the monetary medium. He was also among the first to perceive of what is today referred to as macroeconomic analysis, and he developed a primitive idea of the central microeconomic concepts of marginality and elasticity of supply and demand.

53. Spengler observed that among the concepts Boisguillebert entertained were "division of labor, circular flow, velocity of money, hoarding, confidence, the multiplier, and variability of employment; supply and demand, diminishing utility, elasticity of demand, natural and market price, price variability, price flexibility, cobweb price-model, cost of production, diminishing returns, labor supply curve, bargaining range, impulse propagation, economic equilibrium, optimum and suboptimum price structures, and competition" (Spengler 1984, 77).

7.3 *The Emergence of Physiocracy*

It is common to date the Peace of Aix-la-Chapelle in 1748, ending the War of Austrian Succession, as the time when the French socio-politico-economic structure began to change. The "Age of Reason" is the commonly viewed outcome of the collapse of the old order. The philosopher-jurist Charles Louis de Secondat, Baron de la Brède et de Montesquieu (1689–1755) published his authoritative *De l'Esprit des Lois* (the *Spirit of the Laws*) in 1748, and Denis Diderot (1713–84) and Jean le Rond d'Alembert (1717–83) began publishing their *Encyclopédie, ou Dictionnaire raisonné des arts, des sciences et des métiers* in 1751. While Bodin championed monarchy and so takes on the persona of a French version of Hobbes, Montesquieu, with his notion of a separation of government powers as a means to assure individual freedom, reflected the position of Locke (whom he regarded as his intellectual mentor). As Montesquieu's position gained popularity—more in the United States than in his native France—the idea of absolutist monarchy became less and less supportable.

In any event, whatever the impetus behind the social metamorphosis, the institutional order was changing as these men wrote. France's economy was beginning to recover from the wars of Louis XIV and Louis XV. (Louis XV reigned at the time of the ill-fated colonial struggle against Britain, known variously as the Seven Years' War or the French and Indian Wars.) Thus the environment arose for a rethinking of the policies of industrialization and militarization, and the very basis of the French state. One answer to the questions plaguing France was provided by the physiocrats.

As we mentioned above, "Physiocracy" means literally "natural rule." But just what was the doctrine of Physiocracy? Max Beer viewed it as a reaction to Mercantilism, becoming a social philosophy that maintained "a compound of inconsistent views and contradictory tenets, yoking together most modern and strictly medieval doctrines" (Beer 1939, 16).[54] Pribram esteemed it as "an outstanding achievement as an attempt

---

54. "Physiocracy would thus appear to be a system of advanced liberalism or a foundation for a constitution of a peasant democracy. So, indeed, it appeared to some French historians, who regarded the physiocrats as precursors of the French Revolution. Yet the same school held absolute authority (*despotisme légal, autorité tutélaire*) as the best form of government, and advocated the total exclusion of all the three orders of society—nobility, merchants and manufacturers, the peasantry and the labouring population—from participation in political matters. It extolled unrestricted competition in all commercial dealings and exchanges, and at the same time it refused liberty to moneylending, and advocated governmental fixing of the rate of interest. It regarded commerce as necessary and beneficial, and at the same time as a financial burden upon the people; none the less, it exempted the merchants from all taxation. In the midst of the industrial revolution which opened up new and abundant sources of wealth, the physiocrats tenaciously maintained that manufacture was sterile. The school worked for the free exportation of all produce, and

to establish a generally valid system of social relationships in accordance with Cartesian philosophy" (Pribram 1983, 103). Charles Gide and Charles Rist maintained that "The essence of the Physiocratic system lay in their conception of the 'natural order' " (Gide and Rist 1947, 25), by which is meant not the "order" that exists in the pristine (read pre-civilized) state, nor the order that obtains in the physical universe; rather the "natural order" (as Gide and Rist interpreted it) "was that order which seemed obviously the best, not to any individual whomsoever, but to rational, cultured, liberal-minded men like the Physiocrats. It was not the product of the observation of external facts; it was the revelation of a principle within" (29). The physiocratic principle of the "natural order" then amounts to an innate, patristic notion, universally true. While not always obvious or capable of articulation by those who seek to understand its meaning—hence the need for an educational system that is given the task of instructing those with insufficient clarity on the subject—it is nonetheless divinely ordained. The philosophical underpinnings of the doctrine, in this interpretation, were of a rigorous mathematical type, the desire being to explain the functionings of the social order in as rational a manner as possible, stripped of all the details. The doctrine "seemed to them [the physiocrats] to be endowed with all the grandeur of the geometrical order" (29).

In a less philosophical light, the principal defining elements of this theory of economic and political relationships may be stated as combining (1) the special place of land as a factor of production; (2) the importance given to the circular flow between goods and money, an idea first enunciated by Cantillon, a true precursor of the physiocrats; and (3) the centrality of the principle of laissez-faire and the acceptance of Natural Law as a unifying force. Adam Smith, who accepted as true many of the tenets of the school, saw Physiocracy, or "the agricultural systems of political occonomy," as fundamentally worthwhile. In *The Wealth of Nations,* Smith maintained that the theory was "perhaps, the nearest approximation to the truth that has yet been published upon the subject of political oeconomy, and is upon that account well worth the consideration of every man who wishes to examine with attention the principles of that very important science" (book IV, chap. IX, 642). Specifically, Smith noted that Physiocracy as a doctrine of political economy held (1) that wealth did not consist solely of monetary riches, but instead is defined in terms of the total amount of goods produced in the society; and (2) that the basis of the theory was individual liberty, this being "the only effectual expedient for rendering this annual reproduction the greatest

---

yet they regarded foreign trade or traffic as a *pis-aller,* a necessary evil. Finally, physiocracy glorified tillage as the only productive work, and yet it assigned the *produit net,* the net income or the profit of tillage, not to the cultivators as reward of their labour, but as a tribute to be paid to the landlords" (Beer 1939, 15–16).

possible" (642).[55] Karl Marx, in *A History of Economic Theories* (1952),[56] maintained that the physiocrats were "the true creators of modern economics" (25), in that they were the first to treat explicitly of the nature of capital. He regarded Physiocracy as being

> truly the first systematic analysis of capitalist production and the first to present as natural and eternal laws of production the conditions under which capital produces and is produced. On the other hand, it bore no slight resemblance to a bourgeois reproduction of the feudal system and of the regime of the landed gentry; and the industrial sphere, where capital begins its autonomous evolution, seemed to it, unproductive branches of labor, mere parasitic complements to agriculture. (30)

Gide and Rist likewise considered the French physiocrats, in particular Quesnay, to have been the true originators of the "science" of political economy, and even though later French economists "very inconsiderately allowed the title to pass to Adam Smith," France eventually retrieved it, "to remain in all probability definitely hers" (Gide and Rist 1947, 22).

Beyond these charitable assessments, we must appraise some basic characteristics. Physiocracy, as we have noted, asserted that economic laws were *part of* and *derived from* the natural order, so that economics could be considered an abstract and perhaps even deductive science along Cartesian lines.[57] This is not to imply that these laws were derived from an appeal to Natural Law, although indeed some physiocratic writers did hold to this belief (for example, du Pont); it simply means that the system as it is naturally ordered is the most rational. Economics was not on this view institutional-order bound. The truths of the Physiocrats pertained not only to their beloved France, but to universal history.

To comprehend Physiocracy, one needs first to understand the philosophy of Jean-Jacques Rousseau (1712–78)[58] and its contrast to the

---

55. Smith continued, noting that any system that favored one sector of the economy over any other would only retard progress in the very sector it meant to promote. His preference was for the government to favor no sector, but to let natural forces determine the share of the total income that should go to any single one.

56. This was also published under the title by which it is better known, *Theories of Surplus Value.*

57. "To them, bourgeois forms of production necessarily resembled natural forms. Their especial merit lies in their grasp of these forms as the physiological forms of society, determined by the natural necessities of production, independent of politics or will, etc. They are material laws. The Physiocrats' sole error was of seeing in this material law of an historically determined stage of society an abstract law controlling all forms of society equally" (Marx 1952, 25).

58. Rousseau was born in Switzerland and raised as a Calvinist; later (1728) he was to convert to Catholicism as a result of his acquaintance with Madame de Warens, and still later (1754) he returned to Protestantism. Among his other accomplishments, Rousseau developed a system of musical notation.

prevailing philosophy of the Enlightenment. Rousseau rejected the empirical study of the nature of man in favor of an approach centering on human intuition and individual conscience, stressing the primacy of sentiment and self-love (reminiscent of Smith's *Theory of Moral Sentiments*). His introspective philosophy focused on the notion of absolute moral obligation. In his 1762 *The Social Contract,* he wrote of the place of the *individual* within the general confines of his *society:* because he is a social being, man functions best in a social setting, but is still an individual and perceives himself in this light. In contrast to Locke, Rousseau did not believe in the will of the majority in setting the common good; he rather introduced the notion of the "general will." Freedom, equality, justice— the basic demands of free men—are bound to hold irrespective of the capricious will of the current majority. The social contract emerged as a means of advancing the general will: each individual must surrender *individual* sovereignty to the state, since only the state as a collective can ensure the achievement of the general will.

The philosophy of Physiocracy also held that man was first and foremost a moral individual; indeed, his role in the economy and as part of the state could be perceived only in that way. Absent the intrusion of government, the "natural order" would be revitalized, with private property serving in the role of Rousseau's contract (Gide and Rist 1947, 26n.). Individual liberty means the minimum of governmental control (perhaps explaining the attractiveness of the doctrine to Thomas Jefferson, the chief American advocate of a limited national government). Governmental regulation was in any event self-defeating since the regulated had every incentive to become the regulators (begging the question, *Quis custodiet ipsos custodes?*).

Physiocracy developed as the antithesis of Mercantilism. On the physiocratic model, the pursuit of foreign trade and the buildup of bullion stocks as the means to national power and wealth—the basis of mercantilist credo—could only lead to long-term economic degradation. The mercantilist preoccupation with treating bullion as synonymous with wealth carried with it a fundamental contradiction: to acquire bullion with goods meant producing ever-larger quantities of manufactures without purchasing anything in return; it meant selling with no consequent purchasing. The question asked by the physiocrats was, What does one *do* with the bullion so acquired? The circular flow that demands purchases follow sales (or vice versa), not one to the exclusion of the other. To favor any one side of the equation was proof of a serious deficiency in the model, a deficiency exacerbated by the mercantilists' unalterable belief in the position of manufacturing as the sole productive sector. Of necessity, the model had to be redefined to account for the dictates of the circular flow framework; the focus had to be placed not on sales but on production. Thus the physiocrats were led to rely on the agricultural sector as the prime area of wealth creation.

In an effort to reinvigorate the agricultural sector, the predominant sector of the economy and source of wealth (given the expulsion of the Huguenots), France had to emulate the example of Britain. One of the principles of the doctrine of Physiocracy was that only extractive industry was "productive"; one derived more value from the extractive industries than one put in.[59] Everything else was priced in the long run (meaning "naturally") by the costs of production. Thus, all value derived from the soil. Acceptance of this "fact" meant the elimination of the feudal agricultural system, at the time still existing in France, and the implementation of policies designed to encourage free trade. Specifically, the state had to remove restrictions on the trade of agricultural commodities, much as the British later deregulated the corn trade. The state must also allow consolidation of agricultural holdings, while acknowledging the important role of private property rights, founded on an Aristotelian belief in private ownership but common use (or rather private ownership in concert with the promotion of the public good).

8   Physiocratic Writers

8.1   Quesnay

The physiocrats as a doctrinal group had many devotees and important adherents, but none could surpass François Quesnay (1694–1774).[60] Schumpeter in fact opined that the entire school reduced itself to Quesnay alone, a man "to whom all economists look up as one of the greatest figures of their science" (Schumpeter 1954, 223).[61]

A physician and surgeon who had served as General Secretary of the Academy of Surgery, Quesnay's philosophical beliefs, upon which were based his economic and political ideas, were shaped by the teachings of Nicolas de Malebranche (1638–1715), the French rationalist philosopher. As did Descartes, Malebranche insisted on the primacy of ideas over sensory data: the only reality was the reality of the mind. With this foundation Quesnay was led to consider Natural Law as something

59. Note Marx: "Therefore, the Physiocrats believed agricultural labor to be the only productive labor, because they saw it as the only labor which produces surplus value and because they knew no other form of surplus value than ground rent . . ." (Marx 1952, 27).

60. Quesnay was the son of a lawyer. Apparently self-taught—he did not learn to read until the age of 12!—he began practicing medicine at the age of 24 and actually wrote several tracts on the subject.

61. No small part of Quesnay's influence seems to be associated with his being the physician to Madame Pompadour, Louis XV's mistress, and a prominent intellectual. Louis XV was something of an intellectual himself. While he is famous for his remark, *Après moi, la deluge,* an even more insightful remark, one revealing his cynical realism, was that were he not king he would be a Republican.

real, intuitively true. Just as with the fundamental, analytic truths (axioms) of mathematics, so economics and all human sciences were subject to these same structures.[62] He was also connected with, but never actually became a part of, the group known as the *Encyclopédistes,* which included Voltaire, Helvétius, Diderot, and many other luminaries. Their epistemological position of Cartesian-Platonist rationality coincided with his own.[63]

Quesnay's magnum opus was his 1758 essay, *Tableau Économique,* the work that more than any other epitomizes the thought of the physiocrats. It illustrated both a perception of the national economy organized by economic function and the system of interdependent circular flow to which it gives rise. So persuasive were the views set forth in this and his other works that Quesnay, enjoying the protection of Madame de Pompadour, developed this "school" of economic, political, and social thought to propound his views. These were the first individuals to call themselves "economists." An interesting facet of the school was that its success relied on a form of "bandwagon" effect: not only were the members of this group led by a charismatic person (Quesnay), but each was convinced that membership in the group conferred charisma on him.

The *Tableau Économique* is very simply a formal economic model—actually a diagrammatic representation of the workings of an economy[64]—through which Quesnay sought to demonstrate the manner in which income is generated and shifted from sector to sector in the national economy, and to highlight the mechanics behind the process of wealth creation.[65] In the *Tableau Économique,* Quesnay distinguished between agricultural and manufacturing employments, or what he termed productive and sterile expenditures.

---

62. Pribram (1983, 103–4) presents a more elaborate discussion of Quesnay's philosophical background.

63. His encyclopedia articles were on Evidence (1754), Farmers (1756), Grains (1757), and Men (1757). He also contributed to the articles on Natural Law (1765), a doctrine of which he was a forceful advocate, and Commerce (1766). In 1767 he wrote on despotism in China. In addition, he published considerable medical research and earlier wrote a book on animal husbandry, *Essai physique sur l'economie animale* (1736). In his encyclopedia articles, he offered empirical generalizations (something he had not done in his earlier medical research), granting such bits of policy wisdom as horses were more cost-efficient than oxen, *grand culture* was more cost-efficient than *petit culture* (where *grand culture* refers to the capitalist mode of farming, while *petit culture* refers to the share-cropping, or *métayer,* system), the countryside had to be repopulated, legislation relating to farming was counterproductive, and the cultivation of wine and corn was more cost-effective than the cultivation of mulberry bushes and silk.

64. See Vernard Foley (1973) for the thesis that the *tableau* actually grew out of Quesnay's medical work, with the bifurcation of the economy into two sectors and the flows within and between having derived from his understanding of the flow of blood in the human body.

65. A "refined" version of this diagrammatic analysis is represented by Wassily Leontief's input-output matrix. Shigeto Tsuru (1956) in particular has made this observation.

Productive expenditure is employed in agriculture, grasslands, pastures, forests, mines, fishing, etc., in order to perpetuate wealth in the form of corn, drink, wood, livestock, raw materials for manufactured goods, etc.

Sterile expenditure is on manufactured commodities, house-room, clothing, interest on money, servants, commercial costs, foreign produce, etc. (Quesnay 1758–59, i; emphasis in original)

In addition to the classification of types of expenditure, Quesnay identified three classes of individuals within the economy who held claims to them: (1) the productive, or cultivator, class; (2) the proprietor, or landowning, class; and (3) the sterile, or artisan-manufacturing, class (Quesnay 1758–59, i).

The production process begins with the creation of output and income from the productive sector of the economy. The *Tableau* itself is merely a three-column table that demonstrates the interrelationships among the three classes of economic actors. The first column shows the annual advances to the productive class, taken on the "sale of the net product which the cultivator has generated in the previous year" (1758–59, i). This value gives a payment or revenue to the proprietor (the values in the second column, also taken as additions to net revenue). In column three are listed the annual advances of the sterile class, "employed for the capital and costs of trade, for the purchase of raw materials for manufactured goods, and for the subsistence and other needs of the artisan until he has completed and sold his work" (i). The revenue, paid to the proprietor at the outset of the process, is spent, one-half going to the purchase of goods from the productive class, one-half to the purchase of goods from the sterile class. The advances to the productive class return to the proprietor in the form of monetary payments, a form of return on the surplus from production. This surplus is again spent, one-half for the consumption of cultivated goods, one-half for sterile expenditure. The process continues ad infinitum.

The produce of land, the most "natural" and original of the factors of production, was viewed as the only true generator of wealth; farmers made up the productive class, and the output of their labor was responsible for setting the economic process in motion. Only the cultivator class could add anything in the way of a true surplus to the national income. The proprietor class, for instance, engaged merely in an exchange of value, not in an increase in net national wealth. Capital was not an original factor, so the produce of manufacturing industry could only be of *indirect* import in national wealth expansion. Agriculture, unlike manufacturing, produces net additions to the national income, hence agriculture is productive, manufacturing sterile. This is not to say that capital did not have an important role to play in the *process behind* the generation of national income; it is just that the *process of income generation* itself has to begin with the productive sector of the economy.

The physiocrats were fixated on agriculture as the sole basis of productive wealth, this deriving from their emphasis on the enhancement of state power. In this connection, the institution of private property was given center stage. Quesnay's view of property was that, while there was indeed a natural right to the accumulation of property, this acquisition must be tempered by the ability to use in an efficient manner the amount acquired. As with Aristotle, Quesnay distinguished *ownership* from *use,* although he did not require any restrictions on an individual's personal use of his own possessions. While private property rights were upheld and enforced, indeed lauded, the reasoning was as much for the protection and preservation of national power as it was due to a belief in a natural right to property. Even this "natural right" had to be restricted, as did the other "natural rights," in order to promote the greater state interest. Should the individual be allowed to engage in activities that enhanced his personal wealth, producing for his own remuneration instead of for the national good, the state would be the worse off for such "selfishness." As agriculture was deemed the mainstay of the economy (and hence, by extension, the well-being of the nation), anything that hindered its development or lessened its efficiency (such as smallholder agriculture managed by individual profit seekers), was seen as detrimental to the security of the state.

Since all wealth is derived from the productive (agricultural) sector, this is the area in which the state should center its efforts. Quesnay's advocacy of a strong *state* as opposed to a focus on *individual* initiative as the basis of an economic, political, and social system is well-expressed in his maxim 18: "That means to meet the extraordinary needs of the State are expected to be found only in the prosperity of the nation and not in the credit of financiers; for *monetary fortunes are a clandestine form of wealth which knows neither king nor country*" (1758–59, 13; emphasis in original).

In addition, by forging large agricultural plots and a national policy to guide their production decisions, the state in effect had created a more efficient base for the collection of revenue and the administration of the countryside. As expressed in maxim 21, farms should be collectivized because such collectivization leads to economies of scale. Small-plot agriculture, requiring a "multiplicity of farmers," is "less favourable to population than is the increase of revenue" that collectivization would provide (Quesnay 1758–59, 15).

While in maxim 22 Quesnay accepted "[t]hat each person is free to cultivate in his fields such products as his interests, his means, and the nature of the land suggest to him, in order that he may extract from them the greatest possible product" (16), this should not be seen as license to produce anything in abundance. After all, "[i]t is revenue and taxes which are the wealth of primary necessity in a State." Presumably the farmer is to be aware of the supply of any commodity on the market and so will be able to adjust his own planting decisions accordingly. He is to do this for the good of the state, and of course in his own best interest; the two are coincident. The capacity for knowledge on the part of the "physiocratic farmer" is immense; he is expected to predict with incredible accuracy the production decisions of others, as well as the demand conditions of the populace at large, and to undertake the decisions that best serve himself and the nation. Of course the "typical" peasant farmer cannot be expected to have reached this level of skill. The peasant farmer is only a marginal worker who is expendable for the betterment of the collective. To generate the greatest degree of wealth for the state takes the skills of a superior class: "Thus it is wealthy men whom you should put in charge of the enterprises of agriculture and rural trade, in order to enrich yourselves, to enrich the State, and to enable inexhaustible wealth to be generated" (20). Thus did the physiocrats' model of economic production provide a rationale for the economic inequality of the citizenry.

All of these maxims, actually more in the line of rationalizations for the expansion of the powers of an absolute monarch, were predicated on Quesnay's belief in the inviolability of Natural Law. Natural Law institutions he held to be invariant in their fundamental importance to society. It was no historical accident that private property institutions, or the French monarchy for that matter, emerged as the dominant forces in French society, both in the political sphere and the intellectual; these institutional arrangements came about because they were the most naturally conducive to the human condition.

8.2 Turgot

Anne Robert Jacques Turgot, Baron d'Aulne (1727–81)[66] was not exactly a member of the physiocratic clan; he was too much a man of practical affairs to be tied to any identifiable school of economic, political, or social thought. As Finance Minister, Turgot was able to accomplish reforms in the direction of physiocratic policies, including deregulating the corn trade and initiating a broad-based tax that everyone, including the upper classes, had to pay.[67]

Turgot's 1770 essay, *Reflexions sur la formation et la distribution*

---

66. Turgot was born into a well-to-do Norman bourgeois family, and was educated at the Sorbonne. From 1761 to 1774 he served as the general administrator for Limoges; in 1774 he served as Minister of the Navy, and Minister of Finance and Commerce and Commissioner of Public Works.

67. For his efforts Turgot was relieved of his duties by Louis XVI at the behest of Marie Antoinette, and his measures were repealed. They were for the most part reinstituted by the Revolutionary government.

des richesses, the work for which he is best known, built on Quesnay's brand of thinking in setting forth a coherent theory of the formation of a capitalist economy from the basic foundation of a right to property.[68] Turgot began with an analysis of the social division of labor. Commerce, he maintained, had to reflect the initial unequal distribution of land, diversity of soils, multiplicity of human needs, and the advantages of the division of labor. Should it be the case that lands are divided equally among the citizenry,

> it is evident that, all being equal, no one would be willing to work for others. No one, besides, would possess anything with which to pay for the labour of another; for each, having only as much land as he needed to produce his subsistence, would consume all that he had gathered, and would have nothing that he could exchange for the labour of the others. (Turgot 1770, 3)

Thus, inequality in the distribution of property is a necessary condition for the development of specialized production; with an equal distribution there would be no production in the economy beyond the level of subsistence, since there would be no incentive for anyone to work in the employ of another.

Moreover, since lands differ in quality, it is by no means clear that anyone could, under an equal distribution, be reasonably expected to provide for himself even the barest level of subsistence. To accomplish this feat would require that each farmer cultivate a wide variety of crops capable of serving all his various needs, something which simply could not be accomplished on a single plot of land. Thus even *should* there have been an initial equality in distribution—something Turgot denied, since cultivation preceded division, and cultivation originated in unequal distribution—the system would have collapsed due to the necessity to specialize in production. Thus trade and exchange became necessary from the outset, generated by the need to specialize in agriculture.

Agriculture was for Turgot the basis of national prosperity. While it is obvious that a principal reason for this conclusion is that nations must have an adequate food supply, there is a much more important reason for the reliance on agricultural output: it provides the wherewithal for industrial production. The produce of the agricultural sector for the most part "must undergo various changes and be prepared by art" before it is consumed (1770, 5). Just as each producer discovered that by specializing

---

68. In his introduction to the English language translation (1898), William Ashley noted that the *Reflections* was prepared "for the benefit of two young Chinese, who having been educated in France were returning to their country with a pension from the crown. China was commonly regarded by the French economists of the time as the peculiar home of enlightened government. . . . Turgot drew up a list of questions for them to answer, and prepared the *Reflections* to enable them the better to understand the purpose of his interrogations" (Turgot 1770, viii).

in the production of a certain crop and trading with others he could better meet his basic needs, so must there develop specialized occupations relating to the *preparation* of the agricultural output to satisfy other material wants. This need for the transformation of agricultural produce brings about an exchange of produce for labor—the husbandman (cultivator) exchanging his surplus product for the labor of another specializing in the production of a finished good. This exchange engenders the rise of a new class of skilled workers, an artisan or "stipendiary" class, consisting of millers, bakers, tanners, smiths, weavers, spinners, leatherworkers, and a multitude of other craftsmen.

From the evolution of the division of labor, Turgot next considered the evolution of social or class divisions. In the chain of importance, the husbandman is accorded first rank. He is "the first mover in the circulation of labours," who provides "all with the most important and most considerable article of their consumption," namely, "their food and also the materials of almost every industry" (1770, 7). Without the husbandman, no one else in the chain can earn a livelihood (although the farmer himself is dependent on no one for his own well-being). It is he, by producing beyond his own requirements, who establishes the fund of wages "which all the other members of the society receive in exchange for their labour" (7–8). The husbandman purchases the goods provided by the artisans with the proceeds from his surplus, which is for Turgot then the source of the wages fund for the economy; the nonagricultural laborers "only return to him exactly what they have received from him" (8). It must be true then that the husbandman is "the sole source of the riches, which, by their circulation, animate all the labours of the society; because he is the only one whose labour produces over and above the wages of the labour" (9).

It is here we see the development of economic classes. The husbandman, as the "sole source of riches," can afford to purchase with his surplus the labor of others, and in so doing amass "a wealth which is independent and disposable, which he has not bought and which he sells" (Turgot 1770, 9). But the "mere Workman, who has only his arms and his industry, has nothing except in so far as he succeeds in selling his toil to others" (8). Thus there appeared, as an inevitable consequence of the initial inequality in land ownership, an economic inequality as well. It is for this reason that society became divided into two classes, the productive (cultivators) and the stipendiary (artisans), a division based solely on original (agricultural) production. The productive class "draws from the land, riches which are continually springing up afresh, and which supply the whole society with its subsistence and with the materials for all its needs," while the stipendiary class is "occupied in giving to materials thus produced the preparations and the forms which render them suitable for the use of men" (10).

Having defined the social class division and the bifurcation of society into two distinct entities, Turgot then described the emergence of a third economic class. Also derived from the situation with respect to agriculture, a proprietary class results from the role of the husbandman as employer of labor. While initially the proprietor and the husbandman were in many ways indistinguishable, the legal institution of private property ultimately led to the creation of a new and distinct class, consisting of the owners of land who did not themselves engage directly in production. As the husbandman gained a surplus over production and could afford to hire wage-labor to do the actual cultivation of his lands, ownership of land became separated from use; more importantly, the land itself became an object of commerce (1770, 13). The produce could then be divided into the cultivator's part—including his subsistence and "profit"—and a disposable part, "which the land gives as a pure gift to him who cultivates it, over and above his advances and the wages of his trouble"—accruing to the proprietor (14). The proprietor thus gains a net product (produit net), allowing him to "live without labour"; he reaps profits (rents) from the work of the tenant-cultivators (either employees or sharecropper farmers) (14).[69]

From this description of the evolution of the economy, Turgot was led to refine his definition of economic classes: the cultivators still comprised the sole *productive* class—the true working class—while the artisans (stipendiary class) and the proprietors (disposable class) jointly comprised the *sterile* class. While the husbandman and artisans were still "bound by the need of subsistence to a particular labour," the proprietors, being removed from the need for physical labor, "can be employed for the general needs of the Society, such as war and the administration of justice . . ." (1770, 15). Plato's Ideal republic was thus shown to have a historical basis in fact.

But Turgot did not confine his discussion of the division of classes solely to agriculture; he considered class divisions as they had developed in the manufacturing sector as well. The assurance of an annual revenue from property and the accumulation of wealth that resulted therefrom ("moveable riches") served as the advance fund, as we have already seen. For Turgot, advances were necessary not only in agriculture but in all areas of commerce; thus the "moveable riches" served also as the fund in support of manufacturing, acting the role of industrial capital (1770, 52–54).

In the use of this advance fund as capital we see the emergence within *industrial* society of a two-class system, as had developed in agriculture; the division here is between those who possess advance capital

---

69. Turgot held there to be five methods used by proprietors for the cultivation of their lands: (1) the paying of fixed wages to workers; (2) slavery; (3) the abandoning of the estate altogether to the cultivators in return for a portion of the produce; (4) the making of advances to the cultivator in return for a fixed share of the output (the *métayer* system); and (5) the letting out the land in return for rent, with the cultivator himself making the advances (the capitalist farming system) (Turgot 1770, 18–25).

(the "Undertakers, Manufacturers, Employers"), and the artisans "who advance only their daily labour, and receive no profit but their wages" (Turgot 1770, 54). As agriculture has its productive and sterile classes, industry has its capitalists and wage-earners.

Also in the development of a manufacturing sector we see effects on agriculture and on the earnings of those employed there. Manufacturing being very lucrative, it may be that few wealthy entrepreneurs remain to provide the advances necessary to agriculture; the profit margins are simply too small. Should this occur, Turgot reasoned, the result would be a further division of classes within agriculture itself: capitalists who make the advances, and wage-earners who differ from the earlier class of cultivators in that they no longer have title to a portion of their produce.

Turgot was of two minds, two loyalties. While he was essentially antimonarchist, meaning that he doubted that the monarch and the bureaucracy could handle their respective roles in a sufficiently efficient manner to make the system work, he was nonetheless loyal to his king. As Finance Minister under Louis XVI, he took it upon himself to suggest that various actions he thought necessary to the efficient administration of the nation be decreed by the monarch. The specific recommendations, however, were not popular with the French Parlement, nor with the nobility and the moneyed elites, and Louis refused to issue the necessary royal decrees. Turgot's first impulse was to push for implementation, whatever the cost. In any event, Turgot eventually lost clout with the king, and by the time of the Revolution (after he had passed from the scene) his reputation appears to have been unaffected by the association.[70]

---

70. Given the foregoing, it is little wonder Turgot was not trusted by the ruling castes. One who distrusted him most was Victor Riqueti, Marquis de Mirabeau (1715–89), an aristocrat, publicist, and fellow physiocrat, as well as a friend and admirer of Quesnay. Mirabeau was involved in the movement at the beginning, having met Quesnay in 1757 when the latter had just commenced his work on economic problems; it is Mirabeau who more than anyone else can be held responsible for the birth of the movement and for its evolution into a force of cultlike proportion. Mirabeau's *Théorie de l'impot* (*Theory of Taxes*) and *L'Ami des hommes* (*Friend of Mankind*) became well-known physiocratic tracts, the latter being influenced by the writings of Cantillon. Among the prescriptions of Mirabeau was the idea of a single tax on agricultural output. His outspokenness, and the lack on his part of a political support base, led to his arrest and imprisonment for a brief time for attacks on the king and his ministers. Turgot had used Mirabeau as his contact with the ruling groups outside of France.

Pierre-Paul Mercier de la Rivière (1720–93) was another such personage, but his interest in Physiocracy was more on the political than the economic-theoretical side. His principal work is *L'Order naturel et essential des Societés politiques* (Natural and essential order of political societies) (1767).

François de Forbonnais (1722–1800) published a major criticism of the physiocrats in 1767, *Principes et observations économiques* (Economic principles and observations), which attacked their antimanufacturing bias (value can also come out of things other than the soil), and their opposition to regulations such as tariffs, and he consequently urged a much broader basis for taxation.

Du Pont   *8.3*

The last of the physiocratic writers with whom we shall deal is Pierre Samuel du Pont de Nemours (1739–1817), a student of both Quesnay and Turgot, a biographer of Turgot[71] and the editor of his *Reflexions.*[72] As a teenager, du Pont read Vauban's book with its recommendation for changes in the French tax system and even served as assistant to Turgot when the latter was finance minister under Louis XVI.[73]

It was as an editor that du Pont's influence was most profound. He edited the *Journal de l'Agriculture* (for only a year until it folded), and then the *Ephémérides du Citoyen,* the two journals that served as organs of the physiocratic movement. This capacity served du Pont well, as it provided him a forum for the promotion of physiocratic ideas. As editor of the journals, he was able to expose the ideas of the physiocratic movement to a larger audience than would be possible in any other venue; he may very well have contributed far more to the movement in this capacity than he could have as a writer or government bureaucrat. The journals of opinion also promulgated his views of Natural Law and the basis of their "discovery." He believed not that Natural Laws were "discoverable" in the scientific sense, through investigation of phenomena, but rather that they were already known, having been identified by, among others, Quesnay; all that remained was the task of advertising, meaning the promotion of their status as laws through the continuing process of intellectual discourse. As du Pont framed it:

> Our work falls naturally into three parts; the first historical, the second descriptive, and the third one intended to spread an interest in and contribute to the progress of the *science of economics,* through the example and the help of good and wise Citizens who will be willing to communicate their enlightenment and to use us to publish their writings. (Cited in McLain 1977, 72; emphasis in original)

In 1763, du Pont published *Réflexions sur l'écrit intitulé: Richesse de l'Etat,* a tract on taxation. Here he argued that the tax system should

---

71. Du Pont published *Mémoires sur la vie et les ouvrages de M. Turgot* in 1782.

72. Du Pont did not simply edit Turgot; he made substantial alterations to the text, adding his own ideas to those of the author, which annoyed Turgot.

73. Suffering through many years of changing regimes (he returned as an assistant to Jacques Necker, who had replaced Turgot in the position, continuing in this capacity under Charles Alexandre de Calonne), du Pont was imprisoned briefly by the Revolutionary government.

In 1799, he arrived in the United States (in Kentucky) with his family, with the hope of founding an agricultural community based on physiocratic principles. The plan failed. As a result of continuing disastrous business ventures, he returned to France in 1802, where he stayed until 1815. He eventually returned to the United States (settling in Wilmington, Delaware), where his son, Eleuthère Irenée du Pont, had established a gunpowder business. For particulars on du Pont see Schumpeter (1954, 225–27) and James McLain (1977).

be radically simplified, reduced to a single tax levied on the owners of land. This publication served as du Pont's entry to the world of the physiocrats, as it caught the attention of Mirabeau, and eventually Quesnay himself.[74]

His first book-length work, *De l'exportation et de l'importation des grains* (1764), focused on the subject of international trade, again from the physiocratic standpoint. The position taken in this work on the desirability of laissez-faire policies, especially in the area of agriculture, was essentially that taken by Cantillon and Quesnay. But then, throughout his career du Pont's motivation had been more to expand on the works of others than to be creative in his own right.

His last two efforts demonstrate his ability as a historian of thought and an integrator and synthesizer of ideas. From 1782 to 1811, du Pont published his edition of the works of Turgot (*Oeuvres de Turgot*). In 1817 he published *Examen du livre de M. Malthus sur le principe de population; auquel on a joint la traduction de quatre chapitres de ce livre supprimés dans l'edition française; et une lettre à M. Say sur son Traité d'économie politique*, a critical essay on the population theory of Malthus and the economic theory of Say, and also a translation of the parts of Malthus's *Principles of Population* that had previously been neglected.[75]

As for du Pont's influence on physiocratic thought, it appears to have been minimal, although his importance as a popularizer and tireless proponent of physiocratic ideas cannot be overestimated. Schumpeter considered him to be "by far the ablest of the lot," but added that his "talents were those of the pianist and not those of the composer" (Schumpeter 1954, 226).

8.4 Remarks on the Physiocratic School

The physiocrats in France were of the consultant-administrator mode (as was Steuart in England), except that they eschewed questions of morality

---

74. The description of social and economic ills and the prescriptions for their treatment that du Pont offered in this work were so much in tune with the work of Quesnay that it was thought that he must have read the latter's works. He always insisted, however, that the ideas presented were original with him and just happened to emerge at the same time in the minds of others. On this controversy, see McLain 1977, 56–57.

75. In this work, du Pont suggested that Malthus's theory of population was flawed by his failure to note the limiting role of food production on population growth. The population growth rate cannot exceed the growth rate of agricultural production, since, according to du Pont, that rate of growth is dependent upon the availability of the food supply for sustenance. As soon as population pressures begin to exceed this level, this excess in growth would be immediately met with a limiting factor, that being the availability of foodstuffs, which would halt the rise. But of course du Pont failed to realize, in his zeal to promote physiocratic ideas, that Malthus had in fact said this same thing, that the supply of food was the factor that would ultimately reduce population increase.

and oligarchic social stewardship. Their doctrines were not empirically verified (although they were verifiable) and were often wrong. Their assumptions thus bore little resemblance to the observable world. This lack of an empirical commitment on the part of the physiocrats was not the result of being empirically skeptical, but rather reflected their belief that the underlying Natural Laws would work to introduce something approximating either stability or equilibrium. They, too, were interested in social efficiency and the economic growth of the nation-state. A revitalized central state was seen as needed to correct the evils of a corrupt and particularly inefficient tax system, a necessary reform to maintain the social and governmental contracts. Untouched by the Lockean argument that labor-input is the ultimate rationale for the existence of private property, they clung instead to the belief that land was the source of all value, which made the Roman rule of prior possession a natural expression of their views. Theirs was a world built principally on agricultural estates, in most cases worked not by the owners, but rather by tenants. Thus, they envisioned a type of nation-state concerned with population maintenance and the capacity to engage in international relations (includ ing the fighting of political wars). As consultant-administrators they were specialists; they were far more focused on one objective, fiscal efficiency, than they were on more sociological or ethical questions, as seems implicit in Steuart's consultant-administrators. The physiocrats' rhetoric was far less historical, that is, example-oriented, than Steuart's; doubtless impressed by or of one mind with Cantillon, their rhetoric relied on abstraction. Why did the physiocrats think so little about trade and manufacturing? Perhaps the answer lies in the pressing governmental problems and the *Weltanschauung* of the rulers. The *ancien régime* was interested in the preservation of status and the property concept that status implied; status was in estates, not in trade or manufactures functions which had been driven into disrepute because they had been defined as Protestant rather than "true French."

In the end Physiocracy failed in large measure because it could not advance the "coalescence" of the public around state action; the physiocrats failed to gain the support of the populace in whose name the programs were to be enacted. Since his legitimacy had dissolved, the Hobbesian *sovereign* could no longer be expected to rule; by contrast, the Lockean *individual* had never been empowered. The public remained unconvinced that the policies of the physiocrats were so badly needed as to entail the wholesale disruption of society. As Karl Polanyi phrased the argument:

> the Physiocratic landlords of France and Germany, with their enthusiasm for free trade, were obliterated in the public mind by the modern prejudice of the everlasting backwardness of the rural scene. (Polanyi 1944, 186)

9 The American Scene: Alexander Hamilton

To pursue further the perception of the relative importance of agriculture and manufacturing and their respective roles in the maintenance of a strong national state, we now turn to the argument as it developed in the United States, considering the important contributions of Alexander Hamilton (1757–1804).[76]

Hamilton's contribution to the debate is presented most succinctly in his 1791 *Report on the Subject of Manufactures,* in its own way a vision of the course of the United States as an economic and political power.[77] The expressed purpose of the *Report* was to present before the Congress of the United States a position in favor of the encouragement of a manufacturing base for the American economy. At the time of Hamilton's "essay" the United States was predominantly an agrarian society, agriculture being in many senses identified with self-sufficiency and independence. But Hamilton was keenly aware of developments in Europe and was particularly concerned about the role the United States should and could play in world affairs. With these points in mind, he attempted to impress his views as Secretary of the Treasury upon the Congress.

Hamilton had been familiar with the arguments of the leading British philosophers and political economists on both sides of the mercantilist debate: he had, for example, read Smith, Hume, and Steuart and, more importantly, had *understood* the criticisms put forth.[78] He also under-

---

76. Hamilton was born on the island of Nevis in the West Indies. At the age of twenty he became aide-de-camp to the commander of the Continental Army, General George Washington. From 1782 to 1783, he served as a delegate to the Continental Congress, where he attempted (unsuccessfully) to reform the government established under the Articles of Confederation to a more centralized organization. As it became clear that the Confederation could not stand, he, along with James Madison and John Jay, was instrumental in channeling opinion in support of a strong central government authority; the *Federalist Papers* represent the expression of the thought of these three writers on the matter.

In 1789 Hamilton was appointed Secretary of the Treasury. In this role he advocated the creation of a national bank and pressed for the federal government to assume the war debts incurred by the states.

Hamilton was killed in a duel by Aaron Burr, who was serving as vice president during the first Jefferson Administration.

77. Included in the collection of Hamilton's papers (Volume X) is a draft of a report on manufactures by Tench Coxe, Assistant Secretary of the Treasury under Hamilton. Written in 1790 and lost until discovered by the editors of the papers, this draft can readily be seen to have been incorporated by Hamilton into his own *Report;* the incorporation is especially evident in Hamilton's first draft of 1790.

78. With respect to Smith, Schumpeter opined: Hamilton "was one of those rare practitioners of economic policy who think it worth while to acquire more analytic economics than that smattering that does such good service in addressing audiences of a certain type. He knew Smithian economics well—not only A. Smith himself—so well in fact as to be able to mold it to his own visions of practical possibilities or necessities and to perceive its limitations" (1954, 199n.9).

stood the position of the physiocrats, as it had been explained by Smith.[79] It is particularly clear that Hamilton had a great affinity for the views of Steuart, especially regarding the usefulness of increasing economic wealth to the benefit and enhancement of state power. While he agreed with much of Smith's *economic* position, especially respecting his theory of the division of labor, he took issue with Smith on the role of manufacturing in relation to agriculture. For example, Hamilton did not accept Smith's contention that agricultural production was inherently superior to manufacturing production.

After listing several arguments *against* the policy of the promotion of manufacturing—including (1) the beneficial and productive nature of agricultural employment, especially on the open, fertile lands of the American frontier; (2) the view that agricultural production was somehow a "natural" form to which, if left to its own desires, the nation would gravitate; (3) the notion that a small work force employed in manufacturing would lead to escalating labor costs; and (4) the invariable class differentiation and monopolization brought about by the "misdirection of labor" (Hamilton 1791, 231–35)—Hamilton stated his own position against agriculture's claim to superiority. In this, his position is not unlike Smith's. In opposition to the physiocrats, he required as proof of agriculture's *inherent supremacy* not an appeal to maxims, but rather empirical evidence for the claim; this he did not find forthcoming.

Agriculture, he believed, was important "as the immediate and chief source of subsistence to man—as the principal source of those materials which constitute the nutriment of other kinds of labor—as including a state most favourable to the freedom and independence of the human mind" (Hamilton 1791, 236). But its importance could not be considered in isolation from the importance of manufacturing, especially since the latter had the added advantage of increasing the productivity of the labor force (246). The *positive* impact of a manufacturing-based economy he held consisted of (1) the "perfection" of the division of labor, (2) the improvement of the productivity of the labor force by the employment of machinery, (3) the expansion of employment to businesses that served a support role to manufacturing, (4) the fostering of immigration, (5) the furtherance of diversity in the talents of the labor force, (6) the increase in the "objects of enterprise" brought about by the stimulation of imagination and creativity, and (7) the increase in demand for the agricultural surplus (249–58). But still, Hamilton did not believe that the one could be ranked in importance above the other, if for no other reason than that the two were interdependent.[80]

---

79. We find no evidence that Hamilton had read the works of the French writers.
80. "There seems to be a moral certainty, that the trade of a country which is both manufacturing and Agricultural will be more lucrative and prosperous, than that of a Country, which is, merely Agricultural" (Hamilton 1791, 287).

That its [agriculture's] real interests, precious and important as without the help of exaggeration, they truly are, will be advanced, rather than injured by the due encouragement of manufactures, may, it is believed, be satisfactorily demonstrated. (1791, 236)

He then immediately connected this dual encouragement of agriculture and manufacturing to the promotion of a strong national state:

And it is also believed that the expediency of such encouragement in a general view may be shewn to be recommended by the most cogent and persuasive motives of national policy. (1791, 236)

Thus we see Hamilton taking an even-handed position on the question, refusing to argue the merits of one or the other position on the basis of a moral or natural superiority; his framework was a truly positivistic one, which perhaps explains why, although his *Report* was rejected by the Congress, his ideas are still well worth considering.

10 National Income Accounting[81]

The work of the English political arithmeticians Graunt, Petty, King, and Davenant, bolstered by the philosophical positions, not to exclude the theoretical advances, of the physiocrats and to a lesser extent the later pronouncements of the mercantilists, provided the impetus for the transformation of economics from a rhetorical discipline (in terms of Aristotelian rhetoric) to a more formal, quantitatively grounded and (eventually) practical (meaning politically oriented) discipline. In other words, the evolution of economics from a literary to a scientific endeavor can be traced to the advancements, or perhaps we should say modifications, in approach that occurred during this period. This metamorphosis was brought about with the elucidation of a framework for the numerical analysis of the interactions among the sectors of a national economy, a national income accounting framework.

As Studenski (1958) has very ably demonstrated, national income accounting originated in England with the work of Petty, Davenant, and King. Boisguillebert was the first French economist to consider the construction of a national income account. He was followed in due course by Vauban, Quesnay, Turgot, and even Antoine Lavoisier (1743–94), a scientist whose achievements in the field of chemistry are so well known as to be perhaps unnecessary to mention.[82]

The common thread running through the late-seventeenth- and

---

81. The material of this section is primarily from Schumpeter (1954) and Studenski (1958).

82. A complete list of the French contributors to the creation of a national accounting framework is given in Studenski (1958, 52–77, 119–28).

early-eighteenth-century presentations of national accounting is the effort to systematize the theory of national economies and the process of the production and concentration of wealth. The earlier economic "theories" that are included in the rather broadly defined category of Mercantilism neither required nor allowed a place for any concept so rigidly defined as *national income*. Wealth in these analyses, such as they were, was easily and rather simply defined as a stock of treasure, be it gold or silver or the proceeds from a favorable balance of trade. The Political Arithmeticians and the prephysiocratic French administrators succeeded in changing the argument by reorienting the rhetoric. No longer could wealth be so narrowly defined, divorced from the workings of the productive economy. This new definition required that the concept of *wealth* be redefined to account for its status as a *factor* of production. Wealth was not to be viewed as a sterile commodity, the importance of which rested with its accumulation; it became important for what it could produce in the way of future goods and services, for the role it could play in the expansion of national wealth in addition to itself.

With the emergence of the physiocrats came a second, but perhaps more important theoretical contribution, which assured that national income accounting would be elevated from a mere curiosity to the position of importance that it was eventually to hold. This contribution was the concept of the *circular flow*. Although originally formulated by Cantillon and later Quesnay with the idea of demonstrating the mechanics behind the flow of income in an agriculturally based society—income-as-surplus flowing from the productive class to the proprietor class to the sterile class, and eventually back again—the flow concept of income was complete in itself, valid conceptually irrespective of the basis of the flow. It could be applied equally well to cases in which the initial source of wealth creation was manufacturing (as Smith had demonstrated) or some combination of the two, as would be the case in a contained general economic model.

Conclusion   11

As we have already noted, the systematic collection of statistics on any and all aspects of life was a very important component in the promotion of state power. Before the rulers of a nation could ascertain its strength and potential for expansion—both internally and with respect to rival powers—they had to have some method for determining, in as exact a manner as possible, the composition of the economy and the general population. Figures on population, disease, social status, sex ratios, births and deaths, marriages, life expectancy, housing, the composition of households, industrial and agricultural production and productivity, and so forth, provided for the administrators of the state a statistical base for many critical functions. Included among these are taxation, the calculation of state power (in relation to foreign economies), the facilitation of internal management of the economy and the political environment, and the calculation of the potential for expansion.

Graunt, King, Davenant, and Petty, the chief players in the drama from the British view, provide us with a portrait of the evolution in the collection and analysis of such information for the promotion of state interests; they went further than their predecessors, *identifying* the collection of statistics with the requirements of the state.

With the advent of Political Arithmetic, the rhetoric of political economy was to undergo a revolutionary change. The changes in the constitution of the language and subject matter of economics brought about by the mania for statistical data collection would certainly qualify as among the most profound, and indeed seemingly inevitable, developments in the entire history of the discipline. While this change was slow to materialize, that is, slow to enter the mainstream as a viable alternative to the dominant rhetorical culture, it is nonetheless the case that, once it took hold, it succeeded in dominating the conversation, and for the most part it continues to do so today. This dominion has spread far beyond economics, to encompass fields (allied and not) such as biology, history, sociology, psychology, and numerous other disciplines once thought of as "descriptive." The changes brought about can be described under the general heading of "metrics" and include not only econometrics, but biometrics, cliometrics, sociometrics, and psychometrics, subfields in which the attention is focused on measurement and the analysis of numerical data.

We have already touched on the movement from literary description to numerical description, a movement based on the inductive method providing a type of contingent check on our intuitions. The rhetoric, however, had not changed with the change in method; the rhetoric used was still that of the literary economists, adapted to the new numerical order. It is to the transition to mathematical rhetoric, a language and way of thinking designed to exploit the mounting statistical evidence—to divine from the numbers "the way of the world"—that we must now turn our attention.

Appendix: Chronology of Certain Events in France

1515	Francis I ascends throne; reconquers Milan
1516	Francis I takes over ecclesiastical appointments of bishops and abbots, but recognizes supremacy of the Pope over the Councils; gives first year's revenue of every ecclesiastical domain where he held power of appointment
1520	Meeting with Henry VIII of England at the Field of the Cloth of Gold near Calais; beginning of French Protestantism, condemned alike by the Crown and the various parlements
1547	Henry II, son of Francis I, ascends the throne
1556–59	France defeated in war with Spain
1558	Calais falls to France
1559	Henry II killed in a tournament, succeeded by son, Francis II; Francis marries Mary Stuart of Scotland
1560	Francis II dies and is succeeded by his brother, Charles IX (only 10 years old—mother, Catherine de Medici, becomes Regent)
1562–98	Religious wars
1572	Massacre of St. Bartholomew—Admiral de Coligny assassinated when Henry of Navarre married sister of Charles IX; Henry of Navarre pretends conversion to save his life, but later recants
1589	Charles IX loses his crown, flees to Henry of Navarre, and is murdered
1590	Henry besieges Paris, turns Catholic (involving public penance) and in 1594 is crowned at Chartres
1598	Edict of Nantes
1610	Henry assassinated by François Ravaillac; Louis XIII (son of Henry) ascends throne, at age nine
1624	Cardinal Richelieu takes power
1625	Huguenot revolt (ended in 1628)
1643	Louis XIV (aged 5) becomes king; government is run by Cardinal Mazarin
1648–53	Fronde resistance broken
1659	Louis marries Maria Teresa, eldest daughter of Spanish king, Philip IV
1661	Mazarin dies and Louis takes over government personally; new law with respect to the monarchy: Crown must be Catholic, a male (Salic Law), and cannot alienate his lands
1662	Colbert becomes controller-general of finances (until 1683)
1667–68	War in the Netherlands trying to take land as part of France
1672–78	Successful war against Holland
1685	Revocation of the Edict of Nantes
1689–97	Unsuccessful German War
1701–4	War of the Spanish Succession
1709	Defeat at Malplaquet (by Eugene and Marlborough)
1711	Death of Emperor Joseph II (Austria) shifts power in favor of Louis XIV
1712	French victory at Denain

1713	Treaty of Utrecht—admission of separate crowns in England and France; English king must be Protestant; Spain cedes the Netherlands, Gibraltar, Nova Scotia, and Hudson Bay (holds on to Quebec); Savoy gets Sicily, Prussia gets royal title, Portugal gets boundary adjustment in Brazil
1715	Louis XV (5 years old and great-grandson of Louis XIV) ascends throne; Philip, duke of Orleans becomes regent—rejection of the will of Louis XIV
1718–20	John Law's Mississippi scheme
1748	Peace of Aix-la-Chapelle
1774	Louis XVI (grandson of Louis XV) ascends throne; Turgot becomes finance minister; era of the physiocrats (antiguild, tax reform) begins
1777–81	Necker replaces Turgot
1778–83	France enters American Revolutionary War
1789	Meeting of the Estates General; Fall of the Bastille (symbolic)
1790	Louis XVI accepts constitution
1791	King tries unsuccessfully to flee
1792	Storming of the Tuileries; monarchy abolished
1793	Louis XVI executed; Robespierre and the Reign of Terror
1794	Robespierre falls
1795	Terror ends; Directory established
1799	The Consulate established (Napoleon was first Consul for a 10-year term)
1802	Napoleon becomes Consul for life
1812	Napoleon exiled to Elba
1814	Napoleon becomes Emperor of France
1815	Napoleon defeated at Waterloo; exiled to St. Helena

CHAPTER 5

Data Collection, Statistical Analysis, Econometrics

All science requires mathematics. The knowledge of mathematical things is almost innate in us. . . . This is the easiest of sciences, a fact which is obvious in that no one's brain rejects it; for laymen and people who are utterly illiterate know how to count and reckon.   ROGER BACON, *OPUS MAIUS* (1267)

"A judicious man," says he [the "crabbed satirist"] "looks at Statistics, not to get knowledge but to save himself from having ignorance foisted on him."
THOMAS CARLYLE, *CHARTISM* (1839)

Like dreams, statistics are a form of wish fulfillment.
JEAN BAUDRILLARD, *COOL MEMORIES* (1987)

First came numbers and arithmetic, later came manipulation and algebra, and afterwards came answers of many kinds—some relevant others irrelevant.   ANONYMOUS

Introduction   1

We now pick up the threads originally spun by Francis Bacon and Thomas Hobbes linking scientific advance to systematic investigation. In the previous chapter we described the application of that tradition to the political arithmeticians' efforts at numeracy. What follows is out of chronological order, but we take up the topic at this point because we are stressing intellectual legacies, and this is a fine point to show a seventeenth century legacy 'hopping the years' to appear and develop about two centuries later.

Petty clearly followed Bacon and Hobbes's prescription regarding both systematic data collection and reliance upon cognition. While Petty's personal influence was strong enough to inspire Davenant and King, interest in his system languished. In the early years of the nineteenth century, however, two Englishmen returned to Petty's legacy and made studies of prices and statistical data. Within a few years a Netherlander turned Belgian (Belgium seceded from Holland) revolutionized data handling by introducing a set of constructs that permitted easy analysis. It is to their work and the work of Francis Galton to which we immediately turn.

From an analytical standpoint, the shift in rhetoric foreshadowed by the physiocrats was accompanied by great advances in statistical method. The "statistical method" as perceived here consists of two components: a *framework* for the *collection* of statistical material, and an *analytical structure* by which we may *draw conclusions from* the data. While this latter component, statistical analysis, was very clearly tied in its early stages to demography, it also had direct ties to the study of prices and quantities. In the economic tradition, we need only point to the efforts of Petty, King, and Davenant, and the later extensions by Thomas Tooke (1774–1858)[1] and William Newmarch (1820–82).[2] Although its invention and development was somewhat alien to economics—pride of place in the development of a statistical method should go to the efforts of, among others, Quetelet and Galton—many of the advancements in the techniques of statistical analysis have been made by economists. The tremendous advances in statistical methods since the mid–twentieth century in the field of econometrics is sufficient evidence of this appraisal.

The point of this chapter is to review the "statistical revolution" as it developed within economics. We will begin by examining the rationale for a statistical methodology applicable to economic concerns and turn then to a review of the important concepts developed outside of economics that have served the field (including the ideas of the average man and the representative agent). This is not a diversion; the topic is an important part of the mainstream of economics, and this is the appropriate place to delve into the subject.

2 A Fundamental Shift in Rhetoric

William Newmarch's six-volume *History of Prices and the State of the Circulation from 1792 to 1856* (published over the period 1838 to 1857)

1. Tooke, born in St. Petersburg, Russia (the son of a clergyman), was a businessman, a partner in the firm of Stephen Thornton Bros. Co., and later a partner in the firm of Asteel, Tooke, and Thornton. His involvement in economic matters began in 1819, when he testified before both Houses of the British Parliament on the question of the resumption of cash payments, and later (1820–21) in defense of free trade. He rose to the governorship of the Royal Exchange Assurance Corporation, retiring in 1852 after ten years service. Along with James Mill, Ricardo, and Malthus (among others), he was a founder of the Political Economy Club (1821).

2. Newmarch was born in Yorkshire. Self-educated, he worked in various banking positions, including cashier, before rising to officer at the Agra Bank in 1846. Leaving the bank in 1851, he became secretary of the Globe Insurance Company. From 1862 to 1881 he served as manager of Glyn, Mills, and Co., another banking house, and also served as director of Palmer's Iron and Shipbuilding Company and treasurer of the British Iron Trade Association (until 1880). Newmarch also was on the staff of the *Morning Chronicle*, served as president of the Statistical Society (1869), and was a member of the Political Economy Club. Among his publications are *The New Supplies of Gold: Facts and Statements Relative to Their Actual Amount* (1853), "On Electoral Statistics of the Counties and Boroughs in England and Wales During the Twenty-Five Years from the Reform Act of 1832 to the Present Time" (*Journal of the Statistical Society* 1857), and a pamphlet entitled *The Political Perils of 1859*.

presented a comprehensive collection and systematic display of empirical data. In an 1861 address before Section F (Economic Science and Statistics) of the British Association for the Advancement of Science, Newmarch presented a very interesting interpretation of the evolution of economic doctrine and method up to that time. Reviewing the development of economics from 1830 to 1860, Newmarch reached a then-provocative conclusion. Economics, he wrote

> has ceased to be an abstract science,—it has ceased to be a system of subtle and ingenious reasonings. It has little by little, and by a process cautious and full of promise, become a science almost entirely experimental. We have learned that in all questions relating to human society,—in all controversies where the agency of human beings has to be relied upon for working out even the smallest results—we have learned that in these inquiries the only sound basis on which we can found doctrines, and still more the only safe basis on which we can erect laws, is not hypothetical deduction, however ingenious and subtle, but conclusions and reasoning supported by the largest and most careful investigation of facts. (Newmarch 1861, 452–53)

One reason for this shift in emphasis in economics, moving it from an abstract to an experimental science, was the redefinition by those interested in social affairs of the domain of the subject, a reorientation from theoretical interests to practical ones. This reorientation is especially noticeable in the realization of the social nature of economics and the emphasis on quantification, looking to actual numerical data instead of abstract models. Newmarch listed as within the sphere of "social science" the "five kindred inquiries of Political Economy, Jurisprudence and Amendment of the Law, Education, Sanitary Science, and Statistics" (1861, 456). The first four inquiries had been the centers of attention of pre-Classical and Classical writers on economic questions (as we shall see in the next chapters). The inclusion of statistics within this subject matter is interesting and worth our consideration here not only because of its importance to Newmarch's own work (alone and with Tooke), but also for its importance to those who sought the provision of a sound statistical basis to economic theory and a secure grounding for the often more politically charged policy prescriptions.

As Newmarch understood the field, statistics was not to be confused with a well-defined and intuitively grounded discipline such as mathematics or with any of the mathematical and physical sciences, primarily because of the requirement of the certainty of scientific laws and the rigorous nature of their discovery process—"in Statistics we have no such body of general laws as are to be found in other branches of inquiry, which no one hesitates to describe as sciences" (1861, 457). The rather modest claim Newmarch was to make for statistics—regarding its relevance as part of economics as well as its ambition as a separate field of inquiry—is simply that statistics is a viable tool for the investigation of certain recurring phenomena: "it is the application of the Experimental or Baconian method to the several divisions of inquiry which relate to man in society" (457). Statistics is a *contingent* science, not a demonstrative, deductive one.

The careful use of this tool of investigation is especially important in social applications, since these fields deal with human agents, as opposed to the natural sciences which deal with physical phenomena. The word *statistics* itself derived from the German word *Staatswissenschaft*, meaning the science of governing.[3] The importance of a statistical approach in this regard had already been demonstrated and made manifest by the indispensable charts and tables of Newmarch, Tooke and others; their use of nascent statistical methods for calculation and presentation of figures of an economic and social nature resulted in the publication of an atlas not unlike those which had been held to be the marvels of the physical sciences, especially astronomy.[4]

But with all the usefulness for economics and social sciences generally of a field such as statistics, Newmarch was well aware of the problems involved in attempting to promote the use of a tool in the social realm which is ideally suited to the realm of the experimental sciences. This concern was highlighted in his definitions: "Statistics, as applied to man in society, are no more than carefully recorded observations of occurrences which take place among a certain number of human beings living under certain conditions" (1861, 460). Only in the case of the physical sciences did he believe that statistical reasoning could express findings that may be regarded as lawlike behavior: in these fields, the objects of interest were recurring phenomena, the constants and deviations of which were conformable to strict and definable mathematical formulas. In the social sciences, and in the more general case of observations of a statistical nature, on the other hand, these recurrences were not in evidence; on the social side, the element of "free will" was enough to ensure that such regularity as was observable in physical phenomena would not be forthcoming.[5] Newmarch held that the social scientific researcher should err on the side of caution when seeking to apply statistical methods, and so not ask for too much from, nor overstate the power of, an application designed for other purposes. This is especially evident

---

3. We will deal with *Staatswissenschaft* in chapter 9.

4. "We have, in truth, made no trifling advances towards the construction of an Economical and Statistical Chart, the results of which will be hardly inferior in exactness, as they assuredly will not be inferior in interest or importance, to the admirable charts already constructed of the geology or geography of leading States" (Newmarch 1861, 457).

5. "I confess it has always seemed to me that the great disturber of all statistical uniformity and averages is precisely the uncertain operation of the human will" (Newmarch 1861, 460).

in his definition of a scientific "law," a construct which he saw as tied to a particular definition and use of statistics. In the general case, Newmarch reserved the use of the term *law* to situations in which "there is a power of accurate prediction in individual cases" (461). This "power of individual prediction" was lacking in social scientific endeavors, and so social scientists could not properly consider their results from statistical analyses to be interpretable as "laws" of behavior. However, because of the nature of the variables in the physical scientific domain, the mantle of "law" could be granted very reasonably, and in these instances the term is completely consistent with the analysis of these fields:

> so far as Statistics are concerned I do not consider that any numerical results put forward by Statisticians are entitled to be called or regarded as statistical 'laws.' . . . It appears to me, with all deference, that the term 'law,' as applied to any statistical result whatever, is a misapplication of the term. The utmost that Statistics can do is to express numerically the *average* result of any given series of observations of occurrences taking place under particular conditions among human beings. But in the case of a physical law, I would suggest to the Section that our knowledge is so much superior to any expression of mere average, that we can predict the result of any single event or experiment as confidently and accurately as we can predict the results of series of similar events. (1861, 459; emphasis in original)

Thus are we led in this brief look at Newmarch's review of the appropriateness for economics of a statistical methodology to the subject matter of this chapter—the development of a statistical basis for both testing and theorizing within economics, and the subsequent emergence of economics as a "scientific" approach to the study of society. It is with the development of statistical methods and their use in attempting a better understanding of economic relationships at a formal level that modern economics has been said to have arisen.[6]

The collection and categorization of economic data was but one of the pillars upon which the new structure rested. A second was the identification of mathematical equations taken as governing economic behavior, a third a rhetoric allowing use to be made of the other two. The Newtonian revolution finally enveloped economics. W. Stanley Jevons most clearly understood this problem, and, in the Introduction to his *Theory of Political Economy* (2d ed., 1879), made the following (at the time) astonishing prediction:

> I do not hesitate to say, too, that Economics might be gradually erected into an exact science, if only commercial statistics were far more complete and accurate than they are at present, so that the

---

6. See, e.g., the first paragraph of George J. Stigler (1962).

formulæ could be endowed with exact meaning by the aid of numerical data. These data would consist chiefly in accurate accounts of the quantities of goods possessed and consumed by the community, and the prices at which they are exchanged. There is no reason whatever why we should not have those statistics, except the cost and trouble of collecting them, and the unwillingness of persons to afford information. . . .

The deductive science of Economics must be verified and rendered useful by the purely empirical science of Statistics. Theory must be invested with the reality and life of fact. (Jevons 1879, 21, 90)

The verification of economic theory that Jevons sought as a means for vesting it with a scientific precision would not come to pass until the beginning of the second decade of the twentieth century.[7] One year before this achievement, the possibility of such a radical transformation in technique was ridiculed by one of the then-leading advocates of mathematical economics. Francis Ysidro Edgeworth, an outstanding statistical theoretician in his own right, remarked on Jevons's statement in a survey article on "Curves" written for the original *Palgrave's*. He noted rather blithely that "Jevons's hope of obtaining demand curves by statistical observation . . . may appear chimerical" (Edgeworth 1910, 473). While Edgeworth may indeed have been correct in his estimation of the usefulness of statistical measures, Jevons's conjecture proved to have had an enduring influence on the profession.

Jevons also, some three years earlier, had suggested the need for a science "of commercial fluctuations, which shall inquire why the world is all activity for a few years, and then all inactivity; why, in short, there are such tides in the affairs of men" (Jevons 1876, 631). This, a clear recommendation to his brethren to devote study to the causes of business cycles, had been neglected by his contemporaries. His own work in the area in many ways signaled the beginning of a new economics.

One final statement of the condition of economics during this period was provided by Alfred Marshall, surely one of the greatest economists of the period encompassing the late nineteenth and early twentieth centuries. In attempting to survey the landscape of economic thought and methodology that had been the domain of the classical economists (broadly defined), and daring to chart the new territory that would greet those of the emerging generation, Marshall presented what may be considered the most compact statement that one could hope to find of the competing positions. In an 1896 address to the Cambridge Economic Club, reprinted in 1897 in the *Quarterly Journal of Economics* as "The Old Generation of Economists and the New," Marshall confronted the

---

7. Pribram submitted that "Jevons was perhaps the first economist to suggest the filling of empty boxes of abstract arguments with quantities supplied by statistical investigations" (Pribram 1983, 562).

problems with the methodological position of the old generation and suggested modifications to allow the upcoming generation to rethink and restructure to greater benefit the theories that came before; he was especially concerned that economics should benefit from contact with the physical sciences and in particular with the use in these disciplines of statistical procedures. Marshall wrote:

> it may be said briefly that the latter half of the nineteenth century has thoroughly overhauled the doctrines of the earlier economists as to *tendencies;* and while pruning away much, has set the remainder in order and established them on a firm scientific basis. It has shown, what was perhaps not fully recognized by the older economists themselves, that in their predilection for a study of tendencies, they were really working to obtain just that mastery of knowledge which has laid the foundation of the successive triumphs of physical science. For, when studying particular facts with the purpose of inferring tendencies, they were conforming to the great canon already noticed that in passing from particulars to particulars we must go not directly but by way of generals; and also to a second great canon, that the main importance of the particular facts of nature lies in the light which they throw upon the processes of nature; or in other words that from what *is* we have to learn what *is becoming;* from *das Sein* we have to learn *das Werden.*
>
> And, in the latter half of the century economists have gone one step further and come more into line with physical science by borrowing from it some of those terse and powerful phrases by which it has been long able to describe and explain nature's tendencies more easily and more precisely than is possible in ordinary language. They are facing the fact that at the basis of nearly all modern knowledge there lies a study of tendencies, in the form more or less disguised of a study of the relations between the infinitesimal variations of different things. This is what the shrewd ordinary man does, though he may not know it, any more perhaps than he knows that he is talking prose. The man of science does it, and knows that he does it; though before he addresses a popular audience he may fitly wrap up what he has done in language that is less terse and clear, but more familiar. (Marshall 1897, 122–23; emphasis in original)

The problems facing economists, according to Marshall, are not in structure different from those faced by the physical scientists, nor can the procedure for their solution be held different from the manner of everyday problem solving. At the root of both is a concern with the procedures of statistical analysis, not always of a formal type but nonetheless indicative of a mode of review.

While there were many players whose contributions in this area could be discussed—Gottfried Leibniz (1646–1716), Anton Busching (1724–93), Johann Süssmilch (1707–67), and Johann Goethe (1749–1832) in the German states, and Sir John Sinclair (1754–1835) in Scotland (who is said to have introduced the word "statistics" into the English language)[8]—we will for purposes of the present discussion confine the review to certain key players in the drama. We will then extend the analysis to the development of econometrics in the American context.

3 Precursors: The Idea Men

3.1 *The Setting*

Having identified the importance of statistical *reasoning* in defining a demarcation, so to speak, between the old and the new classical economic thinking, we turn now to a brief introduction of the statistical *method* in economics. The collection of statistical data was only the beginning of the quest to identify certain key indices of national power and to provide the basis for the governors to control the governed. A problem with this simple *collection* of numerical statistics is that, absent some technical apparatus, these raw numerical figures are difficult to *interpret*. Masses of disconnected numbers do not readily lend themselves to interpretation, since to be useful these data must first be placed within a context that allows relationships between disparate series to be recognized. The early generation of innovators in the area of data collection and analysis set the stage; it was left to the later generations to actually invent the apparatus that would make these figures tell a story.

Important in this regard was the development in the late eighteenth century of the graphical method of presentation. Graphs are especially useful in presenting large amounts of numerical data in an orderly fashion, so as to allow ready apprehension of the material and to allow easy comparisons between series of data. One has only to open an introductory economics textbook to understand the value of such instruments for pedagogical purposes. While the development and employment of this method of presentation has itself an interesting history, for purposes of the present we shall confine ourselves to the first use of the technique.[9]

Schumpeter (1954, 526) credits William Playfair (1759–1823) with having introduced graphical methods into economics in his 1786 *Com-*

---

8. On all of these figures and others, see Ian Hacking (1990).

9. As a curiosity, we note that Florence Nightingale (1820–1910) employed the graphical method of statistics to demonstrate the necessity for more efficient nursing techniques in British military hospitals. Her efforts led to an emphasis on professional nursing training.

mercial and Political Atlas.[10] Playfair referred to his graphical presentation of statistical data as the method of "lineal arithmetic." The objective of this technique he explained thus:

> The advantage proposed by this method, is not that of giving a more accurate statement than by figures, but it is to give a more simple and permanent idea of the gradual progress and comparative amounts, at different periods, by presenting to the eye a figure, the proportions of which correspond with the amount of the sums intended to be expressed.

> By this method as much information may be obtained in five minutes as would require whole days to imprint on the memory. . . . (Playfair, *Commercial and Political Atlas,* 3d ed., 1801; as quoted in Funkhouser and Walker 1935, 106)

There are of course many others whose contributions to the foundations of statistics and probability affected the development of statistical methods within economics. These contributions include the development and application of tools of analysis and the introduction of methods for approaching problems. To take just a few examples, Jacob Bernoulli (1654–1705) is generally esteemed to have introduced the mathematical theory of probability, Adrien Marie Legendre (1752–1833) is credited with having devised the method of least squares, Thomas Bayes (1701?–61) is credited with having developed the theory of scientific inference which bears his name, and Pierre Simon Laplace (1749–1827) contributed to virtually all areas of mathematical statistics and probability.

With this in mind, we commence our presentation of this subject with a review of the doctrines of two of the most important, from our point of view, of the early writers on the topic: Quetelet and Galton.

Quetelet and the "Average Man"   3.2

Lambert Adolphe Jacques Quetelet (1796–1874)[11] is a figure of central importance in the movement to introduce an analytic framework into

---

10. In an article in *Economic History* (1935), one of the few to actually look at the work of William Playfair, H. Gray Funkhouser and Helen M. Walker noted that "Playfair's work is noteworthy because it provides one of those rare cases in which an inventor has no important precursors and in which his work is presented in so finished a form that later workers have not materially changed his method" (103).

11. Quetelet, a native of Belgium, was by training a mathematician—he received his doctorate from the University of Ghent, his dissertation being on a topic in analytic geometry, and for the effort was elected to the Belgian Academy. Having acquired instruction in the theory of probability in Paris by the renowned Joseph Fourier, Quetelet tried his hand at many different subjects, including astronomy, meteorology, and sociology. Daniel Boorstin noted that Florence Nightingale considered Quetelet a hero; because "statistics were the measure of God's purpose, the study of statistics became another of her proclaimed religious duties" (Boorstin 1983, 674).

social theory, especially into economics. Despite Quetelet's achievements and his fame in the history of statistics, only Schumpeter among historians of economic thought seems to have recognized him as having brought to economics anything of value:[12] "His vigorous and original investigations into the distribution of human characteristics mark a step in advance that had never to be retraced and, as an example to follow, had eventually also some importance for economics" (Schumpeter 1954, 525). The importance of Quetelet in the present context is not in his technical contributions to the mathematical end of the subject, but rather in his championing of the idea of statistical regularity[13] and in his definition of the concept of *l'homme moyen,* the "average man."

Quetelet's most important work is his two-volume *Sur l'homme et le développment de ses facultés, ou essai de physique sociale,* published in 1835 (translated in 1842 as *A Treatise on Man and the Development of his Faculties*). It was in this work that Quetelet presented his concept of *l'homme moyen,* the "average man." In his *History of Statistics,* the statistician Stephen M. Stigler considered this such an important idea that he described it both as "a vivid and concrete symbol of a society, an embodiment of the target and the ultimate benefactor of nineteenth century social reform" and as a "device for allowing a beginning of a 'social physics,' the gatekeeper to a mathematical social science" (S. M. Stigler 1986, 171).

The method employed by Quetelet is really quite simple. Trained as a scientist, an astronomer to be specific, Quetelet was familiar with the regularities in the positions of stars and planets and other heavenly bodies; these regularities had led scientists to derive laws governing the behavior of astronomical phenomena, laws which could be taken as representative of the mechanism behind celestial motion. The scientific establishment of the time viewed these laws as being objectively real, since they were derived with respect to a real phenomenon, readily observable and measurable.

With this scientific grounding, Quetelet took to the analysis of social data. He began by noting that, in statistical series of social concern, for instance statistics on crime, the relative proportions of various criminal activities held to a nearly constant value. Single elements may prove incommensurable, but a series of observations will generally fit the shape of a normal curve. As the curve itself is derived by reference to mathematical "laws," that is, it has a known mathematically defined underlying frequency distribution, the data also may be subject to this same set of laws. As with astronomical statistics, one should be able to readily discern these regularities and calculate the requisite statistical measures,

---

12. While Schumpeter recognized Quetelet's importance to *economics,* he had to admit that his influence on *economists* was slight.

13. The philosopher Ian Hacking referred to Quetelet as "the greatest regularity salesman of the nineteenth century" (Hacking 1990, 105).

such as the mean and the dispersion from the mean. This led Schumpeter to the following comment on Quetelet's approach:

> he plunged into a philosophy of a sort of statistical determinism by conceiving the theory that those investigations were revealing a stable type of average man whose properties linked up with simple general 'causes,' deviations being of the nature of errors of observation in the Gaussian sense. He thus hoped to reduce, on a statistical basis, the methodology of the social to that of the physical sciences. (Schumpeter 1954, 525–26)

An important consideration in Quetelet's work is the role of probability theory as a basis for statistical reasoning. Critical in this regard is the homogeneity postulate. The "average man" is contingent, bound spatially and temporally to the observations. The rationale for Quetelet's artifact lay with the possibility of the isolation of a single causal factor, with any noticeable variability falling within a normal curve of error. Thus when we speak of the average man, this "creature" must be presented in the context in which he was formed, so that this causal factor may be isolated to the greatest extent possible. We are then faced with the question: is the "average man" defined as the average of military recruits, or the average of bricklayers, or the average of politicians, or the average of bankers, or is the "average man" really the "average woman"? In other words, the statistical artifact we derive is effectively tied to its group. Further, we can relate him only to groups of like constitution. But even so, we *can* still engage in associations, and the average man provided, and still provides today, an interesting basis for these comparisons. Given this figure, calculable from data of other countries and even of other historical time periods, provided we know the composition of the underlying reference class, we can engage in a correlation analysis of those characteristics we deem most important.

What Quetelet did was far more extensive. If the series of observations is homogeneous—comprised of individual elements of the same or similar constitution, so that only minor, trivial variations distinguish them—then the series will follow the normal law of error, that is, it can be represented by a normal or 'bell curve.' The problem, of course, is in defining the appropriate homogeneous collective. Given the state of the art of statistical inference and the theory of probability at the time of Quetelet, such determining conditions were not readily forthcoming. The solution for Quetelet was one which effectively set the stage for a nonprobabilistic statistical theory, one which is maintained up to the present. Even if the set of observations is nonhomogeneous, we can still apply statistical *reasoning*, provided we have at our disposal a sufficiently large amount of observations. The law of large numbers works to ensure that the series can be treated as effectively homogeneous; this will be true so long as one sees no evidence of a "persistence of causes." By reviewing a large-enough observation set, we can effectively eliminate the influence of chance elements, since the observations tend to coalesce about a single "constant cause," with the "chance elements" filtering out away from this central tendency. This Quetelet expressed as follows, declaring it a "fundamental principle":

> The greater the number of individuals observed, the more do individual peculiarities, whether physical or moral, become effaced, and allow the general facts to predominate, by which society exists and is preserved. (Quetelet 1842, 6; quoted in S. M. Stigler 1986, 172)

Thus we are led to the conceptual device of the statistical "average man."[14]

Quetelet then proceeded a step further. The homogeneity postulate led him to the acceptance of the normal curve as the "true" underlying causal factor. But more important, the fitting of the normal curve meant that the data in fact *were* homogeneous; there was no longer any need to seek homogeneity, since the fact of the data having "fit" the curve was establishment enough.

Quetelet had devised the "average man" as a real, objective fact, one which, once developed, could be treated outside of the population from whence it was derived. The average man became an ideal archetype, "occasionally elevated to a standard of beauty at which nature aims, as a marksman aims at the center of a target" (S. M. Stigler 1986, 172).

Eventually, Quetelet was to suffer the wrath of many who thought his new "science" to be destructive of individual will, especially as he sought to extend his observations beyond demographics and into the area of social behavior. If man is under the influence of "laws" of behavior, then he can no longer be said to have the ability to decide on his own between virtue and vice, good and evil. To this Quetelet responded that his method made possible the betterment of society by identifying problem areas in need of institutional reform.

3.3 Galton and the "Representative Man"

Quetelet's elucidation of the concept of *l'homme moyen* set the stage for much of the work in this vein that followed in the social sciences. His conceptual apparatus gave others the impetus to undertake statistical studies that served to better our overall understanding of social concerns. The problem, however, with the definitions of "representative man" and the "normal" value as employed by Quetelet is that, while they may have

---

14. To give an example, begin with observations on height, weight, years of schooling, intelligence scores, speed in the 100-yard dash, and any other desired characteristics, from a randomly chosen sample of an otherwise homogeneous group, say military recruits. The averages of these figures as they fall within a normal distribution give the proportions for the "average man."

originally implied nothing more than a statistical representation of the mean individual in a population, they eventually (and for Quetelet desiredly) took on a much different aura. In other words, a term which originally suggested the normal (meaning statistical mean) value of a population, eventually took on the meaning of a measure of the normal (meaning ethically acceptable) individual in the population.

At this point in the story we are led to the reappraisal of the concept of the "average man" as defined by Sir Francis Galton (1822–1911).[15] As with the contributions to economics of his predecessor Quetelet, Galton's accomplishments in this area are virtually unheralded save for the singular praise of Schumpeter. Galton was, in Schumpeter's considered opinion, "the man whom I should choose as an illustrative example if I were asked to define the specifically English type of great man of science and the specifically English type of scientific creation" (Schumpeter 1954, 790).[16]

As founder of the science of eugenics and the anthropometric laboratory,[17] Galton was fascinated with the notion of constancy of certain general characteristics in each successive generation. From observations of family records, and even of the fossil record, he arrived at a conclusion on the question of stability:

> The processes of heredity are found to be so wonderfully balanced and their equilibrium to be so stable, that they concur in maintaining a perfect statistical resemblance so long as the external conditions remain unaltered. (1877, 492)

This "perfect statistical resemblance" is representable in a straightforward way by the use of the normal curve of distribution, a simple but elegant device with which Galton could readily demonstrate his meaning. In fact, the "law of deviation" and the normal curve became the focus of much of his work: the phrase "reversion to the mean" illustrates his view of the evolution of human types. The law of deviation held very simply "that differences should be wholly due to the collective actions of a host

---

15. Galton, a cousin of Charles Darwin, promoted a heredity view of human nature. Among his more notable works are *Hereditary Genius* (1869), *English Men of Science* (1874), *Inquiries into Human Faculty and Its Development* (1883), and *Natural Inheritance* (1889). Biographical material may be found in F. N. David (1968) and Galton's own *Memories of My Life*. The classic biography is Karl Pearson's three-volume study.

16. Schumpeter listed Galton's contributions to science as: (1) the discovery of correlation, (2) the founding of the Eugenics Laboratory, (3) the founding of a branch of psychology dealing with individual differences, and (4) pioneering ways of handling the nature–nurture problem. These contributions Schumpeter felt assured Galton high rank as a preeminent sociologist—"one of the three greatest sociologists, the other two being Vico and Marx" (Schumpeter 1954, 791)

17. In 1904 Galton established a fellowship in anthropometry and eugenics at the University of London, which later became the Galton Laboratory of National Eugenics. This laboratory was initially under the direction of Galton's student, Karl Pearson, and later under the direction of Ronald Fisher.

of independent *petty* influences as present in various combinations . . ."
(1877, 512), the principal influences holding to a near-constant value.[18]
Thus are we allowed the use of the normal distribution as an approximation to the actual behavior of an empirical data set.

> We see by them that the ordinary genealogical course of a race
> consists in a constant outgrowth from its centre, a constant dying
> away at its margins, and a tendency of the scanty remnants of all
> exceptional stock to revert to that mediocrity, whence the majority
> of their ancestors originally sprang. (1877, 532)

But Galton was quick to remind that by "reversion" he did not
mean to imply anything other than the behavior of "typical" sequences,
those which we are likely to see appearing in nature. "Typical laws" are
then derived with respect to those sequences, holding only to an acceptable degree.

> The typical laws are those which most nearly express what takes
> place in nature generally; they may never be exactly correct in any
> one case, but at the same time they will always be approximately
> true and always serviceable for explanation. (1877, 532)

The philosopher Ian Hacking, in *The Taming of Chance* (his study
of the historical treatment of chance and uncertainty), held that Galton's
view was that statistical laws are autonomous; that is, they are not merely
useful as predictors of phenomena, but are also and more importantly
useful as explanatory devices that allow the investigator to delve into the
essential nature of the phenomena under investigation (Hacking 1990,
182).

As Quetelet was involved in deriving calculations based on the
measurement of physical and other characteristics of various regional and
national populations, and even racial and ethnic types, Galton's interest
likewise was consumed with measurement. But Galton's interests were of
a much different sort than Quetelet's. Where Quetelet had concentrated
his efforts on the identification of "types," Galton had concentrated
instead on how the individuals within each group differed from the "representative" member. Given the identification of a "representative type,"
one could readily "grade" deviations from this average construct, and,
assigning numerical values to these deviations, present a ranking of those
qualities which had been previously thought incapable of measure.[19]

This measurement and comparison of qualities previously believed
to be incommensurable led Galton to a further study of the whole of the
human type. His lifelong interest in anthropometry provided him with
the most detailed measurements of the human body that had yet been

18. "Any selective tendency is ruin to the law of deviation" (Galton 1877, 512).
19. Galton's 1874 "On a Proposed Statistical Scale" presented a sketch of his procedure. See also S. M. Stigler (1986, 271).

attempted; he in fact established the anthropometric laboratory at University College, London, for the express purpose of formalizing and institutionalizing his experimental techniques, and instructing others in the ways of this new approach to social description.[20] He was also very excited about the application of new technologies,[21] such as photography, to this new field; he published many studies, complete with photographs and representations of photographic plates, showing how an average type would look based on superimposition of photographic images. Thus he could show to the public a representative of the average soldier, the average criminal, the average longshoreman, the average farmer, or a representative of whatever group you may want to see.

But Galton's main achievements for purposes of the present discussion were in two areas: the study of natural inheritance and the theory of correlation. We have touched already on the first of these, the theory of natural inheritance. Briefly, Galton held that, in "typical" populations, inheritance led to a "regression to the mean." The import of this observation is that, while certain general characteristics of a population are repeated through successive generations, it is not the case that this outcome can continue unabated. It is not true, for instance, that desirable traits can be guaranteed to survive in a population through successful breeding.[22] Galton, in his heredity and even his eugenics experiments, discovered on the contrary (and at times much to his chagrin) that the rule is toward a regression to mediocrity, not continuance of superiority. This he found somewhat gratifying, in that the laws of heredity indeed follow a normal distribution, wherein "normal" is an ethically neutral term, meaning simply the "usual" outcome.

As Hacking (1990) has noted, Galton was more excited by the dispersion of observations from the mean than he was by the idea of an average value. His 1869 *Hereditary Genius* is perhaps most noteworthy for the appearance of a diagram representing the deviations of observations from the sample's average. This shift of emphasis from the center of the distribution to the extremes is what led Galton to his theory of correlation. The observation that those with "exceptional" traits often have quite "unexceptional" offspring, while those with "unexceptional" traits may produce "exceptional" offspring, gave rise to an understanding that

---

20. F. Y. Edgeworth was particularly impressed with the care Galton took in looking beyond mere measures of central tendency: "Any scruples which he may suggest as to the discrepancy in the values of mean stature determined from his different records are removed by a consideration of the error or diversity to be expected among these results" (Edgeworth 1889a, 604).

21. His own inventions included the quincunx, a device consisting of a square, with a pin at each corner and one in the middle, bounded by glass. Into this device was poured shot. The shot would form, at the bottom of the device, a representation of the normal curve.

22. "Individuals do *not* equally tend to leave their like behind them . . ." (Galton 1877, 492; emphasis in original).

population traits are distributed in accordance with the normal law of error. The meaning of this insight is important: if a given statistical sample is shown to be normally distributed, then a second sample drawn from the same population, or the measures of a second generation of individuals born into this population, will also be normally distributed and possessed of similar characteristics to the first. This identification of regularity and lawlike behavior in observations of human evolution and human behavior was of great import in what Hacking referred to as "the taming of chance."

Also important in this regard is Galton's realization that when presented with a population that was not homogeneous, but was instead a mixture of several populations, each different from the other, the composite population could be represented as being itself homogeneous and following the normal distribution. The mean (or median) and dispersion of the composite population will be, correcting for simple scalar differences, of the same form as each of the individual populations. As Stephen M. Stigler phrased it, Galton's "analogue proof that a normal mixture of normal distributions was itself normal was a stroke of genius. . . . He could conceive of his data as a mixture of very different populations, notwithstanding the unity apparent in its normal outline" (S. M. Stigler 1986, 281).

In the area of correlation, Galton's achievement was in bringing the very idea to the fore, even though he added little beyond this. His student Karl Pearson, himself one of the leading statistical theorists of the twentieth century, credited Galton with having invented the concept.[23] While Pearson may have lavished praise unduly, Galton's connection with the popularization of the concept is important. His anthropometric experiments and his work with fingerprinting and the identification of other notable and measurable characteristics of human beings demonstrated that certain traits appeared together consistently. These "correlated" ("co-related" was the preferred spelling of Galton) measures eventually took on much the same reality as did Quetelet's "average."

4 Henry L. Moore and Statistical Economics

It is difficult to pinpoint the precise moment in which a set of analytical techniques came to be known collectively as econometric analysis. In form if not substance this type of analysis is not far removed from the earlier science of biostatistics, a science which owes its existence to the pioneering work in the field of eugenics by Galton and his student, Karl Pearson. One could also look to the pathbreaking work in statistical

---

23. The concept, however, as S. M. Stigler (1986, 298) observed, may more reasonably be said to have been recognized and expressed in modern form by W. Stanley Jevons in his 1874 *Principles of Science*.

theory of Pearson and Edgeworth, especially in the areas of correlation and the law of error. These studies, which date from the late nineteenth century, developed many of the instruments of mathematical statistics so familiar to modern readers.

In any event, however one seeks to begin, for all intents and purposes the genesis of modern econometrics may be taken to be the publication in 1911 of Henry Ludwell Moore's (1869–1958)[24] *Laws of Wages: An Essay in Statistical Economics*.[25] This book, most of which is devoted to an empirical study of the labor market, specifically to a "test" of John Bates Clark's marginal productivity theory of wages, is important beyond its policy and sociopolitical ramifications. Its true worth lies in the analytical apparatus for the study of empirical problems that it employed, this being the theoretical structure developed by Edgeworth and Pearson. Edgeworth himself praised it as representing "the first time, we believe, that the higher statistics, which are founded on the Calculus of Probabilities, have been used on a large scale as a buttress of economic theory" (Edgeworth 1912a, 66–67).[26] To be sure, the book neither employed nor improved upon the technical apparatus worked out by Edgeworth, Pearson, and others, nor did it present any mathematical model from which could proceed the analysis of data; Moore achieved his results from a contingency table analysis from which he could note deviations from observed trends.[27] But he did succeed in integrating solutions to the analysis of data that had been employed by those earlier generations of pioneers, such as Petty, King, Playfair, Galton, et al.[28]

---

24. Of Moore George J. Stigler remarked, "He had gifted predecessors and contemporaries; but no one else was so persistent, so ambitious, or so influential as he in the development of this new approach [of statistical economics]" (Stigler 1962, 1).

25. In other of his works, Moore, a professor at Columbia University, attempted to apply his statistical work to the analysis of business cycles, with some very interesting (some may say bizarre) results. In *Economic Cycles—Their Law and Cause* (1914) he attempted to connect the periodicity of business cycles to weather patterns (specifically rainfall data). In *Generating Economic Cycles* (1923) he attempted through harmonic analysis to connect cyclic behavior to movements of the planet Venus. Two of his other book-length works were *Forecasting the Yield and Price of Cotton* (1917) and *Synthetic Economics* (1929).

26. It should be noted that Moore's "higher statistics" was devoid of a probability foundation.

27. One of Moore's methods involved plotting a series of data points representing two related series on a scatter diagram. Instead of attempting to plot each and every single point, however, he proposed to consider only "representative facts," a representative fact being one "which for the purpose in hand conveys the maximum of information about the group it represents" (Moore 1911, 15–16). For this purpose, he settled upon various measures of central tendency, including the arithmetic mean, the median, and the mode. In this way, he could reduce the complexity of the problem to a consideration of only a handful of summary measures. The connection to the earlier methods of Quetelet and Galton is obvious.

28. R. J. Epstein (1987) placed Moore in the position of pioneer of econometric analysis. Chapter 1 of his book gives an overview of Moore's work in the area.

Of secondary importance to most investigations, but of prime concern here, the book succeeded in setting forth a methodology, a form of rhetoric, which could be readily exploited by later generations of researchers. It is to this that we now turn.

Moore was concerned with establishing the basis upon which could be founded the new science of statistical economics. For Moore, the new methods for both inquiry and theory-formation called for the skills of a new breed of economic researcher, the "statistical economist." Moore defined statistical economics as having two prime motivations: (1) "to bring to the test of representative facts the hypotheses and theorems of pure economics" and (2) "to supply data, in the form of general facts and empirical laws, for the elaboration of dynamic economics" (Moore 1911, 169–70). Statistical economics thus demanded the services of practitioners who were a composite of both economist and scientist, which roles combined to place economics on a more sound footing than could otherwise have been achieved by those versed solely in the more naive and simplistic analytics of preceding generations. The role of the economist in this effort "is to throw the greatest possible light upon the relation of the economic facts before him," while the role of the scientist is "to achieve this end by summarizing the descriptions of the relations of facts in the simplest and most general formulæ possible" (10). Quantitative measure served as one critical element in this endeavor; the new mathematical framework served as another.

Of far more import, however, was a research methodology that would allow a more complete exploitation of these advances. Theories and explanations based on intuitive judgments or speculative generalizations were no longer acceptable in a discipline that sought to portray itself as "scientific." From this point on, judgments would have to be systematized and formalized in such a manner as to disabuse all notions of doubt and contentions as to their validity. To be sure, the specific purpose of Moore's Laws of Wages was clear-cut:

> to use the newer statistical methods and the more recent economic theory to extract, from data relating to wages, either new truth or else truth in such new form as will admit of its being brought into fruitful relation with the generalizations of economic science. (1911, 6)

As had economists of earlier generations, Moore sought to identify "laws" underlying the behavior of economic phenomena. The progression is one of observation → hypothesis → statistical law (1911, 20). In true inductivist fashion, he believed that the road to this discovery of the ultimate statistical laws lay in the procedure of curve-fitting. In any investigation into the relationship between any two series of data points (just to consider the simplest case), the "law" governing the association (and the surety with which it could be said to hold) "is dependent upon the finding of the simplest curve that will fit satisfactorily the given representative points"[29] (16). But this curve-fitting procedure is not to be used for the purpose of theory *building*; it is to be reserved instead for theory *testing*. We must first *assert* by hypothesis that a particular curve type (linear, log-linear, or any of a number of other functional types) will satisfy the data requirement; we then test with the data itself, by virtue of the goodness-of-fit criterion, whether this relationship in fact holds, that is, whether our alleged relationship between the data sets is the "true" relationship. But we must be mindful that any statements of lawlike behavior are confined to the collective; these "laws" are not valid for *individual* cases, but are rather "laws of mass phenomena," tied to time and place, not in general to be viewed as extendable to other populations.

Moore further insisted that, in arriving at a theory (and a resulting underlying curve) to "explain" the association between data sets, we must invoke Occam's Razor: select the simplest theory that adequately explains the observed correlation. Thus we arrive at Moore's definition of a statistical law: "The statistical law of the association of two series of facts is the hypothesis that satisfies best the imposed conditions of simplicity and excellence of fit to the representative facts" (1911, 17).[30]

As we have discussed already in the previous chapters, the collection of statistical material had been by the nineteenth century a well-established field of inquiry. What remained was the manner for the exploitation of this data. For Moore, one problem with the study of economic and social phenomena involved the interdependence of the variables. The problem was simply enough put:

> Social phenomena are interrelated, are mutually dependent, and the appropriate method of treating such a form of interdependence is the use of a system of simultaneous equations in which the equations are equal in number to the unknown quantities in the problem. (1911, 2)

In an effort to confront the problems that are inevitable in the creation of a "new" science, or a new and different approach to an old one, the pioneer must almost of necessity experiment with alternative modes of inquiry and expression. This often involves the invention of new techniques or the application of techniques borrowed from other disciplines that are taken as being similar in methodological approach. In the present instance, the allied fields of inquiry were those of the physical and natural sciences.

Moore held that the instruments invented for the purpose of data analysis in the physical and natural sciences, and taken for granted as

---

29. "For, a theory or hypothesis as to the association of given facts, in any department of knowledge, may be likened to an hypothesis as to the simplest form of curve that will pass as nearly as possible to given points. . . . The law of the facts and of the points is the supposition that satisfies best the accepted standard of simplicity and excellence of fit of the facts to the hypothesis" (Moore 1911, 20).

30. This "fit" had to satisfy Pearson's "test of excellence of fit."

ideally suited to those subjects, were in fact better suited to application in the social scientific realm. The mathematical tools of the natural sciences, generally termed the "calculus of mass phenomena," were more readily applicable to the type of statistical data collected for social purposes since the time of Petty and Graunt, King and Davenant. The quandary with which Moore had to deal in extending these methods to economics was not that the methods were inappropriate, but rather that social scientific endeavors lacked a means for their successful exploitation. So much effort had been devoted to the collection of statistics on social and economic phenomena; so little had been devoted to procedures for their use in economic investigations:

> The wealth of the statistical material relating to economic questions is itself a source of embarrassment. To utilize it for scientific purposes, it must be described in brief, summary formulæ, and these formulæ must be arranged upon a plan of increasing complexity so that it will be possible to pass from accurate descriptions of mass aggregates to the relations between the aggregates themselves. Now, concurrently with the development of economic and statistical theory and the increasing supply of statistical data, the mathematical instrument for rendering the statistical data available for scientific purposes has been perfected. (1911, 5)

5 Beyond Moore: Haberler, Tinbergen, and Business Cycle Research

5.1 *Haberler's* Prosperity and Depression

Moore's work was indeed important and held significant promise for further research. But it was incomplete and not entirely applicable to problems beyond the simple confines of its charter. To proceed further required a major change in emphasis and approach; in other words, a new rhetoric had to be formulated to analyze more pressing and intricate problems. This new rhetoric was to be realized very quickly thereafter.

Gottfried von Haberler's *Prosperity and Depression* (1937; 3d ed., 1946), a study performed under the auspices of the Economic Intelligence Service of the Secretariat of the League of Nations, was one of the earliest works to state a rationale for the study of business cycles. It was in attempting to test Haberler's "span" of theories that Jan Tinbergen undertook his pioneering statistical investigations of business cycles, *Statistical Testing of Business-Cycle Theories* (1939). It was also published under the auspices of the League of Nations.

Haberler's book presented essentially a survey of business-cycle theories.[31] As he stated in the Introduction, the purpose of the study was very strictly defined. "The present study confines itself to the task of analysing existing theories of the business cycle and deriving therefrom a synthetic account of the nature and possible causes of economic fluctuations" (Haberler 1946, 1). But Haberler immediately made an interesting admission, one which, more than anything else, made clear the confines within which the study was done. The purpose was not for this effort to be a stand-alone work, but rather to provide a platform upon which the next stage of the program could be constructed. This "next stage" was to involve "the application, as far as possible, of quantitative tests to the various causal hypotheses" (1946, 1). Thus the Systematic Analysis of part I of the study was not designed as a historical treatment of business-cycle hypotheses; it was rather designed

> to gather together various hypotheses of explanation, to test their logical consistency and their compatibility with one another and with accepted economic principles. It is intended to give a rounded picture of the possible explanations of economic fluctuations and it is hoped that, by theoretical reasoning, the number of these possibilities can be considerably reduced. (1946, 1)

Tinbergen's Statistical Testing of Business-Cycle Theories   5.2

Once the competing hypotheses had been gathered and their internal logic tested, there remained the task of testing the economic and especially the predictive value of the theories. This was the task of Tinbergen's *Statistical Testing of Business-Cycle Theories* (1939). We are here interested primarily in part I of the study, *A Method and Its Application to Investment Activity.* (Part II is titled *Business Cycles in the United States, 1919–1932,* also published in 1939.)

The stated purpose of part I was simply "to submit to statistical test some of the theories which have been put forward regarding the character and causes of cyclical fluctuation in business activity" (Tinbergen 1939, 11). The problem with undertaking such an exercise is that, in the manner in which Tinbergen proceeded, there had been precious few forerunners. Graunt, Petty, King, Davenant, and subsequently Pigou and Mitchell (to be discussed later) made tremendous advances in the study of statistical data on economic activity; Pigou and Mitchell specifically undertook studies on industrial fluctuations (the business cycle).[32] But these studies for the most part consisted of tabular presentations and

---

31. Originally, the study was divided into two parts, Part I: Systematic Analysis of the Theories of the Business Cycle, and Part II: Systematic Exposition Relating to the Nature and Causes of Business Cycles. A third part, Further Reflections on Recent Developments in Trade Cycle Theory, was added in the 1941 edition.

32. Oddly enough, Tinbergen did not mention any of these forerunners.

graphical "analyses" of series of data, attempting to determine coincident cycles and to "time" the points of inflection so as to identify the constituents of the cycle.

Tinbergen felt he had to proceed further; indeed one may say that he was so mandated by the sponsors of the study. He desired to apply to the data the formal techniques of mathematical statistical analysis. He understood that many of the theories of the business cycle then extant were incomplete or not readily amenable to statistical testing. For this reason he chose to confine his tests to "the relation between certain groups of economic phenomena" (1939, 11).

The method Tinbergen chose for his investigation he described as "econometric business cycle research," defined as "a synthesis of *statistical business cycle research* and *quantitative economic theory*" (1939, 11; emphasis in original). The former program of research was devoted to "the length of cycles, the degree of simple correlation between series and the relative amplitudes of their movements, the decomposition of series into trend, seasonal components, etc." (12). While allowing conclusions to be drawn from the data, this method disguised as much as it highlighted. Patterns and relations between series could be identified, but one may be moved too readily to divine cause–effect relations where none exist, or to overlook "causes" from a failure to specify adequately the constitution of the series. Tinbergen's statistical approach, in his own estimation, was designed specifically to overcome this problem: "what we want to discover is, not merely what causes are operative, but also *with what strength each of them operates*"; he wished "to find out the nature of the combined effect of causes working in opposite directions" (12; emphasis in original).

Because Tinbergen's approach suffered from problems of specification and completeness—as stated above, cause–effect relations are not forthcoming from empirical data—the latter program of quantitative economic theory became fundamental. Statistical testing demands a mathematical, quantitative model of the economy—not simply a formal set of relations, but a model structured parametrically to allow statistical application. More importantly, statistical testing of business cycles requires a *dynamic* mathematical model to allow fluctuation to become manifest. By *dynamic* Tinbergen meant something specific, a theory "which deals with the short-term reactions of one variate upon others, but without neglecting the lapse of time between cause and effect" (1939, 13). This form of modeling he termed "sequence analysis," wherein "[t]he equations in which it [the model] is expressed thus relate to non-simultaneous events . . ." (13).[33]

Together, the statistical research and quantitative theorizing came

33. The approach of "sequence analysis" most probably owes its beginnings to Erik Lindahl. He employed the concept in his 1929 "Prisbildningsproblements uppläggning fran kapitalteoretisk synpunkt."

together to form the basis of the new program of economic analysis, namely, econometric research.

The Need for an Organized Center: 6
The Founding of the Econometric Society

The Econometric Society was founded in 1930 as an association dedicated to research in mathematical and quantitative economics. The desire for such a society began in about 1912 (as suggested by Carl Christ [1952]), when Irving Fisher proposed the creation of an independent international organization, distinct from the more encompassing associations of the time—including but not limited to the American Economic Association, the American Association for the Advancement of Science, the American Statistical Association, as well as the British Association for the Advancement of Science, the Royal Statistical Society, and the Royal Society. Despite his efforts, Fisher could only interest a small group of statistically and mathematically minded economists (and economically minded statisticians) that such a new forum was important and necessary.

It took another sixteen years before the climate would be right for such an organization to flower. In 1928, Fisher, Ragnar Frisch, and Charles F. Roos (a mathematician who had served as secretary of Section K—economics, sociology, and statistics—of the American Association for the Advancement of Science) met to discuss the possibility of establishing the type of society Fisher had earlier envisioned.[34]

With the membership roster complete, the Econometric Society held its first meeting in Cleveland, Ohio, on December 29, 1930—where also were held the joint meetings of the American Economic Association, the American Statistical Association, and the American Association for the Advancement of Science (Section K). At this first meeting, chaired by Joseph Schumpeter, Frisch was named president of the new society.

---

34. This was no easy matter. As Carl Christ recounted the meeting:

> Fisher, mindful of the outcome of his earlier attempt, was pessimistic. At length he said that if Frisch and Roos could name one hundred people in the world who would join a society established for the encouragement of econometric work and the exchange of econometric papers, he would become an enthusiastic partner in organizing such a society. They were very happy with this response, thinking that it would be a simple matter to list a hundred interested people. At first, the list virtually wrote itself, but then the going got harder, and after three days they had to give up with about seventy likely prospects. Fisher looked over their list and suggested about a dozen additional names. He was quite surprised that they had found so many, and he agreed that eighty justified going ahead. The three men drafted a letter of invitation to membership in the proposed society together with a request for the names of others who might be interested. The response to the invitation was excellent and nearly eighty more names were suggested. (Christ 1952, 5–6)

In the first issue of the Society's journal, *Econometrica,* published in January 1933, Frisch[35] (editor of the journal) stated the purpose of the Society, as set forth in its Constitution.

The Econometric Society is an international society for the advancement of economic theory in its relation to statistics and mathematics. The Society shall operate as a completely disinterested, scientific organization without political, social, financial, or nationalistic bias. Its main object shall be to promote studies that aim at a unification of the theoretical-quantitative and the empirical-quantitative approach to economic problems and that are penetrated by constructive and rigorous thinking similar to that which has come to dominate in the natural sciences. Any activity which promises ultimately to further such unification of theoretical and factual studies in economics shall be within the sphere of interest of the Society. (Frisch 1933, 1)

The editors of the journal and the members of the Society were keenly aware of the situation respecting quantitative economic analysis as it had existed prior to the formation of the Society. As we have shown, statistics collection had proceeded from the time of Petty and Graunt with but scant attention paid to the *usefulness* of the numbers; taxation and considerations of political and economic power were important reasons in and of themselves to undertake the task, but the data collected were often too extensive to serve simply these limited purposes, the collection having seemingly assumed a life of its own.

Likewise, the introduction of mathematics into the collection of rhetorical devices available to the economist, coincident with the adoption of a deductive method, served to dichotomize the discipline into quantitative and qualitative branches, each of which granted to itself the mantle of true scientific social science. Each group thought the other somehow "unscientific" and lacking in rigor because it had disavowed an approach to analysis. Deductivists could not be scientific because they tended to eschew the numerical data upon which scientific theories depend. The historical economists could not be scientific because they proceeded without a firm theoretical foundation, instead allowing statistical evidence to establish their conclusions. The Econometric Society ended the charade. The founders recognized explicitly, or rather stated as a matter of course, that economics cannot be understood as "either/or," but must be treated as "this and that." A priori theory and the use of statistical evidence did not conflict, but actually served to strengthen one another. Shades of Newmarch and Jevons appear in the statement of the territory to be covered by this "new" subdiscipline:

---

35. Among the others listed as members of the Advisory Editorial Board in that first issue were A. L. Bowley, Irving Fisher, Harold Hotelling, John Maynard Keynes, Wesley Clair Mitchell, Charles Rist, Henry Schultz, and Joseph Schumpeter.

Experience has shown that each of these three view-points, that of statistics, economic theory, and mathematics, is a necessary, but not by itself a sufficient, condition for a real understanding of the quantitative relations in modern economic life. It is the *unification* of all three that is powerful. And it is this unification that constitutes econometrics. (Frisch 1933, 2; emphasis in original)

Theory should not lead observation, nor observation determine theory.[36]

The historical background to the development of econometrics and statistical economics was covered by Schumpeter in the lead article in the inaugural issue of *Econometrica,* entitled "The Common Sense of Econometrics." This essay was dedicated primarily to answering the query, How did we get to where we are? Schumpeter gave ample credit to the early pioneers of quantitative research and offered an assessment of their inability to achieve their objectives. Petty, King, sixteenth-century Italian writers, even John Stuart Mill's *Principles,* were all "[e]ssentially quantitative analysis, but crippled by the lack both of appropriate technique and of adequate statistical material" (Schumpeter 1933, 7).

What eventually led to the fulfillment of the early promise was the pioneering work of the system-building "geniuses" of economics: Cournot, Jevons, Thünen, Walras, and Marshall.[37] All of these giants engaged in an econometric rhetoric, developing their theories in an econometric phraseology, whether they were aware of the fact or not (and clearly Schumpeter believed they were not).

This is the historical element of Schumpeter's essay. But there was a more important feature that needs to be considered, one that goes to the very meaning of the Society itself. At the outset of his article, Schumpeter proclaimed the Society, and by extension the entire new field of econometrics, to be divorced from any "credo—scientific or otherwise," with but two major exceptions: "economics is a science," and "this science has one very important quantitative aspect" (1933, 5). This of course begs the question, What is a science? a question Schumpeter did not attempt to answer.

Despite the stance that economics is a science, Schumpeter understood the important contributions made to the field of economics by *qualitative* theorists, presumably those not engaged in the *scientific* pursuit of economic truth. The desire of the Econometric Society and those expressing kinship with their aims and methods was not to eclipse the

---

36. Consider Frisch's description of theory: "Theory, in formulating its abstract quantitative notions, must be inspired to a larger extent by the technique of observation. And fresh statistical and other factual studies must be the healthy element of disturbance that constantly threatens and disquiets the theorist and prevents him from coming to rest on some inherited, obsolete set of assumptions" (Frisch 1933, 2).

37. Schumpeter also mentioned the "econometric claims" in the works of Auspitz and Lieben, Wicksell, Edgeworth, and Pareto. He even paid homage to two "living" pioneers, Fisher and Moore.

prevailing "schools of thought," but, on the contrary, to assist them where possible to live in mutual harmony.

> Much of what we want to know about economic phenomena can be discovered and stated without any technical, let alone mathematical, refinements upon ordinary modes of thought, and without elaborate treatment of statistical figures. Nothing is farther from our minds than any acrimonious belief in the exclusive excellence of mathematical methods, or any wish to belittle the work of historians, ethnologists, sociologists, and so on. We do not want to fight anyone, or, beyond dilettantism, anything. We want to *serve* as best we can. (1933, 5)

7 What Has Been Wrought?

As we have seen in the preceding chapters, the physiocrats, mercantilists, and political arithmeticians devised theoretical, albeit empirically based, frameworks that allowed for the use of statistical data in economic applications, specifically economic planning and national accounting. The principal purposes of this significant politicoeconomic tool were to facilitate taxation and champion the augmentation of national power. Their combined legacy is the creation and employment of the framework that is taken here as the foundation of what would come to be known as "macroeconomics"—or the study of the economy as a unified system. It was this progression in the method of economic analysis that led to political economy becoming "scientific," at least insofar as it pertains to analytical method. These new tools demanded nothing less than a change in the rhetoric by which the political and social elites in the epoch of Mercantilism and Physiocracy could fashion the conversation, thereby allowing them to effect policies anchored on a solid position.

As Pribram (1983) suggested, the set of doctrines known as Mercantilism was based on the empirical scientific (or prescientific) philosophical method advanced by Francis Bacon; Physiocracy as a comprehensive economic program was by contrast predicated on Cartesian rationalism. These two philosophical approaches, and the economic views they engendered and helped support, could not have been more different, despite the fact that the outcomes the policies were designed to achieve were so similar. The first of the economic schools, the mercantilist, became, by virtue of its *empirical* basis, a policy-oriented set of doctrines aimed at the objective of national power enhancement; the second, the physiocratic, began, by virtue of its rationalist basis, with a fundamental axiom—that land was the basis of all wealth creation—and from this were *deduced* policies aimed at national power enhancement.

Thus materialized within the nascent "science" of political economy two distinct approaches to method, the statistical and the mathematical. Insofar as the approaches led to a reconsideration of the mode of argumentation—the rhetoric of analysis—they may be deemed "advancements" in the technique of persuasion. They attain importance because these "advancements" followed the emergence of what may be termed the first great "debate" in economics: the Hobbes–Locke contest between communitarianism and individualism, an event that shaped the rhetoric of the early preclassical schools of economic discourse.

The importance of this contest cannot be overestimated. In many regards, the debate surrounding it has continued unabated even to this very day and so still commands our attention. It forces us to confront the important underlying (but still easily neglected) rationale of our economic, social, and political beliefs. We are compelled by virtue of our opinions on this critical question to judge propositions, others' as well as our own, and to lend or withhold support on this basis.

While the Hobbes–Locke question retained its significance in guiding attitudes in political economy, additional concerns were also raised, which, by about the mid–nineteenth century, began to gain prominence. Specifically, we can note a concern with the twin problems of scarcity and uncertainty, problems that we earlier maintained as being the *true* consequence of the fall from grace. While there had of course been recognition of the importance of these factors—especially scarcity and to a lesser extent uncertainty—the ultimate realization of these obstacles as centrally important led to a restructuring of political economy and the general study of society and social relationships. This is evident in the shift from a connection with ethics, the law, and moral philosophy, and toward an alliance with the advocates of a more materialist disposition, those who desired to promote political economy as a more "scientific" endeavor. Here the previously accepted fundamental question did not necessarily change; it simply became submerged beneath a new concern, a concern with questions of far more (apparent) relevance.

While the bases of this change in emphasis within early political economy were firmly established as early as the mid–eighteenth century—in the work of Cantillon, for instance—and are easily identifiable in the works of the Greek contributors and the Scholastics as well, it was not until the emergence of what has become popularly accepted as the classical school, especially within the tradition of the utilitarians and their radical offshoot, the utopian socialists, that political economy could be redirected to incorporate concepts of scarcity and uncertainty as basic. But the process of incorporation was *evolutionary,* not *revolutionary;* one can indeed view, from a distance to be sure, the change that was taking place at the time, and note the difficulty of attaching to the transition a precise date of occurrence. What we can see is that, for the most part, the change occurred within the camp known in general terms as the utilitarians.

To demonstrate better this contention, it is necessary to divide Utilitarianism into two distinct groups. The first grouping of utilitarians may be termed the "ethical utilitarians" or "Natural-Law utilitarians," thus giving them a solid connection to the earlier writers of the preclassical tradition who employed in their studies the rhetoric of the earlier moral philosophers, particularly the Scholastics. This version of utilitarian doctrine continued in the empirical tradition of the political arithmeticians, while including rhetorical connections with the physiocrats, including positions on free trade and much of book V of Smith's *Wealth of Nations*. Only later does the break with this moralistic tradition become evident, as the rhetoric changed to encompass a different, more mechanistic, jargon. By then the rational method can be seen to have emerged triumphant over the empirical, and political economy appears well on its way to becoming scientifically grounded economics. From this break was born Scientific Utilitarianism, with its emphasis on formalism and measurement. Still, the change was evolutionary, albeit perhaps a punctuated evolution, and not a radical departure from the past. In addition, there is within both of these traditions a strong enough link to the past, especially to the moral philosophy tradition, to classify the writers in both camps as "Classical."

British Classical Political Economy
Individualism, Utilitarianism, and Property Rights

In every one of us there are two ruling and directing principles, whose guidance we follow wherever they may lead; the one being an innate desire of pleasure; the other, an acquired judgment which aspires after excellence.   SOCRATES

A man hath no better thing under the sun, than to eat, and to drink, and be merry.   ECCLESIASTES 8:15

The great end of all human industry is the attainment of happiness. For this were arts invented, sciences cultivated, laws ordained, and societies modelled, by the most profound wisdom of patriots and legislators. Even the lonely savage, who lies exposed to the inclemency of the elements and the fury of wild beasts, forgets not, for a moment, this grand object of his being.
DAVID HUME, *ESSAYS, MORAL, POLITICAL, AND LITERARY* (1742)

Introduction   1

The Legacy of Hobbes and Locke   1.1

One of the themes of chapter 2 was that Hobbes not only challenged the most appropriate method of investigation for moral and ethical questions, but also questioned the very nature of some of the more commonly held Christian perceptions of life. The proposed answers to the Hobbes challenge, particularly those emanating from the ecclesiastical advocates, while quickly forthcoming, had an appeal mainly to the faithful, that is, to those who already accepted traditional Christian doctrine. What the ecclesiastics found most offensive in Hobbes was essentially his materialism— his assertion that the essence of good seemed to be, unfortunately to be sure from the Christian standpoint, equivalent to success.

True, High Churchmen (those closest to the Roman Catholic ritual and hierarchical organization) found Hobbes difficult to accept, especially his individualism in the elaboration of the initial compact, and the secular nature of the Leviathan. Still, the Low Churchmen (particularly those closest to the Protestant convictions of Calvin and Knox) found much of Hobbes acceptable, the reason being that Hobbes denied the validity of the "Universal Church," which the Papacy had become. Hobbes in *Leviathan* replaced the Universal Church with an ecclesiastical authority dependent for its legitimacy upon the will of the secular, civil government. Certainly, the widespread popularity among lay parishioners of Locke's views, built on the edifice of Hobbes, seems confirmation of the individualistic emphasis in the initial societal organization, one which Hobbes employed only as a means to the legitimation of the sovereign, but which Locke took as central to a view of societal relationships and governmental organization.

The ultimate acceptance within the British intellectual tradition of the position of Locke, and the subsequent repudiation of the position of Hobbes, can be understood in the manner of the treatment by each of the structure of society as it passes from the base state. Locke's individualism in both ethics and property rights served to make his presentation more palatable to those convinced of the essential role of the individual citizen in providing legitimacy to any governmental form. The apologia for the continuation of the nonrepresentative monarchy presented by Hobbes (established at the expense of the ecclesiastical authorities) did not have the same appeal. The preeminence of Locke's views, while clearly evident in much of British political theory in the eighteenth century, became truly "triumphant" as the espoused rationale behind the American Revolution. Locke was the dominant force in the development of the American constitutional system, having been read and studied by the framers of the Declaration of Independence and the U.S. Constitution. What was seen to replace the old governmental system as perceived and admired by Hobbes, one predicated on a strong, authoritarian sovereign, was, if not Lockean, at least within the confines of a Lockean structure. It encompassed not only the advent of modern republicanism, but included as well a repudiation of the right of the ecclesiastical authorities to any form of political representation or direct influence in the secular affairs of the state.[1] Yet in the absence of ecclesiastical power, there could develop no counterweight to secular materialism—something which no small number of non-Americans found (and still seem to find) most offensive about the American culture.

Whatever else, the Lockean influence that emerged stressed more significantly some form of individualism—albeit an individualism somewhat different from the concept as we know it today. For Locke (and for many others still), the "individual" is really the household, not the single human actor. It is for this reason that Locke cannot be viewed as the father of the utilitarian tradition. In addition, one finds in Locke no

---

1. The obverse side of the Great Seal of the United States contains not only a Masonic symbol (anti–Roman Catholic hierarchy, to say the very least), but also the original motto of the American republic, "Novus Ordo Seclorum" (A New Secular Order). In addition, the all-seeing eye hovering over a pyramid, plus the phrase, *Annuit cæptus* ("He Has Freed Us"), is a simile, comparing George III to the Pharaoh.

elaboration of a utilitarian ethic. For the genesis of this doctrine, we must indeed look elsewhere.[2]

Another, perhaps unintended, consequence of the Hobbes–Locke contest was in the fostering of a political-economic rhetoric based on moral, ethical, and legal discourse; rationalizations for proposals could be found given a correct interpretation of the jurisprudential traditions of a people. It is thus within the context of this debate that we see the development of notions of property, ownership, use, control, utility, and a host of other concepts that we today seem to take for granted but which have not always been central to the economic and political debate. It is also in this context that we see the basis for the emergence of British classical political economy, in the ethical program that became known as Utilitarianism.

Utilitarianism Defined   1.2

Following the Hobbes–Locke debate on the nature of society, there developed a system of ethics which eventually was to be termed *Utilitarianism*. Utilitarianism may be defined in the manner of John Stuart Mill, "as a name for one single opinion, not a set of opinions—to denote the recognition of utility as the standard, not any particular way of applying it . . ." (J. S. Mill 1861, 394n.). Schumpeter proclaimed it "nothing but another natural-law system," characterizing it as "a philosophy of life," "a normative system with a strong legal slant," and "a comprehensive system of social science embodying a uniform method of analysis" (Schumpeter 1954, 132–33).[3] It differed from the ethical doctrine of the Scholastics only to the extent

> that the doctors confined the utilitarian point of view to purely utilitarian activity where it is (nearly—not even there wholly) adequate, whereas the utilitarians reduced the whole world of human values to the same schema, ruling out, as contrary to reason, all that really matters to man. (Schumpeter 1954, 133)

Elie Halévy—whose 1928 classic *The Growth of Philosophic Radicalism* is perhaps the most comprehensive work on the subject—maintained that the "moral arithmeticians" of the Utilitarian School did not so much succeed at establishing a moral theory as they did "at founding a science of law, at providing a mathematical basis for the theory of legal punishment" (Halévy 1928, xvii). Smith, Malthus, and Ricardo were to Halévy important parts of the tradition. More importantly, since it was at once a system predicated on moral/legal principles

---

2. This point was ably made by Elie Halévy (1928, 7).

3. Schumpeter later in the same work characterized Utilitarianism thus: "No philosophy at all in the technical sense, unsurpassably shallow as a 'philosophy of life,' it fitted to perfection the streak of materialistic (antimetaphysical) rationalism that may be associated with liberalism and the business mind" (Schumpeter 1954, 407–8).

and a system of social-scientific analysis, it could (and did) continue to be accepted as an analytical device even after its political and philosophical underpinnings were rejected. This is what made Utilitarianism so compelling and has led to its signal place in the history of philosophical and economic thought.

To understand Utilitarianism as a philosophical movement, one must first understand the importance of the term *utility*. Utility (as per David Lyons 1965) is a *teleological* notion, in that the judgment of the rightness of an action is entirely dependent on the *consequences* of that action. This is in stark contrast to a *deontological* theory, which argues that the criterion of rightness applies to the acts themselves. (To the extent that actions are identified with consequences, this form of utilitarianism is often referred to as *act-utilitarianism,* to distinguish it from *rule-utilitarianism,* a hybrid wherein acts are deemed right only to the extent they conform to rules that themselves can be supported on utilitarian grounds. Here only the rule requires justification, not the acts themselves [Lyons 1965, vii].)

The philosopher Ernest Albee, in his 1902 *History of English Utilitarianism,* held that Richard Cumberland, Bishop of Peterborough, in his 1672 *De legibus naturae,* presented the first statement of English Utilitarianism, in the context of a refutation of the views of Hobbes. Hobbes had maintained that the interminable struggle of man against man, brought about as a result of his egoistic nature, had led, out of a desire for survival, to the institution of a social arrangement whereby the individuals in the "society" agreed to be subjected to the rule of a single sovereign. Cumberland held this view to be erroneous, arguing instead that the society could be more readily understood as an organism, not a mere collection of atomistic individuals intent on the pursuit of their own base self-interests. The organic social whole is composed of sympathetic and, indeed, altruistic, individual members. While for Hobbes, society was necessary but artificial, for Cumberland society was the most natural of arrangements. Further, as the interests of the individual and the society appear to coincide, the happiness of the one is manifest in the promotion of the happiness of the other.

> No one does truly observe the law unless he sincerely propose the same end with the legislator. But, if he directly and constantly aim at this end, it is no diminution to the sincerity of his obedience that, at the instigation of his own happiness, he first perceived that his sovereign commanded him to respect a higher end. (Cumberland, quoted in Albee 1902, 26)

As Cumberland proposed what would eventually become the utilitarian credo—the promotion of the greatest happiness of the greatest number as a means to the common good—the "happiness" to be maximized is the happiness or welfare of the *society*, not that of each *individual member* of that society:

> I proceed more fully to explain the common, which also I call the public good. By these words I understand the aggregate or sum of all those good things which either we can contribute towards, or are necessary to, the *happiness* of all rational beings, considered as collected into one body, each in his proper order. (30; emphasis in original)

Beyond the work of Cumberland, there were others concerned with the basis of social welfare. Before we review this work, we should perhaps clarify an important point. Utilitarianism is not simply an ethical doctrine; in fact, within the British utilitarian tradition specifically, early on there developed a concern with problems beyond those treated as part of traditional ethics. Indeed, Albee noted the distinction between Utilitarianism as an ethical doctrine and the later practical theory predicated on the more "scientific" notion of "utility." Albee commented thus on the problem one encounters when approaching the topic:

> When one speaks of English Utilitarianism . . . it is not wholly evident, without explanation, whether one mainly refers to a very important practical movement of English thought, extending through the closing years of the eighteenth century and about the first half of the nineteenth century, or to a very familiar, to us probably the most familiar, type of abstract ethical theory. (Albee 1902, xi)

Albee maintained that those commonly held to have been the leaders of the early utilitarian movement—principally Bentham and James Mill—were concerned solely with the *practical* side of the theory and not with the theory itself as a part of ethics, this latter being what Henry Sidgwick termed *Universalistic Hedonism*. In the ethical tradition of Utilitarianism, we are very much involved with the Hobbes question of the nature of man and the role of the state, and with the role of the community versus the importance of the individual. On the practical side, such topics are still of great importance, but concerns with the promotion of the greatest pleasure (happiness) as a social objective—one which can be measured and seen as an index of social welfare—seem to take on an even greater significance. It is in the promotion of Utilitarianism as an ethical theory that Hume and Smith and Mandeville must be given credit for having advanced ideas that are evident in the understandings of the later British utilitarians, especially in providing the moral base of the doctrine. Francis Hutcheson surely ranks as one of the originators of this tradition, and his important work will be touched on briefly later. There are those who have argued that the roots of Utilitarianism may be traced also to the writings of Hobbes and Claude Adrien Helvétius

(1715–71),[4] generally, and Cesare Beccaria (1738–94),[5] specifically; in fact, the fundamental axiom of Utilitarianism—that the proper measure of right and wrong is the greatest happiness of the greatest number—is found in both Beccaria and Joseph Priestly (1733–1804).[6] Joseph Schumpeter (1954), and even the philosopher Bertrand Russell (1945), noted the debt owed to Helvétius by the practical philosophers of the utilitarian school, the so-called Philosophic Radicals.

To the extent that the writers in practical Utilitarianism extended the focus of their arguments from ethics to a concern with consequentialism as it affects the society as a whole, there developed from this reorientation the classical British political economy we know and understand today. To a definition of this economic movement we now turn.

1.3 Classical Political Economy Defined

While it is customary to accept the view that there was a single identifiable entity known as the Classical School of Political Economy, a look at the literature reveals this generalization to be more apparent than real. The "classical" British economic literature is just as diffuse and difficult to catalog and categorize as was the mercantilist. As with the mercantilist "school," we can identify within the "classical tradition" not only differences in approach, but also distinct conflicts concerning the expression of the characteristic elements that serve to define the school; this is probably inevitable, given that the classical tradition was neither as monolithic as the physiocratic, nor as idiosyncratic as the mercantilist. It is, however,

---

4. Helvétius's important work is De l'Esprit. Halévy (1928, 18) noted that Helvétius's influence was great in Europe, and especially in England, as he held himself to be a disciple of Hume.

5. Schumpeter (1954) referred to Beccaria as "the Italian A. Smith" (179n.).

6. In Beccaria's 1764 On Crimes and Punishments, we see the following: "Sometimes laws arise from a fortuitous and transient necessity, but they have never been dictated by an impartial observer of human nature who can grasp the actions of a multitude of men and consider them from this point of view: the greatest happiness shared among the greatest number. Happy are those very few nations that have not waited for the slow movement of happenstance and human vicissitudes to make excessive evil give way to progress toward goodness but that have accelerated the intermediate stages with good laws!" (Beccaria 1764, 3; emphasis in original).

In Priestley's 1768 An Essay on the First Principles of Government; and on the Nature of Political, Civil, and Religious Liberty, we have the following, obviously a comment on Hobbes: "It must necessarily be understood, therefore, whether it be expressed or not, that all people live in society for their mutual advantage; so that the good and happiness of the members, that is the majority of the members of any state, is the great standard by which every thing relating to that state must finally be determined. And though it may be supposed, that a body of people may be bound by a voluntary resignation of all their interests (which they have been so infatuated as to make) to a single person, or to a few, it can never be supposed that the resignation is obligatory to their posterity; because it is manifestly contrary to the good of the whole that it should be so" (Priestley 1768, 17; emphasis in original).

possible despite the lack of a coherent, definable, delineable tradition, to identify a cluster of thinking as Classical Economics. As any such identification will be somewhat subjective, the reader must accept that this is but one of many possible groupings, but the one which serves the present purposes rather well.

There have been many attempts at the identification of a Classical School of Economic Thought. Karl Marx (1890) argued that the school commenced with the work of Petty and terminated with the work of Ricardo, while making a grand sweep through the work of French economists from Boisguillebert to Sismondi. James Bonar (1910) held that it comprised the works of Smith and his "successors," namely, Malthus, James Mill, Ricardo, McCulloch, and Senior. John Maynard Keynes (1936a) felt that it had started with Ricardo and ended with Arthur Cecil Pigou, encompassing writers who had failed to abandon Say's Law. Lujo Brentano (1888) compared Classical Political Economy to classical sculpture, noting that it was the general abstractions that were important, not the peculiarities of any individual statement of principles; thus Classical Political Economy is defined with respect to those economists who attempted to draw conclusions from the abstracted "economic man."[7] Schumpeter (1954) defined the period as spanning the years 1798 through 1871, beginning with Thomas Robert Malthus and ending with William Stanley Jevons. For Mitchell (1967, 1969) it seems to have centered around Ricardo and Malthus. Thomas Sowell noted that in economics, the term *classical* "usually implies something that has established an authoritative tradition that serves as a point of departure for later developments in the same field" (Sowell 1974, 6), and thus the classical economists represented "a certain small core shading off into a larger penumbra . . ." (7); the classical period thus defined extends from Smith to the beginning of the marginal revolution of 1871.[8] Denis O'Brien (1975) handled it from a sociological standpoint. On this view, the heyday of Classical Economics extended from 1800 to 1850. While he considered that its origins could be traced to about 1750—Smith's lectures at Edinburgh began in 1748, and Hume's *Essays* were published in 1752—the importance of the School did not become clear until 1800, with the eclipse of the physiocratic movement. As to its eventual decline, O'Brien attributed this to the work of Jevons, among others, who by 1870 had overrun the barricades with the machinery of marginalism.[9] Finally,

---

7. This was noted by Bonar (1910, 303).

8. Included would be Smith, Ricardo, James and John Stuart Mill, McCulloch, Say, Malthus, West, Torrens, Senior, and Marx.

9. O'Brien's "classical" political economy has three groups: Smith and Ricardo; Malthus, Say, James Mill, John Stuart Mill, McCulloch, Senior, Torrens, Tooke, Cairnes, and Fawcett; Henry Drummond, Thomas Joplin, George Norman, Samuel Loyd, Lord Overstone, Henry Thornton, William Blake, Francis Horner, John Wheatley, Newmarch, Richard Page, Thomas De Quincey, Samuel Bailey, Mountifort Longfield, Edward West,

Mark Blaug (1987) noted that the label *classical* typically applies to the development of economic thought from 1750 to 1870, the period "in which a group of predominantly British economists used Adam Smith's *Wealth of Nations* as a springboard for analysing the production, distribution and exchange of goods and services in a capitalist economy" (Blaug 1987, 434).[10]

Here we employ a narrower definition than that offered by Schumpeter, but a broader one than that offered by Mitchell, one which stresses the effort to distinguish economic analysis from its moral and philosophical roots. Thus for the present purposes, the Classical School—the *British* Classical School—is perceived as quite doctrinal (although the doctrine is not always consistent among those considered classical political economists); it begins by taking up the central questions of the place of the property right and the status of the individual in society—concerns, that is, from the tradition of ethical Utilitarianism. The Classical School considered that once these relationships were established, accepted, and adhered to by the participants in the system, the remainder of the pieces would fall into place. It is thus that, in conjunction with the definition and demarcation of the property right and the position of the individual vis-à-vis the community interest, the defining characteristic of the Classical school is a belief in the system as predicated on a Natural Law foundation.

While we could justify beginning the discussion of the British Classical school with Smith, we prefer to define it with respect to the philosophical principles underlying the Hobbes–Locke debate. Important in this regard are the pre-Smithian interpretations of man in society given by the philosophers Hume and Hutcheson.[11] (We have already covered the major contributions in this context of Hobbes, Locke, Mandeville, and others, who also could easily have been included.) Smith himself, we have previously noted, made a significant contribution to the debate centering around the problem set forth by Hobbes and is included here again as an important figure in the rise of ethical Utilitarianism.

The focus of Utilitarianism as a shaper and organizer of classical British economic thought is thus a critical element in our interpretation. In general, we find in the British case that empiricism in a more refined form was combined with elements of rationalism to provide a method-

---

James Maitland, and John Barton. The significance of the writers in the last group "is that they were men of considerable intellectual ability, sometimes highly influential over a narrow field of thought and policy, but men who did not attempt to exercise a broad general influence over large areas of economics and did not, with one or two exceptions, attempt comprehensive treatises, unlike virtually every writer in Group II except Tooke" (O'Brien 1975, 5).

10. Although *The Wealth of Nations* did not appear until 1776!

11. On the importance of Hutcheson and Hume as predecessors of Smith, see especially W. L. Taylor (1965).

ological foundation for economics. This is more true of the later form of scientific Utilitarianism than of the ethical variant, for in the scientific form utility was given a central place in analysis. While it may be true that Smith and those before him had a grasp of the concept of utility as an abstract quality, it is equally evident that, in framing their dialogues in a political, ethical, moral, legal, and social nomenclature, they reserved no expressions in their lexicons for describing the justification behind the value process. As George J. Stigler observed in his famous articles on the development of utility theory (1950), while Smith, for example, may have *identified* and *proposed a solution to* the water–diamond paradox, he maintained no technical apparatus actually to *do* anything with it beyond the exposition; while he could argue that value in use and value in exchange were two entirely different and distinct concepts, his rhetoric allowed no more than the offering of a "moral judgment" since it could provide "no basis . . . on which he could compare such heterogeneous quantities" (Stigler 1950, 308). While this led Stigler to pronounce that "Smith's statement deserves neither criticism nor quotation" (308), this may be too uncharitable a conclusion. Still, it is apparent that Smith's *language* (in the sense of the form of rhetoric he employed to persuade his audience) prevented him from "seeing" certain subtleties that his theory clearly implied. Smith's rhetoric was more conducive to the descriptive than to the analytical.

Classical Political Economy is so characterized because it succeeded eventually in *creating* a language conducive to an analytical discussion. The classical economists, while adhering to a moral and ethical and legal rhetoric, nevertheless found a central place for an analytical concept that grounded their system, that being utility. This single notion made classical political economy more than simply a revision or reinterpretation of preceding doctrines, for example, Physiocracy with a manufacturing base. The concept of utility allowed Classical Political Economy to serve as a bridge between moral philosophy and mathematical analytics.

We are thus led to contemplate two great watersheds in the development of British Classical Political Economy. The first of these is the passage from an ethical to a scientific rhetoric, beginning in earnest with the work of Jeremy Bentham and continuing through the ethical utilitarian tradition, even to the inclusion of Ricardo. Thus by this period the moral philosophy of Hume, Hutcheson, and Smith began to be recast in a more scientific and less philosophical light. While one might reasonably argue that Bentham and others of his time were not in fact economists but rather moral philosophers, writing in the physiocratic mold, the problems on which they wrote and the terminology they employed are indeed central to much that later was accepted as the corpus of scientific economic thought. To quote Stigler again, "Jeremy Bentham brought the principle of utility (to be understood much more broadly than is customary in economics) to the forefront of discussion in

England at the beginning of the nineteenth century" (1950, 307–8). Even today, the problems about which economists write and argue are based, with perhaps little or no realization of the fact, on the early writings of these moral philosophers.

But this "early" classical school, still embracing the doctrines of the early moral philosophers, did much more than simply realize the importance of the concept of utility in a theory of value. It also provided the foundation for the second watershed, this being the scientific Utilitarianism of Jevons, Edgeworth, Marshall, and Wicksteed.

Yet a definition of classical British political economy must include much more than this. It must account for alternative explanations of events, framed in a clearly identifiable classical economic rhetorical form. It must, in other words, include, for reasons of completeness and topical agreement, the works of antagonists to classical political economy such as Karl Marx and Robert Owen, and even touch on the lesser known but nonetheless very important work of Thomas Hodgskin. While these writers are in virtually complete disagreement with any of the others of the utilitarian (ethical or scientific) tradition, and have major areas of disagreement among themselves, they are united in handling the question of the place of the institution of property and the question of the role of the individual in a society. Although their conclusions, and even their approaches, differ radically from the others, and at times from one another, the fact that they tackled many of the same problems at about the same time, and even recognized each other's contributions, seems reason enough to expand the traditional definition of Classical Political Economy to include their moral philosophies. Thus the "early" classical school will be said here to encompass the works of Hume, Hutcheson, Bentham, Smith, Ricardo, James Mill, John Ramsey McCulloch, Malthus, John Stuart Mill, Owen, Hodgskin, and Marx.[12]

The "early" classical period is important also because it served as a precursor of the next three definable "schools" or factional groupings of economics, each of which emerged at about the same time. These are (1) the "later" classical, or "scientific utilitarian" orientation; (2) the Austrian school; and (3) the Lausanne school of general equilibrium. With the reorientation from a moral to a scientific discipline came a consequent change in the focus of economics, that is, the questions that were of interest to economists. It is this change in the basic questions that has altered economics, shaping it to the form we know today. Specifically, the interest changed from Natural Law and the centrality of the property right to a reliance on something intangible called "utility" as the basis of an analytic science.

---

12. Walt W. Rostow (1990) proclaimed the classical school to have encompassed the works of Hume and Marx.

The Focus of This Chapter 1.4

This chapter then focuses on the competing views of human nature and the institutional structures for the promotion of social welfare compatible with these views. The disputes arising during this period mirrored those we treated earlier, namely, individualism versus communitarianism, and Natural Law principles versus positivist propositions. In the present context, the specific arguments center around Free Will versus instructed morality, and private property versus communal ownership. The principal players in this drama are a rather odd lot, with, at first glance, very little in common. As we will show, the links among these thinkers are more solid than may be evident from a first view.

Hutcheson, Hume, and Smith: Moral Economy 2

Hutcheson as the Father of the Utilitarian Principle 2.1

While pride of place in histories of economic thought on the question of the modern ethical basis of economics is usually reserved for the likes of Smith and even Mandeville, there is much to recommend at least a part of the credit be given to Francis Hutcheson (1694–1746),[13] teacher and predecessor of Smith in the Glasgow Chair of Moral Philosophy, who surely ranks as one of the originators of this tradition. In his 1725 *An Inquiry into the Original of Our Ideas of Beauty and Virtue*, he laid out what may be the first attempt at a "mathematical" theory of morality.

Hutcheson's expressed purpose in the *Inquiry* was to defend the position of the first Earl of Shaftesbury[14] against the position of Mandeville.[15] The "second treatise" of this work—*An Inquiry Concerning the Original of Our Ideas of Virtue or Moral Good*—is of concern for us here, as it was in this part of the essay that Hutcheson identified the "moral sense," through which we perceive virtue and vice. This sense allows us to acknowledge a "moral good" as distinct from a "natural good," the difference being that the former does not demand a tangible

---

13. Hutcheson was the son of an Irish Presbyterian minister. From 1710 to 1716 he studied at the University of Glasgow. He founded a private academy in 1719 in Dublin, the same year he was licensed a preacher by the Irish Presbyterians in Ulster. His opinions on religion placed his position in the church in jeopardy, and eventually he returned to Glasgow (1729) where he remained.

14. See the discussion in chapter 2.

15. The full title of the essay is: *An Inquiry into the Original of Our Ideas of Beauty and Virtue; In Two Treatises. In Which the Principles of the Late Earl of Shaftesbury are Explain'd and Defended, Against the Author of the Fable of the Bees: and the Ideas of Moral Good and Evil are Establish'd, According to the Sentiments of the Antient Moralists. With an Attempt to Introduce a Mathematical Calculation in Subjects of Morality.*

benefit with its procurement: while "it procures Love toward those we apprehend possess'd of it," there is no expectation of benefit on the part of those demonstrating a moral good. On the other hand, the natural good, or happiness, is merely reflective of "our sensible Perceptions of any kind" which give rise to an excitation of pleasure (Hutcheson 1725, Second Treatise, Introduction, 101–3). It is in our perception of the natural good that advantage and interest enter, in the manner of the pleasure engendered. As "Our *Sense* of Pleasure is antecedent to *Advantage* and *Interest*," it is also then true that pleasure "is the Foundation of them" (103; emphasis in original). The perception of pleasure is not direct, but is derived from the advantages we gain through possession and use of material objects (the gratification engendered) (103).

In this part of the *Inquiry* Hutcheson introduced in explicit terms what would later be heralded as the first principle of Utilitarianism, the principle of the greatest happiness of the greatest number:[16]

> In comparing the *moral Qualitys* of Actions, in order to regulate our Election among various Actions propos'd, or to find which of them has the greatest *moral Excellency,* we are led by *our moral Sense* of *Virtue* thus to judge, that in *equal Degrees* of Happiness, expected to proceed from the Action, the *Virtue* is in proportion to the *Number* of Persons to whom the Happiness shall extend: And here the *Dignity,* or *moral Importance* of Persons, may compensate Numbers; and in equal *Numbers,* the *Virtue* is as the *Quantity* of the Happiness, or natural Good; or that the *Virtue* is in a *compound Ratio* of the *Quantity* of Good, and *Number* of Enjoyers: And in the same manner, the *moral Evil,* or *Vice,* is as the *Degree* of Misery, and *Number* of Sufferers; so that, *that Action* is *best,* which accomplishes the *greatest Happiness* for the *greatest Numbers;* and *that, worst,* which, in *like manner,* occasions *Misery.* (1725, sec. III, §VIII, 163–64; emphasis in original)

From this definition followed the mathematical calculus of Utilitarianism. Hutcheson advanced five propositions (axioms), designed to be "a *universal Canon* to compute the *Morality* of any Actions, with all their Circumstances, when we judge of the Actions done by our selves, or by others" (1725, §XI, 168). First, let M denote "the *Moment* of *Good,*" A denote Ability, and B denote Benevolence, where Benevolence excludes self-interest, and is "design'd for the *Good* of others" (1725, sec. II, §III, 129). Thus:

PROPOSITION 1. "The *moral Importance* of any Character, or the *Quantity* of *publick Good* produc'd by him, is in a *compound Ratio* of his *Benevolence* and *Abilitys,*" that is, $M = BA$ (1725, sec. III, §XI, 168).

16. In his 1728 *An Essay on the Nature and Conduct of the Passions and Affections, with Illustrations on the Moral Sense,* he extended the program begun in the earlier work.

PROPOSITION 2. If the abilities of two agents are equal, then Benevolence is the "Moment of publick Good," or $B = M$.

PROPOSITION 3. If the benevolence of two agents are equal, then Ability is the "Moment of publick Good," or $M = A$.

PROPOSITION 4. Virtue or Benevolence "is always *directly* as the *Moment* of *Good* produc'd in like Circumstances, and *inversely* as their *Abilitys*," or $B = M/A$ (1725, 169).[17]

As the consequences of actions are not always determinate—"some *good* to our selves, and *evil* to the Publick, and others *evil* to our selves, and *good* to the Publick; or either *useful* both to our selves and others, or *pernicious* to both" (1725, 169)—Benevolence cannot be the sole motivation to action. We must include self-love as "conspiring" with Benevolence to inspire action. This leads to

PROPOSITION 5. "When the *Moment* in one Action, partly intended for the *Good* of the *Agent,* is but equal to the *Moment* in the Action of *another Agent* influenc'd only by *Benevolence,* the former is less *virtuous;* and in his Case the *Interest* must be deducted to find the true Effect of the *Benevolence* or *Virtue*" (1725, 170; emphasis in original). Thus, in the instance where the agent takes action not out of Benevolence alone, but in concert with the self-interest motive, his "advantageous Virtue" is less than the value afforded by true Benevolence by the measure of his personal interest, that is, $B = (M - 1)/A$.

Hutcheson thus went a great way toward providing the foundation for a calculus of utility. While work in this area of Utilitarianism would be neglected until the later period—the period of scientific Utilitarianism—it is of interest here in demonstrating an appreciation of the motivation behind efforts to formalize (mathematize or quantify) the study of utilitarian ethics.

Hume as Progenitor of Smith and the Utilitarians   2.2

The second important figure in establishing the basis of utilitarian doctrine and thus the basis of British Classical Political Economy is David Hume (1711–76).[18] In his seminal *A Treatise of Human Nature,* published from

---

17. Thus *M,* as the moment of happiness, must be a known quantity; on this see also Albee 1902, 61.

18. Rostow noted, "David Hume has a quite strong—but not exclusive—claim to being the first modern economist" (1990, 18). Hume was the son of Joseph Hume, lord of Ninewells, a small estate in Scotland, and Catherine Falconer, a daughter of Sir David Falconer, president of the Scottish Court of Session. He entered Edinburgh University at age 12, completing his studies at 15. From 1734 to 1737 he lived in France, where he wrote most of his *Treatise.*

1739 to 1740, Hume set out the philosophical principle upon which the current notion of positivism is based, namely, his devastating critique of induction as a valid principle of argument. In so doing, he actually established the bases upon which Smith, and many of the later utilitarian philosophers, would construct their systems. Halévy (1928) indeed credited Hume with the invention of the term *utility.*[19]

In the third book of the *Treatise,* Hume set himself the task of discovering from whence derived the principles of morality upon which laws and rules of conduct, including relations respecting the ownership of property, could be based. His first task was to show that, contrary to the beliefs of the rationalist philosophers, principles of morality did not, indeed could not, derive from some innate sense. Morals impact greatly on our actions, influencing us in everything we choose to do. In fact, the single strongest motivation to action is selfishness—a desire to attend to the welfare of ourselves and our immediate families before we attend to the welfare of others not so connected with ourselves. For this reason alone, the idea that morals can be predicated on our *reason* is absurd; they are based entirely on the *passions:* "Morals excite passions, and produce or prevent actions. Reason of itself is utterly impotent in this particular. The rules of morality, therefore, are not conclusions of our reason" (Hume, 1739–40, bk. III, pt. II, §I, 509). Certainly reason has a role to play, but this role is a secondary one, confined to "prompting," or "directing a passion" (514).

Hume then established that man, at his core, distinguishes between the twin inducements to action of virtue and vice, and seeks to pursue that which is virtuous while minimizing his exposure to that which is vicious. But from whence do these judgments originate? Hume had denied that they are judged from reason, leaving only *impressions* as the means for their adjudgment. "Morality, therefore, is more properly felt than judg'd of" (1739–40, bk. III, pt. II, 522). How are these impressions made known? Hume answered that, upon asking the question, we "pronounce the impression arising from virtue, to be agreeable, and that proceeding from vice to be uneasy" (522).

> An action, or sentiment, or character is virtuous or vicious; why? because its view causes a pleasure or uneasiness of a particular kind. In giving a reason, therefore, for the pleasure or uneasiness, we sufficiently explain the vice or virtue. . . . We do not infer a character to be virtuous, because it pleases: But in feeling that it pleases after such a particular manner, we in effect feel that it is virtuous. (523)

---

19. Hume employed it, for example, in his discussion of the place of property in relation to justice. See Hume (1739–40, bk. II, pt. I, §X, 362).

Yet the answer Hume gave appears unacceptable, for it seems to beg the question: from whence derive the principles of morality that enable us to distinguish good from evil? Hume, it seems, needed to discover the general principles upon which are founded the rules of conduct and morality. Rejecting natural laws and natural rights as the basis for morality, in contradistinction to the design of Smith discussed earlier, he needed to fall back on an empirically derived code in his definition of virtue and vice, one contingent on the consequences of actions: *"virtue is distinguished by the pleasure, and vice by the pain, that any action, sentiment or character gives us by the mere view and contemplation"* (1739–40, 527; emphasis added). Thus Hume introduced into his argument the idea of the pleasure/pain calculus as a means for the determination of the presence of virtue or vice, and in so doing established a basis for the subsequently defined utilitarian ethic.

The next step in the deontological theory of Hume involved the definition of justice (in its ethical as opposed to legal sense). Having identified the distinguishing characteristics of virtue and vice, justice is then defined with respect to virtue; in fact, justice is merely a special kind of virtue, one arising "from the circumstances and necessity of mankind" (1739–40, bk. III, pt. II, sec. I, 529). Justice is of necessity fashioned by man—it is not a "natural virtue"—in an effort to restrain selfishness and promote generosity. This fashioning must be purposeful in order that it be considered virtuous, for indeed *"no action can be virtuous, or morally good, unless there be in human nature some motive to produce it, distinct from the sense of its morality"* (531; emphasis in original). Rules and modes of behavior, which we collectively subsume under the term *justice*, are thus artificial contrivances, but contrivances designed for a purpose. They are neither constructed nor administered haphazardly. *Justice,* motivated by feelings of self-interest and sympathy,[20] precedes any discussion of individual and societal rights, including the right of security in ownership of property. Thus did Hume arrive at what may be termed his primary proposition, *"that 'tis only from the selfishness and confin'd generosity of men, along with the scanty provision nature has made for his wants, that justice derives its origin"* (bk. III, pt. II, §II, 547; emphasis in original).

From justice derives the right of property, one of Hume's "inviolable relations." The selfish motive, in concert with a sympathetic feeling, together instill a feeling that property relations are inviolable: to demand that we have a right to our own possessions, we must accept that others have the same right to theirs. This understanding leads to the establishment of social conventions, which the members of society enter

20. *"Thus self-interest is the original motive to the* establishment *of justice: but a* sympathy *with public interest is the source of the* moral approbation, *which attends that virtue"* (Hume 1739–40, bk. III, pt. II, §II, 551; emphasis in original).

into as a matter of course in order to promote security and hence stability, and to guarantee that certain social relations are legally protected. Conventions become necessary as a means of restricting the baser instincts of man, that is, they serve to restrain the passions "in their partial and contradictory motions" (1739–40, 541). Among the more important of the conventions Hume offered is one by which the members accept and respect individual rights of ownership and possession. For Hume, this particular convention works to the benefit of *all* the parties, and so it is in the interest of all for the promotion of social stability to adhere to it.[21]

To understand better the necessity for convention and especially the importance of the protection of the property right, we must first understand the *place* of property in Hume's system. Property is first and foremost "*a relation betwixt a person and an object as permits him, but forbids any other, the free use and possession of it, without violating the laws of justice and moral equity*" (1739–40, bk. II, pt. I, §X, 360; emphasis in original). In Hume's relational rhetoric, property and the holder of property are naturally related; they are in constant conjunction. Furthermore, the relation "produces a transition of affections," so that it must be true that "whenever any pleasure or pain arises from an object, connected with us by property, we may be certain, that either pride or humility must arise from this conjunction of relations" (361). But for this relation to manifest itself, there must be established a legal foundation for the preservation of the right to ownership. The social (legal) convention must then *precede* the institution of property and in fact is the basis for the *existence* of property. Property then "is nothing but those goods, whose constant possession is establish'd by the laws of society; that is, by the laws of justice" (bk. III, §II, 542).

With the clarification of his view of justice and the place of property and self-interest, Hume cleared the way for a discussion of the necessity of and the means for the establishment of government. Hume considered that it was part of the nature of man to prefer that which was contiguous to himself to that which was more remote. As action is dependent upon the passions, not reason, "men are mightily govern'd by the imagination" and so at times appear to act against their own best interests (1739–40, §VII, 586). This explained for Hume the necessity for the establishment of a system of government: to provide the means for an impartial (i.e., remote) spectator to judge of our actions toward others.

Here we have in Hume already the basic principles found later in Smith. This is not to denigrate the accomplishments of Smith, but rather

---

21. "Instead of departing from our own interest, or from that of our nearest friends, by abstaining from the possessions of others, we cannot better consult both these interests, than by such a convention; because it is by that means we maintain society, which is so necessary to their well-being and subsistence, as well as to our own" (Hume 1739–40, bk. III, §2, 541).

to point to his refinements of principles that served to promote the ideas later called Utilitarianism. Before getting into a discussion of these theories, however, it is necessary to look once again at Smith's contributions.

Smith's Utilitarianism   2.3

Earlier (in chapter 2) the point was made that Smith's *homo economicus* was not a simple, grubby, selfish utility maximizer. On the contrary he was a man with a temporal sense, a man with loyalties, a man who clearly understood that he was part of a larger social collective. What Smith's man wanted and needed was the responsibility for making his own decisions and accepting the consequences of those decisions. This responsibility had to be understood as existing in concert with the twin principles of self-love and sympathy, for all were combined in the Smithian calculus. In brief, in modern parlance what was to be maximized by Smith's man was the right of self-determination, while still allowing a place for both moral and social sensibilities and even expressions of altruism. It is in this sense that Smith made a lasting contribution to our present understanding of the building blocks of the open market system.

Smith suggested that he may have been the first to discover that an act may be valued more highly than the consequences of that act; the means are often held in more regard than the ends. Indeed, this is the basis for the invisible hand, guiding actions of those seeking "what is most precious and agreeable, . . . the gratification of their own vain and insatiable desires," without regard for "advancing the interest of the society" (1790, pt. IV, chap. I, 184–85). This concern with acts, and the understanding that such acts will lead "naturally" to socially beneficial consequences, means that the consequences themselves need be of no concern.

By extension, then, we can see that Smith also understood the problem with the consequentialism of Utilitarianism. In fact he sought to identify the problem posed in the choice of a deontological (ethical) theory over a utilitarian (consequentialist) one:

> With regard to all such [unsocial] passions, our sympathy is divided between the person who feels them, and the person who is the object of them. The interests of these two are directly opposite. What our sympathy with the person who feels them would prompt us to wish for, our fellow-feeling with the other would lead us to fear. As they are both men, we are concerned for both, and our fear for what the one may suffer, damps our resentment for what the other has suffered. Our sympathy, therefore, with the man who has received the provocation, necessarily falls short of the passion which naturally animates him, not only upon account of those general causes which render all sympathetic passions inferior to the

original ones, but upon account of that particular cause which is peculiar to itself, our opposite sympathy with another person. . . .

But though the utility of those passions to the individual, by rendering it dangerous to insult or injure him, be acknowledged; and though their utility to the public, as the guardians of justice, and of the equality of its administration, be not less considerable, as shall be shewn hereafter; yet there is still something disagreeable in the passions themselves, which makes the appearance of them in other men the natural object of our aversion. . . . It is the remote effects of these passions which are agreeable; the immediate effects are mischief to the person against whom they are directed. But it is the immediate, and not the remote effects of objects which render them agreeable or disagreeable to the imagination. (1790, pt. I, sec. ii, chap. III, 34, 35)

Smith did not hold to the view that the promotion of social welfare was or "should be the sole virtuous motive of action." On the contrary, "it ought to cast the balance against all other motives" (1790, pt. VII, sec. ii, chap. III, 304–5). Systems that stress virtue must place equal stress on propriety, not simply virtue or utility in the promotion of individual happiness. The appropriateness of action then is moderation:

But the agreeableness or utility of any affection depends upon the degree which it is allowed to subsist in. Every affection is useful when it is confined to a certain degree of moderation; and every affection is disadvantageous when it exceeds the proper bounds. According to this system therefore, virtue consists not in any one affection, but in the proper degree of all the affections. The only difference between it and that which I have been endeavouring to establish, is, that it makes utility, and not sympathy, or the correspondent affection of the spectator, the natural and original measure of this proper degree. (306)

Thus we see that, although Smith appears to have anticipated some of the later utilitarian arguments, especially in the sense of Bentham (as we shall see later), he also took pains to set boundaries. One final example will make the point more pronounced:

One individual must never prefer himself so much even to any other individual, as to hurt or injure that other, in order to benefit himself, though the benefit to the one should be much greater than the hurt or injury to the other. The poor man must neither defraud nor steal from the rich, though the acquisition might be much more beneficial to the one than the loss could be hurtful to the other. (1790, pt. III, chap. 3, 138)

A Summary of the Positions of the Scottish Philosophers   2.4

Hutcheson, Hume, and Smith formed part of a patristic tradition that came to be known as the Scottish Enlightenment. Alongside such figures as Adam Ferguson and Sir James Steuart, these writers ruminated on the general material conditions affecting social progress.[22]

The Scottish Enlightenment ranged from about 1740 to 1790 and was a variant of the European Enlightenment that had swept England, France, and the German states. The roots of the early European Enlightenment, often described as the "Age of Reason," lay in the philosophical writings of Descartes, Montesquieu, Hobbes, and Locke, and extended to the science of Newton and Watt. The philosophers declared that reason held the key to understanding the workings of nature, and by extension the nature of society and the mind of man, and thus there was little need to resort to religion or theology to provide answers to basic questions concerning the physical or the moral world. Deism—a movement advocating "natural" religion based on reason as opposed to revelation—promoted the idea that, while God may have indeed set the world in motion, man could nonetheless discover the laws of the universe.

By the late eighteenth century, the focus had changed somewhat from a reliance on reason, to include emotion and sentiment. Hume's *Treatise* reflected and encouraged this aspect of late Enlightenment thought. Hume was indeed fortunate, since the intellectual and religious climate in Scotland at the time he wrote was particularly conducive to such an approach. While the English universities continued to preach Christian Rationalism (relying on the patristic influence of Aristotle), Scottish universities had relieved themselves of the shackles of religious orthodoxy and had taken a more secular humanist position.

The philosophers of the Scottish Enlightenment based their views of society on a historical and moral footing, much in the tradition of Hobbes and Locke, a tradition that can be traced to the jurisprudential writings of the late seventeenth century. The Scots accepted the position of Locke that the property right emerged historically as a consequence of the evolution of social arrangements. The right of possession derived not from any agreement among those in the base state that henceforth a "social contract" would countenance private holdings; rather possession derived from the facts of appropriation and scarcity, and its protection required the institution of the contract. From this foundation the Scottish writers determined that society had undergone a natural and inevitable progression from tribal hunting communities to the commercial economy. The property relation and the respective roles of the individual and

22. For general treatments of the Scottish Enlightenment, see Anand Chitnis (1976), R. H. Campbell and Andrew Skinner (1982), the collection edited by Istvan Hont and Michael Ignatieff (1983), and the article in the *New Palgrave* by John Robertson (1987).

the state assumed their contemporary guises as a consequence of, and became the catalyst for, the evolution of society.

From Hobbes the Scots took the notion that, in matters of economic distribution, Aristotle had allowed his attachment to justice to lead him too far astray. Wants no longer had to be constrained to mere need or subsistence, so wealth-holding could actually be virtuous (although not all, including Hume, agreed). The concept of justice, it was said, has no place in discussions of distribution. Justice was identified with virtue; it was employed to justify the property relation and so safeguard the right of individual private holdings. To serve such a role, justice cannot then be applied to *distribution,* for were it to be so extended, one must deny it a role in maintaining the property arrangement. Were wealth and the property distribution taken to be unequal, it may be argued that this was unjust. But justice was the rationale behind private wealth and was to be the instrument for its protection. One cannot then employ the same instrument as a remedy.

In economic matters, the Scottish philosophers were most concerned with the conditions underlying economic improvement, especially the moral and political dimensions. Scotland, despite the Treaty of Union of 1707 whereby Scotland and England became united, managed to achieve a modest rate of economic growth, not all of which could be explained by the gains from trade. Perhaps the lack of an independent parliament, and the ingrained belief that somehow Scotland was little more than an English territory, compelled the Scottish writers to analyze the problems besetting a poor country under the influence of a major economic and political power. Certainly Hume directed much of his energy to the question of the exploitation by a great power of the resources of the colony. He and Smith, however, perceived the opportunities for development and the potential for growth from an expansion of free trade, while Steuart, the odd man out, advocated protectionist measures. While free trade may have the immediate effect of generating more inequality, the long-run economic growth would more than compensate. Viewing the economy in physical terms, Smith could attribute to the market those qualities of a benevolent creator. The market was the single most efficient mechanism for the promotion of economic and social welfare, and while we may not always be cognizant of its benevolence (just as we are not aware of the force of gravity, while we know very well its consequences), in the end the "invisible hand" would guarantee the protection of the poor as it increased the wealth of the rich.

But at the same time, Smith and Hume were keenly aware of the necessity of a legal system that acted to protect ownership rights and of a government that did not interfere in the free exercise of economic activity. The institutional dimension thus played a major role in the Scottish view. The Scots then may be said to have begun in a formal sense what is now known as Institutionalism.

The Calculus of Jeremy Bentham 3

For the most part, the material presented thus far has focused on the periphery of Classical Political Economy, on the *ethical* variant of Utilitarianism. It is to the more *practical* side that we now turn, with the man generally held to have been the "founder" of the utilitarian movement, Jeremy Bentham (1748–1832).[23]

Bentham actually began his career writing on problems of ethics and conduct, on the government and the law. Yet early on Bentham became interested in political economy, perhaps seeing in its approach to problems a potential framework for the amelioration of social ills, a concern which he had long maintained. In 1776 he published his *Fragment on Government*, the work which in many ways set the tone for his life's output. The essay—a broad-based attack on the jurisprudential views of his former teacher in the law, the British legal authority Sir William Blackstone—was regarded as a first-rate commentary on the laws, and served to reorient critical discussion in the area. In 1787, while visiting his brother in Russia, he wrote *Defence of Usury*,[24] a copy of which he sent to Smith. This tract presented Bentham's views on liberty and the right of contract, arguing that anyone should be granted the ability to use his resources to whatever advantage he desires.

The philosophy of Bentham derived from the philosophical stances of Helvétius and Locke, and one can in his writings discern the mathematical morality of Hutcheson as well. From Helvétius and Hutcheson he derived his basic principles of Utilitarianism: pleasure and happiness are good and should be pursued, while pain and sorrow are bad and should be avoided. From Locke and Montesquieu he derived his beliefs regarding the appropriate form of government and the basis of law, and his views on the individualist ethic and the importance of property rights. The *Fragment* commences with the statement of a "fundamental axiom,"

---

23. Bentham was a lawyer, the son and grandson of lawyers. His early education (from the age of four) included training in Latin, Greek, and French (one of the books he is said to have read was Mandeville's *Fable of the Bees*). In 1760 (at age 12!) he began his formal studies at Queen's College, Oxford, where he studied with the great British legal authority Sir William Blackstone. Unlike his familial predecessors, Bentham was interested in improving the law, not profiting from its practice. Of course, he accepted his legacy, so his emphasis on social improvement rather than on personal profits was more an example of satiation or satisficing than a public lesson on moral improvement. Yet for all his venality, Bentham not only wrote on the subject of social betterment, but actually spent his own time and money on worthy projects, such as the founding of University College of the University of London, where he remains to this day. (Bentham bequeathed his skeletal remains to the Hospital of University College. The frame was built up and clothed in a suit of Bentham's choosing, seated in a chair with his cane and table placed in front of him, and housed in a wardrobe-like cabinet.

24. The book was a great success initially on the Continent, but in Britain only after 1802, from which time forward Bentham had an audience among those creating Classical Economics.

from which the framework of his system could be derived. This axiom holds, as it did in Hume, that it is the balance of pleasure over pain which is the most appropriate determinant of welfare. Bentham reiterated the importance of this axiom in his *Theory of Legislation* (1802), connecting it to the very important principle of utility:

> Nature has placed man under the empire of *pleasure* and of *pain*. We owe to them all our ideas; we refer to them all our judgments, and all the determinations of our life. He who pretends to withdraw himself from this subjection knows not what he says. His only object is to seek pleasure and to shun pain, even at the very instant that he rejects the greatest pleasures or embraces pains the most acute. These eternal and irresistible sentiments ought to be the great study of the moralist and the legislator. The *principle of utility* subjects everything to these two motives. (Bentham 1802b, 2; emphasis in original)

Thus the principle of utility is the instrument by which man can administer the pleasure/pain principle; Max Beer in fact regarded Bentham's use of utility as "the moral test of individual and government actions" (Beer 1940, vol. I, 104). But what precisely is utility? It is significant in this regard to quote Bentham's definition, again from his *Theory of Legislation:*

> *Utility* is an abstract term. It expresses the property or tendency of a thing to prevent some evil or to procure some good. *Evil* is pain, or the cause of pain. *Good* is pleasure, or the cause of pleasure. That which is conformable to the utility, or the interest of an individual, is what tends to augment the total sum of his happiness. That which is conformable to the utility, or the interest of a community, is what tends to augment the total sum of the happiness of the individuals that compose it. (Bentham 1802b, 2; emphasis in original)

Given two similar scenarios, the one which results in the greater happiness, that is, provides the greatest *utility,* is, for the *individual,* to be preferred. The individual is the fundamental unit of Bentham's society, and hence the needs of the individual in the provision of his personal welfare are granted primacy. Extended to the society as a whole, *social welfare* calls for the promotion of the greatest happiness of the greatest number (the maximization of individual welfare), since the interest of society is defined as the sum of the individual interests of the citizens; the social interest is nothing but "the sum of the interests of the several members who compose it" (Bentham 1789, 2), and thus social welfare is measured as the total of individual welfare. In fact, the ethical nature of Bentham's system is noticeable by virtue of the interpretation of "the greatest happiness of the greatest number" as the appropriate measure of right and wrong;[25] in other words, in a Rawlsian sense, justice is synonymous with equality of *result*.[26] Paradoxically, the uncritical acceptance of this consequentialist principle, while ostensibly leading to a democratic outcome, one consistent with the solution proposed by Locke, in fact denies the validity of the doctrine of the Rights of Man (since Bentham's Ideal is security, not the pursuance of liberty), and so is fundamentally anti-Lockean (but perhaps pro-Hobbesian).

In light of the above, Bentham seems to have been more in line with the position of Mandeville than with that of Smith, although he employed Hume's and Smith's notions of sympathy.[27] In terms of his epistemology, he accepted Locke's view of the mind as a tabula rasa. Morals and codes of conduct can be encoded onto these "blank slates," suggesting that man was not born with a moral sense. To the extent that he held this position, Bentham then could not accept the Smithian argument in favor of Natural Law and moral imperatives, but instead had to accept a more humanistic, legislative stance, one consistent with the argument of Hume: laws are enacted by man, not God, so they are not natural and so cannot be intuited. Passions rein in reason. Once again, Bentham's own words, this time from his *Theory of Legislation*, are to the point:

> He who adopts the *principle of utility*, esteems virtue to be a good only on account of the pleasures which result from it; he regards vice as an evil only because of the pains which it produces. Moral good is *good* only by its tendency to produce physical good. Moral evil is *evil* only by its tendency to produce physical evil. (1802b, 3; emphasis in original)

---

25. As Mitchell (vol. II, 1969, 41) noted, "The 'greatest happiness' principle with Bentham is not so much part of his psychology as of his ethics."

26. One of John Rawls's problems with classical Utilitarianism was that "there is no reason in principle why the greater gains of some should not compensate for the lesser losses of others; or more importantly, why the violation of the liberty of a few might not be made right by the greater good shared by many" (Rawls 1971, 26). Rawls accepted that the problem could be lessened, although not completely ameliorated, by the acceptance of natural rights, but that the utilitarian rationale for this admission was the utility derived from such acceptance (1971, 28). The doctrine of Utilitarianism relies on acceptance of Natural Laws and Natural Rights which serve to reward moral choices and punish (or deny) choices which, if engaged in, would reduce the net happiness of society (1971, 32). Utility simply replaces Natural Law and natural rights as a first principle. Yet both Rawls's theory and utilitarian theories are consequentialist, i.e., predicated on the consequences of actions, not the morality of the actions themselves.

27. "The principle which has exercised the greatest influence upon governments, is that of sympathy and antipathy. In fact, we must refer to that principle all those specious objects which governments pursue, without having the general good for a single and independent aim; such as good morals, equality, liberty, justice, power, commerce, religion; objects respectable in themselves, and which ought to enter into the views of the legislator; but which too often lead him astray, because he regards them as ends, not as means. He substitutes them for public happiness, instead of making them subordinate to it" (Bentham 1802b, 14).

The application of the principle to the administration of the state—extending the doctrine from the happiness of the individual to the welfare of the community—is then readily made. The task of the good administrator is to activate and enforce codes designed to promote a harmonious attitude between and among the citizenry. Bentham argued that the "right kind" of legislation ("right" seen in the foregoing sense) was that which not only makes for happiness, but which also provides a justification for legislation itself. So among the first points to conclude about Bentham is that he was not a free-marketeer in the strict libertarian sense of the term, even though he did accept that there were likely to be allocative distortions if and when state intervention occurred. But make no mistake, some form of legislative remedy was eventually going to be necessary. Man is essentially good; the problem lay in legislating the "right" and "proper" type of law.[28]

This rejection of Natural Law and the necessity for a civil law foundation for the promotion of individual happiness and social welfare is especially evident in his theory of property. In his *Principles of the Civil Code* (1802), Bentham expressly denied the concept of "natural property," maintaining instead that property "is entirely the creature of law" (Bentham 1802a, 308). More importantly, property is defined epistemically. Property is above all else an *idea,* not a concrete reality; it is the means to the achievement of utility, where utility is a subjective concept understandable solely with respect to individual desires.

> Property is only a foundation of expectation—the expectation of deriving certain advantages from the thing said to be possessed, in consequence of the relations in which one already stands to it.
>
> There is no form, or colour, or visible trace, by which it is possible to express the relation which constitutes property. It belongs not to physics, but to metaphysics: it is altogether a creature of the mind. (1802a, 308)

The import of the law is in promoting and securing this expectation, in introducing security into the equation. We can see here shades of Hobbes: for Hobbes, the need for security is the basis for the establishment of the political order; for Bentham, the need for security is the basis of the legal assurance of property ownership.[29] One can expect to reap the benefits of one's possessions only so long as title is assured, that is, protections are made against encroachment (presumably not only from the encroachment of others, but by the state as well); it is the law which guarantees that surety, and so protects those rights of ownership and use:

28. Getting good men to obey good legislation was not an insurmountable problem. (Later J. S. Mill was to make a similar point—a modern example is that it is not hard to get good men to accept the arbitrariness of traffic lights when traffic is heavy.)

29. On this question of the relationship between the Hobbesian and the Benthamite views on the nature of the state, see Nancy Rosenblum (1978).

It is the law alone which allows me to forget my natural weakness: it is from the law alone that I can enclose a field and give myself to its cultivation, in the distant hope of the harvest. (1802a, 308)

Pleasure being the enjoyment of an expectation, property is thus nothing more than an *established* expectation, the instrument of its establishment being the law.[30]

Having rejected the intuitive nature of the "naturalness" of first principles upon which rules of human conduct must be predicated, Bentham went even further and denounced the entire idea of Natural Law and natural rights as nothing more than fictions, man-made inventions endowed with a real existence beyond the temporal:

> The primitive sense of the word *law,* and the ordinary meaning of the word, is—the will or command of a legislator. The *law of nature* is a figurative expression, in which nature is represented as a being. . . . In this sense, all the general inclinations of men, all those which appear to exist independently of human societies, and from which must proceed the establishment of political and civil law, are called *laws of nature.* This is the true sense of the phrase.
>
> But this is not the way in which it is understood. Authors have taken it in a direct sense; as if there had been a real code of natural laws. . . . They do not see that these natural laws are laws of their own invention. (Bentham 1802b, 82–83)

Even Bentham's ethics and morals could not stand alone as boundaries to action, without being subjected to proof. The same held true for those activities condemned as breaches of societal normality. Criminal activity, for instance, must not be proscribed absent an empirical examination of the relative merits resulting from the activity; that is, even criminal activity, not to mention ethical and moral standards, must be subjected to the rigors of the pleasure/pain calculus.

There followed a derivation of the relative pleasures and pains resulting from a criminal act, predicated on "the laws of human feeling" (essentially Bentham's First Cause).[31] If the pains of the victim outweighed the

---

30. Beer concluded that Bentham "regarded private property as the only possible basis of social life, and whenever it came into conflict with equality, the latter should forthwith be abandoned" (Beer 1940, vol. I, 104).

31. As John Stuart Mill pointed out in his biographical treatment of Bentham (1838):

> . . . he will distinguish all the different mischiefs of a crime, whether of the *first,* the *second,* or the *third* order, namely 1. the evil to the sufferer, and to his personal connections; 2. the *danger* from example, and the *alarm* or painful feeling of insecurity; and 3. the discouragement to industry and useful pursuits arising from the *alarm,* and the trouble and resources which must be expended in warding off the *danger.* (Mill 1838, 139; emphasis in original)

pleasure derived by the perpetrator of the act, punishment was indeed warranted. If not, the punishment should be revoked.[32]

Thus did Bentham "propose a treaty of conciliation with the partisans of natural rights" (1802b, 86). However, if it was meant to assuage those advocates of the principle, it did so by simply moving the discussion to another level, by urging them to make known the author of these principles. Bentham's conciliation merely moved the First Cause to a position demanding empirical elucidation and confirmation:

> If *nature* has made such or such a law, those who cite it with so much confidence, those who have modestly taken upon themselves to be its interpreters, must suppose that nature had some reasons for her law. Would it not be surer, shorter and more persuasive, to give us those reasons directly, instead of urging upon us the will of this unknown legislator, as itself an authority? (1802b, 86–87)

Yet despite his denial of the use of moral precepts and Natural Law foundations for his system, Benthamite Utilitarianism (as with Utilitarianism generally) is beyond question a system predicated on moral imperatives, and Bentham seems to have at times at least implicitly (and perhaps unknowingly) accepted this. The concepts of *good* and *bad* are themselves ethical judgments which require a moral basis for their definition and elucidation.[33] Further, Bentham expressly accepted that "sentiments of pleasure or pain" are natural to man (1802b, 82), while refusing to call them "laws."

> What is natural to man is sentiments of pleasure or pain, what are called inclinations. But to call these sentiments and these inclinations *laws,* is to introduce a false and dangerous idea. It is to set language in opposition to itself; for it is necessary to make *laws* precisely for the purpose of restraining these inclinations. Instead of regarding them as laws, they must be submitted to laws. (1802b, 83; emphasis in original)

---

32. Cf. the treatment of punishment by Smith in his *Theory of Moral Sentiments:* "Justice . . . is the main pillar that upholds the whole edifice. If it is removed, the great, the immense fabric of human society, that fabric which to raise and support seems in this world . . . to have been the peculiar and darling care of Nature, must in a moment crumble into atoms. In order to enforce the observation of justice, therefore, Nature has implanted in the human breast that consciousness of ill-desert, those terrors of merited punishment which attend upon its violation, as the great safe-guards of the association of mankind, to protect the weak, to curb the violent, and to chastise the guilty" (Smith 1790, pt. II, sec. ii, chap. 3, 86).

33. As Schumpeter noted: "The essential point to grasp is that utilitarianism was nothing but another natural-law system" (Schumpeter 1954, 132). Further: "The program of deriving, by the light of reason, 'laws' about man in society from a very stable and highly simplified human nature fits the utilitarians not less well than the philosophers or the scholastics . . ." (132).

Despite the apparent hedonistic aspects of Bentham's system—and there are certainly elements of hedonism present in his social and individual philosophy—it does not allow for unrestricted behavior. While hedonism in its original variant stressed the inviolate pursuit of pleasure by the individual, without concern for his role within the society, Bentham's Utilitarianism is far more restrictive. It seeks the "greatest happiness of the greatest number," thereby expanding the horizon of the individual beyond himself to encompass society as a whole; Bentham's Utilitarianism is fundamentally communitarian.

It is the role of *society* to promote the general welfare, to maximize the general happiness. This can be accomplished through the rule of law, through moral persuasion, through religious sanctions, through social ostracism, or through any of a number of other means to channel activity to the furtherance of the social role.[34] But there must be a rationale for the enactment of laws. Bentham himself sincerely believed that "every law is contrary to liberty," since to believe otherwise is to become hopelessly embroiled in consequentialism.[35] Thus was Bentham moved to set out his propositions respecting the role of government:

1. "The only object of government ought to be the greatest possible happiness of the community."
2. "The happiness of an individual is increased in proportion as his sufferings are lighter and fewer, and his enjoyments greater and more numerous."
3. "The care of his enjoyments ought to be left almost entirely to the individual. The principal function of government is to guard against pains."
4. "It fulfils this object by creating rights, which it confers upon individuals: rights of personal security, rights of protection for honour, rights of property, rights of receiving aid in case of need. To these rights correspond offences of different kinds. The law cannot create rights except by creating corresponding obligations. It cannot create rights and obligations without creating offences. It cannot command nor forbid without restraining the liberty of individuals." (1802b, 95)

---

34. "As between individual and individual, the pleasure to the superior, to the power-holder, from the possession and exercise of the power, is not so great as the pain experienced by the party subjected.

"Therefore, only when converted into extra-benefiting by appropriate obligation, can it be conducive to greatest happiness. . . .

"The principle corresponding to these axioms, as to equality, is *the inequality-minimizing principle*" (Bentham, "The Philosophy of Economic Science," in Bentham 1952, 117; emphasis in original).

35. According to the advocates of the principle of unfettered liberty, "*Liberty consists in the right of doing everything which is not injurious to another*" (Bentham 1802b, 94; emphasis in original). But a strict adherence to this principle demands that actions be suspended until all the consequences are known (95).

Before the government could take it upon itself to promulgate new rules and regulations designed to restrict individual behavior, it should be required to provide to the citizenry the reasons behind the necessity of the rules. In *Defence of Usury,* for example, Bentham argued that with respect to the regulation of usury, the state should be agnostic; the interest rate was simply a price, no different from any other commodity price, and the consequence of setting it artificially was the same with that of any other commodity—prices could be set, but the artificial valuation distorted the allocation process. Further, and perhaps more important, was the need to consider the evolution of the concept of usury. Usury has a legal definition and a moral one; the legal definition serves only to codify the moral one, where the moral definition is derived from custom and convention. Thus the actions of the government in the prohibition of usury implicitly accept that there could be defined a moral or natural rate of interest, any rate above which society could not accept (Bentham 1787, 131). But any individual should be free to engage in the taking of (usurious) interest, so long as there is someone who wishes to pay the price. The reason, then, for defending usury rests on (1) a view of the individual as free to engage in activities so long as they are not harmful to others, and (2) the need to restrict governmental interference to those areas in which it can reasonably be shown to be necessary.[36]

Bentham held a lifelong interest in social problems, the solutions to which could be expressed in terms familiar to those then engaged in political-economic arguments (at the time mere pamphleteers) as well as social philosophers; thus the solution proposed need not have been an economic one. Yet the solutions often were predicated on the promotion of efficiency and rationality. For example, in 1791, while in St. Petersburg (where he had written his *Defence of Usury*), he authored a pamphlet proposing a more efficient prison system. His proposal involved abandoning penal colonies such as that in New South Wales and substituting a central physical prison structure organized on the order of a hub, with the guards in the center and cell blocks radiating outward. The idea met with public enthusiasm, and a bill appropriating money for the purpose of construction sailed through Parliament; unfortunately, King George III was not impressed, and the design was not immediately implemented.[37] The important thing to note from this episode, however, is that what interested Bentham was not only such marvelous mechanisms as the self-

---

36. As Bentham stated with respect to usury: "... *no man of ripe years and of sound mind, acting freely, and with his eyes open, ought to be hindered, with a view to his advantage, from making such bargains, in the way of obtaining money, as he thinks fit: nor,* (what is a necessary consequence) *any body hindered from supplying him, upon any terms he thinks proper to accede to*" (Bentham 1787, 129; emphasis in original).

37. George III desired to remove the convicts from England, wishing the navy to get the "contract" for so doing. In time Bentham's design was erected in the United States as the Illinois State Penitentiary at Joliet.

regulating market, but also, as much or perhaps even more, the efficient use of governmental intervention in matters of social policy, areas where the market had not or could not, left to its own devices, arrive at a solution.

Perhaps the best way of ending this discussion of Bentham is to quote from the tribute paid him by John Stuart Mill:

> Bentham's idea of the world is that of a collection of persons pursuing each his separate interest or pleasure, and the prevention of whom from jostling one another more than is unavoidable may be attempted by hopes and fears derived from three sources—the law, religion, and public opinion. To these three powers, considered as binding human conduct, he gave the name of *sanctions:* the *political* sanction, operating by the rewards and penalties of the law; the *religious* sanction, by those expected from the Ruler of the Universe; and the *popular,* which he characteristically calls the *moral* sanction, operating through the pains and pleasures arising from the favour or disfavour of our fellow creatures. (J. S. Mill 1838, 155; emphasis in original)

Malthus and the Fear of Social Unrest   4

All in all, Bentham imagined a world of hope. Man acting in his own interest, maximizing his own net pleasure, constrained only by rules aimed at the protection of the social welfare (defined of course with respect to the individual citizen), would guarantee a smooth-functioning society. This is as obvious a result as if it had been dictated by Natural Law!

However, the picture of harmony painted by Bentham was not admired by all. While Bentham's view held valid within its own closed (ethical) sphere, other real-world economic considerations that he had overlooked seriously affected his conclusions. It is these considerations which became the concern of a parson-turned-teacher, Thomas Robert Malthus (1766–1834).[38] It is with Malthus that we begin to see the emergence of *economic* analysis as derivative from *ethical* concerns.

---

38. Malthus was very clearly a member of the gentry. Perhaps as a result of his father's admiration for Rousseau's views on education, he was initially given liberal schooling, and he went off to Jesus College, Cambridge, where he took both a B.A. (Ninth Wrangler) and a master's degree, and received holy orders in the Church of England. In 1805 he became Professor of General History, Politics, Commerce and Finance (later altered to Professor of History and Political Economy) at the East India College at Haileybury, an academy established to educate the sons of East India Company officials as well as potential officials (much in the way of an elite modern high school).

A political conservative, Malthus may be said to have advanced theories and advocated policies furthering the interests of the landed classes, and in this position began advocating social reform (perhaps as much as anything the result of the fact that he was much afraid of the violence in the streets, which had reached high levels due to the continuous problems of war and impressment).

Malthus's economics were very Smithian, but promoted always with an eye to refinement so as to be applicable especially to the alleviation of social ills. Nowhere is this refinement more evident than in Malthus's description of the nature of man himself. Whereas Smith allowed that man, in pursuing his own self-interest, constrained by the precepts of Natural Law, would be guided to the solution of the fundamental economic question of scarcity, Malthus took a more dismal view, one not necessarily discordant with Hobbes. Outward constraints beyond the control of the individual actor serve to thwart the otherwise natural tendencies discussed by Smith for the generation of growth and the expansion of economic well-being. *An Essay on the Principles of Population* (1798, hereafter to be known as *First Essay*),[39] more of an attack on Marie Jean Antoine Nicolas Caritat, the Marquis de Condorcet (1743–94)[40] and William Godwin (1756–1836)[41] than on Smith, expressed Malthus's pessimistic view of the economic process and the nature of man as *homo economicus*. While he did not deny the validity of the concept of the "economic man," his perception of "economic man" was subordinated to a larger grasp of human interest.

The genesis of the *First Essay* was Malthus's objection to the eternal optimism of Condorcet and Godwin and its Rousseauian underpinnings: Godwin believed that social and economic policy could be so structured as to achieve a utopian result, and Condorcet held an unfailing belief in the ability of man to solve his problems through an appeal to science and reason. Both Godwin and Condorcet advocated a form of socialism as a means of advancing economic equality—the need to provide everyone with a comfortable standard of living—predicated on a view of man as inherently good. Godwin had, according to Malthus, attributed the ills of society to the dominant institution of private property and the political system which served to promote and protect it (Malthus 1798, 176–77); given the nature of the property structure, natural forces would guide the society to ever greater levels of inequality. Malthus, however, believed just the opposite about the nature of man and his ultimate condition. Contrary to the thesis advanced by Godwin that property was the immediate and proximate cause of all degradation, Malthus held that selfishness and covetousness would rule to the detriment of society should the institution of private property be *abolished*

---

39. The full title of the essay is *An Essay on the Principle of Population, as It Affects the Future Improvement of Society, with Remarks on the Speculations of Mr. Godwin, M. Condorcet, and Other Writers.*

40. Condorcet was a mathematician, who studied at the Collège de Paris. In 1782 he was elected to the Académie Française. He is known today for his employment of the probability calculus in the study of political problems.

41. Godwin, an anarchist, is known for his antidemocratic political views. His wife, Mary Wollstonecraft, was another famous radical. Their daughter, Mary, was a major literary figure, wife of Percy Shelley, and author of *Frankenstein*. Godwin is best known for his *Enquiry Concerning Political Justice*, published in 1793.

(1798, 179), since, given private property relations, self-interest (self-love), as per Smith and Hume, guarantees an optimal social outcome. Property serves to unleash the best that man has to offer, allowing him to attain his present state of civilization:

> It is to the established administration of property, and to the apparently narrow principle of self-love, that we are indebted for all the noblest exertions of human genius, all the finer and more delicate emotions of the soul, for every thing, indeed, that distinguishes the civilized, from the savage state. (1798, 286–87)

The social fabric simply could not tolerate an equal distribution of income and goods, nor could the government under these terms introduce effective measures for the provision of peace, social security, and abundance. The very same principles that underlay Aristotle's belief in the deleterious effects of a communitarian redistribution scheme, namely complete equality in the division of property, also implicitly underlay Malthus's model.[42] In a state such as would emerge given a complete equality in the distribution of property, there would also be no limit to population increase; the restructured society would in a very few generations collapse into an anarchic nightmare.[43]

Malthus considered that the root of Godwin's philosophy was a consequentialism not different from that advanced by Bentham. "Morality, according to Mr. Godwin, is a calculation of consequences . . ." (1798, 213). Morality is defined on this view (or at least on Malthus's apprehension of this view) as arising from the determination of the greatest pleasure. For Malthus, *reason* was essential as the guide in the calculation of the consequences of actions: "In the pursuit of every enjoyment, whether sensual or intellectual, Reason, that faculty which enables us to calculate consequences, is the proper corrective and guide" (215–16). Thus Benthamite utilitarianism must be denied in favor of a less hedonistic, more intellectual and spiritual, economic calculus.

Given his social consciousness, Malthus was active in the move-

---

42. Cf. Aristotle: "There is an absurdity, too, in equalizing the property and not regulating the number of citizens. . . . One would have thought that it was even more necessary to limit population than property. . . . The neglect of this subject, which in existing states is so common, is a never-failing cause of poverty among the citizens; and poverty is the parent of revolution and crime" (*Politics* 1265a38–1265b12). And: "But those who make such laws [respecting the equal division of property] should remember what they are apt to forget—that the legislator who fixes the amount of property should also fix the number of children; for, if the children are too many for the property, the law must be broken" (1266b9–12).

43. "In a state therefore of great equality and virtue, where pure and simple manners prevailed, and where the means of subsistence were so abundant, that no part of the society could have any fears about providing amply for a family, the power of population being left to exert itself unchecked, the increase of the human species would evidently be much greater than any increase that has been hitherto known" (Malthus 1798, 20).

ment to change the "Poor Laws." As he viewed them, the Poor Laws did not act to ameliorate, but served only to exacerbate, the plight of the poor, for reasons which appear to be very "classical." Under the Poor Laws, the poor as a group was allotted an annual amount for its subsistence, which was to be used to purchase foodstuffs. But the result of the allotment was that prices of all foodstuffs, and consequently all commodities in general, rose, since demand for food increased while production was held constant given the limited resources which could be brought to its cultivation. Further, society as a whole was harmed, as the subsidy promoted idleness in what had been a potentially worthwhile work force. In Malthus's mind, by not requiring the poor to provide a service in return for the welfare payment, the government placed a premium on idleness and hence assured that more would be forthcoming. The irony then of the Poor Laws was that the poor (and so society in general) were made worse off for the interference of the government in devising and implementing a program ostensibly designed to improve their lot.

> It may at first appear strange, but I believe it is true, that I cannot by means of money raise a poor man, and enable him to live much better than he did before, without proportionably depressing others in the same class. If I retrench the quantity of food consumed in my house, and give him what I have cut off, I then benefit him, without depressing any but myself and family, who, perhaps, may be well able to bear it. If I turn up a piece of uncultivated land, and give him the produce, I then benefit both him, and all the members of the society, because what he before consumed is thrown into the common stock, and probably some of the new produce with it. But if I only give him money, supposing the produce of the country to remain the same, I give him a title to a larger share of that produce than formerly, which share he cannot receive without diminishing the shares of others. It is evident that this effect, in individual instances, must be so small as to be totally imperceptible; but still it must exist, as many other effects do, which like some of the insects that people the air, elude our grosser perceptions.
>
> But whether a government could with advantage to society actively interfere to repress inequality of fortunes, may be a matter of doubt. (1798, 79–80, 287–88n.)

The Malthusian world represents a zero-sum game, played on the field of survival. The poor cannot be relieved of their misery and squalor by monetary handouts from the government, but may be relieved only by their own industry. But the adage, "It avails the poor not-at-all to build them cottages; better they should be confined to poor houses where their behavior can be controlled," was also not for Malthus a solution, for he

considered two ways in which the Poor Laws resulted in a more depressed condition for the poor: (1) population increases geometrically
while food production increases arithmetically; and (2) provisions for the
poor who seek the "refuge" of workhouses cannot be expanded because
the inhabitants of the workhouses are marginal workers, so that to increase the quantity allotted to them takes away from the more productive
members of the society a share of a finite pie, and, in consequence, leads
to dependence on the part of the poor in the workhouses (1798, 83–84).
Thus in actuality there is no program or policy that can be implemented
by the government which would effect a reduction in the number of the
poor, or further an alleviation of their condition.

But for Malthus, dependence, the potential for a general price infla-
tion, and even the creation of a permanent underclass, were not the
primary objections to the Poor Laws. One of the principal objections was
even more profound than survival itself. This objection was that the
institution of the Poor Laws served to subjugate the poor as a class to the
control of the state:

> for this assistance which some of the poor receive, in itself almost a
> doubtful blessing, the whole class of the common people of En-
> gland, is subjected to a set of grating, inconvenient, and tyrannical
> laws, totally inconsistent with the genuine spirit of the constitution.
> The whole business of settlements, even in its present amended
> state, is utterly contradictory to all ideas of freedom. . . . And the
> obstructions continually occasioned in the market of labour by
> these laws, have a constant tendency to add to the difficulties of
> those who are struggling to support themselves without assistance.
> (1798, 92)

The true objection of Malthus to government action in the alleviation of
social ills was thus not that the policies would not work or would have
but marginal impact; the real reason for advocating repeal was that the
legislation served to insinuate the government into society, in an area for
which it was ill-suited and not legally and morally entitled. By so doing,
the government had violated the social contract, leaving the poor, who
had upheld their obligations, with no recourse (1798, 98–99).

Having achieved some fame (and notoriety) on the topic, Malthus
was led to ask whether his predictions had worked out. He traveled
widely in Europe and discovered that they had not. He then began to
back away from the simplicity of his original formula. In 1803 Malthus
published *An Essay on the Principle of Population, or a View of Its Past
and Present Effects on Human Happiness, with an Inquiry into Our
Prospects Respecting the Future Removal or Mitigation of the Evils
which it Occasions* (hereafter the *Second Essay*), essentially a revision of
the earlier *First Essay*, but more in the way of a revised treatise on the

subject of population.[44] In this work, Malthus continued in his critique of the utopians in their insistence that an equal distribution of property held the key to man's escape from despair and degradation, and their belief that the nature of man was such that moral constraints, particularly in regard to the institution of marriage, were unnecessary.

Malthus identified two "fundamental laws of society," these being "the security of property and the institution of marriage" (Malthus 1872, bk. III, chap. II, 20). The denial of the validity and universality of these "laws," as the utopians were desirous of achieving, insured that inequality *of result* would follow. Respecting the property right, the utopian socialist solution of redistribution struck Malthus as being peculiar to a philosophy described as egalitarianism. Malthus's reasoning was that, as the property had been allotted, the allotment must remain fixed; it would be a violation of the preconditions of the allotment and a breach of the (tacit) agreement between the populace and the state, if the initial distribution could be subjected to continuous alteration. But such continuous alteration must occur if future generations are to share a claim in the distribution of property, and so be on an equal footing with earlier generations. The problem is then obvious: the mere fact of equalization of property rights denies that right to future generations, and it further results in a more unjust distribution of resources than under the regime of private property:

> We have seen the fatal effects that would result to society if every man had a valid claim to an equal share of the produce of the earth. The members of a family which was grown too large for the original division of land appropriated to it could not then demand a part of the surplus produce of others as a debt of justice. (1872, 20)

Furthermore, the mere fact of the *protection* of the rights of private property is enough to guarantee that the society would be more secure, and not simply more just, than under a system of equal distribution. The very notion of equalization breeds selfishness and stifles the very processes of thought, while the adherence to Natural Laws, the right of private ownership and the ability to dispose of the surplus produced as the owner sees fit, encourages a greater feeling of community as it ensures a greater degree of individual security:

> Were there no established administration of property, every man would be obliged to guard with force his little store. Selfishness would be triumphant. The subjects of contention would be perpetual. Every individual would be under a constant anxiety about corporal support, and not a single intellect would be left free to expatiate in the field of thought. (1872, 13)

44. We use here the 7th edition (1872), which in structure is essentially the 2nd edition.

The constancy of the laws of nature, and of effects and causes, is the foundation of all human knowledge. . . . (1872, bk. III, chap. I, 6)

In the area of morality, Malthus held that moral restraint played a greater role in controlling population increase than he had previously acknowledged: "All the immediate checks to population, which have been observed to prevail in the same and different countries, seem to be resolvable into moral restraint, vice and misery" (1872, bk. IV, chap. I, 151). The utopian programs of Condorcet and Godwin (and others) with respect to socialization of the ownership of property and the denial of the supremacy of Natural Law, he reiterated, serve only to debase the society.[45] A society attuned to the protection of property rights, adhering to the dictates of Natural Law, would by definition be sympathetic to and encouraging of moral restraint and hence inducements to a slower rate of population increase would be engendered. The socialized society would need to promulgate and enforce some type of laws for the restraint of individuals no longer subject to Natural Law proscriptions (read religious-based teachings). But these laws would be so "unnatural" and "shocking" to the sensibilities of all men as to be completely impossible to legislate:

And yet, if it be absolutely necessary, in order to prevent the most overwhelming wretchedness, that there should be some restraint on the tendency to early marriages, . . . can the most fertile imagination conceive one at once so natural, so just, so consonant to the laws of God and to the best laws framed by the most enlightened men, as that each individual should be responsible for the maintenance of his own children; that is, that he should be subjected to the natural inconveniences and difficulties arising from the indulgence of his inclinations, and to no other whatever? . . .

. . . But the operation of this natural check depends exclusively upon the existence of the laws of property and succession; and in a state of equality and community of property could only be replaced by some artificial regulation of a very different stamp and a much more unnatural character. (1872, bk. III, chap. III, 28)

Thus, as in the earlier essay, Malthus recommended as a remedy to unchecked population increase, the inducements of celibacy and "delayed gratification."[46]

---

45. "Natural and moral evil seem to be the instruments employed by the Deity in admonishing us to avoid any mode of conduct which is not suited to our being, and will consequently injure our happiness.

"Diseases have been generally considered as the inevitable inflictions of Providence; but, perhaps, a great part of them may more justly be considered as indications that we have offended against some of the laws of nature" (Malthus 1872, bk. IV, chap. I, 151-52).

46. In fact, Malthus admitted he had nothing to substitute for his previous theory—and that bothered him. What can be substituted for it is the view of Simon Kuznets. Kuznets argued that the capacity for genius (the capacity for invention) is allocated to a steady but

The role of the civil government in all this is rather interesting. Malthus began by noting that the powers of civil government are determined and granted (since we must submit to them, they cannot simply be assumed) on the grounds of "general expediency" (1872, bk. IV, chap. VI, 188). But liberty was not among the things which a government, any government, was disposed to protect; on the contrary, the citizens, especially those of the landed classes, need be constantly vigilant against governmental usurpation of individual rights and liberties. The government, the power and legitimacy of which is granted by the people, must be constantly scrutinized by the citizenry to prevent abuse:

> The checks, which are necessary to secure the liberty of the subject, will always in some degree embarrass and delay the operations of the executive government. The members of this government feeling these inconveniences, while they are exerting themselves, as they conceive, in the service of their country, . . . will naturally be disposed, on every occasion, to demand the suspension or abolition of these checks; but if once the convenience of ministers be put in competition with the liberties of the people, and we get into a habit of relying on fair assurances and personal character, instead of examining, with the most scrupulous and jealous care, the merits of each particular case, there is an end of British freedom. If we once admit the principle that the government must know better with regard to the quantity of power which it wants than we can possibly do with our limited means of information, and that, therefore, it is our duty to surrender up our private judgments, we may just as well at the same time surrender up the whole of our constitution. (1872, bk. IV, chap. VI, 189)

Even more egregious than the usurpation of individual rights by the governing elite was the passing of laws in contradiction to the laws of nature; for Malthus, there simply is no right, for example, to subsistence, and to allege one, and worse yet to codify it as law, is detrimental to society and especially the poor, the very element that the law is supposed to help. Thus every aspect of society that is subject to analysis is, on the position of Malthus, characterizable as impinging on either the right to property or the limitations of ameliorations of poverty brought about by the dictates of population pressures.

---

very small portion of the population. What counts is not simply the number of geniuses, but rather the opportunities for interaction between them. Given pressure, these geniuses will invent substitutes for scarce resources. Whence comes this pressure? Kuznets suggested it was the pricing system and a freedom to let incentives drive the geniuses on. Thus, the argument that the resource supply will increase only at a comparatively slow rate is offset by the history of technological change; geniuses expand the capacity to produce as fast or faster than the population seems to be able to assimilate the product. See M. Perlman (1981).

So much of Malthus's early writing fitted into the *Wealth of Nations* pattern that this was what came through most strongly. In fact, it was Malthus's intent to rewrite *The Wealth of Nations* that led him to develop his *Principles of Political Economy* (1820; 2d ed., 1836), which we shall discuss here briefly in regard to Malthus's idea of the method of political economy.[47]

In the *Principles* Malthus placed political economy in the realm of the moral sciences, not the "certain" sciences such as mathematics. The "general rules" of political economy are often "found to resemble in most particulars the great general rules in morals and politics founded upon the known passions and propensities of human nature" (Malthus 1836, 1). Wary of the tendency of his contemporaries to draw hasty generalizations from fragmentary evidence, he declared such practices improper, as they did not "allow of modifications, limitations, and exceptions to any rule or proposition, than to admit the operation of more causes than one" (1836, 6). Indeed, he proclaimed the "first business of philosophy" to be simply "to account for things as they are" (8). This suggests that such general rules as are stipulated in political economy must be qualified sufficiently to be of practical use in providing an explanation of the continually changing structure of human society. This he felt he had accomplished in his theory of population, a universal theory derived through an analysis of, and confirmed by reference to, "the state of society as it actually exists in every country with which we are acquainted" (8).

The Rational Political Economy of James Mill   5

The paradox which Bentham *seems* to have created, wherein a system predicated upon a principle of individuality leads to a nondemocratic outcome, was tied to his belief in the underlying axiomatic importance of the individual felicific calculus (the cornerstone of individualism as well as "vulgar self-interest") in concert with his antimarket posture regarding social solutions to social problems. A satisfactory solution to the apparent puzzle may be found in ascribing to Bentham an instrumentalist, rather than a consistent philosophical, role. Because there are in Bentham many lines of argument—pro- and anti–Natural Law, democratic and nondemocratic outcomes, hedonism and bounded Utilitarianism—it may be that he did not hold to any position with a dogmatic conviction. But this answer is less than acceptable because while it may explain Bentham in the sense of *Expliquer c'est pardonner,* it does not begin to explain the

47. Malthus's *Principles of Political Economy* will be discussed in more detail later (in the companion volume), in respect to the factors of labor and land.

influence that James Mill's admiration (perhaps distorted) had on the development of classical economics.

James Mill (1773–1836),[48] a former divinity student and admirer of Plato, is of central import in our discussion of Utilitarianism, nearly as much as Bentham himself; Halévy went so far as to categorize him as Bentham's St. Paul (Halévy 1928, xix). Bentham and Mill actually met in 1808, when Mill was trying to reduce Bentham's adaptation of Smith's economics to a set of coherent principles,[49] and he soon became one of Bentham's closest and most trusted disciples. It was Bentham who is credited (or blamed) with Mill's forced abandonment of his former stance with respect to Christianity and to religion in general.[50] Like Bentham, Mill admired Helvétius and accepted the centrality of the principle behind hedonistic Utilitarianism: men act in their own best interests, and these interests can be analyzed in terms of the Benthamite pleasure/pain calculus. In his essay on government, written as a supplement to the *Encyclopædia Britannica* (and published in *Essays on Government, Jurisprudence, Liberty of the Press, and Law of Nations* in 1825, hereafter

---

48. James Mill was born into a long line of Scottish thinkers whose influence on early economic thought was profound. He entered the University of Edinburgh in 1790. From 1794 to 1798, he undertook studies as a divinity student, but never took his religious orders. He decided instead "to be a poor man, rather than be dishonest, either to my own mind, by smothering my convictions, or to my fellow creatures by using language at variance with my convictions" (Letter from Mill to Ricardo, in *The Works and Correspondence of David Ricardo,* vol. VII, 213; the sketch in the *Dictionary of National Biography* noted that he "was licensed to preach on 4 Oct. 1798 . . ."). In 1802, he accompanied Sir John Stuart, an acquaintance from Scotland who had been elected to Parliament, to London. In 1804, he published a tract on the ill effects of the reinstitution of the grain bounty, this being his first important economic work. In 1807 he published his very important *Commerce Defended,* in which he challenged the bases for both the mercantilist and physiocratic systems of political economy and advanced a proposition very similar in design to what is now known as Say's Law. But it was his 1818 *History of British India,* a work actually begun as early as 1806, which led to his prominence and acclaim as an intellectual force (this despite the fact that he had never traveled to India). It also led to a very lucrative appointment in the India House, partly secured with the help of Ricardo. Material on Mill's life may be found in article in the *Dictionary of National Biography,* written by Leslie Stephen; Alexander Bain (1882); and the *Introduction* by Donald Winch to Mill's selected economic writings.

49. This program involved Mill's son, John Stuart Mill, in the transcribing of James's tutorial lectures on the subject, which volume became James Mill's *Principles of Political Economy.* In other words, the ideas were Bentham's, the editor was James Mill, and the amanuensis was John Stuart Mill.

50. John Stuart Mill in his *Autobiography* identified his father's moral convictions as having derived from the works of the Greek philosophers: "My father's moral inculcations were at all times mainly those of the 'Socratici viri'; justice, temperance (to which he gave a very extended application), veracity, perseverance, readiness to encounter pain and especially labour; regard for the public good; estimation of persons according to their merits, and of things according to their intrinsic usefulness; a life of exertion in contradiction to one of self-indulgent sloth" (J. S. Mill 1873, 31–32).

known as *Essay on Government*), Mill desired to know the composition
of the happiness of individuals in order to explore the most appropriate
form for government.

Given that "the lot of every human being is determined by his pains
and pleasures" (James Mill 1825, 4), we must inquire as to the source of
these pains and pleasures. For Mill, they are either (1) produced "by our
fellow-men," or (2) produced "by causes independent of other men"
(1825, 4). Once the sources are known, the appropriate measures for the
alleviation of pain and the promotion of pleasure (so as to maximize net
pleasure) can be taken. If independent of other men, the pains and pleasures must originate with ourselves, and so we should be held responsible
for efforts taken, for our own benefit, for the maximization of net pleasure; if not, then government must become involved in promoting measures for redress, since the "business [of the government] is to increase to
the utmost the pleasures, and diminish to the utmost the pains, which
men derive from one another" (4).

Having set out to delimit the rationale for the existence of
government—this being to act as a facilitator and coordinator in instances which cannot be handled by individual means—Mill identified
several "natural laws" which serve to identify the most just and least
invasive form of government. The first of these laws, the "primary cause
of Government," "is the necessity of labour for obtaining the means of
subsistence, as well as the means of the greatest part of our pleasures"
(1825, 4). That the resources of the earth are limited, while our desires
are limitless, means that government of some sort becomes necessary if
we are to exist in any situation other than a constant state of warfare for
conquest of the possessions of others. Government becomes a "means"
to guarantee the "greatest sum" of happiness to the community, "preventing every individual, or combination of individuals, from interfering
with that distribution, or making any man to have less than his share"
(4). The important thing to note here is that Mill does not require the
state to allocate the produce of the community equally among all the
members, whether or not they are engaged in its production. It is *labor*
that is the vehicle for production and distribution of the goods in the
society, and so happiness is directly related to the production of goods
and the acquisition of the fruits of that labor. As Mill stated the utilitarian credo, "The greatest possible happiness of society is, therefore, attained by insuring to every man the greatest possible quantity of the
produce of his labour" (5).

The way in which this protection can best be achieved is through
a collective agreement of those in the community with like interests.
As to the degree of collectivization required, it is obvious that the collective must include all within the society, to prevent both the usurpation of power by a few, and the confiscation of the property of those

outside of the power structure by those granted the right to make and enforce laws.[51]

This leads to Mill's second law of human nature, "that a man, if able, will take from others any thing which they have and he desires" (1825, 8). The attribution by Mill of the desire on the part of any single individual, or narrowly defined interest group, for power and dominion over others in the community, an opinion of human nature not different from that of Hobbes, led Mill to his conclusion, in direct opposition to the conclusion drawn by Hobbes from the same premises, that the only legitimate form of government, one protective of the rights of all members of the community and least likely to usurp those rights (especially the property right), was that of a representative democracy.[52]

The "economic man" of Mill, being a rational (albeit modestly hedonistic) calculator, can exist only in an unfettered state, albeit one bounded by organization and structure designed to govern interpersonal interactions. The primacy of the individual was as central to Mill as it had been to Bentham, the expression of his interests a necessary prerequisite for the establishment of law and behavioral codes. Man is on this view the prisoner of his interests:

> It is indisputable that the acts of men follow their will; that their will follows their desires; and that their desires are generated by their apprehensions of good or evil; in other words, by their interests. (1825, 28)

Therefore the Hobbesian Leviathan, with its autocratic (although perhaps benevolent) sovereign, must be seen as anathema to Mill, since it allowed only for the airing of the views of the monarch, ignoring those of the governed. The interests of the masses could be furthered only through the creation of a popularly elected representative assembly.

Finally, Mill drew from Bentham the following ideas as basic economic propositions, which we know today as the heart of classical economic theory.[53]

---

51. "That one human being will desire to render the person and property of another subservient to his pleasures, notwithstanding the pain or loss of pleasure which it may occasion to that other individual, is the foundation of Government" (James Mill 1825, 9).

52. "A disposition to overrate one's own advantages, and underrate those of other men" is a third law (James Mill 1825, 15). A fourth law holds that "the great majority of old men have sons, whose interest they regard as an essential part of their own" (22).

53. James Mill, as any number of modern economists, was intrigued by Bentham's rhetorical devices. While his chosen method for the elucidation of first principles was empiricism—making the principles synthetic, inductive generalizations—Bentham's rhetoric was squarely in the tradition of Euclid, which serves as the basis of the modern passion among social scientists for mathematical (logical) modeling: A must be equal to, more than, or less than B. If it is not equal to or less than B, then it must be more than B. *Q.e.d.!* (Halévy argued that it was James Mill who "introduced for the first time into the language of political economy the Euclidean metaphor, which is even more audacious than the Newtonian metaphor" [Halévy 1928, 272].)

1. The ultimate purpose of economic activity is the individuals' consumption;

2. Optimal individual consumption is in a direct way attached to the individual's felicific calculus;

3. The individual's felicific calculus is self-determined, and this self-determination can best be described as self-interest;

4. The appropriate analog for the economic system is physics. Men's decisions are best seen to be consistent, and so logic is the best analytical tool. There is a science to men's decision making, and that science is essentially deductive;

5. Institutions merely reflect men's reason; institutions are in no way natural, nor do they have a life of their own.

The Utilitarianism of David Ricardo   6

David Ricardo (1772–1823),[54] a student of James Mill,[55] is a pivotal figure in the history of economic thought. His views, while steeped in the

---

But, as in Bentham's manner, the assertion was allowed that there could, for instance, only be eight objections to a given proposition, for our exhaustive search for possibilities has turned up only these and so we can allow of no more. If one can then dispose of all eight objections to the proposition, the proposition itself must be valid. (This was also the basis of the deductive approach of Arthur Conan Doyle's detective, Sherlock Holmes.) Bentham then did as he proposed—all eight objections were shown either to be false or irrelevant. Ergo, the proposition is valid. Q.e.d. But the problem immediately arose that there was at least one more objection, which somehow someone overlooked. James Mill, with his belief in Natural Law and as an avowed deductivist whose first principles were intuited (in contrast to Bentham's inductivist stance), followed a similar procedure, and so he argued conclusively what should only have been discussed contingently.

54. Ricardo was the third of at least seventeen children. His father, an immigrant from Holland, was a very successful London stockbroker. As a Jewish boy of an observant family, he was not sent to a "public school"; rather, he had house tutors and spent at least two years (from the ages of 12 to 13) at one of the *yeshivoth* (academies of Jewish studies) in Amsterdam. After his return to London, at the age of 14, he entered the family business. Apparently little or no time was spent on his being an adolescent.

Not content with mere material pursuits, Ricardo engaged in other areas which had piqued his interest. An interest in rocks and minerals led to his becoming a founding member of the Geological Society. Upon reading Smith's *Wealth of Nations,* he developed a lifelong interest in the subject of economics. In 1809 he published several letters in the *Morning Chronicle* on the subject of currency depreciation, which attracted the attention of the Bullion Committee of Parliament (whose position was in substantial agreement with Ricardo's). In 1815, he published another essay showing an inconsistency between Malthus's theory of rent and his posture of protection for agriculture. By this time, Ricardo had acquired a reputation as an authority on all matters economic.

Ricardo was elected to Parliament in 1819, when he bought a listing in a "rotten" borough in Portarlington, Ireland (where there were only 12 electors). He remained at Parliament until his death in 1823.

55. The relationship with James Mill was an interesting one: Ricardo was the willing student, while Mill played the role of a stern and sometimes unpleasant writing-master. It was Mill who urged Ricardo to stand for Parliament, where many of his views on property and government were actually expounded.

Utilitarianism of Bentham and James Mill, nonetheless led to different conclusions and even prompted a group of followers known as the Ricardian Socialists.

Ricardo's view of property kept with the tradition of the Philosophic Radicals, perhaps due (as much as anything) to his relationship and frequent communications with Bentham and James Mill. Property was a thing to be held sacrosanct. Additionally, Ricardo's economic theories—directed to the problem of *distribution* and not *production*—were predicated on a Natural Law foundation, so that, for instance, distribution of the product would, in the absence of inhibiting factors, be socially equitable.[56] Like Bentham, he maintained a belief in individual actions being the result of a calculation of self-interest, with institutions serving to shape individual interests. His position on property was intimately tied to his view of the role of government, which he developed not only through his discussions with his acquaintances, but also through his personal experiences in the House of Commons. These firsthand observations of the workings of government must be examined in some detail, as they are important in understanding Ricardo's views on property and the role of the individual in economic and social relations.

Ricardo was uncomfortable with the governmental situation in Britain in the early nineteenth century.[57] While the power of the monarchy was held in check by the countervailing (actually superior) power of the House of Commons, the Commons itself had become a tool of the aristocracy. Thus it came to be that an implicit compact, an "understanding," had been reached between the aristocracy and the monarchy for a division of power in the running of the affairs of the government. This power structure was maintained by trading favors with the ruling party in Commons. Although the situation had continued for many years with no serious breakdown in the "democratic tradition" of Great Britain, for Ricardo the situation could very easily and very rapidly decline, creating a despotic regime, absent an explicit constitutional check on the monarch *and* on the members of Parliament.

This check Ricardo held to be already in existence in a somewhat informal way, being held in the hands of (1) the people themselves, for whom government is established and from whom it derives its legitimacy, and (2) the information-dissemination power of a free and unfettered (vigilant and independent) press. The combined influence of these two forces "resolves itself into the fear which government and the aristocracy have of an insurrection of the people, by which their power might be overturned, and which alone keeps them within the bounds which now appear to arrest them" ("Observations on Parliamentary Reform," 497).

56. See Ricardo 1821, chapter IV; see also Beer 1940, vol. I, 148.
57. On this, see Ricardo's "Observations on Parliamentary Reform," in *The Works and Correspondence of David Ricardo,* vol. V, 495–503.

But given the nature of the ruling elites, these checks, while necessary, were not at all sufficient to restrain the government from involvement in actions detrimental to the overall well-being of the citizenry. While the press may rightly protest that an action taken by the government may be unjust or unlawful or hurtful to the general interests of liberty, the average citizen may not perceive it that way, or the authorities may simply find it expedient to ignore the commentaries, thinking (perhaps rightly) that the clamor will soon fade.

Thus was Ricardo to argue for the establishment of a truly representative House of Commons, one more conducive to the promotion of the "general happiness" of the citizenry as a whole. The franchise would be of the "average" people, neither the aristocracy nor the special interests, nor in fact those who were not in a position to understand the process. The House of Commons would be "chosen by the people, excluding all those, whether high or low, who had interests separate and distinct from the general interest . . ." ("Observations on Parliamentary Reform," 498). It also, evidently, was not to be a universal suffrage.[58]

Apart from the question of the suffrage, Ricardo accepted that the government had actually been performing well *as constituted*. The British government had not taken actions detrimental to the welfare of its citizens, and the kingdom was prosperous and growing economically, despite the sometimes self-centered motivations of the governors. However, for Ricardo, the issue was more important than the apparent smooth functioning of the system; the issue went to the design of the system itself, the principles which lay at its base. Ricardo needed as a basis for legitimization of the government a set of principles of governance—a physical document, constitution or other such social compact—which could be referenced to ensure the system functioned the way that the people stated that it *should* function, thus guaranteeing an outcome more favorable to the majority of the governed. The codification, or express stipulation of government authority and the extent of its power, was missing in the case of Great Britain, but was, for Ricardo, a necessary statement of rights and responsibilities of the citizenry, and limitations and restrictions on governmental interference in individual affairs.

The most important aspect of this constitution was the protection afforded to the right to property; after all, the rationale behind the compact was the promotion of rights of contract, and the protection of the means to carry out the provisions of any contract; "it must be shewn that such a constitution of it is favourable to the prosperity of the country, before such an argument can be admitted for its continuance" ("Observations on Parliamentary Reform," 499). Property rights were for Ricardo

---

58. "I am convinced that an extension of the suffrage, far short of making it universal, will substantially secure to the people the good government they wish for, and therefore I deprecate the demand for the universality of the elective franchise. . . ." ("Observations on Parliamentary Reform," 502).

the most fundamental of rights. "So essential does it appear to me, to the cause of good government, that the rights of property should be held sacred, that I would agree to deprive those of the elective franchise against whom it could justly be alleged that they considered it their interest to invade them" ("Observations on Parliamentary Reform," 501).

In his 1816 *Proposals for an Economical and Secure Currency,* Ricardo extolled the virtues of a free and unrestricted trade. Consistent with the themes taken up by Smith and the utilitarians, Ricardo demanded as little government intervention as possible in the affairs of commerce. Constraints on commerce, on the free exercise of individual liberty, stifle creativity and initiative and imagination, crucial components to social and economic advancement. Only when restrictions are removed so as to allow the full talents of the individual to be exercised, will the economy and the state flourish.

> Much has been ably written on the benefits resulting to a country from the liberty of trade, leaving every man to employ his talents, and capital, as to him may seem best, unshackled by restrictions of every kind. . . . It is with pleasure, that I see the progress which this great principle is making amongst those whom we should have expected to clinge the longest to old prejudices. In the petitions to parliament against the corn bill, the advantages of an unrestricted trade were generally recognized; . . . These are principles which cannot be too widely extended, nor too generally adopted in practice. . . . (Ricardo 1816, 70–71)

But despite his enthusiastic advocacy, Ricardo freely admitted the defects in free trade. The government may be required, as part of its legitimate supervisory function, to intervene in two specific instances, these being (1) to protect the public from fraud and abuse, and (2) to "certify a fact" (1816, 71).

The achievement for which Ricardo is today best known is *The Principles of Political Economy and Taxation,* published in 1817 (3d ed., 1821). While begun as the expansion of a tract on the need to abolish the Corn Laws, and expanded into a treatise at the behest of James Mill, this work established much more convincingly than did Smith the idea that labor was the ultimate expression of value, and in so doing it provided the impetus for the later socialist challenges to the system of capitalist production and Classical Political Economy.[59] Here it will be noted that, once again, Ricardo in this work took the occasion to advocate the primacy of the individual in the system and the inviolability of the property right.

Ricardo, attuned to Natural Law, held a great deal of faith in the

---

59. Ricardo's contribution to this area will be discussed in a companion volume, treating labor as a factor of production.

ability of the market to regulate economic activity through the working of immutable laws. Wages are in essence stipulated by contracts between employer and employee, and such an agreement should not be interfered with by the government or any other outside authority. "Like all other contracts, wages should be left to the fair and free competition of the market, and should never be controlled by the interference of the legislature" (Ricardo 1821, 61). The Poor Laws supplied the perfect example of the results of interference by the government in the workings of the free market. Intended as a program for the alleviation of poverty in England by establishing and maintaining a subsistence level, the result was precisely the opposite of the intention. The laws served:

> to deteriorate the condition of both poor and rich; instead of making the poor rich, they are calculated to make the rich poor; and whilst the present laws are in force, it is quite in the natural order of things that the fund for the maintenance of the poor should progressively increase till it has absorbed all the net revenue of the country, or at least so much of it as the state shall leave to us, after satisfying its own never-failing demands for the public expenditure. (1821, 61)

In this Ricardo agreed with Malthus. But he accepted that the abolition of the Poor Laws could not take place immediately given the entrenchment of these programs and the dependence they fostered. The social consequences of an immediate rejection would be severe. Nonetheless, their abolition is required if the society is to have any hope of prospering, for only in the absence of such pernicious legislation could the industry of the individual be returned.

Perhaps the most amazing of Ricardo's contributions is his rhetoric—abstract statements designed for ready application and implementation. His method, as with that of James Mill, involved the employment of abstract models combined with logical reasoning, with an emphasis on rational, deductive argumentation. Once the terms of the debate had been defined (also in a rather abstract manner), the results desired could with little effort be obtained, and be applicable to policy problems as well. While it is of course the case that there were earlier promoters of a deductive approach to economics (for example, Dudley North and John Locke), the movement of economics from a moral to a Cartesian science will be here taken to begin with James Mill, and to achieve its apotheosis with the work of Ricardo and the later materialist philosophy of Marx. As Halévy stated the position, "What for Adam Smith had been a preliminary became, for Ricardo, the essence of political economy. Political economy was now a theory detached from practice, whatever might subsequently be its practical consequences" (Halévy 1928, 267).[60]

---

60. Beer, however, concluded that, of all political economists, "there has been none more inductive, and less abstract in method, than Ricardo" (1940, vol. I, 147).

7 The Return of Political Arithmetic: J. R. McCulloch

One may suspect from the presentation to this point that the important work of the political arithmeticians lay forgotten while the philosophic radicals pursued their hedonical studies. Thus the impression may be that there came with Bentham a sharp and decisive break with the more scientifically minded, statistically oriented, British political economists of previous generations. As we shall presently see, however, such a hasty conclusion would be in error, for there were indeed efforts made to fulfill Bentham's dream and create a "moral arithmetic." The connection between the two groups was made by one of the most influential writers of the Philosophic Radical tradition,[61] a man known more in his time as a statistician than a political economist, John Ramsay McCulloch (1789–1864).[62]

As a disciple of Ricardo, McCulloch took (with vigor) to the task of extending Ricardian economics beyond the restrictive realm of Ricardo himself; Halévy went so far as to claim that McCulloch and James Mill "systematically neglected all these restrictions [of Ricardo], and became, so to speak, more Ricardian than Ricardo himself" (1928, 343).[63] However, it was after the manner of Graunt, Petty, and the political arithmeticians, especially Davenant and King, and the later work of Tooke and Newmarch, that McCulloch published his statistical collections, a task which some believe was of more importance than his economic investigations. (With the specifics of McCulloch's economic views we will deal at a

---

61. While McCulloch had a great *affinity* for the views of the philosophic radicals, he was not a formal member of the group.

62. McCulloch, born in Scotland, was the son of Edward, the laird of Auchengool. Having studied at Edinburgh University, he left without a degree, served briefly in "the office of a writer to the signet" (what we may today call a prothonotary), and thereafter took up the study of economics.

Between 1818 and 1829 he served as editor of *The Scotsman,* contributing also significant pieces to the *Edinburgh Review* and the *Encyclopædia Britannica.*

With the assistance of James Mill, McCulloch was appointed in 1828 to the Chair of Political Economy at the University of London (now University College), a position he held until 1831. Halévy proclaimed that McCulloch and Mill "were two intransigent disciples who brought to bear on their economic propaganda the zeal of the Scottish religious enthusiast" (Halévy 1928, 343).

McCulloch, with Tooke, James Mill, Malthus, and Ricardo, was a founding member of the Political Economy Club. In 1838, he was appointed Comptroller of the Stationery Office, where he remained until his death; in 1843 he was elected an associate to the Institute of France.

In 1846, he undertook to produce the first collection of Ricardo's works, and from 1856 to 1858 edited five collections of scarce tracts in economics.

63. Mitchell, however, characterized McCulloch as "a man of mediocre talent," distinguished only by the fact that "[f]ew economists, even among the Germans, have achieved a greater output with less intellectual distinction" (1967, vol. I, 301, 302). He then bestowed upon him the distinction of having been "one of the first men to make his living as an economist" (301).

later time.) His first such collection was the 1832 *A Dictionary, Practical, Theoretical, and Historical, of Commerce and Commercial Navigation.*[64] His second collection (1837) was *A Statistical Account of the British Empire: Exhibiting Its Extent, Physical Capacities, Population, Industry, and Civil and Religious Institutions.*[65] In this two-volume compilation, McCulloch endeavored not to deliver a work confined "to mere statements of results, or to the detail of such information as might have been mostly thrown into a tabular form." Nor was he especially interested "in giving an account of any branch of industry, with stating the value of its products, the number and wages of the people engaged in it, and so forth." He sought instead to present his material in a readable fashion, complete with commentary, to provide for the reader "some notices of its history, and of the more prominent of the circumstances that have accelerated or retarded its progress" (McCulloch 1837, vi). The work is actually the production of a number of authors, each a specialist in his area. Subject headings include Geology; Climate; Botany; Zoology; the English Constitution and System of Law; Corporations; the Scot and Irish Constitutions and Systems of Courts; Education in Ireland, England, Scotland, and Wales; Vital Statistics; Provision for the Poor; and even the Origin and Progress of the English Language.

Despite the sheer breadth of the project, McCulloch despaired over the paucity of the statistical information available upon which to draw authoritative conclusions. "Few, indeed, would imagine, *à priori,* how ill supplied British writers are with the means necessary to throw light on some of the most interesting departments of statistical inquiry" (1837, viii). This did not prevent him from drawing conclusions; he simply desired to point out to his readers their conditionality.[66]

McCulloch's best-known work in economics is *The Principles of Political Economy: with Some Inquiries Respecting their Application, and a Sketch of the Rise and Progress of the Science* (1825),[67] essentially an expansion of his 1824 *A Discourse on the Rise, Progress, Peculiar Objects and Importance of Political Economy.* Until the publication of

---

64. This was his *statistical* work. In 1816, he published his first work, *An Essay on a Reduction of the Interest of the National Debt, proving that this is the only possible means of Relieving the Distresses of the Commercial and Agricultural Interests; and Establishing the Justice of that Measure on the Surest Principles of Political Economy,* a work whose title pretty much explains the thesis. Of the proposals in this essay, Ricardo, whom McCulloch held in the highest regard as his mentor, wrote that, "though such a measure might be beneficial to one class at the expense of another, it would afford very little relief to the country, and would be a precedent of a most alarming and dangerous nature" (quoted in Mitchell 1967, vol. I, 300).

65. This two-volume work was published "under the superintendence of the Society for the Diffusion of Useful Knowledge."

66. Finally, in 1841, McCulloch published *A Dictionary, Geographical, Statistical, and Historical, of the Various Countries, Places, and Principal Natural Objects of the World.*

67. The edition used here is the fifth, of 1864.

John Stuart Mill's *Principles,* this work was the standard authority in political economy, its influence notable in the fact that it was translated into French, German, and Spanish.

To set the stage for his presentation, McCulloch felt it necessary to identify the realm of economics, so as to provide some sense of the subject matter and to show what must be excluded from the discussion. For McCulloch, "economy" in its Greek derivation meant literally "the government of a family"; "political economy" was therefore and by extension "to the State what domestic economy is to a family" (McCulloch 1864, 1n.1). In utilitarian fashion, he then defined economics as "the science of the laws which regulate the production, accumulation, distribution, and consumption of these articles or products that are necessary, useful, or agreeable to man, and which at the same time possess exchangeable value" (1864, 1).[68]

Employing the Smithian argument, McCulloch directed that an object could possess "utility" without having "exchangeable value"; *utility* means simply the "power or capacity which particular articles or products have of satisfying one or more of the various wants and desires of which man is susceptible." Without the labor content, however, no good can ever become *valuable:*

> A commodity or product, is not valuable merely because it is useful or desirable; but it is valuable when, besides being possessed of these qualities, it can only be procured through the intervention of labour. (1864, 2)

For this reason, he maintained that "political economy" was "the *science of values*" (1864, 3; emphasis in original), by which he meant value in *exchange,* and not utility or value in *use.*[69]

McCulloch identified three phenomena instrumental in the evolution from a primitive to a productive (capitalistic) state. These are (1) the right of property (not the right *to* property), (2) the emergence of an exchange economy (including the ability to engage in pursuits in which the individual has a comparative advantage), and (3) the accumulation of capital (which he held to be the embodiment of past labor exertions).[70] We will only be concerned at the present with the first of these phenomena, the right of property.

The right of property is, as McCulloch approached it, a proposition

---

68. As McCulloch held to a form of the labor theory of value, he defined "exchangeable value" as meaning "that there are individuals disposed to give some quantity of labour, or of some other article or product, obtainable only by means of labour, in exchange for it" (McCulloch 1864, 1).

69. McCulloch was not always consistent, as is clear a mere two pages later when he writes of "the production of utility, and consequently of value . . ." (McCulloch 1864, 5).

70. In this McCulloch was in agreement with the view of Robert Torrens (1780–1864), a critic of Ricardo and James Mill.

intuitively obvious: "All the rude products furnished by nature have to be appropriated," this being necessary in order to allow the natural resources of the earth to be fashioned in a manner usable by man (1864, 25–26). To ensure that a man be able to control and protect the fruits of his labor, so that his efforts will not be appropriated by others, is a proposition "so obvious and urgent, that it must have been all but coeval with the formation of societies" (26). The right of property "is, in truth, the foundation on which the other institutions of society mainly rest" (28). It is for the protection and the guarantee of the right of property that governments are needed.

As societies evolved, so did the meaning of the property right. Originally confined to the spoils from hunting and gathering, it gradually expanded in scope to include land, as population growth and territorial expansion led to the development of agriculture and the domestication of animals (1864, 27). But it meant much more. By "property" and "right of property," McCulloch did not mean simply ownership of objects for use; property included intellectual output and physical abilities as well. In libertarian fashion, McCulloch held that "[o]f all the species of property which a man can possess, the faculties of his mind and the powers of his body are most particularly his own; and these he should be permitted to enjoy, that is, to use or exert, at his discretion" (29). From this belief he advanced a fundamental right of trade, this being a natural prohibition of monopoly (whether state sponsored or commercial) and other restrictions on the free exercise of one's natural abilities. It is then a violation of the natural order for restraints and regulations on the activities of individuals in their capacities as trading agents to be proposed and implemented, including but not limited to government decrees restricting use rights (including zoning ordinances), usury regulations, cartelization, wage restrictions, and presumably restraints on occupations such as prostitution. Nothing, on McCulloch's view, is more destructive than a government which violates or attempts to restrain the right of property.[71]

Government has, of course, a function to perform with respect to property. In general terms, McCulloch held that the government "will fail of its duty if it do not exert itself to prevent that confusion and disorder in the distribution of property, and in the prosecution of employments, that could either not be prevented without its interference, or not so easily and completely" (1864, 190). Government specifically has six principal functions: (1) to provide for the security of its citizens, against threats foreign and domestic; (2) to give legal sanction to contracts, including testaments and wills; (3) to adjudicate disputes and enforce contracts; (4) to provide protection against fraud; (5) to sanction industrial activity, including the

---

71. "... without security of property, and freedom to engage in every employment not hurtful to others, society can make no considerable advances. Government is, therefore, bound to take such measures as may be effectual to secure these objects" (McCulloch 1864, 190).

construction of necessary infrastructure, and the explicit involvement in certain basic industries; and (6) to protect property and persons from casualty (190–231).

Finally, McCulloch felt obliged to counter the criticism that private ownership would leave some with great wealth and others, perhaps the majority, in great poverty. To this he responded that the property right is a catalyst for industry and the creation of wealth, and has no role whatsoever in the generation of poverty. "The establishment of a right of property enables exertion, invention and enterprise, forethought and economy, to reap their due reward. But it does this without inflicting the smallest imaginable injury upon anything else." Without property rights, "all would sink to the same bottomless abyss of barbarism and poverty" (1864, 36).

8 A Summary of Classical British Economic Orthodoxy: Nassau Senior

Having come this far, we are now in a position to state some general propositions of political economy as it developed to this point. These propositions were stated by Nassau William Senior (1790–1864)[72] in his 1836 *An Outline of the Science of Political Economy*. Briefly, the four propositions are: (1) the principle of individual maximization; (2) the Malthusian law of population; (3) increasing returns to industry; and (4) decreasing returns to agriculture. Only the first two relate to the present interpretation of the history of economic thought, so the last two will be merely stated.

The first proposition—"that every man desires to obtain additional wealth with as little sacrifice as posible"—Senior made clear was a subjective principle, "a matter of conscience." As such it implies only "that no person feels his whole wants to be adequately supplied; that every person has some unsatisfied desires which he believes that additional wealth would satisfy" (Senior 1836, 27). Senior defined wealth utilitarianly, as "all those things, and those things only, which are transferable, are limited in supply, and are directly or indirectly productive of pleasure or preventive of pain" (1836, 6). Money, as "abstract wealth," is the most universally desired object. It can assist the individual in satisfying "at will his ambition, or vanity, or indolence, his public spirit or his private be-

72. Senior, son of the vicar of Durnford, Wiltshire, was educated at Eton and Magdalen College, Oxford, his training being in the law. With the assistance of James Mill, he was elected to the Political Economy Club (1823) and subsequently became Drummond Professor of Political Economy at Oxford (1825–30). Following his service there, he became active in public affairs—as an adviser to the Whigs—but returned to academia, again as Drummond Professor (1847–52). The classic reference on Senior is Marian Bowley (1937).

nevolence" and allow him to "multiply the means of obtaining bodily pleasure, or of avoiding bodily evil, or the still more expensive amusements of the mind" (27).

As for other desires, the sacrifices necessary to achieve them differ both relatively and absolutely. In fact, Senior regarded these differences as forming "some of the principal distinctions in individual and national character" (1836, 27). Important here is the security of property: where property rights are secured, so the populace is free to pursue wealth and opulence; where they are not, poverty is manifest (although the *desire* is still evident). Thus the first proposition accounts for the utilitarian pleasure principle and the individualist pursuit of property, as developed through the work of the philosophers of the Scottish Enlightenment.

The second proposition—"that the population of the world, or, in other words, the number of persons inhabiting it, is limited only by moral or physical evil, or by fear of the deficiency of those articles of wealth which the habits of the individuals of each class of its inhabitants lead them to require" (1836, 30)—reflects Malthus's population principle. Again, the basis of this "empirical" proposition is the pleasure principle. Resources are finite, wants are not. As economic development proceeds, and national wealth expands, so do the demands of the population. But an expanding population reduces the individual share of the existing product, while wants continue to increase. Eventually the two collide. Population is therefore limited out of a concern that, were it not, there would be repercussions on the expansion and distribution of wealth.

The third proposition—"That the Powers of Labour, and of the other Instruments which produce Wealth, may be indefinitely increased by using their Products as the means of further Production" (1836, 50)— and the fourth—"That Agricultural Skill remaining the same, Additional Labour employed on the Land within a given district, produces in general a Less Proportionate Return" (81)—are also empirical propositions that reflect the state of the theory of capital and labor in industry and agriculture, respectively. However, as their importance to the present discussion is marginal at best, we shall leave them for the companion volume.

The Importance of John Stuart Mill   9

Mill's Utilitarianism   9.1

We have already adverted to John Stuart Mill (1806–73),[73] the son of James Mill. The younger Mill's influence greatly surpassed that of his

73. Born in London, Mill was educated by his father, by all accounts a stern taskmaster. The regimen included intensive study of Greek and of the classical Greek literature, which Mill himself recollected having been told occurred by the age of three. In his eighth year, he began instruction in Latin and soon had become familiar with the classical Latin

father, and even defined political economy: his classic *Principles of Political Economy,* first published in 1848, remained the dominant statement of the subject in the English language until the publication in 1890 of Marshall's *Principles of Economics.* Thus Mill's understanding of the essentials of Utilitarianism and the concerns we have addressed here as underlying the Hobbes–Locke debate did much to fashion the understandings of the mainstream of classical and postclassical economic thought through the end of the nineteenth century. For this reason alone, Mill's place as a pivotal figure in the history of Classical Political Economy is assured.

We begin this presentation of the place of John Stuart Mill in the history of Utilitarianism and Classical Political Economy with Mill's most authoritative statement of the philosophy of Utilitarianism: his essay entitled, simply enough, "Utilitarianism."[74] While he considered his reading of Bentham's *Theory of Legislation* to have been a turning point in his intellectual growth,[75] as it was this work perhaps more than any other that directed his attention to the philosophy of Utilitarianism, Mill nonetheless took great care to differentiate his preference for "ethical

works; also at eight he was set to the difficult task of mastering algebra, geometry, and differential calculus. His instruction in logic commenced at age twelve and included the study of Aristotle and Hobbes. (He had already completed the study of Herodotus and the first six books of Plato before his eighth birthday.) It was also about this time that he became acquainted with the field of political economy.

Returning to England from a brief stay in France, during which he felt the "free and genial atmosphere of Continental life" (Mill 1873, 38), Mill read briefly for the law. In 1822, he planned for the creation of the Utilitarian Society (according to Mill the first time the term had been used), a short-lived (three years) group which had no effect on the transmission of the ideas of the movement as it later developed. Having decided against the practice of law, he instead (in 1823) took a position as junior clerk at India House, in the office of Examiner of India Correspondence, the office where his father also worked and under whom he served. (He became head of the office in 1856.)

From about 1822 to 1830, Mill was engaged in various pursuits, including writing for the *Traveller* (an evening newspaper owned by the economist Robert Torrens), the *Westminster Review,* and the *Parliamentary History and Review* (as well as contributing letters to the *Morning Chronicle*); later (in his *Autobiography*) he referred to this episode as his period of "youthful propagandism." It was also at this time that he took to editing Bentham's *Treatise Upon Evidence.*

At about this time (1826) Mill suffered a nervous breakdown, which he attributed to his intense schedule from the age of three. Following a later illness in 1836, he seems to have changed his views of human behavior, moving away from a means–end framework to a belief in achieving "happiness," the ultimate end, through indirect (not "rational" in the accepted sense of the term) means.

In 1865, he was elected to Parliament from Westminster, serving only until 1868 when he was defeated for reelection. After his defeat, he retired to an estate in Avignon, France.

74. This essay first appeared in 1861 as a series of three articles in *Fraser's Magazine.* This is the edition we use here, and not the 1871 reprint.

75. Mill lived for a while with Bentham, working as an amanuensis, and not only absorbed his thinking (which was his father's intent) but seems also to have developed a contempt for Bentham's epicurean life-style.

Utilitarianism" as distinct from the "hedonistic Utilitarianism" he (and others) associated with Bentham.[76]

Mill's morality and ethics were not predicated on Natural Law, as were Smith's. Rather, as with Bentham, they were predicated on the principle of utility and so could be rationally determined and debated. Mill accepted Bentham's definition of utility, and indeed his requirement to derive a first principle that could be accepted, once made known, as self-evident. From this principle, Mill (like Bentham) then "could attach all his other doctrines as logical consequences" (Mill 1838, 171). Mill's ethics were on this account synthetic, predicated on secular-humanistic and not religiously derived principles; thus the notion of "ethical Utilitarianism," an ethics derived from reflection on the conduct of the individual as he actually exists in the society and interacts with others, is clearly descriptive of Mill's view. Morals are not on this view the codes handed down as religious commandments, but instead are in no small sense evolutionary codes, capable of change as times and conditions warrant.

Despite his agreement with the basics of Bentham's social philosophy—he accepted Bentham's general premise of the equation of the rightness of actions with the happiness they engender, that is, Bentham's consequentialism—Mill did not believe that action was dictated by self-interest alone. For Mill, as with Bentham, "right" implies the promotion of pleasure, "wrong" the promotion of pain or the denial of pleasure. The difference between the two writers is that while Bentham advanced a seemingly crude pleasure calculus, looking only at the net value (where calculable) of pleasure, Mill felt the need to inquire as to its composition, that is, as to the *quality* of the pleasure. This is intimately connected with the distinction between the crude valuation and its composition, the whole as opposed to the sum of the parts. There were also the additional factors of individual morality, ethics, and a sense of belonging to a community to which Bentham gave but little attention, but which were to Mill at least equally as important in the determination of the overall pleasure calculation as were the more hedonistic factors. Mill indeed lamented "that utilitarian writers in general have placed the superiority of mental over bodily pleasures chiefly in the greater permanency, safety, uncostliness, &c., of the former—that is, in their circumstantial advantages rather that in their intrinsic nature" (J. S. Mill 1861, 395).

While Bentham's calculus demanded that all pleasures be treated as equal in substance and worth, so that total community pleasure is the summation of individual pleasures, Mill allowed for a more discriminatory attitude. Pleasure calculations need not be comparable interpersonally, as the individual rankings are little more than personal value judgments. But it was just as evident to Mill that the philosophy of Utilitarianism in no way

---

76. Thus Schumpeter claimed that J. S. Mill was merely a "qualified" utilitarian (Schumpeter 1954, 408).

denied the validity of the ethical statement "that some *kinds* of pleasure are more desirable and more valuable than others" (1861, 395; emphasis in original). Indeed a person possessed of the "higher faculties" is more finely attuned to the appreciation of the better things in life and so "requires more to make him happy, is capable probably of more acute suffering, and is certainly accessible to it at more points, than one of an inferior type" (396). The very attainment of the "higher faculties" means that the person so endowed is less easily satiated, or pleased only incompletely. But this is not enough to make the "superior being" envious of the "inferior," for "in spite of these liabilities, he can never really wish to sink into what he feels to be a lower grade of existence" (396).[77] Thus we see here an elitism in the view that the educated (higher classes) are able to evaluate the utilities of the lower, uneducated, classes.

"Moral feelings" for Mill are not innate, but are acquired, and therefore are capable of development and direction. As with other beliefs which are learned, morality is furthered by a desire for community, a "social state" that "is at once so natural, so necessary, and so habitual to man, that, except in some unusual circumstances or by an effort of voluntary abstraction, he never conceives himself otherwise than as a member of a body" (1861, 528). That we cannot in fact think of ourselves otherwise reinforces a capacity within us to act in accordance with the requirements of a societal framework. This acceptance of a community interest leads us to identify our own ends with the ends of others in the community, and vice versa.

But this framework from which are derived the morals and beliefs of the community was not itself derived haphazardly, with no reflection as to its constitution; it was not something erected for the sake of expediency or practicality, without a purpose. All of the institutions developed by man have some purpose at their core, and the consolidation of a code of morals and ethics is not substantially different.

> Whether happiness be or be not the end to which morality should be referred—that it be referred to an *end* of some sort, and not left in the dominion of vague feeling or inexplicable internal conviction, that it be made a matter of reason and calculation, and not merely of sentiment, is essential to the very idea of moral philosophy. . . .
> (J. S. Mill 1838, 171; emphasis in original)

Standards are an essential ingredient then in the Millian scheme for the advancement of an ethical and moral base. An appeal to pragmatism will not suffice, since this appeal is too subjective. Mill in fact held that man has some control over his actions, but did not admit that he has any

---

77. Then follows the famous line: "It is better to be a human being dissatisfied than a pig satisfied; better to be Socrates dissatisfied than a fool satisfied. And if the fool, or the pig, are of a different opinion, it is because they only know their own side of the question. The other party to the comparison knows both sides" (J. S. Mill 1861, 396).

control over the *consequences* of those actions.[78] Thus there needs to be some reliance on rules of behavior to serve as guideposts that may channel those attributes regarded most highly by society in terms of their utility-enhancement (although it is perhaps going a bit too far to classify Mill as a strict rule-utilitarian).

Consider as an example Mill's stance on education. Education is important because it inculcates a standard to which the individual will seek to adhere. It trains the mind to obey, to accept certain moral and ethical principles that an untrained, simple utility calculator would neglect in a strictly hedonistic approach to Utilitarianism.[79] Education, while important to the growth of the individual in training him to employ more effectively his given talents, also serves a social purpose by instilling a sense of community and social purpose. But Mill also required the individual to be wary of the dangers of "following the herd." While useful as a tool for the direction of individual motivations to the pursuit of the common good, mass education has the potential for abuse by the authorities, as it can very easily be converted to a forum for propagandizing and proselytizing, and the pursuit of an agenda taken as representative of the "popular will." Mill did not accept the Benthamist position that the popular will should always be followed, but remained skeptical, urging a pursuit of individuality as a bulwark against the force of opinion.

While respecting the role that education can play in the socializing process, Mill was not sanguine about accepting the simplistic view of the nurture argument as expressed by the utopian socialist Robert Owen (about whom more later). Owen, he thought, was no more than a fatalist, holding that man could be molded in any way desired simply by educating him in the proper manner. The possibility of achieving this Mill vehemently denied, insisting that this doctrine neglected the significant role of the individual in forming his own character; man has as much to do with shaping his character, and perhaps more so, as does the environment. Consider the following from *The Logic of the Moral Sciences*, book VI of Mill's *A System of Logic* (1843):

> A Fatalist believes, or half believes, (for nobody is a consistent Fatalist,) not only that whatever is about to happen will be the infallible result of the causes which produce it, (which is the true Necessitarian doctrine,) but, moreover, that there is no use in struggling against it; that it will happen however we may strive to prevent it. Now, a Necessitarian, believing that our actions follow from our characters, and that our characters follow from our organisation, our education, and

---

78. See *Principles of Political Economy*: "Human beings can control their own acts, but not the consequences of their acts either to themselves or to others" (J. S. Mill 1871, bk. II, chap. I, §1, 200–201).

79. "A cultivated mind . . . finds sources of inexhaustible interest in all that surrounds it . . ." (J. S. Mill 1861, 399).

our circumstances, is apt to be, with more or less of consciousness on his part, a Fatalist as to his own actions, and to believe that his nature is such, or that his education and circumstances have so moulded his character, that nothing can now prevent him from feeling and acting in a particular way, or at least that no effort of his own can hinder it. In the words of the sect which in our own day has most perseveringly inculcated and most perversely misunderstood this great doctrine, his character is formed *for* him, and not *by* him; therefore his wishing that it had been formed differently is of no use; he has no power to alter it. But this is a grand error. He has, to a certain extent, a power to alter his character. Its being, in the ultimate resort, formed for him, is not inconsistent with its being, in part, formed *by* him as one of the intermediate agents. His character is formed by his circumstances, (including among these his particular organisation,) but his own desire to mould it in a particular way is one of those circumstances, and by no means one of the least influential. . . . We are exactly as capable of making our own character, *if we will,* as others are of making it for us. (J. S. Mill 1872, 26–27; emphasis in original)

In his 1859 *On Liberty* Mill expressed most succinctly his perceptions of human will, human action, and the place of the individual in society. He proclaimed most passionately that all human faculties—including "perception, judgment, discriminative feeling, mental activity, and even moral preference"—result from, and can best be maintained by, the individual being allowed free choice (J. S. Mill 1859, 71). Individualism was in fact the center of Mill's intellectual universe: "The initiative of all wise or noble things comes and must come from individuals" (1859, 81). Society will progress only so long as this fundamental notion is understood; society will cease to progress "[w]hen it ceases to possess individuality" (86).

Yet Mill accepted the necessity for individuals, as part of society, to abide by general rules of conduct (not to be confused with *customs,* which he regarded as pernicious).[80] Rules of conduct shape expectations while allowing an otherwise free interplay of human actions:

In the conduct of human beings toward one another it is necessary that general rules should for the most part be observed in order that people may know what they have to expect; but in each person's own concerns his individual spontaneity is entitled to free exercise. (1859, 93)

Thus emerged Mill's views on liberty, combining a strong civil libertarian position, predicated on a refined Benthamism, with a belief that

---

80. "The despotism of custom is everywhere the standing hindrance to human advancement, being in unceasing antagonism to that disposition to aim at something better than customary, which is called, according to circumstances, the spirit of liberty, or that of progress or improvement" (Mill 1859, 85).

there existed, nonetheless, an ethical ordering. There must be a qualitative element to decision making: good and wise men *should* instruct those less good and less wise as to what they ought to be doing and believing. While everyone had a right to his opinion, opinions can and should be judged, and those whose positions have been defeated should accept that judgment as final.[81]

Wary of the potential for the subjugation of the individual by the group, Mill professed a general disdain for the interference of government in the affairs of the people. Government has an important and obvious role to play as an agent of acculturation, but it should not be forgotten that government is a necessary evil. There is no reason to believe that the government is any better equipped to impose moral and ethical systems of conduct on the populace than the people themselves can devise. While social reformers may desire governmental action on the grounds that it can more immediately redress social problems than, for instance, education could by altering attitudes and behaviors, it should never be forgotten that the public has become wary of government intrusion in their lives and so in most instances profoundly seeks to resist it (J. S. Mill 1871, bk. V, chap. I, sec. 1, 795).[82]

Despite his wariness, John Stuart Mill, in the manner of Bentham, McCulloch, and James Mill, held that government has *necessary* functions to perform, including taxation (as revenue generation, not as a social expedient for income distribution purposes), protection of persons and property, and the enforcement of contracts. But there were also other functions that had been over the years appropriated by government, duties for which a utilitarian basis could not be found. These "optional" interferences (typically based on "erroneous" theories) include, for example, protectionism and usury laws (1871, chaps. X and XI of bk. V). So, while the function and intrusion of government is important for the health and well-being of the society, its institutions should be subject to the following important stricture:

> Whatever theory we adopt respecting the foundation of the social union, and under whatever political institutions we live, there is a circle around every individual human being which no government,

---

81. Does one have the right to suicide? Yes, if no one will be the loser in the commission of the act. But how does one know whether there will be losers? Socrates could perhaps tell; others can not.

82. Mill offered three objections to government interference: (1) individuals are likely to perform tasks more efficiently than is government ("there is no one so fit to conduct any business, or to determine how or by whom it shall be conducted, as those who are personally interested in it" [J. S. Mill 1859, 133]); (2) individuals should assume tasks "as a means to their own mental education" (133); and (3) government should be restricted in its scope to avoid increasing unnecessarily its power ("Every function superadded to those already exercised by the government causes its influence over hopes and fears to be more widely diffused, and converts, more and more, the active and ambitious part of the public into hangers-on of the government, or of some party which aims at becoming the government" [134–35]).

be it that of one, of a few, or of the many, ought to be permitted to overstep: there is a part of the life of every person who has come to years of discretion, within which the individuality of that person ought to reign uncontrolled either by any other individual or by the public collectively. (1871, bk. V, ch. XI, sec. 2, 943)

To explain better his position, so as to reiterate that government had important and legitimate functions, and so not to give the impression that he was advocating anarchy, Mill identified two types of governmental intervention: the *authoritative* and the *advisory*. Authoritative interference in the affairs of the individual seeks to restrict activity, to prevent the free exercise of individual liberty; it is the coercive form of interference in individual life, demanding strict adherence to the laws and fiats and decrees of the rulers of the society, under penalty of punishment. As there is the potential in undertaking the authoritative role for the government to demand too severe a restriction of liberty, and especially of individuality, as the government attempts to exercise functions for which it was never intended, its legitimacy becomes severely limited.

The advisory role is the more acceptable from the point of view of the protection of individual rights, although it is rarely followed in practice because it does not employ oppressive legislation; the "reforms" which it seeks to institute can be accomplished in a fraction of the time through more compulsory means. The advisory role is one of positive reinforcement and so involves only the setting of bounds or limitations on behavior, not proscriptions or prohibitions. In performing this role, the government can legitimately, according to Mill, establish rules and definitions of what constitutes acceptable behavior, and even institutions for the provision of services, so long as it does not interfere with the ability of others in the provision of these same services.

When a government provides means for fulfilling a certain end, leaving individuals free to avail themselves of different means if in their opinion preferable, there is no infringement of liberty, no irksome or degrading restraint. One of the principal objections to government interference is then absent. (1871, 944)

Mill did not object, for instance, to the government establishing a postal system, or a school system, or even a religion, so long as the private, individual citizen is not prohibited from establishing without interference his own alongside that of the government. Whether this could actually work Mill did not say; still, it should be an available option.

Mill was as much concerned about the *quality* of government as he was about the *process* of governing. In principle he saw little wrong with benevolent dictatorship, but worried about its implementation. If the dictator performed as the people wished and did not behave in a coercive manner, he was not really a dictator (or was he?), since the actions taken would, after all, be in the interest of the majority. The important thing is that the measures dictated cannot be oppressive or compulsive (which coercion actually defines a dictator). If the dictator did not do as the people willed but rather did as he pleased (even if it was ostensibly for improvement of the social welfare), the people would be losers in the *process*, even if not in the direct programmatic results; if the results are such as to increase the social welfare, but the interests and opinions of the individual are excluded from the process, the system is illegitimate. Above all, Mill seemed to believe in all kinds of persuasion—almost anything *absent force* was acceptable. In the end, either a consensus had to be forged, or government would cease to exist.

It was as an *institutional* form that Mill regarded private property, a position not in essentials different from that of Bentham and James Mill. He freely admitted that his view of property was predicated on a different foundation from that underlying his theory of the production of wealth: the latter is positive—laws of production "partake of the character of physical truths" (1871, bk. II, chap. I, §1, 199)—while the former depends entirely upon human design and "the permission of society" (200). Such laws of distribution, being artificial, are also capricious and so bound to the place and time of their construction. This extends even to the fruits of the production of one's own labor:

> Even what a person has produced by his individual toil, unaided by any one, he cannot keep, unless by the permission of society. . . . The distribution of wealth, therefore, depends on the laws and customs of society. The rules by which it is determined are what the opinions and feelings of the ruling portion of the community make them, and are very different in different ages and countries; and might be still more different, if mankind so chose. (1871, 200)

Given the conflicts involved in the manner of the governance of property, society must choose the manner of distribution. Here Mill considered two possibilities: individual ownership and community (social) ownership. To the first, if it should be adopted—and Mill expressed his hope that, if it were, "it would be accompanied by none of the initial inequalities and injustices which obstruct the beneficial operation of the principle in old societies" (1871, §2, 202)—it must be understood by all concerned that the compact would be inviolate: "the division, once made, would not again be interfered with; individuals would be left to their own exertions and to the ordinary chances, for making an advantageous use of what was assigned to them" (202).[83]

---

83. Mill defined property rights thus: "The institution of property, when limited to its essential elements, consists in the recognition, in each person, of a right to the exclusive disposal of what he or she produced by their own exertions, or received either by gift or by fair agreement, without force or fraud, from those who produced it" (Mill 1871, bk. II, chap. ii, 218).

Should the society choose instead the regime of social property—in which "the land and all instruments of production [were held] as the joint property of the community" (1871, 202)—then the governance of the use of property would become all the more complicated. Under this arrangement, every aspect of the use of the community resource, including individual labor, would be guided, placed under the direction of "a magistrate or magistrates, whom we may suppose elected by the suffrages of the community," whose direction "we must assume to be voluntarily obeyed by them." This would be also the manner for the direction of distribution, which "would in like manner be a public act" (202).

Mill himself was rather agnostic on the approach to be chosen, since the form was to be determined through a social compact, although he did consider both the positive and negative aspects of various communitarian schemes. On the whole, Mill was sensitive to the same social impact elements that had worried Malthus, but unlike Malthus he had a tremendous faith in the socialization process as applied to the impecunious; he was certain that the iron law of wages would not apply, once workers had been educated, generally, and instructed to the use of birth control, specifically. It is not the fall in the wage rate which brings on a fall of population growth, but rather it is economic stagnation which leads to a fall in the profit rate. When that occurs, Mill expressed confidence that workers would turn their time to greater self-improvement. To facilitate this last, he was willing to accept public expenditure as a means to its attainment.

In all, Mill was a classical economist in the sense of Smith and Bentham, an ethical utilitarian who, underneath it all, believed that knowing the nature of *moral* value was more important than knowing the determinants of *price*. While he was clearly interested in economic growth, he was so opposed to the inequality of the English institutions of the time that he could not bear to think that there was anything inherently scientific about the then current accepted "laws" of allocation and reallocation.[84]

The "Chapters on Socialism"   9.2

In 1879 there appeared in the *Fortnightly Review* a series of articles entitled "Chapters on Socialism," by John Stuart Mill. Part of a proposed book on the subject, which never materialized, the completed chapters were offered by Helen Taylor (Mill's stepdaughter) after Mill's death as evidence of his contribution to the discussion of the positive and negative attributes of socialism.

Mill began by noting that, with the inevitability of universal suffrage,

84. For this and other reasons, Beer asserted that Mill, from the second edition of his *Principles* (1849), advocated proposals which "were all in favour of socialism" (Beer 1940, vol. II, 188n.1).

a paramount concern would be the distribution of wealth, especially the position in society of the right of property and individual ownership. The impecunious would, as a matter of course, most certainly not be mollified by arguments for the protection of the right to individual ownership of something to which there is a *social* benefit. They would insist on a reconsideration of the very notion of private property as the center of the social relationship and would almost certainly be disposed to accept any politicoeconomic solution which had as its central tenet communal ownership.

Of all the countries in which such "antiproperty doctrines" had taken hold, the leading proponents called themselves socialists, which Mill described as "a designation under which schemes of very diverse character are comprehended and confounded, but which implies at least a remodelling generally approaching to abolition of the institution of private property" (Mill 1879, 221). To the extent that there should be a debate over the merits of socialist versus private ownership—and given that, in his estimation, much of the leadership of the British labor movement was indeed disposed to socialist solutions, such a debate was indeed necessary—Mill felt there should be as impartial a demonstration of relative merits as possible. To this task he set himself.

To commence his task, Mill noted socialist objections to the structure of a property-based order. First, the socialists contend, property as an institution "is upheld and commended principally as being the means by which labour and frugality are insured their reward, and mankind enabled to emerge from indigence" (1879, 224). The problem, say the socialists, is that, in this regard, it has failed as a means of reducing poverty: the population has not received any substantial benefits from the current distribution. The mantra—that those best fit for the challenge will survive, and those unfit to the challenge will perish—is not a philosophy worthy of an enlightened people; in the "right state" the prosperous would take the initiative in insisting that, in exchange for the continuance of their prosperity, those in their charge would be granted an opportunity of "obtaining a desirable existence" (225) (although it seems as though they insist on the *guarantee* of a desirable outcome).

The socialist solution is to accept that "every one who was willing to undergo a fair share of this labour and abstinence could attain a fair share of the fruits" (1879, 226). That this does not occur, say the socialists, is further evidence of the bankruptcy of the social and economic structure. The existing property arrangement only succeeded in separating reward from effort.

The second failure of the existing arrangement is "human misconduct," including "crime, vice, and folly, with all the sufferings which follow in their train" (1879, 227). To the socialists, these "failures" are the result of poverty, idleness, and "bad" education. Poverty and idleness are "failures in the social arrangements," while "bad" education is "the fault of those arrangements—it may almost be said the crime" (227). At fault, insist the socialists, is the entire structure of society, including the structure of production, which "is essentially vicious and anti-social." Specifically, the culprits are individualism and competitive self-interest:

> It is the principle of individualism, competition, each one for him-self and against all the rest. It is grounded on opposition of interests, not harmony of interests, and under it every one is required to find his place by a struggle, by pushing others back or being pushed back by them. Socialists consider this system of private war (as it may be termed) between every one and every one, especially fatal in an economical point of view and in a moral. Morally considered, its evils are obvious. It is the parent of envy, hatred, and all unchari-tableness; it makes every one the natural enemy of all others who cross his path, and every one's path is constantly liable to be crossed. Under the present system hardly any one can gain except by the loss or disappointment of one or of many others. (1879, 227)

The socialist "solution" is communitarianism, a complete recon-figuration of the social structure to ensure a community of interests and a consequent community of feeling: "In a well-constituted community ev-ery one would be a gainer by every other person's successful exertions" (1879, 227–28).

These statements of the socialist ideal Mill attributed to errors in their understanding of political economy—"ignorance of economic facts, and of the causes by which the economic phenomena of society as it is, are actually determined" (1879, 373). Contrary to the assertions of the socialists, Mill in these Chapters of 1879 held that wages in the advanced economies had been increasing steadily as had the general standard of living.

Secondly, the socialists misunderstood the very nature of competi-tion. Competition in fact achieved some socialist designs: under competi-tion, remuneration as between occupations was not exaggerated, but rather was equalized "to a general average" (1879, 375). Further, to the extent that prices are kept low by competition, workers benefit in that their purchasing power is maintained; and to the extent that competition drives out inefficient producers, the advantage accrues to consumers and society as a whole, as resources are no longer wasted and "the parasites of industry" are eliminated (376).[85]

Withal, Mill did not in these ruminations dispute the *practicability* of socialism: ownership of consumables and individual plots of land (residential property) was allowed, with the means of production being common property (the idea of the state as a community of communal

---

85. Mill accepted, though, that one by-product of low prices may be low quality, as the one is a trade-off for the other. His solutions were greater enforcement of the statutes against fraud, and the opening of consumer cooperatives, a concession to the communi-tarianism of the socialists.

villages). What Mill objected to was the attempt to run the entire national economy through a state bureaucratic organization. Further, he questioned whether state bureaucratic management would ever realize the efficiencies of private enterprise. The motivation to succeed under free enterprise is paramount; under socialism (Mill used the foil of communism as defined by Louis Blanc), there is no such motivation, as the proceeds are divided equally irrespective of merit.[86] Mill concluded:

> We must therefore expect, unless we are operating upon a select portion of the population, that personal interest will for a long time be a more effective stimulus to the most vigorous and careful conduct of the industrial business of society than motives of a higher character. (1879, 516)

This is true of managers and laborers alike—and even under communism there would remain such a distinction.

One solution offered by Mill, which seemed to ameliorate the ills of capitalism while promoting the advantages of socialism, was the "industrial partnership." Under this arrangement, the firm would be restructured so as to allow the workers to participate in the distribution of profits, after the capitalist (who would retain title to the capital) received a fixed portion to cover his risk and a suitable profit. Where it had been tried, "it has very materially increased the remuneration of every description of labour" (1879, 519). From this he concluded that the property right could legitimately be retained, while the more socially undesirable consequences of free-market capitalism could be rectified: "Communism has no advantage which may not be reached under private property, while as respects the managing heads it is at a considerable disadvantage" (520).

For Mill, the most important element in favor of free enterprise was the exercise of individual human freedom.

> The obstacles to human progression are always great, and require a concurrence of favourable circumstances to overcome them; but an indispensable condition of their being overcome is, that human nature should have freedom to expand spontaneously in various directions, both in thought and practice; that people should both think for themselves and try experiments for themselves, and should not resign into the hands of rulers, whether acting in the name of a few or of the majority, the business of thinking for them, and of prescribing how they shall act. But in Communist associations private life would be brought in a most unexampled degree within the dominion of public authority, and there would be less scope for the

---

86. While such intangibles as public spirit, conscience, and credit for a job well done are, under socialism, replacements for the rewards of free enterprise, they seemed to Mill to serve "a restraining" not an "impelling" role (1879, 516).

development of individual character and individual preferences than has hitherto existed among the full citizens of any state belonging to the progressive branches of the human family. Already in all societies the compression of individuality by the majority is a great and growing evil; it would probably be much greater under Communism, except so far as it might be in the power of individuals to set bounds to it by selecting to belong to a community of persons like-minded with themselves. (1879, 522)

Having examined Mill's arguments on the subject of socialism, we turn now to the figures on the left of British Classical Political Economy who espoused such beliefs, these being Owen, Hodgskin, and Marx.

10 The Rise of the Utopian Socialists

10.1 Owen as Practical Socialist

Robert Owen (1771–1858) is generally regarded as the father of English Socialism, an appellation bestowed upon him by Friedrich Engels. Owen's early reputation was made in the manufacturing sector, particularly the cotton mills of New Lanark, Scotland, where he learned the fundamentals of business management and gained in the process a fair amount of personal wealth. In his capacity as the "lord" of the mills at New Lanark, he had managed to secure a laboratory of sorts in which he could apply his ideas of human behavior to the problems of the productivity of the work force; this he achieved with amazing success. The motivations behind the increases in productivity were a mixture of Skinnerianism[87] (positive reinforcement) and paternalism, emphasizing regular performance evaluations and strict rules against unacceptable behavior, such as drunkenness and tardiness, with a strong emphasis on education in the formation of character. (One of Owen's partners in the New Lanark venture was Jeremy Bentham.)

In 1825, Owen attempted to export his philosophy to the United States, having purchased a site in Indiana for a communal society which he named New Harmony; a second such community was established in Orbiston, Scotland. These experiments at establishing a socialist community built on rational principles failed, mainly because of a lack of social cohesion and commitment to principle. By 1827 the New Harmony community had dissolved into several factional groups; the failure nearly bankrupted Owen. (In 1832 he founded the National Equitable Labour Exchange, which also failed.)

But what were the underlying principles which Owen felt could be

87. The psychologist B. F. Skinner employed a similar tactic in his novel, *Walden Two*.

applied to the betterment of society? Gide and Rist placed him in the camp of the Associative Socialists, a group whose central tenet was "that voluntary association on the basis of some preconceived plan is sufficient for the solution of all social problems" (Gide and Rist 1947, 242).[88] Owen's interest was in attempting to fashion the character of the individual by providing an environment that promoted the traits he wished to encourage: morality, kindness, motivation, selflessness, and a sense of community. His "new views" on the correct form for society, which developed into his essays of the same name[89] (published from 1813 to 1816), stressed that the best way to further these traits was to promote the twin themes of education and management as tools for the formation of a more humane civil society.

As a means of setting up the argument, Owen expressed what he took to be a self-evident principle of human nature, incontrovertibly true, having passed every test of its validity throughout the ages:

> This principle is, that *"Any general character, from the best to the worst, from the most ignorant to the most enlightened, may be given to any community, even to the world at large, by the application of proper means; which means are to a great extent at the command and under the control of those who have influence in the affairs of men."* (Owen 1813–16, 12; emphasis in original)

Man is not, on the Owen view, born into a given, unalterable state; nor is he endowed by nature with the free will and independence of thought and action supposed of him by the earlier utilitarians and political economists and philosophers of the classical tradition. On the contrary, man is a product entirely of his environment, his social and political and economic milieu. His constitution is not the product of his birth; it is rather shaped by factors to which he is constantly exposed but of whose significance he may not be consciously aware.[90]

---

88. Gide and Rist also contrasted Associationism with Saint-Simonianism or socialization: "The advocates of socialization always thought of 'Society' with a capital S, and of all the members of the nation as included in one collective organization. The term 'nationalization' much better describes what they sought. Associationism, on the other hand, more individualistic in character and fearing lest the individual should be merged in the mass, would have him safeguarded by means of small autonomous groups, where federation would be entirely voluntary, and any unity that might exist would be prompted from within rather than imposed from without" (Gide and Rist 1947, 242).

89. The full title of Owen's essays is *A New View of Society, or, Essays on the Principle of the Formation of the Human Character, and the Application of the Principle to Practice*.

90. Gide and Rist called Owen the father of etiology, the part of sociology "which treats of the subordination and adaptation of man to his environment" (Gide and Rist 1947, 248). Alexander Gray contended that Owen's entire philosophy can be reduced to the proposition "that our characters are made for us, and that accordingly we are in no way responsible for what we are" (Gray 1946, 203).

From the earliest ages it has been the practice of the world to act on the supposition that each individual man forms his own character, and that therefore he is accountable for all his sentiments and habits, and consequently merits reward for some and punishment for others. Every system which has been established among men has been founded on these erroneous principles. When, however, they shall be brought to the test of fair examination, they will be found not only unsupported, but in direct opposition to all experience, and to the evidence of our senses.

This error cannot much longer exist; for every day will make it more and more evident *that the character of man is, without a single exception, always formed for him; that it may be, and is, chiefly created by his predecessors; that they give him, or may give him, his ideas and habits, which are the powers that govern and direct his conduct. Man therefore, never did, nor is it possible he ever can, form his own character.* (1813–16, 43; emphasis in original)

This was for Owen an undeniable truth, a principle not derived from abstract reasoning but from an appeal to all empirical data from the beginning of time to the present. It amounts to his Aristotelian First Principle. This proposition is in fact so indubitable that Owen considered it unnecessary to spend much time on the proof of its validity; he is so certain of the self-evidence of the proposition that he considers that "it cannot now be necessary to enter into the detail of acts to prove that children can be trained to acquire '*any language, sentiments, belief, or any bodily habits and manners, not contrary to human nature*' " (1813–16, 13; emphasis in original).[91] Its confirmation is already abundantly clear to anyone with any sense of history whatever.

There was no question for Owen but that nature has very little role to play in the molding of the character and morality of individuals in society. Man is not destined to remain a product of his nature; on the contrary, he can be trained and manipulated in his behavior and character. He can be shaped and molded to behave as a model community citizen, respectful of others, hard-working, of the highest moral fiber—a person whose happiness is the happiness of the community. This process of changing the way the individual perceives of the world and his role in it is not an easy one and is particularly difficult in adults, who have been affected by their environment to an extent not readily reversible. Owen had the greatest faith in his

---

91. Later Owen clarified his statement: "The knowledge of this important fact has not been derived from any of the wild and heated speculations of an ardent and ungoverned imagination; on the contrary, it proceeds from a long and patient study of the theory and practice of human nature, under many varied circumstances; it will be found to be a deduction drawn from such a multiplicity of facts, as to afford the most complete demonstration" (1813–16, 44). Thus did Owen employ an early version of the well-known principle of induction, the Principle of Limited Independent Variety.

program when it could engage the individual at an early age, early enough
so that he has not been previously influenced by any notions contrary to
those that Owen deems the most worthy. Thus the education of children is
the building block of the new Owenian order:

> Children are, without exception, passive and wonderfully contrived
> compounds; which, by an accurate previous and subsequent atten-
> tion, *founded on a correct knowledge of the subject,* may be formed
> collectively to have any human character.

> Let truth unaccompanied with *error* be placed before them; give
> them time to examine it and to see that it is in unison with all
> previously ascertained truths; and conviction and acknowledge-
> ment of it will follow of course. It is weakness itself to require assent
> *before* conviction; and *afterwards* it will not be withheld. (1813–
> 16, 19, 21; emphasis in original)

Having established that nature is not the motive force behind the
shaping of character and behavior, but on the contrary that man is ma-
nipulable and so his actions can be altered to the designs of the state,
Owen declared it "the highest interest, and consequently the first and
most important duty, of every state, to form the individual characters of
which the state is composed" (1813–16, 73). The state therefore must, if
there is to be any legitimate rationale for its existence, keep as the primary goal the fostering of a desirable social climate by training its citizens
through universal education to be socially conscious.

Owen's second principle, actually a "single principle of action"
(1813–16, 14), is similar to the guiding principle of the utilitarians: the
principle of the greatest happiness of the greatest number, or, as Owen
phrased it, "*the happiness of self, clearly understood and uniformly
practised; which can only be attained by conduct that must promote the
happiness of the community*" (14; emphasis in original). This "greatest
happiness," however, differs from the principle as enunciated by Bentham
and James Mill, and even Hume. For Owen, the good of the *community* is
given precedence over the happiness of the *individual,* and the property
rights considered essential to the ideas of the utilitarians were anathema to
Owen.[92] The paramount duty of the state is to promote and protect the
interests of the community, even above that of the individual. Taken in
concert with the requirement that the state indoctrinate the citizenry to
accept the provision of the good of the community over and above any
egoistic demands, the individual interest and the interest of the social
collective will be one and the same.

Owen's economic theories followed on his ideas concerning the

---

92. Owen stated the principle later in the essay in more Benthamite terms: "That
government, then, is the best, which in practice produces the greatest happiness to the
greatest number; including those who govern, and those who obey" (1813–16, 62).

desirability and efficacy of education. He opposed the Poor Laws, primarily on the ground that they promoted idleness, which itself encouraged antisocial behavior. He felt these laws to be mere expedients or political palliatives, established in lieu of any real reform measures designed to facilitate the employment of the chronically unemployed. The same admonishment he directed to the programs established for these purposes by church authorities.

> Many of these laws, by their never-failing effects, speak in a language which no one can misunderstand, and say to the unprotected and untaught, '*Remain in ignorance, and let your labour be directed by that ignorance; for while you can procure what is sufficient to support life by such labour, although that life should be an existence in abject poverty, disease, and misery, we will not trouble ourselves with you, or any of your proceedings; when, however, you can no longer procure work, or obtain the means to support nature, then apply for relief to the parish, and you shall be maintained in idleness.* (1813–16, 85; emphasis in original)

In his opposition to legislative approaches to alleviate poverty, Owen did not promote massive public works or public employment schemes as a solution to the unemployment problem. He proposed only to make the working classes more productive through education; once the population had been properly educated, employment opportunities would follow (1813–16, 87).

Owen's view of the efficacy of training and education in the formation of a socially productive citizenry had the added benefit (at least in theory) of continually increasing the productivity of not only manufacturing industries but of agriculture as well. He accepted Malthus's claim "that the population of the world is ever adapting itself to the quantity of food raised for its support," but rejected the inevitability of the situation. Malthus's position, he claimed, had been predicated on a view of man as in a perpetual state of ignorance. Owen's man would be enlightened and therefore industrious, and so would produce, not indeed for his own selfish needs, but for the overall needs of the collective. The result would be production in relation to an "ignorant and ill-governed" people, "as one to infinity" (1813–16, 86). Malthusian despair thus would be transformed into the Owenian millennium.

Owen eventually realized that his efforts to institute through governmental means his social agenda, including a Factory Act designed to improve working conditions by imposing constraints on employers, were not going to come to fruition. In 1820 he published his *Report to the County of Lanark,* in which he proposed a radical restructuring of society, a revolutionary program which has come to be termed "socialism." At the outset of this reorganization scheme, Owen offered a new unit of value to replace the use of precious metals or paper money which served (and still

serve) as the basic unit of exchange. These traditional units of valuation
Owen considered to be artificial contrivances; they did not and could not
represent the true value of goods and services but only the value of the
units themselves as defined by the private concerns whose interests were
furthered by their use. For Owen the only "natural standard of value" is
labor (Owen 1820, 256). But the legitimation of labor as a standard of
valuation requires a means for the determination of labor values in the
goods and services produced. This Owen believed had been established
already, in a sense, in scientific applications; the principle of the average
physical power of man was one widely used example of the procedure. So,
as labor is the source of all wealth in the community (Owen's First Cause),
and there exists a procedure for the determination of "the average of
human labour," it is but a small step to the calculation of the value of
labor present in every good offered for sale. From this can be derived
comparative values for all the goods traded in the economy, akin to the
process employed in the determination of index numbers (1820, 256).

This most "natural" form for the valuation of production allows
for the constant reevaluation of goods-values, as more productivity-
enhancing methods are introduced. It also removes the artificial impediments to goods-supply, allowing a greater degree of economic expansion.
The wage structure would by the employment of this technique be made
more "natural" and rational, wage negotiations would become anachronistic, the education (i.e., socialization) of the workers would be enhanced as they attempted to improve their labor-value, and altogether
greater happiness would be promoted (1820, 257).

Recommendations made by Owen for the promotion of his
scheme included (1) an immediate halt to cash payments for services, (2)
the implementation of measures for the employment of the "labouring
unoccupied poor," (3) and the institution of the labor-value plan in
place of the money-value system (1820, 257–58). In regard to the social
arrangements Owen intended to implement, the plan revolved around
the idea of planned villages or communes, centered around spade agriculture (as Owen believed the plow to be a tool inimical to productive
agriculture and the promotion of social cohesion). The communes themselves would be shaped in the form of a parallelogram, with population
limited to from 300 to 2000 persons, with from 800 to 1200 being the
most desirable number. Property, labor, and privileges would be shared
equally, so as to instill within the members of the community a feeling
of social consciousness.[93]

---

93. Owen went so far as to design the layouts of each house (apartment) and the dress
of the inhabitants of the community. The apartments would have no kitchen facilities (the
cooking and food preparation would be handled in a communal room), heating and cooling
of the individual apartments would be directed to each through a central system, and the type
of clothing worn would be such as to express the beauty of the human form while being
utilitarian in design (patterned on the dress of the Romans and Scots) [1820, 284].

The principle of individual self-interest, taken as the centerpiece of Classical Economics, would be replaced by the principle of community. Self-interest was for Owen a distasteful principle: "opposed as it is perpetually to the public good," it is "the sole cause of poverty" (1820, 276–77). The remedy Owen prescribed was to instill within each individual a desire to act in unison, as one, for the good of the society. As the principle had a proven record of success—it clearly works to the advantage of a nation in time of war—so should it (logically, for Owen) be advantageous in the creation of social wealth and collective happiness. But Owen realized the process of instilling a new ethic would be no easy matter; it must be accompanied by nothing less than a new social compact (278). The result would be a new community that would be so socially conscious that courts of law and other enforcement mechanisms would be entirely unnecessary.

10.2 Hodgskin: Natural and Artificial Rights

While Owen may be understood in the tradition of Bentham, others of the utopian socialists reflected the logical extension of the position on the labor theory of value advanced by Ricardo and so are identified with his name. In her 1911 *The Ricardian Socialists,* Esther Lowenthal (as did H. S. Foxwell in his 1899 Introduction to Anton Menger's *The Right to the Whole Produce of Labour*) identified four men as pivotal in the development of British Socialism: John Francis Bray (1809–97),[94] John Gray (1799–1883),[95] William Thompson (1775–1833),[96] and Thomas Hodgskin (1787–1869). We will focus here on Hodgskin.[97]

Hodgskin is perhaps the best known and certainly the most interesting of the so-called Ricardian socialists in the sense that he formulated a theory of social welfare and distribution along individualist lines. A former naval lieutenant, he was instrumental in the founding of the London Mechanics' Institute (later the Birkbeck Institute, which was to become Birkbeck College) in an effort to improve the plight of the working

---

94. Bray was born in Washington, D.C., into a theatrical family, and worked as a printer and farmer. He lived in England from 1822 to 1842 and while there published *Labour's Wrongs and Labour's Remedy* (1839).

95. Gray was a clerk in London who eventually became wealthy as a publisher. His 1825 *Lecture on Human Happiness* is a proposal for radical change in the economic relations of society.

96. Thompson was an Irish landowner. His 1824 *Inquiry into the Principles of the Distribution of Wealth* treated rent and interest as inherently unjust. He is said to have coined the phrase "surplus value."

97. Beer noted that Hodgskin met Ricardo about 1820, "misunderstood and disparaged" him, but eventually accepted Ricardo's brilliance and ingeniousness. See Beer 1940, vol. I, 259.

class.[98] His 1827 *Popular Political Economy* is notable for its thesis that wealth production is regulated by "natural laws." On this basis, Hodgskin was able to reinterpret Smith's labor theory of value into a statement to the effect that labor is the sole producer of wealth.[99]

Hodgskin's direct connection to Utilitarianism is through his relationship with Francis Place (1771–1854), a disciple of Bentham. But Hodgskin early on rejected the hedonistic basis of Benthamism—the consequentialism of the "greatest happiness" formula—and chose instead to focus on the importance of Natural Law and natural rights as the foundation for social rules and order. In his 1832 *The Natural and Artificial Right of Property Contrasted,* he presented his clearest statement of the origin and constitution of the property right. The property right was for Hodgskin a "first principle" upon which society and social relations were structured; in fact, he went so far as to maintain that "[p]olitical organization depends very much on the mode in which property is distributed" (Hodgskin 1832, 12). The consequences of an improper foundation for the property right were dire indeed, a position for which he found a basis in Locke, Bentham, and James Mill:

> Wherever the right of property is placed on a proper foundation, slavery, with all its hateful consequences, is unknown:—wherever this foundation is rotten, freedom cannot exist, nor justice be administered. (1832, 12)

Having accepted the *importance* of the property right, Hodgskin then delved into the *origin* of that right, and here he maintained a fundamental distinction, between the "natural" and the "artificial" rights of property. Under this conception, we see the basis of a fundamental disagreement between the views of Locke and those of the Philosophic Radicals. Locke had maintained that property antedated government, and that indeed government developed as a means to protect the property right and the subsequent distribution; Mill and Bentham, by contrast, held that property relations were the creation of law. This difference as to the very rationale underlying the property right Hodgskin took to be a

98. Gray (1946, 277) noted that Hodgskin's naval career was finished after he published *An Essay on Naval Discipline, Showing Part of its Evil Effects on the Minds of the Officers and the Minds of the Men and on the Community; with an Amended System by Which Pressing May be Immediately Abolished* (1813), a tract, as suggested by the title, relating the injustices of British naval life.

99. N. W. Thompson opined that Adam Smith was the most important influence on the thought of Hodgskin. "From Smith he believed he had derived the central tenet of his social and economic philosophy, namely that the material world was shaped by natural laws, emanating from an omniscient and beneficent Providence, all interference with which was either superfluous or pernicious" (Thompson 1987, 666). Gray (1946, 278) insisted that Hodgskin professed a mix of the views of Smith and Godwin and held to an individualist ethic that was tantamount to anarchism. Hunt (1977, 322) esteemed Hodgskin a "loyal disciple of Smith."

major concern, one which went to the basis of the law and indeed extended to "the very foundation of the whole political edifice" (1832, 17):

> If a right of property be a natural right, not created by legislation, if it be a principle of society, derived immediately and directly from the laws of the universe, all its results will be determined, at all times, by those laws; and the legislator ought to ascertain these results, before he dreams of making decrees, to enforce them. Before he takes any steps to protect the right of property, he must, on Mr. Locke's principles, find out in what it consists. If, on the other hand, a right of property be altogether the creature and work of laws, as the legislator seems to suppose, he may at all times determine all its consequences. He will have no occasion to inquire into any circumstances foreign to his own enactments; he will only have to frame his decrees with logical accuracy from the principles he lays down. One system looks on the legislator as an ally, in enforcing the laws of nature, to do which he must know them; the other denies that there are any such laws, which in fact its authors do in express terms, and they look on enactments as determining the welfare and destiny of mankind. (1832, 16–17)

Apart from its significance in legitimizing a "natural" basis of the property right, this statement is important as a critique of Utilitarianism. While a system based on Natural Law allows a universal derivation of law, one based on a utilitarian design allows only that laws be logical deductions from stated premises, which premises are themselves idiosyncratic and based on little more than opinion. As a legal doctrine, Utilitarianism—as identified with Bentham and James Mill—denied the necessity for Natural Law and natural rights, focusing instead on legislative enactment as the proper mechanism for the promotion of order in society. This for Hodgskin was an invitation to caprice in the order of the state and so led to an increased apprehension on the part of the governed as to the motives behind the legislation. He thus condemned the utilitarian model as having been predicated on an "incorrect and insecure foundation"—this foundation being the notion "that all the rights of man are derived from the legislator" (1832, 17). To Hodgskin a reliance on this understanding of the basis of the social contract was nothing less than an invitation to despotism:

> Man, having naturally no rights, may be experimented on, imprisoned, expatriated or even exterminated, as the legislator pleases. Life and property being his [the legislator's] gift, he may resume them at pleasure; and hence he never classes the executions and wholesale slaughters, he continually commands, with murder—nor the forcible appropriation of property he sanctions, under the name of taxes, tithes, &c., with larceny or high-way robbery. (1832, 21)

To sum up Hodgskin's position, without a secure Natural Law basis, including an understanding of the importance of natural rights (especially the right of property) as a first principle, society—meaning the free association of individuals in pursuit of personal goals and interests— could not continue to function. Hodgskin's Utopianism was predicated on individualist, not communitarian, grounds, and this distinction is critical to his views on the importance of natural rights. The consequences for human freedom of the abandonment of a belief in such necessary guiding first principles would be catastrophic:

> I am satisfied that it is not possible to meliorate our political condition, or even to save society from convulsions, more terrible perhaps than have ever been known, unless all classes attain correct notions of the natural right of property, and endeavour gradually to adapt their conduct and social institutions to what nature decrees. (1832, 24)

The most extreme statement of Hodgskin's economic views is contained in his 1825 *Labour Defended Against the Claims of Capital, or the Unproductiveness of Capital Proved,* an anticapitalist diatribe (published anonymously) devoted to a proof that the classical argument for the existence of profit was fundamentally wrong. According to Hodgskin, profit is pernicious because it is a violation of Natural Law. Profit is not a reward for entrepreneurial risk or for waiting, but is rather the produce of the laborer, expropriated by the capitalist in his role as "owner" of the means of production; since capital is nothing more than the embodiment of past labor input, deriving its utility from present labor input, profit amounts to nothing but an exploitation of past labor exertions.

Hodgskin's version of socialism differed markedly from that of Owen, in that it was based on the *legitimation* of the private property right and not its replacement. Owen's utopia was communal; Hodgskin's centered on the primacy of the individual. He thus distinguished himself from Owen, Saint-Simon, Rousseau, and others especially on this score, maintaining

> the right of individuals, to have and to own, for their own separate and selfish use and enjoyment, the produce of their own industry, with power freely to dispose of the whole of that in the manner most agreeable to themselves, as essential to the welfare and even to the continued existence of society. (Hodgskin 1832, 24)

Hodgskin thus appropriated the Lockean position on the right of property, including the right to the produce of one's own labor,[100] and in

---

100. "I heartily and cordially concur with Mr. Locke, in his view of the origin and foundation of a right of property" (Hodgskin 1832, 25). Beer noted that Hodgskin "rea-

so doing arrived at a more solidly grounded economic understanding of the process than is to be found in other presentations which treated labor as being somehow unique. While Schumpeter (1954, 479) regarded Hodgskin as having enunciated an economic theory of exploitation recognizably Marxian in content, Beer went so far as to suggest that Hodgskin was not a socialist at all, since he "preferred competition in the midst of institutions and opinions as free as man can form them" (Beer 1940, vol. I, 266).[101] Hodgskin may properly be termed, within his own restrictive Natural Law framework, as a free-market laborist for whom capital and labor were seen as inextricably connected.

10.3 Summary

The proposals put forth by the utopian socialists alarmed the Philosophic Radicals, since the doctrine of Utopian Socialism (especially as enunciated by Owen) suggested in essence that man was not responsible for the consequences of his own actions. If this were taken seriously as a basis for the construction of a system of government, the result would be completely unworkable, given the utilitarian ethic, since it would demand more government intrusion into the social arrangements hitherto left to the devices of the individual citizen. James Mill—to whom Hodgskin owed his position as a reporter at the *Morning Chronicle*—expressed the utilitarian rebuttal thus:

> Their notions of property look ugly; . . . they seem to think that it should not exist, and that the existence of it is an evil to them. Rascals, I have no doubt, are at work among them. . . . The fools, not to see that what they madly desire would be such a calamity to them as no hands but their own could bring upon them.

And, in a later letter:

> These opinions, if they were to spread, would be the subversion of civilized society; worse than the overwhelming deluge of Huns and Tartars. (James Mill, cited in Russell 1945, 781–82)

With these comments in mind, we turn attention now to the most notorious figure in this group, Karl Marx.

---

soned in all matters concerning government and property in the sense of Locke" (Beer 1940, 259). See also N. W. Thompson (1987).

101. Gray commented: "Among the English forerunners of Marx, it is Thomas Hodgskin . . . who gives most clearly the impression of intellectual eminence and distinction, and who leaves most acutely a feeling that here was one designed for greatness which, owing to the misfits of time and of life, was never attained" (1946, 277).

The Great Satan: Karl Marx and the Development of Scientific Socialism

The work of Karl Heinrich Marx (1818–83)[102] can be considered in different ways.[103] Here we wish to stress that he appropriated from Utilitarianism the emphasis on a property-rights framework and in effect, by restating the fundamentals, proceeded (in a Ricardian fashion) to transform the nature of economics.[104] Not a conscious utilitarian—he took great pains to deprecate the notions of the utilitarians, maintaining that

---

102. Marx was born during the Great Reaction in Trier to a son of a rabbi who had converted to Lutheranism in 1824. His mother was Dutch, also from a Jewish family.

In Berlin, where he studied jurisprudence, Marx became attracted to the philosophical doctrine of Hegelianism. As he had his doubts about getting his initial doctorate in Berlin, he submitted his dissertation in 1839 at the University of Jena on the differences between Democritean (materialist) and Epicurean rational philosophy; this study was intended to be the first part of a whole study of Greek philosophy.

Exiled by the German government, he chose to relocate to Paris, where he remained until exiled by the French on the petition of the Prussian government for reason of his revolutionary writing. Typical of his temperament and no doubt bothered by his Jewish heritage, Marx at the time chose to write an anti-Jewish essay, "On the Jewish Question." This theme of personal anti-Semitism was not all that unknown among those in his status, but the vitriol of his language was unusual.

Marx's friendship with Friedrich Engels, the revolutionary son of a cotton mill owner from Wuppertal, led to their great lifetime cooperation. Together they attacked the likes of Bruno Bauer, Moses Hess, and later Karl Eugen Dühring. The bitterness and *ad hominem* nature of these attacks presage much of the snarl in the socialist movement, suggesting that Marx knew neither gratitude nor kindliness. Overkill was the name of the game for these two writers.

Visiting London in 1847, Marx was "instructed" by the Communist League to write, with Engels, a Manifesto. The tract, published in 1848, was designed to thwart the plans of the anarchist Mikhail Aleksandrovich Bakunin (1814–76). After the revolution in 1848 in France (deposing the last of the Bourbons, Philippe Auguste) and Marx's exile from Belgium, he returned to France. Advised to keep out of Paris, he decided to move to Cologne. Marx was later denaturalized by Prussia and expelled, surfacing in London, where he remained for the rest of his career—which from a pecuniary standpoint consisted of some newspaper writing (he was from 1851 to 1861 the London correspondent of the *New York Tribune*) and a great deal of largesse from Engels. He was attracted to British labor union leaders (by current standards rather right-wing) and was intent on using that connection to shore his programmatic institution, the first Working Man's International. An indefatigable reader and writer, he showed up daily at the British Museum for years.

103. Part of the problem in understanding his work is that Marx wrote a very difficult German, and when some of his works, particularly his masterwork, *Capital,* were translated, the translators did a miserable job. No small part of the opaqueness of Marxian theory should be laid to the inadequacies of the translations.

For many years the "standard" English translation was that of Samuel Moore and Edward Aveling. This edition was actually edited by Engels, who "sanitized" the work to make it more accessible to readers, but in the process removed much of the flavor of Marx. We use here a more modern and complete translation (1977) of the fourth edition of 1890, translated by Ben Fowkes.

104. Beer regarded Marx as "the last great disciple of Ricardo who developed the labour value theory to its final consequences" (Beer 1940, vol. I, 188).

they had, in their reliance on consequences, neglected to actually *deal* with any aspect of human behavior and human nature[105]—his insistence on property rights as the cornerstone of economic system-building and his use of a moralistic rhetoric within which to present his doctrine are evidence for his inheritance from the utilitarians. Likewise, his appropriation of the labor theory of value (evident in Locke, Smith, and Ricardo, among others) places him squarely within the classical tradition.[106]

But for all this, it is his theory of history that most Marxians embrace on their way to conversion. Central to this view is materialism, itself a variant of Hegelianism, that is, Hegel's dialectic applied to Platonic essences. Marxism is essentially a doctrine stressing both materialism and determinism: there are no accidents in history. Influenced by Moses Hess, Marx employed Ludwig Feuerbach's materialist interpretation of history to flesh out the dynamics of the social record. Where Hegel had relied upon transcendental theses altered by transcendental antitheses to form new transcendental syntheses, Marx challenged *existing* material orders with *new* (usually technologically inspired) material orders, with the result being the emergence of a third, or *synthetical,* material order.[107]

Marx's basic historical unit was the social class. A social class is a group of people with the same value system who are usually operating in a similar phase of a productive process. These value systems were super-structures atop a given material production process; they were the mores or the institutions that those who dominated the system used to keep the underclasses in line. Of course, when the production system was chal-

---

105. "To know what is useful for a dog, one must investigate the nature of dogs. This nature is not itself deducible from the principle of utility. Applying this to man, he that would judge all human acts, movements, relations, etc. according to the principle of utility would first have to deal with human nature in general, and then with human nature as historically modified in each epoch. Bentham does not trouble himself with this. With the dryest naïveté he assumes that the modern petty bourgeois, especially the English petty bourgeois, is the normal man. Whatever is useful to this peculiar kind of normal man, and to his world, is useful in and for itself. He applies this yardstick to the past, the present and the future" (Marx 1890, vol. I, chap. 24, 758–59n.51).

106. Marx let loose his venom on the classical economists. For example, he referred to Malthus as "that master in plagiarism (his whole population theory is a shameless plagiarism)" (Marx 1890, vol. I, 639n.49). He also claimed that Smith had committed plagiarism, having copied verbatim from Mandeville (see Marx 1890, 475n.33). Bentham he described as "that soberly pedantic and heavy-footed oracle of the 'common sense' of the nineteenth-century bourgeoisie" (758), as well as "a genius in the way of bourgeois stupidity" (759n.51).

107. Marx's materialism and the dialectic came together in his discussion of the role of education: "The materialist doctrine that men are products of circumstances and upbringing, and that, therefore, changed men are products of other circumstances and changed upbringing, forgets that it is man that changes circumstances, and that the educator himself needs educating. Hence this doctrine necessarily arrives at dividing society into two parts, of which one is superior to society (in Robert Owen, for example)" (Marx, "Theses on Feuerbach," in Marx and Engels 1959, 244).

lenged (in Marx's view, always by technological change), a new dominant class emerged, complete with its own useful-to-its-ends value system. Thus it was that the bourgeoisie, capitalizing on the destructive powers of "gunpowder wars," emerged to wrest economic and political control from the landed nobility. That transfer involved replacing not only the form of government (*parliamentary debate* rather than *Privy Council discussion*) and the basis of law (*contract* emerging over *status*), but required as well a wholesale cultural shift, from chivalry and courtoisie as well as total deference to civil and ecclesiastical authority, to individualism, the Common Law, and the predominance of materialism and choice of consumption goods and services.[108]

According to Marx's reading of the historical record, the original structure of social organization took the form of the common ownership of property: "Man is in the most literal sense of the word a *zoon politikon,* not only a social animal, but an animal which can develop into an individual only in society" (Marx 1904, 268). In this Marx was neither unique nor particularly unusual, but rather was within the communitarian orbit of many of the utilitarian school. The concept of property, even in this elementary state of social organization, is thus seen as an important one; indeed, the very notion of property and its importance in the social structure is such that to deny it leads to an absurdity, for property by its very nature is essential to the existence of society. As Marx stated: "it is a tautology to say that property (appropriation) is a condition of production" (1904, 273).

For Marx, while the property concept is fundamental, "property relations" is a mere legal concept, not different in form from the manner of Bentham's legal conception of usury, as the relations are meant to correspond to the essential nature of the productive structure. Much in the manner of Bentham and James Mill, the property relation for Marx is an artificial construct imposed upon an existing economic and social structure (and so is subject to the same objections posed by Hodgskin). The productive structure of the society—this being identified as the social relations existing between individuals as they are engaged in the process of production—is determined in large part by the particular stage of economic development in which the society finds itself. The relations among those engaged in production and the form of property arrangement that thus obtains are intimately connected to and determined by the economic structure in place. Marx insisted that the legal relationships of property are not more than fabrications, and thus not inherent in the nature of social relationships. This is evident from the fact that certain social structures, such as the familial unit, and power relations which serve to identify and codify class differences, must have

---

108. This was spelled out in his 1859 *A Contribution to the Critique of Political Economy.*

of necessity and by definition existed prior to the emergence of private property.[109]

In order to avoid what could very easily have become an overwhelming confusion as to just what is meant by property, Marx in the *Critique* attempted a clarification. In his discussion of property and the relations it engenders, Marx felt it necessary to distinguish between *property* and *possessions*. Possessions he defined as having been with us from the earliest times; in many ways they serve to define and delimit familial and social relations, since their existence implies no more than "a relation of simple family or tribal communities to property" (1904, 207). Possessions require no legal superstructure to define their existence; only the most basic social unit of organization is required. Possessions are then those objects we identify as *personal* property, in contrast with *real* property, a legal fiction. While personal property is defined independently of any social, economic, or political arrangement, real property can only arise given the legal framework that serves to promote and encourage its existence. Consistent with Hodgskin's definition of the "artificial" form of property, real property does not and cannot have an existence or even a meaning divorced from this legal context.

Yet even these categories are defined too broadly to be meaningful; certain covering propositions and definitions are required to allow them any substantive meaning. One of these refinements clarifies the idea of the property *right*. The development and nature of property rights, as they were understood by Marx, are a creation of capitalist society, and so are at least in this respect defined with reference to the individual and his legal attachment to those goods upon which he has or can declare dominion. To satisfy his own sensibilities, however, Marx held that property rights are not definable with reference to the individual; the individual on this account holds *possessions* only. For the phrase "property rights" to have any meaning in the Marxian sense, it must be understood that the right of ownership applies solely to the social collective, not to the single individual; the community determines ownership and control of all but the most basic of goods. Thus do possessions and real property attain a connection to the form of the economic structure and the set of existing economic and social (including legal) relations. Possessions may then be defined more precisely, for legalistic purposes, as property for use in *consumption*—the Marxian form of private property. By contrast we are now asked to consider "social property," or property for use in *production*, which entails the ownership of the means of producing the goods required in any complex (not merely capitalist) society. Both represent a form of private ownership, but the former has a natural basis for its

---

109. As Marx noted, "But there is no such thing as possession before the family or the relations of lord and serf . . ." (Marx 1904, 295). See also John Torrance (1995), especially pages 185–89.

existence, based on the rights of ownership of the individual, while the latter is artificial, manufactured by imposing legal restrictions on the criteria for ownership within a social collective. This is the definition of property as expressed by Marx in *Capital,* and is worth quoting *in extenso:*

> Private property, as the antithesis to social, collective property, exists only where the means of labour and the external conditions of labour belong to private individuals. But according to whether these private individuals are workers or non-workers, private property has a different character. The innumerable different shades of private property which appear at first sight are only reflections of the intermediate situations which lie between the two extremes.
>
> The private property of the worker in his means of production is the foundation of small-scale industry, and small-scale industry is a necessary condition for the development of social production and of the free individuality of the worker himself. Of course, this mode of production also exists under slavery, serfdom and other situations of dependence. But it flourishes, unleashes the whole of its energy, attains its adequate classical form, only where the worker is the free proprietor of the conditions of his labour, and sets them in motion himself: where the peasant owns the land he cultivates, or the artisan owns the tool with which he is an accomplished performer. (Marx 1890, vol. I, chap. XXXII, 927)

Here we confront the notion of historical determinism. As society advances, the means of production necessarily evolves from one based on individual, proprietary means to one founded on a communitarian base. What emerges is the capitalist form of industrial production. While in the earliest stages of society, understood to be within the confines of a familial social structure, each individual member could conceivably provide for his own needs and welfare using only his labor skills and possessions. The social arrangements brought about by the further evolution of the economic system engender an ever greater degree of dependence. The single individual can no longer continue to function outside of an increasingly interdependent social and economic structure. The individual, in other words, is no longer of primary significance for himself, as he must become incorporated into the larger economic and social collective. The ultimate form of economic structure that emerges is one based on industrial production, a truly social form of production that demands a ready supply of labor with specific and necessarily interchangeable skills. But this arrangement makes it impossible to consider that there is any role whatever for private property in production. As production is now social, so the relation of property or capital must follow and take on the same character. The only impediment to this evolution in the nature of property relations is the legal establishment of property rights as a simple extension of the right of ownership of consumer possessions, this extension having been promoted by those holding capital.

It was in his *Economic and Philosophic Manuscripts of 1844,* his most complete presentation of the subject, that Marx connected his theory of property more explicitly to his philosophical beliefs predicated on the Hegelian dialectic.[110] Here Marx employed a much more refined terminology than he had done in his other, better known, works.[111] He began his discussion of property by distinguishing between "immovable private property," more properly termed "landed property," and "movable private property," or capital. While ultimately both appear as forms of capital, the differences are readily apparent. Landed property is more properly a form of possession; it has a localized character and so cannot be shifted spatially; it is "the first form of private property" (Marx 1844, 131). As such, it has not realized a social role, nor has it been imbued with a social meaning, and it is thus properly termed *private property* in the sense of possessions.

> *Landed property* in its distinction from capital is private property— capital—still afflicted with *local* and political prejudices; it is capital which has not yet regained itself from its entanglement with the world—capital not yet *fully developed.* It must achieve its abstract, that is, its *pure,* expression in the course of its *world-wide development.* (1844, 126; emphasis in original)

It was in this context that Marx specified that property is endowed with both a subjective and an objective character. In this regard, the society is assumed to have evolved to the stage of capitalist development. Under the capitalist production structure, the "subjective essence" of private property is labor. At this stage, it is no longer true that wealth is determined from outside the means of its production. As labor becomes in capitalist society the source of wealth, it is the central organizing factor around which all production decisions must revolve. Thus could Marx then consider that the only valid science of political economy was that which gave central place to labor. Adam Smith had on this issue, according to Marx, got it right.

> It is therefore evident that only the political economy which acknowledged *labor* as its principle (Adam Smith), and which therefore no

110. Frederick Copleston (1965) noted the contrasting views of Hegel and Marx: For Hegel, the state, "as the full expression of the Idea in the form of objective Spirit," is the subject, while the family is the predicate. For Marx, the family is the subject, the state the predicate. See especially Copleston 1965, vol. VII, 307.

111. At about the time of the writing of the *Economic and Philosophic Manuscripts,* Marx also composed fragments of commentary on James Mill's *Elements of Political Economy* (published in Marx 1975). These comments are essentially identical with the *Economic and Philosophic Manuscripts* but not as detailed, so we will concentrate on the more detailed work.

longer looked upon private property as a mere *condition* external to man—that it is this political economy which has to be regarded on the one hand as a product of the real *energy* and the real *movement* of private property—as a product of modern *industry*—and on the other hand, as a force which has quickened and glorified the energy and development of modern *industry* and made it a power in the realm of *consciousness*. (1844, 128; emphasis in original)

The genius of Smith, on Marx's interpretation of the historical literature, was in his having "discovered within private property the *subjective essence* of wealth." This Marx contrasted to the mercantilist argument against which Smith himself railed, an argument in which the protagonists (the mercantilist writers) "look upon private property *only as an objective* substance confronting man . . ." (1844, 128; emphasis in original); he thus followed Smith by allying himself with the physiocrats, who accepted that "labor is from the outset only the *subjective essence* of landed property" (131; emphasis in original). This rubric (subjectification) of private property Marx took to be akin to Martin Luther's break with the then-dominant Catholic authority in Rome. As Luther "internalized" religion to make every man in essence his own priest, Marx viewed the prophets of the "enlightened" political economy, predicated on the labor theory of value, as having abandoned the principle of wealth as an external *object,* replacing it with the notion of man as key to the "essence" of private property.

Private property is thus fundamental to human existence; man creates the arrangements that make it possible for property to exist, and its realization in turn serves to identify him. This subjectification presented Marx with a paradox: while property relations form and characterize man, they also in the end serve to alienate him from his social nature and even from himself:

Under the semblance of recognizing man, political economy, whose principle is labor, rather carries to its logical conclusion the denial of man, since man himself no longer stands in an external relation of tension to the external substance of private property, but has himself become this essence of private property. (1844, 128–29)

This is especially so with respect to "movable property." Movable property, or capital, serves a social purpose in that it promotes human labor as the source of all wealth. Movable property, however, alienates the laborer, since it results in a social production process (identified with the mass-production techniques that have become the hallmark of industrial society), while at the same time leaving the worker alienated from the process of production; the product of the laborer is disconnected from the being of the laborer. But this alienation is a necessary concomitant to the movement to a truly communistic society. Capital gives life to "landed property" by replacing land with labor as the source of all wealth-creation. This Marx referred to as movable property's "civilized victory" (1844, 125). Once again to quote Marx at length:

> This political economy begins by seeming to acknowledge man (his independence, spontaneity, etc.); then locating private property in man's own being, it can no longer be conditioned by the local, national or other *characteristics of private property* as of *something existing outside itself.* This political economy, consequently, displays a *cosmopolitan,* universal energy which overthrows every restriction and bond so as to establish itself instead as the *sole* politics, the sole universality, the sole limit and sole bond. Hence it must throw aside this *hypocrisy* in the course of its further development and come out *in its complete cynicism.* And this it does—untroubled by all the apparent contradictions in which it becomes involved—by developing the idea of *labor* much *more one-sidedly,* and therefore *more sharply* and *more consistently,* as the sole *essence of wealth;* by proving the implications of this theory to be *anti-human* in character, in contrast to the other, original approach. Finally, by dealing the deathblow to ground rent—that last, *individual, natural* mode of private property and source of wealth existing independently of the movement of labor, that expression of feudal property, an expression which has already become wholly economic in character and therefore incapable of resisting political economy. (The *Ricardo* school.) (1844, 129; emphasis in original)

This "overthrow" of the "hypocrisy" of social production and private wealth accumulation resolves itself in the ultimate triumph of communism, whereby social production is attuned to social ownership and the social control and distribution of wealth. Communism becomes "the *positive* expression of annulled private property" (1844, 132; emphasis in original);[112] it is "the *positive* transcendence of *private property,* as *human self-estrangement,* and therefore as the real *appropriation of the human* essence by and for man. Communism therefore is the complete return of man to himself as a *social* (i.e., human) being—a return become conscious, and accomplished within the entire wealth of previous development" (135; emphasis in original). Under this reorientation of the social, economic, and political structures of society, the community, motivated by something other than a rate of profit, plans production according to the needs of the working class.

---

112. "The first positive annulment of private property—*crude* communism—is thus merely one *form* in which the vileness of private property, which wants to set itself up as the *positive community, comes to the surface*" (Marx 1844, 134–35; emphasis in original).

The transcendence of private property is therefore the complete *emancipation* of all human senses and qualities, but it is this emancipation precisely because these senses and attributes have become, subjectively and objectively, *human*. (1844, 139; emphasis in original)

Marx did not, then, we may surmise, embrace socialism and communism on the basis of any *ethical* argument, but rather on the grounds of *inevitability*. However, he must have believed socialism and communism to be ethically "better" or "purer" than the earlier stages of societal and economic development, feudalism and capitalism. Without the later stages of the evolution of the social system being of a more pure and correct form, the dialectic would not have chosen objectively these societal configurations as the ultimate form.

Marx's economics were worked out over a great number of years. The first volume of *Capital* was published in 1867; volume II (refined by Engels) came out in 1883, after Marx's death. (Engels also brought out volume III in 1894, while the "missing" fourth volume was published in 1904 as *A History of Economic Theories*, edited by Karl Kautsky [English translation, 1952].)[113] The specifics of Marx's contributions to economics will be discussed in turn, in the companion volume's chapter dealing with labor as a factor of production.

Conclusion 12

While one's initial feeling may be that the economists and otherwise economically minded writers reviewed in this chapter may have had little in common, least of all anything that could allow them to be included together under the heading of "Utilitarianism," the fact remains that the basic posture of each relies on the fundamental propositions regarding property rights and the role of the individual in their social, political, and economic systems. They range, in fact, across the entire spectrum of thought on the matter, from the libertarian positions of Bentham, Ricardo, James Mill, and McCulloch, to the more cautious attitudes of Malthus and John Stuart Mill, and finally to the restrictive stances of Owen, Hodgskin, and Marx. These actors are in fact the progenitors of much of the debate that still rages, a debate between those who believe that the individual is capable of responsible action if left to his own devices (with government as a central authority having

---

113. Thus the appearance of the book covered a span of almost 30 years. Some have found numerous contradictions between what was written in volume I and what appeared in volumes II and III; but such exegesis is not always that simple. In one famous comment, Böhm-Bawerk noted that Marx undid himself in volume III. However, what appeared in volume III had been written well before the appearance of volume I; the later version of Marx's thought was most likely represented in the material appearing in volume I. He might never have included the offending chapter, which Engels published in volume III.

the sole function of ascribing bounds to that behavior) and those who cannot fathom that government has any less a role than the enumeration of personal rights and privileges (functioning as a channel for what a majority of the representatives has decided are the best and most efficient methods for the attainment of a good and just society).

Before proceeding to the next act in this drama, it should be noted that the Utilitarianism expressed here—ethical Utilitarianism—is not a set of defunct economic (and political) theories, but is still with us today, alive and flourishing in the Law and Economics discipline, associated most strongly with the University of Chicago. In this connection, one need only mention the names of Nobel laureates George J. Stigler (1911–91), Ronald Coase, and Gary Becker.

Portrait Gallery

**St. Thomas Aquinas
(1225–1274)**

Horst-Claus Recktenwald-Archiv,
Lehrstuhl Professor K.-D. Grüske, Nürnberg

**Francis Bacon
(1561–1626)**

Horst-Claus Recktenwald-Archiv,
Lehrstuhl Professor K.-D. Grüske, Nürnberg

**Thomas Hobbes
(1588–1679)**

Horst-Claus Recktenwald-Archiv,
Lehrstuhl Professor K.-D. Grüske, Nürnberg

John Locke
(1632–1704)

Horst-Claus Recktenwald-Archiv,
Lehrstuhl Professor K.-D. Grüske, Nürnberg

Adam Smith
(1723–1790)

Horst-Claus Recktenwald-Archiv,
Lehrstuhl Professor K.-D. Grüske, Nürnberg

Sir James Steuart-Denham
(1712–1780)

Horst-Claus Recktenwald-Archiv,
Lehrstuhl Professor K.-D. Grüske, Nürnberg

Sir William Petty
(1623–1687)
Horst-Claus Recktenwald-Archiv,
Lehrstuhl Professor K.-D. Gruske, Nürnberg

Jonathan Swift
(1667–1745)
Horst-Claus Recktenwald-Archiv,
Lehrstuhl Professor K.-D. Grüske, Nürnberg

Jean-Jacques Rousseau
(1712–1778)
Horst-Claus Recktenwald-Archiv,
Lehrstuhl Professor K.-D. Grüske, Nürnberg

François Quesnay
(1694–1774)

Horst-Claus Recktenwald-Archiv,
Lehrstuhl Professor K.-D. Grüske, Nürnberg

Anne Robert Jacques Turgot
(1727–1781)

Horst-Claus Recktenwald-Archiv,
Lehrstuhl Professor K.-D. Grüske, Nürnberg

Thomas Tooke
(1774–1858)

Horst-Claus Recktenwald-Archiv,
Lehrstuhl Professor K.-D. Grüske, Nürnberg

Francis Hutcheson
(1694–1746)

Horst-Claus Recktenwald-Archiv,
Lehrstuhl Professor K.-D. Grüske, Nürnberg

Jeremy Bentham
(1748–1832)

"The Auto-Icon of Jeremy Bentham with
Bentham's Head" © The College Shop,
University College, London

David Hume
(1711–1776)

Horst-Claus Recktenwald-Archiv,
Lehrstuhl Professor K.-D. Grüske, Nürnberg

Thomas Robert Malthus
(1766–1834)

Horst-Claus Recktenwald-Archiv,
Lehrstuhl Professor K.-D. Grüske, Nürnberg

David Ricardo
(1772–1823)

Horst-Claus Recktenwald-Archiv,
Lehrstuhl Professor K.-D. Grüske, Nürnberg

John Ramsay McCulloch
(1789–1864)

Horst-Claus Recktenwald-Archiv,
Lehrstuhl Professor K.-D. Grüske, Nürnberg

John Stuart Mill
(1806–1873)

Horst-Claus Recktenwald-Archiv,
Lehrstuhl Professor K.-D. Grüske, Nürnberg

Thomas Hodgskin
(1787–1869)

The Historical Society of Pennsylvania

Karl Marx
(1818–1883)

Horst-Claus Recktenwald-Archiv,
Lehrstuhl Professor K.-D. Grüske, Nürnberg

William Stanley Jevons
(1835–1882)

Horst-Claus Recktenwald-Archiv,
Lehrstuhl Professor K.-D. Grüske, Nürnberg

Francis Ysidro Edgeworth
(1845–1926)

Horst-Claus Recktenwald-Archiv,
Lehrstuhl Professor K.-D. Grüske, Nürnberg

Arthur Cecil Pigou
(1877–1959)

Horst-Claus Recktenwald-Archiv,
Lehrstuhl Professor K.-D. Grüske, Nürnberg

Adam Müller
(1779–1829)

Horst-Claus Recktenwald-Archiv,
Lehrstuhl Professor K.-D. Grüske, Nürnberg

Friedrich List
(1789–1846)

Horst-Claus Recktenwald-Archiv,
Lehrstuhl Professor K.-D. Grüske, Nürnberg

Wilhelm Georg Friedrich Roscher
(1817–1894)

Horst-Claus Recktenwald-Archiv,
Lehrstuhl Professor K.-D. Grüske, Nürnberg

Gustav von Schmoller
(1838–1917)

Horst-Claus Recktenwald-Archiv,
Lehrstuhl Professor K.-D. Grüske, Nürnberg

Carl Menger
(1840–1921)

Horst-Claus Recktenwald-Archiv,
Lehrstuhl Professor K.-D. Grüske, Nürnberg

Eugen von Böhm-Bawerk
(1851–1914)

Horst-Claus Recktenwald-Archiv,
Lehrstuhl Professor K.-D. Grüske, Nürnberg

Friedrich von Wieser
(1851–1926)

Horst-Claus Recktenwald-Archiv,
Lehrstuhl Professor K.-D. Grüske, Nürnberg

Ludwig Edler von Mises
(1881–1973)

Horst-Claus Recktenwald-Archiv,
Lehrstuhl Professor K.-D. Grüske, Nürnberg

Jean-Baptiste Say
(1767–1832)

Horst-Claus Recktenwald-Archiv,
Lehrstuhl Professor K.-D. Grüske, Nürnberg

Antoine Augustin Cournot
(1801–1877)

Horst-Claus Recktenwald-Archiv,
Lehrstuhl Professor K.-D. Grüske, Nürnberg

Marie Ésprit Léon Walras
(1834–1910)

Horst-Claus Recktenwald-Archiv,
Lehrstuhl Professor K.-D. Grüske, Nürnberg

Arsène Jules Étienne
Juvénal Dupuit
(1804–1866)

Collection École nationale des
ponts et chaussées

John Bates Clark
(1847–1938)

Horst-Claus Recktenwald-Archiv,
Lehrstuhl Professor K.-D. Grüske, Nürnberg

Thorstein Bunde Veblen
(1857–1929)

Horst-Claus Recktenwald-Archiv,
Lehrstuhl Professor K.-D. Grüske, Nürnberg

Wesley Clair Mitchell
(1874–1948)

Horst-Claus Recktenwald-Archiv,
Lehrstuhl Professor K.-D. Grüske, Nürnberg

John Rogers Commons
(1862–1945)

Courtesy of Mark Perlman

Vilfredo Federico Damaso Pareto
(1848–1923)

Horst-Claus Recktenwald-Archiv,
Lehrstuhl Professor K.-D. Grüske, Nürnberg

Joseph Schumpeter
(1883–1950)

Horst-Claus Recktenwald-Archiv,
Lehrstuhl Professor K.-D. Grüske, Nürnberg

Karl Pribram
(1877–1973)

Carl Menger Photograph Collection Ms. 153,
Special Collections, Milton S. Eisenhower
Library, The Johns Hopkins University

Lionel Charles Robbins
(1898–1984)

Horst-Claus Recktenwald-Archiv,
Lehrstuhl Professor K.-D. Grüske, Nürnberg

CHAPTER 7

Utilitarianism as the Basis for "Scientific" Economics
The Emergence of Neoclassicism

Life admits not of delays; when pleasure can be had, it is fit to
catch it: every hour takes away part of the things that please us,
and perhaps part of the disposition to be pleased.
SAMUEL JOHNSON, LETTER TO JAMES BOSWELL
(SEPT. 1, 1791)

Every reasonable human being should be a moderate
Socialist.
THOMAS MANN, *NEW YORK TIMES* (JUNE 18, 1950)

Real socialism in inside man. It wasn't born with Marx. It was
in the communes of Italy in the Middle Ages. You can't say it is
finished.   DARIO FO, *LONDON TIMES* (APRIL 6, 1992)

Introduction   1

The ethical utilitarian tradition—of which Bentham, James and John
Stuart Mill, and even Malthus and Ricardo are taken here as having been
leading intellectual spokesmen—established a theoretical framework for
the analysis of social and economic problems. As we have seen, these
moral philosophers tackled themes reminiscent of the basic problems
confronting Hobbes and Locke, and their analyses of social affairs reflected this concern. In attempting to rationalize inquiry, they proceeded
in defining the terms, establishing the parameters of discussion, and even
suggesting the manner of the appropriate study of human behavior.

While they may have succeeded in framing the *intellectual* questions,
what they did not provide was any formula, or even general set of methodological principles, with which an *empirical* analysis of individual economic behavior could be conducted. In other words, while establishing the
guidelines and setting forth the philosophical precepts of Utilitarianism,
and even cataloging those constituents deemed necessary and sufficient for
inclusion in and exclusion from an economic calculus, they provided little
or no guidance as to the mechanics underlying the measurement and calculation of "utility."

It was left to what may be regarded as the "scientific" school of utilitarians to complete the task, to erect an analytical edifice on the ethical foundation laid by the older school. While the early Utilitarianism was concerned with ethical and moral problems, the new group was more committed to the employment of a refined version of Utilitarianism that could serve as a practical, ethically neutral, or "scientific" tool for decision making (and could serve as an analytical tool for the social scientist). The group's members seemed disinclined to further the quest for a rational philosophical system devoted to the understanding of moral and ethical problems. The earlier school—moral philosophers trained in the rationality of the law rather than concerned with anything so pedestrian as the worldly concerns of political economy—had, after all, advanced notions consistent with this base. The later school, being more scientifically minded and mathematically versed, redefined the problems so as to make them conform to a new rhetoric with which they were conversant. This new approach employed a structural framework upon which individual behavior could be rigorously evaluated, one amenable to a "quantitative" expression, however one may choose to define the term.

In effecting the evolution from doctrine to analytical instrument, the "scientific" utilitarians restructured the very approach to economics, changing it from a moral and ethical discipline grounded on legal foundations to one more closely akin to the natural sciences grounded on objective scientific principles. In so doing they also laid the groundwork for the transformation of economics into a truly experimental science. As Alfred Marshall noted with respect to the changing of a later economic old guard, "The generation of students of social science which is now passing away has striven to deal with the problem on a broader basis; and your generation is called on to continue that work with greater knowledge and with greater resources" (Marshall 1897, 134). While the era was different, the sentiment remains valid.

This is where the story continues. The major protagonists of the younger school of Utilitarianism are four: William Stanley Jevons, Alfred Marshall, Francis Ysidro Edgeworth, and Philip Henry Wicksteed.

2 Jevons's Individualism: The Role of Mathematical Formalism

2.1 Jevons and the Theory of Marginal Utility

William Stanley Jevons (1835–82)[1] was (in his time) and is today rightly regarded by many as the father of the modern form of "scientific" Utili-

---

1. Jevons was born in Liverpool, England, the ninth child in an established Unitarian family. His father, Thomas, an iron merchant, is reputed to have built the first ocean-capable iron boat and was something of a writer on issues in law and economics. Stanley (as

tarianism. A true polymath, he studied, worked, and wrote in areas as diverse as meteorology, chemistry, statistics, biology, metallurgy, and logic. Of Jevons, Schumpeter opined he was "without any doubt one of the most genuinely original economists who ever lived" (Schumpeter 1954, 826). John Maynard Keynes esteemed him "the first theoretical economist to survey his material with the prying eyes and fertile, controlled imagination of the natural scientist" (Keynes 1936b, 524). Together with Menger and Walras, he is granted the appellation of one of the inventors of the theory of marginal utility.[2]

Whatever mark Jevons may have made in the physical sciences— and certainly his 1874 *Principles of Science* ranks as an achievement in this area—it was in the area of economics that he made his most profound and lasting contributions, specifically in the realm of value theory. It was in this field that his mathematical intuitions had the greatest impact and led to conceptualizations that forever transformed mainstream economics from a moral discipline into a logico-mathematical one, albeit one predicated on a utilitarian base. His 1871 *Theory of Political Economy*[3]—esteemed by Keynes as "[t]he first modern book on economics" (Keynes 1936b, 533–34)—grew out of his 1862 paper, "Notice of a General Mathematical Theory of Political Economy," read before Section F of the British Association.[4] In this work, Jevons claimed that he was

he was known) studied chemistry and botany at University College, London, but family poverty led him to seek employment before finishing his courses, and he took a well paying job as an assayer in the Sydney (Australia) mint. (He had in preparation for the position studied assaying at the Paris mint.) While in Australia (where he spent five years) he studied botany and meteorology in his spare time, publishing a pamphlet entitled "Some Data Concerning the Climate of Australia and New Zealand," but eventually became interested in the "study of man." After fulfilling his contract with the mint in 1859, he returned to London, enrolling at University College and completing the requirements for a B.A. degree in 1860 and an M.A. in 1863 (earning the Gold Medal in political economy and philosophy). He initially sought (unsuccessfully) employment as a journalist, but later accepted a position as general tutor at Owens College, Manchester. In 1866 he was appointed Cobden lecturer in Political Economy at Owens and in 1872 was elected to the Royal Society.

Jevons chose to resign his Manchester professorship in 1875 for health reasons, but later that year took up a professorship of political economy at University College, London, resigning the position in 1880 in order to devote himself to writing. Jevons died in a drowning accident at age 47.

2. We note here that earlier writers could also be granted the title of "instigator" of the marginal revolution (cf. Blaug 1972). Mountifort Longfield (1802–84) wrote in 1834 of the distinction between total and marginal utility, and Nassau Senior (1790–1864) also contributed to the foundation of the theory. Jevons himself read Richard Jennings's 1855 *Natural Elements of Political Economy,* which presented an early form of the theory.

3. Jevons himself prepared a second edition only (1879). The edition used here is the fourth, of 1911, edited by his son, H. S. Jevons. (We use the reprint, introduced by R. D. C. Black in 1970.)

4. The paper itself, little more than an outline of the theory to come, elicited no response and was not published until 1866 in the *Journal of the Statistical Society.* Keynes noted that at Cambridge in that year, where the paper was read, Marshall was in his first year as an undergraduate. See Keynes 1936b, 532.

"led . . . to the somewhat novel opinion, that *value depends entirely upon utility*" (Jevons 1911, 77; emphasis in original). The "novel" aspect of this interpretation of the criterion for value theory lay in the development and eventual acceptance of a new approach, the marginal utility interpretation of value.[5]

As Pribram noted, in the *Theory of Political Economy* Jevons "attempted to preserve, as far as possible, the utilitarian foundations of economics and the Ricardian formulation of the problems of distribution" (Pribram 1983, 283). As did Bentham, Jevons identified pleasure and pain as the primary quantities of importance to an economic calculus: "Pleasure and pain are undoubtedly the ultimate objects of the calculus of economics" (Jevons 1911, 101). In fact, he went so far as to quote Bentham as to the composition of the quantities that should enter into the calculus, considering Bentham's words "too grand and too full of truth to be omitted" (91).[6] But Jevons was not of a kind to rest arguments on authority, even when the authority was Bentham, and so he took to the task of refining the basis of the utilitarian calculus.[7] Bentham had argued (according to Jevons) that pleasure and pain—the arguments, in a sense, of the individual's preference function—should be defined in as broad a manner as possible. Given that Bentham had desired a theory of *ethics,* not a theory of *political economy,* it seemed reasonable that he should then take pleasure and pain as inclusive of "all the forces which drive us to action. They are explicitly or implicitly the matter of all our calculations, and form the ultimate quantities to be treated in all the moral sciences" (91).

Jevons desired a different interpretation. Unlike Bentham, but more consistent with the position of John Stuart Mill, Jevons believed that pleasures and pains were of different degrees: "the feelings of which a man is capable are of various grades" (1911, 92).[8] The categorization of motives

---

5. Howey (1972, 283) praised Jevons as having been the only marginal utility theorist in the 1860s.

6. R. D. Collison Black maintained that it was his attachment to Benthamism that "may well have been a main reason for Jevons's oft-remarked failure to construct a complete and consistent marginal theory of value and distribution" (Black 1972b, 374).

7. In a section entitled "The Noxious Influence of Authority," Jevons proclaimed: ". . . I think there is some fear of the too great influence of authoritative writers in political economy. I protest against deference for any man, whether John Stuart Mill, or Adam Smith, or Aristotle, being allowed to check inquiry" (1911, 261). The reason was strictly utilitarian: "In the republic of the sciences sedition and even anarchy are beneficial in the long run to the greatest happiness of the greatest number" (260).

8. Cf. Mitchell: ". . . motivating the individual to action is the only problem that Jevons wants to throw light on by using the felicific calculus. . . . Jevons is using the calculus in a spirit quite different from Bentham. To Bentham it was a scheme for showing both how people act and what the net results are. . . . Jevons, remember, had comparatively slight interest, as far as one can judge, in the general issues of welfare. . . . The more limited range of the problem which Jevons has in view accounts for this important difference between his and Bentham's employment of the felicific calculus" (1969, vol. II, 42–43).

as dependent on the pursuit of pleasure and the rejection of pain is not one of functional significance for economics, for the fact that man can experience gradations of pleasure and pain implies that all pleasure and pain are not equal in kind—there exists lower and higher forms. To Jevons, the higher form serves as the immediate guide to action, with the latter tending to drive us toward apprehension and acceptance of a moral code of behavior. More specifically, he classified gradations of feeling as those (1) emanating from "bodily wants and susceptibilities" (the "lower" motives), and (2) those evolving from "mental and moral feelings of several degrees of elevation" (the "higher" motives) (92). Significantly, Jevons held that it is not possible to "balance" the different motives; rather, higher motives are comparable only with higher motives, lower with lower, a procedure which eliminates the possibility that "a single higher pleasure will sometimes neutralize a vast extent and continuance of lower pains" (93).

To ensure comparability—and to allay fears of the theory becoming tautological (since without refinement we may "[c]all any motive which attracts us to a certain course of conduct, pleasure; and call any motive which deters us from that conduct, pain")—Jevons felt that the proper scope of economics was to treat of the "lowest rank of feelings" (1911, 93), meaning feelings associated with physical desire. By so doing, he could concentrate on the labor effort needed to secure *physical* objects which serve to satisfy that desire, and the need of the laborer to "devote his energy to the accumulation of wealth" (93). Thus Jevons in effect decided that, in order to ensure comparability and commensurability in his theory of utility, he must endeavor to hold moral values constant. The higher values are of course necessary in providing a basis for a social and moral contract and the fulfillment of conditions for the realization of Smith's "sympathetic" motivation, but cannot easily be handled by a theory predicated on the calculus of self-interest. While the moral problem is important, it is the baser feelings which should be looked upon by economists (in their guise as objective social investigators) as being the more appropriate guides to action:[9] "we need the lower calculus to gain us the utmost good in matters of moral indifference" (93). It is here that Jevons's place in the history of economic thought is secured, for by dividing motives into higher and lower orders, and developing a procedure for handling quantitatively those lower values associated with the provision of base wants, he in effect removed the moral component from Utilitarianism. This left for the "scientific" economist the task of analyzing the structure for the provision of base needs; in other words, "economics" could now be free of questions of social morality, and free to concentrate

9. Again, cf. Mitchell: ". . . Jevons imputes to the human mind ability not to measure pleasures and pains but to discriminate among relations of equality or inequality among different pleasures, among different pains and among different pleasures as compared with different pains. . . . The modest ability to recognize relations of equality or inequality among pleasures and pains is sufficient" (1969, vol. II, 45).

on prices and quantities, production and consumption—those elements amenable to measure.

Perhaps the single detail that set Jevons apart from the utilitarians of the Philosophic Radical tradition was his desire to move Utilitarianism in a more empirical direction, while retaining a rationalist foundation.[10] This he began with a reexamination of the very idea of utility. Having partitioned the class of motives, Jevons proceeded along the lines of Bentham's general definition. He wrote that Bentham's definition of utility "perfectly expresses the meaning of the word in economics, provided that the will or inclination of the person immediately concerned is taken as the sole criterion, for the time, of what is or is not useful" (1911, 102). In Benthamite fashion, Jevons held that utility should signify "the abstract quality whereby an object serves our purposes, and becomes entitled to rank as a commodity," where a *commodity* is "any object, substance, action or service, which can afford pleasure or ward off pain" (101). A few pages on, he refined his definition, treating the concept more precisely as "*a circumstance of things* arising from their relation to man's requirements" (105; emphasis in original). The utility derived from an object may be positive (producing pleasure) or negative (producing pain). Thus we must consider not only commodities, but discommodities as well (114). The important point is that utility is *derived*, not *inherent*. The utility afforded by an object (as we seek to objectify the utility we derive) is entirely subjectively ascertained and is not an objective quality which itself defines the object; utility is most assuredly *not* a property of the object itself, but relates to our individual (even idiosyncratic) apprehensions of the usefulness to be derived from it. "We can never, therefore, say absolutely that some objects have utility and others have not. . . . Nor, when we consider the matter closely, can we say that all portions of the same commodity possess equal utility" (105).[11]

This leads us to perhaps the most important aspect of Jevons's theory—the theory of diminishing marginal utility. While *utility* reflects the total amount of pleasure induced by an object, the important aspect for economists is the *incremental* increase in pleasure. Jevons held that "the continued uniform application of an useful object to the senses or the desires, will not commonly produce uniform amounts of pleasure"

---

10. "Such complicated laws as those of economy cannot be accurately traced in individual cases. Their operation can only be detailed in aggregates and by the method of averages. *We must think under the forms of these laws in their theoretic perfection and complication; in practice we must be content with approximate and empirical laws*" (Jevons 1866, 285; emphasis in original).

11. As Margaret Schabas observed, "Jevons was the one who released economics from its material constraints and shifted the focus to the deliberations of the mind. The economist would henceforth look to psychology rather that to physics for his fundamental principles" (1990, 53). This should not be taken to suggest that Jevons believed economists should take the *approach* of psychology in their work, but rather should be cognizant of *aspects* of human psychology.

(Jevons 1866, 283). His explanation is more clearly expressed in his 1862 paper (Jevons 1866) than in his later works, where the clarity is sometimes obscured by the symbolism:

> Every appetite or sense is more or less rapidly satiated. A certain quantity of an object received, a further quantity is indifferent to us, or may even excite disgust. Every successive application will commonly excite the feelings less intensely than the previous application. The utility of the last supply of an object, then, usually decreases in some proportion, or as some function of the whole quantity received. This variation theoretically existing even in the smallest quantities, we must recede to infinitesimals, and what we shall call the *coefficient of utility*, is the ratio between the last increment or infinitely small supply of the object, and the increment of pleasure which it occasions, both, of course, estimated in their appropriate units. (1866, 283; emphasis in original)

While here we find one of the earliest statements of the rationale behind the theory of marginal utility, Jevons the scientist desired a *measure* of utility. To facilitate measurement, he needed a means to quantify human motives. To Jevons, the only impediment to economics being an "exact science" was a method for using the vast quantity of statistical and other economic-related data that had been collected over the decades and even centuries prior to his time. The "numerical data" required for making precise calculations of economic well-being, Bentham's felicific calculus, were available in great quantities; they were simply not prepared in a form that would allow their exploitation by economists. Yet a problem remained. While Jevons did not question the ability to gather adequate data on human behavior (he considered the task as having been well accomplished), he did question the viability of a method allowing its use (1911, 83). He noted that *direct* measures of motives, beliefs, and feelings were (probably) not achievable, since neither a unit of measurement nor a scale of comparability had been or could be devised which would allow for such a direct comparison: "I have granted that we can hardly form the conception of a unit of pleasure or pain, so that the numerical expression of quantitative feelings seems to be out of the question" (84). Barring direct measures, he found that *indirect* measures were available that could achieve the same purpose: "it is the amount of these feelings which is continually prompting us to buying and selling, borrowing and lending, labouring and resting, producing and consuming; and *it is from the quantitative effects of the feelings that we must estimate their comparative amounts*" (83; emphasis in original).[12]

---

12. As George Stigler (1950, pt. II, 317) noted, Jevons denied that utility was measurable in the first edition of his *Principles,* but acquiesced in the second edition, considering that money could be employed as a measuring rod. We need only note that this measure was held to be an *indirect* one.

It is here that the work of the German psychophysicists Gustav Theodor Fechner (1801–87) and Ernst Heinrich Weber (1795–1878) enters the picture. In his 1851 *Der Tastsinn und das Gemeingefühl* (*The Sense of Touch and the Common Sensibility*) and the earlier (1834) *De Tactu*, Weber—an anatomist and psychologist—promoted the concept of the just-noticeable difference. In brief, he observed that in experimental situations his subjects did not immediately perceive the intensity of a stimulus, but rather did so only after a threshold of sensation had been passed. This he termed the "just-noticeable" difference. He also noted that the difference was not linear, but differed depending on the base: an addition of one degree in temperature Fahrenheit from a base of ten degrees is more noticeable than a similar increase from a base of 100 degrees. Weber's insights were formalized by Fechner. In his 1860 *Elemente der Psychophysik,* Fechner—a physicist and philosopher—suggested that while "sensations" could not be measured directly—we have no gauge by which to quantify "feelings"—one could proceed to an indirect gauge by measuring responses to stimuli. From this application in psychology, a route to economics was clear.

Jevons, keenly interested in physics and psychology, should have been impressed with the work of Fechner and the elucidation of the Weber–Fechner Law relating stimulus to response. Jevons did not judge all human *motives* as within the domain of economic analysis, only the *consequences* of actions.[13] So, if efforts could be directed from focusing on direct measures of happiness and welfare to more indirect measures, that is, from attempting to measure "feelings" and emotions and motives, the alleged "causes" of actions, to measurement of the more numerically tractable "effects" or "consequences" of those actions, we would more likely be successful in our efforts to establish economics as a mathematical discipline and an exact science.[14] The marketplace, in generating numerical data such as prices and quantities, could therefore reflect a type of empirical laboratory, from which data on human behavior (beliefs, emotions, etc.) may be derived indirectly as responses to market signals and stimuli. (Jevons would probably have been intrigued and delighted with the possibility of a device such as the British mathematician Frank Ramsey's [1926] proposed psychogalvanometer, with which

13. "Economy investigates the relations of ordinary pleasures and pains thus arising, and it has a wide enough field of inquiry. But economy does not treat of all human motives. There are motives nearly always present with us, arising from conscience, compassion, or from some moral or religious source, which economy cannot and does not pretend to treat. These will remain to us as outstanding and disturbing forces; they must be treated, if at all, by other appropriate branches of knowledge" (Jevons 1866, 282).

14. "We can no more know nor measure gravity in its own nature than we can measure a feeling; but, just as we measure gravity by its effects in the motion of a pendulum, so we may estimate the equality or inequality of feelings by the decisions of the human mind. The will is our pendulum, and its oscillations are minutely registered in the price lists of the markets" (Jevons 1911, 83–84).

one could presumably "measure" feelings.) For this reason alone, one can hold Jevons to have been the father of the current economic vogue, experimental economics.

So to the question of "how pleasure and pain can be estimated as magnitudes" (1911, 94), Jevons, interested more in measurement than in the elucidation of a psychological theory of human behavior, maintained that "feelings" have two dimensions, duration and intensity;[15] this point he discovered in Hutcheson's *Essay*.[16] Should one of these qualities be the same in each of two instances, the other becomes important as the gauge of greater or less (95). Jevons could then construct a diagram in which the horizontal axis measured duration and the vertical intensity, so that the "aggregate quantity of feeling" could be measured as the area under a curve. Likewise, the utility afforded by a commodity could be identified as having two dimensions, quantity and intensity of effect (108).

While Jevons allowed that the measurement of pleasure and pain was possible—albeit only indirectly in terms of greater or less, and then only as regards effects, not causes—he did not believe that this measurement could be extended to interpersonal comparisons: "The reader will find, again, that there is never, in any single instance, an attempt made to compare the amount of feeling in one mind with that in another. I see no means by which such comparison can be accomplished" (1911, 85). His mathematical exposition of the relation between marginal utilities and prices, for instance, is valid only for an *individual* confronted with a set of prices; his equations are not in general extendable to an economy peopled by multiple agents (which is, after all, the *definition* of an *economy*).[17] This conviction is fundamentally connected to Jevons's belief in the ultimately subjective nature of aspects of human behavior. Differentials in individual abilities, wishes, desires, motivations, and so on, militate against the establishment of a consistent and viable set of units, a prerequisite for comparison. As with John Stuart Mill's insistence on the impossibility of deriving an objective measure of goods value, Jevons maintained the impossibility of arriving at an objective measure of interpersonal utility. Interpersonal comparisons of value simply can not be made, as there exists no basis upon which they may be founded. In effect, however, the impossibility of interpersonal comparisons did not really bear on the theory of utility. Jevons required only *personal* measures of utility, from which he could discern the behavior of a "representative" or average agent. The laws of probability guaranteed (to an acceptable degree) that differences

---

15. Jevons actually accepted the first four of Bentham's criteria for measurement: (1) intensity, (2) duration, (3) certainty, and (4) propinquity (Jevons 1911, 94).

16. Jevons held that Hutcheson "thoroughly anticipates the foundations of Bentham's moral system, showing that the 'moment of good or evil' is, in a compound proportion of the 'duration' and 'intenseness', affected also by the 'hazard' or uncertainty of our existence" (Jevons 1911, 55).

17. G. J. Stigler (1950, 318) made this observation.

among individuals would balance out over the long run and in the aggregate (86).

> The use of an average, or, what is the same, an aggregate result, depends upon the high probability that accidental and disturbing causes will operate, in the long run, as often in one direction as the other, so as to neutralize each other. Provided that we have a sufficient number of independent cases, we may then detect the effect of any *tendency,* however slight. Accordingly, questions which appear, and perhaps are, quite indeterminate as regards individuals, may be capable of exact investigation and solution in regard to great masses and wide averages. (1911, 86; emphasis in original)

Yet, despite his admonitions, Jevons held that such problems as those inherent in interpersonal comparisons are really somewhat illusory. His reasoning was identical to that employed earlier by Mill. Averaging over the aggregate (that is, using data from the macroeconomy), a procedure with which Jevons was particularly familiar given his abiding interest in analyzing statistical time series, removes the effects of the extraneous influences which may exist at the level of the individual. The individual distinctions are of course important at the microanalytic level, but simply cancel out over the aggregate. Given a large enough sample size, the tendencies become demonstrably evident. And it is these tendencies that interest economists. In this respect Jevons postulated the "trading body" as a single homogeneous grouping about which he could speak as though it were a single agent. But one need remember that the aggregate is composed of individuals and so must conform to the laws of economics established for the individual case.[18] So although there simply is no means, even theoretical, for making *individual* comparisons of subjective calculations of value and utility, even from an analysis of consequences and effects, (1911, 85), considerations of the *aggregate* were of a different type.

While the *Theory of Political Economy* represents the kernel of Jevons's thought on utility, a second but unfinished work should also be discussed. *The Principles of Economics* was edited and published by Henry Higgs in 1905 from Jevons's unpublished manuscripts. Consistent with his earlier work, here Jevons again defined utility (or usefulness, which he took as synonymous) as "the power of directly or indirectly producing pleasure or preventing pain" (Jevons 1905, 2). Utility was taken to be an umbrella, "under which we may, following [Nassau W.] Senior, sum up all the qualities which enable a thing to give pleasure or prevent pain" (2).[19]

---

18. "But the laws of the aggregate depend of course upon the laws applying to individual cases" (Jevons 1911, 109).

19. Jevons regarded Senior as having presented "the best exposition of the basis of economics" (Jevons 1905, 1). Senior's "invention" of marginal utility was quite advanced, but it was a device in search of a theory.

The important thing to remember in this regard is that Jevons assumed, or rather asserted as an axiom, that utility was to be defined conceptually only in reference to those commodities (in the broadest sense) that are useful, as determined subjectively. Wealth is desired because it allows us to procure that which is useful: "All that is not useful to us must be indifferent; nobody would take any pains to procure or to exchange a useless article" (1905, 2). Further, and more importantly, this utility is not an attribute of the commodity itself, something objectively present that causes it to be desired; utility is expressed as a subjective feeling one has about the increase of pleasure or reduction of pain brought about by the possession or use of the object.

This subjectivity of utility provides the conditions for exchange. If utility were an objective aspect of a commodity, everyone would derive the same satisfaction from a given amount. But then exchange would not take place. The subjectivity fosters exchange by allowing different people to value the same quantity of a good differently; the exchange thus increases not only an individual's utility, but the total (community) utility as well. With each exchange is engendered an increase in the total utility, the felt satisfaction, afforded by the good.

Jevons's Method of Science   2.2

The theory of economics that Jevons put forth he deemed "purely mathematical in character" (Jevons 1911, 78). All attempts by economists to deny this fact were futile: "Economists cannot alter their nature by denying them the name; they might as well try to alter red light by calling it blue" (78). Yet opposition to Jevons's theory was indeed pronounced. The reason for the antipathy is that economists up to that time had little interest in a new rhetorical form; the literary form had served them well. Jevons viewed this as a gross mistake, since these critics had conflated formalism with the rigor of mathematical calculation.[20] The subject matter of economics, according to Jevons, is well suited to the use of the formalism of the mathematical calculus; its laws are in the nature of self-evident truths.[21] Because of the logical nature of economic truths, the

20. "Economy, indeed, being concerned with quantities, has always of necessity been mathematical in its subject, but the strict and general statement, and the easy comprehension of its quantitative laws has been prevented by a neglect of those powerful methods of expression which have been applied to most other sciences with so much success. It is not to be supposed, however, that because economy becomes mathematical in form, it will, therefore, become a matter of rigorous calculation. Its mathematical principles may become formal and certain, while its individual data remain as inexact as ever" (Jevons 1866, 282).

21. Jevons also expressed at least a flirtation with some idiosyncratic concept of Natural Law, especially in his 1865 *The Coal Question*: "But the statement *that living beings of the same nature and in the same circumstances multiply in the same geometrical ratio* is self-evident when the meaning of the words is once properly understood" (1865, 194; emphasis in original). In fact, chapter IX of this work is entitled "Of the Natural Law of Social Growth."

theories put forth by economists, such as they are, can be more accurately expressed in symbolic form than through the use of "ordinary language." In other words, economics requires the strictures of a mathematical rhetoric, not the looseness of a literary exposition. Nonetheless, and despite the *methodological* position taken by Jevons as to the nature of economic truths, he did not regard this reduction of economic propositions to a logical form as necessary for the employment of the mathematical method. Mathematics could be applied even in a less demonstrative discipline; exactness is not required for a discipline to employ the precision found in such a tool.[22] All that is required is that the variables be expressible in terms of greater or less, not that the concepts themselves be rigorous or even exactly measurable. Thus he was led once again to refine his definition of utility:

> Utility must be considered as measured by, or even as actually identical with, the addition made to a person's happiness. It is a convenient name for the aggregate of the favourable balance of feeling produced—the sum of the pleasure created and the pain prevented. (1911, 106)

In his *Principles of Science,* written from 1867 to 1872, Jevons presented his systemic structure. One can see that Jevons's treatment of the subject was in opposition to that of John Stuart Mill, whose 1843 *System of Logic* he sought to replace. While Mill took a decidedly different, justificationist, approach to the subject, Jevons desired to combine a deductive logic predicated on Boolean mathematics with an inductive logic.[23] Scientific rigor and deductive reasoning would provide to econom-

---

22. This contention will arise again in the discussion of Edgeworth.

23. Mill's logic was primarily evidentiary: his "inductive logic" presupposed that the field of logic was itself an empirical discipline. But enumerative empiricism or historical episodic empiricism he ridiculed as insufficient in providing a basis for the *derivation* of laws. Mill's system thus began with his elucidation of rules that must govern a system of scientific logic.

While both Mill and Jevons were empiricists, the differences in approach were great. Fundamentally, while Mill found it necessary to analyze the preconditions under which knowledge emerges and ideas originate, Jevons by contrast simply asserted that knowledge derived from experience. As did Kant, Jevons believed that our apprehension of the world followed from our belief system: we view the world through a predefined set of perception-spectacles. Jevons's definition of induction likewise put him at odds with Mill. For Mill, induction is a useful scientific rule. For Jevons, induction is valid only because the laws that govern it are derived from the laws governing deduction. In fact, the syllogism formed the basis of Jevons's method, wherein he invoked the axiom of the substitution of similars—the condition that, if two things (propositions, etc.) are such as to be indistinguishable in all particulars, then what is true of the first is also true of the second. This he combined with three "generally received" axioms of existence, to wit, "whatever is, is," "a thing cannot both be and not be," and "a thing must either be or not be" (Wicksteed 1910a, 475). This allowed him to reduce the analysis of propositions to a mere process of the algebraic manipulation of stipulated terms.

ics the same cachet as they had given to physics. However, with the introduction of the new rhetoric, Jevons was led to impose on economics a structure that was either unaccepting of or unable to accommodate the cultural richness of Bentham's or John Stuart Mill's versions of Utilitarianism. Either Jevons had failed to acknowledge the fullness of Mill's presentation, or his rhetoric was incapable of incorporating anything as broad and encompassing.[24]

Perhaps the clearest statement by Jevons of his approach to economics—his methodological stance—appears in "The Future of Political Economy," a lecture he presented at University College, London, and published in the *Fortnightly Review* in 1876. Here Jevons proclaimed himself troubled by those who committed the logical blunder he termed the "fallacy of exclusiveness," meaning the devotion to a single method of demonstration, often to the complete disregard of any other. Theorists decry historical and institutional inquiry as an attempt to assemble facts in the absence of any theoretical design; historians and sociologists distrust theoretical investigation as vacuous. Seldom do the two groups realize the complementarity of their methods, feeling compelled to argue that one is superior to the other.

> There are too many in the present day who advocate the teaching of physical science, and imply in the mode of their advocacy that moral, classical, or other studies are to be discountenanced. It is most common to find people speaking of inductive reasoning, as if it were entirely distinct and opposite to deductive reasoning, the fact being, however, as I believe, that deduction is a necessary element of induction. (Jevons 1876, 623)

The historical and the "scientific" (axiomatic, a priori) must be seen as mutually reinforcing in economics, as they are in virtually all sciences. Merely because a science develops a specialty of a historical nature is not to suggest that the more theoretical aspects no longer provide valid avenues of research. The two deal with different aspects of the same problem: "Any group of objects may be studied, either as regards the laws of action of their component parts, irrespective of time, or as regards the successive forms produced from time to time under the action of those laws" (1876, 623).

Political economy is no exception. It seeks to identify basic laws of human nature, laws "so simple in their foundation that they would apply, more or less completely, to all human beings of whom we have any knowledge" (1876, 623). Political economy further seeks to apply

---

24. Indeed, in many respects Jevons despised Mill. Keynes noted, "Jevons's aversion to Mill [was] pursued almost to the point of morbidity" (1936b, 538). In that attitude, one can find much to explain Jevons's own disposition.

historical analysis, first to a verification of these laws, and second to their extension to areas beyond the ones to which they have traditionally been applied.[25]

Another interesting aspect of this essay is the advice Jevons offered for the future instruction of economics. To begin, there was no reason to believe that economics could any longer be understood as it had been at the time of Smith and John Stuart Mill. The changes in rhetoric and substance were coming far too fast and carrying the subject too far afield. For instance, in the traditional mode of inquiry, political economy had been understood to encompass four foci—production, exchange, distribution, and consumption—with different laws respecting each division. It soon became evident that consumption, ignored by British economists in favor of production, could in fact be given first importance in a reorganization that understood that goods were not produced absent a perceived demand. In a similar manner each of the four divisions could be reduced to a single unified theoretical core. Likewise, should these conventional divisions be replaced with theories of utility, labor, capital, and exchange, it is certainly feasible to integrate them into one general theoretical edifice. This Jevons succeeded in doing in his *Theory of Political Economy*.

His second point in regard to economics instruction condemned the preoccupation of mainstream British academic economists with literary exposition and their consequent eschewal of mathematical symbolism. This meant to Jevons that British economics risked losing its preeminence to the Continental economists who had no such hesitations and who were pushing on the mathematical front.[26] Absent a concerted effort to seek out foreign publications (such as those of Léon Walras, Jules Dupuit, and Johann von Thünen, to name but a few) and provide a comprehensive appraisal of the neglected British work in this area (such as that of William Whewell, Dionysius Lardner, Fleeming Jenkin, and Alfred Marshall), the promise of this redirection of effort would be lost. Without a collection of the efforts of those working on the frontier, placed in a form understandable to succeeding generations of students of economics, and without training in the requisite methods of inquiry, the discipline would deprive itself of a potentially valuable mode of expression. In the British case, given the hostility in general quarters to the mathematical method, this inability to understand and so communicate in the new rhetoric would severely handicap British economics, reducing it to an ineffectual position in the intellectual arena. Jevons feared it would be-

---

25. Jevons noted that many of these same theoretical principles of human behavior, such as the law of property, are equally applicable to an explanation of the behavior of animals (1876, 624).

26. The interested reader should peruse the bibliography of mathematical writings in the second edition of Jevons's *Theory of Political Economy*.

come evident very quickly that British political economists simply had nothing of interest to say.[27]

Jevons's third point was that the practical element of political economy had been ignored. Each of the branches of the subject—money and banking, public finance, capital theory, welfare, trade, labor studies, and so forth—functions under the regulation of identical laws, despite the apparent complexity of the interactions. There is, in other words, a method underlying the chaos. The problem is that the complexities are such that it is no longer feasible for a single person to profess proficiency in each specialty; as with any other field, economics had simply become too complex and too specialized to allow anyone more than a passing familiarity with all of its disparate aspects.

Jevons's Place in Utilitarianism   2.3

While Jevons is commonly perceived by modern English and American economists as the father of marginal utility analysis, his contributions involve much more, including the introduction of a methodology that reestablished Utilitarianism as a dominant economic and social (and even moral) philosophy. Thus did Jevons devote some of his energy to the identification and solution of the discipline's problems. It is in his attitude toward the amelioration of social ills that we see his return to his Benthamite roots. Utilitarian criteria can be used effectively to judge the merits of social reform policies. In his 1882 *The State in Relation to Labour*, he justified state intervention so long as the legislation "adds to the sum total of human happiness" (Jevons 1882, 12). The basis for such action rested on the failure of individual choice. While he saw the Poor Laws as an example of enlightened social policy (since they could lead to the promotion of individual initiative), he also understood that individual initiatives could lead to combinations which could negatively affect other classes or interests. For this reason, legislative involvement became imperative.[28]

As an example of Jevons's program for social reform, consider his 1878 "Amusements of the People," part of a series of essays on methods of social reform written for the *Contemporary Review*.[29] Jevons began the essay by maintaining that the complexities of modern society necessitated an expansion of the legislative role in an effort to increase social welfare:

> As society becomes more complex and the forms of human activity multiply, so must multiply also the points at which careful legislation

27. Jevons had added much to the literature on logic. In 1864 he published his *Pure Logic, or the Logic of Quality Apart from Quantity*. This work seems to have been mostly an effort to transform logical verbal expression into mathematical terms, thus enabling one to use mathematical substitutions easily.

28. On Jevons's ideas of policy reform, see Roger Backhouse (1985, 74–75).

29. We use here the version reprinted in *Methods of Social Reform* (1883).

and continuous social effort are required to prevent abuse, and secure the best utilisation of resources. (Jevons 1883, 1)

But an understanding of the legislative role was itself not sufficient.
Of paramount importance was the need to engage in *concerted* efforts at
reform, not piecemeal legislation designed to correct one or a few social
ills. It must be acknowledged that reforms take time, and that there is
simply no palliative for the amelioration of societal problems. As Jevons
phrased it,

> If the citadel of poverty and ignorance and vice is to be taken at all, it
> must be besieged from every point of the compass—from below,
> from above, from within; and no kind of arm must be neglected
> which will tend to secure the ultimate victory of morality and culture.
> (1883, 2)

Among the "arms" to be taken up in the fight, Jevons proclaimed
that the simplest one, and the one which held the possibility of the greatest achievement, was the provision of public amusements. Amusements
broadly defined—and they could consist of public concerts, museums,
galleries, and so forth—he felt served a necessary function in the promotion of the betterment of life, a fact that had been little appreciated by the
"upper" classes as they sought their own amusement while disparaging
that of the "lower" ranks as not conducive to individual effort or social
morality. "The old idea of keeping people moral by keeping their noses to
the grindstone must be abandoned" (1883, 7). His other ideas for social
reform proceeded along the same lines—always with the understanding
that mere efficiency criteria alone could not advance modern society. In
advocating measures aimed at the expansion of production, one must be
aware of the human toll involved. To Jevons, it was the insensitivity to
such human concerns that produced the problems of social decay and
immorality, problems which became so ingrained in the society that only
state action could now control them.

3 The Synthesis of Marshall

3.1 Marshall's Utilitarianism

While Jevons is credited with the elevation of economics to a scientific
discipline—and with the beginning of the marginal revolution in Britain—
it would be left to another figure to advance these ideas in the intellectual
marketplace. Of all the British economists of this period, undoubtedly the
most celebrated was the father of the Cambridge School of Economics,

Alfred Marshall (1842–1924).[30] Marshall's influence was so great that his teachings dominated English economics (and American as well) for a generation after his death.[31] His student, John Maynard Keynes, went so far as

30. Marshall was born in Bermondsey, England, a suburb of London and at the time a center of the leather tanning industry. His father served for many years as a clerk at the Bank of England; his mother was born to a working-class family. Despite his humble origins, Marshall is said to have peddled a somewhat romanticized version of them. Ronald Coase (1984) identified several inaccuracies in the generally accepted accounts of Marshall's life, including the account given by Keynes (1924). For example, he discovered that Marshall was born in Bermondsey, not Clapham as Keynes contended; that Marshall's father was a clerk and not a cashier at the Bank; and that his mother was the daughter of a butcher, not a chemist.

In 1862 Marshall matriculated at St. John's College, Cambridge, a move purportedly disapproved of by his father, who apparently wished him to study classics at Oxford. He was graduated from Cambridge in 1865 (Second Wrangler) in mathematics, a discipline for which his father had expressed the utmost contempt. Upon completion of his studies, he was elected to a fellowship.

To repay accumulated debts and as a way to earn a living following his graduation, Marshall briefly accepted a position as mathematical master at Clifton College. It was through the contacts made here that he was to gain entry to the intellectual circles which would serve him well in later life. In 1868, he was appointed a lecturer in political economy in the moral science faculty at St. John's.

In 1875 Marshall embarked on a four-month tour of the United States, the purpose of which was to gain an understanding of the intricacies involved in the question of protectionism, an idea which at the time had been little understood within the conventional British economics establishment. As he spoke not merely to academics, but to politicians and businessmen as well, thus gaining from the experience a firsthand knowledge of the policies, the reasonings behind them, and the ensuing effects on the business climate, Marshall felt the educational value of the enterprise was incalculable. (Keynes quoted from a letter by Marshall: "In Philadelphia I spent many hours in conversation with the leading protectionists. And now I think, as soon as I have read some books they have recommended me to read, I shall really know the whole of their case; and I do not believe there is or ever has been another Englishman who could say the same" [Keynes 1924, 324].)

He then accepted a position in the political economy department of University College, Bristol, serving first as principal and then as professor of political economy. In 1883, at the death of Arnold Toynbee, Marshall accepted a lectureship at Balliol College, Oxford, a position the duties of which included lecturing to candidates for the Indian Civil Service. At the death of Henry Fawcett in 1884, he was elected professor of political economy at Cambridge, a position he held from January 1885 until his retirement in 1908. Upon his return he saw that economics was elevated to the status of a separate course of study. To this end, he was instrumental in the establishment of the Cambridge Economics Tripos, a dream which was finally realized in 1903.

Marshall continued an active pursuit of writing up to the end of his life. In 1923 he published his last book, a long-overdue work on monetary theory, *Money, Credit and Commerce*, a project that actually began to take shape between the years 1867 and 1877. Details of Marshall's life are from John Maynard Keynes (1924), Ronald H. Coase (1984), John K. Whitaker (1987), and Peter Groenewegen (1995).

31. A list of Marshall's students at both Oxford and Cambridge reads as a "who's who" of British economists: Herbert Foxwell, John Neville Keynes, John Maynard Keynes, Arthur Bowley, Arthur Cecil Pigou, and Arthur W. Flux are just a few of the names associated with the teachings of Marshall.

to describe him thus: "As a scientist he was, within his own field, the greatest in the world for a hundred years" (1924, 321).[32]

In 1867 Marshall became a member of the "Grote Club," an informal "discussion group" organized by the Reverend John Grote, then the Knightbridge Professor of Moral Philosophy. The group included such personages as Henry Sidgwick and the logician John Venn. The discussions there shifted Marshall's interest from molecular physics—his first choice of vocation—to ethical and epistemological studies. This period also marked a dramatic change in his attitude toward theology. His earlier ambition for a clerical career waned, and he became much more agnostic in outlook, accepting what was at the time emerging as vogue in Cambridge academic circles. As J. M. Keynes suggested, "Marshall's Cambridge career came just at the date which will, I think, be regarded by the historians of opinion as the critical moment at which Christian dogma fell away from the serious philosophical world of England, or at any rate of Cambridge" (Keynes 1924, 317).[33] It was also in 1867 that he became familiar with the economic works of John Stuart Mill, an acquaintanceship which was to have a profound effect on his life, as it was this reading that ultimately led to his decision to turn to the study of political economy.[34]

Marshall's first published book[35] was The Economics of Industry (1879). Originally the product of his wife, Mary Paley Marshall[36]— described by Schumpeter as "the tutelary deity of his life" (1954, 834)[37]—it was to arrive as a joint intellectual effort, one which Alfred Marshall later took great steps to suppress.[38] Marshall himself described

---

32. Yet Keynes later paid an even greater tribute to Jevons, maintaining that in the *Theory of Political Economy* he presented a theory that was "simple, lucid, unfaltering, chiselled in stone where Marshall knits in wool" (Keynes 1936b, 534).

33. Keynes quickly added, however, that Marshall never went so far as to adopt "an 'anti-religious' attitude" (Keynes 1924, 317).

34. The influence of Mill's works on Marshall has been suggested by some to have been more than insightful. Consider Schumpeter's statement that Marshall "need only have allowed his mind to play on Mill's loose statements and to work out their exact model (system of equations) in order to arrive at a point where the purely theoretical parts of the *Principles* came in sight. The incidental innovations would then naturally appear to him as mere developments from Mill instead of as 'revolutionary' " (1954, 838).

35. His first published article was a review of Jevons's *Theory of Political Economy*, published in *The Academy* in 1872.

36. Mary Paley was asked by James Stuart to write the book as a text for a series of extension lectures, primarily aimed at a non-university audience—one including the worker-intellectuals in the blue-collar labor force.

37. His marriage to her in 1871 forced him to resign his Cambridge fellowship because of the then-prevailing rules of celibacy.

38. After publication of his great *Principles of Economics*, Marshall published a more elementary version of the great work, *Elements of the Economics of Industry*, apparently with the intent of denying a market to the earlier joint effort. Marshall later expressed his loathing for *The Economics of Industry*, which he described as "a cheap popular book, which was necessarily superficial" (1933, 222). On his attitude toward the book, see Rita McWilliams-Tullberg (1992) and Peter Groenewegen (1995).

the book as an introduction to the economics of John Stuart Mill. In fact, the material on value follows closely the treatment by Marshall in his 1876 "On Mr. Mill's Theory of Value," published in the *Fortnightly Review*. The essay defended John Stuart Mill's economic theory against attacks launched by, among others, John Elliott Cairnes and Jevons. It was in this essay that Marshall took an important step in demonstrating, as Jevons had done in his *Theory of Political Economy*, that economics could command the status of "scientific" endeavor and so be separated from the realm of ethics. As Marshall stated the case:

> The pure science of Ethics halts for lack of a system of measurement of efforts, sacrifices, desires, &c., fit for her wide purposes. But the pure science of Political Economy has found a system that will subserve her narrower aims. This discovery, rather than any particular proposition, is the great fact of the pure science. (Marshall 1876, 597)

The principal element allowing for such a transformation was the measurement of utility.

> Proceeding from its new point of view, Political Economy has analysed the efforts and sacrifices that are required for the production of a commodity for a given market at a given time; she has found a measure for them in their *cost to the person who will purchase them*, and then enunciated her central truth. This central truth is that producers, each governed under the sway of free competition by calculations of his own interest, will endeavour so to regulate the amount of any commodity which is produced for a given market during a given period, that this amount shall be just capable on the average of finding purchasers during this period at a remunerative price: a remunerative price being defined to be a price which shall be just equal to the sum of the exchange measures of those efforts and sacrifices which are required for the production of the commodity when this particular amount is produced, *i.e.*, to the sum of the expenses which must be incurred by a person who would purchase the performance of these efforts and sacrifices. (1876, 597; emphasis in original)

Now we are led to consider Marshall's greatest contribution to economics, his *Principles of Economics*.[39] First published in 1890 as the proposed initial volume of a major economics work, the *Principles* never really fulfilled that dream, which nonetheless was not finally surrendered until the fifth edition of the work. As it grew through seven successive

---

39. In 1890, the year of publication of his masterwork *Principles of Economics*, Marshall was elected president of Section F of the British Association for the Advancement of Science. In this capacity he initiated the movement for the creation of a separate British Economic Association, later to be renamed the Royal Economic Society.

editions (1891, 1895, 1898, 1907, 1910, 1916, and 1920),[40] the scope and thoroughness of the coverage changed, but it had been from the beginning already a truly comprehensive treatise. Of this magisterial production much has been said, so much that we may forgive those who assume it to be Marshall's only book-length effort. Keynes went so far as to consider its publication the first of three definitive events that brought about the "modern age of British economics," the other two being the founding of the British Economic Association and the publication of the first true economics compendium, Palgrave's[41] *Dictionary of Political Economy* (Keynes 1940, 409).[42] With this in mind, we turn now to a look at Marshall's phenomenal work.

With the fifth edition (1907) of the *Principles,* Marshall included a statement of purpose, a brief methodological interlude, designed to sketch out what he considered a serious defect in the then-contemporary economic discourse.[43] While Jevons had insisted on introducing formalism into the economic dialogue, Marshall felt that the pendulum had swung too far in that direction and had consequently not only affected the quality of work in the field, but also threatened to undermine the entire program to which economics as a discipline was devoted. What was missing from the economics of Jevons and even Ricardo (who we have seen insisted on a deductive economics) was a recognized connection between formalism and the ethical and moral bases upon which the fundamental propositions of economics had, since before the time of Smith, been predicated. To this end Marshall's work achieved a synthesis and an integration.

An important additional ingredient was his introduction into economic theory of the biological analogy. Well-known to readers of Marshall is his statement, "The Mecca of the economist lies in economic

---

40. A variorum edition was published in 1961, edited by Marshall's nephew, Claude Guillebaud.

41. Robert Harry Inglis Palgrave (1827–1919), a banker and editor (at *The Economist* and *Banker's Magazine*), became a Fellow of the Royal Society in 1882, with the support of Jevons.

42. Keynes's praise for the book was lavish indeed: "A student can read the *Principles,* be fascinated by its persuading charm, think that he comprehends it, and, yet, a week later, know but little about it. How often has it not happened even to those who have been brought up on the *Principles,* lighting upon what seems a new problem or a new solution, to go back to it and to find, after all, that the problem and a better solution have been always there, yet quite escaping notice! It needs much study and independent thought on the reader's part, before he can know the half of what is contained in the concealed crevices of that rounded globe of knowledge, which is Marshall's *Principles of Economics*" (1924, 356). Thus was born the idea that "it's all in Marshall"!

Schumpeter, however, took a slightly different view, suggesting that to understand fully Marshall's contributions to economics, it was necessary to become acquainted with the whole of his work: "nobody knows Marshall who knows only the *Principles*" (1954, 834).

43. The first edition began with an outline of economic history, which in later editions was relegated to the appendixes.

biology rather than in economic dynamics" (1920, xiv). Specifically, what intrigued Marshall was the notion of evolution. Biological systems are dynamic and evolve in a continuous and gradual manner (with episodes of punctuated change). Marshall believed the same mechanism underlay the development of economies and so envisioned the economics discipline developing along similar lines to that of biology. He criticized earlier economic writers for having ignored the obvious symmetries between biology and economics in favor of mechanical analogies, and even considered that progress on the economic front had been hindered by this lack of attention:[44]

> [B]iology itself teaches us that the vertebrate organisms are the most highly developed. The modern economic organism is vertebrate; and the science which deals with it should not be invertebrate. It should have that delicacy and sensitiveness of touch which are required for enabling it to adapt itself closely to the real phenomena of the world; but none the less must it have a firm backbone of careful reasoning and analysis. (1920, app. B, §8, 769)

He too for the most part reverted to the use of the mechanical analogy in his theoretical analysis; he suggested at the outset that this was due to the realization that "biological conceptions are more complex than those of mechanics" and so "a volume on Foundations must therefore give a relatively large place to mechanical analogies" (1920, Preface to 8th ed., xiv). While "it is especially needful to remember that economic problems are imperfectly presented when they are treated as problems of statical equilibrium, and not of organic growth," it is nonetheless also clear that "the statical treatment alone can give us definiteness and precision of thought" (bk.V, chap. XII, §3, 461). To understand the functioning of an economy, it is necessary to reduce the complexities to simple components, each analyzable separately and capable of integration into a whole. The physical science analogue is more appropriate to this tack that is the biological, since the structures involved in the physical sciences can be compartmentalized and then aggregated. Biological analogies serve a useful function, and we must be cognizant of their importance in the study of economic evolution; but for the sake of deliberative reasoning, the mechanical analogy is more appropriate (as is the static method) in clarifying statements of principle.[45]

---

44. He also made use of a military analogy, especially in 1920, appendix C, §4, 776–77.

45. Marshall did, however, secure a place for biological analogies in the study of institutions: "The qualities which a breeder or a gardener notices as eminently adapted to enable an animal or a plant to thrive in its environment, are for that very reason likely to have been developed in comparatively recent times. And in like manner those properties of an economic institution which play the most important part in fitting it for the work which it has to do now, are for that very reason likely to be in a great measure of recent growth" (1920, bk. II, chap. I, §2, 50).

To illustrate Marshall's concerns, consider the primary motivation behind the *Principles*. In the preface to the first edition, Marshall declared that in the current practice of economic inquiry, the concept of the individual as a rational, deliberative being had undergone such a metamorphosis as to produce a creature unrecognizable as human. This he felt was unacceptable; it raised concerns as to the purpose of the science of economics and by extension the methodology which directs that study. Marshall faced the question first as a problem of ascertaining the correct place within scientific study of observation and of formal analytics, a question which has been central to all that has come before. He began:

> the function of the science [of economics] is to collect, arrange and analyse economic facts, and to apply the knowledge, gained by observation and experience, in determining what are likely to be the immediate and ultimate effects of various groups of causes; and it is held that the Laws of Economics are statements of tendencies expressed in the indicative mood, and not ethical precepts in the imperative. Economic laws and reasonings in fact are merely a part of the material which Conscience and Common-sense have to turn to account in solving practical problems, and in laying down rules which may be a guide in life. (1920, Preface to 1st ed., v–vi)

He took issue immediately with the attempts of some writers to abstract the motives and ethical behaviors of man into a conceptual "economic man," for whom ethics, morality, obligation, and motivation to action are quite irrelevant and so can be readily dismissed from the reflections of the "scientist." Marshall felt that the failure of these attempts was due precisely to the fact that, absent a moral and ethical base, "economic man" must be governed entirely by selfish motives and desires.[46] The classical conception was an individual "who is under no ethical influences and who pursues pecuniary gain warily and energetically, but mechanically and selfishly" (1920, vi). Yet he is also defined as a social creature. Thus economists had been forced to confront a paradox of their own making: while stipulating "economic man" as egoistically constituted, they had then been compelled to introduce into his constitution attributes of sacrifice, family affections and obligations, and community relationships, which serve to instill altruistic and communal, but certainly not egoistic, motives.

Marshall desired to avoid the inconsistency by avoiding the abstraction of man into "economic man." To this end, he redefined actions according to nonselfish (nonrational?) motives: "in the present book normal action is taken to be that which may be expected, under certain conditions, from the members of an industrial group; and no attempt is made to exclude the influence of any motives, the action of which is

---

46. On Marshall's rejection of "economic man," see Whitaker (1977).

regular, merely because they are altruistic" (1920, vi).[47] The actions of the individual stem not from egoistic motives alone, but also from adopted habits. It matters not "whether these impulses are an expression of his higher nature or not; whether they spring from mandates of his conscience, the pressure of social connection, or the claims of his bodily wants," for in any case

> he yields a certain relative precedence to them without reflection now, because on previous occasions he has decided deliberately to yield that relative precedence. The predominant attractiveness of one course of action over others, even when not the result of calcula-tion at the time, is the product of more or less deliberate decisions made by him before in somewhat similar cases. (1920, bk. I, chap. II, §3, 20n.1)

He later extended his depiction to account for the evolution within mankind of a feeling of sympathy, an emotion he felt to be at the heart of collective activities (and which certainly can be completely consistent with the moral philosophy of Smith). Wrote Marshall:

> Gradually the unreasoning sympathy, of which there are germs in the lower animals, extends its area and gets to be deliberately adopted as a basis of action: tribal affection, starting from a level hardly higher than that which prevails in a pack of wolves or a horde of banditti, gradually grows into a noble patriotism; and religious ideals are raised and purified. . . . Thus the struggle for existence causes in the long run those races of men to survive in which the individual is most willing to sacrifice himself for the benefit of those around him; and which are consequently the best adapted collectively to make use of their environment. (1920, bk. IV, chap. VIII, §2, 243)

Thus we see Marshall defining his "representative man" not as the classical automaton or quintessential Benthamite calculator, devoid of purpose and any sense of ethics and community, but rather as a Smithian proxy defined with respect to the modal ethical and moral temperament of the community. He is possessed of those qualities which define him as human. Thus interpreted, Marshall's man can be seen as centered within a particular ethical milieu.[48] Marshall's representative in this connection—

---

47. Note in this context the extension of the biological analogy: "partly through the suggestions of biological study, the influence of circumstances in fashioning character is generally recognized as the dominant fact in social science. Economists have accordingly now learnt to take a larger and more hopeful view of the possibilities of human progress. They have learnt to trust that the human will, guided by careful thought, can so modify cir-cumstances as largely to modify character; and thus to bring about new conditions of life still more favourable to character; and therefore to the economic, as well as the moral, well-being of the masses of the people" (Marshall 1920, bk. I, chap. IV, §5, 48).

48. Cf. Isaiah Berlin, particularly 1958, 1980.

his "economic man"—is then a true statistical representative of an actual community-oriented being, one not divorced from but rather defined by the very social and moral sphere of which he is a part.[49]

Implicit in the conception of the "representative agent" is the Marshallian concept of "normal." In introducing the idea into economics, Marshall implied that the terms *normal* and *abnormal* were not to be viewed within any ethical context; the terms themselves hold no moral connotation, but rather are statistical artifacts. Surprisingly, the ethical utility of the terms derives from their value-free nature; they allow the "economic man" to be defined with reference only to the domain in which he is situated, and so to be imbued with the ethical and moral values and constraints typified in the "average" citizen. "Normal" values so interpreted are then "those which would be ultimately attained, if the economic conditions under view had time to work out undisturbed their full effect," while "abnormal" values are "those values in which the accidents of the moment exert a preponderating influence" (1920, vii).

Marshall's definitions are then intimately connected to statistical theory.[50] Normal and abnormal (or "current") values "shade into one another by continuous gradations." While the normal is akin to a statistical average, the very definition is dependent on the length of time which we consider relevant for study. What was once "normal" becomes "current" when we extend the period under analysis: "The values which we may regard as normal if we are thinking of the changes from hour to hour on a Produce Exchange, do but indicate current variations with regard to the year's history" (1920, vii).[51]

One of the extensions of this interpretation of economic man arises in the consideration of the element of time in economic analysis. Should we choose a restrictive-enough time interval, we can regard tastes, expectations and a whole sequence of other inputs as fixed, and so handle the analytics in a highly abstract manner. The short run was thus stipulated by Marshall so as to "take a man as he is, without allowing time for any change in his character" (1920, bk. III, chap. III, §2, 94). The reference to

49. "In all this they [economists] deal with man as he is: not with an abstract or 'economic' man; but a man of flesh and blood. They deal with a man who is largely influenced by egoistic motives in his business life to a great extent with reference to them; but who is neither above vanity and recklessness, nor below delight in doing his work well for its own sake, or in sacrificing himself for the good of his family, his neighbours, or his country; a man who is not below the love of a virtuous life for its own sake" (Marshall 1920, bk. I, chap. II, §7, 26–27).

50. Marshall was a close friend of Edgeworth, who produced a great deal in the areas of statistics and probability. Also, given that Marshall was a member of the Grote Club—membership included the father of the frequency interpretation of probability, John Venn—it is likely that this was another influence.

51. Marshall's "normal" should be contrasted with Max Weber's Ideal Type and Arthur Spiethoff's Representative Type. Marshall's concept was in the medieval nominalist (empirical) tradition, the tradition of Galton. Weber and Spiethoff were more in the Platonic-transcendental-medieval realist tradition.

character once again suggests that *his* economic man was founded on an ethical base. Interestingly enough, if we extend the time period to the infinite (or at any rate to an exceptionally long period), we may also for the sake of the analysis abstract from certain identifying characteristics and so cast our analysis in an abstract fashion.

In all, Marshall declared that economics could never attain the status of the physical sciences, since "it deals with the ever changing and subtle forces of human nature" (1920, bk. I, chap. II, §1, 14). In treating of the "Substance of Economics" (the title of bk. I, chap. II of the *Principles*), Marshall harkened back to a theme identified by the early utilitarian writers and by Jevons, this being the measurement of motives. Economics "concerns itself chiefly with those motives which affect, most powerfully and most steadily, man's conduct in the business part of his life" (14). In economics, the apprehensible motives to action are generally taken to be measurable by the device of money, and this device makes economics unique among the social sciences in respect to quantification. Marshall in fact held that economics is unique because it

> concerns itself chiefly with those desires, aspirations and other affections of human nature, the outward manifestations of which appear as incentives to action in such a form that the force or quantity of the incentives can be estimated and measured with some approach to accuracy; and which therefore are in some degree amenable to treatment by scientific machinery. An opening is made for the methods and the tests of science as soon as the force of a person's motives—*not* the motives themselves—can be approximately measured by the sum of money, which we will just give up to secure a desired satisfaction; or again by the sum which is just required to induce him to undergo a certain fatigue. (1920, 15)

The coincidence with the views of Jevons is obvious. *Direct* measures of motives are not possible; only the *effects* of actions are amenable to measurement. Further, the rule of measure is that pleasures can be ranked based on the desire to forgo one item for another, comparisons being made "indirectly by the incentives which they [physical gratifications] afford to action" (1920, 15–16). Marshall then, in Jevonsian terms, identified the nature of motives as higher and lower, but unlike Jevons, he did not hold economics to be interested in the latter only. For Marshall,

> the economist studies mental states rather through their manifestations than in themselves; and if he finds they afford evenly balanced incentives to action, he treats them *primâ facie* as for his purpose equal. He follows indeed in a more patient and thoughtful way, and with greater precautions, what everybody is always doing every day in ordinary life. He does not attempt to weigh the real

value of the higher affections of our nature against those of our lower: he does not balance the love for virtue against the desire for agreeable food. He estimates the incentives to action by their effects just in the same way as people do in common life. He follows the course of ordinary conversation, differing from it only in taking more precautions to make clear the limits of his knowledge as he goes. He reaches his provisional conclusions by observations of men in general under given conditions without attempting to fathom the mental and spiritual characteristics of individuals. But he does not ignore the mental and spiritual side of life. On the contrary, even for the narrower uses of economic studies, it is important to know whether the desires which prevail are such as will help to build up a strong and righteous character. And in the broader uses of those studies, when they are being applied to practical problems, the economist, like every one else, must concern himself with the ultimate aims of man, and take account of differences in real value between gratifications that are equally powerful incentives to action and have therefore equal economic measures. A study of these measures is only the starting-point of economics: but it is the starting-point. (1920, 16–17)

While Marshall did express concern about interpersonal comparisons, he felt the problem could be overcome by the judicious use of averages. He was quite willing to offer the argument that the "source of error . . . is lessened when we are able to consider the actions and the motives of large groups of people" (1920, §2, 19). This discounted the effects on *individuals,* allowing the economist to employ the tools of the utility calculus on matters of social concern. The point appears to have been to gauge *social* utility, and the example he employed concerns the relative injury from the application of a tax (18–19). But Marshall also made clear that in maintaining his indirect measure of motives, he was not implying that the actions taken were necessarily the result of deliberation or rational calculation; he noted that it is typically the case that "people do not weigh beforehand the results of every action, whether the impulses to it come from their higher nature or their lower" (§3, 20). The import of this observation was in the allowance for altruism, actions for which no "rational" deliberation seems to occur. Thus while Jevons dismissed the higher motives as incapable of incorporation into an economic calculus, Marshall held just the opposite view, insisting that it was the higher motives that justified the economic study of human behavior.

In the *Principles* Marshall cultivated, and introduced into economics, ideas which have become commonplace as analytical tools. To take an example, he extended the concepts of elasticity of demand and of supply, concepts which had been developed a half-century before by

Cournot.[52] Marshall's role lay in extending the conceptual apparatus beyond its original use; elasticity achieved with Marshall the mathematical form by which we know it today.[53] Again, the forerunner of Marshall's description of elasticity in the *Principles* was in the area of statistical theory, specifically his 1885 "On the Graphic Method of Statistics," the essay in which Keynes maintained the definition of elasticity of demand first appeared.[54] Here he displayed in a different rhetoric the derivation and use of the elasticity measure.

One of the interesting, and at the same time disappointing, aspects of the *Principles* is in Marshall's handling of utility. His positive insight on this question can be seen in note I of the mathematical appendix (1920, 838). Given a utility function, denoted by $U = f(x)$, marginal utility is then defined as the total differential, $dU = (\partial U/\partial x)dx$. What previous writers on the matter had done, especially Jevons (whom Marshall singled out for identification by name), was to identify (in equilibrium) dU/dx as the "final degree of utility." This is the change in total utility brought about by an incremental change in the holding of a good; it is the rate of change of total utility. This was an unfortunate choice of terminology, for it leads to great confusion as to just what is meant by "final degree" and how this is related to marginal valuations; Marshall himself referred to dU/dx as the *marginal degree* of utility (although even today the expression dU/dx is described as marginal utility). While Marshall added, "There is room for doubt as to which mode of expression is the more convenient: no question of principle is involved in the decision," clearly the problem is a real one. If the choice is made to employ the "final degree of utility," then total utility is merely the utility derived from any unit of the good (since no one unit can be designated as the final one from the standpoint of the consumer's calculus); total utility is then the product of the single value of marginal utility and the total number of units of the good. If the Marshallian definition of marginal utility (as dU) is instead employed, then total utility is the integral, $\int(\partial U/\partial x)dx$.[55]

The disappointing aspects of Marshall's utility theory are his choice

52. Whitaker (1987) noted that Marshall read the *Récherches* around 1868. There is some recent scholarship which has hinted at the influence on Marshall of the work of William Whewell (1794–1866), professor of moral philosophy at Cambridge from 1838 to 1855, and Master of Trinity from 1841 until his death. While Schumpeter (1954, 448n.7) dismissed Whewell's early attempts at the mathematization of economics which appeared in the *Cambridge Philosophical Transactions* (1829, 1831, 1850) as displaying no mathematical *reasoning*, there is much to suggest that Marshall was aware of Whewell's work in respect to the elasticity of supply and demand, even though he did not refer to it as a precursor of his own views. On this see D. P. O'Brien (1975) and Robert W. Dimand (1993).

53. On the elasticity of demand, see 1920, bk. III, chap. IV, §§1 and 2, 102–4; on the elasticity of supply, see bk. V, chap. XII, §1, 456–57.

54. See Keynes's list of Marshall's writings in Marshall 1925.

55. On this, see Blaug (1985, 310n.1).

of utility function and his attempt to base his subsequent analysis on a flawed and incomplete form. His demand analysis was expressed to allow the ceteris paribus assumption to apply to the *average* of the prices of all other goods, not merely each price individually (an advance over previous interpretations), and he made explicit reference to the purchasing power of money, not merely the aggregate of money balances (another plus). But his utility function was defined so as to ignore interdependencies among and between goods; in other words, he omitted from his utility theory consideration of the cross-partial derivatives.[56] The result of his stipulations was that Marshall *required* for his theoretical analysis an additively separable utility function, not different in design in general from the descriptions given by the early ethical utilitarians, but too narrowly conceived to be of use in a general theory of value. Thus was he led to the erroneous conclusion that the "marginal utility of a thing to anyone diminishes with every increase in the amount of it he already has" (1920, bk. III, chap. III, §1, 93), a statement he took as a general law.[57]

3.2 Marshall's "Tendency to Socialism"

In his 1919 *Industry and Trade* (4th ed., 1923), Marshall identified certain aspects of what we have here termed the Hobbes question. Specifically, in book III, chapter XI, he invoked the spirits of Hobbes, Locke, and the early utilitarian writers on the role of the individual in society. He noted that the principal asset to the economic development of Britain was a strong sense of individuality on the part of the citizenry:

> Each man settled his own affairs, subject to but little discipline save that of custom. And since the shackles of custom were not felt, they merely narrowed the range of action of individuality: they did not destroy it. (Marshall 1923a, bk. III, chap. XI, §2, 580)

It was this individualistic nature that indeed prevented the decay of British society into tyranny, for it fostered a mutual respect for individual rights. In Marshall's words, "He, who respects his own individuality, is unlikely to be a tyrant. . . . [R]efusing to be regimented, he is unlikely to regiment others" (1923a, 580). Most important for Marshall was the ability of the individual to be tolerant and assimilative, traits we find in Smith's compassionate man. These traits he felt were significant in the stability and growth not only of society, but of business enterprises as well. Individuality (represented by the pioneering entrepreneur) may have been the source of enterprise, but continued existence (social stability) required a willingness to cooperate in the formation of business associa-

---

56. On this point see George J. Stigler (1950).

57. A second aspect is in Marshall's characterization of the demand function as $p = f(q)$. Note that, by holding quantity to be exogenous, Marshall then does not need to specify *in advance of a theory of demand* a theory of consumer choice!

tions (promoting "orderly cooperation"). These could serve as a bulwark (in the preservation of social cohesion) against more powerful industrial combines (as invasive forces).

Finally, and in the context of the above, we shall mention some aspects of Marshall's social position with respect to property. In *Industry and Trade* he noted that the institution of private ownership served to perform "a great and necessary work" (as had the notion of individuality) (1923a, app. A, §1, 675). British society had flourished as a result of the security of such relations, and the age of private capital and individual industry combined to make Britain the dominant economic force in the world. Yet Marshall argued that social evolution had made unworkable a rigid interpretation of private ownership rights and the social relations engendered by them and to a large extent had led to inequitable distributions of the "social" product (not Marshall's term). He maintained "that social benefit would result from some softening of these rights in such ways as would promote the more equal distribution of wealth" (675). It was in respect to this reappraisal of the social effects of individual ownership rights on an "advanced" economy that he expressed his "tendency to socialism." Consider his own expression of his "conversion":

> Nearly half a century has passed since I set myself to obtain some insight into industrial problems by obtaining leave to visit one or more representative works in each chief industry. I tried to get such a knowledge of mechanical technique ... as would enable me to understand the resources and the mode of operation of all elementary plants in general use: I sought also to study the relations between technique and the conditions of employment for men and for women.
>
> ... The result was a conviction that inequalities of pay were less arbitrary than was often asserted, and were more directly under the influence of broad "natural" causes.
>
> But I believed that the causes of these causes were not wholly beyond human control; and that they might probably be so modified as to bring about a nearer approach to equality of conditions, and a better use of the products of human effort for the benefit of humanity. I developed a tendency to socialism; which was fortified later on by Mill's essays in the *Fortnightly Review* in 1879. Thus for more than a decade, I remained under the conviction that the suggestions, which are associated with the word "socialism," were the most important subject of study, if not in the world, yet at all events for me. But the writings of socialists generally repelled me, almost as much as they attracted me; because they seemed far out of touch with realities: and, partly for that reason, I decided to say little on the matter, till I had thought much longer. (1923a, vii)

As Rita McWilliams-Tullberg (1975) and Peter Groenewegen (1995) noted, Marshall's "tendency to socialism" could be seen as early as the 1870s, when he read a paper before the Cambridge Reform Club entitled "The Future of the Working Classes."[58] The expressed purpose in writing the essay was to see "whether the amelioration of the working classes has limits beyond which it cannot pass" (Marshall 1925, 102). Marshall believed that continuous strenuous labor limited the ability of the working classes to pursue intellectual interests or any endeavor leading to self-improvement—"the rougher the work of the body, the lower the condition of the mind" (107)—and that this fact was responsible for the continuing degradation of those in the working classes. As an example of a more "desirable" society, Marshall offered the picture painted by the socialists, "who attributed to every man an unlimited capacity for those self-forgetting virtues that they found in their own breasts" (but who nonetheless "recklessly suggested means which were always insufficient and not seldom pernicious" [109]). His interpretation of the Utopia, however, was markedly different from that identified with the socialist writers: while the utopians desired "a subversion of existing arrangements" (choice of occupation and wages determined through the workings of the free market), Marshall required only "that no one in it should have any occupation which tends to make him anything less than a gentleman" (109–10).

To fulfill the dream in his "fancied country," Marshall offered four proposals: wealth would be equalized (each would have a "fair share"); population would be held to a manageable level; education would be provided for all, and would be continued through the higher grades; and work hours would be shortened to allow for "intellectual and artistic enjoyment in the evening" (1925, 110).[59] These conditions would serve to promote *individual* development, and by extension the development of the *society* (making it less "coarse and unrefined" [111]). For Marshall, "material welfare, as well as spiritual, will be the lot of that country which, by public and private action, devotes its full energies to raising the standard of the culture of the people" (118).

It is also important in understanding the preceding to understand the period in which Marshall wrote his essay. The Christian Social Movement was flourishing at the time, and such prominent figures as John Ruskin (1819–1900) were pursuing a socialist economics. Marshall (according to Groenewegen 1995) was active briefly in organizing rural workers into unions and even wrote for a labor newspaper, the *Bee-Hive*,

---

58. The essay was published in *The Eagle* in 1873. We use here the reprint in *Memorials of Alfred Marshall* (Marshall 1925).

59. Marshall accepted the position of John Stuart Mill and Harriet Taylor (who was the influence behind Mill's chapter on the future of the laboring classes), that labor associations—in which workers owned the means of production and had the authority to remove management—would effectively keep capital from fleeing the country, while promoting labor (and hence societal) interests.

all the while insisting that the interests of the working classes be handled through the application of sound economic principles.

Marshall declared himself to have been a "socialist" of the John Stuart Mill variety, one who advocated socialism as a reform system and not a revolutionary doctrine; he is said to have preferred Mill's *On Liberty* to his "Chapters on Socialism." While both offer support for free enterprise and individual initiative, the former identifies clearly the limits of government interference with individual choice and action, holding collective action to be stifling of both human creativity and human freedom. In his 1907 "The Social Possibilities of Economic Chivalry," Marshall noted that if socialism were taken to be doctrine aimed at the amelioration of social ills through concerted action, he indeed had been a socialist "before I knew anything of economics" (Marshall 1907, 17). The problem with socialism arose with its extension into areas in which individual initiative and the higher qualities of human nature could better handle affairs.[60]

In a letter to Lord Reay, dated November 12, 1909,[61] Marshall defined socialism as "a movement for taking the responsibility for a man's life and work, as far as possible, off his shoulders and putting it on to the State" (Marshall 1925, 462). To the extent that there were in society, especially in British society, those "incapable of caring for themselves," he thought it prudent for Britain to copy the German plan of social insurance. However, beyond support for the indigent and the infirm, he did not favor state intervention in individual affairs; in fact, he held socialism as a movement to be "not merely a danger, but by far the greatest present danger to human well-being." He believed that socialistic programs "weaken character by limiting initiative and dulling aspiration; and that they lower character by diverting energy from creation to wirepulling" (462). Thus did Marshall, as did Mill before him, eventually abandon the formal principles of the socialist cause upon recognizing that it was a demoralizing system which crippled individual will and initiative.[62]

Withal, Marshall concluded that, while in the development of society he saw "a broader and firmer foundation for socialistic schemes than existed when Mill wrote," in fact it was the development of society along capitalistic, free-market lines which served to ameliorate social ills. Referring to *Industry and Trade,* and completing the thought expressed above,

---

60. "I submit, therefore, that if collectivism is to work even fairly well, there must be ample provision for enabling anyone who thinks his lot unduly hard to find relief in some way that has not as yet been discovered. It is true that ingenious suggestions have been made for automatically regulating the work and pay in different occupations under a collectivist *régime.* They are perhaps not likely to approve themselves to anyone who has followed closely the working of co-operative and competitive businesses" (Marshall 1907, 25).

61. Published in *Memorials of Alfred Marshall* (Marshall 1925), 461–65.

62. On this see also Groenewegen 1995, chapter 16.

we see Marshall's intellectual evolution in his expression of the economic reasoning behind the failure of socialist experiments:

> But no socialistic scheme, yet advanced, seems to make adequate provision for the maintenance of high enterprise, and individual strength of character; nor to promise a sufficiently rapid increase in the business plant and other material implements of production, to enable the real incomes of the manual labour classes to continue to increase as fast as they have done in the recent past, even if the total income of the country be shared equally by all. The average level of human nature in the western world has risen rapidly during the last fifty years. But it has seemed to me that those have made most real progress towards the distant goal of ideally perfect social organization, who have concentrated their energies on some particular difficulties in the way, and not spent strength on endeavouring to rush past them. (Marshall 1923, viii)

3.3 The Marshallian Rhetoric

While trained as a mathematician—Second Wrangler in Mathematics at St. John's, Cambridge, 1865—and so possessing the insights which this training instills, Marshall was quick to realize the limitations of the mathematical rhetoric. His writings were after all intended for the likes of businessmen and others for whom a formal analytical presentation would have been beyond comprehension.

One of Marshall's outstanding accomplishments in economics was the manner of his presentation, his rhetorical style. Indeed, Marshall had entered economics via the mathematical route, having been introduced to Mill's *Principles* during his tenure as mathematical master at Clifton, and so had read it through his mathematical prism. In a remembrance of his early career (contained in a letter published only after his death), he commented: "as I thought much more easily in mathematics at that time than in English, I tried to translate him [Mill] into mathematics before forming an opinion as to the validity of his work" (Marshall 1933, 221). For Marshall, the reasoning process took place through the filter of mathematics, with the literary presentation coming only later. The "skeleton" of the *Principles,* for instance, Marshall felt had been completed *before* the publication of Jevons's *Theory of Political Economy* in 1871, but had remained unpublished for a number of reasons, not the least of which was the need to reexpress his mathematical results into a literary and diagrammatical form. He in fact criticized Jevons's *Theory* thus: "The main value of the book, however, does not lie in its more prominent theories, but in its original treatment of a number of minor points, its suggestive remarks and careful analyses. . . . The book before us would be improved if the mathematics were omitted, but the diagrams retained"

(Marshall 1872, 131, 132). But Jevons's work proved useful, in that it allowed Marshall to restructure his argument in light of a newly available mathematical theory of utility, a tool to which he did not have access at the time of his earlier efforts. In this regard Marshall's success lay in the instrumental use of diagrammatic analysis as a means of explaining economic theory and showing the structure of his theoretical models. While today this may seem a rather pedestrian concern, it was at the time viewed as a breakthrough that introduced a degree of clarity and precision into the then-dominant classical literary explication of economic theory. As Keynes expressed it:

> Marshall's mathematical and diagrammatic exercises in Economic Theory were of such a character in their grasp, comprehensiveness and scientific accuracy and went so far beyond the 'bright ideas' of his predecessors, that we may justly claim him as the founder of modern diagrammatic economics—that elegant apparatus which generally exercises a powerful attraction on clever beginners, which all of us use as an inspirer of, and a check on, our intuitions and as a shorthand record of our results, but which generally falls into the background as we penetrate further into the recesses of the subject. (J. M. Keynes 1924, 332–33)

But Marshall's employment of the diagrammatic method was not confined to economics; it was rather a part of the technical apparatus that served him in expressing and even apprehending concepts generally. As evidence one has only to look at an example of Marshall's excursion into the theory of statistics, expressed in his 1885 "On the Graphic Method of Statistics."

Marshall clearly wrote within the utilitarian tradition, which at the time dominated British political economy. Nonetheless, his particular form of Utilitarianism was not of the same form as that of Bentham, the Mills, or even Jevons. On the contrary, while man may be seen as tied to his moral and ethical milieu, Marshall's Utilitarianism was not predicated on any ethical base or for that matter on any definable criterion whatever. John Maynard Keynes characterized Marshall's position as anethical, that is, as not deviating from the ideas and ideals of classical Utilitarianism, while at the same time showing a great degree of agnosticism in regard to the study of the motivation behind the hedonic calculus. "The solution of economic problems was for Marshall, not an application of the hedonistic calculus, but a prior condition of the exercise of man's higher faculties, irrespective, almost, of what we mean by 'higher' " (J. M. Keynes 1924, 319). John K. Whitaker (1977) held that a minor source of Marshall's ethical views may have been a combination of the philosophies of the German and English Historical Schools, the individualist Herbert Spencer, and the communitarian T. H. Green. From the Historical philosophers and economists, he appropriated a scheme for the classification of motives;

from Spencer he gained an appreciation for the doctrine of social evolution; and from Green he gained an insight into Philosophic Idealism. Most important was the influence of Henry Sidgwick, from whom Marshall gained an appreciation of Utilitarianism.

That Marshall published so little in the way of formal theoretical economic analysis is perhaps due to his insistence on having worked out completely the consequences of a proposal, and carefully investigating the nuances associated with any proposition. His *Principles* of 1890 and *Money, Credit and Commerce* of 1923 appeared decades after their original insights had been disseminated throughout the economic community in other venues. But by that time the innovativeness behind the presentations had dissolved into a routine survey of things past and accepted as dogma. Keynes put it well: "Inevitably when the books themselves appeared, they lacked the novelty and path-breaking powers which would have been acclaimed in them a generation earlier, and those economists all over the world who know Marshall only by his published work may find it difficult to understand the extraordinary position claimed for him by his English contemporaries and successors" (1924, 327). Schumpeter, however, thought a delay brought about by the desire to produce as thoroughgoing and complete a treatise as possible was a credit to Marshall and was clearly the mark of a patient and careful mind. This attitude he likened to Smith:

> both the *Wealth* and the *Principles* are what they are, partly at least, because they are the result of the work of decades and fully matured, the products of minds that took infinite care, were patient of labor, and indifferent to the lapse of years. This is all the more remarkable because both Smith and Marshall were extremely anxious to preach their wisdom and to influence political practice—yet neither of them allowed himself to be hurried into print before his manuscripts were as perfect as he felt able to make them. (Schumpeter 1954, 835)

Thus in the end we are presented with two opposed views on the status of perhaps the single most important work of English political economy—Keynes's claim to its being, after all is said, a book too long in the making and too sparing of novelty, and Schumpeter's response that it was well worth the wait.[63]

3.4 *An Appraisal*

Marshall was undoubtedly the most influential economist of the late nineteenth and early twentieth centuries. Even today he is considered as having been among the greatest economists who ever lived.

---

63. In response to Keynes's conjecture, Schumpeter opined, "The position of the *Principles* would, in this respect [of a claim to priority], be no different if it had appeared in 1880" (1954, 835n.9).

Be that as it may, it is difficult to appraise Marshall's contributions to economics, for much of what he wrote has been accepted as conventional wisdom. Throughout his writings, and especially in the *Principles,* we see the explicit use of the static model, but always in the background is the dynamic general equilibrium form. In his relegation of mathematics to notes in appendixes, Marshall offered the reader clarity of exposition and at the same time an appreciation of the rigor and robustness of his analysis. Marshall, as Edgeworth phrased it, "renders to the queen of the sciences the things which belong to her province, and to the spiritual side of our nature things which transcend man's power of calculation" (Edgeworth 1890a, 364). More importantly, in his use of the biological analogy Marshall began to shift economics away from the stultifying influence of the physical sciences toward a more evolutionary-developmental approach. As we have seen, this was of greater importance than could have been known at the time.

In his obituary article on Marshall, J. M. Keynes identified what he considered to have been the original elements in Marshall's economics. In the realm of monetary theory, the seven original contributions included: (1) the incorporation of the quantity theory of money into the general theory of value; (2) the distinction between real and nominal rates of interest; (3) the effect on prices of an increase in the money supply; (4) the theory of purchasing power parity; (5) the "chain method" for computing index numbers; (6) a proposal for use of a paper currency based on a gold–silver standard (what Keynes called symmetallism); and (7) a proposal for the publication of a standard table of purchasing power to facilitate business contracting (J. M. Keynes 1924, 337–41).

In terms of the *Principles,* Keynes related seven more contributions: (1) clarifying the role of the theory of demand and cost of production into a general theory of value;[64] (2) the application of the concept of general equilibrium in value theory; (3) the introduction of the time element into economic analysis; (4) the introduction of consumer's surplus; (5) the analysis of monopoly and increasing returns, with an extension to the cases of external and internal economies; (6) the use of the term *elasticity;* and (7) the explicit acknowledgment of the historical background of economics and its significance for contemporary work (1924, 349–54).

Keynes, of course, was kind to his teacher and mentor. Schumpeter, however, held no such loyalties. While admitting that Marshall "pointed beyond himself," he nonetheless took him to task for failing to make original contributions to economics and instead suggested he merely synthesized the work of others:

According to what I believe to be the ordinary standards of scientific historiography, such merit as there was in the rediscovery of the

---

64. Of this Keynes commented, "After Marshall's analysis there was nothing more to be said" (1924, 350).

marginal utility principle is Jevons'; the system of general equilibrium (including the theory of barter) is Walras'; the principle of
substitution and the marginal productivity theory are Thünen's; the
demand and supply curves and the static theory of monopoly are
Cournot's (as is the concept, though not the word, price elasticity);
the consumers' rent is Dupuit's; the 'diagrammatic method' of presentation is also Dupuit's or else Jenkin's. If this had been always
clearly understood, there would be no more to be said. But it has
not been generally understood—perhaps it is not even understood
now by *all* economists—with the result that the reputation of others
has suffered and that there exists, in many minds, a picture of the
scientific situation of that time that it is the duty of the historian to
correct. (Schumpeter 1954, 838–39; emphasis in original)

Yet despite Schumpeter's protestations, the achievements of Marshall, even if relegated to the mere creation of a new economic edifice based
on the synthesis of the methods, concepts, and approaches of others, can
not be minimized. Even if his contributions were limited to placing the
received theory of his time in a new guise, he nonetheless succeeded in
revolutionizing the approach to economics for half a century.

4 Edgeworth and the Development of "Psychical Economics"

4.1 The Basis of Edgeworth's Thought

A friend of both Jevons and Marshall, Francis Ysidro Edgeworth (1845–
1926)[65] continued in the "scientific" utilitarian tradition, but followed a

---

65. Edgeworth was born Ysidro Francis Edgeworth in Edgeworthstown, County
Longford, Ireland, into a family which traced its roots to the time of Henry VIII. (The
novelist Maria Edgeworth, who had been an acquaintance of Ricardo, among others, was
Francis's aunt.) Educated at Trinity College, Dublin, in the classics, he later went to
Magdalen College, Oxford, and finally to Balliol College, taking a First in *Literis Hu-
manioribus;* he was not, however, granted his degree for another four years. His early career
was spent in the law (in his early writings he is cited merely as Barrister-at-Law). Despite
having been called to the Bar in 1877, he never actually practiced.

After having served in various capacities—including a lectureship in logic and metaphysics at a private London school—he eventually accepted a lectureship in logic at King's
College, London, and later (1890) became Tooke Professor in Political Economy. In 1891,
he became Drummond Professor at Oxford (All Souls College), retiring in 1922.

In 1891, Edgeworth became editor of the newly founded *Economic Journal,* a position
he held until his death. (For a time he held the post of editor alone, then later shared joint
editorship with J. M. Keynes.) This is generally regarded as one of his most significant
contributions to the field of economics. From 1912 to 1914 he served as president of the
Royal Statistical Society. Biographical information on Edgeworth is from the article in the
Dictionary of National Biography, written by J. M. Keynes, and from Stephen M. Stigler
(1978) and Peter Newman (1987).

somewhat different approach. Trained in the law and the classics, and apparently self-taught in mathematics, he sought to promote an economics grounded on a "mathematical ethics." In so doing, he took the program of Jevons to a new and more rigorous level. With Edgeworth, it became possible to think of utilitarian concerns as ethical problems restated in the rhetoric of mathematical statistics, a rhetoric not distinguishable from that employed in the physical sciences.

In 1877 Edgeworth published his first book, *New and Old Methods of Ethics,* a largely forgotten work in the utilitarian tradition. Consistent with Jevons's program, Edgeworth concentrated on the hedonic side of ethics while considering the ramifications of the use of the utility calculus. In this respect, he relied, as did Jevons, on the work of Fechner. Edgeworth took pleasure to be fundamental, and defined it as a "cause of action." In Jevonsian fashion, he justified the employment of the principles of Fechnerian psychophysics, with its emphasis on the promotion of maximum net pleasure, to the realm of utilitarian ethics. The correspondence is easily made: "the intensity of sensations is deducible from the intensity of stimulus, according to the Fechnerian law; and in so far as the Fechnerian or a similar law . . . is applicable to pleasures, the conditions favourable to the production of the greatest quality of pleasure from a given stimulus may be deduced" (Edgeworth 1877, 19). Pleasure is simply one form of sensation, the measurement of which can be accomplished through a proven experimental design.

In all, the thesis of this early work we see repeated throughout Edgeworth's writings: while utility could indeed be expressed in a mathematical formalism, this did not imply that precise numerical measurements could be obtained. As we shall see below, Edgeworth did not need to rely on numerical measures as the basis for his quantitative Utilitarianism; he consistently maintained that only a quantitative *relationship* was necessary in studies of ethics and the moral sciences. It was enough to identify a mathematical relationship, without confounding matters through resort to numerical comparisons.

Before reviewing his approach to Utilitarianism, it may serve to set the stage by briefly discussing Edgeworth's contributions to the fields of mathematical statistics and probability.[66] Among his achievements in these fields was an interpretation of probability defined with respect to a logic of partial or incomplete belief, in opposition to the then-dominant materialistic frequency interpretation identified with his contemporary, the logician John Venn (to whom we nodded earlier in the discussion of Marshall). While being in substantial agreement with Venn

---

66. From 1883 until his death in 1926, Edgeworth published nearly 100 articles in probability and statistical theory and their applications (counting as separate those multipart contributions for which he was and is famous, and including reviews of statistical works).

as to the foundation of a theory of probability—Edgeworth accepted that the basis of a probability calculus was statistical uniformity—he nonetheless disputed the point made by Venn that belief was necessarily of the same form as chance (Edgeworth 1884, 223–24).[67] Edgeworth demanded that probability be defined subjectively, viewing it as an epistemic concern and not an ontologic one.[68] He further noted, taking a suggestion from Jevons, that there is no "particular difficulty in extending the statistical method to unnumerical quantities . . ." (228). In the case of "complicated beliefs," we may be able to discern "important quantitative, although not numerical, estimates" of our degree of belief in any proposition (225). This theory of Edgeworth's foreshadowed later attempts by, among others, Emile Borel, Frank P. Ramsey, and Leonard J. Savage, to develop what has become known as a personalistic theory of probability.[69]

But for all his abilities, Edgeworth's contributions to probability and statistics lay for many years forgotten, eclipsed by the work of Karl Pearson, among others. Perhaps the reason for his lack of influence in these areas is that, despite his lifelong interest and the totality of his writings in the field, his presentations were often written in a very difficult prose, including not infrequent use of literary allusions. He also had a penchant for inventing terms, mostly ignored and even misunderstood by others. In addition, his presentations were often accompanied by mathematics and notations not accessible to many writing in what was regarded as the mainstream of the discipline. As Arthur Bowley, considered to be Edgeworth's only disciple, commented in a slim volume dedicated to Edgeworth's thought in this area (published in 1928), Edgeworth wrote from the standpoint of a philosopher at a time when others who regarded themselves as statisticians took a much more pragmatic tack. He continued in his investigations apparently indifferent to the fact of his standing outside the mainstream.[70]

---

67. Predominantly Bayesian in his outlook, Edgeworth advanced what he termed the "inverse method" as his primary approach to statistical analysis. This method involved the use of a nonuniform a priori distribution that would generate an a posteriori value, a procedure most useful in the case of small sample size. But even this method assumed that there was some knowledge on the part of the individual as to the form of the distribution; for the most part Edgeworth believed that fundamental ignorance would prevent the individual from having any information at all on the form of the prior distribution. This led him to look at substitutes, such as the trend.

While his economic writings were published in three volumes in 1925, Edgeworth's statistical writings have only recently been collected. See Edgeworth (1994 and 1996).

68. "There is only one class of practical problems to which the subjective view is exclusively applicable; those actions which cannot be regarded as forming part of a 'series' in Mr. Venn's sense . . ." (Edgeworth 1884, 224).

69. Neither Ramsey nor Savage acknowledged Edgeworth as a precursor.

70. On Edgeworth's abilities in these areas, see Stephen Stigler (1986). See also the Introductory essay by McCann in Edgeworth (1996).

Edgeworthian Utilitarianism: 4.2
Hedonics and Mathematical Psychics

Regarding the study of economics proper, while Edgeworth was responsible for some novel developments, he has nonetheless remained in the
shadow of Marshall and Jevons. Marshall's theoretical framework—more
of a metaphorical presentation of the subject along biological lines—
allowed better understanding and a more intuitive grasp of the arcana
involved than did the highly systematic, abstract and symbolic treatment
of Edgeworth. By contrast, Jevons's mathematical formalism, and his use
of the calculus to identify the conditions for utility comparisons, foreshadowed Edgeworth's excursions into these same areas. Yet despite the lack of
a core following, it is the contributions of Edgeworth in the formalistic
reinterpretation of the theory of utility that have survived and flourished,
albeit in a highly modified fashion, to the present day.

For Edgeworth, "hedonics" was the broad category of which economics, or political economy, was a mere "arbitrarily selected fragment":
political economy he held to be nothing more or less than "an ill-defined
tract of speculation irregularly grouped about a central spot, the theory
of exchange, which is distinguished from the general phenomena of human life by the same attribute as the statistically measured belief, namely
a certain quasi-mathematical precision" (1884, 225–26). On the other
hand, hedonics, as a general field of inquiry, he felt was amenable to strict
analytical presentation, as the terms employed could be rigorously defined and the techniques of mathematical analysis could be easily applied.

In an 1879 article for the British journal *Mind*, entitled "The
Hedonical Calculus," Edgeworth presented his definitions for the constituent parts of a utilitarian theory. His characterization of the utilitarian
axiom, "greatest possible happiness," for example, derived directly from
the principal notion of "pleasure" from *New and Old Methods of Ethics:*

> *Pleasure* is used for "preferable feeling" in general (in deference to
> high authority, though the general term does not appear to call up
> with equal facility all the particulars which are meant to be included
> under it, but rather the grosser feelings than for instance the "joy
> and felicity" of devotion). The term includes absence of pain. *Great-
> est possible happiness* is the greatest possible integral of the differ-
> ential "Number of enjoyers X duration of enjoyment X degree
> thereof." (Edgeworth 1879, 394; emphasis in original)

With his statement of the characteristics of "pleasure," Edgeworth
established the primitive concept needed for an axiomatization of utilitarian economics. He then identified a single fundamental axiom and six
subsidiary postulates. The primary axiom reads: "Pleasure is measurable,
and all pleasures are commensurable; so much of one sort of pleasure felt

by one sentient being equateable to so much of other sorts of pleasure felt by other sentients" (1879, 396). The postulates concerning pleasure are:

(1) While pleasure is a "good" (as opposed to a "bad," not a commodity), nonetheless it shows decreasing returns: "The rate of increase of pleasure decreases as its means increase." Further, "the second differential of pleasure with regard to means is continually negative." (But this is not to imply "that the first differential is continually positive" [1879, 397].)

(2) Pain or fatigue is an increasing function of work done ("the rate of increase of fatigue increases as the work done increases" [399]).

(3) There is in human beings an "evolutionary" basis for the theory expounded. In terms of qualitative improvement, the "capacity for pleasure and capacity for work generally speaking go together" (400). This also in turn becomes something of a social Darwinian criterion, since as Edgeworth noted, "In the general advance the most advanced should advance most."

(4) The Malthusian postulate: "as population increases, means . . . increase at a decreasing rate" (400).

(5) The "evolution" postulate: "to substitute in one generation for any number of parents an equal number each superior in capacity (evolution) is beneficial for the next generation" (401).

(6) A corollary to postulate (5): "To substitute in one generation for any number of parents an equal number each superior in capacity (evolution) is beneficial for all time" (402).

Having stated the axioms of Utilitarianism, Edgeworth succeeded in creating the necessary framework of his analysis. But "The Hedonical Calculus" and *New and Old Methods of Ethics* were but prelude to the great work to come. His expressed purpose for the 1881 *Mathematical Psychics: An Essay on the Application of Mathematics to the Moral Sciences,* the work for which he is best known in economic circles, was to extend his preliminary work and to propose a "calculus of *Feeling,* of Pleasure and Pain" (1881, 1).[71] Jevons, in reviewing it for *Mind,* considered the book "a very remarkable one," which, although "one of the most difficult to read which we ever came across," nonetheless would eventually "be recognised in the future as containing new and most important suggestions" (Jevons 1881b, 581). Marshall declared, "This book shows clear signs of genius, and is a promise of great things to come" (Marshall 1881, 457).[72]

---

71. Much of this essay by Edgeworth reprints his earlier statement of utilitarian principle, "The Hedonical Calculus."

72. But Marshall offered that the work may have been better received, and more understandable, had Edgeworth "kept his work by him a little longer till he had worked it out more fully, and obtained that simplicity which comes only through long labour" (Mar-

In establishing his version of a formal utilitarian calculus, Edgeworth took the position that the mathematical method was ideally suited to a discipline such as economics. His reasoning did not rely on the fact that economic data are numerical, for he held the method to be applicable throughout the social sciences. The important point is the employment of the appropriate *method* alone, mathematics:

> The science of quantity is not alien to the study of man, it will be generally admitted, in so far as actions and effective desires can be *numerically* measured by way of statistics—that is, very far, as Professor Jevons anticipates. But in so far as our *data* may consist of estimates other than *numerical,* observations that some conditions are accompanied with *greater* or *less* pleasure than others, it is necessary to realise that mathematical reasoning is not, as commonly supposed, limited to subjects where numerical data are attainable. Where there are data which, though not *numerical* are *quantitative*—for example, that a quantity is *greater* or *less* than another, *increases* or *decreases,* is *positive* or *negative,* a *maximum* or *minimum,* there mathematical reasoning is possible and may be indispensable. (Edgeworth 1881, 2; emphasis in original)

To be a quantitative discipline, it is enough that the data generated can be related by way of an order. He thus reiterated his position in *New and Old Methods of Ethics,* that so long as it can be shown that certain relationships—transitivity, irreflexivity, and so on—hold, mathematical *reasoning* can be applied to aid in the solution of problems, even if *numerical valuation* is not possible.[73]

It is the *reasoning* of mathematics, rather than the employment of mathematical symbols, that is important. The mathematical reasoning served in other disciplines to remove the obstacles in the way of attaining "truth"—structures hidden when alternative methods of rhetoric were exercised.[74] "Common sense" and the rhetoric it requires may provide equally valid conclusions; but common sense may also, because of the lack of a disciplined rhetorical structure, lead us astray in our quest for

---

shall 1881, 457). Interestingly enough, Edgeworth reviewed the first edition of Marshall's *Principles* twice, a technical review for *Nature,* and a more "general" review for the literature section of *The Academy.* He also reviewed subsequent editions of the work, notably in the *Economic Journal.*

73. Edgeworth considered Cournot to have been particularly well-informed with respect to this type of reasoning (Edgeworth 1881, 2 n.2).

74. Consider this from Edgeworth's 1889 address, reprinted in *Nature:* "But, indeed, even the limited degree of arithmetical precision which is proper to statistical generalizations need not be claimed by our mathematical method rightly understood. It is concerned with quantity, indeed, but not necessarily with number. It is not so much a political arithmetic as a sort of economical algebra, in which the problem is not to find x and y in terms of given quantities, but rather to discover loose quantitative relations of the form: x is greater or less than y, and increases or decreases with the increase of z" (Edgeworth 1889c, 497).

valid deducible conclusions. The method of mathematics prevents this from occurring, as it forces rigor and discipline on our otherwise capricious thought.

> He that will not verify his conclusions as far as possible by mathematics, as it were bringing the ingots of common sense to be assayed and coined at the mint of the sovereign science, will hardly realize the full value of what he holds, will want a measure of what it will be worth in however slightly altered circumstances, a means of conveying and making it current. (1881, 3)

As an illustration of the use of the mathematical method, take the problem of exchange. With a multitude of agents interacting in the making of contracts to buy and sell,

> it is possible to imagine a mechanism of many parts where the law of motion, which particular part moves off with which, is not precisely given—with symbols, arbitrary functions, representing not merely *not numerical knowledge* but *ignorance*—where, though the mode of motion towards equilibrium is indeterminate, the position of equilibrium is mathematically determined. (1881, 4; emphasis in original)

Significant for the development of Utilitarianism, Edgeworth viewed the measurement of pleasure and pain as especially amenable to mathematical treatment. The fact that these magnitudes are of a generally quantitative nature means that individual utility calculations can be made, as the "values" allow the application of mathematical reasoning. The basic problems of economics (and social sciences in general) are *maximum* problems (1881, 6). Optimization procedures need not give numerical solutions, and as applied in economics to the question of utility it is indeed unnecessary that they do; all we need is to demonstrate a *relationship*. The social sciences Edgeworth held to be similar to the calculus of variations—both move from reliance on "loose quantitative relations" to the determination of a maximum. The basic principle of Utilitarianism, for example, is the maximization of pleasure and the minimization of pain, or, in the more refined variants, the maximization of net pleasure, that is, utility:

> Economics investigates the arrangements between agents each tending to his own *maximum* utility; and Politics and (Utilitarian) Ethics investigate arrangements which conduce to the *maximum* sum total of utility. (1881, 6; emphasis in original)

While in his "Hedonical Calculus" Edgeworth identified his method, in *Mathematical Psychics* he took the problem a step beyond Jevons and Marshall to demonstrate the possibility of calculation of *social* utility. To perform such a calculation, one must first account for *interpersonal* differences, "if there is to be any systematic morality at all." *Individual* actions have *social* consequences, and these consequences must be accounted for in order to gauge the full "cost" of an increase in personal utility. "You cannot spend sixpence utilitarianly, without having considered whether your action tends to increase the comfort of a limited number, or numbers with limited comfort; without having compared such alternative utilities" (1881, 6–7).

To provide a basis for interpersonal comparisons, Edgeworth had to extend the dimensionality suggested by Jevons. Whereas Jevons held that "feelings" had two principal dimensions, duration (time) and intensity, Edgeworth added the third dimension of number, the units of each dimension being "the just perceivable increment" (1881, 6). "Intensity" refers to a subjective "feeling," or an apprehension of "atoms of pleasure"; "time"—"an affair of clockwork"—refers to Jevons's dimension of duration, suggesting that all satisfaction is temporally related; "number" Edgeworth defines merely as "an affair of the census" (7). Of the three, it is *intensity* that suggests a problem. With intensity "we leave the safe ground of the objective, equating to unity each *minimum sensibile*."

> *Atoms of pleasure* are not easy to distinguish and discern; more continuous than sand, more discrete than liquid; as it were nuclei of the just-perceivable, embedded in circumambient semi-consciousness. (1881, 7; emphasis in original)

Edgeworth then expressed a "solution" in terms of order:

> We cannot *count* the golden sands of life; we cannot *number* the "innumerable smile" of seas of love; but we seem to be capable of observing that there is here a *greater*, there a *less*, multitude of pleasure-units, mass of happiness, and that is enough. (1881, 7; emphasis in original)

Guided by this characterization of the foundation of social science, especially of the fundamentals of a Benthamite Utilitarianism, and postulating the basic mathematical conditions of transitivity and order, we can then speak of a mathematical theory of utility. But Edgeworth went further. Taking cues from the psychological theories of Fechner (as he had in his early work), Edgeworth incorporated into his hedonics principles developed in the mathematical theory of energy. Declaring that "every psychical phenomenon is the concomitant, and in some sense the other side of a physical phenomenon," he maintained that indeed "Pleasure is the concomitant of Energy" (1881, 7). To explain and understand Edgeworth fully in this regard, it is necessary to quote *in extenso*:

> Now this accumulation (or time-integral) of energy which thus becomes the principal object of the physical investigation is analogous to that accumulation of pleasure which is constituted by bringing together in prospect the pleasure existing at each instant of time, the

end of rational action, whether self-interested or benevolent. The central conception of Dynamics and (in virtue of the pervading analogies it may be said) in general of Mathematical Physics is *other-sidedly identical* with the central conception of Ethics; and a solution practical and philosophical, although not numerical and precise, as it exists for the problem of the interaction of bodies, so is possible for the problem of the interaction of souls.

This general solution, it may be thought, at most is applicable to the utilitarian problem of which the object is the greatest possible sum total of universal happiness. But it deserves consideration that an object of Economics also, the arrangement to which contracting agents actuated only by self-interest tend is capable of being regarded upon the psychophysical hypothesis here entertained as the realisation of the maximum sum-total of happiness, the *relative maximum,* or that which is *consistent with certain conditions.* There is dimly discerned the Divine idea of a power tending to the greatest possible quantity of happiness *under conditions;* whether the condition of that perfect disintegration and unsympathetic isolation abstractedly assumed in Economics, or those intermediate conditions of what Herbert Spencer might term integration on to that perfected utilitarian sympathy in which the pleasures of another are accounted equal with one's own. There are diversities of conditions, but one maximum-principle; many stages of evolution, but "one increasing purpose." (1881, 9–10; emphasis in original)

With the fundamentals stated, Edgeworth then proceeded to divide the subject matter of Utilitarianism into two groups. The first, the Economical Calculus, deals with "maximum individual utility," while the second, Utilitarian Ethics, deals with the system in which the whole tends to an equilibrium, characterized by "maximum universal utility" (1881, 13). To the first, the Economical Calculus, Edgeworth began with the postulate that actions are dictated by self-interest—his "first principle of Economics" (14). With this first principle, one can proceed with the mathematical statement of the basic principles of a theory of value. The fundamental building block of this science is the contract, essentially an agreement stipulating the distribution of goods and services, and the amount of sacrifice to be undertaken by each party (15). Employing the contract as the centerpiece of the Economical Calculus, Edgeworth presented what has since come to be known as the contract curve, or Edgeworth diagram,[75] a tool for demonstrating his theory of Utilitarianism.

---

75. The familiar "Edgeworth Box" diagram, while suggested in *Mathematical Psychics,* was actually first drawn in its present form by Pareto. Edgeworth's own diagrammatic exposition, which preceded Pareto's reinvention, appeared in *Mathematical Psychics,* but was recast in refined form in his 1889 Opening Address to Section F of the British Association, published in *Nature.* Here he employed the two-axis quadrant, not the four-axis "box," to analyze simple exchange, variations in supply, gains of trade, equilibrium,

The structure of the contract curve as Edgeworth envisioned it is actually quite simple. Consider the situation of bilateral exchange, within an economy consisting of two individuals and two goods for trade (but otherwise no production). (See fig. 1.) From the locus of points representing combinations of these two goods, each allowing the individual equal utility, we can construct indifference curves (or surfaces, when considering greater dimensions). Now consider the graph space. Let the vertical axis represent the amount of the first good (good I) offered by person A, in exchange for the good (good II) held by person B, and let the horizontal axis represent the amount of the good offered by person B for that held by person A. From this specification, we have two sets of indifference curves, each convex to its respective axis. The points of tangency comprise the contract curve: neither party can improve his position without harming the other, and should the initial allocation be off the contract curve, at least one party can gain by recontracting and moving to an allocation on the curve.

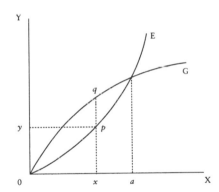

FIGURE 1. Edgeworth's Box
     Diagram

Extending his system to the whole of society, Edgeworth presented (as listed above) his six postulates concerning pleasure, predicated on a contractual Utilitarianism and expressed in a mathematical rhetoric. In addition to his contributions in the Economical Calculus, Edgeworth generalized the utility function that had been formalized mathematically by Jevons so as to make it more intuitively apparent. Jevons had been content with an additive utility function, accompanied by stipulations of diminishing marginal utility and negatively sloped (convex to the origin) indifference curves. While pedagogically elegant, the analysis of choice which was ostensibly the purpose of this device was correspondingly restricted (it excluded such things as complementary goods) by the selection of a

complex exchange, commercial competition, industrial competition, theories of business profits, and the determinateness of equilibrium. Vincent Tarascio (1972, 1980), in noting the genealogy of the diagram, suggested it be called the Jevons-Edgeworth-Fisher-Pareto-Bowley-Lerner diagram, but inexplicably preferred the designation Pareto Box.

specific function. By generalizing to a functional notation and so not being wedded to any single empirical form, Edgeworth no longer needed to stipulate ad hoc any restrictions on the form of the function; the utility function could take on any form and so generate indifference curves of any shape whatever. This allowed, as was discovered only much later, for utility theory to develop and attain its current dominant status within price (microeconomic) theory. However, despite the elegance of the discovery and the fecundity of such a revolutionary advance in theory, Edgeworth could not escape the restrictions placed on utility theory by his predecessors, so powerful was the force of their rhetoric. He continued to adhere to the restrictions of diminishing marginal utility and convex indifference surfaces as a matter of course, despite the fact that he need not have been so confined.[76]

Having dispensed with the technical details of the Economical Calculus, Edgeworth turned next to the Utilitarian Calculus, revisiting the problem of the determination of the "greatest possible happiness" and in so doing revisiting his Fechnerian roots. Pleasure he defined (yet again) as

> "preferable feeling" in general (in deference to high authority, though the general term does not appear to call up with equal facility all the particulars which are meant to be included under it, but rather the grosser feelings than for instance the "joy and felicity" of devotion). The term includes absence of pain. (1881, 44)

Under such a definition of pleasure, the "greatest possible happiness" is then derived as $\int\int\int dp\ dn\ dt$, where dp "corresponds to a just perceivable increment of pleasure," dn to "a sentient individual," and dt to "an instant of time" (1881, 44n.2). Having identified mathematically the form of *individual* utility, he then allowed for *interpersonal comparisons* of utility:

> An individual has greater *capacity for happiness* than another, when for the same amount whatsoever of means he obtains a greater amount of pleasure, *and also* for the same increment (to the same amount) whatsoever of means a greater increment of pleasure. (1881, 44; emphasis in original)

While Edgeworth was quick to realize the problems associated with such comparisons, he just as readily dismissed them, noting that "if one individual has the advantages in respect of most and the greatest pleasures, he may be treated as having more capacity for pleasure in general" (1881, 45). In effect, he was willing to argue that some people are inherently better than others, a condition expressed as the third postulate of

---

76. G. J. Stigler (1950, 322–23) stressed this point at length.

his "Hedonical Calculus." Thus did Edgeworth come to state his utilitarian axiom:

> Pleasure is measurable, and all pleasures are commensurable; so
> much of one sort of pleasure felt by one sentient being equateable to
> so much of other sorts of pleasure felt by other sentients. (1881, 46)

Edgeworth had then come full circle. Beginning with individual
utility rankings, he readily moved to interpersonal rankings, and even to
social rankings not necessarily grounded on democratic ideals. He professed acceptance of the position of Alexander Bain, in showing "how
one may correct one's estimate of one's own pleasures upon much the
same principle as the observations made with one's senses; how one may
correctly estimate the pleasures of others upon the principle 'Accept identical objective marks as showing identical subjective states,' notwithstanding personal differences, as of activity or demonstrativeness" (1881,
46).[77] He was, in other words, willing to accept that the utilitarian calculus made it possible to move from the subjectivist realm of Bentham et al.
to an objective characterization of social utility. Bain's "moral arithmetic" and Fechner's "moral differential calculus" could then be combined
to create a viable, *objective* utilitarian calculus.

In 1887 Edgeworth published *Metretike, or the Method of Measuring Probability and Utility*, a work devoted to the determination of a
technique for the simultaneous (abstract) measurement of utility and
probability. Edgeworth began by noting the similarities between probability and Utilitarianism, and the way in which probability concepts can be
utilized by economists and other social scientists. As physical scientists
often appeal to the mean of observations as representing a more accurate
point-value, social scientists often revert to the use of means of the testi-
mony of competent experts in ascertaining the "correct" interpretation of
events, or otherwise employ the concept in gauging an Ideal. In addition,
social scientists employ the categories of time, intensity (of enjoyment),
and multitude as hedonic dimensions, comparable to physical dimensions, to which mean calculations can be applied in order to determine an
expression of pleasure-value.

But for all his preparation, Edgeworth was never able to complete his
task of the simultaneous measurement of probability and utility; in fact,
the program was not actually achieved until the work of Ramsey in the late
1920s and Savage in the 1950s, although the idea of a simultaneous *axiomatization* had been suggested by John von Neumann and Oskar
Morgenstern in their 1944 *Theory of Games and Economic Behavior*.[78]

---

77. Cf. the basis for the "rational expectations" revolution initiated in 1961 by John
Muth.

78. One should not forget the earlier effort by Emile Borel in 1924, a work which
Savage had not acknowledged until the second edition (1972) of his book.

4.3 Edgeworth's Rhetoric

Finally, some mention must be made of Edgeworth's connection to the ethical brand of Utilitarianism of the Philosophic Radicals. Edgeworth held that the utilitarian philosophy of, among others, Bentham and John Stuart Mill could have been improved upon, and indeed strengthened with respect to its conclusions, had it been expressed in mathematical rhetoric (with or without recourse to the physics analog) and not through literary and legal analogies. For instance, he stated (in sympathy with Jevons) that Bentham's catchphrase, "the greatest good of the greatest number," was essentially vacuous, since the terms and concepts had not been rigorously defined. (Of course, this begs the question whether Edgeworth actually understood Bentham's meaning. Edgeworth sensed the meaning as concerning the maximum of total happiness, which may be detrimental when a few hold a greater portion of the total than others. See especially Edgeworth 1881, 117–18.)

Edgeworth's contributions to economics were somewhat overshadowed by his commitment to an abstract and mathematical method, which he also applied to the study of probability and statistics. This method, more than his theoretical advancements, is what separated him from others of his generation, in both economics and statistics. In fact, the bulk of his efforts was devoted to the elaboration and practical application of this abstract method, instead of to the development of any theoretical disciplinary school. It was his commitment to the method that served to give a permanence and importance to his accomplishments.

In regard to his theory of probability, Edgeworth could easily make the connection to utility by considering that both utility and probability dealt with variables that were inherently non-(numerically) measurable. The expression of utility as a quantity then involved epistemic considerations. As Edgeworth remarked, "in the absence of definite calculations of utility, it may be found necessary often to fall back upon those analogies confirmed by general experience which constitute intellectual probability" (Edgeworth 1884, 233–34), where "intellectual probability" is comprised of "a more diffused sort of matter" than material probability (230); it may even be a form of intuition. Edgeworth viewed this as being part and parcel of Jevonsian Utilitarianism, whereby it is considered " 'fair' to treat as equals those between whom no material difference is discerned" (234).

5 Jevons's Legacy and Wicksteed

In discussing Jevons, we noted the very technical nature of his contributions to economics. His choice of presentation indeed limited the extent to which his ideas could gain an audience; his 1862 paper, as we have mentioned, gathered no response at its initial reading. Thus, to gain an audience, Jevons required a popularizer. No small part of Jevons's reputation is built on the foundations constructed by his disciple and "interpreter," a former Unitarian minister, Philip Henry Wicksteed (1844–1927).[79]

In about 1882 Wicksteed became perhaps forever saddled with the title of "Jevons's only disciple." Schumpeter (1954, 832) went so far as to characterize him as being "the only Jevonian theorist of note," correcting and supplementing Jevons's economic analytics with reference to the advances of the Austrians. Despite these intellectual relations, his first appreciation of economics came after reading Henry George's 1879 *Progress and Poverty,* a tract which proposed reasons for economic downturns and the irremediability of income inequality, and which promoted, among other things, such policies as land reform (including nationalization) and the Single Tax. He was also active in other more socialist-oriented economics circles—he was a close friend of the playwright George Bernard Shaw, Graham Wallas (of "The Great Society" fame), and other Fabian socialists. Yet, notwithstanding his connections in these circles, Wicksteed remained more of an observer than an activist.

In 1884 Wicksteed published a critique of the first volume of Marx's *Capital* in *To-day,* a journal devoted to writings on the topic of socialism. In this venue, he actually launched an attack on the foundations of Marx's theories. He put to his readers two important questions, both central to Marx's theoretical foundation: (1) *Is there any validity to the concept of the "labor theory of value"?* (that is, does the time-element of labor determine the exchange-value of goods?) and (2) *What is the value of the labor force?* To the first question, Wicksteed attacked Marx's arbitrarily stipulated view that only "socially useful" objects can be appraised when determining labor-time. This artificial, and not particularly useful, concept unnecessarily complicated matters. Wicksteed proposed the concept of "abstract utility" to replace Marx's "abstract labor" as the appropriate measure of the value of commodities, produced and not. Through Wicksteed's interpretation, one could transform Marx after a fashion into a utilitarian. In response to the second question, Wicksteed criticized Marx's notion of profit as being determined solely by surplus labor, a fundamental criterion in Marx's system.

---

79. Wicksteed was the son of a Unitarian minister. Having studied at University College, London, where he took an M.A. (with Gold Medal) in classics (1867), he afterward followed in his father's footsteps, becoming a Unitarian minister. In 1897 he chose to leave the ministry.

Although he was never granted what is today considered necessary as a validator for scholarship, a university position, Wicksteed nevertheless made his marks in the fields of classical literature and economics. Wicksteed had a great gift for languages and was recognized as an important translator of Dante. A contemporary and "intellectual fellow" of John Ruskin, the critic, Wicksteed wrote extensively on Dante and Aquinas, and on the general theme of Greek tragedy.

Of all Wicksteed's works, his 1888 *The Alphabet of Economic Science* represents the truest personal achievement. Of this book Edgeworth wrote: "Mr. Wicksteed brings the science of Jevons down to earth. How many tedious controversies about value might have been cut short, if the disputants had seized the points which he puts so clearly! How much more economic science is contained in this little textbook than in almost all the ponderous mass of German literature which relates to the theory of worth!" (Edgeworth 1889a, 71). Subtitled "Elements of the Theory of Value or Worth," the expressed purpose of the work was

> in the first place to explain the meaning and demonstrate the truth of the proposition, that *the value in use and the value in exchange of any commodity are two distinct, but connected, functions of the quantity of the commodity possessed by the persons or the community to whom it is valuable,* and in the second place, so to familiarise the reader with some of the methods and results that necessarily flow from that proposition as to make it impossible for him unconsciously to accept arguments and statements which are inconsistent with it. (Wicksteed 1888, 1; emphasis in original)

The "methods" Wicksteed chose to employ were those of mathematics, especially the calculus. The first 67 pages are a mixture of an introduction to the fundamentals of the calculus and a mathematical presentation of value theory as it applies to the individual; the remainder is devoted to an extension of the theory to society, and to an understanding of, among other things, the topics of exchange and equilibrium.[80]

Wicksteed's reason for beginning the work with a presentation of a mathematical framework hinged on his view of economics as a deductive science, one so structured as to demand for its comprehension a serious and disciplined mind: "a firm grasp of the elementary truths of Political Economy cannot be got without the same kind of severe and sustained mental application which is necessary in all other serious studies" (1888, ix). It was just this lack of a "seriousness" on the part of many of the earlier political economists that led to their inability to perceive the inadequacies of their methods and the fruitlessness of their prescriptions. But Wicksteed's use of mathematics was not to be relegated to an elucidation of theoretical arguments alone; he was first and foremost interested in demonstrating how the theory could be applied to the workaday world. The theory is not important in itself, but only to the extent that it assists us in understanding actual economic relations. The mathematical struc-

---

80. In the Preface to this book, Wicksteed recounted a comment by a friend who had read the proofs. The acquaintance "dwelt in glowing terms on the pleasure and profit that my reader would derive from them, 'if only he survived the first cold plunge into "functions."'" Another equally candid friend to whom I reported the remark exclaimed, '*Survive* it indeed! Why, what on earth is to induce him to *take* it?'" (1888, ix).

ture, insofar as it brought a certain clarity to the exposition of the subject, he deemed indispensable to this charge:

> my object is to bring Economics down from the clouds and make the study throw light on our daily doings and experiences, as well as on the great commercial and industrial machinery of the world. But in order to get this light some mathematical knowledge is needed, which it would be difficult to pick out of the standard treatises as it is wanted. (1888, x)

Among the more interesting sidelights of the *Alphabet* is Wicksteed's expressed desire to move economics from the realm of ethics (a normative domain) to that of science (a positive one). He would continue along the trail blazed by Jevons to redirect economics away from the Benthamite path.

> Economics, it is said, have nothing to do with ethics, since they deal, not with the legitimacy of human desires, but with the means of satisfying them by human effort. (1888, 8)

This effort at redirection must begin with an alteration of our vocabulary, replacing terms which have an ethical meaning with ethically neutral ones; this is but the first step in changing economics from a normative to a positive discipline. Such words as "advantageous" and "useful" must be purged from the economics lexicon, replaced with neutral terms and phrases such as "worth" and "value in use." Hence the title of the book, *The Alphabet of Economic Science*.

Wicksteed applied this search for an ethically neutral terminology to the case of utility; his preferred descriptions were "marginal effectiveness" (see, for example, 40, 45) and "marginal usefulness" (e.g., 41, 45). He did, however, also employ the now-conventional term "marginal utility," rather than Jevons's preferred phrase, "final degree of utility" (45) But note this proviso: marginal *usefulness* or *effectiveness* refers to commodities, while marginal *utility* or *effect* refers to *units* of the commodities, the distinction being related to the increment under consideration.[81]

In defining utility, the subjective element was not lost on Wicksteed. He denied, for instance, in sympathy with Jevons, that there could be interpersonal comparisons of utility: "by no possibility can desires or wants, even for one and the same thing, which exist *in different minds,* be measured against one another or reduced to a common measure" and "it is impossible to establish any scientific comparison between the wants and desires of two or more separate individuals" (1888, 68, 69). Yet to speak at all of the "community," one has to be able to make just such comparisons. Wicksteed's answer, consistent with that of Jevons, was to

---

81. Marginal effectiveness is "the *rate* per unit at which the commodity is satisfying desire," while the marginal effect is "the actual result which it produces when applied at the margin" (Wicksteed 1888, 46).

express desires in terms of a common measure, for example, gold (or any other form of acceptable monetary unit); this commodity would then serve the function of an "objective scale of equivalence" (77). The reasoning was entirely instrumental, not out of line with usual scientific procedure: this objective measure is artificial and should not be taken as anything other than a proxy for the real, but unknown, unit of comparison.[82] If there was a problem with the work, it lay in the limitation of its scope to value alone. As Edgeworth remarked, "His treatise is the alpha and beta, but hardly the omega, of economic science" (Edgeworth 1889a, 71). Nonetheless, even Edgeworth was led to conclude that, "on the important subject which this manual introduces, it is the best educational treatise known to us" (71).

While a Jevons disciple, Wicksteed nonetheless found it necessary at times to "correct" certain statements in Jevons's work. One of the most widely read of Wicksteed's contributions to the economics literature was his 1889 *Quarterly Journal of Economics* article, "On Certain Passages in Jevons's *Theory of Political Economy.*" Here he took issue with certain points made by the master in his *Theory,* showing them as minor flaws in an otherwise brilliant effort.

Wicksteed began by critiquing data which Jevons employed to formulate an empirical relationship between price and the quantity of wheat demanded.[83] Wicksteed insisted that data relating the wheat harvest to price (estimates originally derived by Gregory King, but which Wicksteed attributed to Davenant) could only be valid under the assumption that all other things were held constant (the ceteris paribus assumption). In the case of wheat, the curve relating quantity and price is only legitimate under the assumption that wheat is used solely and exclusively for *human* consumption. Any and all other uses must be eliminated from consideration, as these apply to total demand and so must include such possibilities as substitution between goods and the interaction of complementary goods.

A second problem Wicksteed identified related to the shape of the curve itself. While Jevons's curve was asymptotic to both the price and quantity axes, Wicksteed felt that this was clearly a mistake. In regard to quantity, since the marginal utility of wheat would be zero at some given level (that is, everyone would eventually reach a level of satiation), the curve would eventually cut the quantity (x) axis. As regards price, Wicksteed argued that an infinite price could not exist, for two reasons: (1) at a high enough price, demand ceases to be effective, and (2) before

---

82. "Money is the symbol of the exact balancing and setting off one against the other of services rendered or goods exchanged; and this balancing can only be affected by absolutely renouncing all attempts to arrive at a *real* equivalence of effort or sacrifice, and adopting in its place an external and mechanical equivalence which has no tendency to conform to the real equivalence" (Wicksteed 1888, 77).

83. Jevons held that the relationship was $p = f(q)$. Thus we see that, as with Marshall, Jevons really did not have at hand a theory of consumer choice.

the price gets too high, there will be efforts to substitute other similar goods. Together these two conditions suggest that the curve would also intersect the price (y) axis.[84] Thus Wicksteed was led to look for a "law" relating the King data. This he achieved by suggesting an equation (a cubic equation) that fitted the data well.

The third, more troubling, aspect of Jevons's method was his perceived incorrect use of the "theory of dimensions." For Wicksteed, the theory of dimensions was of the utmost importance in standardizing certain of the relationships among economic variables, something which had been accomplished long before in the physical sciences. One can only make clear the underlying relations among disparate concepts once the units of comparison have been well-defined and the correspondences between the concepts have been made. (Today we would refer to this as the "measurement problem," as it relates to the selection of appropriate units for the representation of data; it is a fundamental criterion of graph theory. Wicksteed discussed this also throughout the *Alphabet*.)

> It is of vital consequence that we should have a precise conception of our several units and their relations to each other, if the mathematical method of economic study is to make any real progress; and the careful student will very rapidly learn to recognize in the theory of dimensions a valuable means of elucidating and checking his processes and results. (Wicksteed 1889, 298)

This correspondence Wicksteed felt Jevons failed to achieve. It was this singular error, this failure of coordination, which he maintained had led to the flaws in Jevons's scheme of economics.

In 1894 Wicksteed published *An Essay on the Co-ordination of the Laws of Distribution*,[85] an outgrowth of his 1889 *QJE* article on Jevons's marginal productivity theory. This paper offered what Schumpeter (1954, 1051) regarded as the first explicit recognition of the production function and was itself an effort to apply Jevons's theory of utility to the problem of distribution.

Wicksteed began the *Essay* with what may be regarded as a statement of method, in this instance concerning the use of mathematics as a rhetorical device, albeit one more systematic and thereby more convincing from a logical standpoint than the merely literary. Mathematical recasting of economic theory does not, he suggested, make the statements and propositions of economics more definite or definitive than does a purely literary rendering; what the mathematical phrasing does is to make known to the audience the *definiteness* of the propositions.

---

84. "Indeed, it is pitiable to think how slight the rise would probably have to be in order to induce incipient 'famine,' and how false the inference that if people are dying for want of a thing the price of that thing must be 'infinite' " (Wicksteed 1889, 296).

85. Schumpeter (1954, 831) ranked this as "his most original piece of work," although he lamented that only two copies were sold.

My contention is that the proposition stated in this mathematical form is not more definite or more bold than it is in the form in which it is generally assumed by the economists, but that its mathematical form forces its definiteness and its boldness upon us, makes us realise what we are doing in assuming it and therefore gives us pause. (Wicksteed 1894, 52)

Mathematical phrasing of economic propositions serves two principal purposes: (1) it serves "as a safeguard against unconscious assumptions," and (2) it allows that conclusions drawn are not beyond the premises. Mathematical reasoning, in other words, allows us to better see the assumptions we normally take for granted or set out haphazardly in an ad hoc fashion, and it forces us to rely on deductions the validity of which is dependent upon the premises alone and not on our interpretations of what the premises should demonstrate (1894, 52–53). We are only allowed deductions from established premises, and, according to the deductive method, those premises cannot give more than they contain. This form of reasoning thus assists the economist in his quest to reduce to a minimum the error of his deductions.[86]

Consistent with his desire for a rhetoric which could focus attention on the essentials of any (not simply economic) theoretical presentation, Wicksteed sought to define the laws of distribution. Previously, there could not be said to have existed a single "law" of distribution, in the same form and of the same rigor as the "laws" of exchange, for the fashion was to view factors as being unique in nature, requiring the elucidation of "special" laws governing their roles in production. Labor was seen as a unique factor by Locke, Smith, Ricardo, and Marx, who granted it center stage in the economic scheme. Capital and land also could only be understood as factors with special characteristics in regard to both their composition and their role in the valuation of product.

Wicksteed assigned himself the task of coordination of the disparate laws in an effort to determine the relative shares accruing to each (1894, 55). What was needed was a common set of terms in which the concern of distribution and the relative importance of each factor in production could be expressed, such commonality being a prerequisite to comparison. For Wicksteed, "[t]he very term 'distribution of the product' is a tacit acknowledgement of the obligation to co-ordinate the laws of distribution" (55).

To see what Wicksteed considered his challenge, it makes sense to review the theory as he presented it. Let P represent the total product, with $P = f(a_1, a_2, a_3, \ldots, a_n)$, and where a_i is a factor of production.

---

86. "For it is one thing to be practically familiar with a principle and to assume it in special cases as a matter of course, and it is another thing to grasp it so consciously and so firmly as never to lose hold of it or admit anything inconsistent with it, however remote from familiar experience and however complicated and abstract may be the regions of enquiry in which we need it as our clue" (Wicksteed 1894, 59).

Further, let us assume that f is homogeneous of degree one, a condition he maintained perhaps without being fully cognizant of its importance.[87] Quite simply, Wicksteed then argued, although due to his professed lack of knowledge of the mathematical literature rather painstakingly derived in the essay, that the share of any factor in the total product will equal $(\partial P/\partial a_i)a_i$, and so $\Delta(\partial P/\partial a_i)a_i = P$.

The result is of course Euler's theorem applied to the distribution of the product. All this result means is, as Wicksteed phrased it:

> That the share in the product which falls to any factor, no matter what be the character of that factor or of the service which it renders, is determined by the amount per unit which the concern, as a whole, would find it pays to allow to that factor sooner than have a portion of it withdrawn from co-operation. So stated the theorem may seem self-evident. And so indeed it is. (1894, 58–59)

In addition to formulating (actually reformulating) the law in a "correct" way, Wicksteed's derivation also made comparisons between factors unit-free, so that we no longer have to seek comparisons between money values which may be, in any event, arbitrarily assigned. "Each factor is expressed in its own unit and treated as having its independent influence, at the margin, on the increment or decrement of the product" (1894, 61).

It should also be noted in respect to the *Essay* that Wicksteed's theory included a place for risk as a factor of production, a possibility mentioned earlier (1850) by Thünen and even Cantillon, and expanded upon later (1921) by Frank Knight and John Maynard Keynes. In Wicksteed's presentation, speculation resolves itself into two categories: (1) risk-compensation, and (2) a reward for speculating (1894, 93). Knight (1921) termed this the distinction between risk and true uncertainty. Wicksteed was content, however, with mere mention of the distinction and did not see fit to extend it into a more comprehensive theory of the *motives* behind enterprise and profit. But the fact that he noted it at all is certainly evidence of his abilities, and his intuitions.

Likewise with the idea of "goodwill." Usually associated with the work of the American Institutionalist John R. Commons, the concept of goodwill is most often connected with institutional models of economics. Wicksteed made mention of the fact that goodwill served an important function in its own right (1894, 99), independent of the influence of any concrete, tangible, or measurable productive factor. Yet he again failed to realize the full import of what he had "discovered."

---

87. In an 1894 *Economic Journal* article, Alfred William Flux, an "applied economist," showed that Euler's Theorem for homogeneous functions in the two-variable case was the appropriate proof of this proposition. The solution follows immediately given homogeneity of degree one. The simplest case in economics is that of the Cobb-Douglas production function.

It can be argued that Wicksteed bridged the differences between the utilitarian marginalism of Jevons and the subjective marginalism of the Austrian Carl Menger.[88] Wicksteed's 1910 *The Common Sense of Political Economy* stressed the importance of a subjective approach to all economic life: the key to understanding the economic problem is in accepting that the foremost issue is the *selection between alternatives*.

To Wicksteed, choice was based on a scale of preferences. Nonetheless, Wicksteed's economic man had a very broad horizon. Economic laws, he thought, are the laws of life, applying as much to the choice between prayer and friendship as to the choice between bread and milk.

6 Conclusion

The thought of this, the second generation of utilitarian thinkers—the "scientific" utilitarians—expresses great similarities and differences in presentation and rhetoric. Jevons and Marshall both expressed an understanding of and a sympathy to the remediation of social problems. In this they harkened back to the roots of ethical Utilitarianism with its emphasis on the betterment of society. Knowing their audience, they chose to express themselves in a readily understandable literary rhetoric. Edgeworth and Wicksteed, by contrast, were more inclined to concentrate efforts on the positive role of economic science (perhaps taking to heart Jevons's own idea of the proper role for a scientific economics). Jevons, Edgeworth, and Wicksteed all sought to express the postulates of economics in a mathematical form, in some sense divorced from any literary exposition; the emphasis was always on the positive, at times at the expense of the normative.

Marshall, on the other hand, sought to *understand* the mathematical structure of economic postulates, while expressing this structure in a rhetoric understandable to others of less mathematical ability and insight. He was also keenly aware that economics began as a moral science, not a positive one, and so economists should be mindful always of their roots. One cannot deny the impact of Marshall on the development of British and American economic thought, especially in regard to the rhetoric. Mitchell is said to have had such a distaste for theory precisely because of the absence in his graduate education of a text such as Marshall's *Principles* (Schumpeter 1951, 241–43). It remained the leading and most influential text until the end of World War II.[89]

It is no small wonder that Marshall became the champion of nineteenth-century British economics, the great expositor of the subject

88. See chapter 9.

89. Although Keynes's *General Theory* was published in 1936, the true import of the message of this new approach was not to be felt until after the war, and particularly, in the United States at least, in the 1950s and 1960s.

and its intricacies. However, it is also no small wonder that the others have endured to the present day, their legends carved in the stone of theorems and propositions, while Marshall is more the darling of the historian of thought. Rarely is there to be found among academics of a theoretical stripe any mention of the Marshallian basis for a postulate or principle, while at the same time the names of Jevons, Edgeworth, and even Wicksteed are to be found scattered throughout the references and indexes of these same works. The positive revolution has indeed become the dominant evolutionary trend.

CHAPTER 8

The British Historical School and the Post-Marshallian Cambridge Tradition
A Reinterpretation of Utilitarianism

A university should be a place of light, or liberty, and of learning.
BENJAMIN DISRAELI, *HOUSE OF COMMONS* (MARCH 11, 1873)

All human knowledge takes the form of interpretation.
WALTER BENJAMIN, *BRIEFE* 126 (DECEMBER 9, 1923)

The Politicoeconomic Background   I

It is generally acknowledged that the era of the British Classical School of Economics coincided with the great glory days of the intellectual leadership of Britain. The nineteenth century, during which the classical school developed and flourished, produced some of the major intellectual achievements in British philosophy, as well as in political, social, and economic theory. James and John Stuart Mill, Ricardo, and Malthus wrote pamphlets and treatises of a type little known before or since, covering every aspect of social, political, and economic life. Ricardo and J. S. Mill not only wrote of the social and political conditions of the country, but as parliamentarians placed themselves in a position to act on these beliefs, to actually implement their policy positions and determine empirically whether in fact they had merit. Great social groupings and political associations—from the Philosophic Radicals to the Fabian Socialists—defined for their era an intellectual climate within which social and political reform movements could thrive. The explosion in the number and variety of journals designed to appeal to every type of political persuasion, and the interest shown by the British intellectual elites in

employing these forums for the free exchange of information and intellectual positions, led to a flourishing of debate.

This is not, however, the only way of describing the milieu of
nineteenth-century British culture. An opposing view is that by 1851 it
had become abundantly clear that the sheer cruelty of the industrialization process, superimposed as it was on the cruelty of the British class
system, had engendered the beginnings of a movement dedicated to the
proposition that "economic progress" was not as advertised. In the coal
mines, for example, children as young as eight years of age (and perhaps
even younger) were employed, the rationale being that the temperament
needed for mining was a quality which had to be bred, not a trait in
abundance throughout the general population. Yet the realization that
the society had underlying flaws had been a long time coming. The Ludd-
ites of 1811, who sought to follow the advice of their (fictitious) leader
Ned Ludd and destroy their machinery as a means of mobilizing discon-
tented workers disgusted with the excesses of employers, were actually
following in the path of the Newcastle miners of 1765.[1] Thus the Dicken-
sian horrors were not the imaginary ruminations of a depressed novelist,
but were accurate portrayals of conditions as they actually appeared. Into
this scenario emerged those who sought to explain the situation as the
inevitable consequence of the capitalist mode of production, the stratified
culture, or the fanatic adherence to the individualist ethos. Here we need
only mention the names of Owen, Hodgskin, Marx, and Engels.

The Great Exhibition of 1851 celebrated Britain's economic progress and served to vindicate the champions of free trade. This may have
been the high-water mark of British scientific-intellectual supremacy.
Thereafter, reform movements began to challenge the foundations of the
previously accepted near-total faith in the desirability of British scientific
advancement and its impact on industrial leadership. Although the Great
Reform Bill of 1832 had been successful in restricting if not eliminating
the rule of squirarchy (the archaic system of representation involved in
the Commons) and thereby extending the suffrage, there was increasing
doubt as to whether the established parliamentary leadership was running the country and the empire in a beneficent manner, or indeed ever
could. Among the reform movements[2] of this period were efforts at
broadening suffrage to include all male citizens, moves toward the recognition of legal unionism, the legislating of minimum environmental stan-

---

1. For an excellent discussion of this period, and the particulars above, see M. J.
Daunton 1995.

2. What is most interesting is that the major reforms were undertaken by the Conservative Party. Benjamin Disraeli, in most senses an outsider, captured control of the party
and substituted his New Conservatism (a generous state paternalism) for the free-marketism
of the Liberals (a policy still known in Europe as Liberalism) and the social indifference of
the Wellington era of Conservative Party leadership. Disraeli's cleverness is very well represented in his novels—of these, two, *Conningsby* and *Sybil*, should be read by those interested in the nature of political reconstruction.

dards for workers, and the institution of the Factory Act (1844) and the Ten Hour Act (1847).[3] Reformers also sought to broaden opportunity for the poor by instituting free schooling, and reform the public health service to include central registration of disease experience as well as vital statistics. These measures served to ameliorate the more obvious excesses.

Withal, throughout this period Britain remained a very class-structured society. Nowhere was this more evident than in the great universities of Oxford, Cambridge, and London. Change there required not only a fundamental alteration in the very nature of university education, but also specific reforms in the curricula which would allow realization of this end.

In the specific area of the teaching of political economy, the intellectual *Methodenstreit* that accompanied this intellectual revolution led ultimately to a kind of armed neutrality, with some antagonists devoted to historical economics, others devoted to theoretical economics, and most not desirous of airing their preferences. One way to handle the matter was to argue that, at the current knowledge frontier, most economic questions should be handled positively—establish the parameters of the debate and settle on a scientifically grounded solution. If norms are to be invoked, others could worry about them later.[4]

As Britain entered the twentieth century, the collapse of its intellectual, cultural, and even political and military dominance was becoming more obvious. While it is true that signs of the decline were evident well before this time, the beginning of a new century served to heighten awareness. Events in the first decades served as witness to the new reality, and in an effort to forestall the inevitable, the decline was attributed to all manner of causes. The loss of British industrial and economic hegemony, for example, was attributed to the exhaustion caused by the First World War, rather than by a failure of intellectual policy formation. The rise of American economic power, in like manner, was seen principally as a result of its war experience—an experience which occupied it for only one year, as opposed to the four-year drain on England and the continental powers—rather than by a shift in the intellectual center.

The 1920s again brought social conflict, much of it associated with a desire for socialist reforms. The Great War not only hastened the demise of the remnants of the old feudal class structure, but forced the middle class to reconsider its objectives. Technological change wreaked havoc with the old social structure, and a worldwide Depression caused

---

3. The Factory Act limited children under the age of thirteen to no more than six and one-half hours of labor a day and those under the age of eighteen (and women) to twelve hours. The Ten Hour Act limited the workday to ten hours for women and children.

4. For example, if heredity is a factor in behavior, so is the environment. Since one could *do* something about the environment, we need to focus more closely on it. This is not the same thing as denying heredity; instrumentally it amounts only to postponing discussions which lead to conflict.

devastating unemployment and a falling price level; both served to create tastes for new forms of economic relations. These changes led the intellectual elites to take a far more critical look at the nature of corporations, and centrally organized units generally, than had previously been the tradition. It also led to efforts at repackaging the old abandoned utopian positions of the past century. As the actual situation changed, suggesting in the eyes of many the need for a reexamination of the laissez-faire, individualistic ethic of the past, so did the general mood concerning the viability of alternatives.

There was, to be sure, a change in the nature of the socialist threat that made the shift all the more palatable—anarchism (in terms of its socialist manifestations) tended to disappear, replaced by a widening base for reform along the social democrat model. But the true depth of reaction proved even more extensive. The collapse of the credit market and then of the agricultural economy in the 1920s, leading to the worldwide Great Depression of the 1930s, engendered a loss of faith in the efficacy of economics as an engine of change: the belief that scientific precision in the manipulation of social and economic conditions was within the realm of possibility, which the public had taken for granted, was shown finally to be mere pretense. This loss of faith by the public in the prescriptive ability of economics led in turn to an eventual realization that the discipline itself needed rehabilitation and reinvigoration, since the theories taught for so long as dogma had little relevance to the reality of the changed world.[5]

The year 1885 marked the beginning of the Marshallian Age, this being the year Alfred Marshall delivered his Cambridge Inaugural Lecture. Marshall held that economics should be concerned with life as it was led by the ordinary man; men were motivated by approbation as well as by a desire for money and purchases, and so the artificial construct of the *homo economicus* held little interest as a viable economic principle. Being nurture-, not nature-, minded, he also believed that poverty was the great curable evil of civilization. Although he was well aware of the heuristic value of models and generalizations, Marshall was, as we have seen, fascinated with institutions and the way they worked; economics should follow a *biological,* not a *physical* or *chemical,* analogue. He was not, however, able to create the sort of synthesis he desired, nor was he particularly sanguine that it could in fact be accomplished. The *Principles* dealt primarily with static analysis, and while his 1919 *Industry and*

---

5. This restructure took several forms: (1) a turn from the method of statics to that of dynamics; (2) a turn to the study of competitive market imperfections (the study of imperfect competition); (3) a turn to the study of the causes and controls of economic depressions; (4) a turn to the study of the endogenous causes of economic growth; (5) a turn to the causes of price instability; and finally (6) a turn to systems of macroeconomic monitoring (including national accounting systems, progress in the formalization of microeconomics, and efforts to formalize the study of macroeconomics).

Trade was a brilliant, if incomplete, effort at describing and generalizing a dynamic economics, the synthesis was never fulfilled. He never completely succeeded in imposing his understanding of the changes required of political economy on those who would eventually take the mantle of leadership from him.

The eventual breakdown of the Marshallian synthesis involves many points, only a few of which can be discussed here.[6] For one, there is the argument that, taken on its own terms, Marshall's program disintegrated primarily because of its own inadequacy. In particular, the key assumptions of the Marshallian model, including free competition (not to be confused with perfect competition) and perfect knowledge, served best as pedagogical devices rather than as analytical starting points.

Secondly, Marshall's economics focused most clearly on static, rather than truly dynamic, analysis. The introduction of the time element in the classification of market behavior swept most of the interesting problems into the "fourth state," that of secular change. Even *Industry and Trade* offered no analytical schema comparable to that of the *Principles* within which to construct a dynamic theory. This lack of a "universal" (beyond time and place) analytical framework limited the extension of Marshall's influence.

Thirdly, taken on its own terms, the Marshallian synthesis was deprived of its canonical authority by the subsequent Pigovian analysis of the causes of unemployment. By 1908 Pigou had succeeded in finally demolishing what later became known as the "Treasury View" (by the late 1920s, the "Treasury Orthodoxy"), this being that tax-financed public expenditures succeed only in misallocating resources (especially labor) from productive to unproductive employment. With the collapse of an intellectual basis for this tenet of classical economics that had lasted from the time of Smith and Ricardo, classical doctrine was itself called into question.[7] Marshall had in effect been rendered irrelevant and had simply outlived his usefulness to a new generation beset by the complications of a changed world.[8]

6. Marshall's schemata for market analysis is presented in the companion volume.

7. No doctrine ever truly disappears. In the 1970s a form of the "Treasury View" reemerged as the Ricardian Equivalence theorem.

8. In *The Years of High Theory* (1967) G. L. S. Shackle saw the breakdown of the Marshallian synthesis as tied up with the inadequacy of two of its assumptions: (1) that most firms are driven to produce in the area of *increasing* costs (decreasing returns), and (2) that economics deals with a *knowable* spectrum of costs and prices. If neither of these assumptions was significantly mistaken, both were remarkably naive. The Marshallian inability or unwillingness to face the problems of redrawing the assumptions inevitably and irretrievably led the Marshallian synthesis to crash. Thus, it was only an indirect variant of the Wicksteed insight about the lack of congruence between the real vs. the money economy which spelled analytical disaster to the Marshallian hegemony (a point which Keynes was later to articulate). To Shackle the more basic fault was an apparently intentional ignoring of the general principle of uncertainty, a concept which Marshall clearly had derived from Thünen.

2 The Intellectual Reform Movement: English Historical
Economics and the London School of Economics

2.1 *Maine, Cliffe Leslie, and the English Historical School*

By the 1870s there had developed a widespread belief in Britain that the
teachings of the Classical School held little value for the contemporary
society. Deductions from fundamental postulates could not explain the
growing political, social, and economic tensions, especially the growing
poverty that had enveloped Ireland.

It was in this environment that there emerged the English Historical
School, the tenets of which perhaps inevitably precipitated a *Methodenstreit* with the deductivists of the Classical Political Economy. The chief
protagonist in the battle with the deductivists was Thomas Edward Cliffe
Leslie (1827–82),[9] an Irish student of the classics, ethics, logic, and law.
While he never produced a comprehensive treatise on political economy,
his scattered essays on the appropriate methods for the study of economic
problems provide an insight into his approach, one based on the "historical jurisprudence" of Henry James Sumner Maine (1822–88),[10] to which
we shall briefly turn.

Maine is considered to have been the founder of anthropological
jurisprudence and served as lecturer at both Oxford and Cambridge. His
approach to the law was in opposition to the analytical method of
Bentham and John Austin (1790–1859), an approach which (we have
seen) relied on an understanding of rational principles as the foundation
of law. In his 1861 *Ancient Law* (5th ed., 1873), Maine declared, after an
exhaustive review of the historical development of Greek and Roman law
codes, that legal codes did not simply materialize, but rather were the
result of an evolutionary process that was itself site-bound: each society
had a unique primitive beginning and laws developed within the confines
of a specific social (national) arrangement. Maine argued that primitive
man established social relations on the basis of status—defined as "a
condition of society in which all the relations of Persons are summed up
in the relations of Family" (Maine 1873, 163)[11]—while, in more complex
societies, social relations were made on the basis of contract—an agree-

---

9. Leslie was educated at Trinity College, Dublin. Following graduation, he studied
law in London, attending the lectures of Maine. He was appointed to the chair of jurisprudence and political science at Queen's College, Belfast, in 1853, where he remained until his
death. Excellent general treatments of Leslie include John K. Ingram (1879) and Gerard M.
Koot (1975).

10. Maine was a graduate of Christ's Hospital and Pembroke College, Cambridge.
He served as Regius Professor of Civil Law (1847–54), Corpus Professor of Jurisprudence
(Oxford) (1869–77), and Master of Trinity Hall College (1877–88).

11. "All the forms of Status taken notice of in the Law of Persons were derived from,
and to some extent are still coloured by, the powers and privileges anciently residing in the
Family" (Maine 1873, 164–65).

ment or promise of obligation reached through the free interaction of individuals, and granted legal enforcement by the instruments of government. In the movement from status to contract, we see a gradual but sure change in the respective roles of the individual and the community: the "individual is steadily substituted for the Family, as the unit of which civil laws take account" (163).

While Maine believed in laissez-faire and the right of property, his historical approach nonetheless led him to conclude that the property right, of central import in the philosophy of laissez-faire, was not in fact universal in origin, but was a product of "modern" society. More importantly, he did not accept the received wisdom of an individual taking possession of a *res nullium*—something which does not now nor did ever have an owner—as the basis for the property right; the idea of an individualistic contract *assumes* the existence of property relations. The *family* (community) unit was for Maine the fundamental social unit in ancient times, and so the right of ownership must have pertained to the family as representative of a collective, and not the individual. It was the institution of Roman law which gave credence to the notion of the individual acquiring ownership through occupation, a thesis which had become persuasive to, and was given license by, both Hobbes and Locke.

Maine held that the evolution of society from status-based to contract-based was important for another reason, that in shifting the central focus from the family to the individual, it made political economy possible. The movement from status to contract led, as a by-product, to the need for a contract-based law, independent of the civil code, upon which to ground the relations among *individuals* in the disposition of affairs. Political economy then concentrated all efforts on analyzing the constitution of the latter, thus ignoring the foundation which had been laid by the former:

> It is certain that the science of Political Economy, the only department of moral inquiry which has made any considerable progress in our day, would fail to correspond with the facts of life if it were not true that Imperative Law had abandoned the largest part of the field which it once occupied, and had left men to settle rules of conduct for themselves with a liberty never allowed to them till recently. The bias indeed of most persons trained in political economy is to consider the general truth on which their science reposes as entitled to become universal, and, when they apply it as an art, their efforts are ordinarily directed to enlarging the province of Contract and to curtailing that of Imperative Law, except so far as law is necessary to enforce the performance of Contracts. (1873, 296)

Yet Maine did not seek to condemn completely the orthodox economics (at the time the economics of John Stuart Mill). The problem lay in accepting that there existed contemporaneously a mix of the (modern) contract-based society, and the (ancient) custom-based society. The ortho-dox economics had been predicated on the former, but had neglected the still-evident place of the latter, leaving it as an anachronism. This is obvious in the characterization of the market. The market began not as an organized arena for individual merchants interested in buying and selling, but as a consequence of the convergence of proximate village communities exchanging communal goods. Maine argued that political economists had chosen to ignore the role of the community in the estab-lishment of the marketplace since it no longer fitted into the grand design. Yet the communal origin of the market was still alive (albeit unrecog-nized) in the philosophical underpinnings of economics as a "moral sci-ence." Maine's criticism touched on this observation, that "the vague moral sentiments which obstruct the complete reception of their [the political economists] principles" were just those ancient doctrines of vil-lage communities (Maine 1889, 195), to which the "modern" economic scientist was oblivious. Despite the tensions evident in Classical Econom-ics, time would eventually serve to resurrect the efficacy of the classical model, as society moved more completely from status to contract, from community-based to individual-based:

> Everything which has helped to convert society into a collection of individuals from being an assemblage of families, has helped to add to the truth of the assertion made of human nature by the Political Economists. (1889, 197)

With this introduction to the jurisprudential work of Maine, we are led to the foundations of the English Historical School of Economics and to its founder, T. E. Cliffe Leslie.[12] A disciple of Maine—in his 1875 "review" of Maine's *Early History of Institutions* Leslie remarked, "it is not a rash prediction that one of the results of his works on the history of law will be the application of the historical method to political economy" (Leslie 1875a, 320)—Leslie sought to apply the inductive method of historical analysis to the study of economic science. In his first foray into the subject, a methodological essay published in *The Fortnightly Review* as "The Political Economy of Adam Smith" (1870), Leslie attributed the tensions in economic methodology to the very structure of Smith's work itself. Smith believed that society was driven to "a beneficial and harmo-nious natural order" in the absence of any external guidance (Leslie 1870, 551); individuals acting in their own best interests, and possessed of the twin attributes of sympathy and self-love, would, unknowingly but assuredly, promote the common welfare. It was this "natural order," seen as having been composed of "a body of necessary and universal truths, founded on invariable laws of nature, and deduced from the constitution

---

12. Spiegel declared Leslie to have been "the first English writer to produce a system-atic statement of the philosophic foundation of the historical method as the appropriate instrument of economic research" (Spiegel 1991, 403).

of the human mind," which had formed the basis for the deductive economics of Ricardo and James Mill (among others) (1870, 549). Yet while pretending to necessary truth, the *foundation* of Smith's method was inductivism, which had led him to promulgate the existence of natural laws and the ideal order on the basis of experiential evidence. With these generalizations at hand, Smith then could proceed to his deductions. Hence the problem and the tension.

Leslie proceeded to condemn the a priori reasoning of Smith as moving "not by the interrogation but by the anticipation of nature" (1870, 551). In his use of Natural Law and the mechanism of the "invisible hand," Smith had merely *assumed* an underlying natural order and had chosen from the evidence those elements which could serve as support. Leslie, by contrast, proposed

> that Political Economy is not a body of natural laws in the true sense, or of universal and immutable truths, but an assemblage of speculations and doctrines which are the result of a particular history, coloured even by the history and character of its chief writers; that, so far from being of no country, and unchangeable from age to age, it has varied much in different ages and countries, and even with different expositors in the same age and country; that, in fact, its expositors, since the time of Adam Smith, are substantially divisible into two schools, following opposite methods; and that the method of one of them, of which the fundamental conception is, that their political economy *is* an ascertained body of laws of nature, is an offshoot of the ancient fiction of a Code of Nature, and a natural order of things, in a form given to that fiction in modern times, by theology on one hand, and a revolt against the tyranny of the folly and inequality of such human codes as the world had known on the other. (1870, 549)

But it was his 1875 "On the Philosophical Method of Political Economy" which actually provided the impetus to the development of the English Historical School. Here Leslie attacked directly the classical postulate of rational economic man. Man is not a rational maximizer pursuing economic goods and satisfactions through the use of the Benthamite calculus, but rather, as with Smith's and Hume's men, is motivated by "passions, appetites, affections, moral and religious sentiments, family feelings, aesthetical tastes, and intellectual wants," in other words, Hume's passions (Leslie 1875b, 230). He likewise attacked the basis of classical orthodoxy, namely, the place of the individual in the center of society and the workings of laissez-faire. Along the lines of Maine, he maintained that it was not the individual who was responsible for the evolution of the market and thus the maintenance of the social order, but rather it was "the primitive community—a community one in blood, property, thought, moral responsibility, and manner of life" that was the basis for social interaction. Individuals in pursuit of self-interest do not direct as if by the "invisible hand" the achievement of a social outcome; rather the "individual interest itself, and the desires, aims, and pursuits of every man and woman in the nation have been molded by, and received their direction and form from, the history of that community" (230).

2.2 The London School of Economics: A Citadel for Social Change

With Maine and Leslie, British economics had been confronted with an alternative method of analysis. Through the use of historical materials, the record of the development of civilizations could be made to provide essential insights into the workings of modern society. The inductions, moreover, need not be in conflict with the classical philosophical notions of laissez-faire and the inviolable right of ownership of property, but could on the contrary provide the support needed to buttress these fundamental classical political economic ideals. The "fact" of a communal form of ownership preceding the protection of property rights by contract in no way invalidated the significance of the latter, but rather pointed to an evolution in social arrangements devoid of any ethical foundation. Individualism as the intellectual basis of social organization became dominant over the communal identity of the family. In any event, for Classical Political Economy, the change in method was revolutionary.

By the 1880s Britain had begun to experience an intellectual revolution of another kind, this one a frontal assault on the very notion of individualism itself. Nowhere is this more evident than in the founding of the London School of Economics and Political Science, the LSE.[13] Founded in 1895 with the proceeds from the estate of a prominent supporter of the Fabian movement, Henry Hunt Hutchinson, the LSE became synonymous with the goals of the Fabian membership; Sidney and Beatrice Webb, George Bernard Shaw, Graham Wallas, and G. D. H. Cole were but a few of the more well-known members who were influential in its establishment.

The "method" of the LSE was to be historical research into social and economic problems:

> the special aim of the School will be, from the first, the study and investigation of the concrete facts of industrial life and the actual working of economic and political relations as they exist or have existed, in the United Kingdom and in foreign countries. (From an undated LSE prospectus; quoted in Dahrendorf 1995, 20)

---

13. The essential reference on the founding of the LSE is Ralf Dahrendorf (1995). See also the excellent essay by F. A. von Hayek (1946), in commemoration of the fiftieth anniversary of the institution.

Significantly, the choice to head the new institution was W. A. S. Newins, a mathematician by training (Pembroke College, Oxford) who had also studied history.[14] While not himself a Fabian (or a socialist for that matter), Newins was a devotee of the doctrines of the German Historical School, a mercantilist, and a protectionist.[15]

While "ostensibly" nonpolitical—Sidney Webb noted that all "sensible" persons would eventually come to conclude that socialism afforded the best solution to economic problems, making any formal inculcation unnecessary—the driving force of the school was an opposition to the individualism and abstract method of the classical economists, especially Ricardo. To this end, political predispositions would be neglected in exchange for a committed opposition to the established orthodoxy.[16]

But this was all to change. In 1929 Lionel Robbins returned to the LSE from Oxford (he had been at the LSE from 1925 to 1927), with F. A. von Hayek arriving in 1931 (later to become Tooke Professor). Hayek brought to the LSE a decidedly Austrian approach to economics, emphasizing individuality, subjectivism, and a general equilibrium approach to the subject, as well as an aversion to the tenets of socialism. Robbins was also much inclined to this approach, making him everything the founders of the school had opposed. Robbins was but a qualified utilitarian, for whom the "greatest happiness" principle was held to be along the lines of a working rule by which to judge legislation; he went so far as to write a laudatory book on the twentieth-century influence of Bentham (Robbins 1965). In this vein, the utilitarian principle was, among all other ethical structures, "better, more sensible, more humane, more agreeable to the moral conscience if you like, than any other I can think of" (Robbins 1970, 80). Worse, in his 1932 *An Essay on the Nature and Significance of Economic Science*, he undertook the task of separating economics from ethics, arguing that economics should be a positive, value-free discipline in terms of the methods of its analysis. He thus took up the banner of Ricardo and James Mill and carried it proudly through the halls of the new school, changing the character of the one institution devoted to countering the Ricardian heresy. The influence of Hayek and Robbins was also evident in the figures they would to bring to the school—such luminaries as John R. Hicks, James Meade, W. Arthur Lewis, and Ronald Coase—all of whom would later be awarded Nobel Prizes. (We will discuss in greater detail the beliefs of Hayek and Robbins in the following chapter.)

---

14. In 1892 Newins published *English Trade and Finance, Chiefly in the Seventeenth Century*.

15. As Schumpeter noted, Sidney Webb, in lectures at the LSE (1906), focused his efforts on method, a method much in line with that of the German Historical School. Schumpeter went so far as to call Webb an "anti-theorist" (1954, 832).

16. See especially Hayek 1946, 5.

3 Marshall's Successor: Pigou and Welfare Economics

3.1 The Nature of Economics

The credit for the establishment of what has become known as the Marshallian School of Economics goes not to Marshall himself, but to a student and his eventual successor at Cambridge, Arthur Cecil Pigou (1877–1959).[17] Indeed, as Austin Robinson opined, "It was Pigou, more than any other, who brought up a generation of Cambridge economists in the conviction that (in his often-repeated words) 'it's all in Marshall' and the belief that if they were in error, it was because they had misunderstood Marshall or had overlooked some essential passage in the holy writ" (A. Robinson 1968, 91). Interestingly enough, it was Pigou who also was responsible for its eventual eclipse.

As successor to Marshall in the Chair of Political Economy at Cambridge, Pigou owed his career as a professor to Marshall's sponsorship

---

17. Pigou was born on the Isle of Wight, the eldest son of an army officer who descended from a well-to-do Huguenot family. Educated at Harrow—Champernowne described him there "as a god among mortals" (Champernowne 1959, 264)—Pigou won a scholarship to King's College, Cambridge, majoring for the first two years in history and only later taking up the study of economics. (He took a First in the Historical Tripos in 1899.) At Cambridge, he developed his rhetorical skills as a member of the Union Debating Society. While a student, he won both the Chancellor's Prize (1899) for English verse (with an ode on Alfred the Great), and the Adam Smith Prize (1903) for an essay on industrial peace, an effort which he later expanded into *Principles and Methods of Industrial Peace* (1905). (Johnson [1960, 151] noted that Pigou sold the Chancellor's gold medal after World War I to provide famine relief to the Georgians.)

In 1900, Pigou took a First in Part II of the Moral Sciences Tripos (this time focusing on Political Economy) and in addition was named a Fellow of the Royal Statistical Society; in 1901 he began lecturing in economics at Cambridge. This latter date also marked the publication of his first book, *Robert Browning as a Religious Teacher,* originally written to satisfy the requirements for a fellowship (and awarded the Burney Prize). While that second essay failed to get him a King's Fellowship, the next year (1902) he was elected Fellow on the basis of his Cobden Prize Essay, describing movements in agricultural prices during the previous half century. (The prize-winning essay was entitled "The Causes and Effects of Changes in the Relative Values of Agricultural Produce in the United Kingdom During the Last Fifty Years.") By 1904, he had been named Girdler's Lecturer (1904–8), succeeding Marshall in 1908.

At the outbreak of World War I, Pigou was a conscientious objector. In a patriotic move, he volunteered for service during his vacations from Cambridge as an ambulance driver. It is generally acknowledged that his firsthand experiences in the war changed forever his outlook on the world. He became dour and inclined to the study of such topics as war finance and the war economy.

For a period after the war, Pigou served as a civil servant on the Board of Trade; in the period 1918 to 1919 he served on the Cunliffe Committee on the Foreign Exchanges; from 1919 to 1920 he served on the Royal Commission on the Income Tax; and from 1924 to 1925 he served on the Chamberlain Committee on the Currency and Bank of England Note Issues.

Details of Pigou's life are from D. G. Champernowne (1959), Harry G. Johnson (1960), and Austin Robinson (1968).

and was conscientious in popularizing Marshall's work; his 1908 Inaugural Lecture, "Economic Theory in Relation to Practice," in which he made the argument for increased public expenditures as a means of expanding employment, is in many respects a Marshallian interpretation of the basis of economic knowledge. However, while Pigou may have seemed content to be the "moon" to Marshall's "sun," if truth be told, Pigou created his own light and so was a good deal more than a mere reflector.[18]

In terms of the present effort, what is important is Pigou's Utilitarianism and his interest in social problems, and here the influence of Marshall is less evident than is the influence of Henry Sidgwick. Marshall was content with an extension of the ideas of laissez-faire economics, while obviously aware of its limitations; Sidgwick returned to the approach of John Stuart Mill in emphasizing the economic and social distortions of laissez-faire capitalism and the capacity of state action in rectifying such distortions.[19] Yet Sidgwick proceeded with both hope and alarm. The alarm lay in the worldwide movement toward socialism—"the more and more extensive intervention of Government with a view to palliate the inequities in the distribution of wealth"—while the hope lay with the possibility that socialism would moderate and become "purely beneficent, and bring improvement at every stage" (Sidgwick and Sidgwick 1906, 441). It was this moderating tendency that proved to be attractive to Pigou's sensibilities.

Pigou's interests in social policies surfaced in his 1912 *Wealth and Welfare*, a book Schumpeter referred to as "the greatest venture in labor economics ever undertaken by a man who was primarily a theorist" (Schumpeter 1954, 948). Viewed by Pigou as a supplement to the work of Marshall, *Wealth and Welfare* actually extended Marshall's "proof" that the free competition (laissez-faire) model is invalid under certain conditions and undertook to demonstrate more completely the consequences of this for social and economic policy. Designed originally as a statement of the causes of and remedies for unemployment, this important work became instead one of the first comprehensive treatments of the problem of economic welfare.

The arguments presented in *Wealth and Welfare* were more comprehensively laid out in Pigou's 1920 *Economics of Welfare*, an extension of his earlier work.[20] (We use here the fourth edition of 1932.) It was there

---

18. Champernowne opined, "Pigou's strength lay in his sure grasp of logical relations and his fanatical intellectual honesty. Had Pigou written *The Principles of Economics* or *The General Theory of Employment*, they might have been less attractive works, but there would have been far less ambiguity left for lesser economists to resolve" (1959, 264).

19. On this see Margaret O'Donnell 1979.

20. In his review of the second edition of *The Economics of Welfare* (1924), Frank Knight summed up quite succinctly the magnitude of the work: "It continues and develops the 'Cambridge Economics,' which continues and develops English Political Economy, ex-

that he addressed the question of the purpose behind intellectual inquiry. Dividing intellectual inquiries into light-bearing and fruit-bearing, he placed Classical Economics with the latter, allowing that economics was much more than a classificatory discipline; there was in the study of economics the potential for the solution to practical concerns. In so situating economics as an extensive (ampliative) science, Pigou desired to remove it from identification with the natural sciences, suggesting instead a connection to physiology:[21]

> If it were not for the hope that a scientific study of men's social actions may lead, not necessarily directly or immediately, but at some time and in some way, to practical results in social improvement, not a few students of these actions would regard the time devoted to their study as time misspent. That is true of all social sciences, but especially true of Economics. . . . When we elect to watch the play of human motives that are ordinary—that are sometimes mean and dismal and ignoble—our impulse is not the philosopher's impulse, knowledge for the sake of knowledge, but rather the physiologist's, knowledge for the healing that knowledge may help to bring. (Pigou 1932, 4–5)

In terms of its foundations, economics for Pigou was not a branch of logic. Neither could its postulates be expressed in terms of the physical analogue. Economics is fundamentally distinguishable from the implicative sciences of logic and mathematics, and is by contrast an experimental science, emphasizing realism as opposed to abstraction. Economics is fundamentally concerned with "the world known in experience, and in nowise extends to the commercial doings of a community of angels" (1932, 6). From this view of the domain of the subject,

> it follows that the type of science that the economist will endeavour to develop must be one adapted to form the basis of an art. It will not, indeed, itself be an art, or directly enunciate precepts of government. It is a positive science of what is and tends to be, not a normative science of what ought to be. Nor will it limit itself to those fields of positive scientific inquiry which have an obvious relevance to immediate practical problems . . . . But, though wholly independent in its tactics and its strategy, it will be guided in general

---

pounding its achieved results with a sure touch and marshalling them to bear explicitly in the real objective of all social science,—the wealth of nations or general human well-being. The doctrine is essentially that of Dr. Alfred Marshall; Pigou's exposition is less deliberate and more readable than that of his teacher, but lacks a certain touch of realism, the evidence of vast knowledge of detail acquired through first-hand observation. To the reviewer, the book represents the science of economics at its best so far; no work in the field known to him is its equal in the combination of scholarship, analytical penetration and lucidity of exposition" (Knight 1926, 51).

21. Thus one can see in Pigou's work a similarity with the approach of Hobbes.

direction by practical interest. This decides its choice of essential form. (1932, 5)

So understanding the nature of the "science" of economics is not to deny its chief function—to view problems with an eye to the "practical interest." "Positive" sciences, including economics, need not be abstract, sterile, and descriptive, concerned mainly with deductions from established and accepted premises; they can be positive and yet be classed as either formal or realistic, or contain elements of both. The formal side seeks logical inquiry in an effort "to discover *implications*"; the realistic side is, by contrast, "concerned with actualities" (1932, 5). Economics is unique with respect to the other sciences, in that it can be understood in either guise.

To clarify, consider the characterizations of motives in economics. As a pure, formal science, economics "would study equilibria and disturbances of equilibria among groups of persons actuated by any set of motives x" (1932, 6). Schools of economic thought could then be distinguished by their definitions of x. As an applied, realistic science, economics is governed by laws relating to the *actual* world, and not to any sequence of *possible* worlds. We must be cognizant of the fact that economic theories must have some application to the solution of real problems. This should not be taken, however, to imply theorizing based on a simple enumeration of instances; we must always remember to meet the facts with reason.

> In realistic science facts are not simply brought together; they are compelled by thought to *speak*. . . . Rather, every science, through examination and cross-examination of the particular facts which it is able to ascertain, seeks to discover the general laws of whose operation these particular facts are instances. . . . These laws, furthermore, are not merely summaries of the observed facts re-stated in a shorthand form. They are *generalisations,* and, as such, extend our knowledge to facts that have not been observed, may be, that have not as yet even occurred. (1932, 7; emphasis in original)

A realistic science must be not only rationally sound, but its inductions must be ampliative (capable of extension) as well.

Utility and Satisfaction and the Social Welfare 3.2

While fundamentally in Pigou's view a quantitative science, economics suffers from the fact that the individuals about whose actions it seeks explanation are each given to subjective utility judgments, not necessarily compatible with one another: "the fundamental things in the economic world—the schedules expressing the desires or aversions of groups of people for different sorts of commodities and services—are not thus simple and uniform" (1932, 8). This subjective aspect of the fundamental concerns of the discipline suggests that economics, while perhaps a *scientific* endeavor, cannot be treated with the same methodological structure as the "hard" sciences of physics and chemistry. Specifically, it is simply not possible to engage in controlled scientific experiments designed to test the validity of hypotheses.[22]

> But the economic constants—these elasticities of demand and supply—depending, as they do, upon human consciousness, are liable to vary. The constitution of the molecule, as it were, and not merely its position, changes under the influence of environment. . . . This malleability in the actual substance with which economic study deals means that the goal sought is itself perpetually shifting, so that, even if it were possible by experiment exactly to determine the values of the economic constants to-day, we could not say with confidence that this determination would hold good also of to-morrow. Hence the inevitable shortcomings of our science. (1932, 9–10)

Consider the application of this concern to the problem of the economics of social welfare. Pigou at the outset eschewed any formal statement of *individual* action in favor of a concern with *social* outcomes. He concentrated his efforts on the analysis of community welfare, maintaining that the basis of economics lay in "the social enthusiasm which revolts from the sordidness of mean streets and the joylessness of withered lives" (1932, 5). Economics is by its very nature concerned not with a description of the bases of individual decision making, but rather with the amelioration of social ills. While the promotion of social welfare remained an *end* to be achieved, to understand that end and to demonstrate the manner in which it could be attained required the analysis be predicated on the interpersonal comparisons of individual utility decisions. "The goal sought [for economics] is to make more easy practical measures to promote welfare" (10). To achieve this goal, the economist must be cognizant of two fundamental propositions, propositions of an entirely utilitarian nature:

> first, that the elements of welfare are states of consciousness and, perhaps, their relations; secondly, that welfare can be brought under the category of greater and less. (1932, 10)

The propositions of a utilitarian welfare economics, evident in the literature from (at least) the time of Bentham through John Stuart Mill, were held by Pigou to be too ambiguous to be of practical use, and thus he sought a redirection in the scope of the terms. Pigou's use of the term

---

22. "In economics, for the simple reason that its subject-matter is living and free men, direct experiment under conditions adequately controlled is hardly ever feasible" (Pigou [1920] 1932, 9).

"welfare," for example, did not necessarily imply *material* welfare. Rather, welfare could better be characterized as having a moral foundation and a central epistemic core. Welfare in fact must be understood on two different levels, as "goodness" and as "satisfaction." Goodness is a subjective and undefinable concept, commonly held to be identical with welfare; satisfaction is by contrast merely an effort to get around the complexities of utility.

One readily sees that Pigou consistently phrased his version of Utilitarianism in moral terms reminiscent of the ethical utilitarians; throughout, one sees reminders of an ethical base, as he classes "ethically inferior" satisfactions, and "debasing" and "elevating" influences (1932, 17). This is especially evident in the identification of the "good" as a normative social welfare criterion, the maximand in a social welfare calculus.[23] "Goodness" in fact replaces the Benthamite "satisfaction" or "happiness" as the basis of social welfare. In promoting the social welfare, the state must aim for the promotion of welfare as social "goodness" rather than welfare as the sum of individual "satisfactions," since it is always possible to be satisfied in ways injurious to the overall community good. As Pigou himself expressed the point in his 1951 "Some Aspects of Welfare Economics,"[24]

> welfare must be taken to refer either to the goodness of a man's state of mind or to the satisfactions embodied in it. . . . For the present purpose, I propose to make welfare refer to satisfactions, not goodness, thus leaving it possible that in certain circumstances, a government "ought"—granted that it "ought" to promote goodness—to foster a situation embodying less welfare (but more goodness) in preference to one embodying more welfare. (Pigou 1951, 288)

In his 1951 essay, in which he reiterated the position of *The Economics of Welfare,* Pigou defined the domain of the new subject as "concerned to investigate the dominant influence through which the economic welfare of the world, or of a particular country, is likely to be increased," with the role of the economist being "to suggest lines of action—or non-action—on the part of the State or of private persons that might foster such influences" (1951, 287). Welfare he defined here with respect to the *individual;* welfare resides in a "state of mind or consciousness," and it is most assuredly not to be conflated with material

---

23. Desirous of promoting social welfare, Pigou wished also to work within the confines of the existing social, political, and economic structure. In his 1939 "State Action and Laissez-Faire," Pigou gave the following justification for state action:

> The moral is plain. The issue about which popular writers argue—the principle of laissez-faire versus the principle of state action—is not an issue at all. There is no principle involved on either side. Each particular case must be decided on its own merits in all details of its concrete circumstances. (Pigou 1939, 217–18)

24. This essay was appended to later printings of *The Economics of Welfare.*

objects, which themselves are merely a *means* to welfare (288). "Satisfaction" and "utility" to Pigou represented the same concept, but were not synonymous with happiness or pleasure, since "a man's desires may be directed to other things than these and may be satisfied." In all, "a man's economic welfare is made up of his utilities" (288–89). As satisfactions embody more than simply the utilitarian foci of pleasure and happiness, there was more to the analysis of satisfaction than the mere identification of a correspondence between a Fechnerian stimulus and a response. Pigou was quite willing to accept that satisfaction and intensity of desire were not proportionate, since it is often the case that "people make mistakes, desiring certain objects in the hope of satisfactions which they do not in fact yield" (288). But as a fuller study would have taken him into areas he wished not to go, such as the foundations of morals and ethics, he limited his appraisal of this area. So welfare, the promotion of the greatest satisfaction, became nothing but the maximization of utility.

In general, satisfactions, pleasure, and utility, being intensive magnitudes (as opposed to length, temperature and height, which are extensive magnitudes), are not amenable to measure: "They are not the sort of thing that we can correlate with a series of cardinal numbers" (1951, 289). Yet for economics as a practical discipline, one needs to develop some device by which to quantify, both in individual and social terms, the utilitarian ends of happiness, well-being, and the good. This is not to claim that the state has no interest in the pursuit of other ideals—"liberty, for instance, the amenities of the family, spiritual needs and so on"—but rather to insist that these are ends in themselves and are outside the scope of welfare economics. Thus in an effort to facilitate study, Pigou needed to narrow the compass of welfare economics, and so constrain *welfare* to be *economic* welfare—"that part of welfare that is associated with the economic aspects of life" (287)—an area akin to satisfaction. The reason for the constraint was to provide a suitably compact field to which the tools of measurement could be applied:

> Hence, the range of our inquiry becomes restricted to that part of social welfare that can be brought directly or indirectly into relation with the measuring-rod of money. This part of welfare may be called economic welfare. (Pigou 1932, 11)

While one may thus conclude that, for Pigou, money afforded a means of measuring satisfaction, he offered a clarification. Money serves as an intermediary of sorts and does not serve as a direct measure of satisfaction; "the money which a person is prepared to offer for a thing measures directly, not the satisfaction he will get from the thing, but the intensity of his desire for it" (1932, 23). While satisfaction and utility could be (as we have seen above) taken to be associated concepts, intensity of desire was of an entirely different character, more consistent with the promotion of happiness or pleasure, but in any event an ethically neutral concept. Having clarified the problem, Pigou then stated his main point, this being

> that we are entitled to use the comparative amounts of money which a person is prepared to offer for two different things as a test of the comparative satisfactions which these things will yield to him, only on condition that the ratio between the intensities of desire that he feels for the two is equal to the ratio between the amounts of satisfaction which their possession will yield to him. (1932, 23)

Yet he was not sanguine about the possibility of such an objective measure, for he did not subscribe to the Fechnerian psychophysical approach. Nonetheless, he understood the implications of the use of such a measure, confident that, by employing it, one could succeed in establishing an *index* of welfare:

> What we wish to learn is, not how large welfare is, or has been, but how its magnitude would be affected by the introduction of causes which it is in the power of statesmen or private persons to call into being. . . . It will not, indeed, tell us how total welfare, after the introduction of an economic cause, will differ from what it was before; but it will tell us how total welfare will differ from what it would have been if that cause had not been introduced: and this, and not the other, is the information of which we are in search. (1932, 12)

With Marshall, Pigou agreed that such a measuring device as money could not in any event allow "us to measure anything more than small parts of a man's satisfaction," and even then it is valid only for small, incremental comparisons. Yet, while money "does not, therefore, enable us to correlate satisfactions with a series of cardinal numbers," it can nonetheless afford a means of *comparability* (Pigou 1951, 289–90). All that is required is a relation of greater or less, that will enable the economist to demonstrate relative differences. Comparability was likewise the rationale behind the use of marginal utility analysis; utility is not measurable (it represents a "feeling" of satisfaction), but in order to demonstrate interpersonal comparisons of satisfaction graphically (and algebraically),

> it is still legitimate in principle to imagine a marginal utilities curve and to say, not merely that it slopes down or up, but also that it slopes more or less steeply as we move along it from right to left. (1951, 290)

While suggesting that welfare may be measured indirectly by monetary expenditures, Pigou felt it to be more directly related to the size of the "national dividend" (national income) and to be in direct correspondence to the absolute share of income that accrues to the poor. The national dividend provides a suitable indicator of national welfare, since its maximization implies that the marginal social benefits of resources are equalized. In terms of the accrual of income to the poor, given separable and additive utility functions (allowing interpersonal comparisons of utility), one may reasonably equate welfare improvements and income transfers. Any "cause" which results in a greater distribution to the poor, "provided that it does not lead to a contraction in the size of the national dividend from any point of view, will, in general, increase economic welfare" (Pigou 1932, 89).[25]

3.3 Pigou's Method

Pigou's 1914 *Unemployment* is a particularly interesting work, in which he explicitly stated his views on the role of the economist. He identified the economist not as an unbiased, disinterested, outside observer and commentator on conditions as they appear, but rather as a compassionate and engaged social actor, along the lines of a social reformer. This compassion, akin to Smith's "sympathy," is the motivation behind the economist's study. He is not drawn to the subject out of some intellectual desire to apply the rules of dispassionate logic to an analysis of market forces and trading blocs; his motivation to study political economy had a larger, social dimension in which the application of sound principles could lead to a greater overall sense of material welfare. The economist's motivation thus develops from a

> sense that, in the world of business and of labour, justice stands with biassed scales; that men, women and children stagger often into an abyss that *might* be fenced and guarded; that the lives of many are darker than they need be; that the wealth, on which western nations pride themselves, bears but a faded flower of welfare. In these things lies the impulse to economic investigation; and the removal, or at least the mitigation, of the evils they portray is the goal of the economist's search. (Pigou 1914, 9–10; emphasis in original)

Yet the public persona of the economist has always been one of the distant, coldhearted scientific observer, a practitioner of the "dismal science," interested in the consequences of social and economic policy only to the extent that they represent deviations from an expected and perceived norm. Despite his description of the economist as a compassionate reformer with a clear, social conscience, Pigou did not dissent from the

---

25. "In other words, a larger proportion of the satisfaction yielded by the incomes of rich people comes from their *relative*, rather than from their absolute, amount. This part of it will not be destroyed if the incomes of all rich people are diminished together" (Pigou [1920] 1932, 90).

interpretation of economics as a rational, scientific discipline, but instead embraced it as the correct one. The sympathetic reformer can only succeed if he can base his reform proposals on rational scientific principles, divorced from personal feelings and the goals of political and social movements. The aloofness of the economic scientist he held to be a necessary condition, a condition which allowed him to act from reason and not from emotion:

> If the "art" of social reform is to be effective, the basis of it must be laid in a "science." . . . Their effort, though it may well be roused to action by the emotions, itself necessarily lies within the sphere of the intellect. Resentment at the evils investigated must be controlled, lest it militate against scientific exactitude in our study of their causes. (1914, 10–11)

This "art" can best be pursued through a rigorous process of definition and delineation. One must first define the subject matter so as to allow the audience to discern those aspects deemed important and appropriate for study, and those perceived as irrelevant and so beyond the focus of study. But one must also be mindful not to restrict the definition too greatly from its accepted usage so as to create more confusion than light. Indeed, Pigou began the analytical portion of the book by narrowing the field of inquiry through just such a definition of terms:

> There is no matter of principle involved: it is simply a question of the precise sense in which it is most convenient to use a particular common word. Hence, there are two conditions, and only two, that our definition must obey. It must be so fashioned as to prove a useful tool in the investigation we have in hand; and it must, subject to that condition, conform as closely as possible to the general drift of common usage. (1914, 13)

This statement of method, beginning with the clarification of concepts, was to set the tone for other of his works.

It was in his 1933 *The Theory of Unemployment* that Pigou expressed some distance from Marshall's overall approach. As with Marshall, Pigou held that theoretical economic models were best understood when constructed around a "mathematical skeleton." Marshall's *Principles* succeeded both as a "scientific" and as an instructive (practical) work precisely because of its internal structure, fleshed out and concealed by a literary narrative. But Pigou had reservations about Marshall's approach; the advantages gained by the general public through the clarity of literary exposition may have been at the expense of a true grasp by academic and other professional economists of Marshall's underlying process of thought, a dilemma that could have been rectified easily had he chosen to announce his mathematical structure more explicitly.[26] This Pigou thought his own work had succeeded in accomplishing.[27]

4 Keynes and the Eclipse of Benthamite Utilitarianism

4.1 The Roots of Reform

Although it is certainly true that Pigou has been and continues to be grossly underrated in respect to his impact on the development of Cambridge economics, the indisputable fact is that most people believe it was John Maynard (Lord) Keynes, Baron of Tilton (1883–1946),[28] who

---

26. "Would they [the readers of the *Principles*] not in the end have been better off had mathematical ideas been presented to them in mathematical form: and had they been advised to acquire a mastery of these few and simple tools?" (Pigou 1933, vi).

27. In the Preface to the second edition of his *Industrial Fluctuations*, Pigou stressed that the method of his study was that of "graphic representation" of the time-series data. While he may have preferred to employ numerical statistical analysis to handle the data, he chose instead this method for a very good reason: his "mastery of modern statistical technique" he felt was wanting (1929, vi). But he had another reason for relying on the graphic and not the numerical method, beyond that of his own limitations: he was interested in demonstrating "broad movements" of statistical series, not annual differences or exact relations:

> The precise quantitative relation between the movements of production indices and of employment indices does not greatly concern us. The point of practical importance is that, even when the trend is eliminated, production indices and employment indices have swings of *different* amplitude. (11; emphasis in original).
>
> It was these "swings" Pigou was most anxious to present and discuss, and the graphic method seemed the best means to the task.

28. As there are many biographies of Keynes, including R. F. Harrod (1951), Robert Skidelsky (1983, 1994), and Donald Moggridge (1992), we will present here only a few pertinent details of his life.

Keynes was the son of John Neville Keynes and Florence Ada Brown. Neville Keynes (1852–1949) was a graduate of University College, London, and Pembroke College, Cambridge. He served as University Lecturer in Moral Science at Cambridge from 1884 to 1911 and University registrar from 1910 to 1925. Neville Keynes is best known for his 1891 *The Scope and Method of Political Economy*. Florence Keynes (1861–1958) was very active politically, serving as mayor of Cambridge from 1932 to 1933.

Maynard was educated at Eton and King's College, Cambridge (Twelfth Wrangler, 1905). His first book, *Indian Currency and Finance*, derived from his work with the India Office following his graduation. His work at the Versailles Peace Conference ending World War I led to his 1919 *The Economic Consequences of the Peace*, a book which established his reputation as a profound economic and political intellectual force.

His fame was worldwide, and his interests extended far beyond economics. A member of the Bloomsbury Group (which also included Leonard and Virginia Woolf, Clive and Vanessa Bell, and Lytton Strachey), Keynes became an influential social force. In 1925, he married Lydia Lopokova, a Russian ballerina who had been a leading dancer in the Diaghilev company.

During the Second World War, Keynes was instrumental in the establishment of the international monetary framework arrangement agreed to at Bretton Woods.

ranks as the true architect of the new Cambridge School. While such a supposition may be far from the mark, it is nonetheless true that Keynes exerted a tremendous influence on Cambridge thought and on economic thought generally; for better or worse, his influence is being felt still.

It was Keynes's membership in the Apostles—technically, the Cambridge Conversazione Society, an august, secret, and self-selected assemblage of Cambridge philosophers, economists, metaphysicians, historians, et al., the self-consciously intellectual elite (including in their ranks privileged undergraduates)[29]—which is credited with the shaping of his intellectual outlook.[30] At a meeting of the Apostles in January 1904 Keynes read a very important paper, "Ethics in Relation to Conduct," which is telling as an antecedent to his later work in probability and his subsequent commentaries on Utilitarianism and ethics. R. M. O'Donnell, whose discovery of Keynes's early unpublished letters and manuscripts has led to a general recasting of his philosophical and economic roots, labeled the years 1903 through 1908 as "Keynes's philosophical apprenticeship, during which time, if he had an intended career, it was either that of philosopher, or, in common with the role models surrounding him, of moral scientist combining philosophy and economics" (R. M. O'Donnell 1989, 16).

Influenced greatly in his undergraduate education by the work of the philosophers George Edward Moore[31] (who in his 1903 *Principia Ethica* sought to provide a logical structure to ethics) and Bertrand Russell[32] (who attempted a similar program first with his 1903 *Principles of Mathematics* and later with Alfred North Whitehead[33] in the

---

29. The Society had been founded in 1820 by George Tomlinson, Bishop of Gibraltar, at St. John's College. Its membership included such "greats" as Henry Sidgwick, Alfred (Lord) Tennyson, Henry Maine, Alfred North Whitehead, Bertrand Russell, G. E. Moore, G. H. Hardy, Ludwig Wittgenstein, Frank P. Ramsey, R. B. Braithwaite, F. W. Maitland, and Ralph Hawtrey.

30. Two excellent book-length studies of the philosophical foundations of Keynes's economics are Anna Carabelli (1988) and Rod O'Donnell (1989), both extended versions of earlier doctoral dissertations at Cambridge. These accounts draw not only on Keynes's published work, but on unpublished archival material at King's College.

In addition, much work in this area has been undertaken at Cambridge University, particularly by Tony Lawson and Jochen Runde. See especially Lawson (1988) and Runde (1990, 1991). See also McCann (1994).

31. Moore (1873–1958) was graduated from Trinity College, Cambridge. He served as University Lecturer in Moral Science at Cambridge (1911–25) and Professor of Philosophy (1925–39).

32. Bertrand Arthur William (the third Earl) Russell (1872–1970) was tutored at home before attending Cambridge (Trinity College, Seventh Wrangler, 1893). He was a Fellow at Trinity from 1895 through 1901 and 1944 through 1970, serving as Lecturer from 1910 through 1916. Among his other works are *A History of Western Philosophy* (1945) and *Human Knowledge: Its Scope and Limits* (1948). He was awarded the Nobel Prize in Literature in 1950.

33. Whitehead (1861–1947) was educated at Trinity College, Cambridge (Fellow 1884–1947). He served as Professor of Applied Mathematics at Imperial College (1914–24) and Professor of Philosophy at Harvard (1924–37).

monumental [1910–13] *Principia Mathematica*), Keynes applied the same rigor to the subject of probability, desiring to give to the subject a solid logical structure.[34]

Keynes's economics were clearly rooted in the tradition of Marshall, his teacher at Cambridge. The identifying marks of the Marshallian tradition included its Victorian concern with the amelioration of social ills, especially in regard to the distribution of wealth, and the use of the biological analogy. We have already discussed the former, noting Marshall's sympathy for social movements, including efforts at wealth redistribution and his support of various cooperative ventures. It was the biological analogy that Marshall exploited so thoroughly in promoting a theory of moral evolution, wherein want-satisfaction would apply not to the base needs of survival, but to the higher (ethical and moral) aspects of life. The model also lent itself to the use of the historical method, but only in conjunction with an analytical framework. For Marshall, the methods of the Historical schools showed great promise in placing in context the theories of the economist, especially insofar as they could be made to relate to the concerns of the poor and the lower classes, the moral concerns he took to be the basis of the discipline.

Despite his Marshallian roots, Keynes understood economics somewhat differently from either Marshall or Pigou. In a letter to Roy Harrod dated July 4, 1938, he maintained that, in terms of analog, economics is akin neither to the biological nor the physical sciences, but rather is "a branch of logic, a way of thinking."[35] Economics is indeed an evolutionary discipline, as Marshall insisted, but as a *logical* discipline the evolutionary progress in economics applies not to the actors or to the constitution of the society, but applies instead to the manner of our understanding of the matter of economics. Economics is fundamentally a ratiocinative science, one which proceeds in a punctuated manner from abstract model to better abstract model. Progress is impeded when this punctuated movement is misunderstood and the evolution in the application of explanatory means becomes one of gradual, incremental change. One is then left with analytical tools inappropriate to the new reality.

> *Progress* in economics consists almost entirely in a progressive improvement in the choice of models. The grave fault of the later classical school, exemplified by Pigou, has been to overwork a too simple or out-of-date model, and in not seeing that progress lay in improving the model; whilst Marshall often confused his models,

---

34. The effort was not immediately accepted at Cambridge, due principally to the revolutionary thesis it set forth. (Of his examiners, Whitehead expressed reservations, while the logician W. E. Johnson found it overall a satisfactory effort.) After a series of major revisions, Keynes finally received his fellowship in 1909.

35. This passage and the following quotation are from the letter of July 4, 1938. It is reprinted in volume XIV of the *Collected Writings*, 295–97.

for devising which he had great genius, by wanting to be realistic and by being unnecessarily ashamed of lean and abstract outlines.

Just twelve days later, however, in another letter to Harrod, Keynes reflected not on the nature of the economic *model* but rather on the nature of the economic *agent*. Here he expressed a need "to emphasise strongly the point about economics being a moral science . . . [which] deals with introspection and with values . . . [and] with motives, expectation, psychological uncertainties."[36] The *form* of economics is logical and abstract; the *nature* of economics is the moral dimension as understood by the utilitarian ethicists. Again we see in evidence the Marshallian influence. Economics is a moral discipline, one which analyzes moral development through the use of analytical techniques.

Keynes and Utilitarianism   4.2

Keynes's economic, political, and social beliefs derived from his ethical views, specifically his understanding of Utilitarianism. In his 1921 *Treatise on Probability,* Keynes presented a philosophy of conduct consistent with a version of act-consequentialism, a form of Utilitarianism not inconsistent in many respects from that of Hutcheson and Bentham. There are, however, two major differences between Keynes's understanding of Utilitarianism and that of the Philosophic Radicals: the first deals with basing actions on *immediate* consequences, and the second involves Keynes's incorporation into utilitarian doctrine of his logical conception of probability.

Bentham, Hutcheson, et al. held the fundamental axiom of Utilitarianism to be the promotion of the greatest happiness of the greatest number. Under this description of the basis of action, as each agent could readily and mechanically determine those actions producing for him the greatest utility, the problem was determinate and had a mechanical solution. In Keynes's version, individuals are not assumed to be knowledgeable of the consequences of actions, or even necessarily cognizant of their own best interests; in short, the outcome of the application of the utility calculus is a contingent, probabilistic one.

Keynes readily admitted he was not the first to note the necessity of employing the probability calculus to utilitarian concerns. In chapter 26 of the *Treatise,* "The Application of Probability to Conduct," he maintained that the philosophers of the Port Royal had hit on the "correct" means of analyzing human action. He quoted approvingly from the *Port Royal Logic* of 1662 the statement,

> In order to judge of what we ought to do in order to obtain a good and to avoid an evil, it is necessary to consider not only the good and evil in themselves, but also the probability of their happening

---

36. In volume XIV of the *Collected Writings,* 299–301.

and not happening, and to regard geometrically the proportion
which all these things have, taken together. (Quoted in Keynes
1921, 340)

Along with the Port Royal philosophers, others such as Locke, Leibniz,
and Bishop Butler had likewise championed the importance of probability in such judgments. Butler's phrase, "To us probability is the very guide
of life" is indeed well known, and Keynes quoted it admiringly in support
of his contention.

It was the Philosophic Radicals and the later Cambridge realist
philosophers (such as Moore) who, Keynes insisted, had taken the use of
probability in analyzing judgments and beliefs to a new level, but had
nonetheless left large aspects of the problem unaddressed:

> With the development of a utilitarian ethics largely concerned with
> the summing up of consequences, the place of probability in ethical
> theory has become much more explicit. But although the general
> outlines of the problem are now clear, there are some elements of
> confusion not yet dispersed. (1921, 341)

To understand Keynes's views of Utilitarianism, we must begin with
a brief characterization of Moore's ethical system, to which Keynes posi-
tioned his own as a counter. In *Principia Ethica*, Moore maintained that
"the good" was a simple, undefined notion, known intuitively. In contrast to Sidgwick's "common sense" morality—basically a form of hedonistic Utilitarianism, but with an intuitionist base—Moore held that right
conduct should be predicated on the consequences of action.[37] The good
cannot be identified with pleasure or with any metaphysical entity, for to
do so would be to commit the "naturalistic fallacy." He thus rejected the
pleasure principle as a basis for Utilitarianism, arguing instead for a form
of "ideal" or "nonhedonistic" Utilitarianism, wherein "states of consciousness" are the important determinants of utility. In addition, Moore
held that "right" action is that action which leads to the greatest sum of
universal good through all future time, and that, given perfect foresight,
we could in fact have knowledge of the objective good. Thus under *ideal*
conditions, act-consequentialism (act-Utilitarianism) becomes the foundation of an ethical system, and general rules of conduct are irrelevant.

However, Moore was quick to point out the problem with act-
consequentialism: we are *not* capable of perfect foresight or foreknowledge. Since consequences extend through an infinite future and we can
have no knowledge of that future, it is impossible to know beforehand

---

37. On the relation between the philosophies of Sidgwick, Moore, and Keynes, see
Yuichi Shionoya (1991). Shionoya and Anna Carabelli (1988) denied that Keynes was a
consequentialist; Rod O'Donnell held that Keynes could not be understood otherwise than
as a consequentialist.

An excellent essay on the relation between Moore's philosophy and Keynes's economics
is Lawson (1993), which takes a position similar to that offered here.

which actions are "right" and allow of the greatest good. As foresight is unobtainable, it follows that we cannot attain even an *understanding* of the universal good. This unknowability led Moore to advocate a form of rule-Utilitarianism, a reliance on ethical strictures which must be followed in all cases; in adhering to the rules, the probability of promoting "right" conduct is greater than if we act according to circumstances.[38]

Whereas Moore had allowed that objects may be associated with "the good," for Keynes it is the resulting states of mind that are important. Further, knowledge of "good" states of mind "was a matter of direct inspection, of direct unanalysable intuition about which it is useless and impossible to argue" (Keynes 1938, 84). This is a legacy of Moore. Keynes regarded Moore's ethics as "nothing more than the application of logic and rational analysis to the material presented as sense-data"; this logical system of conduct allows that the "apprehension of good is exactly the same as our apprehension of green" as the essential apparatus involved is identical (86).

Yet Keynes proclaimed himself to have been at odds with Moore, in that Moore's advocacy of rules of conduct (a position in sympathy with Sidgwick and Bentham) was a position Keynes simply could not accept. He agreed with Moore's "religion," while rejecting his "morals," believing that "one of the greatest advantages of his religion, was that it made morals unnecessary" (1938, 82).[39] Specifically, he proclaimed to have ignored Moore's discussion of rules, since he (and others of his generation of Apostles) "entirely repudiated a personal liability on us to obey general rules. We claimed the right to judge every individual case on its merits, and the wisdom, experience and self-control to do so successfully" (97). This "judgment" of actions on their "merits" (which must include at least the immediate consequences of those actions), combined with "wisdom, experience and self-control" in making such judgments (suggesting that Keynes and his circle considered themselves capable of a greater degree of foreknowledge than the average mortal) is entirely consistent with act-consequentialism. While his interpretation of Moore caused him to in effect reduce Moore's philosophy to one of act-Utilitarianism (as Keynes claimed to have rejected the rule-utilitarian aspects of Moore's ethical theory), Keynes nonetheless regarded it as superior to Bentham's design, a philosophy of ethics which he claimed had been at the very root of societal ills:

> I do now regard that [Benthamite Utilitarianism] as the worm which has been gnawing at the insides of modern civilisation and is

---

38. For an excellent introduction to Moore's philosophy, including the problems involved, see A. J. Ayer (1984).

39. Moore "had one foot on the threshold of the new heaven, but the other foot in Sidgwick and the Benthamite calculus and the general rules of correct behaviour" (Keynes 1938, 82).

responsible for its present moral decay. We used to regard the Christians as the enemy, because they appeared as the representatives of tradition, convention and hocus-pocus. In truth it was the Benthamite calculus, based on an over-valuation of the economic criterion, which was destroying the quality of the popular Ideal. (1938, 96–97)

For Keynes the break was cathartic: "it was this escape from Bentham, joined with the unsurpassable individualism of our philosophy, which has served to protect the whole lot of us from the final *reductio ad absurdum* of Benthamism known as Marxism" (1938, 97). Nonetheless, as we shall see later, despite his denials, Keynes ultimately accepted even Moore's "morals," as he came to regard certain general rules of conduct—conventions—as necessary to rational deliberation.

Keynes's difficulty with ethical philosophy, from Benthamite Utilitarianism to the ethics of Moore, revolved around the use of mathematical expectation and the implied correspondence of utility calculations with the calculation of gaming odds:

> Normal ethical theory at the present day, if there can be said to be any such, makes two assumptions: first, that degrees of goodness are numerically measurable and arithmetically additive, and second, that degrees of probability also are numerically measurable. This theory goes on to maintain that what we ought to add together, when, in order to decide between two courses of action, we sum up the results of each, are the "mathematical expectations" of the several results. "Mathematical expectation" is a technical expression originally derived from the scientific study of gambling and games of chance, and stands for the product of the possible gain with the probability of attaining it. In order to obtain, therefore, a measure of what ought to be our preference in regard to various alternative courses of action, we must sum for each course of action a series of terms made up of the amounts of good which may attach to each of its possible consequences, each multiplied by its appropriate probability. (Keynes 1921, 343–44)

Keynes reserved doubt as to the validity of the first assumption, that goodness is a quality amenable to arithmetic expression. To the second assumption—that probabilities are by nature numerically measurable—he was emphatically opposed, noting that (as we have seen was maintained by Edgeworth) beliefs are such that any attempt at measurement is futile and may be meaningless, and going further to insist that even a ranking may not be possible.[40] In respect to Moore's ethics, since the past

---

40. In his 1930 *Treatise on Money* he revisited the problem of the indeterminacy of numerical comparisons and the problem of the aggregation of dissimilar magnitudes:

> This difficulty in making precise quantitative comparisons is the same as arises in the case of many other famous concepts, namely all of those which are

is not necessarily a guide to the future, one cannot evaluate future consequences of present acts, but can only evaluate actions on the basis of current knowledge and immediate consequences. All of these "difficulties" at arriving at a consistent, reasonable index of comparison lead to the abandonment of efforts to gauge in any objective and definite way a value for future actions. Thus was Keynes led to his critique of rule-Utilitarianism, the "morals" of Moore; since one cannot revert to mathematical expectation in evaluating the consequences of actions, one cannot require adherence to ethical rules based on the premise that such rules will lead to the maximization of "the good." Absent such an index one is led to rely on current experience.

Yet in the 1936 *General Theory of Employment, Interest, and Money* Keynes can be seen to have retreated somewhat from his position in the *Treatise on Probability*. By 1936 he was willing to acknowledge circumstances in which rules played an important, indeed critical, role in decision making, and he thus no longer felt obliged to dismiss so cavalierly Moore's "morals." In general terms, Keynes was willing to concede that the following of general rules of conduct—"customs" or "conventions"—could be rational and may even lead to socially beneficial outcomes. In the *General Theory* he accepted, for example, that it may be a prudent course of action for investors to adhere to conventions in the face of an unpredictable and volatile market: one may be rational in assuming that certain patterns of behavior will persist absent some motivation for considering a change:

> In practice we have tacitly agreed, as a rule, to fall back on what is, in truth, a *convention*. The essence of this convention . . . lies in assuming that the existing state of affairs will continue indefinitely, except in so far as we have specific reasons to expect a change. This does not mean that we really believe that the existing state of affairs will continue indefinitely. . . . We are assuming, in effect, that the existing market valuation, however arrived at, is uniquely *correct* in relation to our existing knowledge of the facts . . . , and that it will only change in proportion to changes in this knowledge.
>
> Nonetheless the above conventional method of calculation will be compatible with a considerable measure of continuity and stability in our affairs, *so long as we can rely on the maintenance of the convention.* (Keynes 1936a, 152; emphasis in original)

Conventions are useful heuristic devices which aid the individual in the decision process. For example, a convention may be accepted so long

---

complex or manifold in the sense that they are capable of variations of degree in more than one mutually incommensurable direction at the same time. . . . The same difficulty arises whenever we ask whether one thing is superior in degree to another *on the whole,* the superiority depending on the resultant of several attributes which are each variable in degree but in ways not commensurable with one another. (Keynes 1930, 88; emphasis in original)

as it is believed that exogenous "shocks" are of little import, and that the market will maintain the convention irrespective of the expectations of the individual participants. The trend of current opinion, thus, is *not* the sum of the opinions of the individual participants; it is not a measure derived with respect to individual beliefs and anticipations, but is rather an aggregate measure. The problem with relying on such a convention is that it is highly tenuous, subject to "waves of optimistic and pessimistic sentiment" (1936a, 154). What we may come to accept as a rule for action may itself come to be unreliable as a guide to action, as "the psychology of a large number of ignorant individuals is liable to change violently as the result of a sudden fluctuation of opinion due to factors which do not really make much difference . . . ; since there will be no strong roots of conviction to hold it steady" (154).[41]

It is in the realm of conventions that we see emerge Keynes's concept of "economic man." Of interest here is his sympathy to the proposition of Hume, that reason supports the passions and does not drive them. Hume's argument rested on the fundamental nature of our uncertainty as to the consequences of our actions (epistemic uncertainty), an understanding which Keynes shared. This in turn molded Keynes's interpretation of "economic man" as a being incapable of rigorous utilitarian calculations. Consider the following from a letter to Hugh Townshend dated February 7, 1938:[42]

> Generally speaking, in making a decision we have before us a large number of alternatives, none of which is demonstrably more "rational" than the others, in the sense that we can arrange in order of

---

41. In his 1923 *A Tract on Monetary Reform,* his first major reflection on the role of expectations in economics following the philosophical treatment in the *Treatise on Probability,* Keynes wrote what has become one of the most popular quotations in the whole of the Keynesian literature. The passage, a disquisition on the meaning of the long run in economic life, reads as follows:

> But this *long run* is a misleading guide to current affairs. *In the long run* we are all dead. Economists set themselves too easy, too useless a task if in tempestuous seasons they can only tell us that when the storm is long past the ocean is flat again. (Keynes 1923, 65; emphasis in original)

Keynes was ultimately led to consider that expectations were the result of "animal spirits" and not a systematic calculation of mathematical expectation. It is to "animal spirits," for instance, that one can point in order to explain the volatility of investment spending. It is for this reason that Keynes suggested the state exercise some control over investment, thus mitigating the fluctuations caused by such unpredictable waves of investor behavior (1936a, 164). But he also realized that "animal spirits" were necessary to the investment process. Lacking these capricious impulses, there would no longer exist the vital, energetic, entrepreneurial spirit, the spirit of enterprise. "Thus if the animal spirits are dimmed and the spontaneous optimism falters, leaving us to depend on nothing but a mathematical expectation, enterprise will fade and die" (162). Opinions are by themselves factors of significance in economic valuation.

42. Published in volume XXIX of the *Collected Writings,* 293–94.

merit the sum aggregate of the benefits obtainable from the complete consequences of each. To avoid being in the position of Buridan's ass, we fall back, therefore, and necessarily do so, on motives of another kind, which are not "rational" in the sense of being concerned with the evaluation of consequences, but are decided by habit, instinct, preference, desire, will, etc.

Thus, given the inability to calculate on the basis of the utilitarian calculus, we must of necessity relate to the Humean expedient, a second-best solution.

Acts, Rules, and Communitarianism   4.3

While Keynes's economics was influenced by Marshall, and his ethical philosophy derived from Moore, his political views were shaped in large measure by the political philosophy of Edmund Burke (1729–97). From Burke Keynes appropriated the doctrine of means and, oddly enough, his view of the necessity for following moral conventions—"those classes of action which lead to good results in the vast majority of cases" (1936a, 277). This extended to his understanding of Utilitarianism. Whereas Hume had interpreted utilitarianism as an *ethical* principle, Burke (and Keynes) viewed it as *political* one, oriented to means rather than ends. As we have seen above, Keynes focused his analysis on a form of act-Utilitarianism, wherein actions are understood to be related to circumstances. His dispute with Moore lay in a belief that rules need not be followed blindly (a position Moore did not in fact hold), since the rules themselves are contingent. Yet we have also seen Keynes willing to adhere to rules (in the form of conventions) as guides to behavior in the presence of variability, as a means of reducing epistemic uncertainty. As quoted in O'Donnell's study of the foundations of Keynes's thought, Keynes gave, in an unpublished 1905 essay entitled "Modern Civilisation," the following justification for in effect accepting Moore's "morals" in following rules of conduct:

> There are rules, which though not immutable have nevertheless so wide and general a validity that they ought to be obeyed as universally as if they were themselves universal. We may accept the experience of the race in certain matters—in fact we *ought* so to accept it—and not all cases of action ought to be decided by us individually. We shall do well, as Burke says, to avail ourselves of the general bank and capital of nations and of ages. It is out of this that arises that class of actions commonly known as duties. . . . (Keynes 1905; in R. M. O'Donnell 1989, 110; emphasis in original).

It is evident from this passage, as O'Donnell noted, that Keynes held there to be "no universally true political principles, no abstract political ends, and no ideal political systems or forms of government. . . . His political philosophy was thus corollary to his theory of practical reason" (R. M. O'Donnell 1989, 273–74). The foundation of political "truths" lay in ethics, specifically in the form of act-Utilitarianism he espoused in the *Treatise on Probability* and his early efforts at confronting Moore and Burke. Keynes's political writings, in fact, demonstrate his lack of a guiding political philosophy, as he variously stressed themes of individualism and communitarianism, but always as means rather than as ends in themselves. His motive was to transform the debate through a persuasive rhetoric. As O'Donnell suggested:

> The central presuppositions of his view were that *in the long run* the most powerful motive forces in politics were centred on ideas, opinion, persuasion and reason, and that to effect lasting, non-violent social change it was sufficient patiently to disseminate reasonable views which addressed and persuaded the intelligence of those who influenced affairs at whatever level. (R. M. O'Donnell 1989, 274; emphasis in original)

The contrast with Hume is instructive. Hume's statement that reason should only be a tool to ("a slave of") the advancement of "the passions"—meaning that motives were and should be the driving instrument in action—did not imply that selfishness would inevitably rule over altruistic tendencies. Rather, *any* "passion" whatever could be sufficient to justify actions. In Hume's memorable (but often imperfectly quoted) phrase, "'Tis not contrary to reason to prefer the destruction of the whole world to the scratching of my finger. 'Tis not contrary to reason for me to chuse my total ruin, to prevent the least uneasiness of an *Indian* or person wholly unknown to me" (Hume, 1739/40, Bk.II, §III, 463; emphasis in original). Yet consistent with his own views on probability and expectations, Keynes, like Burke, ultimately preferred the known present to the unknown past, and thus he could not but be disposed to an adherence to stabilizing rules of conduct, while being at the same time reform-minded (meaning opposed to stasis):

> Burke ever held, and held rightly, that it can seldom be right to sacrifice the well-being of a nation for a generation, to plunge whole communities in distress, or to destroy a beneficent institution for the sake of a supposed millennium in the comparatively remote future. We can never know enough to make the chance worth taking, and the fact that cataclysms in the past have sometimes inaugurated lasting benefits is no argument for cataclysms in general. (O'Donnell 1989, 278; quoting Keynes, "The Political Doctrines of Edmund Burke," 1904)

As against Hume, Keynes thus held to a more socially responsible, community ethic; given insufficient foresight with which to arrive at

individual utility values, "[i]t is therefore the happiness of our own contemporaries that is our main concern; we should be very chary of sacrificing large numbers of people for the sake of a contingent end, however
advantageous that may appear" (Keynes, quoted in Skidelsky 1994, 62).

In the 1924 Sidney Ball Lecture at Oxford, entitled "The End of
Laissez-Faire,"[43] Keynes addressed directly the topic of the place of the
individual versus the community, what we have here identified as the
Hobbes problem. In this essay, Keynes began by noting the evolution of
utilitarian ideas. The seventeenth-century notions of the social compact
and Natural Rights had eclipsed the divine right of kings, and these
important notions were buttressed in the mid–eighteenth century by the
utilitarian ideal. Locke and Hume (among others) employed the new
ethic of utility, in conjunction with the social compact, to give structure to
their notions of individual rights.

> The compact presumed rights in the individual; the new ethics,
> being no more than a scientific study of the consequences of ra-
> tional self-love, placed the individual at the centre. (Keynes 1926,
> 13)

This placement was important because it "furnished a satisfactory intellectual foundation to the rights of property and to the liberty of the
individual in possession to do what he liked with himself and with his
own" (1926, 13).

For Keynes, while Utilitarianism provided a vehicle for the enlargement of individual rights and a means to the establishment of an individualist ethic, it also laid the foundation for the collectivist state. Despite
being synonymous with individual actions, Bentham's interpretation of
the maxim "the greatest happiness of the greatest number" actually applied to *community* ends, in contrast to Hume's conception as a means to
the promotion of *individual* ends, and so moved Utilitarianism from an
ethical doctrine into the realm of social welfare. Thus, with Bentham we
see the change in design, as from utilitarian doctrine emerged the *social*
contract and the perception of the *general* will.

Further, Utilitarianism actually became useful as a justification for
communitarian and socialist programs. In Keynes's phrase, "[i]t harmonized the conservative individualism of Locke and Hume with the socialism and democratic equality of Rousseau and Paley" (1926, 14). Mandeville's "private vices, public virtues" and Smith's "invisible hand" were, as
we have seen, different interpretations of the movement toward a social
harmony (although in his essay Keynes ignored Mandeville). This "harmony" of the private and the public good Keynes held had been enshrined
in classical economic doctrine as the principle of laissez-faire, a "scientific"

---

43. "The End of Laissez-Faire" was published in *The New Republic* in 1924 and
released as a pamphlet in 1926. We use here *The New Republic* article.

principle designed to demonstrate the "inexpediency" of governmental interference with the activities of individuals in everyday affairs.

> The principle of laissez-faire had arrived to harmonize individualism and socialism, and to make at one Hume's egoism with the greatest good of the greatest number. The political philosopher could retire in favor of the business man—for the latter could attain the philosopher's summum bonum by just pursuing his own private profit. (1926, 14)

In addition to the *economic* justification of laissez-faire, Keynes pointed to the emergence of a *scientific* one as well. By the mid–nineteenth century (at the end of the first phase of the industrial revolution) Charles Darwin had arrived on the scene with a theory that would serve as a scientific buttress to the economics of laissez-faire. Not only could the "scientific" explanation of the origin of species explain the development of mankind—implying the illegitimacy of the old philosophy of a divine hand in the creation of the universe—but it could also provide justification for the current social order:

> The economists were teaching that wealth, commerce and machinery were the children of free competition—that free competition built London. But the Darwinians could go one better than that— free competition had built Man. The human eye was no longer the demonstration of design, miraculously contriving all things for the best; it was the supreme achievement of chance, operating under conditions of free competition and laissez-faire. The principle of the survival of the fittest could be regarded as a vast generalization of the Ricardian economics. (1926, 14)

With such a firm foundation upon which to structure an individualist ethic, one could only conclude (as indeed the classical economists did) that schemes of centralized control were not only unnecessary, but were perhaps contrary to universal design:

> Socialistic interferences became, in the light of this grander synthesis, not merely inexpedient, but impious, as calculated to retard the onward movement of the mighty process by which we ourselves had risen like Aphrodite out of the primeval slime of Ocean. (1926, 14)

Thus, efforts at coordination of individual effort to the promotion of social welfare were seen by the ethical utilitarians and the classical political economists as not only unnecessary, but (as in Mandeville) counterproductive as well. The laissez-faire approach could achieve the goal of social welfare not through design, but through the random workings of spontaneous order.

Having set forth a sequence of events and ideas which he suggested had led to the contemporary understanding of the principle of laissez-faire and to a general distrust of governmental action and motive, Keynes felt compelled to clarify the record (and in the process absolve the economists of any guilt in the matter). Smith, for one, was exonerated by the claim that he never really advocated a utilitarian ethic, but rather had a theistic foundation to his system of natural order. The real culprits in the current misunderstanding were Bentham—"not an economist at all"—and the popularizers of early political economy—Jane Marcet and Harriet Martineau—who had incompletely distilled the essence of Utilitarianism as an ethical and moral system into a few popular but misleading phrases and presented it as a statement of economic and social welfare. In so removing the philosophy from its ethical moorings, what was left was a superstructure in search of a foundation, and any foundation would suffice. In addition, each of the competing visions—Marxism and protectionism, specifically—was logically flawed and so acted to reinforce the legitimacy of laissez-faire by failing to provide a cogent alternative vision.[44]

The fallacy of laissez-faire Keynes himself believed was based on three misperceptions: (1) production and consumption are mechanical, not organic; (2) agents have foresight and foreknowledge; and (3) agents can *acquire* foreknowledge (1926, 38). In addition, he attacked the very citadel of Classical Political Economy in questioning the validity of the notion of the "invisible hand" and spontaneous order as necessarily conducive to the social interest. Smith's sympathy and self-love are not sufficient motivations to guarantee a just social order. Nor is it clear (as we have shown above) that the individual actor is even aware of his own self-interest, let alone competent enough to pursue it. Classical economic theory simply did not for Keynes provide any intellectual basis for the deduction of such propositions concerning the creation and management of social order:

> It is *not* a correct deduction from the principles of economics that enlightened self-interest always operates in the public interest. Nor is it true that self-interest generally *is* enlightened; more often individuals acting separately to promote their own ends are too ignorant or too weak to attain even these. Experience does *not* show that individuals, when they make up a social unit, are always less clear-sighted than when they act separately. (1926, 39)

(Of course, as we have mentioned, Keynes did not consider Mandeville's "solution," wherein it became unnecessary and indeed counterproductive to reform individual virtue in order to promote the social good.)

Again, Keynes turned to Burke to make his key points, this time on

---

44. Keynes wrote of Marxism: "Marxian socialism must always remain a portent to the historians of opinion—how a doctrine so illogical and so dull can have exercised so powerful and enduring an influence over the minds of men, and, through them, the events of history" (1926, 38).

the question of the role of government. Keynes quoted Burke to the effect that the problem to be addressed was one of coordination, that is, " 'to determine what the state ought to take upon itself to direct by the public wisdom, and what it ought to leave, with as little interference as possible, to individual exertion' " (1926, 39). Individual initiative and private enterprise have crucial roles in society and the economy, and the state should most assuredly not endeavor to take on those roles for which the private sector has an obvious and demonstrable advantage. The key for Keynes was to distinguish the sphere of government and the sphere of private industry, so as to allow the government a role in the activities for which the private sector is either ineffective or uninterested. But he was not necessarily resigned to state interferences as an alternative to private action; rather Keynes's "solution" was interesting, insofar as it relied on an evolution of institutions that was already evident. Instead of focusing on a delineation of state and private interests and control, with interests clearly defined, he suggested the creation of "semi-autonomous bodies within the state—bodies whose criterion of action within their own field is solely the public good as they understand it, and from whose deliberations motives of private advantage are excluded" (39). To this end he suggested the model of the joint-stock company, that is, a socialized private enterprise, wherein ownership has been divorced from control. Thus the model of the modern corporation amounted to a reconstitution of "mediæval conceptions of separate autonomies," a preferable alternative to "organs of the central government" (39–40).

Keynes's desire in all this was to eliminate variability in social and economic affairs, a theme evident in his early work in probability. The control of credit, the dissemination of business "facts," the direction of saving and investment, and even efforts at directing the "quality" of the population (a question of eugenics) were concerns Keynes felt could be better handled by a centralized authority than by individual initiatives. The consultant-administrator, as a disinterested party desiring only the most efficient means for the achievement of a social end, could serve to limit the wild gyrations that seemed endemic to uncoordinated individual interactions (of the Mandevillian type). Yet Keynes's suggestions were not designed to *replace* the capitalist, free-market economy with a centralized command system, but rather to *reinforce* it, to make it socially responsible while still allowing a central role to individual action. The administrator was not to control *all* economic activity, merely that activity prone to the greatest variability.

As Robert Skidelsky remarked, "The End of Laissez-Faire" did not succeed in its indictment of classical Utilitarianism because Keynes presented mere summary statements of a host of objections to the doctrine. Keynes gave no indication as to the specifics of his disagreement with laissez-faire, instead resorting to sweeping generalizations regarding "obvious" excesses resulting from unconstrained individualism. "As a result we are left in the dark about whether the *laissez-faire* project cannot, as a matter of fact, be realised in given circumstances, whether it cannot be realised under any conceivable or probable set of circumstances, or whether it would be wrong to try to realise it, even if it could be" (Skidelsky 1994, 225).[45]

In "The Dilemma of Modern Socialism" (1932), Keynes commented more explicitly on the appropriate route to socialism. Noting that socialists in general had always been willing to pursue "economically unsound" policies in the quest for the revolutionary ideal and in the pursuit of "higher goods" such as "justice, equality, beauty, or the greater glory of the republic," his own desire was "to define the socialist programme as aiming at political power, with a view to doing in the first instance what is economically sound, in order that, later on, the community may become rich enough to *afford* what is economically unsound" (Keynes 1932, 155–56; emphasis in original). The capitalist system of production was simply the most efficient means for the creation of wealth ever devised, and it was *within* this system that Keynes thought the realization of the grand ideal should be made. "For it will have to be on the basis of increased resources, not on the basis of poverty, that the grand experiment of the ideal republic will have to be made" (156). The problem lay in education, and in keeping to the ideal of the betterment of the community, despite the fact that material progress is being made. He saw the task as being "to thrive, not on the vapours of misery and discontent, but on the living energy of the passion for right construction and the right building up of a worthy society" (157).[46]

By 1933 Keynes had changed somewhat his outlook. In a lecture of April 19, 1933, entitled "National Self-Sufficiency,"[47] he criticized the appeal to the accountant's calculus "as a test of the advisability of any course of action sponsored by private or by collective action" (Keynes 1933, 763). Such a criterion had led to the creation of lucrative "slums" instead of extravagant "wonder cities," and to a general "distrust [of] conclusions which should be obvious, out of a reliance on a system of financial accounting which casts doubt on whether such an operation will 'pay' " (764). It is this "rule of self-destructive financial calculation" which led us to "destroy the beauty of the countryside because the unappropriated splendors of nature have no economic value" (764). It is the sacrifice of "other values" to the economic which had led to the inability

---

45. Skidelsky further argued that Keynes had an "anti-market, anti-democratic bias," one which "was driven by a belief in scientific expertise and personal disinterestedness" (1994, 228).

46. In response, A. L. Rowse, a Labour Party apologist and Shakespeare scholar, proclaimed Keynes's position to be "so closely allied to socialism as to be hardly distinguishable from it" (1932, 409). He maintained that the Labour Party Keynes criticized in fact no longer really existed.

47. This was published in *The New Statesman and Nation* and *The Yale Review*. We use the version in the latter.

of the system "to exploit to the utmost the possibilities for economic wealth afforded by the progress of our technique" (765). The remedy Keynes perceived to be the promotion of cultural values, with the "accountant's profit" being afforded secondary status:

> If I had the power to-day, I would most deliberately set out to endow our capital cities with all the appurtenances of art and civilization on the highest standards of which the citizens of each were individually capable, convinced that what I could create, I could afford—and believing that money thus spent not only would be better than any dole but would make unnecessary any dole. For with what we have spent on the dole in England since the War we could have made our cities the greatest works of man in the world. (1933, 764)

Thus we see that the change of emphasis has to be with respect to the *state,* and not the individual.

> It is the state, rather than the individual, which needs to change its criterion. It is the conception of the Secretary of the Treasury as the chairman of a sort of joint stock company which has to be discarded. Now, if the functions and purposes of the state are to be thus enlarged, the decision as to what, broadly speaking, shall be produced within the nation and what shall be exchanged with abroad, must stand high among the objects of policy. (1933, 765)

We come now to the place in all this of the *General Theory,* a work which has been described as "a variegated patchwork applied to the classical coat, which had become frayed and torn by the wear and strain of a society growing and changing too rapidly to be well suited with the same old clothes" (E. S. Johnson and H. G. Johnson 1974, 262). The Victorian ethic is discernible throughout the *General Theory,* especially in chapter 24, "Concluding Notes on the Social Philosophy Towards Which the General Theory Might Lead." Here Keynes reiterated his earlier comments concerning the positive attributes of private wealth-creation and property-holding, and even pointed to the deleterious social effects which their removal might occasion:

> There are valuable human activities which require the motive of money-making and the environment of private wealth-ownership for their full fruition. Moreover, dangerous human proclivities can be canalised into comparatively harmless channels by the existence of opportunities for money-making and private wealth, which, if they cannot be satisfied in this way, may find their outlet in cruelty, the reckless pursuit of personal power and authority, and other forms of self-aggrandisement. (Keynes 1936a, 374)

So the pursuit of personal wealth and private, individual gain is a civilizing influence, and the state would be well-advised to encourage such activity. While not exactly a rephrasing of Mandeville's position, it is not difficult to see in Keynes's statement a Mandevillian presence. Unlike Mandeville's hive, however, Keynes envisioned for his society a critical role for the state, this being the *management* for social purposes of human nature. It is not conceivable that in the immediate or foreseeable future man's nature can be altered to induce a more communitarian attitude, so we must be resigned to the need for the exploitation of pecuniary motivation in the pursuit of social betterment:

> Though in the ideal commonwealth men may have been taught or inspired or bred to take no interest in the stakes, it may still be wise and prudent statesmanship to allow the game to be played, subject to rules and limitations, so long as the average man, or even a significant section of the community, is in fact strongly addicted to the money-making passion. (1936a, 374)

Not unlike the ethical utilitarians (the Philosophic Radicals) and even the utopian socialists, Keynes accepted that state action was absolutely crucial in "guiding" certain aspects of individual initiative in the promotion of a social goal. In Keynes's case, the goals were an increase in the propensity to consume, and the channeling of investment in more efficient and socially desirable directions: "I conceive . . . that a somewhat comprehensive socialisation of investment will prove the only means of securing an approximation to full employment" (1936a, 378). But he was not above combining state action and private initiative in handling social and efficiency problems, a position we have seen presented in "The End of Laissez-Faire." In the *General Theory* Keynes again made his case, this time being abundantly clear that he was not advocating state control over industry or individual private initiative; the fundamental principles of ownership of productive means and the right of property were too important in promoting an efficient use of resources to replace them with a central authority the motives of which were at best suspect and at worst could lead to tyranny. State responsibility was in guiding action, not in compelling it:

> . . . no obvious case is made out for a system of State Socialism which would embrace most of the economic life of the community. It is not the ownership of the instruments of production which it is important for the State to assume. If the State is able to determine the aggregate amount of resources devoted to augmenting the instruments and the basic rate of reward to those who own them, it will have accomplished all that is necessary. Moreover, the necessary measures of socialisation can be introduced gradually and without a break in the general traditions of society. (1936a, 378)

Despite his protestations against the Classical Economics, Keynes viewed his prescriptions as a means not to its overthrow but rather to the assurance of its continued existence. While Classical Economics had been predicated on an individualist ethic, the social harmony envisioned simply did not emerge as a spontaneous order. Thus Keynes felt that some sort of order must be instituted *before* the classical structure could function to produce the desired and promised harmony. Specifically, the problem lay in the establishment of a level of output consistent with full employment. The actions of the state he felt were necessary in order to secure this level of output; after this was achieved,

> then there is no objection to be raised against the classical analysis of the manner in which private self-interest will determine what in particular is produced, in what proportions the factors of production will be combined to produce it, and how the value of the final product will be distributed between them. (1936a, 378–79)

The *economy* need not be socialized; the state need confine its activities to providing a starting point for the exercise of individual initiative. This Keynes felt was completely consistent with classical teaching:

> the modern classical theory has itself called attention to various conditions in which the free play of economic forces may need to be curbed or guided. But there will still remain a wide field for the exercise of private initiative and responsibility. Within this field the traditional advantages of individualism will still hold good. (1936a, 379–80)

5 Joan Robinson and Cambridge Socialism

Much of twentieth-century economics developed directly along Keynesian lines or as a result of a challenge to Keynesian ideas. Within Cambridge itself, there emerged a strain of thought along the lines of Keynes's philosophy but with a decidedly more communitarian flavor. Of those in the Keynesian "Cambridge" circus—a discussion group gathered for the express purpose of critiquing Keynes's *A Treatise on Money,* but which extended its mandate and offered theoretical insights which Keynes himself eventually incorporated into the structure of the *General Theory*—Joan Violet (Maurice) Robinson (1903–83)[48] and Piero Sraffa (1898–

---

48. Joan Robinson was the great-granddaughter of Frederic Maurice (1805–72), a nineteenth-century Cantabrigian Christian Socialist and Apostle who served as professor of moral philosophy (1866–72). A graduate of St. Paul's School and Girton College, Cambridge (1927), she was appointed assistant lecturer in 1931, but it took another six years before she would reach the rank of lecturer, and it was not until 1949 that she attained the position of reader. In 1965, she became a full professor, and was named an honorary fellow of King's in 1970.

1983)[49] may be viewed as the most significant exemplars of this approach. We will focus attention here on the role played by Robinson.

Best known for her exposition of a theory of monopolistic competition, the 1933 *The Economics of Imperfect Competition* (which she was later to all but repudiate), Robinson later attempted to integrate the capital theory of the brilliant Marxian writers Rosa Luxemburg (1870–1919) and Michal Kalecki (1899–1970)[50] with Keynes's efforts at a dynamic macroeconomics. She and a coterie of devoted students eventually turned to the theories of Kalecki as their preferred extension of the Keynesian model. Robinson in fact described herself as a "left-wing Keynesian":

> You might about say that I am the archetypal left-wing Keynesian. I was drawing pinkish rather than bluish conclusions from the *General Theory* long before it was published. (Robinson 1951, vol. 4, 264)

In line with her "left-wing Keynesianism" was the strong belief that property should be subject to state control and the income derived be subject to redistribution efforts. As capital reflects the stock of technical knowledge in a society, a base which is in effect a social good, it follows that the fruits arising from the exploitation of this social good should accrue not to any single individual who happens to hold title to the productive resource, but to society as a whole. Thus productive factors should be held socially, not individually.

At Cambridge, Robinson fell under the influence of Marshall, Pigou, and Keynes. Her expressed purpose in pursuing the study of economics

---

49. Born in Italy, Sraffa obtained a doctorate in law at the University of Turin in 1920, under Luigi Einaudi. After a period at the LSE (1921–22), he held several university positions (including lecturer at the University of Perugia [1923] and a chair at the University of Cagliari [1926], which he continued to hold until his death). He came to Cambridge at the behest of Keynes in 1927.

His most important work came after being named librarian of the Marshall Library, in which capacity he undertook the collection of Ricardo's works. In 1934 he was elected a fellow of Trinity College.

50. Born in Poland, Kalecki began his academic studies in engineering at the Warsaw and Gdansk Polytechic Institutes. In 1929 he took a position at the Institute for Research on Business Cycles and Prices in Warsaw, where he published an important pamphlet entitled *Essays on Business Cycle Theory*. (The importance of this work lies in its statement of the theory of effective demand, which predates the theory as stated by Keynes in 1936.) With the assistance of a Rockefeller grant, he traveled to Sweden and Britain, where he made the acquaintance of Gunnar Myrdal, Bertil Ohlin, Keynes, Joan Robinson, and Sraffa.

For political reasons, Kalecki left the Institute and returned to England. He accepted a position at the Institute of Economics and Statistics at Oxford, where he worked from 1940 to 1945, after which he worked at the United Nations in New York (1946–54). Returning to Poland in 1955, he became chairman of the Commission on Perspective Planning, and later (1961) the Central School of Planning and Statistics.

was a very Pigovian one, namely, to understand the reasons behind the persistence of poverty and unemployment.

In her commencement address given at the University of Maine (1977), Robinson took up the question of the place of morality in economics. She agreed that Smith had been credited (or blamed) wrongly with having advocated the philosophy of laissez-faire as the means to social betterment and an increase in social welfare. As we have seen, while he indeed suggested that the pursuit of self-interest would lead to a social optimum, it had generally been forgotten by interpreters of his work that Smith also required the individuals in the society to have a moral compass; he actually assumed this to be the case. He did not argue "that individuals have no need to consider the collective results of their behaviour," but instead "took it for granted that there is an ethical foundation for society" (1951, vol. V, 44–45). Robinson, in quoting with approval Smith's understanding of economic man, took his argument to imply not merely that naked self-interest is not necessarily conducive to natural order (and in fact is mostly destructive in its effects), but also that moral consciousness is an important, if neglected, moderating factor, akin to social institutions; it was the misperception of the importance of this factor that led to misunderstandings in the orthodox interpretations of Smith. To rephrase her argument in terms of the theme of the present work, Robinson railed against the fact that the orthodoxy had unwittingly accepted the Mandevillian "invisible hand" as an expression of the Smithian "invisible hand," and had in the process eliminated from Smith's laissez-faire the vital component of individual morality.

Always there was in Robinson's economics a social and political element, and this generally took central importance in fashioning her outlook. As Gram and Walsh suggested,

> For Joan Robinson, it is the political aspects of economic problems which have always motivated her interest in formal theory. . . . [T]he purpose of her argument was often to bring into the open those political, social, and moral dimensions of the economic issues under discussion which she felt were being systematically ignored. (Gram and Walsh 1983, 518–19)

That Robinson held many of the tenets of Marxian doctrine does not imply that she accepted that doctrine. Her famous statement in "An Open Letter from a Keynesian to a Marxist" (1953)—"I understand Marx far and away better than you do. . . . I have Marx in my bones and you have him in your mouth" (Robinson 1951, vol. 4, 265)—merely reflected her belief that any economic analysis, Marxian or laissez-faire, must, in order to be viable, meet the strictures of classical economic methodology; she believed she could arrive at Marxist conclusions without the encumbrance of the Marxian framework, which many times seemed to her to be tautological.

Conclusion   6

To conclude this excursion into British economic thought, it may be useful to catalog the theories presented in a simple format. One can see in
the evolution of British economic thought—from ethical to scientific
Utilitarianism and the various approaches to socialism—an emphasis on
communitarianism as at least a consequence. The philosophies of Locke
and Smith were seen as compatible with the labor theory of value (which
they both propounded to varying degrees), which led via Ricardo and his
socialist followers to societal solutions along collectivist lines. Thus the
philosophies underlying these economic theories can be categorized along
the lines of socialist theory, with many of those with whom we have dealt
serving as exemplars.

In *A Theory of the Labor Movement* (1928), Selig Perlman described three types of left-wing intellectuals: ethical, efficiency, and
historico-determinist. The last category clearly includes Marx, but also
could reasonably be extended to include Sraffa, Kalecki, and Robinson.
Keynes most likely falls into the second category, as does John Stuart
Mill, Marshall, Pigou, the Fabian Socialists, and even Bentham. Into the
first category we could include James Mill, Owen, Hodgskin, and the
Christian Socialists.

However we choose to proceed, it is clear that those in the "utilitarian tradition" do not fit easily into any compartment—utilitarian principles lead as easily to individual as to communitarian solutions, and even
an advocacy of the protection of property rights is not enough to classify
one as individualist or collectivist (note Hodgskin and the interpretations
of Locke, who is generally regarded as a leading advocate of individualism but held by some to be an advocate of the *social* good). As we
proceed, the lines of demarcation among advocates of each position will
become more obvious, but keep in mind how they continually refer to
these early writers for justification of their views. Thus the import of the
previous chapters is not so much in what those covered have themselves
proclaimed their positions to be as it is in how they have been interpreted
by others.

CHAPTER 9

From Müller to Schumpeter and Menger to Robbins
The German and Austrian Traditions

History is philosophy teaching by examples.   THUCYDIDES

Histories make men wise; poets witty; the mathematics subtle; natural philosophy deep; moral, grave; logic and rhetoric, able to contend.   FRANCIS BACON

The mind is not a hermit's cell, but a place of hospitality and intercourse.
CHARLES HORTON COOLEY, *HUMAN NATURE AND THE SOCIAL ORDER* (1903)

Introduction   I

The previous two chapters addressed the development of a self-conscious British "scientific" Utilitarianism, a tradition that began with and built upon the work of Jevons in pursuit of a marginalist approach to the study of economics. There it was argued that, while the *essentials* of scientific Utilitarianism may not have been significantly different from those of its ethical heritage as exemplified in the works of Bentham et al. (throughout the later works one sees an emphasis on the same ethical problems dealt with by the Philosophic Radicals and their predecessors), the *form of the argument*—the rhetoric employed in the debate—was markedly distinct. There was still a critical focus on individualism and a basic acceptance of the property right, with the state acting in a benign, supporting role. The most notable difference lay in the movement from a moral-ethical-legal rhetoric to a mathematical rhetoric: while perhaps only marginally affecting the choice of the fundamental issues, this change did affect greatly the bases upon which the arguments rested and so, ipso facto, influenced the conclusions derived. It is this rhetoric more than any fundamental advancement that serves to differentiate the two approaches. The choice of rhetoric also redefined to a large extent the scope of the subject matter to which the later variants of the utilitarian doctrine were deemed relevant.

In this chapter, we take up the development of a second, and markedly distinct, tradition of second-generation Utilitarianism, this one constructed on the teachings of the second of the three popularly cited developers of the concept of marginal utility, Carl Menger. This is the Austrian school of economics. In comparison with the British scientific heritage, it is difficult to recognize the Austrian school as having developed from the same essential framework, so different are the two. The distinctions between these two refinements of the original precepts of Utilitarianism will be seen to be stark indeed, especially in regard to the premises upon which each school was founded and the rhetoric employed in an effort to persuade the faithful. The immediate difference can be seen as a technical distinction. Jevons et al. employed the concept of marginal utility as a shorthand mathematical device that allowed them to get at the problem of the determinants of exchange. The process underlying *valuation* (or rather the calculation of value) was deemed subservient to the process underlying *exchange*. For the Austrians, by contrast, value became fundamental, everything else being determined analytically from this central concept. The Austrian theory of value is not connected directly with the analytics of exchange; it rather allows valuation to occur independently of whether exchanges in fact even take place.

This is not to imply that the Austrian school denied that exchange had any role to play in economic valuation; exchange in the Austrian conception serves the function of determining *price*. *Value,* however, being subjectively determined, has its realization in the theory of marginal utility. Value descends from knowledge on the part of economic agents of the relationship between the available quantities of commodities and the wants (demands) of the actors for those commodities. A "want" in Austrian terminology is not a simple desire for a thing, but is rather a desire actuated by a felt need. Goods acquire value by virtue of their ability to satisfy this subjectively ascertained need. Thus Austrian economics was (and is) inextricably linked with the process or logic of choice; the Austrian value process, in the words of G. L. S. Shackle (1972), takes place entirely in the imagination.

The differences between the two versions of marginal utility theory, the British and the Austrian, are not confined to this seemingly inconsequential distinction underlying value, but rather continue in the choice of presentation. While the British school shifted to a scientific rhetoric, the Austrians continued in the Benthamite tradition; this difference alone allows a clear apprehension of just how economics may have developed had the ethical foundation not been demolished in favor of a more rigorous standard. The British school demanded as the basis of its economic theories the employment of a formal mathematical logic; even Marshall, as we have seen, began his deliberations with a mathematical framework, distilling the essence of the argument in a symbolic functional form and only later translating it to prose. The Austrians for the most part eschewed mathematical (notational) *formalism* in their presentations of the theory of value, although in the spirit of Edgeworth they maintained a form of mathematical (logical, rigorous) *rhetoric* in their expositions. The general theories they put forth emphasized subjective valuations of utility as the rationale behind the process of exchange, valuations not subject to the universal implications inherent in a formal mathematical logic.

Perhaps more importantly, the Austrian perspective developed alongside, and as an antithesis to, the German tradition. The Austrian tradition tended to highlight the place of the individual within the larger social context, but developed along Smithian lines: the controlling force was a form of Smithian sympathy—a moral dimension—and not state interference in organizing individual activity. The Austrian focus was on the society as a collection of atomistic individuals.

The German conception developed quite differently. Much that served to define German culture and values, as well as German economic philosophy, was forged in Prussia. Nowhere is this more apparent than in the Prussian influence on the formation of the bureaucratic state, the single most important element of Prussian culture to survive the Revolution of 1848. The Prussian "high official," who retained status and respect in the civil service even after the upheavals of the Revolution, was (as noted by Herrmann Beck) the embodiment of the Prussian *Staatsgedanke*: he represented the order that resulted from state control and was seen as the promoter of the commonweal (as the state promoted the welfare of the citizenry) (Beck 1995, viii). These differences are critical to the interpretation of the role of the state with respect to the individual and shaped the *Weltanschauung* of the respective schools.

With this brief orientation, we turn now to a review of the development of economic and social concepts of the German and Austrian traditions, their similarities and differences.

The Inductivism of the German Historical School   2

The Romantic Movement   2.1

The place of the German "Romantic" movement in the history of economic thought is not at all secure. While Pribram felt it was indeed a significant intellectual movement, Schumpeter remained unconvinced. The important point to emphasize is that the early nineteenth century was an era of Romantic nationalism, which saw the emergence of movements to identify (metaphorically) states and cultures with an emphasis more on *feeling* than on *definition*. In any event, the "movement" is seen here as important in providing the impetus to the German Historical School.

We will concentrate in this investigation of the German Romantic movement on the work of Adam Heinrich Müller, Ritter von Nittendorf (1779–1829),[1] an Austrian civil servant, lecturer in political economy (Dresden), and acquaintance of the Austrian politician Clemens von Metternich. Müller, whose greatest work was his 1809 *Die Elemente der Staatskunst*, was influenced by the work of the philosopher Johann Gottlieb Fichte (1762–1814). Fichte promoted the ideas of classical individualism and subjectivism,[2] with the "self" being the only ultimate reality. At the same time he held that the individual, as a part of an organic whole— a social organism—is obligated to the fulfillment of moral responsibilities toward the collective. As the organic whole (the "nation") came before the individual (a belief we have seen was shared by the cameralists), it only stands to reason that the individual must place his own self-interest in a secondary position to that of the collective.

For his part, Müller took up the economic philosophy of Fichte and Edmund Burke to advocate a form of feudalism as an example of a unifying form of social organization. In Fichte he discovered the conception of the state as an organic whole; from Burke he gained an appreciation of the corporatist state, in which rights derive from group membership, and the state as a means to preserve the cultural interest and to ensure internal order (Burke of course was a monarchist). All elements of individuality were to be subordinate to the promotion of a spirit of nationhood; even his concept of capital was not confined to material productive goods, but took the form of "spiritual capital" including the political, cultural, social, religious, moral, and ethical traditions of the society.

Yet, despite his statist views, he considered himself to be a follower of Smith and in fact accepted Smith's basic principles while at the same time rejecting those of Smith's German disciples. So far as Müller was concerned, the German interpreters of Smith were simply attempting to apply to the German situation principles which in their qualified form were applicable only to the British; that is, they took Smith's principles as

1. Müller was born in Berlin and studied at the University of Göttingen. From 1805 to 1809 he served as tutor to Prince Bernhard of Saxe-Weimar, after which time he lectured in Dresden and Berlin. He was very active in politics, taking on the causes of the landlords against the reformers. Because of his political activities he was denied a post in the Prussian bureaucracy and so entered the Austrian civil service (1813). Through his acquaintance with the founder of the German Romantic movement, Friedrich Gentz (1764–1832), Müller became known to Metternich, for whom he undertook many diplomatic endeavors. Among his publications are *Die Elemente der Staatskunst* (1809), *Versuche einer neuen Theorie des Geldes* (1816), and *Von der Notwendigkeit einer theologischen Grundlage der gesamten Staatswissenschaften* (1819).

2. Russell proclaimed, Fichte "carried subjectivism to a point which seems almost to involve a kind of insanity" (1945, 718).

objective economic truths, instead of understanding the historical and cultural bases of the propositions.[3]

While professing general agreement with Smith, Müller nonetheless considered him to have erred in his overextension of Natural Law principles to include basic economic observations. He held that Smith's political economy was founded on the principles of selfishness and self-love (apparently neglecting Smith's discussions of sympathy which carried over from *The Theory of Moral Sentiments*) and regarded his own system as being superior in that it was fashioned on a religious foundation, as was necessary to provide structure and purpose to society.[4] True to the line of Fichte, Müller proclaimed society to be an organic whole, with the individuals comprising this whole defined by, and existing for the sake of, the collective. Individual actions are taken with an understanding of their moral implications, suggesting that Smith's sympathy is not innate, but is instead a duty to be fulfilled. Reminiscent of the statist theory of the cameralists, wherein the state and the economy are a single organic entity, Müller's (supposed) ethical reconstitution of Smith's economics maintained that each member of the society knows and accepts his place in the social setting, and willingly subordinates his own interest to that of the state.

List and the Development of German Nationalism   2.2

Although something of a precursor to the German Historical movement, Friedrich List (1789–1846)[5] serves here as a bridge between the Romantics and the Historicists. His two best-known works—*Outline of American Political Economy* (1827) and *Das nationale System der politischen*

---

3. Müller thought that Smith himself had erred in stating general principles which were derived from and so only applicable to the specific experiences of Britain.

4. In 1805 Müller was received into the Roman Catholic Church.

5. List served as professor of political economy at the University of Tübingen. A liberal (in the European sense), he railed against the pernicious influence of the bureaucracy, and for his efforts he incurred the wrath of the authorities. In 1820 he was elected to the legislature at Württemberg. Following his imprisonment—on the charge of advocating local self-government—he fled Germany, but returned in 1824, only to be arrested. On the assurance he would go to the United States—he had been invited by the Marquis de Lafayette—he was allowed to leave Germany, arriving in New York in 1825.

In the United States, List gained a following. He lived for a time in Pennsylvania, serving as editor of the German-language newspaper *Der Adler* in Reading. In 1831 he founded the Little Schuylkill Navigation Railroad and Canal Company. In 1832 he supported Andrew Jackson in the election for president and for his efforts was named consul to Germany. Following a personal financial disaster—he proposed a German railway system which left him bankrupt—he moved to France where he wrote *Le système naturel de l'économie politique* (1837) and *The National System of Political Economy* (1841), the former only discovered in 1925. In 1840 he returned to Germany, but his inability to see through his ambitious plans for the German economy led him to commit suicide.

Ökonomie (1841)[6]—provide the reader with a glimpse into the evolution of his thought.

List criticized Smith and the English classical economists for their reliance on the individual as the center of the economy and society, and for their failure to account for the political reality of foreign trading practices that impinged on the domestic national economy. As did the Romantics, List conceived of the state as an organic unity, endowed with an independent existence and pursuing its own definable ends. He specifically denied the possibility that a society of individuals, each pursuing his own self-interest, could be driven to the social good, meaning in List's case the material and physical well-being of the state; he claimed to have proven historically "that the unity of the nation forms the fundamental condition of lasting national prosperity" (List 1885, 163) and concluded that "individual liberty is in general a good thing so long only as it does not run counter to the interests of society" (172).

Despite his belief in the importance of the individual as the center of social organization, List was not above introducing the power of the state into those areas where efficiency could be achieved only through the managed coordination of economic forces. He insisted that the only way in which the "productive forces" (*Produktionskräfte*) of a nation—including not only the capital structure and raw material base, but also the talents and abilities of the people—could be marshaled to the cause of economic growth was if the state took the initiative; as a force for the aggregation of resources to a specified end, the coercive power of the state was unmatched.[7] Having visited the United States during the period of intense economic expansion (fueled by state financing), he became convinced of the efficacy of financing major economic projects through state issuance of bank notes. His advocacy of "managed" trade likewise followed along these lines. The classical argument in favor of free and open trade could be valid only for an economy already well along the development path; for a developing economy, state intervention held the key to national prosperity. To this end, he proposed protective tariffs for the benefit of "infant industries," as insulation from the obviously unfair position of the more advanced economies.[8]

Given the place and the period in which List wrote—nineteenth-century Germany, a "nation" composed of independent principalities

6. We use here the translation of the 1885 edition.

7. "[W]e have shown that only where the interest of individuals has been subordinated to those of the nation, and where successive generations have striven for one and the same object, the nations have been brought to harmonious development of their productive powers, and how little private industry can prosper without the united efforts both of the individuals who are living at the time, and of successive generations directed to one common object" (List 1885, 163).

8. Schumpeter argued that List's advocacy of "infant industry" protection did not vitiate a free-trade position, since John Stuart Mill had done likewise. See Schumpeter 1954, 505.

experiencing the very earliest stages of development—and the intellectual environment in which he thrived—one in which the basic tenets of Cameralism and the philosophical doctrines of Immanuel Kant,[9] Georg Hegel,[10] and Fichte were in dominance—it is little wonder such ideas took hold and indeed dominated debate and policy. His philosophy led to the creation of institutional arrangements that furthered the foundation of a unified and centralized German state. List himself was responsible for the creation of the *Zollverein,* the German customs union, one of the causes of German coalescence leading to nationhood.[11]

List was not of course alone in his understanding of the workings of an efficient state. Ludwig von Gerlach (1790–1861) held to a feudal conception of society, wherein property-holding implied a reciprocal duty to the welfare of the state. More importantly, the political nature of the property right was complemented by the theological basis for its existence. The very idea of property is "a political concept, an office established by God, in order to keep God's law for the state alive . . ." (quoted in Beck 1995, 81).

9. Kant (1724–1804), with whom we have dealt previously, was born in Königsberg, East Prussia. His parents were Pietists—a sect of Lutheranism—and enrolled him in a Pietist school, where he obtained a thorough grounding in Latin. Following completion of his preparatory studies, he entered the University of Königsberg (1740) to study theology. He quickly came to realize, however, that his true interest lay in the study of mathematics and the physical sciences. Upon graduation he worked as a tutor to several socially prominent families until 1755, when he completed the formal requirements and was appointed *Privatdozent* at Königsberg. In 1770 he took up the chair of logic and mathematics.

Kant's most important works include *Kritik der reinen Vernunft (Critique of Pure Reason,* 1781), *Kritik der praktischen Vernunft (Critique of Practical Reason,* 1788), and *Kritik der Urteilskraft (Critique of Judgment,* 1790). The publication of these three important works established Kant as the leading philosopher in Prussia. Throughout his works he consistently attacked the prevailing philosophy, that of Leibniz, and for this he is usually referred to as the founder of German Idealism (although the 1787 edition of the *Critique of Pure Reason* allows of a realist interpretation). Hume's influence on him was profound, as was the science of Newton, especially as regards his subjectivism. Yet he rejected Hume's approach as leading to solipsism and instead offered an account of rationality as consistency. In addition, Kant confronted Leibniz's analytic philosophy with a twofold distinction: analytic vs. synthetic propositions, and empirical vs. *a priori* propositions. He concluded that analytic *a priori* propositions need not be the only form of premise, for one could arrive at *a priori* statements based on knowledge of the external world. Philosophy may be analytic, but much of the natural sciences, and mathematics, he felt were not. See the discussion on the philosophy of Mises.

10. Georg Wilhelm Friedrich Hegel (1770–1831) grew up in Württemberg and was educated at Tübingen (1788–93). He served as *Privatdozent* at Jena, and later professor of philosophy at the University of Heidelberg. Hegel was responsible for the prominence in German academic circles of the notion of organic unity. "Facts" have no meaning unless related to the circumstances of the whole of which they are part. His important works include *Phänomenologie des Geistes (Phenomenology of Mind,* 1807) and *Wissenschaft der Logik* (1812–16).

11. Schumpeter suggested that List and Daniel Raymond (1786–1849), by whose writings List was quite impressed, actually extended the pioneering work of Alexander Hamilton (Schumpeter 1954, 199).

Similarly, Viktor Aimé Huber (1800–1869) promoted the cause of state intervention in the provision of the material needs of the "proletariat," but in partnership with workers' associations. The state could not take the responsibility for directing the activities of the citizenry, but it could and should exercise a coordinating role, allowing individuals the freedom of action and association while providing some large measure of poor relief, perhaps through a ministry or department designed to that end (Beck 1995, 89).

It was Johann Karl Rodbertus (1805–75), a Ricardian of sorts, who advocated direct state intervention as the solution to poverty. A proponent of state socialism, Rodbertus proposed centralized control of the economy, allowing that the state should take measures designed to increase national output and redistribute land for the common benefit.

2.3 The German Historical School: Roscher and Schmoller

While the cameralists, Fichte, Müller, and List set the early intellectual agenda, the actual foundation of the German Historical School can be traced to the publication in 1843 of *Grundriss zu Vorlesungen über die Staatswirtschaft Nach geschichlicher Methode* by Wilhelm Georg Friedrich Roscher (1817–1894), professor of political economy at the University of Leipzig.[12] The importance of this work, as suggested by Karl Milford, was that it "brought to an end an individualistic development in German economics which started in 1807 with the works of Hufeland" (Milford 1995, 29). From this point on, German economics could be characterized as promoting "methodological collectivism and a theory of subjective evaluations" (30).

The most comprehensive presentation of Roscher's economics appeared as the two-volume *Die Grundlagen der Nationalökonomie* (1854; the thirteenth edition was translated as *Principles of Political Economy* in 1878). This is the work we shall rely on. In the *Grundlagen,* Roscher characterized his aim as

> to describe man's economic nature and economic wants, to investigate the laws and the character of the institutions which are adapted to the satisfaction of these wants, and the greater or less amount of success by which they have been attended. Our task is, therefore, so to speak, the anatomy and physiology of social or national economy! (Roscher 1878, chap. III, §XXVI, 111)

The method Roscher followed in his economic researches involved historical comparisons of national economies. As with Petty, he held the proper method of scientific investigation to be akin to anatomical research.

---

12. Schumpeter felt Roscher should be esteemed "as a very meritorious follower of the English 'classics,' though a follower who happened to have a particularly strong taste for historical illustration" (Schumpeter 1954, 508).

One experiments with a sufficiently large sample of the population—under the assumption, of course, of regularity—and, from the observations gathered, puts forth general propositions as to the nature of the species. However, while the method is ideal in biology and other of the natural sciences, Roscher saw a difficulty in applying it directly to the study of national economies. For one thing, while the anatomist, in studying a certain species of animal, can "make a hundred or a thousand experiments, and use a hundred or a thousand individuals for his purpose," the economist must be content with the observation of existing institutions drawn from a limited universe. He does not have the option of choosing a "representative sample" from which to work. Yet the fact of a universe of finite size is all the better, since it allows the possibility of examining the totality of elements, and not relying on inferences from a subset to the whole; the limited number of observable economies reduces the complexities of the analysis and also limits the error inherent in extrapolating from the historical record of one subset to the pattern of historical development of the whole. In this way, the economist can form his "laws," generalizations that may be treated as universal statements of economic evolution (1878, chap. III, §XXVI, 112).[13]

Taking his cue from the earlier philosophical conceptions of the state as an organic whole, Roscher maintained that each nation had a unique construction. The function of the economist cum historian is to ascertain the unique institutional relationships existing within each nation and so determine for each specific case the cause of economic growth and the promotion of the social welfare. Roscher identified an important aspect of economic development, that of the simultaneity and the mutuality of events: "in the public economy of every people, patient thought soon shows the observer, that the most important simultaneous events or phenomena mutually condition one another" (1878, chap. I, §XIII, 81). This mutual conditioning poses a problem: if events are mutually conditioning, how are we to determine cause and effect in arriving at economic laws? If everything seems to determine, and to be determined by, everything else, how do we disentangle the web of interactions so as to determine the First Cause? His answer was to posit the existence of "an organic life, of which every individual fact is only the manifestation" (82). Roscher's "organic life" was not dissimilar to any other First Cause, including those underlying religious belief.[14]

---

13. Despite his reliance on an institutional-historical approach to economic analysis, Roscher actually was responsible for the importation into German economic thought of the methods of Ricardo.

14. "Whether we call the unknown and inexplicable ground back of all analysis, and which our analysis cannot reach, vital force, generic form, spirit of the nation, or God's thought, is for the present a matter of scientific indifference. All the more necessary are the self-knowledge and honesty, in general, which admit the existence of this background, and which do not, by denying it, deny the connection of the whole, which is, for the most part, much more important than the analyzed parts" (Roscher 1878, chap. I, §13, 82).

In explaining his First Cause, Roscher insisted he was not stipulating a "natural necessity," but rather was describing empirical regularities, or "harmonies," which he identified with Natural Laws. These laws are not, to be sure, the Natural Laws of Smith et al. They are not ethical or moral constraints on individual freedom of action, nor are they legislative codes. They are merely the recognized outcomes of collective action, statistical constructs, uniformities "not dependent on human design" but discernible as empirical regularities governed by the law of large numbers. They are in effect laws "whose operation does not depend on their recognition by individuals, and, over which, only he can obtain power who has learned to obey them" (1878, chap. I, §XIII, 83 and n.4).[15]

In defining the area of his scientific interest, Roscher appealed to the notions of classical Greek thought. His search for the First Cause led him to conclude that economies are "the natural product of the faculties and propensities which make man man" (1878, chap. I, §XIV, 84), a comment reminiscent of the basis of the economy of Aristotle's *Politics* (which Roscher quotes approvingly). Any nation's economy begins (as in Aristotle) with the family unit, and "every independent household management contains the germs of all politico-economical activity" (84). Note that he does not begin with the *individual,* but with the *family* as the basic unit. This is consistent with his belief in an organic polity. It also inspired his definition of the science of economics. Economics is "the science which has to do with the laws of the development of the economy of a nation, or with its economic national life" (chap. II, §XVI, 87). Here the phrase "national life" is especially interesting and important. The "national life" is multifaceted, but, as defined by Roscher, has seven sides of special significance: language, religion, art, science, law, the state, and economy. Of these seven—ranked in ascending order of significance— special importance is given to a "family" of relationships—law, state, economy—which together are more closely aligned than any of the others. These three are of critical importance; they "have their roots so deep in the physical and intellectual imperfection of man, that we can scarcely imagine their continuance beyond his life on earth" (89).[16] As the economic interest is granted the highest order in this scheme,[17] political economy represents, above any other intellectual endeavor, the vehicle for the most complete explanation of the rationale behind social and individual action.

Having granted such a place for political economy, Roscher then maintained its intimate connection to politics. Politics—concerned with

---

15. "They have to do with free rational beings, who, because they are thus free and rational, are responsible to God and their conscience, and constitute in their aggregate a species capable of progress" (Roscher 1878, chap. I, §XIII, 84).

16. Roscher derived this phrase from Matthew 22:30.

17. "Indeed, there is no human relation, not even the highest and the sweetest, but has its economic interests" (Roscher 1878, chap. II, §XVI, 88).

the "administration of public affairs"—is a part of national economy (*Volkswirtschaft*), itself synonymous with state economy (*Staatswirtschaft*). Politics is actually indistinguishable from the affairs of the nation, be they social or economic; it is politics that serves to guide the organism of the state. One cannot, then, attempt to understand the economy and the workings of the society without first understanding the important roles of politics and the state:

> As the physiologist cannot understand the action of the human body, without understanding that of the head; so we would not be able to grasp the organic whole of national economy, if we were to leave the state, the greatest economy of all, the one which uninterruptedly and irresistibly acts on all others, out of consideration. (1878, chap. II, §XVII, 91–92)

While others may also be mentioned as having made important contributions to the older German Historical School—including Bruno Hildebrand (1812–78) and Karl Knies (1821–98)—the kernel of thought is well represented by Roscher. It is to the "younger" school that we now turn.

As the "older" German Historical School owes its founding to Roscher, the "younger" school owes its development to Gustav von Schmoller (1838–1917). This "school," somewhat along the lines of a social reform movement, had as its principal goal the inductive determination of "laws" of social development, laws granted the status of a priori propositions and from which could be deduced the necessary conditions behind historical evolution. Schmoller—having studied *Staatswissenschaften* at the University of Tübingen, and so being educated in the fundamentals of Cameralism—came to view economic analysis through the lenses of Fichte, List, and Roscher. His great work was the massive *Grundriss der allgemeinen Volkswirtschaftslehre* (1900–1904).

Schmoller's difficulty with classical economic orthodoxy lay not with its analytical methodology, but with its concentration only on select aspects of the workings of society. The orthodox economists tended to treat production, distribution, and economic growth apart from the institutional, religious, political, and ethical base, that is, to see the economy as separate from the state as an organic entity. Schmoller felt the emphasis should be on the society as a unit. To this end he insisted the analysis commence with the vast collection of material relating to the institutional history of the nation, with the understanding that only after such data had been collected could one proceed in deriving the laws of the evolution of the society.

Schmoller is typically characterized as a representative of the Historical School, but it is questionable as to whether he really ever advocated a "historical approach" to economics or to the study of the affairs of the state. Kurt Dopfer concluded that Schmoller's approach, while emphasizing the historical nature of economic processes, was nonetheless theoretical and empirico-deductive, not historical and evolutionary (Dopfer 1988, 552). The *Methodenstreit* centered on "the question of how economic reality could be better comprehended and more adequately transformed methodologically into theoretically meaningful statements," and so the debate reduced to "the *appropriate use of a transformation rule*" (555; emphasis in original). Schumpeter disagreed, holding that Schmoller's school had really a historico-ethical base. Schmoller "professed to study *all* the facets of an economic phenomenon; hence *all* the facets of economic behavior and not merely the economic logic of it; hence the *whole* of human motivations as historically displayed, the specifically economic ones not more than the rest for which the term 'ethical' was made to serve, presumably because it seems to stress hyperindividual components" (Schumpeter 1954, 812). While Dopfer conceded that Schmoller believed that the "truth" would "reveal itself if only the entire statistical material is collected and comprehended" (Dopfer 1988, 556), he actually employed the historical method only to the extent that it allowed him to draw lawlike conclusions—empirical regularities—from which his theory could proceed. His economics was thus both nonhysteretic—it did not support nonrepeatable temporal processes, allowing that history *could* repeat itself—and nonteleological (566).

Schmoller's generation of the Historical School became known as *Kathedersozialisten*—academic socialists, who made their economic and political appeals on the basis of social justice. They were also known as Socialists of the Chair, because of their academic affiliations.

3 The Founder of Austrian Economics: Carl Menger

3.1 *An Austrian Theory of Value*

The chronological and intellectual beginning of the Austrian school of economics can be traced to the efforts of a single thinker whose writings and teachings proved truly seminal. Carl Menger (1840–1921), the founder of the Austrian school, actually began in the study of law at the Universities of Vienna (1859–60) and Prague (1860–63), completing a doctorate at the University of Cracow with the intention of becoming a journalist. It was while in the Austrian civil service (1871)—in the influential Ministerratsprasedium, the central cabinet office—that he became interested in economics and economic theory, at which time he published his *Grundsätze der Volkswirtschaftslehre,* later translated as *The Principles of Economics.* (This, his single most important economics work, served as his habilitation [second doctoral] dissertation.)[18]

---

18. With the success of the *Grundsätze,* he secured a position as *Privatdozent*— more or less the equivalent of an assistant professor, a position which entitled him occasion-

In the *Grundsätze,* his most complete presentation of his theory of economics (published, coincidentally, in the same year as Jevons's *Theory of Political Economy*), Menger offered what has since come to be regarded as *the* statement of the Austrian version of the theory of utility and value. In this work, Menger set out to show (1) that Aristotle's view that exchange involved equivalent (objective) values was wrong, (2) that capital (in addition to labor) was productive,[19] and (3) that the value of money was *sui generis.* The form of rhetoric he employed was designed to persuade historical-type economists that scientific economics (by which he meant an economics that was universal) was possible, and to that end he dedicated the book to Wilhelm Roscher.

The key to Menger's *Grundsätze* is his theory of value. In this regard, the paramount question concerns the process by which a "thing" becomes valued. Menger saw the acquisition of "value" by an object, or in fact by anything, as a process which needed to be better understood, which means that all aspects of the valuation needed to be strictly defined. After all, an object cannot be valued or judged to be valuable merely because of the fact of its existence. Value is not in these terms definable outside of the apprehensions by the individual of what we may loosely refer to as utility; certainly the preclassical economic attempts at providing a solution to the water–diamond paradox make the point. Value exists only so long as the person can establish a connection between the object and the satisfaction of some need or desire. The first paragraph of the work is instructive as to Menger's view of the process in which he is interested:

> All things are subject to the law of cause and effect. This great principle knows no exception, and we would search in vain in the realm of experience for an example to the contrary. Human progress has no tendency to cast it in doubt, but rather the effect of confirming it and of always further widening knowledge of the scope of its validity. Its continued and growing recognition is therefore closely linked to human progress. (Menger 1871, 51)

It is the confirmation of this "causal connection" between things and needs-satisfaction that leads to a "thing" being designated a "useful thing." But "useful things" do not attain the level of "goods" unless and

---

ally to lecture, but mostly to tutor students—and he left the civil service. In 1873 he became, at the University of Vienna, an "Extraordinary Professor," a position which provided him a title but no salary, as such, or faculty vote. However, he did manage to serve as the tutor to the Austrian Imperial Crown Prince (Rudolf) during the period 1876 through 1888.

In 1879, well before the Crown Prince's murder-suicide, an event known as the "Mayerling incident," Menger received the coveted appointment of *Professor ordinarius* at the University, a position which gave him both a salary and a faculty vote. In this capacity, he gave lectures to the students in the Faculty of Law.

19. This is a very important point, because what Menger was rejecting was the exclusivity of the Lockean labor theory of value.

until the individual has "the power actually to direct the useful things to the satisfaction of . . . needs" (Menger 1871, 52). For Menger, this meant that the "thing" and the individual "needs" had to fulfill four fundamental conditions:

(1) there must *be* a human need;

(2) the "thing" that is to fulfill the need must be possessed of properties that enable the individual to form a causal connection between it and satisfaction;

(3) the individual must "know" of this connection;

(4) the individual must be able to command access to the "thing" and be able to direct it to the satisfaction of the need (1871, 52).

All four of these conditions must be met for a thing to be endowed with goods-character. Should any one fail to hold, the goods-character and hence value is lost.[20]

For a "thing" to have a "goods-character," therefore, it must be seen to meet the test of a causal connection between itself and the satisfaction of a need. Further, this definition applies not merely to commodities or physical *objects*, those things usually considered as "goods." A material aspect need not in fact be present; what applies to goods per se could just as readily apply to services, or any other intangible. Menger actually listed quite a few of these intangibles, including goodwill, monopoly rights, patent rights, and even social activities, which he placed under the heading of "useful actions." These "useful actions" merely comprise a subset of the more general category of "goods." They satisfy the four fundamental conditions, although they do so in a psychic as opposed to a physical or materialistic way.[21] Recognizing that the distinction between physical and psychical goods was specious, Menger's inclusion of non-material "things" into his calculus went a long way toward refining the concepts of value and utility (1871, 54–55).

Menger rejected what he interpreted as the British economists' (our "ethical" utilitarians) equation of utility with use-value. This equation allowed that (as per John Stuart Mill) exchange value refers only to price (1871, 307–8). As Menger perceived the concepts of utility and use-value, they are fundamentally different, for they derive from two entirely different bases. *Value* emerges "from the relationship . . . be-

20. Menger considered a "special situation" that could exist should the causal connection be missing, but nonetheless the classification of "goods-character" is made. This "special situation" would hold if either (1) "attributes, and therefore capacities, are erroneously ascribed to things that do not really possess them," or (2) "non-existent human needs are mistakenly assumed to exist" (Menger 1871, 53). Thus we may act "irrationally" in subjectively ascribing value to something that clearly does not, in any objective sense, fulfill the conditions of being valuable.

21. Thus did Menger provide an additional reason for the invalidation of the labor theory of value.

tween requirements for and available quantities of goods" (115). Thus only economic goods can be valuable, or possess what we may call value-character (116). But value itself must be viewed as determined by our subjective apprehensions of our own needs and our apprehensions of the ability of a good to satisfy those needs. Value is defined with respect to the four previously mentioned fundamental conditions. "Value is therefore nothing inherent in goods, no property of them, but merely the importance that we first attribute to the satisfaction of our needs, that is, to our lives and well-being, and in consequence carry over to economic goods as the exclusive causes of the satisfaction of our needs" (116). Thus the concept of subjective valuation as a fundamental proposition for a theory of economics, while seemingly a self-evident proposition, proved to be critical in advancing a structure meant to provide explanations for the functioning of the market.[22] It allowed within economics a role for psychological motivations, and more importantly it offered an explanation for valuation extending beyond material transactions, to one which stressed the role of imagination. It is also in this area that Menger's theory afforded a central role to uncertainty as an epistemic concept, a problem handled only in an aleatory form by the "scientific" utilitarians, with the possible single exception of Edgeworth, who wrote from the standpoint of a probability theorist. By restricting their analytics to an empirically based theory, the "scientific" utilitarians could only handle uncertainty objectively as a figment of the environment and were simply not equipped to handle uncertainty as the subjective apprehension by individual actors in that environment.

For Menger, utility is synonymous with a good itself; it is part of the makeup—the "essence"—of the goods-character of a "thing." Utility is *not* to be equated with use-value, for utility is the objective essence or quality of the "thing" itself. Although only economic goods have value, all goods, economic or not, possess utility (1871, 119, 294). Air and water, the quintessential "free" goods, possess utility, but not necessarily value, since, while they are essential to life, they can be obtained at

22. Consider Schumpeter's statement: "The critics of Menger's theory have always maintained that no one could ever have been unaware of the fact of subjective valuation, and that nothing could be more unfair than to put forward such a triviality as an objection to the Classics. But the answer is very simple: it can be demonstrated that almost every one of the classical economists tried to start with this recognition and then threw it aside because he could make no progress with it, because he believed that, in the mechanism of the capitalist economy, subjective valuation had lost its function as the engine of the vehicle. And like subjective valuation itself, so also the phenomena of demand based on it were regarded as useless in comparison to the objective facts of costs. . . .

What matters, therefore, is not the discovery that people buy, sell, or produce goods because and in so far as they value them from the point of view of satisfaction of needs, but a discovery of quite a different kind: the discovery that this simple fact and its sources in the laws of human needs are wholly sufficient to explain the basic facts about all the complex phenomena of the modern exchange economy . . ." (Schumpeter 1951, 83–84).

virtually no cost.[23] Neither is the amount of sacrifice necessary to gain command over a good a mark of value, since "nothing is more certain than that there are numerous economic goods that come into the command of men without the least sacrifice (alluvial land, for instance), and still other economic goods that cannot be attained by any economic sacrifice at all (inborn talents, for example)" (294). Value is thus entirely subjective and is *not* built around utility as understood by the British classical economists. Rather, value is a consideration of our individual and subjective dependence upon something. A good may have multiple uses for any individual and the order in which the buyer uses the goods reveals his preferences.

Price determination may be a market phenomenon and has been so treated in classical economics, but in principle it serves an even more important function, this being the role of the equilibrator of subjective valuations.[24] The pricing process, while predicated on the subjective theory of value, becomes a condition from which statements of economic conditions may be derived. Menger thus accepted that men may rationally maximize, but the basis for their maximization is objective, not subjective; price serves as this objective basis. This is true even though the pricing *process* is itself based on subjective considerations. Prices do not equate the values of different quantities of goods; they serve merely as guides to exchange. Menger analyzed several pricing situations, according to the number of parties on each side in the market. In each instance, however, the pricing policy reverts to the mechanical equilibration of the bargaining parties. From this, one can infer that Menger believed that the equilibration usually associated with the end result of the interactions in a market could take place in the individual's mind, even before he entered the marketplace.

3.2 The Place of the Property Right

Menger argued that individuals arrange their consumption with full (or an effort at full) consciousness of time. Thus, information gathering is an inherent part of the value system. But individuals do not figure on the satisfaction of their future wants under the assumption of stasis; they allow as well for a change in preferences. This last condition allows for a reorganization of production processes. Menger's economizing process involves both a maximization of consumption according to present preferences and a maximization of consumption according to some perception of preference shifts. All of this leads him to explain the evolution of

---

23. This is not to imply that "clean" air and "pure" water can be so obtained.

24. "Prices are only incidental manifestations of these [exchange] activities, symptoms of an economic equilibrium between the economies of individuals" (Menger 1871, 191).

interests and demands, that is, how noneconomic goods can become economic. Into this structure he incorporated the property right.

Menger's position on the role of property derived from his definition of an economic good and the individualistic nature of his analysis. Individual requirements are satisfied not by separate goods, but by the entirety of the goods at our disposal. Menger's definition of property then follows from this understanding: "[t]he entire sum of goods at an economizing individual's command for the satisfaction of his needs." This is not, to be sure, any mere *arbitrary* combination of goods, but on the contrary is "a direct reflection of his needs, an integrated whole, no essential part of which can be diminished or increased without affecting realization of the end it serves" (1871, 76).

To understand Menger's views on property and the role it played in Austrian theory requires that we return to his theory of value, especially his notion of goods-order. Goods, once defined, can be ranked according to their capacity to satisfy wants. Consumer goods are "first order goods" since they serve the direct satisfaction of needs. "Higher order" goods are then those that only indirectly satisfy needs. (The value of the latter is thus merely derivative, since there is no "causal connection" between the holding of the good and the satisfaction derived from the good itself.) Uncertainty in regard to the quantity and quality of goods arises in those individuals who have at their disposal only intermediate goods, those of a high order, since these goods allow only an indirect claim to goods of the first order, consumer goods (1871, 69–70). Menger then dismissed Smith's explanation of exchange as resulting from a human "innate propensity to truck and barter"; rather men exchange because they have a capacity and propensity for rational maximization.[25]

In attempting to satisfy their "wants" (the English-language translation of Menger consistently references "needs," but "wants" is actually a better characterization), individuals in the economy are said by Menger to follow a set of four conditions, which he maintained were in accordance with his previously quoted postulate. The individual will seek: (1) to retain that which he controls that satisfies his wants (needs) either directly or indirectly, (2) to retain the useful properties of the goods under his control, (3) to order wants such that the most important are satisfied with the available quantities of goods at his disposal, and (4) to maximize the result (for the classical economist, read "level of utility") given the available quantities of goods at his command, or to minimize the quantity of goods needed to achieve a given result (1871, 55–56).

In adhering to this form of the *individual* utility calculus, Menger

---

25. Thus, Menger moves from an empirical assessment of the way men behave, to a logical assessment of what they have reason to do. At first glance this move seems to validate the proposition that *homo economicus* is a Bentham-like reasoning machine; but this is misleading. Bentham's man reasons objectively; Menger's man does not require the analytical capacity of Bentham's.

believed that there would be among the *group* the potential for conflict. Social norms—laws—need to be enacted to preserve the individual from having his possessions confiscated by force. That these legal relationships should emerge as a consequence of individual economic relations he saw not as arbitrary or ad hoc, but rather as being in "the nature of things" (1871, 97). They emerge as a natural result of wants exceeding supplies and simply cannot be otherwise. Redistribution and other utopian schemes regarding property are doomed to failure because they deny a central tenet of the economizing process—the centrality of the institution of property. All other arrangements are subsidiary to this most basic of human institutions. As Menger observed:

> it is impossible to abolish the institution of property without remov-
> ing the causes that of necessity bring it about—that is, without
> simultaneously increasing the available quantities of all economic
> goods to such an extent that the requirements of all members of
> society can be met completely, or without reducing the needs of men
> far enough to make the available goods suffice for the complete
> satisfaction of their needs. Without establishing such an equilibrium
> between requirements and available amounts, a new social order
> could indeed ensure that the available quantities of economic goods
> would be used for the satisfaction of the needs of different persons
> than at present. But by such a redistribution it could never sur-
> mount the fact that there would be persons whose requirements for
> economic goods would either not be met at all, or met only incom-
> pletely, and against whose potential acts of force, the possessors of
> economic goods would have to be protected. Property, in this sense,
> is therefore inseparable from human economy in its social form,
> and all plans of social reform can reasonably be directed only to-
> ward an appropriate distribution of economic goods but never to
> the abolition of the institution of property itself. (1871, 97–98)

In other areas of economics, Menger proceeded under the same assumptions he had stipulated for his basic theoretical model. His ratio-nale for the existence of money, for example, is that some commodities are more tradable than others; money is simply the most tradable of them all. Money, therefore, is not a creation of the state, although the state by coining money may draw upon a prior need for the existence of a highly tradable thing; money is rather a commodity that is "naturally" endowed with properties making it more conducive to serve an exchange function (as well as the other functions typically ascribed to money). In other words, money exists to fulfill a universal economic function: if the state coins or prints money, the value of that money relates to the underlying market need rather than to the power of the sovereign.

Economic development is likewise viewed as derivative of the basic process. Development is simply the phenomenon resulting from better information being brought to the trading process. Thus, the economics of development is a subset of the creation of markets for information.

The Methodology of Menger 3.3

As we noted at the outset of this chapter, the German Historical School as it developed under Roscher combined a methodological collectivism with a subjective value theory. There it was mentioned that this represented a fundamental shift in German economic methodology, which had previously been based on methodological individualism. Menger sought in the *Grundsätze* a return to the methodological program of the past, an approach that is evident in his interpretation of the emergence of institutional forms as the spontaneous (uncoordinated) outgrowth of individual actions. He thus in effect reinvigorated Smith's concept of sympathy as an ethical force in guiding the self-interest of the individual to the pursuance of the social good.[26]

In 1883 Menger published his second important work, the *Untersuchungen über die Methode der Socialwissenschaften und der politischen Ökonomie insbesondere* (1883), translated as *Problems of Economics and Sociology*, a work devoted to the idea that theory is *at least as important* in explaining and understanding social phenomena as is the analysis of the historical record. This put him again in conflict with the then-dominant methodological position of the German Historical School and particularly Schmoller. Menger strongly disagreed with the Historical School on the nature of economic laws, arguing that laws of social development are not synthetic; any statement given the status of "law" must be analytic in order to allow deductions that could be taken as necessary. More importantly, Menger in this work developed a truly *micro*-economic, or atomistic, approach to the subject, the approach of methodological individualism. The entire episode that resulted—the (German) *Methodenstreit*, a debate which carried on unabated for several decades—centered on the question of whether the study of economics should include the entire social, political, economic, religious, and moral record of a society (Schmoller's practice) or whether it should focus on distilling from the totality the essential features of economic life, while eliminating the accidental or extraneous elements (much as physicists deal with ideal gases). In other words, the problem centered around the difference between comprehensiveness and the isolation of essences.[27]

Menger was well trained in history and philosophy, and he had, in addition, acquired mathematical skills, including a good knowledge of the calculus. He also always held a keen interest in historical analysis, despite the feud with Schmoller that centered more on the latter's

26. Although Menger criticized Roscher, he actually dedicated the *Grundsätze* to him.

27. On this see especially Dopfer 1988.

perceived *misuse* of historical analysis than with any disdain on Menger's part for an historical method.[28] Yet despite (or perhaps because of) his skills and knowledge, he was vehemently opposed to employing mathematics in economic analysis; he thought quite simply and realistically that mathematical formalism was too restrictive, that it necessarily hid from view critical qualitative distinctions, which took on paramount importance in a body of theory predicated on subjective foundations. His son, Karl, a mathematician out of whose seminar emerged much of current game theory, linear programming, etc., always indicated that his father's de-emphasis on mathematical formalism in economics was not to be associated with an ignorance of mathematics; his reasons were tied up not with personal ineptitude, but rather with a fundamental appreciation that qualitative factors should be taken to be at least as important as the quantitative. His objections to the mathematization of economics were grounded in a belief that such methods were simply inappropriate to the task.[29]

3.4 Menger's Influence

Hayek referred to Menger as "both the most influential and the least read of the major figures who gave economic theory the shape it preserved from about 1885 to 1935" (Hayek 1968, 124). Menger's theoretical presentations did more than simply attempt a resurrection or even revision of the then-waning classical economic theory; he opted instead for nothing less than a completely new vision, an entirely new Weltanschauung. As Schumpeter expressed it, "Without external stimulation, and certainly without external *help*, he attacked the half-ruined edifice of economic theory. . . . Menger belongs to those who have demolished the existing structure of a science and put it on entirely new foundations" (Schumpeter 1951, 82–83).

The reason Menger had so little influence on British economic thought is most likely due to the delay in translating adequately his written works, which were relatively few in number.[30] People knew more

28. The conflict with Schmoller was not really on method as much as it was on the reasoning to be employed in constructing foreign trade policy. Menger was a free trader; Schmoller, by way of contrast, influenced the protectionist policies of Hohenzollern Germany—policies which imitated the then-current "American System," involving planned balanced growth with protection of the rapidly growing industrial sector. But their difference was seen by professional economists to relate not to their actual policy differences, but more to their procedural methods. In actual fact, however, both men reduced their quite interesting *policy* differences to a rather sterile discussion of "the right way to think."

29. Interestingly enough, Alfred Marshall (in this case a most distinguished student in mathematics) also shared the same judgments about the relevance of mathematics in economic analysis. In his case the equations were relegated to appendixes. John Maynard Keynes, whose Cambridge undergraduate training was in mathematics, employed formal equations only in the elucidation of economic concepts.

30. Many American economists *were* influenced by Menger because they actually received graduate training in German universities. See the discussion in chapter 11.

about Menger's work than they knew of the works themselves. This is unfortunate, since Menger wrote at about the same time as Jevons, and the debate that would have ensued had both visions been equally available would certainly have been interesting, to say the least.

But Menger did have disciples, two of whom, Böhm-Bawerk and Wieser, will be discussed below. Here it should be remembered that Wieser and Böhm-Bawerk were not really Menger's students—both had left the University of Vienna before Menger began teaching there—although both were "disciples" in the sense that they acknowledged him as their intellectual master. Wieser built on the question of imputation, which led him to coin the phrase "opportunity cost"; he also extended Menger's partial equilibrium analysis to the point of a national economy and general equilibrium. Böhm-Bawerk took up the themes of time and the arrangement of production. Together they kept alive the principles enunciated by the master, and through their students, maintained a tradition that is still very much alive today.

Böhm-Bawerk: The Austrian System-Builder   4

Within the Austrian tradition, the man who may be most clearly identified as a "system-builder" in the sense of Marx is Eugen von Böhm-Bawerk (1851–1914).[31] Menger initiated the program which was to become Austrian economics; Böhm-Bawerk fabricated the superstructure. His genius

---

31. Böhm-Bawerk was born in Moravia of an ennobled civil servant family—his father died in 1856, he being at the time deputy governor and head of the Austrian imperial administration in Moravia (then one of the most developed parts of Central Europe). Following his formal education—he read law at the University of Vienna—in 1872 Böhm-Bawerk entered the civil service (fiscal administration). In 1875 he took a government bursary to prepare himself for a professorship in economics, continuing his studies at Heidelberg with Karl Knies, at Leipzig with Wilhelm Roscher, and at Jena with Bruno Hildebrand.

Returning to fiscal administration for three years (and while there completing in 1880 his habilitation), Böhm-Bawerk accepted a professorship at Innsbruck (the "capital" of the home province of the ruling Hapsburgs), where he remained until 1889. His habilitation thesis became his first book (volume one of *Kapital und Kapitalzins*).

In 1889, Böhm-Bawerk took a position with the commission in the Ministry of Finance that was given the task of reforming the Austrian income tax; he became its permanent secretary in 1891 and its vice president in 1892. By 1893 he had been named Minister of Finance (for the first of his three times). Too highly ranked to return to the commission, he served as president of the three senates of the *Verwaltungsgerichtshof* (the highest court of appeal in administrative matters). In 1896, while honorary professor at the University of Vienna, he wrote one of his most famous works, translated as *Karl Marx and the Close of His System*, a critique of the program of Marx. Intermittently he served again as Minister of Finance and in 1904 brought down the government over the question of the size of the military budget. Apparently weary of public service, he declined a top-paying government job (Governor of the Central Bank) and instead took a full professorship at the University of Vienna. Biographical material is from Schumpeter (1951) and from K. H. Hennings (1987).

and importance lay in the method he chose to follow: he did not initiate the overall plan by following the blueprints of others, but rather proceeded by launching an entirely new design. Of him Schumpeter wrote, "He was an architect, not an interior decorator, a pathbreaker of science, not a salon scientist" (1951, 159). For Böhm-Bawerk, the grandeur of the structure, the construction of the whole edifice, was more important than concern with the mere placing of individual beams.

Böhm-Bawerk supported the Mengerian theoretical side in the *Methodenstreit*, but in the process achieved a reputation for aggressiveness and casuistry—argumentation designed to deceive. It was a reputation that was deserved and in fact cultivated; it was casuistry he was after. He held that to make a theory simple and easily grasped was to make it also more readily misunderstood. By inundating the reader with detail, illustration, facts, and figures on each and every point upon which there could be any question whatever, there simply could be left no room for misjudgment or misapprehension of his central thesis. Böhm-Bawerk himself made this clear when discussing his approach in his three-volume *Capital and Interest:*

> The basic principles of my interest theory are, I believe, uncommonly simple and natural. Had I been content to set forth a condensed alignment of those basic principles and to forgo all detailed and logical demonstration, I should have been offering a theory which would have created within a limited space the impression of a doctrine so simple as to border on the axiomatic. . . . With respect to the theory of capital, beyond all others, so many views have already been presented, and endowed with so great an appearance of truth, only to prove subsequently to be specious, that I must expect to find my public critical. And it is even to be anticipated that my best and most careful readers will be just the ones to be most critical. Under such circumstances it seemed all the more important that my theory be reared as a solid structure rather than as a light and pleasing edifice. Hence I preferred to burden my presentation with numerous and minutely detailed proofs, with a quantity of exact mathematical demonstrations and the like, rather than leave room at critical points for doubt and error. (Böhm-Bawerk 1959, vol. I, 385)

While the reader may.have difficulty in traversing the terrain, there could be no doubt as to where he would find himself at the end of his journey. As Schumpeter maintained, "In the absence of a *communis opinio* in the economics of his time, Böhm-Bawerk found himself faced with the necessity of submitting to the public every assumption and method he used, every link in the chain of his argument, of fighting every step of the way for a clearing on which to build the structure of his system" (Schumpeter 1951, 150).

As with Menger, Böhm-Bawerk sought to uncover the underlying laws of economics, laws valid independent of time and space. Economics then is not an empirical discipline, but is rather a scientific, meaning analytical, one. Empirical conditions provide the economist a means for the distillation of the underlying conditions; once synthesized, these "laws" are then to be regarded as analytic truths. The empirical material nonetheless has an important role to play, since economics relates after all to problems of the "real world." Böhm-Bawerk judged that his theory was ultimately predicated on empirical principles and went so far as to identify three forms of empiricism: (1) historical facts, (2) statistical observations, and (3) observation from life (Böhm-Bawerk 1959, Vol. II, 383).[32] Still, despite the empirical orientation of his theory, the laws which govern the course of empirical events are not subject to change when confronted with newly identified empirical "facts." Since the laws have already been "discovered," the "facts" serve merely to illustrate.

While ostensibly a student and disciple of Menger, Böhm-Bawerk did not seek simply to engage in the enlargement of the Mengerian system; on the contrary, while building on Mengerian principles and along Mengerian lines, he sought to develop a more comprehensive theory of value and interest, one consistent with the basic elements Menger had set forth. Böhm-Bawerk's theory of value was developed in his *Grundzüge der Theorie des wirtschaftlichen Güterwerts* (1886), a work Schumpeter dubbed "that masterful exposition of the theory of value . . . which will perish only with our science" (Schumpeter 1951, 151). It also set forth a framework for the measurement and comparison of utility.

While in the 1886 book Böhm Bawerk laid out his position on the question of the measurability and comparability of utility, the argument can best be demonstrated through an exchange with his student, Franz Čuhel. Čuhel, in his 1907 *Zur Lehre von den Bedürfinissen, Theoretische Untersuchungen über das Grenzgebiet der Ökonomik und der Psychologie,*[33] criticized the position taken by Böhm-Bawerk in the *Güterwert* as to the feasibility of measuring and comparing utilities. Čuhel began by defining "states of welfare" as the feelings engendered by the satisfaction of needs, maintaining that it is these "states of welfare" that we in fact

---

32. "My book will be found to employ predominantly a method of presentation which is customarily termed 'abstract.' And that term is often used in a somewhat condemnatory tone. And yet I maintain that my theory does not contain a single feature which is not reared on a strictly *empirical* foundation" (Böhm-Bawerk 1959, vol. II, 383; emphasis in original).

33. We use here the translation by William Kirby of chapter 6, "On the Theory of Needs," printed in Israel M. Kirzner (ed.) *Classics in Austrian Economics* (1995).

desire. He termed this feeling of "welfare desire" "egence" or "welfare egence," describing it as "the two-dimensional quantity which manifests itself in the present welfare desires and is dependent on the intensity of their drive for satisfaction and on the duration of the increase in welfare which is to be achieved" (Čuhel 1907, 307).[34]

An egence is obviously a subjective, psychological quantity. Čuhel considered several types of egences, in addition to the welfare variety. "Use egence" is what is typically known as "utility," a two-dimensional quantity relating the quantity of the good to the intensity of feeling engendered by it, that is, relating goods-quantity to satisfaction (cf. Jevons); "possession egence" is also a two-dimensional quantity, relating "the intensity of the desire for possession" to "the quantity of the means of satisfaction at which it is directed," and is more commonly known as "subjective value" (1907, 308). (Note here the distinction between use-egence and possession-egence, and the similarity between possession-egence and welfare-egence.)

Having defined egence, Čuhel then suggested a motivation for the use of the concept. He held that, at any given time, in order for an individual to make a decision, it must be the case that (welfare) egences "simultaneously present in the consciousness of the same person" cannot be equal; there must be a greatest or most intense one (which can at any rate be known only ex post), and this egence will become in effect the "will" (1907, 308). This comparison, however, has nothing whatever to do with "intensity of feeling." Compare this with the utilitarian calculus. While pleasures and pains are coincident, they cannot be mutually reinforcing or mutually destructive (they cannot cancel one another), although they can be present together and cause "mixed feelings." Egences—being "directed towards the maintenance of a present or the fulfilment of an imagined state of welfare or, on the other hand, the removal of a present or the non-fulfilment of an imagined state of welfare"—*can* be either mutually re-inforcing (additive) or mutually destructive (self-canceling) (310). Further, it is not necessarily true that intensity of desire is proportional to intensity of feeling (utility and subjective value are not necessarily comparable notions), as intensities of feeling may diminish or be imperceptible.

This suggests that the welfare egences (and hence possession egences) cannot, in any practical sense, be measured, and so the *differential* intensity of needs is also incapable of numerical measure. In short, it is not possible to state that one sensation is a multiple of another. While he agreed with Böhm-Bawerk's assertion that opinion "must be strictly concerned with how many lesser pleasures are equivalent to one greater pleasure," he rejected the extension, that we can then state "how many times

---

34. It should be noted that the label also allowed for the possibility of a "negative egence," in which "negative welfare desires" or "reluctance to achieve certain states of welfare" was the consideration.

greater the one pleasure is than the other" (1907, 319). We can make *comparisons* (as per Edgeworth), while being unable to state *intensities*.[35]

Böhm-Bawerk's response was presented as one of a series of ex-kurses (essays) (specifically, Exkurs X) to the third volume of *Capital and Interest*. Böhm-Bawerk accepted Čuhel's argument as to the nonfeasibility of an objective measure of intensity of feeling, but held that it was irrelevant to the problem at hand: one does not need an objective measure by which to compare intensities of sensation, for, on the contrary, "we are merely concerned with an 'attempt at indication,' which may be based merely on subjective estimates or application of imaginary standards, without claiming preciseness or even correctness" (Böhm-Bawerk 1959, vol. III, 129). Once the "imaginary standard" is applied, one can then always "correct" the (numerical) estimates on the basis of new and more complete information.

More importantly, while it may be the case that "rational" subjective valuation requires only a comparative ranking, it is often the case that cardinal estimates are needed. As Böhm-Bawerk stated his case for such cardinal measures:

> We need these judgments if we are to act rationally; and we form them because we need them. We form them as well as we can; and we err more often than we evaluate correctly. We form them without guaranteed objective tools of measure, merely through vague, subjective, perhaps even deceptive, estimates of the intensity of sensations which we may partially experience, but mainly reproduce in our imagination. Perhaps we give correct consideration, perhaps none at all, to factors that influence the correctness of such intensity estimates like the influence of perspective on our estimates of length or height. (1959, vol. III, 130)

The fact that it may not be objectively possible to arrive at a precise cardinal measure of intensity of belief does not diminish the equally obvious fact that people do indeed make just such *subjective* cardinal valuations all the time, applying their own idiosyncratic units of measure. Böhm-Bawerk held this to be different in kind from the demands of the Weber-Fechner law, as the "law" deals with "the determination of *sensual stimulations and perceptions*," while his subjective valuations were more concerned with "*feelings of enjoyment and uneasiness*" (1959, vol. III, 135; emphasis in original). So long as the individual *believes* he attains an enjoyment from the possession of one good which is *x* times greater than that obtained by the possession of another, how can anyone say he is mistaken?

(Böhm-Bawerk's great contributions to the theory of capital will be

35. Čuhel used the example of the Mohs hardness scale to make the point. The scale allows one to determine degrees of hardness in minerals, but it is a scale of ordinal comparison and does not reflect a cardinal measure.

dealt with in the discussion of the evolution of capital theory in the companion volume.)

5 Wieser's Social Economics

5.1 The Theory of Value

We now turn attention to the second of Menger's disciples, Friedrich, Freiherr von Wieser (1851–1926).[36] Wieser was moved to the study of economics upon reading Menger's *Grundsätze* and elected to complete his habilitation thesis with Menger in 1883. By 1903, he had succeeded Menger in the economics chair in the faculty of law at the University of Vienna.

His principal work, the one that best defines his Weltanschauung, is the *Grundriss der Sozialökonomik,* known in English as *Social Economics* (1914; the edition used here is the English-language translation of 1927). This work is generally regarded not only as the definitive statement of his own theory of social and economic relationships, but also as the definitive statement of the central propositions of the Austrian school of economics.

Characterizing his method as "psychological" (Wieser 1927, 3), Wieser was clearly in this regard at one with Menger. This sympathy extended to his definition of utility and the process underlying valuation. Based loosely on Menger's four fundamental conditions for a "thing" to be granted goods-character, Wieser narrowed the definition of what constitutes commodity-character (his version of goods-character) by considering that only those commodities (goods) with which we are familiar and to which we have access can be truly classed as commodities proper and so can be said to have utility in the classical sense. Commodities are "materials of economic activity," being "useful objects subject to man's power of disposition" (39). Utility is then descriptive of the "essence" of

---

36. Wieser was the son of Baron Leopold von Wieser, a senior Austrian army officer and Privy Councillor who later became the vice president of the Austrian Court of Audit. These honors were not, however, matched by a similar degree of wealth, so the family lived a modest existence. Despite the financial situation, Wieser was able to attend one of Vienna's "elite" *Gymnasia,* the Benedictine *Schottengymnasium,* where one of his classmates was Böhm-Bawerk. Their education and subsequent careers were parallel: both attended the University of Vienna, studying in the Law Faculty; both joined the civil service (serving in the same unit); and both did "the German circuit" together, studying economics at universities in Jena, Heidelberg, and Leipzig. (In an interesting aside, Wieser married Böhm-Bawerk's sister.)

By 1884 he had risen to the rank of associate professor at the University of Prague, and that of *professor-ordinarius* in 1889; he then later (1901–2) served as Rector of the University. In 1917 he became a member of the Herrenhaus (the Austrian House of Lords). From 1917 until the fall of the monarchy (in 1918), Wieser served as the Austrian Minister of Commerce.

a "thing," as utility "embraces every quality that is calculated to bring about the satisfaction of need, or that merely prepares it effectively" (39). In other words, we must know that we indeed have a need or want, that something exists that can satisfy it, just what this need-satisfier is, and be capable of acquiring control of it. Other things may indeed be useful and even classifiable as commodities, but as we are unaware of their existence or are unaware of the manner in which they may be used (or perhaps these things are capable of satisfying needs we currently are not aware that we have), we simply can make no judgment as to their commodity-character. "But those things are not considered as commodities, whose usefulness man has not yet discovered and which have consequently not yet been subjected to his power" (39–40). Unlike Menger, Wieser identified these *potential* commodities as *latent* commodities; the difference between a commodity and a latent commodity lies in the knowledge we possess of availability and our own apprehensions of the needs that this thing at some time may fulfill. Likewise, when we are cognizant of the utility generated by a good, but have no means of its acquisition, or if its usage requires a complementary good that we may not have, then these goods are defined as "commodity elements" (40).

Value derives from utility. "Economic value" is "the value which is assigned to units or groups of commodities and of labors employed in economic transactions" (1927, 143). Economic value is further divided into primary and secondary components; primary economic or need-values are "felt in personal experience," while secondary need-values are defined derivatively (143). But value is more generally defined with respect to our subjective interests. It is that value which we attach to material goods as they satisfy personal requirements: "Economic value is a material value; back of it lies an egoistic love of external things" (144). A good has value when it satisfies a need or desire.[37]

Wieser divided "exchange value"—defined as "an institution arising out of economic exchange" (1927, 229)—into two forms: personal exchange-value (a subjective relation) and social economic exchange-value (an objective relation).[38] The first, personal exchange-value, is fundamental, but is itself deduced from the definition of utility. The personal exchange-value is derived indirectly "from the fact that in exchange one object is received or surrendered for another, the utility of which is then set up as the measure of value" (229). So, even if the holder of a good cannot derive utility from it, he can nonetheless use it to procure goods that have for him such value. As with Menger, utility-value and exchange-value are not synonymous. Utility-value "is experienced without reference

---

37. "Predicating value as an attribute of the means of satisfaction emphasizes the close association between the experience of an estimate of value and the simultaneous concept of the means of satisfaction" (Wieser 1927, 144).

38. Wieser was emphatic in his condemnation of the terms *subjective* and *objective* in reference to these relations, but the sense of the terms is clear enough in this context.

to exchange and is spoken of as value in use. All utility-value of the simple economy is use-value" (229). Exchange-value is derived from the utility engendered through the possibility of exchange.

Social economic exchange-value is synonymous with market-value, being "by the universal confirmation of all parties interested, . . . the first step in their appraisal of exchange value" (1927, 234). Social economic exchange-value is prior to any personal appraisal of exchange-value, and as everything is tied to it, is vitally important for the economy:

> The costs which may be incurred in production are controlled by it. It forms the foundation of the attribution of yields to the actively employed productive agents. Amounts of income are stated in this value. It is subject to discount and capitalization. It fills the accounts of production and acquisition from beginning to end. It may properly be spoken of as social economic exchange value, as the general social value, for it is the basis of the social economic process. All individuals taking part in the latter make exclusive use of this price in all matters related to this process. (1927, 234)

With respect to the differences between individual (personal-exchange) values and the social exchange-value, Wieser concluded that one of the more serious problems with Classical Economics is that the classical writers had failed to extend sufficiently their arguments from the individual to the society, that is, they had failed to account for the influence on social exchange-value of personal exchange-value. They were content with analyzing individual actions—which they succeeded at brilliantly—through the lens of "objective" exchange-values, as though it were possible to arrive at a theory of economic valuation without examining the basis of individual human actions and their effects on the objective measure. This Wieser held to have been a grave mistake:

> The individualistic school reduced everything in the social economy to individual effort and fully recognized the concert of individual action in economic endeavour; yet it failed to realize one truth, that economic action is the confluence of individual valuations. This is the fundamental reason that the classical doctrine of value and of price could never finally solve its problem. The theory of value and of price must penetrate to the personal sources in order to complete its task. (1927, 235)

5.2 The Property Relation

In appraising the institution of private property, Wieser began with a question not at all Austrian, but rather framed in very Marxian power-political terms:

Is private property an institution of economic endeavor or is it not, much more properly, to be called an institution of superior power? Or, to be more precise, is private property an institution subservient to the economic requirements of society, or is it merely the creature and tool of those who wield socio-economic power? (1927, 389)

Wieser maintained that it was possible to arrive at a utility calculation apart from the question of ownership. Absent a personal interest in goods-allocation, such as would be met in a regime of private ownership, the individual, "unaffected by any active interests of his own, attends to his functions and calculates faithfully the relations involved between goods and the labors performed upon them" (1927, 143). He is able to arrive dispassionately at an accounting of the "true" labor value of commodities. Without the relations of private ownership, there is nothing to get in the way of a strict use of the hedonical calculus in the derivation of costs and benefits. This is the type of impersonal calculation required of "economic man," a pure utility maximizer who has no personal attachment but only an analytical one. It is also, ironically enough, the condition underlying the model of the socialist collective, as it allows that an objective calculation of costs and benefits and utility can be made. When ownership is considered, the result changes, because "the owner infuses the vital feelings of personal interest into his computation of utility" (143). Thus ownership introduces a subjective element into the utility calculus; it "is most intimately interwoven with all the implications of the individual economy" (390).

The institution of private property requires a two-way relationship between the utility calculator and the goods under his control; the one defines the other. Only goods that "have entered into the economic quantitative relation" can be said to be private property; private property relations can only endure under the conditions of the actualization of economic goods, which are by definition in scarce supply relative to demand (1927, 390). To the extent that we confer utility value, there must be some mechanism to "vindicate" the holding of property. So the purpose of instituting property rights, rights to ownership and control of economic goods, "is to confer legal security with respect to economic use" (390).

The earlier utilitarians, those of the Philosophic Radical tradition, treated the property right as an institutional arrangement that evolved along with the general evolution of society. Property rights became necessary, and their protection by legal means obligatory, because social arrangements simply could not be maintained in a complex society without them, and without the resultant right to contract. Even Aristotle accepted this as a central concern; he considered it a fatal flaw in the constitution of Plato's ideal republic. Wieser was not necessarily opposed to this view, but had developed it from wildly different premises.

Wieser's definitions hinged on power relationships, whereby blocs instead of individuals competed for domination. Absent a focus on individual interactions and a legal process devoted to the protection of these associations, the Benthamite ideal of property and contract relations breaks down; what remains is a competition among rival bloc interests, whereby competing power centers seek to use their positions and influence to achieve group (collective) objectives.

But this view, of property relations as conflict-based, was itself predicated on an atomistic or individualistic approach to economic and social relations. As with Menger, the individualist basis of Wieser's theory of the economy led him to conclude that the very concept of value (which Wieser subsumed under the general classification of the theory of utility) demands the institution of private property rights and the construction of a legal framework for the preservation of these rights. The situation that will inevitably develop as a result of the emergence of these private property arrangements, however, places the citizenry in conflict with one another. The inherent differences in individual utility-valuations and hence individual demands (needs), and the inherent inequality in the distribution of scarce goods so engendered, produces a struggle for possession of the ownership rights to these scarce goods, thus requiring a legal structure devoted to the protection of property. More generally, the apparatus designed initially for the protection of private property and the rights of ownership could be shown to develop eventually into a more encompassing device for the protection of individual liberties. It is easier to protect one's rights as a member of a collective than as an individual acting alone, despite a legal system devoted to the protection of this ideal. The collective affords a more powerful voice that cannot be ignored.

From this evolution of the legal structure, evolving as it did from the protection of ownership rights to that of personal liberty via the collective, Wieser extended the argument to include the protection of the fruits of personal labor. Without a legal claim on the product of one's own creativity, the individual is susceptible to exploitation by those possessed of greater means, meaning greater power. Legal systems, however, are, according to his argument, created to protect the existing distributions of wealth and property; for Wieser these systems serve to perpetuate *power* relations, not individual liberties. Thus could he promote the concept of unions acting as countervailing centers of power.

5.3 Wieser and Social Movements

Unlike Menger, for whom economics was a positive discipline, Wieser was interested in normative considerations as well. His 1889 *Der Natür-liche Werth* (translated in 1893 as *Natural Value*) set out the conditions under which a competitive society with complete income equality could function. "Natural value" or "social use value" was the term Wieser coined to apply individual-based value concepts to society as a whole. Irrespective of whether the society was market-oriented or communistic, goods would still hold value, as wants would still exist while the means to the satisfaction of those wants would be in scarce supply. In a communal system, the "social relation" between goods supply and goods demand on the community level would determine value.

This Wieser termed *natural value,* aware of its connection to the classical concepts of Natural Law and similar notions thought to structure human affairs. The term itself conjured up ideas of perfection. It seemed ideal for the depiction of the nature of value—a fundamental criterion of every economic system—in such a communitarian sphere. Since under communism—as with other communitarian schemes—the society is viewed as an organic whole, we are given the possibility once and for all to face the dilemma posed by Mandeville of the simultaneous existence of social goodness and personal sin, without reliance on Smith's sympathetic man, upon whose goodness we can in any event not rely. The organic nature of the state is itself enough to counter Mandeville's conjecture, for it generates the sympathy and order required at the most aggregate level and filters it down through the levels of the society.

> In its simplicity, purity, and originality it [the communistic state] is so attractive, and at the same time so contradictory to all experience, that it is doubtful whether it can ever be more than a dream. So too we shall think of the communistic state as the perfect state. Everything will be ordered in the best possible way; there will be no misuse of power on the part of its officials, or selfish isolation on the part of its individual citizens; no error or any other kind of friction will ever occur. Natural value shall be that which would be recognised by a completely organic and most highly rational community. (Wieser 1893, 61)

The problem with the socialist-communist "dream," as Wieser perceived it, was in its unflinching adherence to the fatally flawed labor theory of value. This theory he held in contempt as "utterly" useless because it failed to incorporate as social values the fundamental tenets of value theory as proclaimed by classical economics. But to be fair, he maintained that this was not the fault of the mainstream socialist. Socialists had merely accepted the theories of "bourgeois" writers who maintained the primacy of the laborer and his right to the whole of the product of his efforts, without attempting to analyze the basis of value. Wieser was most emphatic on this point:

> In the socialist theory of value pretty nearly everything is wrong. The origin of value, which lies in utility and not in labour, is mistaken. The relation of supply to demand—that fact which impels us to attribute utility to goods, and upon whose fluctuations depend,

in the last resort, the fluctuations in amount of value—is overlooked. The objects to which value attaches are not at all embraced,
for among those must be included productive land and capital, both
as elements in the calculation of costs, and also *per se*. And the
service rendered by value in economic life is only half understood,
inasmuch as the most essential part of it, the material control of
economy, is neglected. (1893, 66)

Despite his problems with the intellectual foundations of socialist
economics and communitarian Utopianism, Wieser had a weakness for
social movements that seemed new and offered visions. The idea, developed in the period immediately following the defeat of Germany and
Austria in the First World War, of combining nationalism and socialism,
had great appeal. Viennese socialism was at the time a vibrant force, one
stressing community (usually city, but also state) solutions to social problems. Likewise, nationalism, taken away from its traditional European
base (where it had been advanced as a substitute for ecclesiastical authority), has on occasion meant in many non-European societies no more than
a "genos" (tribe) taking responsible care of its own. Wieser perhaps accepted the combination of the two as a superior achievement and may
even have seen Adolf Hitler as something of a nationally benevolent
socialist. While this may appear a quandary, it should be remembered that
academics and other intellectuals, particularly when steeped in too many
theories and too little observation, are often a strangely naive bunch.

Another criticism of Wieser's approach is to be found in Wesley
Clair Mitchell's Introduction to the English-language translation of
Wieser's *Social Economics*. Mitchell was at least partly sympathetic to
the Austrian view that the subjective recesses of the mind contained the
seeds of economic decisions, but complained that the "Austrians," generally, and Wieser, specifically, treated the mind, that is, the process of
thought, as inherently unknowable (sort of the legendary "black box");
Mitchell felt this was not necessarily true. Other Austrians of the period,
such as the psychoanalyst Sigmund Freud, thought that the mind could
indeed be explored, that the origins of decisions could be identified and
the decision-making process traced.

Wieser appeared to be moving (and trying to take the Austrian tradition in Vienna) quite strongly away from the original Mengerian rigor relating to the selection of method, but Wieser was clearly no true empiricist.
Rather he preferred to make his syllogisms more "politically practical."

6 The Karl Menger Seminar

Despite the sometimes antimathematical stance of many of the Austrians,
especially those of the first and second generations, there were those

sympathetic to the cause for whom mathematics showed a great deal of promise both as a rhetorical device and as a utilitarian tool. A few, more in the German tradition than the Austrian, evinced an interest in mathematics for its own sake, or as it could be applied to other fields, such as physics, biology, and psychology. These were the true pioneers, whose accomplishments, having emerged from one tradition, extended the envelope in many directions at once. The most notable of these pioneering figures shared a common heritage beyond nationality: they were all in some sense connected to one of the most significant intellectual circles of the time, the Karl Menger seminar.

Karl Menger (1902–85), the natural son of Carl Menger,[39] was renowned as a mathematician, economist, philosopher, and physicist. As an influential member of the Vienna Circle—the group known as the bastion of logical positivism[40] in the 1930s—and later a geometer at the University of Notre Dame, the younger Menger advanced ideas dedicated to a "scientific" view of the world. Beyond the realm of pure and applied mathematics, which were his fields of choice, the younger Menger also held strong views regarding the logical bases of ethics; specifically he rejected Kant's "categorical imperatives," since he believed they could not provide irrefutable boundaries. As he saw it, they were neither sufficient nor even necessary as the basis for ethical standards. He believed, well within the tradition of logical positivism, that experiments could be run to test the presence and demonstrate the evolution of ethical norms. In the end, he concluded that a subjective (individual) determination was the only true basis of moral ethics.[41]

Menger wrote principally within economics on the topic of uncertainty—indeed, Kenneth Arrow's pioneering work on the same topic (including the very definition of the subject) drew from Menger's approach.[42] From these early efforts one can see elements of what has since come to be known as von Neumann and Morgenstern game theory. In addition, Menger did important work in the areas of diminishing returns and scale economies, something he termed "metaeconomics" ("behind

---

39. Carl Menger retired prematurely from his professorship, presumably to concentrate on the education of Karl.

40. Logical Positivism emerged as a philosophical movement of the 1920s and 1930s, primarily in Germany. It was dedicated to providing a logical structure to scientific theories and so is usually regarded as an empirical philosophy of science. A central tenet is that philosophy should be concerned with the *clarification* of propositions, and so philosophical analysis must strive to reduce the structure of a science to its atomic units.

41. From Karl Menger's standpoint, ethics were subjective and, accordingly, anchored only in the individual's mind. One answer to the question of the manner in which an ethical norm becomes established in the first place is that it is derived from a patristic tradition. While some are born into such a tradition, others are "immigrants" and so may, accordingly, "choose" a tradition; the educational process is important in this regard.

42. Menger's approach is best approached (for heuristic purposes) by way of the contribution of Amos Tverski and Daniel Kahneman on the framing problem, that is, the dependence on perspective in understanding the St. Petersburg Paradox.

economics"), which led to a reinterpretation of production functions. In all, what he sought to establish was a theoretical (logical) fusion of the different versions of the productive process, as maintained by Böhm-Bawerk, Wicksell, and Mises. What the approach did not involve was a positivistic consideration of the data requirements for testing.

The Karl Menger seminar was instituted while Menger was professor of mathematics at Vienna. Among the distinguished participants were Karl Schlesinger (a banker by trade whose mathematical insights led to the extension of the Walrasian general equilibrium model), Abraham Wald (a mathematician who developed sequential analysis), and Oskar Morgenstern and John von Neumann (who collaborated in the founding of the currently dominant branch of game theory), to name but a few. From this list of participants alone one can readily see the importance to economic theory of the seminar; each made major contributions to economic theory, as well as significant contributions in related areas. The important thing to remember is that, beyond the technique, the underlying appeal was to the Austrian tradition; nonetheless, the influence of Karl Menger reflected an approach quite different from the amathematical stance Menger's father had preferred.

7 The Austrian School after World War I: The Mises Tradition

7.1 The Misesian Epistemology

The Karl Menger seminar is important in that it led to significant developments in the modern theory of general economic equilibrium. But this was only one of the areas in which the influence of Carl Menger was felt after the First World War. A second, more recognizably Austrian set of principles emerged from perhaps the most influential of the newer, postwar generation of thinkers. This figure, widely regarded by later generations of "Austrian" writers as the true progenitor of the school, was Ludwig Edler von Mises (1881–1973).[43] Mises perceived himself princi-

---

43. Born in Lemberg, then part of the Austro-Hungarian Empire, Mises was part of a very technically oriented family. His father was a construction engineer for the Austrian railroads (a position that was at the time part of the civil service), who held a doctorate from the Zurich Institute of Technology. Perceived, particularly by others, as rather a business-oriented Jew, Mises was accordingly not socially acceptable at the University of Vienna as regular (*professor ordinarius*) professorial material, although he did lecture in economic theory there as a *Privatdozent*. When in 1938 the political situation threatened to become intolerable, Mises left Austria for Switzerland, where, from 1934 to 1940, he held a teaching post at the Graduate Institute of International Studies in Geneva. He then emigrated to the United States, landing at New York University. His free-market, individualist philosophy also led to his being a founder of the Mont Pelerin Society, and the inspiration behind the Ludwig von Mises Institute at Auburn University.

pally as a follower of and intellectual successor to Carl Menger and Böhm-Bawerk, placing him squarely in the third generation of Austrian economist-scholars.[44]

The importance of Mises's work in economic theory and policy cannot be overestimated. His 1912 *Theorie des Geldes und der Umlaufsmittel* (*Theory of Money and Credit*) became the standard work on monetary theory from an Austrian perspective; his 1920 essay "Die Wirtschaftsrechnung im sozialistischen Gemeinwesen" ("Economic Calculation in the Socialist Commonwealth") established the parameters of the subsequent debate on the possibility of socialist calculation. In line with the theme of the present work, we wish to review Mises's contributions to the understanding of the place of the individual versus the community, and the role of economics as a discipline. We will handle the latter of these first.

Mises interjected himself squarely into the methodological battle, advocating one variant of the rationalist tradition. Given his connection with empirical macroeconomics—as founder of the Austrian Business Cycle Institute—his preference for rationalism at the expense of empiricism may seem peculiar.[45] Nonetheless, Mises insisted that economics commenced with rather simple but fundamental logical premises—man has a purpose and pursues goals. How man attains his purposeful goals given limited means is *the* economic problem.

In his 1949 treatise, *Human Action*,[46] Mises laid out his economic and epistemological structures, which involved combining (1) time preference; (2) a subjective theory of costs (including opportunity costs), profits, and losses as the dynamic elements in the development of economies; (3) the importance of the entrepreneur; and (4) the role of knowledge as the underlying basis for transactions. But this is simply the outward manifestation of what was a much more complicated, and very much misunderstood, approach to economics as a social discipline.

Mises desired first and foremost to establish economics as a deductive science, the "truths" of which would be independent of the historical data of real-world economic situations (or indeed any experiential data), but which would be capable of explaining the existence of such regularities as the data exhibit. Historical events merely follow from the interaction of causal factors and cannot be used to test theories.

---

44. Ludwig's brother, Richard, was a renowned mathematician, statistician, and probability theorist, and was a prominent member of the Vienna Circle.

45. In 1923, Mises set up his famous seminar, known more familiarly as the Mises Circle, a somewhat loosely organized group, the meetings of which were held at his office in the Vienna Chamber of Commerce, where he served as principal economist (and an economic adviser to the Austrian government). That seminar had many subsequently famous students—Friedrich von Hayek, Fritz Machlup, Gottfried von Haberler, Oskar Morgenstern, Wilhelm Roepke, Paul N. Rosenstein-Rodan, and Lionel Robbins were regular attendees. Others who participated included Karl Menger and Karl Schlesinger, participants in the Karl Menger seminar, and the philosophers Felix Kaufmann and Alfred Schütz.

46. We use here the third edition of 1966.

Each specific historical episode thus could not be employed to corroborate or invalidate the propositions so deduced.[47] The historical episodes must rather be viewed as themselves deducible from the formal propositions, and by this view cannot be understood outside of the context of the formal propositions, that is, without reference to the axioms of the system. The sole test of a theory is its own internal logic (immanent criticism), and not some criterion of empirical verification. Economics, should it be so structured, would attain the status of logic and pure (as opposed to applied) mathematics in that the propositions of the science are a priori, formal, and necessary (i.e., analytic), untestable, and indefinable with respect to simpler, atomic propositions.[48] In sum, the fundamental propositions of economics are in the nature of definitions; they are the analytic, atomic properties underlying human behavior.[49] As Mises expressed his position:

> Praxeology is a theoretical and systematic, not a historical, science. . . . Its cognition is purely formal and general without reference to the material content and the particular features of the actual case. It aims at knowledge valid for all instances in which the conditions exactly correspond to those implied in its assumptions and inferences. Its statements and propositions are not derived from experience. They are, like those of logic and mathematics, a priori. They are not subject to verification or falsification on the ground of experience and facts. They are both logically and temporally antecedent to any comprehension of historical facts. They are a necessary requirement of any intellectual grasp of historical events. Without them we should not be able to see in the course of events anything else than kaleidoscopic change and chaotic muddle.

47. As Mises explained in his *Epistemological Problems of Economics* (1933), "a proposition of an aprioristic theory can never be refuted by experience" (28–29), but at the same time acknowledged that "a theory that does not appear to be contradicted by experience is by no means to be regarded as conclusively established" (30). Clearly, if the propositions are *independent* of experience, their establishment conclusively by reference *to* experience is contradictory.

48. Compare the statement of the logical positivist philosopher Moritz Schlick: "The exact sciences . . . do not secure unique coordination of judgment system and reality through maximizing the number of fundamental judgments. On the contrary, they strive to make this number as small as possible, and leave it to the necessary workings of logical interconnection to bring the two systems into unambiguous agreement. . . . The fewer the fundamental judgments which lie at the base of a science, the smaller the number of elementary concepts it needs to designate the world and hence the higher the level of knowledge to which it raises us" (1925, 79).

49. In 1933, Mises explicitly accepted such a nominalist position, noting that "[t]heories about action are implicit in the very words we use in acting," and so "[t]o apply language, with its words and concepts, to anything is at the same time to approach it with a theory" (1933, 28). Cf. Schlick: "Whenever we have at our disposal suitably defined concepts, knowledge becomes possible in a form practically free from doubt" (1925, 27).

The fundamental logical relations are not subject to proof or disproof. Every attempt to prove them must presuppose their validity. It is impossible to explain them to a being who would not possess them on his own account. Efforts to define them according to the rules of definition must fail. They are primary propositions antecedent to any nominal or real definition. They are ultimate unanalyzable categories. The human mind is utterly incapable of imagining logical categories at variance with them. No matter how they may appear to superhuman beings, they are for man inescapable and absolutely necessary. They are the indispensable prerequisites of perception, apperception, and experience. (Mises 1966, 32, 34)[50]

As the Fundamental Axiom is an analytic, tautological proposition intuitively derived, Mises's praxeology (the study of human action) is founded on "purely logical grounds."[51] His method may thus be characterized as Cartesian: "humans act" is tantamount to Descartes's *Cogito* as a first principle.[52] There is in fact no greater rationale for the acceptance of "humans act" (and the *Cogito*) as an intuitive "first principle" than its acceptance as a definition.[53] Yet as a tautology, the first principle "humans act" is devoid of operational content. Mises recognized this fact

---

50. "All that is needed for the deduction of all praxeological theorems is knowledge of the essence of human action" (Mises 1966, 64). If "human action" is not amenable to real definition, does it possess an essence?

Martin Hollis considered Mises to have suggested that "formal systems consist of real definitions of elementary concepts, their implications and application rules governing *ceteris paribus* clauses." So Mises was "dealing with Kantian conditions *a priori* of the possibility of finding a kind of describable order in social experience." Clearly this is precisely what Mises rejected for his praxeology (Hollis 1987, 185).

51. One could indeed assert that the true pioneers in this effort were David Ricardo and Nassau Senior, in that their elaboration of deductive systems emphasized nominalist aspects. John Cairnes's (1888) system represents the most advanced expression of the argument and is the one most in sympathy with that of Mises. Lionel Robbins's 1932 edition of *An Essay on the Nature and Significance of Economic Science* presented an argument consistent with that of Cairnes and Mises; the 1935 edition, however, is much closer to the position of the positivists.

52. In fact, Mises's rationale for its acceptance as such is virtually identical to that of Descartes for the acceptance of the *cogito:* "I think, therefore I am, was so certain and so evident that all the most extravagant suppositions of the sceptics were not capable of shaking it . . ." (Descartes 1637, 53–54). J. Patrick Gunning also referred to Mises's postulates as Cartesian (Gunning 1989, 165).

53. Despite what may seem to be the self-evidence of the concept, as Moritz Schlick, the founder of the Vienna Circle and the school of logical positivism, explained, the *cogito,* although purportedly expressing an "incontrovertible truth," is still no more than a definition (Schlick 1925, 85). The same reasoning holds for the proposition "humans act." But definitions are useful for the attainment of knowledge. "Truth is uniqueness of designation, and uniqueness can be obtained not only through knowledge, but also through definition" (Schlick 1925, 85).

and felt compelled to demonstrate its significance.[54] Mises may be said to have derived his epistemological views from Carl Menger. For Menger, operational significance was achieved by reference to laws derived inductively through the realistic-empirical method. The axioms of pure geometry, for example, are analytic, untestable, and not referable to empirical phenomena; they are in no way synthetic a priori propositions. Such holds as well for the propositions or "exact laws" of economics.[55] But applied geometry requires the addition of empirical postulates, which allow the use of geometrical logic in making inferences to actual objects. Mises in like manner proceeded by stipulating additional postulates, necessary for his system to function.

> All the concepts and theorems of praxeology are implied in the category of human action. The first task is to extract and to deduce them, to expound their implications and to define the universal conditions of acting as such. Having shown what conditions are required by any action, one must go further and define—of course, in a categorical and formal sense—the less general conditions required for special modes of acting. (1966, 64)

It is the nature of these "less general conditions," or subsidiary postulates, that is at issue in classifying the methodology of Mises. If they are tautologies, the system constructed upon them is not operationally valid; if empirical generalizations, contingent on the state of the world for

54. Here Mises actually seemed to express sympathy with the logical positivists. His (at best implicit) acceptance of Ludwig Wittgenstein's dictum that ". . . only tautologies follow from a tautology" (Wittgenstein 1921, prop. 6.126) is expressed thus:

> Aprioristic reasoning is purely conceptual and deductive. It cannot produce anything else but tautologies and analytic judgments. All its implications are logically derived from the premises and were already contained in them. Hence, according to a popular objection, it cannot add anything to our knowledge.
>
> All geometrical theorems are already implied in the axioms. . . . Nonetheless nobody would contend that geometry in general and the theorem of Pythagoras in particular do not enlarge our knowledge. Cognition from purely deductive reasoning is also creative and opens for our mind access to previously barred spheres. The significant task of aprioristic reasoning is on the one hand to bring into relief all that is implied in the categories, concepts, and premises and, on the other hand, to show what they do not imply. (Mises 1966, 38)

55. To quote Menger: "To want to test the pure theory of economy by experience in its full reality is a process analogous to that of the mathematician who wants to correct the principles of geometry by measuring real objects, without reflecting that the latter are indeed not identical with the magnitudes which pure geometry presumes or that every measurement of necessity implies elements of inexactitude" (1883, 70).

This was as well the view of Schlick, who used a similar argument to handle the problem of universals: "It is impossible to imagine a triangle in general, a triangle that is neither scalene nor isosceles nor equilateral, a triangle that possesses all and only the properties that *every* triangle has and yet is without specific properties. As soon as one imagines a triangle, it is already a specific triangle, for in the image its sides and angles must be of some magnitude or other" (1925, 18).

which they are to be utilized, the result is consistent with the tenets of
Logical Positivism; if empirically derived and necessary, but not tautological, the result is Kantian.[56]

So for all his emphasis on rationalism and the use of deductive
reason in the derivation of economic propositions, and for all his denunciation of those who relied on derivation based on the historical data of
economics, Mises still left room for the valid use of empirical data; such
historical data is useful in connecting theory with the corresponding
reality. In so doing he (perhaps inadvertently) demoted economics to a
position below that enjoyed by logic and mathematics as rational, analytic disciplines, and as well supplied the element that allows for a positivist interpretation of the work (as opposed to a Cartesian or Kantian
rationalist view). In other words, Mises explicitly connected the aprioristic theory with the empirical reality and further accepted the contingency of such an endeavor:

> Economics does not follow the procedure of logic and mathematics.
> It does not present an integrated system of pure aprioristic ratio-
> cination severed from any reference to reality. In introducing as-
> sumptions into its reasoning, it satisfies itself that the treatment of
> the assumptions concerned can render useful services for the com-
> prehension of reality.
>
> [P]raxeology restricts its inquiries to the study of acting under those
> conditions and presuppositions which are given in reality. . . . How-
> ever, this reference to experience does not impair the aprioristic
> character of praxeology and economics. Experience merely directs
> our curiosity toward certain problems and diverts it from other
> problems. (1966, 66, 65)

Economics is therefore constrained by the dictates of the real world in
which the individual acts.[57] The primary axiom cannot stand alone; it must

---

56. Gunning implied that the *subsidiary* postulates are synthetic and allow operational significance by referring to the "true" situation as it exists in the real world (Gunning
1989, 172). Don Lavoie interpreted Mises as acknowledging that "it is precisely history that
tells us what parts of our theorizing are applicable to the real world. Thus, theory is not
nearly as insulated from 'the facts' as some of Mises' own pronouncements suggest" (Lavoie
1986, 194). Both views suggest (albeit hesitatingly) a (potential) logical positivist reading of
Mises's work, not out of line with that provided by Machlup. Richard Langlois, on the
other hand, attributed a synthetic *a priori* character to the axioms and so reiterates the
argument that Mises was a Kantian (1985, 228).

57. Consider the axiomatization of economics initiated by Gerard Debreu, himself
very much influenced by the French tradition. In his *Theory of Value*, Debreu dichotomized
theory and practice, desiring to express the theory as "logically entirely disconnected from
its interpretations" (Debreu 1959, x). Debreu recognized the need for empirical generalizations (subsidiary postulates) in order to provide meaningfulness to the theory; in fact, he
allowed that it is possible to extend the analysis "without modification of the theory by
simple reinterpretations of concepts." These reinterpretations would perforce be of the
nature of empirical postulates.

be viewed in concert with ancillary propositions, thus acquiring empirical validity. But these ancillary propositions are not mere modifications to the primary axiom; neither are they restatements that alter the form and substance of the axiom by making it synthetic. They are empirical statements necessary to lend operational meaning to the axiom, without changing its analytic nature. The "action" axiom is valid as an analytic statement *provided there is appended to it the requisite synthetic propositions.*

7.2 *Methodological Individualism and the Meaning of the State*

In the classic *Human Action,* Mises furthered the concept of "methodological individualism" (a term coined by Schumpeter) as the principle behind praxeology. To the extent that "social action" can be said to exist at all, it is not comprehensible outside the boundaries of "human" (meaning individual) action. Mises argued that actions can only be undertaken by individuals. The state, community, family, or any other collective grouping exists and can operate only through the performance of the individual; individual actions are primary, but can be related to the collective in a secondary relationship. This implies that, while actions are taken by individuals, the *meaning* given to those actions may be such as to identify them with the state sanction.[58]

> If we scrutinize the meaning of the various actions performed by individuals we must necessarily learn everything about the actions of collective wholes. For a social collective has no existence and reality outside of the individual members' actions. The life of a collective is lived in the actions of the individuals constituting its body. There is no social collective conceivable which is not operative in the actions of some individuals. The reality of a social integer consists in its directing and releasing definite actions on the part of individuals. Thus the way to a cognition of collective wholes is through an analysis of the individuals' actions. (1966, 42)

This is not to deny that man is a "social" being. On the contrary, the fact of the existence of society—of language, art, science, commerce, and so on—is enough to demonstrate the validity of the argument that indeed he is. Having so stipulated, Mises believed that it served little intellectual value to argue over the priority of the individual or the collective. He was more concerned with the *evolution* of such social organisms. The important aspect emphasized by Mises was that collectives themselves do not engender change; change occurs only through individual behavior, with the collective reflecting such individual changes on the

---

58. "It is the meaning that marks one action as the action of an individual and another action as the action of the state or of the municipality. The hangman, not the state, executes a criminal. It is the meaning of those concerned that discerns in the hangman's action an action of the state" (Mises 1966, 42).

aggregate, or social, level. One can study the evolution of society, but only so long as one is mindful of the *composition* of that society.

While collectives are "real" things, it is nonetheless true that they have no independent existence beyond the individuals comprising them; they cannot themselves be independently examined, for they are but "a part aspect of the actions of various individuals and as such a real thing determining the course of events":

> It is illusory to believe that it is possible to visualize collective wholes. They are never visible; their cognition is always the outcome of the understanding of the meaning which acting men attribute to their acts. We can see a crowd, i.e., a multitude of people. Whether this crowd is a mere gathering or a mass (in the sense in which this term is used in contemporary psychology) or an organized body or any other kind of social entity is a question which can only be answered by understanding the meaning which they themselves attach to their presence. And this meaning is always the meaning of individuals. Not our senses, but understanding, a mental process, makes us recognize social entities. (1966, 43)

Mises took issue with advocates of an organic conception of the state (specifically the German historical philosophers and economists and those of the cameralist and romantic traditions), alleging they resorted to metaphysics in providing an explanation of the forces compelling man to pursue the social good. The utilitarian philosophers (correctly, in Mises's estimation) understood that man, endowed with reason and the ability to recognize his own best interests, will by so doing also fulfill the social welfare. The holistic or metaphysical philosophers (universalists, collectivists, realists, and others), by contrast, were compelled, given their conception of society as an organic whole, to endow this organism with a further existence beyond, and with ends different from, the ends and existence of the individuals comprising it. The collectivist mentality led to countless episodes of civil strife, as physical challenges replaced logical argument in dispute resolution; since the basis of the legitimacy of the collective is a nonrational (or extrarational) one, its acceptance must be forced on an incredulous public.

Only with the coming of the utilitarian philosophy, and the defeat of universalism (including the German Romantic and Historical Schools), could the idea of tolerance prevail, for only then could the individual comprehend that institutions (the state and its bureaucratic apparatus) were the *means* to an end, and not ends in themselves; only with such an understanding of the basis of the collective—as an outgrowth of individual human action, not an organic whole existing temporally prior to humanity—could man begin to perceive and so accept the basis of its legitimacy (1966, 145–48).

Thus those systems based on utilitarian ethics and classical liberalism hold to the conviction that the foundation of society and the state rests with the governed. The "will of the majority" must overthrow any regime not attuned to that will. The universalist (collectivist) systems, by contrast, demand obedience to an ethical code designed not for the benefit of the citizenry as a collection of individual members, but for the furtherance of the organic whole. Under such a structure, as the citizenry no longer need be persuaded of the efficacy of governmental policy—to attempt to do so would in fact run counter to the belief in an organic unity with its own defined ends—the result is an autocracy. The form of the autocracy is irrelevant—oligarchy, plutocracy, theocracy, monarchy, socialist dictatorship (the planned socialist state). The principle underlying each is the possession of the attributes of omniscience, omnipotence, and knowledge of the social good. The moment it is conceded

> that there exists above and beyond the individual's actions an imperishable entity aiming at its own ends, different from those of mortal men, one has already constructed the concept of a superhuman being. Then one cannot evade the question whose ends take precedence whenever an antagonism arises, those of the state or society or those of the individual. The answer to this question is already implied in the very concept of state or society as conceived by collectivism and universalism. (1966, 151)

7.3 Individualism and the Property Right

Perhaps the most important aspect of the economic theory presented in *Human Action,* and the issue most representative of the theme of the book, revolves around Mises's interpretation of the property right. To begin, Mises held private property to be "the institution the presence of which characterizes the market economy as such. Where it is absent, there is no question of a market economy" (Mises 1966, 682).

The property right evolved to comprise two different but not necessarily incompatible notions: the catallactic notion and the legal notion.[59] Mises reasoned that, although the two notions had originally been indistinct—it had been "the idea of legislators and courts to define the legal concept of property is such a way as to give to the proprietor full protection by the governmental apparatus of coercion and compulsion and to prevent anybody from encroaching upon his rights" (1966, 682)—the government was acting increasingly in opposition to its charter, severely limiting the ability of the "proprietor" to do with his property as he wished. The distinction between the catallactic and the legal notion of property was becoming more apparent as society evolved, with the state attempting to replace private with social (public) ownership.

---

59. "[C]atallactics deals with control, not with legal terms, concepts and definitions" (Mises 1966, 683).

The concept of private ownership Mises accepted as artificial, derived legalistically (but predicated on the catallactic notion) as the invention of society, not something stipulated as an axiom of economics. Furthermore, if one could search the history of the title to a property, one would find that, with some few exceptions, "every owner is the direct or indirect legal successor of people who acquired ownership either by arbitrary appropriation of ownerless things or by violent spoliation of their predecessor" (1966, 683).

While perhaps this basis of title would have upset Marx, it had no effect on the conclusion drawn by Mises. The manner of the historical determination of ownership is irrelevant to the current use of property in the market economy; the market is the current, and most efficient and effective, determinant of use and ownership.

> Ownership in the market economy is no longer linked up with the remote origin of private property. Those events in a far-distant past, hidden in the darkness of primitive mankind's history, are no longer of any concern for our day. For in an unhampered market society the consumers daily decide anew who should own and how much he should own. The consumers allot control of the means of production to those who know how to use them best for the satisfaction of the most urgent wants of the consumers. (1966, 683)

In the same vein Mises argued again in a 1947 monograph entitled *Planned Chaos*. Here he stressed his belief, one which has since become a political motivation of the Austrian school, in the superiority of private enterprise over governmental intervention (with its reliance on bureaucratic methods of command and control) in the economy. Mises felt that (at the time) the trend among governments throughout the world was toward an increasing statism, with governmental measures for planning and organizing the economy and society gaining acceptance over individual organizing activity. He expressed the then-dominant mood as follows:

> The dogma that the State or the Government is the embodiment of all that is good and beneficial and that the individuals are wretched underlings, exclusively intent upon inflicting harm upon one another and badly in need of a guardian, is almost unchallenged. It is taboo to question it in the slightest way. He who proclaims the godliness of the State and the infallibility of its priests, the bureaucrats, is considered as an impartial student of the social sciences. All those raising objections are branded as biased and narrow-minded. (Mises 1947, 16)

It was this statist mind-set that above all else Mises wished to challenge. To that end the pamphlet reviewed subjects including the failure of state intervention in the economy and society, the antidemocratic nature of socialism, the equation of socialism and communism with fascism and Nazism, and the non-inevitability of socialism, in effect laying the foundation for the philosophy of *Human Action.*

8 Hayek and the Reemergence of Spontaneous Order

The preeminent scholar among the fourth generation of Austrian economists, and one of the most politically astute commentators of his generation, was Friedrich August von Hayek (1899–1992). Born into a highly motivated intellectual family—his father was a doctor and research botanist, his brothers were professors of anatomy and chemistry—he received two doctorates—in law (1921) and political science (1923)—from the University of Vienna, where Wieser was one of his instructors.

Hayek's relationship with Mises began in 1921, after he had been awarded his law degree. In that year he accepted a position with the Österreichische Abrechnungsamt, the office assigned to handle Austria's prewar debt situation, directed at the time by Mises. Shortly thereafter Hayek became a participant in the Mises seminar, and he eventually accepted the directorship of Mises's Austrian Institute for Business Cycle Research, a post he held until 1932.

In 1931, Hayek went to lecture at the London School of Economics.[60] It was while at the London School that he published one of his best-known and most controversial books, *The Road to Serfdom* (1944). This single work—which he described as "a political book"—set the stage for the classic clash between the proponents of a free society and those advocating a socialist utopia. (He revisited the argument in 1988 with the publication of *The Fatal Conceit.*)

The argument of *The Road to Serfdom* is that socialism and all other forms of rationalist communitarianism would eventually lead to totalitarian dictatorship, while society viewed from the perspective of the individual—seen not as an organic whole but as a collection of atomistic individuals—would lead to freedom-enhancing rules (as opposed to oppressive order) and maintain an emphasis on the coordination properties of the market.

The conflict centered on individualism versus collectivism. Collectivist ideologies require a commitment to a stipulated social goal, toward which all activity is directed.[61] The society (on this understanding) is an organic unity, devoted to the deliberate attainment of that end, unable or unwilling to admit that the individuals comprising the society have different and perhaps competing ends in mind. The end in the collectivist

---

60. He subsequently was awarded the Tooke Professorship, the first foreign professor to be so honored.

61. Hayek recognized that, for different types of collectivism, the goal may vary, but that they all still *direct* efforts toward the achievement of *some* goal (1944, 56).

regimes is typically expressed in some vaguely worded ideal, such as commonweal, social welfare, general good, or public interest, of which it is said that some measure of realization is possible. With this Hayek emphatically disagreed, denying the existence of any such thing as a "complete, ethical code" or a single definable "social" end, abstracted from individual ends. This meant that attempts at directing individual activity to a "social" end must lead to tyranny.

> The welfare of a people, like the happiness of a man, depends on a great many things that can be provided in an infinite variety of combinations. It cannot be adequately expressed as a single end, but only as a hierarchy of ends, a comprehensive scale of values in which every need of every person is given its place. To direct all our activities according to a single plan presupposes that every one of our needs is given its rank in an order of values which must be complete enough to make it possible to decide among all the different courses which the planner has to choose. It presupposes, in short, the existence of a complete ethical code in which all the different human values are allotted their due place. (Hayek 1944, 57)

The counter to socialism and all other communitarian schemes is individualism. Individualism to Hayek was not coincident with egoism or selfishness or self-love, but included also Smith's sympathy or moral sense. More significantly, individualism accepts and makes allowances for the fact that the human imagination is limited in its ability to formulate a "scale of values." This alone suggests "that the individuals should be allowed, within defined limits, to follow their own values and preferences rather than somebody else's; that within these spheres the individual's system of ends should be supreme and not subject to any dictation by others" (1944, 59).

Perhaps the most concise explanation of Hayek's thought on the matter is his 1948 *Individualism and Economic Order,* a collection of previously published essays on the general topic of the role of the individual in society. As we have attempted to do here, Hayek characterized individualism and socialism—which he claimed to have originated with the Saint-Simonians—as polar opposites, their meanings taken literally as promoting an atomistic (individual) or organic (social) conception of the state and society. Hayek defined "true" individualism as "primarily a *theory* of society, an attempt to understand the forces which determine the social life of man" and secondarily "a set of political maxims derived from this view of society" (Hayek 1948, 6; emphasis in original). It is the *social* aspect that is of the utmost importance: "true" individualism does not posit man removed from his place in society, but instead maintains that man's "nature and character" derive from society.

"True" individualism is represented in the philosophies of Locke, Mandeville, Smith, and Burke (among those we have discussed). The "true" view is that individuals, in pursuit of their own self-interest, constrained only by a moral and ethical code, will in the absence of any rational plan produce an ordered society. Here the paradox of Mandeville is seen not as the "special" case, but as a general statement of the nature of social order: the complexity of society belies the fact that the individuals comprising that society are not intent on promoting the social good, but instead are intent only on pursuing their own individual interests, without a preconceived social end in mind. The only *social* restrictions on individual actions are those of folkways, mores, value and ethical systems, and institutions, the creation of which has no rational basis.[62] "True" individualist philosophy thus maintains that order in society is, in the words of Adam Ferguson, "the result of human action, but not the execution of any human design."[63] Order emerges spontaneously as "the unforeseen result of individual actions" (1948, 8).[64]

"False" individualism Hayek defined as the individualism suggested in the writings of the French rationalists, especially Descartes and Rousseau, who were singled out as representatives of the tradition. This "false" view contends that social order is created deliberately and by design (of which the "social contract" is an example) and cannot be the result of spontaneous order. The rationalists simply cannot comprehend an ordered society that emerges through chance interactions; instead man must have understood the savagery of the base state and taken deliberate measures to create an ordered environment.

The difference between the "true" and "false" variants involves the stature and place of reason: in the former, man is *served* by reason, but not guided by it; in the latter, reason *directs* all action. Thus:

> the former [true individualism] is a product of an acute consciousness of the limitations of the individual mind which induces an attitude of humility toward the impersonal and anonymous social processes by which individuals help to create things greater than they know, while the latter is the product of an exaggerated belief in the powers of individual reason and of a consequent contempt for anything which has not been consciously designed by it or is not fully intelligible to it. (1948, 8)

---

62. See especially Hayek's 1966 essay on Mandeville.

63. See Ferguson's 1767 *An Essay on the History of Civil Society* for an early example of the concept of spontaneous order.

64. Spontaneous order should thus be distinguished from the "natural" order of the physical and biological sciences, and the "artificial" or manufactured order represented by planning systems. It should be noted in this regard that Steve Fleetwood (1995) regarded Hayek as having eventually arrived at a quasi-transcendental realist ontology.

The problem with "false" individualism then is its reliance on an artificial, rationally planned design as a motivation to order. It forces one "to the conclusion that social processes can be made to serve human ends only if they are subjected to the control of individual human reason, and thus lead directly to socialism." The antithesis, "true" individualism, the philosophy of unplanned order, holds by contrast that "if left free, men will often achieve more than individual human reason could design or foresee" (1948, 10–11).

In terms of the appropriate method of governance, Hayek distinguished between "government by rules"—"whose main purpose is to inform the individual what is his sphere of responsibility within which he must shape his own life"—and "government by order"—"which impose[s on the individuals] specific duties" (1948, 18). The distinction is fundamental: "It involves nothing less than the distinction between freedom under the law and the use of the legislative machinery, whether democratic or not, to abolish freedom" (18). For Hayek the solution lay not in the establishment of a set of governing principles, but rather on a reading of consequentialism we saw in G. E. Moore: the difference between remote (and indirect) and immediate (or direct) consequences of actions. The role of government

> should be confined to making the individuals observe principles which *they* know and can take into account in *their* decisions. . . .
> [An individual's actions] must depend not on some remote and indirect consequences which his actions may have but on the immediate and readily recognizable circumstances which he can be supposed to know. (1948, 18)

Thus Hayek insisted that such general rules of conduct "be designed to remain valid for long periods" (1948, 20). Long-run policies can be employed as critical guidelines or signposts, upon which the individual relies in forming his plans and expectations. In an obvious aside to Keynes—whose maxim "In the long run we are all dead" Hayek singled out for particular scorn—Hayek concluded that short-term rules or policies would eventually reduce to centralized orders, collapsing the social order to one of rigid command.

Finally, it is interesting to note Hayek's opinion as to the genealogy of the idea of a spontaneous social order. Mandeville he maintained was the originator of the concept in his *Fable*. Hume, Smith, and Ferguson "borrowed" from him themes which they later extended in other directions. Burke likewise continued along the Mandevillian course, and influenced Herder, Vico, and Savigny. Savigny, in turn, influenced Carl Menger, and so began the Austrian intellectual tradition.[65]

---

65. On this see Hayek 1966, 140n.3.

9 Lionel Robbins

9.1 *The Nature of Economics*

The influence of Lionel Charles (Lord) Robbins, Baron of Clare-Market (1898–1984),[66] surfaced most notably at the London School of Economics, particularly in regard to his 1932 *An Essay on the Nature and Significance of the Economic Science.* (We use here the third edition of 1984.) A seminal book as well as lightning rod of sorts, this was another Misesian offshoot; its defense of rationalism in economics drew criticism from the positivists among economists, whose own methodological program was just gaining adherents, and, perhaps more importantly, paved the way for Mises's own treatise, *Human Action.*

Robbins rejected the identification of economics as "the study of the causes of material welfare" as being a mere *classificatory* notion concerned with specific *kinds* of behavior. He preferred a more *analytical* approach, one concerned with *aspects* of behavior as constrained by scarcity.

> The economist studies the disposal of scarce means. He is interested in the way different degrees of scarcity of different goods give rise to different ratios of valuation between them, and he is interested in the way in which changes in conditions of scarcity, whether coming from changes in ends or changes in means—from the demand side or the supply side—affect their ratios. Economics is the science which studies human behaviour as a relationship between ends and scarce means which have alternative uses. (Robbins 1984, 16)

Of fundamental interest to economists is not satisfactions—the "end-product of activity"—but rather the activities themselves (1984, 25). The economist

> is not concerned with ends as such. He is concerned with the way in which the attainment of ends is limited. The ends may be noble or they may be base. They may be "material" or "immaterial"—if ends can be so described. But if the attainment of one set of ends

---

66. Lord Robbins was originally an Oxonian, but left for the London School of Economics where he introduced the Austrian approach (the School had been founded by the Webbs, who had wanted its orientation to be socialist). Robbins was a marvelously tolerant and wise man, a raconteur of record, and an aesthete of note (he served on the Board of Governors of both the National Gallery and Covent Garden). He had been pro-Hayek and manifestly anti-Keynesian until World War II, when he worked with Keynes and readjusted his opposition somewhat. Robbins was much more of a free trader than Keynes, but served with Keynes on the British Bretton Woods Mission which set up the International Monetary Fund and the World Bank.

Robbins received his peerage as recognition for the Robbins Plan, which was the basis for the establishment of the principle that higher education should be available to all who are qualified to benefit from it.

involves the sacrifice of others, then it has an economic aspect. (1984, 25)

Economics "is concerned with ends in so far as they affect the disposition of means. It takes the ends as given in scales of relative valuation, and enquires what consequences follow in regard to certain aspects of behaviour" (1984, 30). Economics is thus not on a par with aesthetics, which is concerned with an end in itself.

While the focus on scarcity, choice under uncertainty, and exchange may lead one to the conclusion that isolated (Robinson Crusoe) and communistic economies must be excluded from the domain of economics, Robbins did not agree. Economics may have the most *utility* in the analysis of exchange economies—requiring "the utmost effort of abstract thought . . . to devise generalisations which enable us to grasp them" (1984, 19)—but in all others there is still the problem of the means–ends framework and the fact of scarcity, which are the basic problems of interest to economists. So long as human behavior focuses on the means–ends relationship, then irrespective of the politicoeconomic structure, the analytical method of economic science has a positive application.

For Robbins, the propositions of economics are derived from fundamental axioms, which are themselves reflective of experience. This suggests that "[e]conomic laws describe inevitable implications" (1984, 121). To the extent that "the premises relate to reality the deductions from them must have a similar point of reference" (104).[67] The generalizations of economics differ from those of logic "by the fact that in some sense their reference is to that which exists, or that which may exist, rather than to purely formal relations" (104). These generalizations "are known to us by immediate acquaintance" (105).

Robbins criticized specifically the German Historical School and the American Institutionalists (the latter the topic of chapter 11) for relying on a method bound in time and place; he singled out Wesley Clair Mitchell as representative of a particularly egregious form of this type of theorizing.[68] The result of the "revolt" against abstraction—begun, according to Robbins, by Josiah Child and Richard Jones—was disappointing for economic theory (to say the least), as it did not seem to lead to the furtherance of analytical economics. Indeed, Robbins was emphatic in his denunciation, announcing boldly that

---

67. Contrast this with the view of Milton Friedman in his 1953 "The Methodology of Positive Economics," wherein Friedman presented the case for making deductions from unrealistic premises. This is held to be valid so long as the model with which we are working predicts well.

68. "Professor Mitchell, who never tires of belittling the methods and results of orthodox analysis, apparently thinks that, by taking them all together and fitting a highly complicated curve to their frequency distribution, he is constructing something significant—something which is more than a series of straight lines and curves on half a page of his celebrated treatise" (Robbins 1984, 113).

not one single "law" deserving of the name, not one quantitative generalisation of permanent validity has emerged from their efforts. A certain amount of interesting statistical material. Many useful monographs on particular historical situations. But of "concrete laws," substantial uniformities of "economic behaviour," not one— all the really interesting applications of modern statistical technique to economic enquiry have been carried through, not by the Institutionalists, but by men who have been themselves adept in the intricacies of the "orthodox" theoretical analysis. (1984, 114–15)

This is not to imply that historical data are unnecessary to the study of economic phenomena; on the contrary, Robbins held that the analytical school had always maintained a place for the data of the "real" world. In fact, just the opposite seems true. The analytical economists were those who were most likely to gain from the use of empirical data, for they (unlike those of the Historical Schools) have a foundation upon which to ground their generalizations:

The fruitful conduct of realistic investigations can only be undertaken by those who have a firm grasp of analytical principles and some notion of what can and what cannot legitimately be expected from activities of this sort. (1984, 116)

Robbins was not sanguine about the possibility of constructing a system of rules, derived from economic theory, which could drive politics, a "system so unequivocal in its prescriptions regarding the conduct of what was conceived as *economic* policy that, within this sphere, its logic, if not its power to coerce unreasoning politicians, might be regarded as all-compelling" (Robbins 1963, 12; emphasis in original). Political objectives seemed always to drive economic and social policy, and even economic and social *analysis*. It seems hard to deny the political component of what is typically perceived as positive economic theory. The classical writers were unable to achieve such a derivation. Their treatises were based instead on political objectives and values; even the "greatest happiness" principle is a political, not an economic, postulate.

Robbins singled out Pigou's *Economics of Welfare* as a modern "scientific" treatment of the problem of social welfare, which nonetheless was predicated on an ideological and political base. The claims of science in the promotion of welfare were merely a masquerade, designed to obscure the fact that the fundamental criterion—interpersonal comparisons of utility—is itself a criterion of a political nature, one which establishes beforehand the conclusions to be derived.

[A]ny claim that its generalizations and norms of measurement are independent of politics is surely based on illusion. For, in the last analysis, any assertions about the movement of welfare as a whole must depend upon assumptions regarding the comparability of one person's welfare with another's; and these, in the nature of things, are matters of political philosophy—conventions imported from outside. (1963, 14)

Yet Robbins was not above crediting those who showed a glimmer of understanding of the problem. Despite his bad press, even Bentham could be acknowledged to have been aware of the political nature and the ramifications of the hypothesis of the "greatest happiness of the greatest number," as Robbins acknowledged. Bentham was keenly aware that interpersonal comparisons, and the notion of additive utility that made such comparisons possible, were little more than fictions, postulates required to further the inquiry. Pigou, on the other hand, according to Robbins, had neglected even this basic understanding of the role played by assumptions in leading analysis.

In the end, it was better to rest with the recognition

> that there can be no question of a theory of economic policy which does not depend in the most intimate way upon political judgments and valuations. . . . [A]ny theory of economic policy must depend partly on conventions and valuations which are imported from outside. (1963, 19)

Utilitarianism and Ethics   9.2

Robbins did not accept the utilitarian belief that economics and ethics were associated.[69] The propositions of economics must be taken as statements of positive science, not normative ethics. In this he was clearly aligned with Jevons:

> Economics deals with ascertainable facts; ethics with valuations and obligations. The two fields of enquiry are not on the same plane of discourse. Between the generalisations of positive and normative studies there is a logical gulf fixed which no ingenuity can disguise and no juxtaposition in space or time bridge over. . . . Propositions involving the verb "ought" are different in kind from propositions involving the verb "is." And it is difficult to see what possible good can be served by not keeping them separate, or failing to recognise their essential difference. (Robbins 1984, 148–49)

This is not to imply that Robbins denied a place for normative statements in economics. To the extent that it is a "policy science" such influence is hardly escapable. He wished merely "to make it clear that statements about the way in which an economic system worked or *could* work did not in themselves carry any presumption that that was the way

---

69. Economics "is incapable of deciding as between the desirability of different ends. It is fundamentally distinct from Ethics" (Robbins 1984, 152).

in which it *should* work" (Robbins 1971, 148; emphasis in original). This requires a clear understanding among economists of the distinction between existential propositions (the "is") and obligatory propositions (the "ought"), a distinction not always made, adhered to, or understood. Economists need not stay removed from issues of social importance; they should, however, before engaging in arguments of an ethical nature, take pains to ensure that they are grounded in an understanding of the mechanism underlying the system.[70]

Consider the way in which this view seems to have colored his interpretation of Utilitarianism. As we saw above, Robbins was rather sympathetic to Bentham's approach. He viewed Bentham quite differently than did Keynes, who portrayed him as something of an extreme individualist. Bentham, according to Robbins, was more in line with Keynes and Marshall in delimiting the respective roles of the individual and the state:

> The fact is that Bentham's conception of the division of function between state and private activity in the economic sphere was essentially one of leaving to the individual and groups of individuals all that area in which individual or group initiative can be made to harmonise with the public good, and assigning to the state all those functions where individual or group action is plainly insufficient and where only central regulation or initiative can be effective. (Robbins 1970, 76)

Bentham's "greatest happiness" principle had likewise been misinterpreted. The principle was for Robbins not the basis of an individualist act-utilitarian ethic, but could instead serve as a rule for the constraint of the legislator, "by which to judge legislative and administrative projects affecting large masses of people" (1970, 80).[71] While the utilitarian ethic was not itself useful as a guide to "private conduct," it could serve as "a good first approximation to many of the workaday problems of social policy" (57n.2), that is, as a criterion to the legislator of the efficacy of legislative enactments designed ostensibly to ameliorate social ills:

> I submit that there is no more salutary thing for a legislator or an administrator to do than continually to be submitting his possible actions to the test they [the utilitarians] pose: how will they affect the happiness, positive or negative, of the different members of the present and future community; where, on balance, does it stand on this criterion? (1970, 81)

70. "[I]t is only if one knows how the machine runs or can run that one is entitled to say how it ought to run" (Robbins 1971, 148).

71. "To ask of any contemplated law or administrative order, will it, on balance, achieve more happiness or less pain than the other possibilities, is a habit which, in my judgement at least, is just as incumbent today as it was at the time of the publication of the *Principles of Morals and Legislation*" (Robbins 1970, 81–82).

This for Robbins was as much an ethical and moral concern as it was a positive one:

> I do not believe, and I have never believed, that in fact men are necessarily equal or should always be judged as such. But I do believe that, in most cases, political calculations which do not treat them *as if* they were equal are morally revolting. (1938, 635; emphasis in original)

He argued that Bentham was aware of the limitations in applying such a procedure as the "greatest happiness" principle to an analysis of public policy proposals. This is clearly evident in Bentham's desire to restrict its use as "a working rule by which to judge generally applicable laws and procedures" or as a basis for the development of such principles of law. The blame for the ill repute of the utilitarian calculus Robbins laid at the feet of "modern" mathematical economists, who took to "making claims which are repugnant to good sense" (1938, 81).

Consider the problem of interpersonal comparisons of utility we touched on above. Robbins held that such comparisons were not in fact valid as "scientific" economic propositions because they were not deductions from the fundamental postulates of economic theory; they had been merely appended to positive economics much in the manner of legal enactments to canon law and had been accepted as part of the conventional understanding of fairness and equity:

> Just as for purposes of justice we assume equality of responsibility in similar situations as between legal subjects, so for purposes of public finance we agree to assume equality of capacity for experiencing satisfaction from equal incomes in similar circumstances as between economic subjects. (Robbins 1984, 140)

As mentioned in respect to Robbins's methodology, the problem with such an extraeconomic assumption is that it tends to drive policy, which should be grounded on sound economic principles. Once accepted as an element of conventional economic theory, the notion of interpersonal comparisons of utility could readily serve as the basis for the calculation of social utility. Yet the very notion of social utility is not scientific. Rather it gains credence by having at the ready a method for its implementation. We assume equal capacity of satisfaction in conjunction with additive utility and interpersonal comparability, and so we can easily arrive at a measure of the social welfare. The problem of course is that the premise is invalid. Interpersonal utility comparability, equal capacity for satisfaction, and additivity are not derived from established axioms, but rather are stipulated as part of an ethical norm and appended to economic theorems; thus the very notion of an objective measure of "social utility" must be also be viewed as invalid. As Robbins characterized it, social utility is simply the accidental deposit of the historical association of English Economics with Utilitarianism: and both the utilitarian postulates from which it derives and the analytical Economics with which it has been associated will be the better and the more convincing if this is clearly recognised. (1984, 141)

It was as a *convention* that the ethical proposition of comparative interpersonal utility had meaning, not as an objective scientific principle. Robbins simply felt that the purveyors of the notion had not adequately made the case for accepting into positive discourse such an obviously normative principle, and he chose to remain skeptical "until someone can demonstrate to me how objectively to judge between Sir Henry Maine's Brahmin who thought he was many times more capable of satisfaction than an Untouchable, and a radical of the Benthamite tradition who assumed equal capacity all round" (Robbins 1971, 148). Interestingly, it was Bentham's "solution" that proved most satisfactory to Robbins. Bentham used the postulate of equal satisfaction as a normative convention, much along the lines of the Principle of Insufficient Reason, justifying it "on the ground that you need something of this sort if you are to proceed to prescribe about almost anything" (148). Robbins even accepted that he himself was willing "to argue from conventions if they are recognized as such" (148–49). It was on this score that he declared himself to be a "provisional" utilitarian, for whom the Benthamite calculus serves well "as a first approximation in handling questions relating to the lives and actions of large masses of people, the approach which counts each man as one, and, on that assumption, asks which way lies the greatest happiness" (1938, 635).

10 Resolution of an Apparent Inconsistency

The Austrian economic school is most readily seen as (1) adhering to a philosophy of methodological individualism, (2) promoting subjectivism and by extension a nonrationalist view of the structure of society, and (3) working within the parameters of the general equilibrium framework. Some may argue that the inclusion within the Austrian model of any mention of the modern general equilibrium framework is, to say the least, out of place. Carl Menger's perceived amathematical stance and Mises's hostility to mathematical statistics, to take just two instances, cannot possibly coexist with the fundamental underlying methodology of the Karl Menger seminar and the Vienna Circle.

But such a belief as this is a misleading characterization of Austrian economics, and of the methodology of mathematical economics as well. No less a distinguished mathematical scholar than Karl Menger himself cited three differences between the Austrians and those economists more mathematically inclined (K. Menger 1973, 52–55): (1) the Austrians believed mathematics to be little more than "a method of presentation" for economics, not "a means of research" (as had been proclaimed, for instance, by Walras);[72] (2) Austrians search for "*causal explanations,*" while mathematically oriented economists search for "*functional relations*"; and (3) Austrians seek "the *essence* (*das Wesen*) of economic phenomena," while the mathematically inclined "pay less attention . . . to the definition of concepts." Thus it is clear that not only did the Austrian school take the lead in the movement to a general equilibrium statement of economic (and social and political, for that matter) relations, but its uses of the concept were much more significantly developed than were those of the later formalist schools.

---

72. Menger stated that "mathematics cannot create any statements about the physical or social universe. It is confined to *transformations* of assertions (formulae, verbal assumptions, etc.)" (K. Menger 1973, 52).

CHAPTER 10

The Triumph of Cartesian Rationalism
The French Tradition

People are governed with the head; kindness of heart is little use
in chess.
SÉBASTIEN-ROCH NICOLAS DE CHAMFORT, *MAXIMS AND
CONSIDERATIONS* (1796)

To him that looks on the world rationally, the world in its turn
presents a rational aspect. The relation is mutual.
GEORG HEGEL, *THE PHILOSOPHY OF HISTORY* (1837)

"Contrariwise," continued Tweedledee, "if it was so, it might be;
and if it were so, it would be: but as it isn't, it ain't. That's
logic."   LEWIS CARROLL, *ALICE IN WONDERLAND*

Introduction   1

In previous chapters we have seen the development of economic doctrines
as the result of attempts to reconcile two opposing views of the nature of
society: individualism and communitarianism. The former led to the British and Austrian traditions, within which the state is held to be the
creation, and to exist in the service, of its members. The latter led to the
German and French physiocratic traditions, within which the state and
the individual comprise a singular whole, and the members exist for the
sustenance of the body.

In the later French tradition this tension continues, but is at the
same time, as we shall see presently, not as clearly focused. More importantly, in defense of the position there developed a new and more powerful form of argument, mathematical general equilibrium theory.

While general equilibrium approaches had of course been employed
in the classical treatments of political economy, their use in the French
tradition was all the more significant because of the use of equation
systems to detail aspects of the model economy. Of all those who anticipated the transformation that would take place in the rhetoric of modern
economic analysis as it evolved from a literary to a mathematical form of

argumentation, and who contributed to altering that rhetoric and so forever changing the character of the discipline, six individuals writing in this tradition figure prominently. They are hereby nominated for inclusion in that select company of innovators in the history of economic thought. These personalities, names well known to economists and even nonspecialists, are Jean-Baptiste Say, J. C. L. Simonde de Sismondi, Augustin Cournot, Jules Dupuit, Léon Walras, and Vilfredo Pareto. While not all of these writers were of French birth—some being of Swiss or Italian parentage—all produced significant contributions while within what at the time was the intellectual orbit of the French culture.

We have discussed many of the French political economists in an earlier chapter on physiocratic doctrine. The significance of the physiocrats is much greater than may be suggested by a review of such narrow doctrinaire policy pronouncements as the protection of agriculture and the establishment of an accounting matrix for production decisions. They set the stage for much that followed in French political economy, especially the central importance given to the mathematical analysis of economic problems. The next movement in French political economy, on which we are here focused, may be said to have built upon that foundation. While renowned for theoretical advancements, the chief accomplishments of this later approach lay in the creation of new and better methods of analysis and in the definitions of new and exciting concepts, not all of which have been recognized as having had their genesis in this group and at this period. But it was in their openness to experimenting with a new mode of expression that they made the greatest difference to the subject, for here they showed a willingness to use abstraction to develop formal laws of utility, demand, and pricing, and they performed this task better and with more refinement and skill than their predecessors. It is because of this that their achievements have stood the test of time.

2 Say and the "Law of Markets"

2.1 Say and the Smithian Method

The first of the post-physiocrat generation of French economists whose achievements we shall review is Jean-Baptiste Say (1767–1832), reputed to have taught the first public course in political economy in France.

In 1803 Say published *Traité d'économie politique* (*A Treatise on Political Economy*),[1] a work dedicated to the promotion of Smith's theo-

---

1. We are using the sixth American edition published in 1834, specifically the 1880 reprint; hence the date stated is 1880.

ries as presented in *The Wealth of Nations.*[2] Say expressed great admiration for Smith's work, especially *The Wealth of Nations,* despite the fact that he thought it a less-than-sufficient work in political economy, more in the realm of speculative philosophy than economic science. The economic material he held to have been of a highly developed type, although it had little new to recommend it, and the statistical material in support of conclusions was also first-rate; the problem lay in the blending of the two. Say felt that Smith's *Wealth of Nations* should

> be considered as an immethodical assemblage of the soundest principles of political economy, supported by luminous illustrations; of highly ingenious researches in statistics, blended with instructive reflections; it is not, however, a complete treatise of either science, but an irregular mass of curious and original speculations, and of known demonstrated truths. (Say 1880, xix)

For his own part, Say chose to define "political economy" as a scientific discipline of a very special sort: political economy is the "science" concerned with questions "of *social wealth* exclusively, which is founded on exchange and the recognition of the right of property, both social regulations" (1880, xv.n.; emphasis in original). As a "science," economics must maintain a clear and precise set of definitions and axioms from which to commence analysis; the principles of political economy must be tantamount to indubitable propositions, "rigorous deductions of undeniable general facts." Principles so derived then rest "upon an immovable foundation" (xx). Say particularly attacked superficial empiricism and for his efforts achieved the (at the time dubious) reputation for being an abstract theorist. This label was not entirely deserved: Say advocated the practice of "good empiricism" and merely maintained that "facts"[3] were the master of any theory. As Pribram remarked, "there is no doubt that Say's strict adherence to vaguely defined Baconian methods prevented the elaboration of concepts of higher abstraction and the development of procedures of refined hypothetical reasoning" (Pribram 1983, 191).

While Say admired the Baconian method—a method which "consists in only admitting facts carefully observed, and the consequences rigorously deduced from them" (Say 1880, xvii)—he nonetheless felt it necessary to distinguish two types of "facts": "*objects that exist, and*

2. Of this work, and of Say generally, Marx proclaimed, "J. B. Say tries to make up for his lack of profundity by enunciating in absolute terms everything that is false and incomplete in Adam Smith" (1952, 129).

3. But for Say, not just any "fact" would do. "To obtain a knowledge of the truth, it is not then so necessary to be acquainted with a great number of facts, as with such as are essential, and have a direct and immediate influence; and, above all, to examine them under all their aspects, to be enabled to deduce from them just conclusions and be assured that the consequences ascribed to them do not in reality proceed from other causes" (1880, xxiii).

events that take place" (xvii). The difference is an important one. Objects that exist, "must be seen exactly as they are, under every point of view, with all their qualities"; this stricture is the basis of the descriptive sciences. The second type of fact, events that take place, "consists of the phenomena exhibited, when we observe the manner in which things take place"; this is the basis of the "experimental sciences," of which political economy is part (xvii–xviii). What Say objected to was unabashed abstraction, abstraction for abstraction's sake, or the use of abstract reasoning (established axioms and postulates from which deductions were to be made, presumably applicable to policy matters) divorced from an appeal to empirical data. In this he expressed particular opposition to Ricardo and his reliance on demonstration from abstract principles, equating him to "a philosophical mechanician, who, from undoubted proofs drawn from the nature of the lever, would demonstrate the impossibility of the vaults daily executed by dancers on the stage" (xlvii).[4] Say's preferred method may then be termed a sort of *advanced* Smithism, a French rationalism that admitted of extrarational considerations; he may even, as suggested by Bruna Ingrao and Giorgio Israel (1990), have advocated a form of "naturalistic" social science.

In building on the foundation laid by Smith, it is important to note Say's position with regard to a principal tenet of Smithian economics: the labor theory of value. Say had expressed some degree of admiration for Smith on this score, especially in regard to method:

> From this fruitful demonstration he deduced numerous and important conclusions respecting the causes which, from checking the development of the productive powers of labor, are prejudicial to the growth of wealth; and as they are rigorous deductions from an indisputable principle, they have only been assailed by individuals, either too careless to have thoroughly understood the principle, or of such perverted understandings as to be wholly incapable of seizing the connexion or relation between any two ideas. (Say 1880, xxxvii–xxxviii)

But despite his admiration for the *method,* he thought the *principle* incomplete and so in error: "A more exact analysis demonstrates . . . that

---

4. Say also showed great hostility to the use of mathematics in the study of political economy: "It would, however, be idle to imagine that greater precision, or a more steady direction could be given to this study, by the application of mathematics to the solution of its problems. The *values* with which political economy is concerned, admitting of the application to them of the terms *plus* and *minus,* are indeed within the range of mathematical inquiry; but being at the same time subject to the influence of the faculties, the wants and the desires of mankind, they are not susceptible of any rigorous appreciation, and cannot, therefore, furnish any *data* for absolute calculations. In political as well as in physical sciences, all that is essential is a knowledge of the connexion between causes and their consequences. Neither the phenomena of the moral or material world are subject to strict arithmetical computation" (1880, xxvi; emphasis in original).

all values are derived from the operation of labour, or rather from the industry of man, combined with the operation of those agents which nature and capital furnish him" (Say 1880, xl).

The Utilitarian Dimension 2.2

For his part, Say held to a more utilitarian theory of value—the value of goods is merely reflective of the utility they offer and does not depend on the imputation of value from input contributions: "It is universally true, that, when men attribute value to any thing, it is in consideration of its useful properties; what is good for nothing they set no price upon" (1880, 62). The very process of production results not in the *creation* of matter, but in its *reformulation,* and this reformulation produces utility. Production is to be estimated solely "by the utility it presents" (62).

Say held valuation to be "vague and arbitrary," since it is by no means assured that any *single* valuation "will be generally acquiesced in by others" (1880, 285). *Relative,* not *absolute,* values are important.[5] Of particular interest here is Say's understanding of the basis of individual desires; wants or desires are conditioned by society:

> The want or desire of any particular object depends upon the physical and moral constitution of man, the climate he may live in, the laws, customs, and manners of the particular society, in which he may happen to be enrolled. He has wants, both corporeal and intellectual, social and individual; wants for himself and for his family. . . . It is not our business here to inquire, wherein these wants originate; we must take them as existing *data,* and reason upon them accordingly. (Say 1880, 285)

Value thus is determined through social interactions. Likewise, utility is determined socially: "The utility of a product is not confined to one human being, but applies to a whole class of society at the least" (1880, 287). As pointed out by Ingrao and Israel (1990), Say's conception of society was an organic one, in which the physical and moral dimensions coincide. If anything, Say was in a sense a Benthamite utilitarian, which made his classical economics a "natural" for those who followed Ricardo.

In the area of the right of property, a singular interest of the utilitarians, Say made little formal statement. He was not particularly interested in the *derivation* of the right of property, or in the philosophical underpinnings which serve, for example, to distinguish Smith and Locke from Owen and Marx. The issue had, he thought, a place in the arena of political economy, specifically as a factor in the growth of wealth. All other aspects belong within the purview of other branches of philosophy:

---

5. Commenting in a footnote, Say recalled disagreeing with his brother, Louis, on this point. Louis felt that *absolute* utility was the relevant determinant of value, not *recognized* utility, a position which Jean-Baptiste dismissed as neglecting a scale of comparison.

> It is the province of speculative philosophy to trace the origin of the
> right of property; of legislation to regulate its transfer; and of politi-
> cal science to devise the surest means of protecting that right. Politi-
> cal economy recognises the right of property solely as the most
> powerful of all encouragements to the multiplication of wealth, and
> is satisfied with its actual stability, without inquiring about its ori-
> gin or its safeguards. (Say 1880, 127)

Say was led to conclude, given the limitations he imposed on the
scope of economic investigation into the matter, that the interest of the
state was often in conflict with the interests of the property holder; for
instance, he held taxation to be nothing more than a violation of the right
of property. There are, however, instances in which the property right
may be circumvented by the state, such as those cases in which the social
interest demands that the private right of ownership be curtailed. These
instances are: (1) when the state deems it necessary to limit the power of a
master over his slave; (2) where the need of the state is paramount, or
when state interference would lead to a greater social output; and (3)
where the public safety is at risk (1880, 130–31).

2.3 Say's Law

The discovery for which Say is best remembered is his law of markets,
presented in book I, chapter XV, "Of the Demand or Market for Products." Whether Say was in fact the first to actually state Say's Law is still
somewhat controversial: James Mill in *Commerce Defended* (1808) suggested a version of it, and Thomas Sowell (1976) remarked that even
Smith had arrived at a form of the law in *The Wealth of Nations* (1776),
as had the physiocrat Mercier de la Rivière in *L'Ordre Naturel* of 1767.
In any event, this "law" has become a central tenet of macroeconomic
theory, afforded the designation of Say's Law.

A simple presentation of the law is that "supply creates its own
demand," a characterization first used by John Maynard Keynes (1936a,
18) to simplify the propositions behind Classical Economics. Specifically,
in the case of Say, the question arose as to whether there was in fact a
limit to the growth of output in a laissez-faire market economy. To answer the question, Say invoked his version of the labor theory of value
within a utilitarian view of demand:

> A man who applies his labour to the investing of objects with value
> by the creation of utility of some sort, can not expect such a value to
> be appreciated and paid for, unless where other men have the means
> of purchasing it. Now, of what do these means consist? Of other
> values of other products, likewise the fruits of industry, capital, and
> land. Which leads us to a conclusion that may at first sight appear

paradoxical, namely, that it is production which opens a demand for products. (1880, 133)

According to Say, we produce not for the sake of monetary remuneration, but so that we may obtain the wherewithal to purchase other goods that themselves satisfy our desires. We produce not for the sake of amassing piles of money, but rather for what the money received will allow us to purchase. Money serves only as

> the agent of the transfer of values. Its whole utility has consisted in conveying to your hands the value of the commodities, which your customer has sold, for the purpose of buying again from you; and the very next purchase you make, it will again convey to a third person the value of the products you may have sold to others.

> It is worth while to remark, that a product is no sooner created, than it, from that instant, affords a market for other products to the full extent of its own value. (1880, 133, 134)

Simonde de Sismondi 3

The New Principles *and the Foundation of Poverty* 3.1

The next important figure in the French tradition was born in Switzerland of an Italian family. Jean Charles Léonard Simonde de Sismondi (1773–1842) was one of the more interesting figures in the history of political economy, but, perhaps because of circumstances, is one of the more neglected.[6]

It was in Tuscany (where the family had fled to escape the excesses of the French Revolution) that Sismondi became interested in agriculture, especially in the legal and institutional apparatus that surrounded it and allowed it to flourish; this concession to the doctrines of the physiocrats would remain for him a lifelong interest and would have a central place in his work.[7] Returning to Geneva in 1800, Sismondi published *Tableau de l'agriculture Toscane,* a study of the system of agricultural support in the Tuscany region.[8]

---

6. His father Gédéon Simonde was well-connected politically, having served in 1782 as a member of the Council of Two Hundred, the Genevan governmental authority.

7. Continuing in the tradition of the physiocrats, Sismondi utilized the model of the circular flow (Sismondi 1827, 101).

8. Having achieved with his early essays some international fame on the role of agricultural development in the maintenance of national wealth, Sismondi embarked on a huge project, *Histoire des républiques Italiennes du moyen âge,* an 18-volume historical study published over the period 1807 through 1818. This work established his reputation as a historian of major significance, while his *Histoire des Français,* a 31-volume work published between 1821 and 1844, and *Histoire de la chute de l'empire romain* (1835) added further to his distinction.

Sismondi's most famous and important work is undoubtedly his *Nouveaux principes d'économie politique,* the *New Principles of Political Economy,* published in 1819.[9] The history of this work is rather interesting. Sismondi had been offered in 1815 the opportunity to write an essay on political economy for the *Edinburgh Encyclopedia.*[10] The result, an essay divided into seven chapters and written to appeal to a popular audience,[11] was a rather noncontroversial simplification of the classical economic *model* (though one not necessarily accepting of all the *conclusions*) of Adam Smith, for whom Sismondi had the utmost respect and held the deepest devotion.[12]

At the time the article was in preparation, Europe was in the midst of a general economic depression, the likes of which had not been seen since the advent of the "new" political economy. The situation appeared to Sismondi the result of good intentions gone seriously awry: "It seemed to me that I saw on all sides well-intentioned people who created evil, patriots who ruined their countries, charitable souls who multiplied poverty" (Sismondi 1827, Foreword to the First Edition of 1819, 2). In an effort to contribute something to the amelioration of the situation, he took to the task of restating the basic principles of Smith that he had previously laid forth in the essay, amending the earlier presentation with new insights and perforce reaching different conclusions than Smith had entertained; each chapter of the original essay became in turn a separate book in the *New Principles.*

Unwilling to accept the rigidity of the Ricardian approach, or the pessimism of the Malthusian doctrine, or the inevitability depicted by Say's model, each a statement predicated on the classical foundation laid by Smith, Sismondi chose to employ an institutional analysis of the fail-

---

9. We shall make use of the English-language translation of the second edition of 1827, published in 1991.

10. An American edition of the essay was published in 1828 and reprinted in 1991.

11. These chapters are: Objects and Origin of the Science, Formation and Progress of Wealth, Of Territorial Wealth, Of Commercial Wealth, Of Money, Of Taxation, and Of Population.

12. Sismondi throughout the *New Principles* fully expressed this sentiment, writing, "I accepted [to write the encyclopedia essay] in the belief that I would have to do no more than to expound universally accepted principles, to show the status the theory had attained, and which I believed to be settled. I was truly convinced that nothing further needed to be done in political economy than to spread among statesmen, and the mass of the people, a doctrine on which all theorists, it seemed to me, were in universal agreement" (Sismondi 1827, Foreword to the First Edition of 1819, 1). "Adam Smith's doctrine is ours; the torch his genius carries to the subject of this science, having shown his followers the true road, all the advances we have made therein since, are owed to him, and it would be childish vanity to strive to expose all points on which his ideas were not yet clarified, because it is to him that we owe the discovery of truths he himself had not known" (Sismondi 1827, 52). Still, he was quick to emphasize that the arguments in the essay and the subsequent book were his own: "I retraced basic assumptions, I drew conclusions in my way, and I began to build the theory as if nothing had been settled as yet" (Foreword to the First Edition, 1).

ures of the classical model, to in effect once again restate the basic principles and divine some hidden meaning from them. That he was proceeding in the spirit of Smith he had no doubt; that Smith's own design could lead in any of a number of directions was equally clear.

> After this profession of our deep admiration of this creative genius, of our keen gratitude for the enlightenment we owe to him alone, one will no doubt be astonished to learn that the practical results of the doctrine we take from him, appeared to us often diametrically opposed to those he drew from it, and that, by combining his very principles with the experience of a half century during which his theory was more or less put into practice, we believe we can show that it was necessary, in more than one instance, to draw from it quite different conclusions. (Sismondi 1827, 52–53)

The result of this effort to improve upon the work of the master was the *Nouveaux principes*.

In line with his institutional approach, Sismondi appears to have viewed the economy in much the same way as did the mercantilist, physiocrat, and romantic writers, as an organic whole whose activities could be channeled toward social welfare. To this end he began the *New Principles* (and the earlier seminal encyclopedia article) with a statement of the appropriate object of government, a statement that lent shape to his economic theories much as it had for those of Bentham and James Mill.

> The object of government is, or ought to be, the happiness of men united in society. It seeks the means of securing to them the highest degree of felicity compatible with their nature, and at the same time of allowing the greatest possible number of individuals to partake in that felicity. (1827, 21)

Here he was in conflict with Smith, who advocated government involvement only in the sense of establishing parameters. As Sismondi himself proclaimed:

> The reader will have noted the main difference between the ideas we are advancing, and those Adam Smith has expounded, is that the latter has always rejected government intervention in everything connected with the increase of national wealth, and we have often asked for it. (1827, 569)

Government for Sismondi is the "protector of the population" and so invests itself with the authority to prevent excessive competition in the promotion of "individual liberty," many parts of which "are social grants" (1827, 570). Government in effect must, in an effort to protect the individual from himself, limit the choices he can make to those which society deems prudent and which are in the interest of the betterment of the nation.[13]

The institutions of government are faced with a dual challenge in seeking to promote the utilitarian end of the greatest happiness of the greatest number: the legislator has to weigh the different competing concerns of the many disparate groups in society, with the interests of the individual and the welfare of the collective (the social whole); that is, he "has to care at one and the same time for the degree of happiness that mankind may attain through social organization, and the equitable participation of everyone in that happiness" (1827, 21). To achieve this goal requires that the "gifted" members of the society not be penalized for achievement, that their advantages in fact be highlighted and singled out for recognition and indeed praise; it also requires that the less advantaged and less "gifted" not be trod upon in the process.

> That nation is but half-civilized in which no individual suffers, but where no one enjoys sufficient leisure or comforts to feel intensely, or to think deeply, even if that nation should offer to its lower classes an adequate opportunity for happiness. That nation is enslaved where the great mass of the people is exposed to constant privation, to painful anxiety about its existence, to anything which will suppress its will, corrupt its morals, stain its character, even though it may count among its upper classes newly successful men who have achieved the highest degree of happiness, whose every ability has been developed, whose every right is guaranteed, whose every enjoyment is assured. (Sismondi 1827, 21)

Thus Sismondi railed against those who would seek to engender equality by eliminating distinctions based on ability and merit; thus he also railed against those who would seek a society of unbridled competition, a society where the rule of advancement is the "survival of the fittest." To achieve both aims—to allow man to achieve and prosper to his utmost ability while protecting the rights and privileges and opportunities of those of lesser means—Sismondi felt to be "the loftiest theory of welfare" (1827, 22). Richard Hyse (1991) went so far as to conclude that this belief was the basis of the Calvinist order, suggesting that Sismondi was the father of Christian Socialism, an important element in the development of American Institutionalist thought.

The most interesting part of the *New Principles* from the standpoint

---

13. "Thus, the task of government, as protector of the population, is to set everywhere limits to the sacrifices which everyone could be forced to make on his own; to prevent that a man, after having worked ten hours daily, would agree to work twelve, fourteen, sixteen, and eighteen hours; to prevent, likewise, that after having demanded substantial nourishment, animal as well as vegetable, he content himself with dry bread, and finally with potatoes and thin gruels; to prevent, finally, that in always outbidding his neighbor, he lowers himself to the most frightful misery" (Sismondi 1827, 570).

of the theoretical model employed throughout is book II: "Formation and Progress of Wealth." Here Sismondi presented a structure that has survived in the works of others to this day, notably the ideas flowing from the works of Marx and Keynes, even though he is almost never credited with having been the true progenitor of the ideas themselves.

Sismondi began the model phase of his treatise by delimiting the nature of the concept of wealth, clearly predicated on a Lockean–Smithian labor theory of value. Man by his nature has wants and desires which he seeks to satisfy; he also has the wherewithal to see to the satisfaction of these wants and desires, through the efforts of his own labor and industry. The primary function of production is to satisfy these wants and desires, but direct satisfaction is not the definition of wealth. There is a period *between* production and consumption when the product of labor is allowed to accumulate: it is this "unconsumed fruit of labor" to which Sismondi refers when he makes reference to "wealth" (1827, 61).[14]

Since wealth is unconsumed production—a surplus of labor inputs— it is clear that wealth requires neither trade nor exchange to exist; to justify its existence it requires simply the labor input, a want or desire that needs to be satisfied, and a temporal dimension, meaning that the labor expenditure is not for the immediate satisfaction of a want or desire. The object of the production by labor input is stored labor value. Thus wealth (and by extension value) is a function of utility and labor input, labor creating utility by providing the means for the satisfaction of wants and desires.[15]

While the classical school held the chief object of economics to be the study of wealth and production, Sismondi held that, on the contrary,

---

14. That Sismondi held to a labor theory of value there can be no doubt. Consider the following passages:

> Since labor alone has the property of creating wealth by shaping objects such that they can satisfy the needs of humanity, all capital must at first be employed to set labor in motion; all wealth which one does not wish to destroy, must be exchanged against a future wealth that labor must produce. (1827, 82)
>
> ... the power of the machine to produce is owed entirely to previous human labor ... (91)
>
> We have recognized but a single source of wealth, which is labor ... (445)

15. Sismondi's example is of a Robinson Crusoe–type economy, wherein Crusoe, even though alone on an island that is for all intents and purposes his property, has title to nothing in the way of wealth. Wealth even here depends on the expenditure of labor inputs. Labor expenditure alone creates wealth by creating a surplus; the scattered provisions of the island are not wealth, and are valueless unless Crusoe takes the effort to manipulate the natural resources in a way that creates something new: planting trees from the seeds of the fruit, building a hut from the palm fronds and tree branches, etc. "The measure of his wealth will not be the price, which he might obtain for his property in exchange, but the length of time during which no farther labour will be requisite to satisfy his wants, compared with the extent of those wants" (1827, 61).

the chief object should be man and the satisfaction of his wants and desires.[16] Sismondi's system—despite his initial emphasis on the central importance of government in marshaling forces to the promotion of the social good—begins with the individual and extends to the society as a whole, with labor being the critical defining element of wealth:

> the wealth of the whole is only the sum of the wealth of each one; it begins for the whole as it has begun for everyone, with labor; it accumulates for the whole as for everyone, by the excess of the products of daily labor over daily needs; it is destined, for the whole, as for each one, to procure enjoyments which must destroy and consume it; if it ceases to provide such enjoyments, if there is no one who can use it for his needs, it would have lost its value, it would not be wealth any more. All that is true of the individual, is true of society, and vice versa. (1827, 62)

The only additional consideration when moving from the study of the individual in isolation to the society as a whole is the fact that, as a social being, the individual must make his decisions based not on his own wants and desires, but with an eye to the general welfare; egoism is replaced with sympathy. (Note here shades of Smith and a subtle deprecation of Mandeville.) Whereas the lone individual had always and only to consider his own utility to be derived from the use of his labor in the creation of wealth, including the leisure time engendered by the creation of a store of surplus labor, the social being has also to account for the utility and well-being of his fellow actors, to whom he is as devoted as they are to him. He must now labor in the knowledge that he is creating a store of wealth precisely "so that others may enjoy and rest," while being assured of "the work of others for his own enjoyment and rest" (1827, 67).

The individual cannot any more be cognizant of working for his own sake, for the provision of his own utility. He cannot even be assured that he *has* any wants and desires for which he can with his own labor provide satisfaction. He is in all senses a *social* creature, unable to so much as ponder individuality.[17]

> Thenceforth, man being a part of society, an abstract being, whose wealth and needs are hypothetical, cannot anymore follow his work to the moment where its fruits are consumed, nor can he judge the needs for which he ought to provide, or the time when he ought to rest; he works without pause to fill the common coffers, leaving to society the worry of finding a use for the things he has made. (1827, 67)

One consequence of man's realization of his social nature is an explosion in wants and desires. The individual in an isolated state works to accumulate for the sole purpose of satisfying his rather limited desires.

16. The point was made by Gide and Rist (1944, 191).
17. The worker, in Marx's phrase, is alienated from his product.

He then ceases to labor when the accumulation of wealth reaches the (low level of) satiation. The socialized laborer faces a very different environment. The birth of trade led to the realization of advantages to be derived from the division of labor. Later, this division of tasks, the breakdown of the production process into simple, repetitive, mechanical movements, led to the employment of machinery (1827, 69). With each task now reduced to its simplest component movements, machinery designed for the purpose of performing the identical task innumerable times with high efficiency could then be employed in production; some machines required no human element at all. Thus it became possible to increase production with less human effort, making it feasible for some to pursue leisure while others worked. This development meant that the individual need labor at only a single intermediate task, perhaps unaware of the contribution he makes to the composition of the final product, thus allowing to be produced an infinite variety of goods. In expanding the wealth of the society, he expands his own happiness by amassing ever greater amounts of leisure as a result of his efforts at greater productive efficiencies. His wants and desires expand as well, reducing the concept of satiety from a pressing problem to an anachronism. "Whatever wealth he might amass, he could never have occasion to say *it is enough;* he still found means to convert it into pleasure, and to imagine at least that he applied it to his service" (73–74; emphasis in original).

The check on a perpetual increase in production and consumption is enjoyment: man accumulates stored labor services only to have more leisure. Part of this leisure involves the apportionment of labor services to the production of luxury goods. There is a level of satiation corresponding to the production and consumption of necessities, simply by virtue of the fact that there is a trade-off between labor expenditure (which provides negative utility) and the utility generated by the production of the requirements to satisfy the basic needs of the society. With workers as a group seeing to the production of necessities, all workers are rewarded with an increasing amount of leisure time. (Here we can readily see a commentary on Say's Law.)[18] It is from the amassing of leisure time that luxuries are demanded, the production of which allows the economy to continually produce and expand (1827, 75). In a memorable sentence, Sismondi summed up his thought: "Man does not tire himself, except to rest thereafter; he does not save except to spend; he does not aspire to wealth except for enjoyment" (74). This is what separates the solitary from the social being:

> The Solitary worked to rest, social man works so that someone may rest; the Solitary gathered to enjoy thereafter, social man

18. In dismissing Say's Law, Sismondi turned the argument around: demand, specifically the individual's desires, the "pleasure of the imagination," determines the level of production (1827, 102–3).

accumulates the fruits of his sweat for him who can enjoy them; but from the moment that he and his peers produce more, and infinitely more than they can consume, then what they produce must be destined for the consumption of people who will live in no manner like him, and will not produce at all. (1827, 75)

Thus is engendered social inequality, as some continue to labor to produce for the benefit of those who do not. Society becomes stratified into providers and users, as the inevitable progression of the society. To Sismondi, the only recourse was for government intervention in the workings of the economy:

The more a nation has progressed in the arts, in the manufactures, the greater is the disproportion between the status of those who labor and those who enjoy; the more the one live in misery, the more the others display luxury, at least until government corrects the distribution and assures to those who create all the means of enjoyment a greater share of such enjoyment through such institutions that seem to be opposed to the purely economic end of increasing wealth. (1827, 76)

We are then left with a slight redefinition of wealth. Under the old definition of Sismondi—wealth as accumulated labor services—the rich who no longer produce will very quickly see the surplus of their own labor reduced as they continue to consume to meet new wants and desires. This depletion of wealth by the idle class will eventually burden the working class. With depleted resources the rich will no longer be in a position to demand luxury goods, leading to unemployment in this sector of the economy. Wealth then must include the element of reproducibility. The wealthy class can then continually augment its store of value indirectly, by relying not on its own labor services but on the labor services of others, as it adds to capital. The resources of the wealthy are increased by the return on capital goods. This is the essence of national prosperity, the ability to augment one's stock of wealth by the income on capital, borne from the labor of others. Thus inequality in income and a stratified society are in fact essential aspects of a prosperous society:

If all of a sudden the wealthy classes resolved to live off their work, just like the poorest, and to add all their income to their capital, the workers, who counted on the exchange of that income for their livelihood, would be reduced to despair and would die of hunger; if, on the other hand, the wealthy class would not content itself to live off its income, but expended also its capital, it would soon find itself without income, and the same exchange, so necessary to the poorer class, would also cease. (1827, 76–77)

The Property Right 3.2

Having presented the highlights of his theory of value and his thoughts on the nature of man and society, we must examine briefly Sismondi's views on property. Despite holding to a labor theory of value, Sismondi did not hold that labor was the source of the property right. Neither did he believe there to be any such thing as a natural right to hold property—"it is a gift of society and in no way a natural right which preexisted" (1827, 138). Rather, he held that it is "the will to work which alone creates all property" (26). As with Bentham and James Mill, he viewed the right of ownership—the property right—as existing solely as a result of social conventions, and so it can be maintained or withdrawn as *society* sees fit. He held that, in utilitarian fashion,

> the division of rights to property is born from special circumstances, from chance schemes, often from passions or vanity. . . . This division has often been replaced by others, entirely different; it must be judged as all the rest of social institutions, by the good or bad that has flowed from them for mankind; by the quantity of happiness they produce, and the number of individuals who participate therein. (1827, 132)

It was in fact the institution of private ownership of property, fixed by institutional rules, that Sismondi felt had allowed the rapid expansion of agricultural output in the western nations. Along with the provision of general social order and security guaranteed by government, the security of the ownership rights allowed development and the expansion of wealth. He even considered that, absent private ownership, such expansion of output and production would not have taken place: such productivity "is only possible because the earth, otherwise captured by the first occupant, or the most powerful, becomes, under the operation of the law, a property not less sacred than if it were itself the work of man." It was indeed the very act of private ownership in land that, while seeming to infringe on the rights of the landless, was nonetheless socially responsible, from a utilitarian perspective: "This is a fortunate usurpation, and society, for the benefit of all, does well to guarantee it" (1827, 138). We may also add that, in addition to the economic argument, from a purely social standpoint, the right of private property is important because it serves a social stabilizing function, as it "inculcates habits of order and economy" (145).

A Summary Statement 3.3

To sum up, we will present some commentary on Sismondi as others have seen him. Richard Hyse, the translator of Sismondi's *New Principles,* described him as "the first non-Utopian, nonsocialist critic of classical political economy who analyzed the first business cycles the Industrial Revolution had produced, and who was *not* dedicated to the proposition that only a new communal order could save society" (Hyse 1991, xxv). Gide and Rist declared, "He is thus the chief of a line of economists whose works never ceased to exercise influence throughout the whole of the nineteenth century, and who, without being socialists on the one hand or totally blind to the vices of *laissez-faire* on the other, sought that happy mean which permits of the correction of the abuses of liberty while retaining the principle" (1944, 187).

Withal, Sismondi was a believer in the efficiency of the state in the promotion of social welfare. He thus seems to have (perhaps unknowingly) applied what was at the time known in Germany as the principle of *Staatskunst* to the Smithian design, to arrive at a uniquely French position as to the constitution of the organic, paternal state.

4 Cournot and the Mathematization of Political Economy

4.1 Cournot's Methodology

Antoine Augustin Cournot (1801–77) is esteemed by many today as having been a thinker of the first rank; Edgeworth (1910a, 445) went so far as to dub him "the first who successfully applied mathematics to political economy." His writings cover a broad range of subjects, including logic, mathematics, statistics, probability, philosophy, and economics. While in his own time his work was little appreciated, even by himself, later generations recognized the genius of his enormous contributions. His economic works, which interest us here, are considered to have been among the earliest to recognize a place for mathematics and to actually demonstrate the manner in which it could be successfully exploited as an analytical tool.

Cournot's preparatory education included studies in mathematics and the law;[19] among his teachers were the great mathematicians Laplace, Lagrange, Poinsot, and Poisson.[20] But it was his acquaintance with the great French military figure Marshall Saint-Cyr, who engaged Cournot as an adviser and critic (as well as tutor to his son), that proved of great importance. In connection with his new position, he expanded his list of acquaintances to include some of the leading French political figures. When St.-Cyr died, Cournot dutifully took over the editorship of his memoirs.

---

19. Henry L. Moore considered this period as having been especially portentous for Cournot, as it developed in him a strong habit for independent thought (see H. L. Moore 1905, 378).

20. Ingrao and Israel suggested it was Poisson who drove Cournot to apply mathematics "outside the canonical boundaries of physics" (Ingrao and Israel 1990, 79).

A look at Cournot's publishing history shows a long interest in problems of mathematical analysis. In 1841 he published *Traité élémentaire de la théorie des fonctions et de calcul infinitésimal;* in 1843, *Exposition de la théorie des chances et des probabilités,* a work that the philosopher Ian Hacking (1990) credited with being one of the earliest attempts at making a formal distinction between chance and probability; in 1851, *Essai sur les fondements de nos connaissances;* in 1861, *Traité de l'énchainement des idées fondamentales dans les sciences et dans l'histoire;* and in 1872, *Considérations sur la marche des idées et des événements dans les temps modernes.* As for his economic works, there is the classic 1838 *Recherches;* the 1863 *Principes de la théorie des richesses* (a nonmathematical presentation of the ideas from 1838); and the 1877 *Revue sommaire des doctrines économiques* (a still more elementary treatment). We shall focus below on the *Recherches.*

For all his intellectual output, Cournot's 1838 *Recherches sur les principes mathématiques de la théorie des richesses* is for economists his greatest effort.[21] Gide and Rist (1944, 499) went so far as to date its publication as marking the beginning of the "mathematical school" of economics; Edgeworth opined that it "is still the best statement in mathematical form of some of the highest generalisations in economic science,"[22] crediting Cournot with having "been the first to represent by means of an equation, or curve, the relation between the price of a commodity and the quantity saleable at that price in a market consisting of purchasers competing with each other" (Edgeworth 1910a, 445). In this work, Cournot held to an opinion of the efficacy of mathematics in economics not different from that of Edgeworth. In the Preface, Cournot noted the similarities between the use of a mathematical framework for the understanding of economics and the use of a similar framework for the study of the calculus of probability and even classical mechanics. The simple numerical calculation of magnitudes is not the point of mathematization; the purpose of formal mathematical presentation is the elaboration of form and structure, the mathematics serving the purpose formerly held by literary rhetoric.

> [T]hose skilled in mathematical analysis know that its object is not simply to calculate numbers, but that it is also employed to find the relations between magnitudes which cannot be expressed in numbers and between *functions* whose law is not capable of algebraic expression. Thus the theory of probabilities furnishes a demonstration of very important propositions, although, without the help of

---

21. In his own time, Cournot's *Recherches* sold very few copies, leading him to recast it (twice) in a less-formal rhetoric. But the book went virtually unnoticed until interest in it was resurrected by Jevons.

22. Edgeworth was led to note, "How much logomachy is saved by this appropriate conception!" (1910a, 445).

experience, it is impossible to give numerical values for contingent events, except in questions of mere curiosity, such as arise from certain games of chance. (Cournot 1838, 2–3; emphasis in original)

Cournot was quick to point out that his mathematical toolbox was equipped solely with the calculus, "that branch of analysis which comprises arbitrary functions, which are merely restricted to satisfying certain conditions" (1838, 3); it most assuredly did not include the more pedestrian algebra. The desire of Cournot was not, as it had been for his predecessors, for numerical calculation, but rather for the demonstration of functional relationships. Algebra has its place, but this place is not in the understanding of the abstract relationships of economic theory. This is where, Cournot held, Ricardo had gone astray, for even though his attempts at a deductive economic theory held far more rigor than the merely literary expositions of Smith and Say, his reliance on a mathematical tool of such limited potential restricted his ability to take his conclusions to a higher level.[23] The "science" of economics for Cournot is a positivistic discipline; economists are compelled on this score "to observe, and not to criticise, the irresistible laws of nature" (7). But political economy cannot stand alone as a deductive science; the relationships among economic variables are simply too complex and contingent to allow consequences of economic actions to be analytically deduced. This realization led Cournot to distinguish the rational nature of the subject from the empirical. Both are necessary to an understanding of the relations of economics: "It is enough to have to guard against errors in logic on the first score; let us avoid encountering passionate declamations and insoluble questions on the other" (11).

The role of the economist as scientist is to "abstract the moral influences which enter into all these questions and which are entirely incapable of measurement" (1838, 11). It is in this respect that Cournot held that "Political Economy is the hygiene and pathology of the social system. It recognizes as its guide experience or rather observation; but sometimes the sagacity of a superior mind can even anticipate the results of experience" (12). The only impediment to economics becoming an analytical (deductive) discipline is that its terms "are not reducible to fixed terms, or because these relations are much too complicated for our powers of combination and analysis" (13).

4.2 The Meaning of Wealth

In the effort to apply to economics some degree of rigor, Cournot had to delimit the topic in much the manner of Sismondi: by reinterpreting

---

23. Note Ingrao and Israel: "The novelty of his [Cournot's] program consisted in his being the first to indicate clearly the way to apply functional analysis to the study of economic problems without having to specify more than the most general properties of the forms of the functions describing the laws analyzed" (1990, 80). See also George Rhodes (1978) for more on Cournot's epistemology.

terms. He held, for instance, that the concept of "wealth" is, in line with the views of the utilitarian philosophers, intimately connected to a set of commercial and institutional relations. While the elements which comprise wealth—these being "[p]roperty, power, the distinctions between masters, servants and slaves, abundance, and poverty, rights and privileges" (1838, 5)—are predicated on Natural Law foundations and so can be found to have existed in all eras and among peoples of very differing constitution, the form in which we perceive these relations is dependent upon custom, habit, and the state of development of the culture and the society.

Wealth in its modern guise (*modern* meaning at the time of Cournot) suggests an ability to accumulate and to engage in *commercial*, as opposed to *simple*, exchange; the idea of exchange Cournot held in fact to be "natural," and even "instinctive." The problem that has to be faced to allow the development of the concept of "value in exchange," however, upon which are derived notions of wealth and value, is the manner in which objects exchange one for another; in other words, the development of a set of "commercial relations" is necessary to the entire concept of value.

But this idea of wealth as derivative does not imply that wealth so defined is anything other than an abstract notion, "for, strictly speaking, of all the things on which we set a price, or to which we attribute a value in exchange, there are none always exchangeable at will for any other commodity of equal price or value" (1838, 6). The greater the sphere of economic activity, the more "abstract" do our ideas of wealth necessarily become; only when the system is reduced to an abstract, "frictionless," model of reality can the complexities be minimized and the essentials laid bare.

> The extension of commerce and the development of commercial facilities tend to bring the actual condition of affairs nearer and nearer to this order of abstract conceptions, on which alone theoretical calculations can be based, in the same way as the skilful engineer approaches nearer to theoretical conditions by diminishing friction through polished bearings and accurate gearing. (1838, 7)

Wealth, as an "abstract idea" that "constitutes a perfectly determinate relation," is a "precise conception," given to numerical precision and determinateness, and "like all precise conceptions it can become the object of theoretical deductions." Should we succeed in so reducing the concept to a system, "it will presumably be advantageous to present this system by itself," complete of course with the usual restrictive caveats (1838, 13).[24] One can readily see in this an understanding of wealth in

---

24. The point of the study of economics Cournot held to be "to know the laws which govern the variation of values, or, in other words, the theory of wealth. This theory alone can make it possible to prove what absolute variations are due the relative variations which come into the field of observation . . ." (1838, 19).

social, and not *individual,* terms. This is important, for it establishes that Cournot, as Sismondi and even the physiocrats, viewed the welfare of society as the ultimate end in the utilitarian calculus. It also clarifies Cournot's motivation, which was to formulate a more efficient method of taxation.

4.3 The Law of Demand

Cournot was quite content to begin from the position of a "very advanced state of civilization" (1838, 36). By so doing, he could ignore such (seemingly) irrelevant topics as the origin of the property right, the genesis of the mechanism of exchange, and the conditions leading to the correct form of commercial relation. But he did need a fundamental axiom with which to begin his deductions; he could not simply assert a theoretical structure absent a first principle. This axiom for Cournot holds "that each one seeks to derive the greatest possible value from his goods or his labour" (36).

To illustrate, take the case considered by Cournot himself, that of the law of demand. While it had been common for statements of the law to be of the form "price is inversely related to quantity demanded," Cournot believed this statement of the law at best misleading and most likely, as a general statement, false. Even such an *apparently* valid, simple, statement required so many ancillary assumptions that "it is a proposition devoid of meaning" (1838, 37). All we can say, as a general statement, about demand is that it is a function of price. "To know the form of this function would be to know what we call *the law of demand* or *of sales*" (38; emphasis in original). But since we do not know the precise form, it makes no difference; all that is required to engage in an analytical discussion is the functional form of the law:

> Since so many moral causes capable of neither enumeration nor measurement affect the law of demand, it is plain that we should no more expect this law to be expressible by an algebraic formula than the law of mortality, and all the laws whose determination enters into the field of statistics, or what is called social arithmetic. (1838, 39)

While a functional form can allow us to derive an empirical representation of a demand curve, it is not necessary that this be done; all that is necessary is that the functional form be stipulated as true.[25] All we need to know about the function are general properties, such as continuity,

---

25. "[I]t would be nevertheless not improper to introduce the unknown law of demand into analytical combinations, by means of an indeterminate symbol; for it is well known that one of the most important functions of analysis consists precisely in assigning determinate relations between quantities to which numerical values and even algebraic forms are absolutely unassignable" (Cournot 1838, 39).

differentiability, and the signs of the derivatives. By then using the mathematical method, Cournot was able to clear up a confusion that had existed in classical discussions of demand: the distinction between *demand* and the *quantity demanded*.[26] With the stipulation of a functional relationship between quantity demanded and price, the distinction became simple to understand and to portray: since $D = F(p)$, a *change* in price that leads to a change in quantity demanded causes a *movement* along the given demand curve; a change in any other variable that alters the function F itself causes a *shift* in the curve. Still, as noted by Ingrao and Israel, Cournot, following "the promptings of *mathématique sociale* in foreseeing the possibility of estimating the function on the basis of statistical tables of consumption and price trends," advanced economic science and made possible the introduction of the concepts of marginal cost and the elasticity of demand (Ingrao and Israel 1990, 82).

The Engineer's Contribution to the Debate: Dupuit   5

Utility as a Measure of the Efficiency   5.1
of Public Works Expenditure

We have seen throughout the history of economic thought that ideas developed from a variety of intellectual sources. Smith was a moral philosopher, Bentham and Edgeworth studied in the law, many of the mercantilists were themselves merchants, many of the physiocrats were pamphleteers, and there were legions of government bureaucrats and social advocates. In many ways these groups are alike, as they all seem to have been concerned with the solution of social and political problems from a normative perspective. One of the more interesting of the figures we will meet came to economics via an entirely different route from the others, a route which instilled in him an analytical foundation that centered his thought on aspects of the economic problem which had all but eluded previous writers.

Arsène Jules Étienne Juvénal Dupuit (1804–66) was, first and foremost, by training, vocation, and temperament as well, an engineer. Educated at the École Polytechnique and the École des Ponts et Chaussées,[27] he pursued his engineering career in such areas as roadway construction, flood control, and the development of water-supply systems, all major areas of public works expenditure.[28]

---

26. Say at times seemed confused about the two: "To determine the *quantity* to be *demanded,* the price at which the commodity can be sold must already be known, as the demand for it will increase in proportion to its cheapness" (1880, xxviin).

27. For an appreciation of the important role played by the École in applied economics, see Ekelund and Hébert (1973).

28. For his engineering efforts he was awarded the Legion of Honour in 1843.

In 1850 Dupuit was appointed chief engineer for Paris, by which time he had developed an interest in economic topics, principally as they concerned issues within the public works domain, such as benefit-cost analysis and the optimal toll and tariff. (His principal works in these areas [to be discussed later] were published in 1844 and 1849.) As an engineer with a mind educated to seek for quantitative solutions to problems and geared to the quantitative expression of concepts, Dupuit became fascinated with what we now call cost-benefit analysis. In 1844 he published in the *Annales des Ponts et Chaussées* a brilliant article entitled "De la Mesure de l'utilité des travaux publics" (translated as "On the Measurement of the Utility of Public Works") the work for which he is best known. Schumpeter (1954, 957) esteemed it as "perhaps the best of all the arguments for the 'mathematical method.' " Here he set forth his ideas on the justification for the construction of public works projects and at the same time addressed a critical problem in economics that had beset pioneers such as Smith and Say.

The expressed purpose of this essay was to address a rather peculiar phenomenon: public works projects had been designated as useful contrivances, as providing a value to the public, by virtue of legal prescription and not by recourse to any economic argument. Legislative enactments frequently at this time were alone maintained as justifications for the undertakings, with little or no consideration as to the economic basis for the project. The problem with this method of justification, as Dupuit saw it, is that it is precisely the *economic* demonstration of the value of a project which should be the criterion by which it is judged. Economic judgments should determine whether and to what extent a project is useful and so should be financed, the legislation required to realize the project being secondary to the rationale for its existence. It was with this idea in mind—that the methodology behind public works financing was fundamentally flawed—that he took to the task of identifying those aspects of value-creation that had been missing from some leading theories of the pricing and costing of projects.

Of the utmost importance in this identification is the possibility of arriving at some measure of the true worth of a project, or the utility it will render. Dupuit disagreed with the then-fashionable definition of utility as it had been put forth by Say, expressing agreement with Smith. Specifically, as we have seen, Say defined utility as existing in a good to the extent that a price could be found for the good, this price serving as a measure of the utility. Demand is determined by utility, and utility sets value, which is equal to the cost of production.

Dupuit took issue particularly with this last declaration. The *price* for which a good is sold (or the value of services rendered by the construction of a public works project, such as a bridge or a road), is not identical with the utility so derived from the existence of the good or project; the utility could in fact be many times greater than the amount actually paid or the cost incurred. All we can say of the price that obtains is that it provides us with a lower bound on the utility derived from the object. The precise measure of the total utility is unknown, but most certainly it is not identical with the lowest possible boundary.[29]

Of equal significance is the fact, not heretofore explicitly acknowledged, that utility is a subjective judgment. The utility derived will in fact be different for different persons, depending upon the wants and desires, that is, the subjective feelings, of each. Some will value an object highly and so will readily pay a high price to obtain it; some will value it less and so will refuse to pay beyond a modest price. While utility varies according to the individual's apprehension of worth, the cost of production and hence the price of the good are given in the marketplace; the consumer simply faces these parameters as he enters the market in an effort to attempt to satisfy his felt needs. At this given price, those whose utility value is at or above the given price will purchase the good; those whose utility value is below the price of the good will choose not to buy.

Should the price of the good be increased (say, because of the imposition of a tax), then those whose utility value is at or above the new price (price + tax) will buy; if below they will not. The tax has the effect of driving some consumers from the market, specifically, those whose utility value for the good was just enough to allow them to purchase the good at the pretax price. But more importantly, as a distinction, the *producers* of the good are in the same situation as they were *before* the imposition of the tax: since the market price had been set by cost of production, the producers derived a utility from the *sale* of the good which equalled market price; after the tax was imposed, even though the market price is now higher, the price the producers receive has not changed, since their utility has not changed.

This led Dupuit to enunciate a very important principle, in two parts: (1) "the utility of everything which is consumed varies according to the person consuming it" and (2) "each consumer himself attaches a different utility to the same thing according to the quantity which he can consume" (Dupuit 1844, 86). Thus to summarize, utility can be measured (or represented) by the demand curve; the demand curve represents mere subjective apprehensions of value.

---

29. Dupuit used the following example to explain his point: "If society is paying 500 million for the services rendered by the road, that only proves one thing—that their utility is *at least* 500 million. But it may be a hundred times or a thousand times greater; we are left in ignorance of this. If you take the above figure as the measure—and not as the lower limit—of a quantity the exact magnitude of which you do not know, you are acting like a man who, wishing to measure the height of a wall in the dark and finding that he cannot reach the top with his arm raised, says: 'This wall is two meters high, for if it were not, my hand would reach above it'. Now, if you say that the wall is at least two meters in height, then we are agreed; but if you go so far as to say that this is the actual measurement, then we are no longer agreed. In daylight, and equipped with a ladder, you will perceive that our alleged two-meter wall is fifty meters high" (1844, 84).

Another important advance in this article is perhaps the earliest statement of the concept labeled two generations later by Marshall as "consumer's surplus."[30] Dupuit defined the idea as suggesting that "every product has a different utility not only for each consumer but for each of the wants for the satisfaction of which he uses it" (1844, 86–87). He identified the concept by reference to an example:[31] at 50 francs, the cost of providing a single hectoliter of water per day, a consumer whose subjective utility valuation of the water is 50 francs will purchase a single hectoliter. Let the cost of provision be reduced (perhaps by a more efficient means of pumping) to 30 francs. This consumer in still demanding a single hectoliter then realizes a "profit" from his consumption of 20 francs, equal to the value of his utility less the cost of procurement. He may then decide to "expend" his profit by the purchase of another unit. If a second unit is worth to him less than 50 but more than 30 francs, he will purchase it; his total outlay for the two hectoliters is now 60 francs, but he receives a value of *at least* 80 francs, equal to the value of 50 francs which he places on the first hectoliter plus the value of at least 30 francs he places on the second (and of course the value he receives may be as high as 100 francs). As the cost of provision continues to decline, the consumer is enabled to increase his consumption and so can satisfy those uses which for him have a lower utility value. His justification for this conclusion, that cost or price is fundamentally different from utility, he quickly pointed out was nothing more significant than Smith's use-exchange distinction, a distinction he felt had been neglected by the later generation of writers and interpreters of Smith (87).

Having laid out some of the nuances of his argument, Dupuit then set to *defining* utility. The utility afforded to a person by an object is defined as "the maximum sacrifice which each consumer would be willing to make in order to acquire the object" (1844, 89). That this is the definition of a committed positivist is shown by the fact that it focuses entirely on the criterion of *desires* and makes no mention of *needs*. Dupuit, ever the calculating engineer, could only lend himself to analyzing what he could measure, and he satisfied himself that he could measure utility by investigating expenditures. To do otherwise, to evince a concern with utility as somehow a measure of the condition of individuals, was not practical, in the first place, and secondly was beyond the purview of the "science" of economics: "it would be difficult to say whose hunger was the greater—the rich man's, who would be willing to give a million for a kilogramme of bread, or the poor man's, who, having nothing else to give, would risk his life for it." As economists face the problem of the measurement of wants and desires, we need to be content with analyzing

30. See R. W. Houghton (1958) on the importance of the work of Dupuit in establishing this concept.

31. The example is Dupuit's own, given on page 86 of Dupuit 1844.

numerically valued quantities that allow of interpersonal comparison, such as monetary expenditure; money provides the yardstick by which we can express this desire. Beyond this, we can say nothing and so must leave the question to others: "Political economy only bakes bread for those who can buy it, and leaves to social economy the care of supplying it to those with nothing of value to give in exchange" (89).

To clarify further his notion of utility, Dupuit distinguished between two forms: absolute and relative. Absolute utility (*utilité absolue*) is the "utility of all things that satisfy our desires" (1844, 89). It is the entire area under the demand curve, bounded on the right by the quantity demanded.[32] (See fig. 2.) Relative utility (*utilité relative*) is the difference between the absolute utility and the expense incurred in obtaining the object. Expense (or cost of production) is represented in the demand diagram as the area of the rectangle that measures price multiplied by quantity demanded. Relative utility, the total area less the cost incurred in its procurement, gives the measure commonly known as consumer's surplus. So, if a person values an object at 30 francs (his absolute utility), but it costs him only 20, the relative utility is 10 francs.

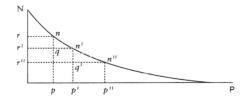

FIGURE 2. Dupuit's Consumers' Surplus Diagram

The importance of this distinction was made clear by Dupuit in its effect on production. Take the case whereby a tax or toll increases the price of an object to such an extent that it exceeds anyone's utility valuation; since no one values the object at that high a price, sales and production cease. The realization of this potentiality led Dupuit to state a corollary to his utility law: "the only real utility is that which people are willing to pay for" (1844, 90). This is important especially in regard to taxation, since it implies that taxes have an effect not typically considered, namely, that by increasing the price of a good, the tax reduces relative utility and removes from the marketplace consumers who would otherwise have purchased the good. There is a twofold loss: there is a loss in utility by those who purchase the good at a higher price than they perhaps could have procured it, and a loss of utility by those who

32. This is of course the case when speaking of the demand curve as it exists in (q,p) space, i.e., as Marshall presented it. Dupuit's curve was stated in (p,q) space, so that the axes are reversed.

would wish to purchase but are precluded from so doing by virtue of the high price. Dupuit held that those who had ignored this important part of the problem did so at great expense: "The fallacy lies in taking account of only one class of citizens—those who pay the charge: account must also be taken of the much greater number who do not pay it because they cannot afford to, and who therefore are no longer consumers" (103).

But utility considerations were not thought by Dupuit to be the sole criterion of price-setting. In the case of a tax or toll, as the rate is reduced, the result is an increase in consumer's surplus or relative utility, as evidenced by the fact that the area under the demand curve but above the revenue rectangle is increased. But it is of course the case that the *maximum* of relative utility will be when the toll is reduced to zero, a case which is obviously not admissible and was certainly ruled out by Dupuit; he was after all not looking for the maximum amount of relative utility, but the *optimum* amount. At a zero rate, there would of course be no income accruing to the state to pay for maintenance and the construction expenses. All Dupuit could say on the matter was that the purpose of a toll was to "produce the greatest possible utility and at the same time a revenue sufficient to cover the cost of upkeep and interest on capital" (1844, 98).

An advance which reduces production costs leads to an increase in relative utility. But the question then arises, how is this change in a relative quantity, itself defined with respect to individual attitudes and beliefs, to be calculated? Dupuit considered two possibilities. In the first, we assume the same quantity demanded as previously, so that the increase in relative utility is simply the reduction in cost multiplied by the quantity demanded. But as with any commodity, a reduction in cost will have the effect of attracting new consumers whose utility was previously just below the offered price, as it makes feasible certain projects which had been prohibitively expensive. Thus the result may be, in the second case, an increase in the quantity demanded of the good.

This raises immediately a problem of the calculation of the new level of utility: not everyone who buys at the lower price holds the same apprehension of the value of utility, and so the fall in price, if it is large enough, will induce consumption not only by those whose utility values were only slightly below the original price, but will also induce consumption by those whose appraisals had been much lower. For example, a fall from 20 to 15 francs will induce consumption from those whose utility had been 19 francs, and 18, and 17, and 16, and 15. Thus to determine accurately the full impact of a drop in price, we must be aware of the differences in subjective appraisals and account for them in our calculations. The conclusion is that, in order to derive accurately a value for relative utility brought about by the reduction in cost, "it would be necessary for each consumer to make known the strength of his desire in terms of the price which would make him cease consuming" (1844, 94). Only then can we gauge fully the extent of the change.

Finally, in this pathbreaking article, Dupuit gave an intuitive feeling for his conjecture that the demand curve is actually convex from below, and not a linear function of price. This belief he stated in the form of two laws: (1) "consumption expands when price falls," and (2) "the increase in consumption due to a price fall will be greater, the lower the initial price" (and conversely, "consumption diminishes less and less rapidly as the tax rises" [1844, 103–4]).

In 1849 Dupuit published "De l'influence des péages sur l'utilité des voies de communication"[33] (translated as "On Tolls and Transport Charges"), an effort to expand upon the propositions expressed in the 1844 article and to respond to criticisms raised with respect to the ideas presented there. While the article itself is basically a restatement of the former work, replete with additional examples that serve to prove the points raised, there are some rather interesting passages that serve to highlight Dupuit's demeanor as an economic theorist. A particularly interesting passage reads as follows:

> Ignorance of the law of consumption is no obstacle to the rational calculation of toll rates. Probability in the place of certainty may render the problem more difficult, but it also lends new charm to the solution. All business calculations turn on conjectures about the law of consumption on the one hand, and, on the other, on the means of making consumers pay for the utility of the products. If the law of consumption were fully known and if the monopoly's sales or production policy were fixed and established, then these calculations would have to do only with perfectly determined problems soluble by the simplest arithmetic. But in the producer's uncertain world the solution depends both on his skill in guessing the needs of the consumers and on his imagination in devising a method of making them pay as much as possible. (Dupuit 1849, 12)

"Skill in guessing," the "uncertain world" of the producer, the fact that the laws of consumption and production are not "fixed and established," and the requirement that the economist understand and make a place in his theoretical model for the workings of the "imagination" are all insights usually credited to others. Dupuit appears to have understood the place for these factors well in advance of the pack.

Dupuit also showed in this article that his economics was positivistic, and utilitarian. This is particularly telling in his account of the basis for tolls and other such levies. Tolls were to be levied based not on ability to pay, but rather on the utility of the transport. He suggested, for in-

---

33. "Communication" as used by Dupuit meant anything providing access between two or more persons. This could include a bridge, a road, a canal, or any other form of conveyance.

stance, that a levy for the transport of manure across a bridge be three times the levy for a good such as coffee. Responding to the perceived inequity of this schedule—that it taxed the poor at a higher rate than the rich—he argued that the transporter of coffee, sugar, and any other "luxury" item need not use the bridge at all; he can always continue to rely on his previous route and mode of travel, even if the time needed for transport is greater than with the bridge. Since a toll is a "voluntary impost, which can be collected only with the personal agreement of the consumers" (1849, 18), the rich will simply refuse to participate, while the poor have little option. In the end, it came down to a simple rule of thumb:

> When establishing a toll schedule, it is therefore best to set aside all philanthropic notions which only harm the interests they are supposed to serve. Goods must be made to pay, not according to their intrinsic nature, but according to the utility of their transport. (1849, 18)

5.2 Other Contributions

Dupuit's accomplishments in economics were not limited to those we have discussed above. In 1860 he published in the *Revue européenne* an article on trade, entitled "La liberté commerciale," which served to establish his credentials as a promoter of free trade. Here he showed a commitment to the doctrine of laissez-faire well within the Smith–Say mold, albeit tinged with a degree of Malthusianism. As a free trader, he was opposed to government influence in commercial affairs. He did, however, advocate government control of prices in the case of a natural monopoly; the economic argument was that only through government intervention would the price result in optimal utility. In addition to developing a theory of marginal utility and the concept of consumer's surplus, he set forth a justification for price discrimination by the monopolist, discussed conditions which would prevent a monopolist from charging an exorbitant price for his product, and at least gave a hint as to the foundation of marginal-cost pricing.

Dupuit took a position on the question of property rights not different from that of James Mill: property rights are to be defined with respect to an established set of governmental rules, which themselves are determined by an existing set of social relations. This led Dupuit to argue in favor of the right to contract, but against an unlimited property right in those instances in which economic efficiency arguments are clearly threatened. (Note again the influence of Aristotle.) His stance on property led him to argue against, among other things, professional licensing, child labor laws, labor unions (which restricted the worker's ability to contract freely for his labor), and in general governmental interferences in areas such as education (where his objective seems to have been focused on state control of the curriculum, and not based on efficiency arguments).

The Grand Equilibrium System of Walras 6

The Methodology of Walras 6.1

Having dispensed with the attempts at creating the building blocks necessary for the construction of a grand theory of economics, we now come to consider a figure who collected the pieces together into a unified whole, presenting in the attempt an elegant framework of interrelated quantities. This system-builder was Léon Walras, among the most acclaimed (by modern scholars) of the economists whose contributions are to be considered in this chapter. His accomplishments have arguably had the most staying power of any of his French predecessors, and his method if not his system is at the heart of virtually all modern economics. Schumpeter went so far as to argue that Walras's "system of equations, defining (static) equilibrium in a system of interdependent quantities, is the Magna Carta of economic theory" (Schumpeter 1954, 242).

Marie Ésprit Léon Walras (1834–1910) was the son of Antoine Auguste Walras (1801–66), himself an economist and a professional metaphysical philosopher and rhetorician.[34] Denied admission to the École Polytechnique because of his lack of mathematical training, Léon embarked on a program of mathematical study, including the study of Cournot's *Recherches*—Cournot had been his father's classmate. (He eventually undertook study at the somewhat less prestigious École des Mines.) In 1860, Walras presented a paper on taxation at Lausanne. At this meeting was one Louis Ruchonnet, the soon-to-be head of the education faculty at the Canton de Vaud, who was very impressed with Walras's abilities. In 1870 Ruchonnet offered him the newly founded chair in political economy (in the law faculty) at the University of Lausanne, a position he held until his retirement in 1892.

Between 1870 and 1878, in a burst of furious activity, Walras turned out the scheme of his general equilibrium theory; it appeared in the first edition of his *Élements d'économie pure*.[35] However, as he was very competitive with Jevons (whose work he understood was similar to

---

34. Antoine Auguste Walras, who studied in the law at the University of Paris, published two important economic works, *De la nature de la richesse et de l'origine de la valeur* (1831), and *Théorie de la richesse sociale* (1849). Léon held that both were important in the foundation of his own theories.

35. Jaffé (1969) mentioned as a possible "progenitor" of Walras one Achylle-Nicolas Isnard (1749–1803), an engineer and graduate of the Ecole des Ponts et Chaussées. He was especially important in that he apparently produced an explanation of the *numéraire* before Walras and did so within a similar framework. Walras was familiar with his approach.

his own, and it was already in press), he published the initial part of the *Élements* in 1874.[36] (We use here the English-language [Jaffé] translation of 1954, based on the "definitive" edition of 1926.)

Walras, as with many of the other figures we have discussed, began his treatise with a brief digression on method and the historical development of the discipline. He held that the pioneers of economics had given insufficient attention to just where the discipline belonged among the sciences. The physiocrats, for example, especially Quesnay, Mercier de la Rivière, and du Pont, had defined the science too broadly; Smith had taken greater care with his definitions, but even these were flawed, since they allowed too readily of normative influences.

To be scientific, the principles of economics had to be stated as positive objects.[37] This is true of all sciences and cannot be disregarded in the case of economics merely because of its social nature. Economics must, as with the other sciences, accept a "complete indifference to consequences, good or bad, with which it carries on the pursuit of pure truth" (Walras 1954, 52). Economists must realize that their primary concerns are not with the means for the provision of revenue or income to the citizenry or the state, as Smith had declared; rather it is more strictly "to pursue and master purely scientific truths" (52). Smith's concerns were those of the applied economist, not of the economist cum scientist.

Walras was equally dismissive of Say's definition of political economy. While Smith had defined political economy as an *art,* Say defined it as a *natural science.* For Walras, this position was untenable, for it ignored the human factor in arriving at decisions regarding production, consumption, and distribution. If for only this reason, Walras declared Say's definition to be "inaccurate and inferior to Adam Smith's which was only incomplete" (1954, 55).

> Man is a creature endowed with reason and freedom, and possessed of a capacity for initiative and progress. In the production and distribution of wealth, and generally in all matters pertaining to social organization, man has the choice between better and worse and tends more and more to choose the better part. Thus man has progressed from a system of guilds, trade regulations and price fixing to a system of freedom of industry and trade, i.e. to a system of *laisser-faire, laisser passer;* he has progressed from slavery to serfdom and from serfdom to the wage system. The superiority of the later forms of organization over the earlier forms lies not in their greater naturalness (both old and new are artificial, the newer forms

36. Walras himself paid for all of his publications—perhaps because he was impatient, but more likely because his efforts to find a regular publishing arrangement were unsuccessful. The historical development of the *Élements* is presented in Jaffé 1977.

37. Walras, citing Plato, held that the purpose of science is the study of universals; the only difference among the sciences is with the facts their practitioners select for their study (Walras 1954, 61).

more so than the old, since they came into existence only by sup-
planting the old); but rather in their closer conformity with material
well-being and justice. (1954, 55)

The problem with the previous definitions is that they did not extend far enough to encompass the nature of economics and the scope of
its problems. Walras considered economics not as being within the confines of a single disciplinary structure, but as having elements belonging
to several. Specifically, he suggested that the subject matter be viewed as
being within the confines of science, art, and ethics. The theory of value
and exchange clearly is in the realm of science; the theory of production
is, however, an art. The theory of distribution, the remaining concern,
must then be in the realm of ethics or "moral science" (1954, 60).

To understand these divisions better, Walras considered how economists order (or should order) their facts. The "facts" of economics are
divisible into two general categories: forces of nature and forces of human will.[38] The first of these, forces of nature, are "blind and ineluc-
table," requiring that when we confront these facts, we restrict ourselves
to identification, verification, and explanation. The second, forces of
human will, are forces "free and cognitive," and so not only can they be
identified, verified, and explained, but they can be controlled as well.
Thus by reference to the "facts of our universe," economics can be understood, first as a pure natural science, and second as both a pure moral
science and as art or ethics.[39] The result is a threefold classification of
economics into natural science, moral science, and ethics. "Their respective *criteria* are the *true*; the *useful* meaning material well-being; and the
good, meaning justice" (1954, 64; emphasis in original).

It was within this threefold classification that Walras introduced his
justification for the use of mathematics in economics. In a letter to Edward Pfeiffer dated 1874, Walras addressed the question of the appropriate place for mathematics in a social discipline such as economics, employing for comparative purposes a slightly modified classification system. In
this scheme the previously listed trichotomy became pure science, applied
science, and practical science. He then argued on the basis of this scheme:

Now the application of mathematics to economics is a very different thing in the first two categories from what it is in the third. In
the first category the use of the language, method, and principles of
mathematics has no other object than to make our analyses more
rigorously accurate and more comprehensive than ordinary logic
can do. It also helps us to reach more rational conclusions. In pure
theory, therefore, our formulas not only may be abstract, but
should be so, in order that they may be general and permanent in

38. Cf. the previous discussion of John Stuart Mill.
39. As to the class "art or ethics," *industry* belongs to the former, *institutions* to the
latter. As persons subordinate things, industry is subordinate to the institutions we erect.

their validity. Our curves and functions ought to be applicable to any commodity which may be exchanged. It is only when we are concerned with problems of the third category, i.e., of practical economics, that our formulas ought to have concrete significance and our formulas or curves ought to have numerical coefficients.

This leaves to the application of mathematics the whole field of pure and applied economics. . . . The application of mathematics to economics consists in discussing and reasoning about *utility, quantity, effective demand, effective supply, price,* etc., which are *magnitudes* . . . , in setting these magnitudes as functions of one another and in making use of a knowledge of the general properties of these functions in a study of economic phenomena.

The application of mathematics to practical economics is quite another thing. In the place of general and abstract formulas, one can, within certain limits and under given conditions, substitute special determinate formulas and obtain a price by calculation instead of waiting for the market to discover these prices. (Quoted in Jaffé 1983, 27–28; emphasis in original)

While it was through the presentation of a formal structure that he made his greatest mark in the development of economics, Walras expressed a sympathetic feeling for the inductivism of the German Historical School. Yet at the same time he rejected the historical school's antitheory bias. Similarly, he accepted the rationalism of Hegel and the Hegelians, but rejected their antihistorical bias. Both theory and history were important for a complete understanding of social processes; to consider one at the expense of the other meant limiting oneself unnecessarily. "For my part, my most deeply felt desire is to see this beautiful scientific and philosophical synthesis accomplished and to share in this accomplishment" (28).

6.2 *Walras and Utility*

One of Walras's innovations in the *Éléments* was in his definitions of scarcity and value, an idea which marked a clear change from the earlier conception of utility as the determinant of value. He began by drawing attention to an error in the work of Dupuit on the question of utility. Dupuit, according to Walras, measured utility "by the sacrifice which the consumer is *willing to* make" instead of the sacrifice he actually *does* make (Walras 1954, 445; emphasis added). The error of Dupuit lay in regarding the sacrifice a person is willing to make to obtain an object as dependent solely on the utility afforded by that object alone. Walras rejected this as incomplete, since it does not account for the effect on this utility value of the utility derived from other goods, or on wealth: "as the utility he derives from other commodities increases or decreases, the maximum sacrifice that he is willing to make . . . will decrease or increase." Further, as his wealth

> is larger or smaller, the sacrifice which he will be ready to make . . . will be larger or smaller. In general, the maximum pecuniary sacrifice which a consumer is willing to make to obtain a unit of a product depends not only on the utility of the product in question, but also on the utility of all the other products in the market, and, finally, on the consumer's means. (1954, 445)

From his father, Walras borrowed the concept of *rareté*, defined as "the intensity of the last want satisfied by any given *quantity consumed* of a commodity" (1954, 119; emphasis in original). It is, in the modern terminology of mathematical economics, the derivative of total utility with respect to the quantity held, and so is a decreasing function of the quantity consumed. *Rareté* causes value in exchange, since it is "synonymous with scarcity" (145). The difference between *rareté* and scarcity is that "*rareté* is taken to be a measurable magnitude which is not only inevitably associated with value in exchange but is also, of necessity, proportionate to this value, in the same way that weight is related to mass" (145). *Exchange value* itself is relative (akin to weight), while *rareté* is absolute (akin to mass). Consider two goods, A and B, which exchange for one another. Should good A become useless or available in unlimited quantity, it would no longer have value in exchange. Good B would then also lose its exchange value, but would not thus be scarce, and it would continue to have "a determinate *rareté*." All that would change would be our ability to measure it.

It is important to note here that *rareté* is not an attribute of any commodity; it is rather a subjective apprehension, defined only for a given individual: "there are no other *raretés* than the *raretés* of (A) or (B) for holders (1), (2), (3) . . . of these commodities, and it is only for these holders that there are ratios of *raretés* of (A) to *raretés* of (B) or of *raretés* of (B) to those of (A)" (1954, 146). Being a subjective quality, *rareté* is "not a measurable quantity; yet we have only to form a conception of it to found the demonstration of the fundamental laws of pure economics upon the fact of its diminution" (463).[40]

Within the confines of the theory of exchange, one can find reflections of the invisible hand and, in turn, see evidence of Smith and Mandeville. In his discussion of the mechanics of the value process, Walras noted that the exchange value of two goods in a market—wheat for money, in his example—is in fact "of the character of a *natural phenomenon*" (1954, 69; emphasis in original). It is not necessary for the buyer or seller to wish this value or even to personally agree to it for it to

---

40. Walras noted the similarity of *rareté* to Jevons's "final degree of utility" (Walras 1954, 463). Note here Walras's statement that *rareté* is "not a measurable *quantity*" and his statement (145) that it is "a measurable *magnitude*." The two are not synonyms.

be so established. The market establishes the value independently of the wishes of the participants (and does so deterministically) much after the fashion of the establishment of social virtue in the absence of individual virtue. As Walras stated:

> Thus any value in exchange, once established, partakes of the character of a natural phenomenon, natural in its origins, natural in its manifestations and natural in essence. If wheat and silver have *any value at all,* it is because they are scarce, that is, useful and limited in quantity—both of these conditions being natural. (1954, 69; emphasis in original)

Walras was keenly aware of the imperfections inherent in the competitive model; still, he believed that the competitive model underlay so much and possessed such an explanatory power that it held a general usefulness. The auction market, for example, could serve as the *example extraordinaire* of the competitive market, with the auctioneer's method, the *tâtonnement* process, an ideal analytical concept for *understanding,* while not actually *describing,* the market process. The introduction of the *tâtonnement* process Walras very clearly stated:

> What must we do in order to prove that the theoretical solution is identically the solution worked out by the market? Our task is very simple: we need only show that the upward and downward movements of prices solve the system of equations of offer and demand by a process of groping. (1954, 170)

In other words, the actual workings of a perfectly competitive market economy can be, under the thesis presented by Walras, demonstrated to be identical with the solution of a system of simultaneous equations. The general system of Walras, then, reduces to an as-if theory: we can accept as a realistic portrayal of the economy a purely abstract set of interdependent equations, since their solution results in an outcome identical to that of the true system.[41]

6.3 Walras and the Property Right

In addition to the preceding, we should mention that Walras also developed the notion that the aggregate of goods in society is the pertinent basis for the property right. Walras held that property derived from appropriability—ownership is nothing but "legalized appropriation" (1954, 67)—and that the specific system of appropriability which a society agrees upon is a social and moral phenomenon, a "relationship among persons," and is intimately connected with questions of distribu-

---

41. Of course, this begs the question, whether the portrayal of the actual economy as perfectly competitive is realistic in and of itself.

tive justice (77). The form of the property right agreed upon by society will thus depend not merely on appropriability, but also on considerations of social justice.

> Property consists in fair and rational appropriation, or rightful appropriation. While appropriation by itself is an objective fact, pure and simple, property, on the other hand, is a phenomenon involving the concept of justice; it is a right. Between the objective fact and the right, there is a place for moral theory. (1954, 78)

Walras held that the problem with discussions of the property right was that they were created by a failure to understand and accept the differences between the *fact* of ownership and the *right*. It is one thing to analyze the historical development of property relations and resource distribution; it is quite another to analyze specific distributive measures (and so to make a moral judgment) on the basis of a criterion such as justice. The historical record is a fact and can be confronted objectively; whether a specific system of ownership and distribution fulfills the criterion of justice is a question to be answered by moral philosophy. The answer to the question of justice will lead to a description of "the only good system" (1954, 78). The two "most prominent" systems of distribution that Walras considered were individualism and communism, the first being championed by Aristotle, the second by Plato. Communism is defined through the collective ownership of goods given initially (in the base state) to all; individualism is defined through personal ownership, based on the understanding of an inherent inequality in virtue, talent, industry, and thrift. Walras (in the *Éléments*) refused to take a position on the matter, but did insist that the

> object [of the problem of property] consists essentially in establishing human relations arising from the appropriation of social wealth so as to achieve a mutual co-ordination of human destinies in conformity with reason and justice. Appropriation being in essence a moral phenomenon, the theory of property must be in essence a moral science. *Ius est suum cuique tribuere*—justice consists in rendering to each that which is properly his. (1954, 79)

Walras extended his appropriation-based theory of property to encompass a theory of taxation. This was a task rather easily performed, for Walras concluded that the two were "simply two aspects of one and the same theory of the distribution of wealth in human society, the first representing this society as composed of separate individuals and the second representing it as a collectivity in the shape of the State" (1954, 55). The role of the state he held to be one of minimal interference: it is "empowered to maintain order and security, to render justice, to guarantee national defence, and to perform many other services besides." But the state is most assuredly not to be involved in the production or distribution of wealth: the state "is not an entrepreneur; it does not sell its services in the market either on the principle of free competition . . . , or on the principle of monopoly." In sum, "the services of the State are meant for collective, and not individual, consumption" (447).

Yet while Walras so defined the limited powers of the state and the necessity of a right of property, he nonetheless accepted, as part of his social-reformist platform, the notion of land as being of such a special nature as to be viewed as a community holding. In his 1896 *Études d'économie sociale* he offered a proposal modeled after one originally suggested by his father, that land should be nationalized (and wage taxation abolished) in order to better promote the end of distributive justice. After all, the fruits of individual effort should accrue to the individual, while at the same time the revenues obtained from a community resource (such as land) should accrue to the community.

This did not, he maintained, suggest his favoring of socialism—he noted that James Mill had advocated just such a scheme—for he did not wish to expropriate the land from its current holders, but rather have the state pay for it. Also, he did not favor the abolition of private property, but only the community holding of a special type of resource—land. Beyond land, the rights to all other property and the rewards therefrom accrued to individuals through appropriability.[42]

6.4 The Influence of Walras

Walras's achievements may be understood as formalism without development. He produced no grand theory of money or distribution or production, but rather limited himself to the presentation of an analytical framework demonstrating the interrelations within an economy. If anything his was a grand theory of *value*. In all, he confined himself to demonstrations of the means to the promotion of social welfare and distributive justice along rational economic lines.

According to Schumpeter (1954, 829) and Mark Blaug (1985, 584), while his work is highly regarded in our time, Walras's personal influence on the profession was in his own time very slight. He had few who were willing or able to follow in his footsteps and preach the doctrine. In Italy, Enrico Barone and Maffeo Panteleoni could be counted as disciples; in England the only one of note was A. L. Bowley, also a disciple of Edgeworth; in the United States, Irving Fisher and Henry L. Moore stand out as followers. Wicksell and even Pareto found his work of immense importance. Schumpeter himself was quite enamored of the approach of Walras, and in fact made it a central theme of his *History of Economic Analysis*.

---

42. On all this see especially Renato Cirillo (1981, 1984).

The Sociological Dimension: Vilfredo Pareto 7

The Political Milieu 7.1

Up to now our discussion in this chapter has focused on the principal economic writers of the late French tradition whose accomplishments were primarily along the lines of technical improvements to an existing theoretical base (that of Adam Smith). There developed, along Smithian lines, a law of markets (Say), a utilitarian revision of the labor theory of value (Sismondi), the mathematization of value theory and a theory of competition in a limited market (Cournot), the invention of the concept of marginal utility (Dupuit), and the workings of a general equilibrium framework (Walras).

The last of our line took a completely different track, seeking to establish economics as a topic within the larger study of social phenomena. As a *social* discipline, economics is institution-bound, something not entirely understood by economists viewing the economic question as somehow separate from social questions. This disconnection led to a narrowing of study, first to problems of value and utility as they affect and are affected by the physical production of goods and wealth, and later to the fixation on mathematical elegance and even numerical calculation of economic magnitudes as a preliminary to theory-building. The sociological dimension is the other side of the coin, and it is to the effort of a lone figure in economic thought, taken by sociologists to be one of their own, that we now turn. This figure is Vilfredo Pareto.

Vilfredo Federico Damaso Pareto (1848–1923) was something of a prodigy, having published his first paper, on the subject of the applications of asymmetric design, at the age of 18. At Turin Polytechnic, he completed his degree in mathematical and physical sciences (1867) and took an advanced degree in engineering (1870).[43] By 1875, having worked as an engineer and director for a private railway, he joined the iron-producing firm of Società Ferriere d'Italia, headed by Ubaldino Peruzzi, the mayor of Florence, who was to become a patron to Pareto. It was this relationship that encouraged Pareto to begin in earnest his writing career.

In 1890, Pareto made the acquaintance of Maffeo Panteleoni (1857–1924),[44] who more than anyone is responsible for having shifted Pareto's interests to the study of economics, especially to the general equilibrium theories of Walras; upon Walras's retirement from the chair of political economy at Lausanne in 1892, Panteleoni arranged for Pareto

---

43. His thesis was entitled "Fundamental Principles of the Theory of Elasticity of Solid Bodies and Fundamental Research into the Integration of the Differential Equations Defining Their Equilibrium."

44. Panteleoni was an economist who is credited with having introduced "modern" economics (i.e., marginalism) into the Italian academic system. He was also a stormy petrel, a supporter of Mussolini, follower of Walras, and something of a Mengerian subjectivist. He has been much better known in Italian academic circles than Pareto, which may say something about those circles.

to fill the vacancy. By 1899 Pareto had become disillusioned with the policies of the Italian government, for two reasons. The basis of Pareto's philosophy at this time was a free-trade, Smithian form of liberalism. To this end he favored limited government intervention in economic affairs, free trade and enterprise, and a decentralized governmental organization. But by the turn of the century the very policies he had supported—anti–interventionist, liberal democracy—had degenerated into bloc-political interests. The result was that the overall situation had not actually changed at all, since democracy had been shunted aside in favor of a simple replacement of one intransigent ruling elite with another. Plutocracy had replaced meritocracy, a state of affairs inconsistent with his own theory of the "circulation" of elites.

The second reason for his disillusionment with the academic and sociopolitical system in Italy at this time was the emergence as a potent political and social force of Marxist philosophy. As Finer (1966) has noted, the poverty of this philosophical, economic, and social paradigm should have made its rejection immediate and complete; the fact that Marxist doctrine was taking hold in Italy at all was something Pareto could not rationalize. Pareto was above all critical of parliamentary systems of governance; as noted by Ingrao and Israel, Pareto "was himself immersed— anti–ideologist par excellence though he was—in a many-sided and ill-defined ideology that has been interpreted both as intransigent liberalism and as its opposite, a legitimization of authoritarian regimes" (Ingrao and Israel 1990, 123). While his individualism verged on the side of libertarianism, he indeed championed the notions of meritocratic order and the hierarchical state. Thus he has been portrayed as believing in an authoritarian political philosophy which held that fascism was preferable as a counter to the decadence that had flourished in the Italy of his time. Yet, at the most fundamental level, Pareto was opposed to the corporatism that is the basis of fascism. He believed in the state as a collection of atomistic individuals, not as an organic whole to the interests of which each member was subservient. It was in fact the Italian flirtation, first with communism and then with fascism that, perhaps more than anything else, led to his interest in developing a general system of sociology that had at its core the analysis of nonrational systems, and to his reorientation of value theory from the abstract concept of *homo economicus* toward a more realistic, socialized economic agent.[45]

7.2 *Paretian Utility: Ophelimité*

Pareto's first book, *Cours d'économie politique*, was published in 1896.[46] A major work in two volumes—reviewed by, among others, Irving

---

45. On this see Cirillo 1983.

46. We use here the translation of selected portions of Pareto's *Cours*, included in a selection of his sociological writings (Pareto 1966), edited by Finer.

Fisher—it had as its object the study of economics as a science, which came to mean the study of *ophélimité,* a term intended by Pareto to replace the concept of utility. Utility as an economic concept had become too trite for economic discussions of the process of choice among alternatives; to promote clarity of exposition, a new, less ambiguous, expression needed to be introduced. *Ophélimité* goes beyond mere utility in the everyday sense of the term, and even in the usual economic sense. For economics to be "scientific," the terms it employs cannot be normative, bound in definition by attitudes or conventions which are tied to a time or place, or which serve to promote a given value judgment. The terms must be value-free. *Ophélimité* is just such a term. *Utility* as it had been employed by the ethical utilitarians became inextricably linked to the goodness or pleasurableness that an object could bring to its holder. Thus could Bentham conclude not only that utility produced happiness, as though it was part of the essential nature of the object, but that indeed utility lay in happiness itself, endowing the concept with an epistemic quality.[47] Later, for example in the hands of Jevons, it was developed into a concept central to the understanding of economic valuation and so became linked inextricably to a numerical decision calculus. The term came to have both physical and psychical qualities, or rather to serve both an epistemic and an ontologic function.

Ophélimité circumvents the objections to the term *utility. Ophélimité* means simply "satisfaction," but without any positive or negative connotation as to what this satisfaction may entail. It is used "to designate the relationship of convenience which makes a thing satisfy a need or a desire, whether legitimate or not" (Pareto 1966, 99 [1896, vol. 1, §5]).[48] An object which causes harm, death, addiction, and so on, or which promotes hatred, abuse, or any of a number of other antisocial activities is, despite the negative consequences of its use, still promoting an end or satisfying a desire. The *attribute* of an object, then, that causes it to be desired, must be separated from the social and individual *consequences* of its desirability, possession, and use. The former is the proper venue for calling an attribute *ophélimité,* the latter is more appropriately designated *utility.* So pleasure is not synonymous with goodness in a social context. Goodness is a positive feeling; pleasure can derive from something which is inherently bad as socially defined.

An important characteristic of *ophélimité* is that it is a "wholly subjective quality" (1966, 99 [1896, §7]). There can be no *ophélimité* without there being a sentient, calculating, rationalizing being as a correspondent: "If the human race were to disappear off the face of the earth, gold would still be a rare metal, soft, and with a specific gravity of 19.26;

---

47. Although it must be noted here that Bentham eventually distanced himself from the term, offering that it was indeed a poor choice.

48. The notation here reflects the Finer edition as well as the corresponding place in the (as yet untranslated) *Cours.*

but its ophelimity would exist not at all" (100 [1896, §7]). But the fact that *ophélimité* is subjective does not militate against its perception as an objective quality. Pareto himself noted that this misapprehension seems to arise from happenstance: for some goods, it appears as though *most,* if not *all,* individuals profess *ophélimité,* that is, the goods produce *ophélimité* for more than one individual (100 [1896, §9]). However, this is of course a mere coincidence and does not, perceptions to the contrary, in any way refute that *ophélimité* is anything but a "wholly subjective" concept. The fact that one man has a feeling for a "thing" does not mean that another cannot experience the same satisfaction (or revulsion, or indifference, for that matter).

In all, the *Cours* is an expression of Walrasian general equilibrium—Schumpeter referred to it as "simply a brilliant Walrasian treatise" (Schumpeter 1954, 860). Equilibrium remained a concern throughout Pareto's writings, not just as a description of the interdependencies of the economic system, but as illustrative of the social structure in its totality. As we can model *economic* activity through reference to a series of interrelated equations of supply and demand, so can we relate the forces at work in the *social* system as a whole. Society he viewed as representable by a mechanical model in which the actions of any single element reverberate throughout the system. But even so, the system is *stable* in the sense that exogenous (and even endogenous—Pareto was keenly aware of the subjective element as a potent force driving change) shocks eventually make their way through the system, balancing out in the end. In the sense that the constituent elements of a stationary statistical series can be regarded as tending to a mean value, or gathering around a measure of central tendency, so did Pareto view the workings of the social system: each constituent of the series can be matched to a countervailing one, over a long period of time canceling the influences of each in favor of the trend of the whole.

> Every society invariably offers considerable resistance to external or internal forces which tend towards its modification. Accidental movements arising in a society are neutralised by the counteracting movements they provoke; and ultimately, as a rule, they die away, and society reverts to its previous state. (Pareto 1966, 104 [1896, vol. II, §585])

While cognizant of the fact that the economy (and by extension the society) is a dynamic system, Pareto held that it is only possible to study it in discrete time, as a series of static equilibrium states. Although economic *dynamics* is the method Pareto would have chosen to employ had the mathematical apparatus been available to him at the time, for practical purposes, and also perhaps because he felt himself constrained by the dictates of Walras's static structure, he had to settle for *representing* dynamic variation by reference to a series of static equilibria.

In the *Manuale di economia politica*,[49] Pareto moved more closely toward a complete subjectivistic theory of economics, one in which psychological factors are granted significance.[50] Once again, as he had in the *Cours,* Pareto refined his notions of utility and *ophélimité,* entirely in keeping with his view that "[s]cientific conceptions are modified little by little so as to come closer to the truth . . ." (Pareto 1971, chap. III, §31, 111). In the *Manuale,* he distinguished between *types* of *ophélimité.* *Elementary ophélimité* is defined as the pleasure given by a small, incremental change in the quantity of an object, divided by the quantity itself. *Weighted ophélimité (ophélimité pondérée)* is this number divided by the price. Again, pleasure is not to be confused with individual or social good or individual or social improvement. Pleasure derives merely from the good being *useful,* from its satisfying a desire of the individual who chooses to use it.

> Thus morphine is not useful, in the ordinary sense of the word, since it is harmful to the morphine addict; on the other hand it is economically *useful* to him, even though it is unhealthful, because it satisfies one of his wants. (1971, 111; emphasis in original)

But Pareto wished to go further, in the manner of Jevons and Edgeworth, and actually provide a means for the measurement of this concept. *Ophélimité* is not asserted to be amenable to cardinal measure, at least in Pareto's textual presentation of the theory, except under conditions where "it is a case of goods of a kind such that the ophelimity of each of them depends only on the quantity of that good, and remains independent of the quantities of other goods consumed" (1971, §35, 112). Comparisons of cardinal measures are strictly determinate only in the case of a single good, since this allows that extraneous factors are controlled; indeterminacy

---

49. This first appeared in 1906. A revised edition of this work was published in French in 1909, entitled *Manuel d'économie politique.* Here lies the genesis of a controversy.

In 1971, Ann S. Schwier translated the 1927 French edition into English. In a review article (1972b), William Jaffé concluded that, in fact, the Italian edition was the definitive one; the French edition was not a very good translation, and an English translation of a bad French translation of an Italian work simply multiplied the difficulties.

In response, Schwier noted that the French edition was a *revision* of the *Manuale* (although it was translated by Alfred Bonnet). She noted further that even Italian economists accepted the French edition as definitive, and it was this edition which many British and American economists relied on in bringing the ideas of Pareto to the English-speaking world. The controversy was summed up nicely by Vincent Tarascio (1974).

The Schwier translation (1971) of the 1927 French edition is the one used here.

50. This work combined economic principles as they would operate in a sociological environment and is the best of his works from the standpoint of current thinking. For instance, Pareto in this book noted correctly the conditions for a general economic equilibrium, emphasized the importance of path-dependency pricing, and proposed a view of optimality which stressed the competitive norm. Schumpeter, however, considered the *Manuale* as "not more than Walras' work done over" (1954, 861).

occurs when comparisons are attempted *between* goods, for under this condition there is no accepted standard of comparison.

For purposes of comparison, we need to construct an appropriate system of indexes. The approach of Pareto, however, was opposed to previous methods of construction. In fact, Pareto went so far as to invert the previously accepted relationship. While earlier proponents of indifference curve analysis, for example Edgeworth, had *derived* indifference curves based on the presumed *existence* of utility, Pareto *assumed* the indifference curves to be existent *prior to* any definition of utility. The definition of utility or *ophélimité* then derived from this initial postulate, namely, from the indifference surface itself (1971, 119). The advantage of this procedure is in eliminating the need for cardinal measures of utility, something which had earlier intrigued Edgeworth. Edgeworth had employed indifference curve analysis to show the manner in which individuals arrange bundles of goods for which they profess indifference as to utility. Pareto's adaptation of this method involved the use of *ophélimité* to order the indifference curves themselves. Choice was to be dependent on the relation between the indifference curves and the *ophélimité* indexes. One must begin with indifference curves and then proceed to a comparison of those combinations which provide for the individual the same degree of *ophélimité*.

It is also in the *Manuale* that there appears one of Pareto's most important, but least acknowledged, contributions to economics. It is in this work that Pareto redefined and so altered the basic structure of Edgeworth's famous diagram, even though this altered version is now (and perhaps forever will be) linked to the name of Edgeworth. Beginning in chapter III, entitled "General Notion of Economic Equilibrium," Pareto extended his indifference curve analysis to account for exchange between two individuals. The description of the process of exchange culminated with the now-famous diagram presented in §116 (138).

While Edgeworth in his original formulation drew only two axes, Pareto thought it more convenient (and probably more rigorous) to require *four* axes to handle the analytics, these representing (1) the amount of good I possessed by person A, (2) the amount of good II possessed by person A, (3) the amount of good I possessed by person B, and (4) the amount of good II possessed by person B. The result is the familiar rectangular "box." An improvement in person A's position is represented by a northeast movement, in person B's position by a southwest movement (see fig. 3).

Using this simple but elegant diagram, Pareto analyzed two important considerations (types of phenomena) in the formulation of economic decisions. Type I attends to the satisfaction of individual tastes, given the constraints placed upon him in the market (chap. III, §41), while type II regards the ability of the individual to modify the market itself to allow better advantage (§42). Considering that each individual behaves in accor-

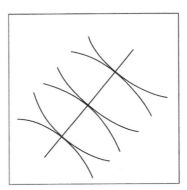

FIGURE 3. Pareto's Box Diagram

dance with type I phenomena, acting in accordance with a utility-maximizing calculus, the point of tangency between two individuals' indifference curves in a situation of exchange will represent an equilib-rium position.[51] Should any one of the two parties behave in accordance with Type II phenomena, attempting to alter the market situation itself to his own benefit, then the equilibrium solution is no longer so neatly identifiable, but rather results in a complicated game scenario. This was the situation Pareto held was most likely to occur. It is this possibility (and a host of other permutations) that shows clearly the genius of his insights.

Later (§49), Pareto extended this typology to a third type of species. Type III relates to the maximization of welfare for all participants and so "corresponds to the collectivist organization of society" (1971, §49, 118). While a typical bargaining situation may then involve two individu-als (or groups), one following in accordance with Type I, and the other Type II, collectivist states that allow free interaction will follow Type III.

The fundamental distinction, then, between Type I and Type III phenomena—since both deal with a specific satisfaction of tastes—is in the distribution of income: Type I distribution "takes place in accordance with all the historical and economic contingencies in which the society has evolved," while Type III distribution "is the result of certain ethico-social principles" (1971, chap. VI, §56, 268).

Of special interest in respect to types of phenomena is the investiga-tion of the form of production. Pareto maintained that "complete transformation"—meaning the relinquishing of one good for another, or the physical transformation of one good into another—is more easily handled under collectivism than under competition. The reason is straight-forward: while private industry in a free-market economy cannot ensure that "complete transformation" ever occurs—that Good A is transformed into Good B with no "residue"—this *can* be ensured in command (collec-tivist) economies simply by levying a tax equal to "overhead expenses" and

51. Pareto did not, however, require that this point be stable. See §§123 and 124.

then selling the output at cost. While from an efficiency standpoint Pareto thought this attractive, he admitted there were drawbacks—including the expense of a bureaucratic state apparatus—which led him to indecision on the matter of the better organization of production.

Interestingly enough, Pareto acknowledged that Type III phenomena may refer to less than the entire social collective. (In the extreme, it collapses to the single individual, and Type III becomes equivalent to Type II.) Thus he could handle with this apparatus (Type III phenomena) not merely the society as a whole, but also such consolidated groupings as labor unions, consumer unions, producer cooperatives, and the like (1971, §§62, 63; 269).

7.3 The Theory of Property

Continuing along these same lines, Pareto also showed an interest in one of the central topics of the earlier school of utilitarians, the right of property.[52] Pareto's view of the institution of property, at the heart of the theories of the Philosophic Radicals, emerged in this work in a much different form than it had been presented in the more legal-oriented works of his predecessors, especially that of Bentham, although it performed essentially the same function. Pareto's presentation is much more of a positivist one, in contradistinction to the more rationalist forms of Bentham and James Mill. It is also tempered by a decidedly socialistic outlook, a philosophy that was anathema to both Bentham and Mill. Distinctions between types of social and political arrangements, however, cannot (and this is also in contradistinction to Bentham and Mill) be made by using any positive criteria:

> pure economics does not give us a truly decisive criterion for choosing between an organization of society based on private property and a socialist organization. (1971, chap. VI, §61, 269)

Pareto readily accepted that private property performed a necessary function: to wit, it created the conditions for a stable social order (1971, chap. VII, §§106–7, 314). So far he appears in agreement with the conten-

---

52. This is not the first appearance of Pareto's interest in property rights; in fact, the theme may be found throughout his earlier works. In the *Cours,* he introduced a sociological interpretation of what Finer (1966, 16) has termed a theory of spoliation. According to this theory, there is in existence at all times a "class" which seeks to enhance its own power and prestige at the expense of others. When a government seeks, by fiat or law, to expropriate the property of one group in order to grant it to another, or seeks to enact policies that have the effect of favoring one group over another, these are examples of legal spoliation and are just as reprehensible as illegal spoliation, or what is commonly referred to as theft. Pareto presented specific examples of legal spoliation, including production subsidies and the Bland and Sherman Acts in the United States (Pareto 1966, 115 [1896, vol. II, §1046]). Today, we may add union exemption from the Sherman and other antitrust legislation, and even affirmative-action legislation.

tions of Bentham and the Mills. But he was not ready to concede that this stability was something that could or should be protected. The stability so engendered by private property as an institution is not necessarily on the Pareto view conducive to a fair and equitable social order, but is rather an element of a system that strives to maintain the existing social situation, including existing social and economic relationships between classes. Private property relations (and presumably, by extension, all contractual arrangements) are ensconced so as to prevent redistribution of both resources and power-relationships. It is not the *sole* criterion that serves to codify social and economic inequities and inequalities; but it is one important and essential facet of the system, one that embraces a governmentally imposed institutional order that serves to maintain the status quo.

> If among our western populations the element of stability were exclusively the result of the institution of private property and inheritance, that would be very strong evidence of the necessity for reducing, or even abolishing, the institution of private property. It is strange that the socialists have not perceived the support which this manner of viewing the phenomena could bring to their theories.
>
> But the element of stability which is opposed to change *via* selection is, in our societies, far from being exclusively the result of the institution of private property. Laws and customs have divided men into classes, and even where these classes have disappeared, as among modern democratic peoples, wealth assures advantages which enable certain individuals to beat back competitors. . . . In general, from ancient times up to our own, the upper classes of society have used political power to despoil the poor classes; but at present, in certain democratic countries, a diametrically opposite phenomenon seems to have begun. We have never been able to observe, for a long enough time period, a state of affairs in which the government remains neutral, neither aiding the latter to despoil the former, nor conversely. Thus we cannot decide empirically whether the considerable strength of the element of stability which opposes selection of elements from the lower classes has its origin in the institution of private property or in political oppression by the upper classes. (1971, chap. VII, §115, 317–18)

Logical versus Nonlogical Behaviors   7.4

One of the most illuminating (albeit ignored among economists) discussions in the *Manuale* pertains to the division of actions into logical and nonlogical forms, or what in modern parlance we distinguish as rational and nonrational (but by no means *irrational*) actions. Logical actions are those predicated on a reasoned analysis of experiential data and are subject to alteration as the data are updated. By *nonlogical* behavior

Pareto meant behavior dictated not by a chain of logical reasoning, but rather influenced by custom, belief, concerns with morality and ethics, even "waves of optimism and pessimism,"[53] anything in fact not involving a formal chain of reason.

It is frequently the case, however, that behavior that has a non-logical basis leads to results which are, after the fact, perceived as logical (rational).[54] Pareto pointed to the example of a beehive: beehives are composed of hexagonal cells, as the hexagon allows the maximum volume with a minimum of surface area. But bees do not *know* this to be the case, so the fact that they have adopted a cell structure that is efficient is a result of nonlogical behavior that leads ironically to a rational outcome. The importance of nonlogical actions is that they are the essence of most decision making. The individual does not, for the most part, calculate the benefits and costs of his actions in the manner of a pure Benthamite optimizer; rather he either pursues actions based on a subjective appraisal of a possible outcome or outcomes, or he may simply act in a certain manner because it is expected of him, or he may even act in what appears to be an "irrational" manner because be believes that others will behave "rationally," thus allowing him to gain an advantage by doing the unexpected. These are all examples of nonlogical behavior, while the *results* engendered may lead to the conclusion that they are the result of rational calculation (Pareto 1971, chap. II, §§2, 3, 4, 29–30).

Pareto made use of the theory of nonlogical behaviors in his two-volume *Les systèmes socialistes* (1902), written to formalize a theory of various types of socialist organization. One important aspect of this work is the recognition that socialism had by this time taken on the trappings of a religion. Although socialism pretends to call on reason as the basis of its conclusions, it is nonetheless propelled by an appeal to the nonlogical "faith" of its followers; and while it proposes to direct social feelings in the name of liberalism, in practice socialist minorities eventually coalesce and assume political power.[55]

---

53. This phrase is borrowed from Keynes (1936a). Keynes's views on the topic under discussion are very similar to those of Pareto, although he never took Pareto as a guide for his own theories of the economic process as motivated for the most part by subjectivistic behavior.

54. George Homans and Charles Curtis (1934) maintained that social stability also played a role. When the social structure appears stable, then we may invoke a form of social ceteris paribus and for the sake of simplicity (i.e., "without loss of generality") view events as having evolved in a logical manner. In times of upheaval, however, when the stability of the system has been compromised, the nonlogical behaviors underlying events are most readily discernible. The authors fault historians and sociologists with failure to recognize in calmer times that these nonlogical behaviors are always at the bottom of social relationships.

55. This was a period when several scholars made significant contributions to the pro- and antisocialism literature, among them Benedetto Croce, Enrico Barone, and Nicolas Gerard Pierson, to say nothing of George Bernard Shaw. Earlier Walras, something of a prosocialist, had written on the topic as well. For translations of the Pierson and the Barone articles, see Friedrich Hayek (ed.), *Collectivist Economic Planning*.

At the time he was preparing this work, Pareto argued that there were clear differences in the epistemological foundations of the competing theories of socialism and a free-market approach to organization, making the appeal on behalf of his behavioral theory. Participation in a market economy requires rationality; participation in a socialist economy means accepting the tenets of a system based on emotional commitment. To accept the market as the dispassionate administrator requires one to use his reason; to accept the socialist alternative of a benign social planner requires one to use his passions. Yet, in the end, each political system (market-based or socialist) requires the same form of economic organization.

The Treatise on General Sociology   7.5

The 1916 *Trattato di Sociologia Generale* was Pareto's most challenging book. (Although literally "Treatise on General Sociology," the title of the English translation is *Mind and Society*, published in 1935.) It is essential to realize that at this time Pareto became thoroughly disillusioned with economics as a science; he thought that economists must become sociologists as well.

The purpose behind the study of human behavior is to distill the fundamental essence of social organization, that is, to identify the motives and predispositions that compel men to arrange themselves into social groupings. In the *Trattato* Pareto extended his earlier presentation (in the *Manuale*) of logical and nonlogical behavior. Pareto's analytical system differentiated between instincts, emotions, and reason. Together there were *residues*, which combine *derivatives* (instincts) and *derivations* (logical rationalizations). These are used to justify our rationalizations, which are themselves cultural.

By the time he wrote the *Trattato*, Pareto had denied the fundamental bases of economic theory—that there is an underlying rationality (cause and effect) in economic decision making. What then, absent logic, can link individual decision making together? Pareto's answer was that the "glue" was a combination of force and cunning, exercised by the governing elite.[56]

For our purposes, the most interesting discussion in this work is that of volume II, "Analysis of Sentiment (Theory of Residues)." Theories (designated by Pareto as *c*) are comprised of two parts, a substantial element (*a*) and a contingent element (*b*) (Pareto 1935, vol. I, §798, 480–81). The distinction draws on his earlier one between logical and non-logical conduct:

The element *a* directly corresponds to non-logical conduct; it is the expression of certain sentiments. The element *b* is the manifestation

---

56. Of course, an elite, much after Hobbes's Leviathan, is self-defined: an elite is what an elite succeeds in doing, while it considers itself being an elite.

of the need of logic that the human being feels. It also partially corresponds to sentiments, to non-logical conduct, but it clothes them with logical or pseudo-logical reasonings. The element *a* is the *principle* . . . existing in the mind of the human being; the element *b* is the explanation (or explanations) of that principle, the inference (or inferences) that he draws from it. (1935, vol. I, §798, 481)

By "principle" Pareto meant "the cause to which an action is to be ascribed" (§306n.2, 199). One begins with the manifestation of a sentiment (the *a*), and then seeks to secure as logical a foundation for this sentiment as possible (the *b*). Finally, the theory that is created to serve the explanatory role is characterized as the *c*.

Pareto (reluctantly) provided labels to these three elements. The element *a*, the constant element, he termed the *residue*; *b*, the deductive element, is the *derivation*; *c*, the theory or resultant, is the *derivative*. (The term *derivative* is little used in Pareto's subsequent presentations, as he frequently employs other terms such as "theory" when discussing this element at all.) The most important element is the residue.

The residue for Pareto is not distinct in many respects from "animal spirits" in Marshall and Keynes. As with anything as ephemeral as a "spirit," a precise definition is wanting. But Pareto attempts one in any event. "Residues correspond to certain instincts in human beings, and for that reason they are usually wanting in definiteness, in exact delimitation" (1935, vol. II, §870, 509). Lacking a specific definition, Pareto instead opted for characterization by example. But he did, prior to this exercise (an exercise which takes up the bulk of volume II), limit the scope of the idea. Residues are not synonymous with instincts or emotions or sentiments. They are rather *indicative* of the existence of a sentiment, "just as the rising of the mercury in a thermometer is a manifestation of the rise in temperature" (1935, §875, 511). Residues point to the existence of an instinct or emotion behind actions; they are consequences, and in effect measure a change in motivation. They are not defined as these ephemeral factors themselves.

7.6 *Pareto's Influence*

Pareto's influence on the discipline of economics is great, although few, if any, of today's economists want to be reminded of what he thought of its shallowness. His work on general equilibrium analysis reflects a marked improvement over the model advanced by Walras, Schumpeter's protestations notwithstanding; indeed, both Gerard Debreu and Maurice Allais received Nobel Awards for the framework introduced by Pareto. His work on ordinal utility came to be one of the chambers of the heart of the theory of economic demand. His work on indifference analysis, ordinal measurement, and efficiency or Paretian optimality are at the "theoretical core" of modern nonnormative welfare economics. His work on income distribution has been refined, but the insight and the methods he suggested remain valid.

What is most incisive and at the same instant most troubling about Pareto was his view that economics when limited to rational models was a sterile subject. He wanted something that could acknowledge and deal with patristic forces, such as the cultural norms within a given society. This implies that economics must be seen not as an independent science of individual rational decision making, but rather as a subdiscipline of sociology. This may be seen as the ramblings of a master; as he was so disillusioned, it is hard for most modern economists (or sociologists, for that matter) to deal with the complexity of his legacy.

Bourbaki: The Essence of Mathematical Formalism 8

In 1939 there appeared the first volume of a soon-to-be masterwork of mathematics. Entitled *Élements de mathématique,* it was ostensibly the work of a Frenchman of Greek descent, one Nicolas Bourbaki. As it turned out, Bourbaki was the pseudonym of a group of French mathematicians—including in their number such well-known figures as André Weil and Jean Dieudonné—who had a singular ambition to systematize the whole of mathematics.[57]

The importance of all this for our purposes is the effect such a grand effort has had on the structure of economics. In his 1959 *Theory of Value,* Gerard Debreu followed Bourbaki in the use of terminology and in the method of presentation. He later described the influence of Bourbaki thus:

> Entering the Ecole Normale Supérieure in the fall of 1941 meant another initiation, this time into living science. The three years during which I studied and lived at the Ecole Normale were rich in revelations. Nicolas Bourbaki was beginning to publish his *Élements de Mathématique,* and his grandiose plan to reconstruct the entire edifice of mathematics commanded instant and total adhesion. Henri Cartan, who represented him at the Ecole Normale, influenced me then as no other faculty member did. . . .
>
> The new levels of abstraction and of purity to which the work of Bourbaki was raising mathematics had won a respect that was not to be withdrawn. (Debreu 1992, 108–9)

Debreu was but one of countless mathematicians drawn to economics who had become enamored of the Bourbaki program. In accepting the

---

57. There was a real Bourbaki—Charles Denis Sauter Bourbaki (1816–97), a French Army officer who declined an offer to become king of Greece. He is immortalized with a statue in Nancy, where many of the members of the Bourbaki group studied and worked.

rigor of Bourbaki as a framework for the study of economics, they succeeded in shifting emphasis within the discipline to formal structure,
including basing economic theory on axiomatic statements of logical
progression. The entire program within economics is not unlike the program of the Bourbaki. As the mathematician Paul Halmos described the
change in mathematics:

> The main features of the Bourbaki approach are a radical attitude
> about the right order for doing things, a dogmatic insistence on a
> privately invented terminology, a clean and economical organiza-
> tion of ideas and a style of presentation which is so bent on saying
> everything that it leaves nothing to the imagination and has, conse-
> quently, a watery, lukewarm effect. (Halmos 1957, 94)

9 An Assessment

With the singular exception of Pareto, we see in the French economic
tradition (including here the earlier physiocratic writers) an understanding of the relations of individuals to the state not much different from
that of the German cameralists and the romantics. Man is not merely a
rational utility calculator, but is also endowed with a social morality and
moral compass that seeks community solutions; he understands implicitly that the state interest is paramount, and his duty lies in its attainment.

For Sismondi and Walras, the right of property derived from society. For Dupuit and Cournot, the efficiency of state taxation was a worthy criterion. Even Say recognized a need for state action in the pursuit of
a greater level of social output.

It was in connection with state considerations that, as with the
physiocrats and the use of the circular flow, these later writers saw the
need to engage in rigorous calculation of relative benefits from social
action, both to demonstrate the *efficacy* and *efficiency* of state action,
and its *feasibility* as well. This explains Pareto's reluctance to accept
homo economicus as any kind of rational maximizer, and his ultimate
decision to forgo economics entirely, in favor of a more general sociological approach, one which forces us to break reliance on a scientific method
of social control and to embrace one that seeks to understand the more
nonrational (and so uncontrollable) aspects of social interactions.

CHAPTER 11

An American Tradition
Institutionalism

The number of new political ideas is very small. . . . But the institutions are found in constant change and must be seized in their own peculiar historical forms.

G. JELLINEK, *DECLARATION OF THE RIGHTS OF MAN* (1895)

No important institution is ever merely what the law makes it. It accumulates about itself traditions, conventions, ways of behavior, which . . . are not less formidable in their influence.

HAROLD LASKI, *THE AMERICAN PRESIDENCY* (1940)

Institutionalism Defined   I

In recent years, American contributions to the economics profession have led the way in the introduction of formalism, in effect extending the legacy of Cartesian rationalism. One need only point to the legacy from Irving Fisher to Paul Samuelson and Kenneth Arrow. But at the same time there has been a longer-standing American cultural emphasis on problem solving, particularly of a social nature. Here the focus is on low-level abstraction, employing generalizations derived ostensibly from an empirical analysis of the environment. This emphasis was notable in economics prior to World War I and has since come to be labeled Institutionalism.

Institutionalism as it developed primarily in the United States (as we shall presently see) was derived in large measure from the German Historical School, the influence of which is clearly evident in the scope of the Institutionalists' programs. This type of Institutionalism flourished from about the 1880s through the Depression of the 1930s, its influence waning by the end of the Second World War. But Institutionalism itself may be seen as having gone through an evolutionary transformation, as the older school was replaced by a new variant, known as Neo-Institutionalism or the New Institutional Economics.

The "older" American Institutional Economics is often perceived and described by neoclassical economists as little more than mono-lithically anti–abstract theory. In fact, it confronted the then-mainstream economics with a set of constraints, in the guise of social and political institutional arrangements, which the received theory had previously ne-glected. In effect, the school succeeded in showing that Pareto's dictum— that rational (economic) and nonrational (sociologic) disciplines must be distinct and separate—simply did not and could not hold.

Defining Institutionalism is not as easy a task as defining Utilitarian-ism; the scope of inclusion is simply too great. The term appears to have been invented by Walton Hamilton in his 1919 "The Institutional Ap-proach to Economic Theory," in which he declared the institutional ap-proach "the only way to the right sort of theory" (Hamilton 1919, 309). We will, in order to effect a workable definition, rely on that of Joseph Dorfman:

> The "institutionalists" had the feeling that traditional economics did not provide effective tools for understanding and dealing with a developing economy and the problems left by the war. They also objected to the inadequate practical recognition given to history, statistics, and such newer group phenomena as trade unions, corpo-rations, and trade associations. They sought not only to broaden the range of economic theory, but also to relate it to the contribu-tions of the other social disciplines. (Dorfman 1959, vol. IV, 352–53)

It has been tradition to identify three kinds of American Institu-tionalism of the "old school": Veblenian, Mitchellian, and Commonsian. While the distinction will continue here, the intent is to note how each interpretation of the institutionalist program, much as with the utilitari-ans, was generated from quite a different source, and to identify their impacts on diverse groups within and without academia. One principal underlying premise of all three interpretations is that the study of eco-nomic relationships (their common point of focus) is generally long-run and contextual, that is, temporally and spatially bound. Each of the three founders was a midwestern American (in temperament as well as by birth), products of the civilization which emerged in the decades follow-ing the American Civil War. A forgotten conflict of that war lay in the conviction that there existed a priority of needs: an economic need for union over a political tradition of voluntary state federalism.

By present standards, each of the three founders was an optimist, particularly in nationalistic American terms. For each, America was a bold experiment in the absorption of European immigrants, in accultura-tion to an English Common Law (preferably Whig) heritage, and in moral improvement. The culture that they understood to be historically basic, but ever adapting to American experience, was an outgrowth of

English political experience during the seventeenth century. Locke, Coke, and (later) Blackstone were seen as important, but not, in the end, definitive influences.

Our treatment of the early American institutionalists focuses on the defining work of Thorstein Veblen, John R. Commons, and Wesley C. Mitchell and extends the discussion to include the contributions to economics of Joseph A. Schumpeter. To set the stage for the American institutionalists, we must begin, however, with the work of another in the American academic economic tradition, John Bates Clark.

John Bates Clark, the "Abraham" of American Economics
2

Early Influences
2.1

The dominant imaginative figure in the economics education of Veblen, Commons, and Mitchell (directly and indirectly) was John Bates Clark (1847–1938),[1] preeminent American economic philosopher and theorist, and critic of classical doctrine. Writing at the time of the three great founders of marginal utility theory—Jevons, Walras, and Menger—Clark himself contributed much to the structure of the concept and so figures prominently in the debate. Schumpeter christened him the "last of the claimants to independent discovery of the principle of marginal analysis and architect of one of its most significant theoretical structures . . ." (Schumpeter 1954, 868).

Clark, born of Puritan stock, began his economics education at Amherst College (Massachusetts). Graduating in 1872, he continued his studies in Europe, at universities in Heidelberg and Zurich; Karl Knies, of the "older" German Historical School, had been one of his instructors. It was in this milieu, dominated by the *Sozialgedanke* of the German economic historicists, that Clark developed his economic and social outlook. It was from the German experience that we see his economics becoming oriented more along social and ethical lines than along the lines of classical economic dogma. In addition, he cultivated an interest in the Christian Socialist approach, an approach predicated on group cooperation within the confines of a corporatist state, later codified in the 1931 papal encyclical *Quadragesimo Anno*.[2]

The Christian Socialist approach and the general tenor of the German social movements had a lasting influence on Clark and American

---

1. Biographical information on Clark beyond that given here can be found in Dorfman (1959, vol. III), and John Maurice Clark (1968).

2. The influence of Christian Socialism, along with his increasingly pacifist outlook, led Clark in 1911 to join the staff of the Carnegie Endowment for International Peace as head of its division of economics and history; he served in this capacity until 1923.

economics generally. Nowhere is this more apparent than in the founding of the American Economic Association (1885). In this regard, Clark played an important, indeed instrumental, role, even serving as its president in 1894. The American Economic Association appears to have been modeled after the German *Verein für Sozialpolitik*. Founded in 1872, the Verein, as an organization of academics—the Socialists of the Chair—was initially dedicated to state action in the advancement of social reform, especially in respect to the protection of labor. Thus the programs offered tended to promote state socialism with a very nationalistic flavor. Such was also the original purpose of the AEA, as is evident from its charter.

> Article III, §1: "We regard the state as an agency whose positive assistance is one of the indispensable conditions of human progress";
> Article III, §2: "We believe that political economy as a science is still in an early stage of its development. While we appreciate the work of former economists, we look not so much to speculation as to the historical and statistical study of actual conditions of economic life for the satisfactory accomplishment of that development";
> Article III, §3: "We hold that the conflict of labor and capital has brought into prominence a vast number of social problems, whose solution requires the united efforts, each in its own sphere, of the church, of the state, and of science";
> Article III, §4: "In the study of the industrial and commercial policy of governments we take no partisan attitude. We believe in a progressive development of economic conditions, which must be met by a corresponding development of legislative policy." (American Economic Association 1887, 35–36)[3]

A more succinct portrayal of the attitude of the German Historical School could not be made.

---

3. To this Ely added, in an accompanying statement: "No one invited to join this association, certainly no one who has been active in calling this meeting, contemplates a form of pure socialism. 'We recognize the necessity of individual initiative.' We would do nothing to weaken individual activity, but we hold that there are certain spheres of activity which do not belong to the individual, certain functions which the great co-operative society, called the state—must perform to keep the avenues open for those who would gain a livelihood by their own exertions."

"We hold that the doctrine of *laissez-faire* is unsafe in politics and unsound in morals, and that it suggests an inadequate explanation of the relations between the state and the citizens. In other words we believe in the existence of a system of social ethics; we do not believe that any man lives for himself alone, nor yet do we believe social classes are devoid of mutual obligations corresponding to their infinitely varied inter-relations. All have duties as well as rights, and, as Emerson said several years ago, it is time we heard more about duties and less about rights. We who have resolved to form an American Economic Association hope to do something towards the development of a system of social ethics" (Ely 1887, 15–17).

The Paradox of Clark's Early Writings   2.2

Mitchell proclaimed, "Anyone who gets into the profound treatises of J. B. Clark . . . will find himself walking in a world of the imagination which is built abstractly of set purpose and for a definite end" (Mitchell 1969, 237). Nowhere is this more in evidence than in *The Philosophy of Wealth: Economic Principles Newly Formulated,*[4] Clark's first book, derived from his early philosophical essays written for *The New Englander* magazine.[5] In the Preface to this work, he set forth the basis of his dissent from the classical doctrine, and established the line of descent for the Institutional School. The theorems of Classical Economics, he held, were invalid because they were but deductions from stipulated premises, not derivations from established facts; any conclusions drawn from premises so stipulated could, he felt, be only contingent at best, and worthless generally. More importantly, the premises accepted were often at variance with known facts, and the human element seemed to be missing entirely from the equation.

> The better elements of human nature were a forgotten factor in certain economic calculations; the man of the scientific formula was more mechanical and more selfish than the man of the actual world. A degraded conception of human nature vitiated the theory of the distribution of wealth. (Clark 1914, iii)

At issue is a methodological debate that continues to this day: the debate centers on the question of whether the propositions of economics need to be observably true to be valid, or whether it is sufficient that they be logically consistent.[6] For Clark, the debate reflected a real concern for the value of results obtained by stipulated and obviously false premises. False premises cannot lead to true conclusions or accurate depictions of the economic process. This is especially true with regard to what had been a central concern of political economists from at least the time of Smith, but which had since, with the emergence of the "scientific" utilitarians and the Classical School, been rendered seemingly inconsequential: the nature of man. "The value of the results of economic reasoning depends on the correctness of its assumptions with regard to the nature of man. If man is not the being he is assumed to be, there is no certainty that the conclusions will be even approximately correct" (1914, 32).[7]

---

4. We use here the 1914 edition.

5. Among his contributions to *The New Englander* magazine were "The New Philosophy of Wealth" (1877), "The Nature and Progress of True Socialism" (1879), and "The Philosophy of Value" (1881).

6. See, for example, the debate that centered around the publication of Milton Friedman's 1953 "The Methodology of Positive Economics."

7. "[T]he true subject of political economy" is "the man whom God has created" (J. B. Clark 1914, 34).

The true nature of man had been consistently neglected, according to Clark, in much classical discourse, in favor of the quest for a scientific (deductive) rhetoric. This quest has led too often to a reliance on artificial constructs, inventions such as the "average man," the "representative agent," and *homo economicus;* this has in turn led economists to look in the wrong place for an acceptable analogue to which our economic postulates could correspond. Economists "have troubled themselves very little with anthropological investigation," but rather "have assumed, as the basis of their science, a certain conception of man, and have employed their acuteness in determining what results will follow from the social labors of this assumed being" (1914, 33). In an obvious reference to the scientific utilitarians, he argued that one of the more "metaphysical" references in accepted theory was of the nature of the human will and the motivations behind human actions.

> Assuming that the will is governed by desires, the metaphysical view most favorable to prediction, we still encounter the fact that the motives of human action are the ultimate determining forces, and that a misconception as to the nature of these motives is liable to vitiate any conclusion which may be attained. (1914, 32)

The stipulation that "the will is governed by desires," no less than the conceptualization of *homo economicus,* is designed to allow mechanical prediction at the expense of explanation and understanding. Simply to accept the validity of such a claim without an adequate foundation—an understanding of the nature of man and his place in society—is to create an intellectual climate which, while pretending to rigor, is nonetheless inherently nonscientific. This is not to imply that Clark dismissed out of hand the value to be derived from deductive reasoning; his early study under Karl Knies instilled in him a sympathy for such reasoning. All he meant to suggest was that the methodology of the German Historical movement, of which he approved, should be emulated, instead of the deductive method of Ricardo, Jevons, and Edgeworth. The adherents of the Historical movement took great pains to develop an approach to economic theory, a formal rhetoric which was at once fact-based, yet in its own way theory-laden: a place was made for both inductive and deductive reasoning:

> Logic must do its work, but its results must be verified. What is here claimed is that its premises need first to be verified. The assumptions of political economy need to be subjected to a comparison with facts. (Clark 1914, 35–36)

Thus must economists become first and foremost, in their investigations of the motivations behind human action and decision, anthropologists.[8]

---

8. "The science, which has rested on a temporary blocking of assumption, needs to be built on a permanent foundation of anthropological fact" (Clark 1914, 34).

As did Marshall, Clark sought to invoke the biological analogy as the appropriate one for the study of economics: "society is an organism, to be treated as a unit in the discussion of many premises affecting wealth" (1914, iii). Thus economists should consider not simply the role of the individual, but also the connection of the individual to all others in the society, and the society itself as an organic whole. "A man is not independent . . . ," but rather "is made, by his relations to others, to be an atomic portion of a higher organism,—society" (1914, 37).

> This universal interdependence of parts is a primary characteristic of social organisms; each member exists and labors, not for himself, but for the whole, and is dependent on the whole for remuneration. The individual man, like the rootlet, produces something, puts it into the circulating system of the organism, and gets from thence that which his being and growth require; he produces for the market, and buys from the market. Every producer is serving the world, and the world is serving every consumer. (1914, 37–38)

As part of the social whole, each individual has a primary responsibility for the welfare of the collective. Thus Clark suggested nothing less than a fundamental reappraisal of the nature of economic and social relationships, toward a more cooperative model; the true unit of study for political economy should be, not the individual, but the society, meaning always the collective.[9] No longer would the individual play the dominant role in human affairs; in terms reminiscent of Müller, Fichte, and even Owen, he related that it is the "higher organism," and not the atomic units which comprise it, which should be the center of the economist's concern. This was not for Clark an opinion about which reasonable men could disagree; it is instead a primary economic fact:

> Political economy treats, not merely of the wealth of individuals who sustain complicated relations with each other, but of the wealth of society as an organic unit. The production and the consumption of wealth by society will be found to embrace its whole subject. The world is before us with its resisting elements, the "thorns and thistles" of Genesis; and we subdue it, not by conquering each his little part, but by collectively subjugating all nature.

> Knowledge of men is the beginning of this science [of economics]; knowledge of the social organism of which men are members is the middle and the end of it. (1914, 39, 55)

---

9. "The great fact that society is an organic unit has been, for the time, forgotten, and the attention has been fixed on individuals and their separate and intricate actions in valuing and exchanging commodities. . . . This subject can never be grasped and understood until the organic whole is made the primary object of attention" (Clark 1914, 70).

Continuing along with his biological analogy of the importance of the individual to the larger society, and of the reciprocal relation, Clark maintained a very strict reading of the anthropological record. The econo-biological model Clark advanced implies that man—"the molecule of society"—is dependent on society not simply for his corporeal existence, but for his intellectual dominance as well; the society, the social "body," establishes in the individual his importance in the whole. Not only is there a mutual dependence developed between man and society, but the social interaction and its influence on individual men determine in large measure their worth to the society. More importantly, the econo-biological model explains very well the formation and importance of social, that is, class, distinctions; in other words, Plato's divisions may well have had a biological foundation:

> The changes which take place in different individuals vary according to the position which each assumes in the organic whole; the man who, in the development of society, becomes a molecule of the brain of the social organism undergoes widely different modifications in his own nature from those experienced by the man who becomes a molecule of the nutritive organ. The scientist differs in mental and physical development from the hand-worker. Apart from frivolous distinctions of caste, there exist classes founded on differences of social function, and accompanied by real differences in the individual. (1914, 40)

As society evolves, man develops "an infinitude of conscious needs" and the society must develop pari passu. But Clark maintained that, along with this evolution of wants and needs brought about by the increasing social complexity, there is an expansion of "specific vices and virtues." The development of the one is inextricably linked to the development of the other. This increasing complexity and concomitant unfolding of certain social pathologies generates "an increasing need of moral force" to hold the system together (1914, 41). Thus does the evolution of society to its "highest type" induce

> increasing division of labor, and a progressive control of the social body by a thinking organ; but there exists, in as marked a degree, a growing subordination of brain and members to the dictates of moral law. This is the great and neglected economic fact of modern times. (1914, 41–42)

Here we see that Clark, not intent on accepting stipulated standards, was content to manage a fact-based theory of the evolution of moral codes and Natural Law.

Individual evolution is promoted and formed by the evolution of the *social* organism. As society becomes increasingly influenced by moral considerations, so too does each member of the collective become increas-

ingly moral, or "spiritualized" (1914, 42). (Whither Mandeville?) All of
the "higher wants" for which the fully evolved man strives—these being
capable of "indefinite" expansion and providing "increased gratification
at each successive attainment of the objects of desire"—are unselfish
wants and so are readily distinguishable from the "lower" wants, which
are capable of "complete satisfaction."

> The true and the beautiful are desired each for its own sake, and
> the desire for personal worthiness opposes self-interest as an equal
> antagonist. Under the influence of such motives, man can never be
> a being striving solely for personal advantage, and society can
> never be wholly given over to an ignoble scramble for profit.
> (1914, 44)

The dominant view in economics at the time, however, could not
comprehend these motives. It ascribed to man—the rational, calculating,
cunning being—only the selfish motive, ignoring the very things that
serve to make him human. The received theory recognized that man seeks
to maximize utility in a rational manner, but it ignored the motives to
altruistic and social behaviors or else treated them as "disturbing elements," exogenous to the system (1914, 45). In other words, economics
had, according to Clark, deviated dramatically from the concerns of the
moral science of Smith with its emphasis on sympathy as a motivating
force, having replaced sentiment with a mechanical calculus said to better
"explain" (read predict) behavior. This Clark felt was unlikely to change
so long as man was regarded as an individual and not as part of an
organic whole.

The underlying philosophical predisposition of *The Philosophy of
Wealth* is Christian Socialism, a doctrine the principles of which have
rarely been better enunciated. We have already seen evidence of Clark's
belief in this doctrine in his rhetoric of organic unities and cooperation, as
opposed to individualism, as the basis of political economy. In his discussion of the theory of value, he invoked

> a beautiful law of society as a whole, which makes the wants of
> every member a matter of decisive interest to all. . . . Independently
> of personal sympathies, society assumes a paternal relation toward
> particular members, buys articles for their use, consigns the articles
> to them, and has no desire to take them again. (1914, 84–85)

In the area of distribution, Clark addressed the problem of the "just
division" of the total aggregate of produced utilities. Having deemed the
"purely competitive system of industry" to have passed away (1914,
150), he went on to introduce (actually to reintroduce, since the concept
had, as we have seen, been an essential part of the philosophy of Smith)
the idea of a "moral force" seeking to restrain competitive ambitions.

We do not realize that moral influences have for their particular and legitimate function to suppress the remnants of natural ferocity which show themselves in the economic dealings of man with man; neither do we realize how radical would be the effect of a comparatively slight reformation in this direction.

Justice in the division of products, equality in exchanges, must become the aim of social effort. The gain will be both material and moral; the change which makes workmen richer will make all classes better; and what is of more importance, it will open the way for continued progress. (1914, 157, 173)

2.3 A Return to the Hobbes Question: Clark's Answer

To understand Clark, one must grasp the essentials of the British (and American) political experience. For this, one must refer back to the discussion of Hobbes and *Leviathan*. In our review of that work, we saw three principal ideas emerge: (1) empiricism is the correct method of discovering sources of truth; (2) without a social contract, man would continue to live in a world of fear, governed by the rule of the survival of the fittest; and (3) without an effective governmental apparatus, the social contract itself is unenforceable.

In a way, Clark wrote as much to address the Hobbes questions as he did to elaborate a theory of economic relations. We have already seen allusions to this in his description of the nature of man and the evolution of society, his emphasis on the collective and the role of the individual in the larger social whole, his invoking of "moral force," and his concern with the "just division." There are, lastly, his choice of rhetoric and methodology. In every sense the response was anti-Mandevillian.

The Distribution of Wealth: A Theory of Wages, Interest, and Profits (1899) was Clark's principal work, the one in which he addressed again (at least in part) these questions and considered others. For example, in the Preface, Clark maintained that the purpose of his endeavor was to examine the "laws" underlying the distribution of income in society, laws which have as their basis a very Hobbesian (and Smithian) character:

It is the purpose of this work to show that the distribution of the income of society is controlled by a natural law, and that this law, if it worked without friction, would give to every agent of production the amount of wealth which that agent creates. (Clark 1899, v)

In the absence of impediments to the smooth functioning of the "natural" economy, wages would tend to equality with the value of the marginal product of labor, and interest would tend to equality with the value of the marginal product of capital. The economic system would then distribute the social product as prescribed in the Ideal, or the natural

analogue, in that it "assigns to every one what he has specifically produced" (1899, v). Distributive justice would then follow from the natural
order of things.

This belief influenced the very model Clark employed, for it forced
reliance on a static description of the economy. But in so doing he did not
believe himself to be engaging in anything revolutionary. Indeed, he held
that the very concept of "natural," which he took as descriptive of his
economics, was identical to the concept employed by the classical economists.[10] It had in these earlier accounts been "unconsciously employed as
an equivalent of the term *static*" (1899, vi). Within this framework, Clark
aimed

> to show to what rates the market prices of goods, the wages of labor
> and the interest on capital would conform, if the changes that are
> going on in the shape of the industrial world and in the character of
> its activities were to cease. It tries completely to isolate the static
> forces that act in distribution from the dynamic forces. Actual soci-
> ety is always dynamic, and the part of it that we are most concerned
> with is highly so. Change and progress are apparent everywhere,
> and industrial society is constantly assuming new forms and dis-
> charging new functions. Because of this continual evolution the
> standards of wages and of interest to-day are not what they will be
> ten years hence. There are, however, normal standards to-day. In
> the midst of all changes there are at work forces that fix rates to
> which, at any one moment, wages and interest tend to conform.
> However stormy may be the ocean, there is an ideal level surface
> projecting itself through the waves, and the actual surface of the
> turbulent water fluctuates about it. There are, likewise, static stan-
> dards with which, in the most turbulent markets, actual values,
> wages and interest tend to coincide. (1899, vi)

These "static standards"—values to which the dynamic process of the
economy converges—are the "natural" values in which Clark was interested and which, he believed, were (or should be) the elements of prime
interest to economists.

An Assessment

2.4

Clark was a man of two sides: the student of the nature of capital, and the
student of catallactics. He was actually the dominant pedagogue for Veblen, and as Mitchell was one of Veblen's students and friends, the filiation
of the Clarkian sets of ideas can be reasonably suggested.[11] To understand
the common linkage between the ideas of Clark and those of the American

---

10. Of interest here is the essay by Joël Jalledeau (1975).

11. For a discussion of Clark's impact on Commons's thinking, see M. Perlman
1991.

institutionalists, it is best to restrict emphasis to Clark's work in the 1880s and 1890s when Veblen, Mitchell, and Commons were in their intellectually most formative years. At that time, a dominant problem in Clark's professorial career involved the defining of rationales for the inclusion of various social classes at the social "bargaining table" (wherein distribution takes place), and for the rights enjoyed by each. His initial desire was to understand the bases for a reasonable and logical formulation of the bargaining place and the right of the owners of capital in the social bargain. Briefly put, the question he pondered was "Is there anything special about capitalists which gave them their uniqueness aside from their holding, according to the institutions of the time, scarce resources?"

In terms of his place in the discovery of marginal utility, he stands apart from the three principal discoverers: while Menger and Jevons applied the concept to the study of exchange, and Walras even more boldly employed it in the analysis of general economic equilibrium, Clark was alone in using it to investigate income distribution. In fact, Clark took distributive justice to be the ultimate end of social evolution, and stated as much in very Benthamite terms, namely, in securing the greatest happiness:

> Society, as an organic unit, has a higher economic end. That end is the attainment of the greatest quantity, the highest quality, and the most just distribution of wealth. It is the true subjection of matter, the placing of it in the most rational condition, absolute and relative. The matter and force of external nature are to be brought into that state which, in itself, is best, and they are to be brought into that relation of ownership which best promotes the general happiness. Matter modified by labor in accordance with enlightened reason may be termed rational wealth; it is this that society is pursuing, and partially realizing. (Clark 1914, 205)

3 The Origins of Veblenian Institutionalism

3.1 Intellectual Influences

Thorstein Bunde Veblen (1857–1929)[12] is one of the more improbable of the personalities we will introduce, despite the fact that his influence was pervasive throughout the American institutionalist movement. John Maurice Clark—son of John Bates Clark, and himself a major Institutional economist—appraised him thus: "He is rated among the great

---

12. Joseph Dorfman's 1934 *Thorstein Veblen and His America* is one of the great classics of American individualism. It is at once readable, scholarly, and generally considered authoritative, a rare combination. For particulars of Veblen's life, see also J. M. Clark (1929), Mitchell (1929b), and Sowell (1987).

economists of history, or as no economist at all; as a great original pioneer or as a critic and satirist without constructive talent or achieve ment" (J. M. Clark 1929, 742). Mitchell opined, "He was an original, whom the discipline of life in a land of 'regular fellows' could not stan dardise" (Mitchell 1929b, 647).[13]

Veblen actually began his academic studies at Carleton College, under the guidance of Clark, who was at that point in his career quite a philosophical type—he was in fact just beginning his work on marginal productivity analysis.[14] At Johns Hopkins, Veblen made the acquaintance of Clark's friend Richard Theodore Ely, himself a devotee of the German philosopher Fichte, who lectured on social responsibility and distributive justice (with a distinct Christian Socialist flavor).[15] After a single term, disillusioned with Ely and the German historical movement, which he felt was too antitheoretical to be of any use in the development of an evolu tionary approach to economics, Veblen left Johns Hopkins and went to Yale where he studied philosophy.

At Yale, the prevalent figure was the sociologist and historian Wil liam Graham Sumner (1840–1910),[16] who preached the philosophy of Herbert Spencer. Yale at that time was a Christian institution, and the students there tended to be Hegelians, holding to a view quite inconsis tent with Spencer's system; the president of Yale, the Reverend Noah Porter, was vehemently opposed to Spencerian philosophy. The antago nism between Porter and Sumner, the most influential of Veblen's instruc tors, exercised a profound influence on his thought. Porter the theologian and traditionalist believed in absolutes and the primacy of Natural Law; Sumner the Spencerian evolutionist viewed the world in relative terms, with the individual raised to a greater level of significance and society in general perceived as an organic whole. (Although both believed in private property and a "natural order," Sumner's belief was based on the prin ciples of evolution leading to the most natural outcome, laissez-faire.)

To this environment Veblen added his own touch. After reading Spencer and Hegel, he then chose to embrace the philosophical ideas of the German philosopher Immanuel Kant. Veblen initially tried to reconcile Kant's idea of immutability with Hume's "Common Sense"

---

13. Mitchell (1969) devoted an entire chapter of 101 pages to Veblen.

14. John Maurice Clark recollected that while at Carleton Veblen asked for, and was granted, permission to take his junior and senior class examinations at the same time. J. B. Clark administered the economics exam, which Veblen passed easily. J. M. Clark noted, "In this manner Thorstein Veblen received his college degree, rated by one at least of his professors as the most brilliant man the college had graduated" (1929, 742).

15. Ely pronounced: "Philosophers like Fichte and Herrmann Lotze must to-day assist economists who are competent to understand them" (1901, 117). Veblen, however, thought Ely superficial, indeed something of a pompous fraud.

16. Sumner's great works in economics were *History of American Currency* (1874) and *History of Banking in the United States* (1896).

philosophy[17]—a reconciliation which really cannot be made. He none-theless made valiant efforts, concluding that Kant's a priori forms were really no more than the collective human experience; at the root of the experiential thinking was a sense of morality.[18] To Veblen, moral respon-sibility was the factor ultimately responsible for individual actions. For his efforts he was granted a doctorate in philosophy in 1884; the title of his dissertation is especially compelling, "Ethical Grounds of a Doctrine of Retribution," a tract questioning the need to believe in God.

After a seven-year hiatus, Veblen entered Cornell as an economics student (1891), where he studied under the tutelage of James Laurence Laughlin.[19] In 1892, Veblen followed Laughlin to the newly renovated University of Chicago, where in 1896 he became an instructor. During the ensuing years promotion came very slowly; he worked after 1899 for the United States Industrial Commission as a research scholar, where his task was to compare the development of Hohenzollern Germany with that of the United States.

During the First World War, Veblen published a comparative study of industrial decision making and control in Hohenzollern Germany and the English-speaking countries, entitled *Imperial Germany and the Indus-trial Revolution* (1915); in 1917 he wrote *An Inquiry into the Nature of Peace and the Terms of Its Perpetuation.* That same year he published an interesting and highly prescient (though now completely forgotten) essay, *The Nature of the Peace,*[20] a social and political commentary on the propo-sitions behind the establishment of the League of Nations (with only obliga-tory references to the fact that there was at the time a war being fought).[21]

---

17. David Hume was a skeptic, which merely suggests that he viewed with an over-whelming caution the products of intellectualizing or intuition. In lieu of excogitation, Hume, characteristic of many but not all skeptics, put his trust in good judgment, a combination of generalization of experience, imaginative insight, and very limited amounts of deduction.

18. This emphasis on morality is important since it places him in the immediate post-Hobbes chain of thinking.

19. Laughlin, incidentally, was the talent behind both Harvard's *Quarterly Journal of Economics* and Chicago's *Journal of Political Economy.* For a life of Laughlin, see Friedman 1987.

20. This essay was reprinted in 1950 as *Elimination of the Unfit.*

21. Among his points in the essay: "The purpose of the projected league is peace and security. . . . It is true, the more genial spokesmen of the project are given to the view that what is to come of it all is a comity of neutral nations, amicably adjusting their own relations among themselves in a spirit of peace and good-will. But this view is over-sanguine, in that it overlooks the point that into this prospective comity of nations Imperial Germany (and Imperial Japan) fit like a drunken savage with a machine gun. It also overlooks the patent fatality that these two are bound to come into a coalition at the next turn, with whatever outside and subsidiary resources they can draw on; provided only that a reasonable opening for further enterprise presents itself" (Veblen 1950, 5).

The United States needed the league, Veblen thought, "as a refuge from otherwise inevitable dangers ahead; and it is only a question of a moderate allowance of time for the American voters to realise that without an adequate copartnership with the other pacific nations the outlook of the Republic is altogether precarious" (53).

After the war, Veblen, with the assistance of Mitchell, secured a professorship at the New School for Social Research in New York (1919); others on the faculty included the historian Charles A. Beard, Mitchell, and Harold J. Laski. In 1926, he declined a nomination for the presidency of the American Economic Association. Said to be an impossible lecturer, he surely became totally, even if he was always slightly, indifferent to the opinions of others. As Mitchell put it,

> Veblen thus brought to economics the detachment of a visitor from Mars, a confirmed habit of ironical expression, a specialist's grounding in philosophy, and the loot of much miscellaneous reading. A man familiar with Kant is not over-awed by the technical parts of economic theory. Nor does he miss the philosophical implications of what is said. (Mitchell 1929b, 647–48)

Thus we see here that Veblen had a thorough grounding in Institutionalist philosophy through his association with the leaders of the early phase of the movement. Yet he was eventually to create his own variant, taking Institutionalism in an entirely different direction.

A Critique of Mainstream Economic Thinking: 3.2
Social Classes

In 1899 Veblen published his first book, *The Theory of the Leisure Class*, a quasi-anthropological attack on capitalism. The thesis is rather simple, and not dissimilar to the structure of society represented by Plato's ideal republic: capitalism tended to make the business leader something of a tribal chieftain, whose goal is to establish a value system designed to keep the workers and others in line. In this work Veblen drew a contrast between business and industry: the former is generally unproductive and more accurately viewed as a game; the latter produces wealth—real physical output—and so is the truly important sector of the economy and society.

Veblen began his disquisition, however, with an indication as to the fundamental nature of the leisure class:

> The institution of a leisure class is found in its best development at the higher stages of the barbarian culture; as, for instance, in feudal Europe or feudal Japan. In such communities the distinction between classes is very rigorously observed; and the feature of most striking economic significance in these class differences is the distinction maintained between the employments proper to the several classes. The upper classes are by custom exempt or excluded from industrial occupations, and are reserved for certain employments to which a degree of honour attaches. . . . The leisure class as a whole comprises the noble and the priestly classes, together with much of

their retinue. The occupations of the class are correspondingly diver-
sified; but they have the common economic characteristic of being
non-industrial. (Veblen 1912, 1–2)

The leisure class is first and foremost an aristocracy, a privileged
group set above the laboring masses. Being "non-industrial" in character,
the members of this class must avail themselves of unproductive, even
frivolous, pursuits, usually represented as having higher social and intellectual status than the pedestrian pursuits of the industrialist and the
wage-earner. Among the "lofty" pursuits Veblen identified with the leisure class are such vocations as "government, warfare, religious obser-
vances, and sports" (1912, 2).

Coincident with the evolution of the leisure class is the emergence of
the institution of private ownership. As with other institutions, private
property is culturally derived, and it evolved along the same lines as did the
class structure of the society. "This is necessarily the case, for these two
institutions result from the same set of economic forces" (1912, 22). While
property began as the result of instinctive drives—competition leading to
the amassing of trophies and even slaves—it took on the special character
of past cultures. Here Veblen evokes the Aristotelian distinction between
ownership and use, noting that in the simplest cultures, it is the case that
"useful things"—the objects of personal consumption—are owned by
those who engage in their appropriation: "The habitual appropriation and
consumption of certain slight personal effects goes on without raising the
question of ownership; that is to say, the question of a conventional,
equitable claim to extraneous things" (23).

But eventually, and inevitably, given "the desire of the successful
men to put their prowess in evidence by exhibiting some durable result of
their exploits," there emerged the convention of private ownership. This
is demonstrated in the coincident shift from the capture of women as
"trophies" to the institution of marriage under male domination. "From
the ownership of women the concept of ownership extends itself to include the products of their industry, and so there arises the ownership of
things as well as of persons" (1912, 24).

The institution of private property becomes "honorific," its very
existence suggesting "a struggle between men for the possession of
goods" (1912, 24). In Veblen's estimation, the "classical" portrayal of
ownership maintained by Smith et al. in their anthropological ruminations (the urge to amass wealth as derived from a preindustrial drive for
subsistence) was simply not convincing; the historical record indicates
that, early on, the level of social wealth was more than adequate to
supply individual needs. The continued "struggle for wealth" proceeded
along different lines, compelled by reasons beyond that of simple subsistence. The chief motive was in fact emulation.

From here Veblen confronted the individual/collective distinction, which has been a constant thread throughout the present work. As the holding of property separated the victor from the vanquished (as individuals) in the early tribal societies, so did it reflect the "prowess" of the group; honor was social. Eventually, the distinction *between* groups as to victor and vanquished was made to extend *within* the dominant group, between those individuals who possessed "trophies" and those who did not. Individual *ownership* gave rise to private property and the individual *interest*. As Veblen interpreted the historical record on the emergence of private ownership and the distinction between the individual and the group:

> The initial phase of ownership, the phase of acquisition by naïve seizure and conversion, begins to pass into the subsequent stage of an incipient organisation of industry on the basis of private property (in slaves); the horde develops into a more or less self-sufficing industrial community; possessions then come to be valued not so much as evidence of successful foray, but rather as evidence of the prepotence of the possessor of these goods over other individuals within the community. The invidious comparison now becomes primarily a comparison of the owner with the other members of the group. Property is still of the nature of trophy, but, with the cultural advance, it becomes more and more a trophy of successes scored in the game of ownership carried on between the members of the group under the quasi-peaceable methods of nomadic life. (1912, 27–28)

This evolution in the nature of society has ramifications for class relations. As society and economic relations evolve, eventually wealth and property become removed from any ethical mooring; their achievement becomes likened less to *reward*, and more to *award*, as the leisure class itself seeks to deemphasize industry while extolling the virtues of pure commerce. The acquisition of wealth by the supreme caste takes the same form in modern industrial society as did the acquisition of trophies in less evolved cultures. These acquisitions serve as measures of success and esteem:

> The possession of wealth, which was at the outset valued simply as an evidence of efficiency, becomes, in popular apprehension, itself a meritorious act. Wealth is now intrinsically honourable and confers honour on its possessor. (1912, 29)

As the society continues to evolve, eventually "property becomes the basis of popular esteem" (1912, 31). As each member continues to accumulate ever-increasing amounts of personal property, the previous "standard" of esteem is eroded, replaced with even higher, more insurmountable levels. This continued "pecuniary emulation" leads to "invidious comparisons" and so to continued dissatisfactions and disaffections.

As the desire for accumulation of wealth for its own sake is insatiable, the fact that the society is structured around the individual can only lead to further attempts at emulation and a more divided social structure. Only when the social whole is viewed as the basis of wealth and welfare can the cycle end.[22]

The interesting idea one should come away with in reviewing the work of Veblen is that, unlike many of the other institutionalist writers, he did not maintain that institutions were necessarily established for rational reasons, or even, for that matter, for the provision of felt or demonstrated needs. An institution, such as private property, could exist simply because of ceremony—as a "trophy"—or in support of the valuation of "trophies."

3.3 A Critique of Mainstream Economic Thinking: The Engineer versus the Business Man

The Theory of Business Enterprise (1904) is generally appraised by economists as Veblen's best book. In it he desired to show the manner in which the modern form of business enterprise influences the culture in which it operates.

Specifically, Veblen held that the modern form of economic organization—capitalistic production—dominates the very social structure in which it flourishes. Two of this system's "features," "the forces by virtue of which it dominates modern culture," are exemplified in the processes of machine production[23] and business investment (1904, 1). The former, the machine process, defines to a large extent the culture; the latter, investment expenditures undertaken with an expectation of profit, is the nature of the business enterprise.

Veblen assumed of the business leader qua cultural revolutionary a great deal of control and therefore power over the society and the individuals within it. He then endeavored to endow him with immense responsibilities commensurate with this power:

------

22. One idea for which Veblen has become popularly known he "borrowed" from John Rae (1796–1872), this being the concept of "conspicuous consumption." While not always understood, this point amounts to an assertion that, if ambitious and successful men are prevented from entering the ranks of the elite (which in his example meant the right to own landed estates), they will then turn to the acquisition of other symbols of wealth and power. These symbols are not, however, genuine, and in the act of acquiring them the nouveaux riches seemingly make a mockery of the system, and parodies of themselves as successes.

23. Veblen defined the "machine process" broadly, more as a state of mind than anything concrete: "Wherever manual dexterity, the rule of thumb, and the fortuitous conjunctures of the seasons have been supplanted by a reasoned procedure on the basis of a systematic knowledge of the forces employed, there the mechanical industry is to be found, even in the absence of intricate mechanical contrivances" (1904, 6).

The business man, especially the business man of wide and authoritative discretion, has become a controlling force in industry, because, through the mechanism of investments and markets, he controls the plants and processes, and these set the pace and determine the direction of movement for the rest. . . . His control of the motions of other men is not strict, . . . but as near as it may be said of any human power in modern times, the large business man controls the exigencies of life under which the community lives. Hence, upon him and his fortunes centres the abiding interest of civilized mankind. (1904, 2–3)

According to Veblen, the chief motive of the businessman in undertaking investment expenditures is the accumulation of wealth, or "pecuniary gain" (1904, 20). He held that the very "method" of modern business had deviated radically from its origin. The historical record clearly established a movement from a merchandise-based system of trade relations—whereby the trader's activity was limited to exploiting the "advantage of the conjunctures offered by the course of the seasons and the fluctuations of demand and supply"—to one in which the actions of the entrepreneur physically altered the environment (including the culture) to assist in his wealth-creation (22). The "machine age" changed this role of the business man from trader to entrepreneur, from a "speculative buyer" to one who manipulates the "conjunctures" to his own benefit and in so doing becomes more a financier than a trader.

But something even more intricate had developed along the way. The new industrial structure itself eventually acquired the nature of a complex mechanical process. As such, it became necessary for its smooth functioning that a delicate balance of forces be maintained. This maintenance requires "adjusting the several industrial processes to one another's work and needs" and is accomplished very simply through "business transactions" (1904, 26). Business is the coordinating factor: "Industry is carried on for the sake of business, and not conversely; and the progress and activity of industry are conditioned by the outlook of the market, which means the presumptive chance of business profits" (26–27).

Thus Veblen (once again) differentiated "business" from "industry." Industry promotes economic welfare; the impact on welfare of business is less readily ascertainable:

The economic welfare of the community at large is best served by a facile and uninterrupted interplay of the various processes which make up the industrial system at large; but the pecuniary interests of the business men in whose hands lies the discretion in the matter are not necessarily best served by an unbroken maintenance of the industrial balance. (1904, 27)

Industry requires a smooth functioning system; economic stability breeds social stability. Business, on the other hand, can succeed under even the most improbable conditions; in fact, it thrives on them, as the businessman (the entrepreneur) exploits weaknesses and turns to his advantage the apprehensions of his rivals.

> Gain may come to them [the business men] from a given disturbance of the system whether the disturbance makes for heightened facility or for wide-spread hardship, very much as a speculator in grain futures may be either a bull or a bear. . . . The end is pecuniary gain, the means is disturbance of the industrial system. . . . [I]t is, by and large, a matter of indifference to him whether his traffic affects the system advantageously or disastrously. His gains (or losses) are related to the magnitude of the disturbances that take place, rather than to their bearing upon the welfare of the community. (1904, 28–29)

The interests of the businessman and the industrialist then are not coincident: the businessman seeks disturbance and volatility; the industrialist seeks stasis and predictability. Veblen thus drew a distinction between the engineer and the financier, the engineer being interested in the creation of a product, while the businessman-financier is interested only in temporary control that he may use to bring about his pecuniary gain.[24] Indeed, while the engineer is actively engaged in the production of output for the ultimate benefit of the society as a whole (in the sense that it expands the social product and hence increases total social wealth), the businessman very often (according to Veblen) will engage in those activities (such as business combinations and other restrictions of competitive output) that promote (personal) financial profit at the expense of industry and social wealth. The engineer produces for society, the businessman exploits for his own selfish ends.

The classical view of the businessman (the entrepreneur) as the coordinator of industrial processes Veblen held to be flawed in its view of business psychology. While he readily accepted that the entrepreneur may indeed undertake financial and industrial processes that may produce greater efficiencies in production and increase factor productivity, and he may even do so with a sincere interest in quality and workmanship and act from a sense of community spirit and equity-promotion in the creation of a genuine business ethic, this does not mitigate the fact that the businessman acts within his *own* ethic and therefore in reality does not abandon the desire for pecuniary gain. Veblen held that the ethic of the businessman is the maxim *caveat emptor,* "let the buyer beware" (1904, 41–43). It is this focus on individual gain at the expense of community

24. The stock market on this view is a fraud, a mirror which not only inaccurately reflects real (productive) values, but more substantively makes no real *attempt* to reflect such values.

welfare, the placing of pecuniary advantage over the social good, that Veblen found to be the mark of the businessman, and indeed found most distasteful. Moreover, it is the entire "modern culture" that "acts to disintegrate the institutional heritage, of all degrees of antiquity and authenticity—whether it be the institutions that embody the principle of natural liberty or those that comprise the residue of more archaic principles of conduct still current in civilized life" (374).

The Veblenian Synthesis   3.4

What dominated Veblen's thinking was a conviction that contemporary economics, as it was then perceived, was a study based on the patristic values of eighteenth- and nineteenth-century England. These values were themselves largely the product of the sixteenth and seventeenth centuries in England, a time in which there was an almost hypnotic fascination with individualism, a tendency Veblen simultaneously both denounced and personally fully observed. Not only did pecuniary society reflect that historic individualism, but everything in that peculiar English world tended to become attuned to pecuniary measures. Veblen himself preferred a society where the making of *things* held greater importance and reward than the making of *money*.

Men, he opined, were forced to fit into the pecuniary system. Institutions such as pecuniary incentives and controls dominated individual choice, with the sad result that men sunk into a kind of value-slavery. Workers lost their desire for creative or perfect workmanship as they were led to think principally in money (economic) rather than in quality (engineering output) terms.

This was particularly true with respect to the economics of Veblen's time, with its slavish commitment to the principles underlying the felicific calculus. The motivations of man, in the mind of the economist, were to be taken for granted; man was taken to be a rational utility-maximizer. The basic principles of rationality could then be employed to reduce human economic activity, in essence motivations to action and responses to stimuli, to the rigors of the calculus. For Veblen, the problems with economics as a discipline began here. Attuned to the analytics of psychological studies, which served in large part to nullify the conclusions about behavior deduced from the Benthamite model, Veblen insisted that economists had paid too little attention to the actual manner in which decisions are made. They rejected inquiry into habits of human conduct, including the grounds for the establishment of institutions designed to channel conduct to constructive purposes; in place of the psychological study of human motivation, the mainstream scholars advocated continued use of the deductive approach, reaching conclusions from established and well-worn premises, which were based not on actual human behavior but on a mechanical model of mankind.

3.5 An Assessment

There have been many to whom Veblen's work has proven attractive. Both Abram Harris (1934) and E. K. Hunt (1979) have suggested affinities between the theories of Veblen and Marx, Hunt going so far as to state that the two are complementary.[25] One common thread linking all converts to Veblen's economics is their disgust for modern neoclassical economics; they own that a theory of price is not a variant of a theory of value—prices cannot explain values.[26] When one considers the richness of the Lockean concept of the place of labor in the theory of value and in the theory of price, and when one realizes that the early formulation of a labor theory of value is *simplice,* it is no wonder they are disappointed. Veblen's teacher, J. B. Clark, tried his hand at coming up with a solution, but was less than successful—the orthodox thought him too mystical, and Veblen thought him too antihistorical.

By way of contrast, Veblen held that the emphasis should be on an essentially instrumentalist right to create goods and services. He approved of and stressed the "engineer," not the "merchant," mentality: the primacy of making things, not money. As he perceived the pecuniary society, the Lockean tradition may have served as an American Zeitgeist, but Veblen wished engineering creativity to serve as the *present* and *future* Zeitgeist. To that end he attempted with his system to explain the psychology of the individual and the behavioral relationship between groups within society. One cannot do justice to the subtlety of Veblen's reasoning in such a brief sketch, but in general he believed the ordinary man to be endowed with four instincts: the acquisitive, reflecting both a desire for personal survival and self-interest as well as a willingness to adapt to the game; the parental, reflecting gregariousness and generosity; workmanship, denoting pride in creation and competency; and idle curiosity, tying imagination to workmanship. Left to his own devices the typical man strives to improve his lot. If for institutional reasons he is unable to advertise his success, he is wont to advertise by more noticeable (conspicuous) consumption. A pecuniary society thus thwarts the more creative and rewards the more selfish instincts.

The simple elements of this schema plus the imaginative use of pseudoscientific rhetoric caught the attention of many, in and out of academia. Many converts were both puzzled and disturbed with the excesses that they associated with a system nominally devoted to free enter-

25. As J. L. Simich and Rick Tilman (1982) suggested, while Veblen took seriously the work of Marx, younger Marxists tended to ignore Veblen, seeing little difference between Veblenian Institutionalism and the emerging Keynesian orthodoxy. Only in the 1970s did the New Left gain an appreciation for Veblen and his contributions to the study of social classes.

26. J. B. Clark had earlier held that prices do not explain real values: his phrase was "prices explain prices."

prise and, in practice, to comparative excesses in consumption. The social irresponsibility of the decades at the end of the nineteenth and the beginning of the twentieth centuries inspired many to form a Veblen "cult."[27]

But there was more to the interest in Veblen's message. Of the many disciples of the Veblenian tradition, probably none surpassed Adolph Berle, a lawyer, and Gardiner C. Means, an economist, who collaborated on what may be called the "jewel of the Veblenian crown," *The Modern Industrial Corporation and Private Property*. Published in 1932, this study extended well beyond the basic Veblenian schema. The work asserted that it was no longer the corporate property owners who ran the modern industrial corporation and benefited from the property rights of corporate ownership; they had been replaced with a managerial class, who, using "Other People's Money" (the title of one of Louis Brandeis's books attacking monopoly power), paid themselves so well as to enjoy virtually unlimited luxuries of economic goods and social power.[28]

While this theme can be seen to exist in Veblen—*The Theory of Business Enterprise* clearly distinguished between owners and managers—some have offered a different interpretation. Malcolm Rutherford, for instance, suggested Veblen was in fact maintaining a distinction between the owners of common stock (corporate voters) and the owners of preferred stock (capital-equipment owners). In any event, Veblen's central message of the disconnect between ownership and control, however defined, is evident not only in the work of Berle and Means, but also in that of John Kenneth Galbraith, especially in *The New Industrial State* (1967).

There is more to the Veblenian tradition than elements of social criticism, for it is also a tradition with its own rhetoric. The power of rhetoric was what Adam Smith was most interested in, and it was the pithiness of his social criticism, found in those excellently phrased first

---

27. William Dugger identified seven concepts by which Veblenian Institutionalism may "guide inquiry." These are "(1) the nature of the socioeconomic context, (2) the dynamic factor in social change, (3) the resistant factor to social change, (4) the locus of value in the social process, (5) the nature of institutions, (6) the role of community (a new element), and (7) the continuation of progress" (1995, 1013).

28. Berle was to play an important role in the Roosevelt administrations of the 1930s, as well as the Temporary National Economic Commission of 1938 to 1940, devoted to illuminating the degree of interactive corporative leadership; this proved to be one logical outcome of the 1932 book. Arthur Robert Burns's scholarly *The Decline of Competition* (1936) and Walton Hamilton and Associates' *Price and Price Policies* (1938) are other critical linkages in the Veblenian tradition, albeit developing analytical frameworks (and even some conclusions) which were not truly envisaged in Veblen's original works. Much of the work going into and the theoretical results arising from the 1938 Temporary National Economic Commission was Veblenian in tone. In the 1940s the leading Veblenian was Clarence Ayres (1891–1972), professor of economics at the University of Texas, Austin. There are many today who still write in the tradition; surely the work of and recognition accorded to John Kenneth Galbraith is *a*, if not *the*, paramount example.

chapters of *The Wealth of Nations,* which made it the inspiring tract that it has become. So, too, with Veblen.[29]

4 Wesley Clair Mitchell, Founder of the School of Modern American Macroeconomic Analysis

4.1 *Mitchell's Intellectual Milieu*

It may be said, without fear of contradiction, that the foremost American macroeconomist of the early twentieth century was Wesley Clair Mitchell (1874–1948). His accomplishments and contributions to the study and teaching of economics included the successful integration of the theoretical and the empirical sides of the discipline. His innovations, especially in the study of business cycles, are with us still, albeit "dressed up" in the guise of intertemporal responses to exogenous shocks. One can readily see the influence of Mitchell, as refined by Fisher and Schumpeter, in modern economic thought.

Mitchell,[30] the eldest son of a physician, enrolled in the first class at the University of Chicago in 1892 (the same year Veblen began teaching there). At Chicago, Mitchell studied with Veblen and the philosopher John Dewey, but his mentor was J. Laurence Laughlin, the department's founder and chairman. At the time, the great economic debate centered around the issue of bimetallism: should the country retain the gold standard or return to a monetary standard based on gold *and* silver? The "free silver" advocates insisted that the deflationary situation set in motion by the Coinage Act of 1873 was the direct result of too little in the way of a metallic standard: by demonetizing silver, the act had the effect of shrinking the monetary base, with the result being, as predicted by the "crude" quantity theory, a decline in the price level.

Laughlin, interested primarily in sound money, rejected the argument, arguing instead that the quantity theory had no basis in fact or logic. Laughlin approached Mitchell, then also working in the area of monetary economics, to assess the validity of the simple mechanical statement of the quantity theory of money. Mitchell published the results in the *Journal of Political Economy* as "The Quantity Theory of the Value of Money" (1896). In 1903 he extended the study as *A History of the*

---

29. So long as Ayres lived in Austin and Allen Gruchy lived in College Park, there were almost daily memorials to Veblen. In addition, there was for years a "living colony" of Veblenites at the University of California, Berkeley.

30. By far the best biography of Mitchell is the one written in 1953 by his wife, Lucy Sprague Mitchell (a preeminent educator in her own right), *Two Lives: The Story of Wesley Clair Mitchell and Myself.* A knowledge of its contents offers some unusual material, since Mitchell at a critical point in his long and difficult courtship of Miss Sprague wrote several detailed letters highly analytical of what interested him in economics and why. See also Dorfman (1949), Schumpeter (1951), and Victor Zarnowitz (1968).

Greenbacks, with Special Reference to the Economic Consequences of Their Issue: 1862–65.

After his graduation in 1896, Mitchell, with the financial help of fellowships obtained with the aid of Laughlin, traveled to Europe, studying at universities in Halle and Vienna (at Vienna with Carl Menger). Upon receiving his doctorate (*summa cum laude*) from Chicago (1899), he worked for a year at the U.S. Census Bureau, returning to Chicago to become a junior member of the staff in 1900. From 1903 to 1913 he taught at the University of California at Berkeley. This proved to be Mitchell's most productive period, as he extended his study to the monetary system as a whole; the result was *Business Cycles* (1913).

Mitchell subsequently worked on various government commissions.[31] In 1913, he accepted a position at Columbia University as the successor to Clark. From 1919 to 1922, he, along with Veblen, Alvin Johnson, and others, served at the New School for Social Research in New York, which he cofounded. Returning to Columbia in 1922 (where he remained until his retirement in 1944), Mitchell again served on various other governmental boards and commissions, including the Committee on Social Trends (1929–33), the National Planning Board, National Resources Board, and the Federal Emergency Administration of Public Works (1933), as well as chairman of the Committee on the Cost of Living (1944). Among the positions he was awarded were the presidencies of the Econometric Society, the American Statistical Association, the American Economic Association, and the American Association for the Advancement of Science.

For all his accomplishments, Mitchell's greatest and longest-lived achievement was his founding of the National Bureau of Economic Research in 1920. Here he was able to realize his ambition of an organization devoted to the quantitative analysis of economic data as a separate field of inquiry, and in so doing was able to direct economics into a more "scientific" mode, with a more direct application to practical issues. His impact as seen in terms of those whom he trained and with whom he collaborated reads like a list of American Empirical Economic Academic Greats: Simon Kuznets, Arthur F. Burns, Milton Friedman, George J. Stigler, Raymond Saulnier, Moses Abramovitz, Geoffrey Moore, and Solomon Fabricant, to name but a few.

Mitchell and A Posteriori Theory 4.2

Mitchell's writings are important not for the development of any philosophical position—it is difficult in any event to discern one—but for his

---

31. In 1908, for example, Mitchell served on the Immigration Commission; during World War I he served in the Bureau of Labor Statistics and headed the Price Section of the Division of Planning and Statistics of the War Industries Board.

approach to the study of economics. This he clearly borrowed from the German Historical School but then developed quite spectacularly along different lines.

In his 1925 "Quantitative Analysis in Economic Theory," Mitchell made the case for a "marriage" of the quantitative and the qualitative approaches. In this essay he presented his thoughts on the role of institutions, suggesting that quantitative analysis could assist in the understanding of Veblen's distinction between the pecuniary and the productive economies. Measurement affords us the opportunity to discern the workings of the "money" economy and the institutions constructed for its continuance. Important in this regard is the basic question of whether individuals form cultures or cultures form the individual. For Mitchell, the answer was obvious, that culture is the source of human social evolution.

The relevance for economists and other social scientists was to encourage them to focus their energies on the study of *institutions* and their behavior as aggregates as opposed to the study of *individuals* in their drive for pecuniary utilitarian gains. The qualitative studies of the classical writers had centered on the motives behind individual actions; these presentations were exercises in the mechanics of decision making. Such exercises were little more than thought experiments, intellectual arguments with limited application to the social arena in which the actions occur. Quantitatively oriented economics is better suited to the handling of economic problems in an institutional setting, providing insights into economic problems that cannot be derived from logical analysis alone. It is in fact the existence of an institutional setting that legitimizes the use of quantitative techniques in the study of economic phenomena, if for no other reason than that the institutions themselves serve to fashion individual and social actions: "institutions standardize behavior, and thereby facilitate statistical procedure" (Mitchell 1925, 8).

In addition to its promise for the movement of the society toward desirable ends, the quantitative method has an equally significant role to play in the shift of focus in economic theory. Classical economic theory had in Mitchell's view been restricted by its Newtonian structure. The classical theory (even up to the time of Jevons and Marshall) had, by focusing on economic behavior as driven by the twin motives of pleasure and pain, simply reinvigorated the Newtonian outlook: "Indeed, any theorist who works by ascribing motives to men and arguing what they will do under guidance of these forces will produce a mechanical type of explanation" (Mitchell 1925, 10). In Mitchell's estimation, quantitative theory was more appropriate, as it represents a "statistical" approach to economic theory, one in which the focus is on observations of "average" behavior, and the discovery of statistical uniformities. The "mechanical" interpretation "involves the notions of sameness, of certainty, of invariant laws," while the "statistical" interpretation "involves the notions of variety, of probability, of approximations" (11).[32]

Further, quantitative institutional analysis allows a deeper understanding of problems of social welfare and provides the means to its improvement. In effect, the use of scientific procedures can assist in fashioning a society in accordance with the dictates of the social utilitarian calculus:

> What quantitative analysis promises here is to increase the range of objective criteria by which we judge welfare, and to study the variations of these criteria in relation to each other. . . . [I]n view of the multiplicity of our competing aims and the limitations of our social resources his [the statistical workers] help in measuring objective costs and objective results is indispensable to convert society's blind fumbling for happiness into an intelligent process of experimentation. (Mitchell 1925, 8)

While admitting that the physical sciences employ both theory and statistical (experimental) methods, Mitchell felt that the application of the statistical method to economic phenomena was fundamentally different from its physical-science counterpart for three reasons: (1) the total number of observations is limited to a small number; (2) economic units are *not* analogous to physical (molecular) units, but are by nature social, meaning defined with respect to the whole; and (3) the economist does not have the luxury of experimentation (he cannot isolate his subjects from the influence of outside forces or study them outside of their social sphere). But these very shortcomings in fact mandate the use of statistical

---

32. In his 1917 essay, "Wieser's Theory of Social Economics," Mitchell suggested the following in "support" of Wieser's method:

"The advantages of Wieser's type of economic theory are evident. To show what economic men logically ought to do is far easier than to show what they do do. For this purpose, as Wieser says, the theorist needs no historical or statistical apparatus; he has simply to analyze that treasure of common experiences that he finds ready within himself. Besides being easy to make, such theory meets the human appeal for guidance toward reform. One has only to accept economic duty as moral duty; then, whenever facts diverge from the theory, the facts are wrong, though none the less facts, and wrong in ways which the theory shows how to correct. Another shift fits the theory to pass as scientific. Grant that men are essentially rational; then the theory reveals substantial economic truth. Discrepancies between this substantial truth and the literal truth are accounted for by showing that existing inequalities imply subordination and that subordination weakens the economic judgment as well as reduces economic power. These three advantages, indeed, are not peculiar to Austrian theory; they are shared by classical economics. But for the Austrians a fourth advantage may be claimed: they seem to be more profound than the classical masters in that they base their whole analysis upon man's ultimate economic interest, the gratification of wants. Finally, as opposed to much modern work, Austrian theory in general and Wieser's version in particular is agreeably realistic; it deals with human planning, not with mathematical abstractions" (1917, 114–15).

theory in economics, for, unlike the physical-science analogues, classical (mechanistic) economic theory and statistical economic theory do not have any close correspondence. Thus Mitchell concluded:

> For these reasons the elements of variety, of uncertainty, of imperfect approximation are more prominent in the statistical work of the social sciences than in the statistical work of the natural sciences. And because our statistical results are so marked by these imperfections they do not approach so closely to the results of our reasoning on the basis of assumed premises. Hence the development of statistical method may be expected to make more radical changes in economic than it makes in physical theory. (1925, 11)

In 1908 Mitchell published a companion volume to his 1903 study of the "greenbacks." This study, entitled *Gold, Prices and Wages Under the Greenback Standard,* included 340 pages of statistical appendixes (not including textual diagrams, charts, and tables) designed to bolster his conclusions. In the last section of this work, Mitchell stated in very general terms the lessons to be learned from the "price-revolutions of the greenback period." These lessons he phrased in Veblenian terms:

> From the point of view of the men who direct it, the production of wealth is nowadays a business process of selling goods for more than they have cost, and is conducted for the sake of getting money profits. . . . It is hardly too much to say that from the standpoint of the business men in control, the production of wealth is simply an incidental feature in the business process of making money.
>
> Alongside these business enterprises . . . stand the business enterprises concerned with finance. . . . These enterprises, like the preceding class, are conducted for the sake of pecuniary profits. . . .
>
> Perhaps the clearest conception of the price-revolutions is gained by regarding them as changes made by the business community in its effort to adapt itself to the monetary conditions created by an inconvertible paper currency . . . . [G]ranted the fluctuations of the premium, the fluctuations in the prices of other goods were the adjustments which men using prices as the basis of their economic relations were constrained to make by circumstances beyond their control. (1908, 280–81)

The influences of Veblen and Clark are clearly present in the notion of a disconnect between business and industry: the emphasis on *business* leads to a myopic concentration on the accumulation of personal wealth. To the extent that there is in the process the generation of social wealth, this is an entirely fortuitous and accidental benefit. Their influence is also readily seen in the idea that the *individual* actions of men taking into account only their pecuniary wants and desires served to cause the fluctuations in the price level: Mandeville's maxim can thus be reconstituted as "Private Vices, Public Vices." It was the lack of a constraint provided by individuals accepting the concept of the "social whole" that Mitchell held had led to the circumstances of the price revolutions. The institutional explanation of events had achieved its empirical verification, and the German organic social ethic had been demonstrated superior to the British and Austrian individualist ethic.

Business Cycles   4.3

Mitchell's postdoctoral research dealt primarily with changes in the overall level of prices and output in the economy; his findings were published in 1913 under the title *Business Cycles* (the analytical section of that book, part III, has been republished numerous times).[33] The aim of this work was to submit the "speculations" of those who would seek to divine truth from the available statistical data on business conditions "to the pragmatic test" (1941, xi).

In the Preface Mitchell attempted a descriptive definition of the "cycle":[34]

> An incipient revival of activity, for example, develops into full prosperity, prosperity gradually breeds a crisis, the crisis merges into depression, depression becomes deeper for a while, but ultimately engenders a fresh revival of activity, which is the beginning of another cycle. (1941, ix)

Having described the cycle, Mitchell then set forth the parameters of business cycle analysis:

> A theory of business cycles must therefore be a descriptive analysis of the cumulative changes by which one set of business conditions transforms itself into another set. (1941, ix)

To Mitchell there was no such general phenomenon as *the* business cycle; he was convinced that the historical record proved that "while business cycles recur decade after decade each new cycle presents idiosyncrasies. Business history repeats itself, but always with a difference" (1941, ix). Each cycle is dependent on the cumulative effects of past economic conditions, which will be different for each cycle. Each cycle is also peculiar to given national and geographic conditions; even the phases are not always orderly and consistent with his descriptive definition. Since there is no ideal type, Mitchell did not need to set himself the task of providing a rigorous theory of the business cycle; in fact, he did

---

33. We will use here the separate edition, published in 1941.

34. These "cycles" or "recurrent phases" Mitchell took, in a manner quite consistent with Veblen, to be inevitable in a system "dominated by the quest of profits" (1941, ix).

not think such an achievement even possible.[35] What he desired was to "single out from the maze of sequences among business phenomena a few that are substantially uniform." These recurrent patterns exhibited by the statistical data could then "be used as guides in forecasting the immediate business future" (1941, x–xi). Thus he could eschew mathematical formalism, as the dating of the cycle became something of a thought experiment. After the fashion of Hume and his notion of constant conjunction, Mitchell sought to advance our understanding:

> Such regular sequences would help us to organize the tangled mass of facts presented by direct observation into coherent clusters. The latter would stimulate the imagination to unravel various lines of causal connection that are jumbled together in the annals of business and in the tables of statistics. Then it might be found that the irregularity of other sequences arises from varying combinations among sequences themselves regular. (1941, xi)

Such a statement of principle is not different in form or substance from the earlier treatments of the problem by Graunt, Petty, King, Davenant, and even Pigou. Each had carried out their analyses in terms of the data, and did not make any serious attempt to manipulate the empirical evidence in support of a preordained theoretical structure. In the past, tensions between the empiricists and the theoreticians erupted in periodic *Methodenstreiten;* with Mitchell, however, the time apparently was right for the acceptance of this method of analysis as scientific rigor.

From his detailed statistical investigations of variations in the output, employment levels (hours worked), and product prices of specific industries, Mitchell in his companion volumes (not unlike Jevons, Pigou, and the other pioneers) constructed detailed statistical charts. From the charts he was then able to identify patterns in the data which he termed "specific cycles" (this was an artistic study even more than it was one of scientific mechanics). The resulting "business cycle" (adjusted for trends) could be dated in terms of peaks, troughs, and points of inflection, and thus measured in terms of duration or amplitude (differences between adjoining peaks and troughs).

Mitchell went on to publish two additional studies of business cycles, the 1927 *Business Cycles: The Problem and Its Setting* and (with Arthur F. Burns) *Measuring Business Cycles.*[36] Mitchell was always interested in generalizing upon his professional perception. Profoundly devoted to empiricism, he constantly worried about the relationship between cognition and cogitation. In his lengthy Columbia University course on "Formative Types of Economic Thought," in which he reviewed his extensive knowledge of post–industrial revolution economic writings both empirical and

---

35. "A thoroughly adequate theory of business cycles, applicable to all cycles, is consequently unattainable" (Mitchell 1941, ix).

36. A third volume was published posthumously.

theoretical, he even attempted to bring some personal order out of what he assessed to be professional chaos.

The Attack on Utilitarianism   4.4

Mitchell, in his 1918 *Political Science Quarterly* article, "Bentham's Felicific Calculus," set forth a very clear statement of his (and by extension the institutionalist) view of the mechanical use of the utility calculus. Here he echoed the sentiments of Clark as to the validity of the rationality postulate, what Mitchell termed the "intellectualist fallacy." The felicific calculus is usually attributed to Bentham, although as we have seen (and as Mitchell gleefully pointed out) others had championed a similar philosophy at least a century earlier. Bentham's role in the extension of the calculus was not so much in offering a statement of the utilitarian philosophy as it was in giving to the doctrine an exactitude previously lacking: "He sought to make legislation, economics, ethics into genuine sciences. His contemporaries were content to talk about utility at large; Bentham insisted upon measuring particular utilities—or rather, the net pleasures on which utilities rest" (Mitchell 1918, 163–64).

In his article, Mitchell held that, while Bentham had indeed arrived at conclusions via an artificial set of constructs, a thorough reading of his work would give pause to the adherents of the "intellectualist fallacy." While Bentham had suggested throughout his writings that pleasures and pains could be measured, and that these quantities could further be used to forge a measure of utility, Mitchell opined that those who would claim Bentham as their intellectual forefather had neglected to heed his admonitions thoroughly. Bentham most assuredly, noted Mitchell, was not advocating cardinal utility comparisons; indeed he did not think them possible. He instead argued the general case for ordinal comparisons.

But Bentham had been unwilling to settle for a mere indifference analysis; he wished to "find a way of reducing qualitatively unlike pleasures and pains to a common denominator, and so of putting figures on felicity" (1918, 169). This "common denominator" was to be the common commodity, money. Yet even this unit of measure had its problems, the most significant being the decreasing marginal utility of money.[37]

Withal, Mitchell believed that Bentham had attempted what modern types decry: he created an amalgam of normative and positive theory (with a heavy emphasis on the normative). "That is, Bentham blends utilitarian ethics with a definite theory of functional psychology" (1918, 172). This psychological theory was comprised of four chief motives: (1) hedonics (the pain and pleasure calculus rule), (2) rationality (including self-interest and pecuniary interest), (3) passivity (motives

---

37. Mitchell, however, felt that Bentham had planted the germ of an idea, to be extended by later generations, of comparing "at the margin," that is, of employing the technique of the calculus.

compel conduct, and interests compel motives), and (4) apprehension (miscalculation is the result of misinterpreting signals or of differences in intellectual abilities) (1918, 172–76).[38]

Thus we see that Bentham, taken by many to have begun the rationalist revolution in economics, indeed set out his theory based on a few simple postulates (a practice denounced by Clark). Mitchell, however, could not bring himself to condemn the entire program. Bentham after all did very clearly consider critical those aspects of society that Clark (and Veblen and Commons and Mitchell) held to be of the utmost importance. For Mitchell, Bentham was not the "Newton of the moral world," but rather was the Linnæus, the great classifier rather than the great calculator. This Mitchell believed to be an even more compelling reason for granting Bentham status as a pioneer in economic thought: "Though he could not literally work out the value of any 'lot' of pain or pleasure, he had a systematic plan for canvassing the probable effects of rival institutions upon the happiness of populations" (1918, 182).

4.5 Institutional Economics: Mitchell's Contributions

For Mitchell, Institutional Economics was the study of the historical context as the basis for and background of the interpretation of economic (production and distribution) phenomena. The study of historical context involved measurement of relevant variables or their proxies. Such measurement was generally quantitative, but never mechanical; the investigator always must stress the logic behind the calculation, which was itself often a cultural phenomenon (for example, the National Bureau defined the timing of business cycles by committee vote, explicitly never depending upon any arithmetic process). Mitchell himself believed economic theory to be simply a set of idiosyncratic explanations of economic events. As they were idiosyncratic, they necessarily reflected essentially personally imagined constructs, the relevance of which would ebb and flow even as they were made quantitatively more reliable.

Yet there is in Mitchell a teleological element which we should mention here, a view evident in his 1929 "review" of Werner Sombart's *Hochkapitalismus*. After presenting a detailed analysis of Sombart's study of the development of capitalism, Mitchell noted its similarity to other theories of evolutionary economic change, such as those of Veblen and Marx. The existence of competing theories of economic evolution, predicated on the same historical evidence, he found "disturbing." Also, Sombart's notion that the evolution of capitalism—including the emergence of the business class, the change in techniques of production, and the evolution of the role of the state—was somehow a "historical accident" did not seem to Mitchell convincing: "I should think it possible to give an account of the development of capitalism in which these phenomena ap-

---

38. Education, however, could work to solve a great many of these conundrums.

pear as inevitable and closely related products in the process of cumulative change" (Mitchell 1929a, 323). Certainly economic *theory* was idiosyncratic, but surely the *facts* of historical development were beyond dispute and would lead one eventually to the discovery of the true path.

An Assessment 4.6

One cannot overestimate Mitchell's impact, for he gave material form to the *soul* of macroeconomic analysis. Ideas cast no shadows; numbers, when tied to ideas, do. Mitchell, like Jacob, begot numerous intellectual sons: Arthur F. Burns and business cycle measurement; Solomon Fabricant and productivity analysis; Milton Friedman and Anna Schwartz and a form of monetary analysis; and so forth. Principal amongst those whom Mitchell begot was Simon Kuznets, whose stock of ideas is legendary.[39]

The major criticism of Mitchell was that he was like Bacon's ant, interested only in accumulating mountains of data and trying to package them. Tjalling Koopmans, in a famous 1946 review article, lambasted Mitchell for eschewing scientific (meaning abstract) analysis in favor of simplistic empirics. The reality was rather different. Mitchell had great use for abstract theory; he just was not convinced that any of the abstract economic theory being distributed as universal wisdom justified that claim. While any perusal of his personal record will reveal how ambitious he was, that same perusal will also reveal intellectual care and modesty.

Mitchell's sources dealt with the great advances in statistical methodology of the turn of the twentieth century. Less imbued with anger at the American social system than Veblen and suffering no personal discriminatory experiences which could have caused that bitterness, Mitchell was trying to call shots as he saw them, particularly as he understood the contemporary development of statistical inference and method.

J. R. Commons: Institutionalism and the Social Bargain 5

Commons's Early Career 5.1

For many, Institutionalism is synonymous with the name of John Rogers Commons (1862–1945).[40] Many of the items held to be on the institutionalist agenda in fact were placed there by Commons himself.

---

39. In addition, there were Robert Nathan and Milton Gilbert and the foundation of modern national income analysis, including modern wartime reallocation; Richard Easterlin and Oded Stark and modern demographic analysis; Jacob Schmookler and the numerical analysis of patents; numerous students producing a variety of measures of income distribution by size; and even more students, including the brilliant if independent-minded Walt Whitman Rostow and the J-shaped economic growth curve.

40. For a discussion of Commons's career and some of his ideas see M. Perlman (1958), Mitchell (1969, 701–36), and Samuels (1987b).

As with other "founders" of the movement, Commons while at Johns Hopkins (1888–90) came under the influence of the German Historical School of Economics, with its emphasis on comparative (historical and statistical) analysis and its decidedly policy-oriented approach.[41] Although he did not do well enough at Hopkins to warrant a fellowship, he was nonetheless placed by his teacher, Richard Ely, at Connecticut Wesleyan (1890) to fill out the contract term of Woodrow Wilson (Wilson had gone off to Princeton to serve as president). From Wesleyan, where he proved a dismal purveyor of the prevailing economic orthodoxy, Commons eventually moved to Syracuse,[42] after which he accepted a position at the newly formed Bureau of Economic Research in New York;[43] his tenure there was short-lived, as the Bureau closed in 1900. Eventually (1904), Ely managed to secure for him an appointment at the University of Wisconsin, where Ely served as Chairman. There Commons remained until 1932, and is credited with having founded the "Wisconsin School" of Institutional Economics.[44]

Commons was always active in social reform movements. Ely prompted him to become a case worker at the Charity Organization Society of Baltimore, in order to gain a more extensive knowledge of social problems. In 1893, Commons helped found the American Proportional Representation League, and (with Ely) the Institute of Christian Sociology. Later he served as vice president of the National League for Promoting the Public Ownership of Monopolies.

5.2 A Reinterpretation of the Rights of the Individual

One of Commons's earliest books was his 1893 treatise *The Distribution of Wealth,* a work Joseph Dorfman proclaimed represented "the foundations of Commons' economics" (Dorfman 1965, xv).[45] An important

41. Dorfman noted that the American variant of the German historical approach "sought to enlarge the hitherto extremely narrow scope of classical economics in order to provide sound guide lines for economic policy; for a policy that would promote orderly industrial growth and equitable distribution of national income but would avoid the extremes of excessive individualism and Marxian socialism" (1965, iii).

42. At Syracuse, Commons "taught ethnology, anthropology, criminology, charity organization, taxation, political economy and city government. He investigated municipal ownership in various small towns around Syracuse. . . . He took his students to visit penitentiaries, reform schools and factories" (Mitchell 1969, 705). For a variety of reasons he proved unsuccessful at Syracuse. His politics had been the issue, but rather than terminate his employment the university governors simply abolished his chair.

43. No relation to the Mitchell-formed National Bureau of Economic Research.

44. It was at Wisconsin that Commons met Wisconsin governor Robert La Follette, widely known as a reform advocate. It was La Follette who commissioned Commons to prepare the civil service laws for the state.

45. Dorfman characterized it as "an ingenious combination of the modern types of economic theory that he had imbibed at Johns Hopkins. It attempted to fuse the Austrian utility theory with an abundance of diagrams and the techniques of the German Historical School with its emphasis on the role of law and the use of statistics" (1965, xi).

element of this book is the central significance granted to the legal and institutional structure within society, and the role of law in economic and political relations. Commons attributed the lack of attention by mainstream economists to questions of law and the legal structure of society to two factors: (1) the focus on "scientific" as opposed to "historical" analysis, and (2) the consideration by the classical theorists of institutional arrangements as given and so exogenous to the determination of economic variables (Commons 1893, 59). This he held to be a mistake, for the legal and institutional relationships of a society are not constant, but change as situations do; they evolve through time and, in so doing, affect economic and social arrangements.

Important as an institutional constraint—institutions being defined as "collective action in control, liberation, and expansion of individual action" (Commons 1950, 21)—are laws respecting contract and the right of property. It must be understood here that Commons held to an organic view of society. The collective molds the individual and, in fact, exerts a dominating influence on human activity; men "become individualized by the rules of collective action" (1950, 21).

Commons viewed this "collective action" as "the means to liberty," and in his understanding, liberty can only be ensured "by imposing duties on others who might interfere with the activity of the 'liberated' individual" (1950, 35). Only under such constraints can the individual actually be free to act in accordance with his will. Absent such specifications, the individuals, whose social interactions define the economy, are prone to too great a level of uncertainty as to the consequences of their actions. The result is a heightened level of instability that may threaten to undermine the existing social and political relations:

> In order that industry may be carried on at all under such complex relations, there must be a very definite understanding by every individual as to what he may expect from others, and what he must do in turn for others. Nothing can be left to chance, fraud, or force. (Commons 1893, 60)

The problem with maintaining such expectations lay in the authority under which such political, social, and economic arrangements would be instituted, and here we see emerge a rationale for his theory of collective action. First, Commons firmly believed, as against the classical economists, that while individual interest and competitive ambition were essential to the functioning of a free society, individual interest of and by itself was too evil a force—"too powerful, or too ignorant, or too immoral" (1893, 61)—to be left to its own designs to channel human behavior. Second, in Hobbesian fashion he held that force and compulsion were necessary to ensure the common good, to check the uncompromising excesses inevitably engendered by a system based on the principles of individual self-government and laissez-faire. Natural Law foundations were not a relevant criterion, since there was neither a compulsion to abide by those dictates nor a penalty should disobedience occur. Finally, the two are combined into a social synthesis. What was needed was a mechanism to channel behavior to the social demands, while at the same time allowing, within prescribed parameters, freedom of individual action. All Commons required was an instrumental test:

> Consequently, there must be found somewhere a supreme authority, with power to define and enforce the rights and duties of individuals. It is not always so important that these rights and duties be based upon ideas of justice as that they be certain. There must be no room for the arbitrary rulings of individuals. This indicates the necessity for law and government. Thus there are in society two lines of economic activity, the voluntary activity of individuals and associations, and the compulsory activity of government. The first is the field of free competition and self-interest; the one hitherto solely treated by the English economists. The second is the field of coercion,—of force. (1893, 60–61)

Commons extended the scope of the argument to cover, among other things, the theory of property. On this issue he clearly held to an Aristotelian distinction between ownership and use, a view nowhere more evident than in his discussion (in 1893, chap. VII, sec. VI) of personal rights. Here he made the point that, while it may be individual abilities which serve to create wealth—"They are the agents whereby man changes the place and arrangement of external objects of nature . . ." (65)— it is the institutional framework that determines who shall partake of this wealth and to what extent.

Thus was Commons led to his view of the role of the legal apparatus of the state in social, political, and economic affairs. This view can be more clearly grasped through the following logical chain. The "fundamental right" is the right to life; the right to life can be upheld only by the provision of a minimum level of subsistence; the state through its power of coercion can provide this subsistence through a redistribution of the total product in the society; the state is compelled morally and ethically to uphold fundamental rights of its citizens; therefore, the state has a moral and ethical obligation to protect the fundamental right of its citizens to life by providing for them a minimum level of subsistence (1893, 66–67).

The conclusion drawn from this chain of reasoning is itself of interest in that it leads to a moral basis of rights. The provision of a "floor" for the maintenance of the population Commons felt was justified at least on altruistic grounds. In a peculiar logic, he first stipulated that the institution of slavery was morally correct—it "marked a long advance-step in human civilisation" (1893, 68)—on the grounds that it led to (1) an expansion of the production of wealth (producing a social surplus that could be used to satisfy basic human wants), and (2) a realization on the part of the slaveholders that it was in their best interests to protect their property (slaves) by providing them with a minimum level of goods and care. This he deemed an improvement over the savage state, since, after all, the "slave had the right to life and personal security, the hired servant had not this most precious of rights" (69). The important thing to remember here is that the institution of slavery engendered a sense of responsibility on the part of the slaveholders. This sense of custodianship continued after the abolition of slavery (generally brought about for economic reasons, as paid labor did not require the employer to provide a "safety net"). Custodianship became codified in a way through the idea of a "right to life" (brought about as much by a perceived ethical and moral responsibility as through a fear of rebellion on the part of the unemployed and the disadvantaged).

Having established a general right to life, Commons then extended it to a *guarantee* of a share of the total output "equal, at least, to his minimum of subsistence" (1893, 70).[46] He then defined a second set of rights, a "bundle" he termed collectively the "right to liberty." Included in this "bundle" of rights are conditions of existence so fundamental that their enumeration seems entirely unnecessary, these being "the right to free motion and locomotion; rights to the uses of the free gifts of nature, air, sunlight, water; rights of free contract, free industry, free belief and worship, free speech and publication; the right to equality, and the right to marriage" (70). But having enumerated these most basic "rights" of human existence, he then immediately extended the list to include the right *to* property (not the right *of* property), and the right to a state-furnished education. In so doing he situated the individual squarely within the social milieu and endowed him with societal obligations.

It is in the distribution of the social product that this enumeration of rights holds the most import. (Interestingly enough, the conclusion was deduced from his premises and not through historical induction.) To demonstrate, consider the position of labor. For Commons, "collective action" is the most basic rule of human society, and it could be applied here as well. The law of diminishing marginal utility suggests that by limiting the supply of a factor, each individual composite element can demand a larger share of the total product. As labor is a primary productive factor, for the laborer such restriction can be most readily achieved through the exercise of (a collective) freedom of contract and freedom of industry; in other words, the laborer achieves the greatest reward through collective action, in this instance through the creation of the

---

46. "[A] right without provisions for its physical enforcement by government is only a moral and abstract right, not a legal and serviceable one" (Commons 1893, 63).

labor union. Thus, the right to combine for the purpose of limiting the size of the labor pool is for the workingman "one of their most important rights of freedom" (1893, 75).

Of course, there are negative social consequences to this form of activity. By combining to limit the numbers of workers employed at a specific task or in a given industry, there is created a larger pool of unemployed, those whose marginal status is too low to qualify for membership. Collective action benefits those in the collective (in this instance the union), but cannot assist those outside. For this contingency, Commons devised yet another right: the right to work. This right had two facets: it had to provide (1) a guard "against arbitrary discharge, as long as one proves efficient and honest," and (2) a requirement on the part of the government to maintain the unemployed by offering useful employment (1893, 81). Collective action in support of specific interest groups thus must itself be supported by the collective action of the state.

It is this last provision that is the most troubling, but also the most telling in Commons's philosophy, at least when compared with the moral and ethical stance of the utilitarians of the Philosophic Radical tradition. The machinery of government in Commons new social contract would thus be used not merely as a last resort, but on the contrary would be used to ameliorate the failures of the private sector. In the case of employment, the government was not to be engaged solely in the provision of public-sector jobs for the unemployed, but would compel private industry to provide employment as well. This required a new coercive mechanism of laws, and a new system of courts to administer not merely legal rulings, but to manage in very significant ways the entire corporate structure as well:

> The new courts that shall enforce the right to employment are courts of arbitration, created by government, and empowered to compel employers to submit to investigation and to suffer punishment for violating the right of employés to work. No man is to be discharged for any cause except inefficiency and dishonesty. Wages, hours of labour, conditions of work, are to be adjudicated by the courts. (1893, 82–83)

In *The Distribution of Wealth*, Commons also presented, within a (property) rights framework, his theory of "goodwill." In order to secure a right of property, it is fundamental that there be, among other things, an object over which the right is to be secured. To be considered legal property a thing must be amenable to appropriation by the person claiming the right to ownership or dominion. But this tangibility requirement does not imply that the object must itself be real in a physical sense; the law does not demand for the granting of a property right a corporeal existence. Thus claims for patent rights, copyrights, mortgages, notes of debt, and so on, are held to be actionable under the law, although they themselves are not tangible property but rather represent *claims* to this property.

The problem as Commons perceived it is that this legal delineation of property excludes important "intangibles" from the equation, one of the more important being business goodwill. Goodwill is incapable of legal protection in terms of the current legal definition of property, while at the same time it is recognized as a transferable business asset:

> But the good-will of a business is both intangible and unrepresented by legal paper, and therefore cannot be reached by the officers. Yet the "good-will" may be transferred by means of a contract, stipulating that the original possessor will abstain from following the same pursuit whose good-will he has sold, and the contract can, of course, be enforced by law. (1893, 91)

Commons approached the problem in a way very different from that of legal scholars and the classical economic writers. He held that property was not a right in and of itself, but rather was to be understood as an abstract collection ("bundle") of rights, similar to the right to liberty (1893, 92). The "property right" then is a single right, with gradations expressible along a continuum that "extends indefinitely not only in the direction of the *use* and *disposition* of the object, but also in the *duration* of the control" (92; emphasis in original).

In this connection, he distinguished between *partial* and *full* rights to property. The partial right is definite and "may be either a right which limits its [the object's] use and disposition by the full owner, or one which merely limits the time over which his full control extends"; the full right is "the indefinite residuum," which remains after deductions for non-proprietary ("definite") claims (1893, 91–92). Partial rights can be traded while the ownership claims to the property remain intact; the full right (the *dominium*) is transferred only upon the sale or bequeathing of the object itself. Among the partial rights are public ones, such as eminent domain, right of way, taxation, public nuisance, and usage "contrary to public policy" (93–95). Other partial rights are private and may be granted by the proprietor; they include such "rights" as lease, mortgage, and inheritance (96–98).

With this redefinition of the property right, Commons could state a legal definition of capital. Capital can be understood to be of two forms, social and private. It can thus be seen from the view of production and society, and from the view of distribution and the individual. From the view of production and society, capital "consists of the instruments and material of production—the things themselves . . ."; social capital, in other words, "creates" utilities. From the standpoint of distribution and the individual, capital "is a historical institution, consisting in the *ownership* of social capital, and comprises both those kinds of partial ownership known as definite rights—*res incorporales*—and that full, indefinite ownership known as *dominium*" (1893, 100). Thus, in Aristotelian fashion, Commons advanced a legal and economic argument for the distinction of ownership and use.

In 1924 Commons published *Legal Foundations of Capitalism*, a very readable history of the reinterpretation of the property rights concept in English and American law. In this landmark work in institutional economic analysis, Commons noted that, in American jurisprudence, the meaning of the idea of property had changed dramatically over the latter part of the nineteenth century. In a series of Supreme Court decisions immediately following the Civil War (the *Slaughter House Cases* of 1872, *Munn v. Illinois* of 1876), the Court held to a definition of property predicated on the Smithian notion of value-in-use and rejected arguments based on the concept of value-in-exchange. The Court had ruled that, while the laws did indeed deprive the plaintiffs in these cases of their ability to engage in a commercial activity (and thus de facto expropriated the exchange-value of their business enterprises), they did not deprive them of their liberty or their personal property, since they were not compelled in any instance to servitude.

By 1890 (in the *First Minnesota Rate Case*), the picture changed dramatically, as the concept of property as exchange value began to be accepted by the Court. Here the Court ruled that the property right as defined (indirectly, in the guise of the liberty clause) in the Fourteenth Amendment applied not only to physical "objects of property," but also to "the *expected earning power* of those things" (Commons 1924, 16; emphasis in original). Property thus no longer could be confined to physical goods, but must be extended to include incorporeal and intangible objects as well: the definition of property then "evolved" from "any tangible thing owned" to "any of the expected activities implied with regard to the thing owned, comprehended in the activities of acquiring, using and disposing of the thing" (18).[47] As Commons asserted, the definition of property underwent a fundamental alteration, from a corporeal to a behavioristic one (19).

These cases and others set the stage for what has become known today as the "takings" controversy: how far can the power of the state police authority extend in regard to the taking of private property without compensation before it becomes illegal confiscation? Commons summed it thus:

> Thus the transition in the definition of property from physical objects to exchange-value was completed. "Title and possession" of

---

47. In his *The Economics of Collective Action*, Commons defined "incorporeal" property as "the duty of the debtor to pay money, known either as a credit or its equivalent debt," and "intangible" property as "the economic power of sellers, buyers, or competitors, in charging against others or paying to others such prices as they wished or could enforce for commodities or services" (1950, 80).

physical property could be taken from its owner for public purposes under the power of eminent domain, but only on condition that equivalent value should be paid, such that the owners' assets should not be reduced; and this equivalent value, or just compensation, is a judicial question. Now it is enlarged to read: The exchange-value of property may be taken from its owners under the police power, but only to the extent that they retain sufficient bargaining power to maintain the same exchange-value that they had, and this also is a judicial question. The definition of property is changed from physical things to the exchange-value of anything, and the federal courts now take jurisdiction. (1924, 16–17)

An Appeal to Method   5.3

In 1934 Commons published a rather intense but opaque book, *Institutional Economics*,[48] in which he presented in detail and with reference to the intellectual historical background his interpretation of the nature of Institutionalism. As much of the material dealt with the topics presented above, we shall deal here with the question of method and the notion of society as a social organism. In respect to the first, he identified four approaches to economics, these being the mechanical, the machinist, the organic, and the going concern. Mechanical theories follow along the analogy of molecular physics, "wherein society is only a population . . . and the blind forces of nature act without cause, effect, or purpose . . ." (Commons 1934, 119). Machine theories by contrast posit the society as an artificial mechanism and came into prominence "on account of the dominance of the Engineer in the business and politics of a Machine Age" (119); adherence to these theories leads to attempts to control the economy and society, variously identified as fascism, communism, and even managerial capitalism. Organic theories derive from biology; they proceed by identifying all activities as collective, positing such things as the "social will." As with machine theories, organic theories can result in fascist remedies, or even "banker capitalism."

The "Going Concern" approach is fundamentally different. This approach views collective institutions as real, not contrived, "with their working rules, in unlimited variety, each looking towards the future, and controlling individual action" (1934, 120). Unlike the "equilibrium" mechanical and machine theories, it is not necessary to invent a purpose for institutions, such as maintaining or providing a harmony of interests. Unlike the "process" organic theories, it is not necessary to rely on

---

48. Mitchell opined that *Institutional Economics* "certainly deserves consideration as a valiant attempt to provide the constructive contribution which has been demanded of institutionalists" (1969, 701). It was in this work that Commons actually defined his idea of Institutional Economics: "Institutional economics is concerned with the Assets and Liabilities of Concerns contrasted with Adam Smith's Wealth of Nations" (Commons 1934, 72).

accidental alterations or shocks to the system to promote evolution. The "Going Concern" approach has elements of both; the difference is that the change is foreseen and purposeful, and indeed managed to the pursuit of equilibrium. All that occurs in the structure of the social institution is by design, the process being shaped toward an end. It is therefore not necessary to invoke "Dramatic or Poetic Analogies" as was the approach of not only the classical economists but also the physiocrats, the mercantilists, and the neoclassical writers as well; all one need do is examine the social, legal, moral, and ethical environments to understand the basis of the social and institutional structure.

Beyond the matter of the appropriate approach to economics, of particular interest in *Institutional Economics* is Commons's understanding of the views of Locke, Smith, and Hume (and Bentham, Blackstone, Quesnay, Malthus, and Peirce) in providing a foundation to his theory of collective action. Commons identified Locke, for one, as having had a profound influence on the intellectual environment of his time and of all time thereafter: "In every branch of learning he epitomized the Seventeenth Century, dominated the Eighteenth, and controlled the institutional and psychological concepts of orthodox economists in the Nineteenth and Twentieth Centuries, after philosophers and psychologists had abandoned them." His legacy "was skepticism in place of knowledge, probability in place of certainty, reason in place of authority, research in place of dogmatism, constitutional government in place of absolutism, independence of the judiciary for the sake of property, liberty, and toleration" (1934, 13). It was in the Lockean legacy that Commons found the basis for an institutional approach to economics, especially in the notion that certainty was not realizable and so one must make due with probable judgments, faith, and opinion. Locke's individualism was centered on the need to remove man from the constrictions of custom and habit, and instead reorient his understanding to that of a rational being who is himself the center of all things. Locke established rational man as a focal point "to which all changes and probabilities might be referred" (22). Once man is so defined, it is but one small step to distinguish *reason* from *reasonableness,* and to establish the rationale for social action: "Reason may give us the immutable laws of God, Nature, Perfection, but Reasonableness gives us mutual assent to the preponderance of probability in the affairs of life" (23). Locke's (and the classical economists' as a whole) professed economic and political individualism Commons defined as "Individual Epistemology and Valuation," wherein the problem centers on the manner in which "an individual [can] *know* and give *value* to anything." In contrast to this view, Commons, by reaffirming Locke's basic philosophical ideals as the grounds of a social ethic, identified his own approach as "a theory of the joint activity and valuations of individuals in all transactions through which the participants mutually induce each other to a consensus of opinion and action" (25). This interpretation he felt was equivalent not to Locke's "theory of Reason," but rather to his "theory of Reasonableness."

According to Commons, Locke and Smith had, in their economic and political writings, divorced ethics and law from economics, with their "assumptions of abundance and divine beneficence" (1934, 143). By contrast, Hume—whom Commons esteemed as a founder of Institutional Economics—had recognized the necessity of "a union of economics, ethics, and jurisprudence" in his understanding that scarcity is the "universal principle," a principle that "operates . . . both as self-interest and self-sacrifice" (143); he "had substituted Scarcity and Public Utility for Locke's Abundance and Commonwealth" (158). Commons readily accepted that Hume's "virtues" were similar to Smith's "sympathy" in the sense that both stood in opposition to the "selfish" morality of Hobbes and Locke. But Hume was prepared to go further and allow for a social ethic, wherein there exist both a private and a public interest and a private and a public sentiment, something which (Commons held) Smith denied was an ineffective restraint on the individual; Commons asserted that in fact the blame lay with the disrepute among classical political economists (meaning Smith, Bentham, and Ricardo) of the entire concept of private collective action, a belief presented most completely in the work of Herbert Spencer. Yet Hume's recognition of public sentiment and the use of the notion of scarcity not as solely applicable to material goods, but rather as applicable to opportunities and conflicting interests, was important in allowing for

> all the economic virtues of honesty, fair dealing, fair competition, reasonable exercise of economic power, equal opportunity, live-and-let-live, good-will, and reasonable value, which subordinate the immediate interests of self to that sharing with others of limited opportunities which makes possible the peaceful conduct of transactions and going concerns. (1934, 143)

For Commons, political economy and economics developed from the acceptance of a conflict of interests and the need to harmonize interests to a social goal (or at least to the prevention of a social breakdown). In fact, he considered collective action to be liberating, not only of individuals from coercion, discrimination, and unfair practices, but also of the individual *will*, as it allows the individual to exercise a force well beyond his physical limitations. This understanding Commons felt was the great significance of Locke's Reasonableness standard.

Commons and Mainstream Economics   5.4

Commons, unlike Veblen, did not spend much time criticizing Marshallian or Austrian economics. That was not his way. He read that material very sympathetically, but thought that empiricism combined with historically based generalizations, not abstract theorizing, was the

preferred method. For him, "institutions" were "collective rules controlling individual actions." He held a somewhat jaundiced view of the general *wisdom* of government, but always held respect for the *power* of
government. The best way to control society, he thought, was to encourage the formation of competing groups (countervailing blocs) in order to
protect the interests of private members. The method he suggested involved publicity—do not forbid people to engage in wicked activities,
merely make their activities public and let them handle the social scorn
that (he was convinced) was sure to follow.

In his early years Commons was something of a reader and thinker
along the Marxian line, but never in a very committed way. The initial
source of Commons's Institutionalism was the same vein as Clark's *Philosophy of Wealth,* but Commons went well beyond Clark, replacing his
Christian Socialist morality with a rhetorically tedious but nonetheless
brilliant episodic empiricism. It has been said that, while Commons was
indeed brilliant and creative, his style and method of persuasion (his
rhetoric) were so "convoluted" as to defy categorization. Even he regarded his theories as so highly personal as to be unexplainable to anyone
else.[49] Commons's later sources came from an autodidactic legal training,
one based on examination of historical prose.

The critical element in Commons's thinking was an effort to make
sense of the historical record. In this sense he was in the tradition of the
seventeenth-century political scientists. One notable difference between
him and the earlier writers was his view that the "culture of the people"
served as part of the "stabilizing morality" aspect of history. On the
positive side, he acknowledged the critical importance of property rights
and was willing to extend them far beyond real estate and chattel. He also
was critically aware of the impact of market extension (usually perceived
as geographic growth): the more extended the market, not only the
greater the opportunity for specialization (*à la* Adam Smith), but also the
greater the likelihood of impersonality and brute market power. Commons feared the brutality of unfettered market forces (as in competition);
he instead favored bilateral bargaining between blocs. Basic to his view
was a conviction—he thought it based on his observed experience—that
within each bloc there were likely differing views, and that the more
mature, moderate view would in time prevail.

For a man who had great success in designing governmental programs, he had relatively little faith in any magic associated with an intellectual (and surely legal) assertion of governmental power, unless it were
backed by sheer force. Even that he believed would prove to be only
temporary (cf. Commons 1919, 1921). Rather, he felt that the owners of
capital and the leadership of the labor movement would come to develop
a capacity to govern industry wisely, with each leadership able to educate

---

49. These points were made by, for example, Yngve Ramstad (1987).

and control the excesses of its own clientele. He favored "voluntaristic industrial government," not "government in industry," and sought to lay out both the patterns that had emerged in his America and his discernment of just what those patterns were. The first, "industrial government," depended upon some *élan vital,* which the accountants and he came to call "goodwill." Goodwill was a possible institutional product of a long series of group interactions. Drawing on Maine and Maitland, he saw not contract (which cannot be effectively enforced in the face of social hatred) replacing traditional status but growing specified agreement.[50] Collective bargaining was a process; if *labor contract* was the name of the result of each stage, the term *contract* was used in a special sense. *Implicit contract* is the phrase now more popularly adopted.

Commons was without question *a,* if not *the,* preeminent *political* economist of his time. Whether what he offered was "scientific" economics is clearly another matter.[51] While he thought that he was being scientific in his labors, his science leaned much more to "episodic empiricism"—arriving at generalizations based on observations of historical patterns—than it did to models or formal logical disquisition. Greatly admired, he was nonetheless something of a withdrawn personality. He needed much personal admiration; during his most active period, from 1904 through 1935, he probably had four or five major nervous breakdowns, for which rest and admiration seem to have been the necessary curative factors. Still, when he received that regard his capacity for work was prodigious. In his own view, his achievements suited his times: he did not believe that one could build for the indefinite future—in that sense he was more of an economic historian than a *"Drang noch Gleichstellung"* ("Urge to Equilibrium") type. Part of the contradiction of our discipline is that the leading theorists thought Commons first-rate—first-rate in what way is, of course, the issue.[52]

---

50. But in his 1934 *Institutional Economics,* Commons expressed disagreement with Maine on the evolution of free contract: custom did not give way to competition and contract, but rather "[c]ustoms have merely changed with changes in economic conditions, and they may today be so mandatory that even a dictator cannot overrule them" (Commons 1934, 72).

51. Ramstad (1995) attempted to answer the question of why Commons has been ignored by the mainstream in economics, providing an explanation for the exclusion of Commonsian constructs in economic theory.

52. By 1931, one of Commons's students, Carl Rauschenbush (the son of the eminent theologian as well as the son-in-law of Justice Brandeis), had designed and managed to get passed by the legislature an operative unemployment insurance system for Wisconsin—one with experience ratings. Another of his students, Edwin E. Witte, chaired the committee which designed the federal social security system; still another, Arthur Altmeyer, was its first administrator. Two more students, Wilbur Cohen and Jacob Perlman, were the originators of the Medicare principles. Some of his students originated the limited interference policies of the National Labor Relations Board (the board was initially so pro-union that Congress threatened to repeal the Wagner Act—ultimately it did the next thing to it, passing the Landrum Griffin Act in 1947).

6 The Austrian Connection: Schumpeter

6.1 Motivations

The one on whom the Veblen mantle fell most squarely, and on whom we have here relied throughout, was Joseph Alois Schumpeter (1883–1950),[53] an Austrian who spent the last two decades of his life at Harvard. Like Veblen, Schumpeter was an outsider (even though he always insisted that he was *la crème de la crème*). Schumpeter, the supreme European iconoclast, may have exhibited just the persona Veblen sought to portray in his America.

Having received a "classical" education at the Theresianum (a school for children of the aristocracy and civil service), Schumpeter continued his studies at the University of Vienna (1901–6) in law and economics; his teachers there included Wieser, Phillipovich, and Böhm-Bawerk. While in Cairo, where he engaged in the practice of law as a junior partner in a firm and amassed a personal fortune,[54] he wrote *Das Wesen und der Hauptinhalt der theoretischen Nationalökonomie (The Nature and Essence of Economic Theory)* (1908), an effort which served as his *habilitation* thesis. One of his concerns in this, his first methodological work, was that economic theory to be viable and timeless had to be value-free; in other words, economics had to viewed as a positive and not a normative discipline, a position consistent with the view of the German Historical School on the necessity of basing theoretical arguments on empirical facts. It was also in this work that Schumpeter reflected admiration for Walras as well as a desire to present his arguments formally (meaning mathematically); it was written to explain to historical inductivists what formalism meant—particularly the importance of equilibrium as an economic concept.

Prior to the First World War, Schumpeter did some of his most profound work. In 1911 he published *Theorie der wirtschaftlichen Entwicklung (The Theory of Economic Development: An Inquiry into Profits, Capital, Credit, Interest, and the Business Cycle)*, in which he emphasized the important but previously neglected role in economic development played by institutional constraints. As an explanation of the capitalist process, the book is unparalleled. In 1914 he published *Epochen der Dogmen- und Methodengeschichte* (translated in 1954 as *Economic Doctrine and Method*), a methodological and historical tract

---

53. Biographical material on Schumpeter may be found in Arthur Smithies (1950), Mitchell (1969, chap. XV), Loring Allen (1991), Richard Swedberg (1991), and Wolfgang Stolper (1968, 1994).

54. Smithies reckoned this as follows: As manager in Cairo of "the financial affairs of an Egyptian princess," Schumpeter "performed the financial miracle of cutting rents on the princess's estates in half and doubling her income—by the simple device of appropriating to his own use no more than he was legally entitled to" (Smithies 1950, 629).

which he later extended into his *History of Economic Analysis* (published after his death by his third wife, Elizabeth Boody Schumpeter).

At the end of the war,[55] Schumpeter was named a member of the German Socialization Commission (1918) and minister of finance in the socialist Austrian government (March to October 1919), despite the fact that he was not a socialist. He was eventually forced from his position for advocating, among other things, that Austria not align herself with Germany but instead seek relations with the western democracies. Later (1921) he was named to the presidency of the Biedermann Bank, which became insolvent within two years of his departure. As a result, he lost a substantial portion of his personal fortune.

Following his appointment and a brief career at the University of Bonn (a chair in public finance, 1925), Schumpeter emigrated to the United States and in 1932 accepted a position at Harvard University, his final academic post.[56] He served as president of the American Economic Association (1948) and was a founder of the Econometric Society and its president from 1937 to 1941.

Schumpeter and Development   6.2

The second of Schumpeter's major books to be discussed is his 1911 *The Theory of Economic Development*.[57] As mentioned above, the book is unsurpassed as a treatise on the role of institutional constraints in economic development. What interests us here, however, is that this work presents Schumpeter's earliest discussion of one of the most important ideas in Schumpeterian economics, what was later termed "creative destruction."

Schumpeter defined his concept of "economic development" as "spontaneous and discontinuous change in the channels of the flow, disturbance of equilibrium, which forever alters and displaces the equilibrium state previously existing" (1934, 64). Defined in this way, it is clear that economic development originates in endogenous change, incorporating "only such changes in economic life as are not forced upon it from without but arise by its own initiative, from within" (63). Economic development is *not* adaptation, given changes in noneconomic forces; neither is its process simply a response to signals in the social environment. These conditions cause mere changes in the *data* of economics, but cannot affect qualitative economic development.

---

55. Schumpeter was by nature a pacifist. During the war he did not participate as a combatant, but apparently had some role in the 1916 attempt to arrange a settlement of hostilities. He continued after the war to insinuate himself into the political aftermath. For instance, in 1918 he published a very interesting book, *Die Krise der Steuerstaats* (*The Crisis of the Tax State*) in which he advocated a program designed to achieve a stable economy in postwar Austria.

56. He had visited Harvard in 1927 and 1930.

57. We use here the English-language edition of 1934.

Given his definition of the concept, it is not surprising that Schumpeter held to a view of development (and hence the business cycle) not unlike that offered by Mitchell, whereby each cycle is dependent upon conditions preceding its emergence, and each cycle consequently derives from the last:

> Every concrete process of development finally rests upon preceding development. . . . Every process of development creates the prerequisites for the following. Thereby the form of the latter is altered, and things will turn out differently from what they would have been if every concrete phase of development had been compelled first to create its own conditions. (1934, 64)

Having explained the concept of "economic development," Schumpeter then proceeded to the important idea of "creative destruction." The economy, to begin with, is on the order of a circular flow (Physiocracy revisited!). The problem with the standard circular model is that it is in essence static; it characterizes movements *within* a given framework of institutions and relationships. *Development* is a different idea altogether: it is "spontaneous and discontinuous *change in the channels of the flow*" (1934, 64; emphasis added). In other words, it involves the transformation of the circular model. Such alterations of the system itself, affecting not merely the data of economics but the interactions among economic variables and groups, represented nothing less than a challenge to the existing orthodoxy. Such a theory as this does not entail consideration of a change in data such as "preferences" or "tastes," but requires something more fundamental; it requires a fundamental alteration "in the sphere of industrial and commercial life" (65).

To take an example of the nature of Schumpeter's theory, consider the basic economic forces of demand and supply. Supply in Schumpeter's model (as in Say's and other of the French economists) is the dynamic force, not demand or changes in wants. Schumpeter insisted that the view that production corresponds to changes in demand was simply wrong: the chain of events begins with production. The producer

> as a rule initiates economic change, and consumers are educated by him if necessary; they are, as it were, taught to want new things, or things which differ in some respect or other from those which they have been in the habit of using. (1934, 65)

Production—the dynamic force inducing change and therefore development in a capitalistic system—consists of a continual recombination of raw materials and the employment of innovative methods of combining factors. It also applies to the invention of a completely new product line.[58] This point is of critical importance. In general, the new

---

58. "Development in our sense is then defined by the carrying out of new combinations" (Schumpeter 1934, 66).

combinations (or new processes or products) represent a radical departure from the methods of the past and so are not simple evolutionary changes in existing methods undertaken by the old producers. The very process which results in the new combination eventually displaces the old, not by having the old conform to the new, but by forcing a "competitive elimination of the old" (1934, 67). This notion led Schumpeter to give yet another definition of development: "development consists primarily in employing existing resources in a different way, in doing new things with them, irrespective of whether those resources increase or not" (68).

In this process of innovation, of replacing the old with the new, the entrepreneur is most important. Unlike the thesis of Veblen, whereby the businessman (entrepreneur) is likened to a parasite on the social body, the entrepreneur for Schumpeter is the very embodiment of the system, "the mechanism of change" (1934, 6n.1). He is critical in forcing the system to undergo wrenching change, to introduce such fundamentally radical ideas into the routine as to destroy it and so allow a rebuilding on the rubble. Such a concept is so compelling, it is little wonder that this idea above all others was embraced so completely by the Japanese after the devastation of World War II and is at the heart of the industrial model known as the Japanese miracle.

Capitalism, Socialism, and Democracy   6.3

Among Schumpeter's greatest works, known even to the nonacademic public, is his 1942 *Capitalism, Socialism, and Democracy.*[59] One of the theses of this work Schumpeter stated in the Preface to the first edition: "I have tried to show that a socialist form of society will inevitably emerge from an equally inevitable decomposition of capitalist society" (Schumpeter 1950, xiii). He quite simply did not believe capitalism could survive, and in fact he explicitly stated so (61).

Not that Schumpeter was a conventional Marxist: he thought Marxism a form of religion, with its adherents dogmatic believers (worshipers at the temple), unwilling to accept dissent "once the Message has been revealed" (1950, 5n.1).[60] But he did appreciate that Marxism proved to be a great achievement, at least as rhetoric. It succeeded

> on the one hand, by formulating with unsurpassed force that feeling of being thwarted and ill treated which is the auto-therapeutic attitude of the unsuccessful many, and, on the other hand, by

59. We use here the third edition of 1950.

60. "To the believer it [Marxism] presents, first, a system of ultimate ends that embody the meaning of life and are absolute standards by which to judge events and actions; and, secondly, a guide to those ends which implies a plan of salvation and the indication of the evil from which mankind, or a chosen section of mankind, is to be saved" (Schumpeter 1950, 5).

proclaiming that socialistic deliverance from those ills was certainly amenable to rational proof. (1950, 6)

Thus did Schumpeter demonstrate the attractiveness of the doctrine of Marxism. He next had to demonstrate the problems associated with capitalism. Capitalism, he opined, would collapse not because of its failures, but rather because of its success: "its very success undermines the social institutions which protect it, and 'inevitably' creates conditions in which it will not be able to live and which strongly point to socialism as the heir apparent" (1950, 61).[61] To an examination of these conditions we now turn.

The problem with capitalism as a special case of a "commercial society" (according to Schumpeter) is that it succeeded in eventually destroying the very institutions responsible for its existence. Included here are the fundamental institutions of the free contract and the right of property, upon which rested private, individual economic activity. In the modern, bureaucratized corporate order, "individual contracting regulated by individual choice between an indefinite number of possibilities" was replaced by the institutionalized bureaucratic contract, "which presents but restricted freedom of choice and mostly turns on a *c'est à prendre ou à laisser*" (1950, 141). Likewise, shareholder capitalism—wherein managers and owners represent two distinct groups, a situation central to Veblen's interpretation of capitalism—had left the notion of property without any substance. The divorce of ownership and control created an environment ill-suited to individual private ownership and individual initiative, conditions basic to an understanding of the Smithian and Mandevillian social arrangement. As Schumpeter characterized it, the resulting institutional shift

> loosens the grip that once was so strong—the grip in the sense of the legal right and the actual ability to do as one pleases with one's own; the grip also in the sense that the holder of the title loses the will to fight, economically, physically, politically, for "his" factory and his control over it, to die if necessary on its steps. And this evaporation of what we may term the material substance of property—its visible and touchable reality—affects not only the attitude of holders but also that of the workmen and of the public in general. Dematerialized, defunctionalized and absentee ownership does not impress and call forth moral allegiance as the vital form of property did. Eventually there will be *nobody* left who really cares to stand for it—nobody within and nobody without the precincts of the big concerns. (1950, 142)

---

61. Schumpeter admitted at this point that his argument was consistent with that of Marxist writers on the subject, but suggested that "in order to accept it one does not need to be a socialist" (1950, 61). He was merely describing the obvious and the inevitable, not desiring the end he predicted.

A second problem lay in the process of capitalist development. By its very nature capitalism is evolutionary. The basis of this evolutionary character is, as we have seen above, creative destruction, a process by which the entrepreneur succeeds in devising new and different methods of production and organization in a continual effort to create new market opportunities where none exist.

It is, moreover, the theory of creative destruction which forces us to rethink the fundamental tenets of both classical and neoclassical value theory. Creative destruction as a viable alternative explanation of the capitalistic process demands an element of monopoly profit, which prevents prices from achieving a "market" equilibrium, prevents free entrance, and is certainly not efficient with resources; it is in fact the very antithesis of an efficient allocation model.[62] The perfectly competitive model of the classical economists is not a plausible archetype of the capitalistic process under these conditions. But capitalism is more than just a system of economic relationships; it represents not simply a theory of production, but is rather nothing less than a total theory of social relationships.

> The capitalist process rationalizes behavior and ideas and by so doing chases from our minds, along with metaphysical belief, mystic and romantic ideas of all sorts. Thus it reshapes not only our methods of attaining our ends but also these ultimate ends themselves. (1950, 127)

The problems leading to capitalism's demise are all of its own making. Taking an extreme example, Schumpeter noted that, should all wants be satisfied and all investment opportunities realized, there would be no reason for capitalism to continue: the entrepreneur would be irrelevant, as we would approach the very ideal of the textbook competitive model. Interest rates and profits would be forced to zero, and business management would be relegated to administration. This is nothing more than a realization of a socialist bureaucratic design.

Even in the "real world" in which this extreme does not hold, the economy nonetheless (according to Schumpeter) seemed to be approaching it or something very like it. Creative destruction, which had been the engine of capitalist progress and economic development, threatened to become routine activity, the progress it generated being more and more

---

62. According to Schumpeter, the perfectly competitive, efficient allocation model has never been itself more than a pedagogic device; it was never meant to describe conditions as they actually exist, since, when confronted with the actual data of economic life, its adherents have always chosen to abandon it.

"The introduction of new methods of production and new commodities is hardly conceivable with perfect—and perfectly prompt—competition from the start. And this means that the bulk of what we call economic progress is incompatible with it. As a matter of fact, perfect competition is and always has been temporarily suspended whenever anything new is being introduced" (1950, 105).

coordinated and managed.[63] The role of the entrepreneur he felt was being diminished, shifting from a revolutionary who takes risks and exploits new innovations, and by so doing generates new products and new markets, to a business specialist who calculates gains based on known costs and benefits. The entrepreneur of the capitalist system, once its very lifeblood, had threatened to become an obstacle to further development and innovation within the system itself.

As an alternative Schumpeter advanced the socialist form of enterprise. Within a centralized command and ownership structure (accepting that under socialism there is a determinate solution—the argument of Enrico Barone), the socialist model leads to greater productive efficiency than does the model of creative destruction:

> Those determinate solutions of the problems of production are rational or optimal from the standpoint of given data, and anything that shortens, smoothens or safeguards the road that leads to them is bound to save human energy and material resources, and to reduce the costs at which a given result is attained. Unless the resources thus saved are completely wasted, efficiency in our sense must necessarily increase. (1950, 194)

But efficiency arguments aside, Schumpeter was not completely sanguine about the transition from capitalism to socialism from a social (human) standpoint: "I have made it abundantly clear that in the nature of things there never can be a general case for socialism but only a case with reference to given social conditions and given historical stages" (1950, 200). "In fact, we need only assume that the ideas prevail which constitute what I have termed idyllic socialism in order to convince ourselves of the likelihood of complete and ludicrous failure" (218).

Nonetheless, Schumpeter believed that the true *essence* of socialism would inevitably prevail. The effects of capitalism would lead ultimately to the erection of institutional arrangements designed to ameliorate the more antisocial elements; government control would be ordained in an effort to give the economy a "human face." In Schumpeter's world, it was the intellectuals with their utopian dreams of a unified social organism in pursuit of a common goal of social betterment who would become disaffected with the capitalists' control of society and would lead the popular rebellion.

6.4 *An Assessment*

In recent years there has been a resurgence of interest in Schumpeter's work; there is even an organization—the International Joseph A. Schumpeter Society—which holds meetings every two years to discuss aspects of

---

63. See especially Schumpeter's chapter XII.

Schumpeter's work and carry on his tradition. He was an early advocate of econometrics (although he did not claim to have the technical capacity), and econometricians rightly claim him as one of their own; he was, after all, a founding member of the Econometric Society. His predictions about the efficiency of capitalism are remembered, while his companion theory of the collapse of capitalism is not. His ideas about the innovative role of the entrepreneur have blocked out his thoughts about the importance of class and the intellectuals. In short, Schumpeter worked both sides of the street. He was clever, and he had an eye for failings in the system.

The "New Institutionalists"   7

The Institutionalism of Commons, Mitchell, Veblen, and Schumpeter had by the mid-1940s been deemed irrelevant, or at least misdirected. While there had been significant achievements—in practice, the creation of social security legislation; in theory, introducing the importance of institutions and the evolutionary nature of economic organizations—the movement had appeared to many, especially those enraptured by the emerging Keynesian orthodoxy, as being too far removed from economic theorizing. In addition, the adherents of the "old" school were too often given to the formation of socialistic schemes in their policy pronouncements, and so were perceived as opponents of free-market individualist solutions.

In the 1970s, there emerged a new form of Institutionalism, the New Institutional Economics. This variant differed in fundamental ways from the original. For one, the perspective shifted from organicism to methodological individualism, as the "new" school adopted the methodological presuppositions of neoclassical (and Austrian) economic theory. Secondly, "economic man" was seen as a utility maximizer, not as one whose actions are the result of social habits; while conventions may constrain actions, man is indeed different from society. Yet the two have in common a disdain for mechanistic equilibrium and abstraction from time and place.[64]

Oliver Williamson is the most notable representative of the "new" variant of Institutionalism. In his 1975 *Markets and Hierarchies*, he argued that, by focusing on transactions as the basic unit of analysis, one could better understand both the firm and the market, and form an integrated theory of the two in contractual terms. This would allow a fuller treatment of such topics as industrial integration and even monopolistic

64. In support of the "old" form, there have sprung up professional societies devoted to the message, including the Association for Evolutionary Economics (which publishes *The Journal of Economic Issues*) and the European Association for Evolutionary Political Economy, as well as the already mentioned International Joseph A. Schumpeter Society (and its journal, *The Journal of Evolutionary Economics*).

competition, both at the level of the firm and the market. His "transactions" approach to economics is thus reminiscent in some respects of Commons's earlier theories, but is based on the neoclassical utility maximization model. Douglass C. North—a pioneer of the "new economic history"—has shown that traditional treatments of institutions have failed to account for the long-term evolution of economic systems and the importance of systemic as opposed to external factors affecting development (see especially North 1990, 1991). Even Hayek's economics, and the economics of Ludwig Lachmann, Israel Kirzner, and others in the Austrian tradition, can be seen as consistent with this "new" approach, as they have struggled with problems of information, custom, laws, rules, and the place of the entrepreneur in their analyses of economic change, problems at the core of the Institutional approach. Thus we see Institutional economics gaining a place as an alternative to the neoclassical model and its rigidity.

CHAPTER 12

What Do We Make of It All?

It is the true office of history to represent the events themselves, together with the counsels, and to leave the observations and conclusions thereupon to the liberty and faculty of every man's judgement.
FRANCIS BACON, *ADVANCEMENT OF LEARNING* (1605)

A book, like a child, needs time to be born. Books written quickly— within a few weeks—make me suspicious of the author. A respectable woman does not bring a child into the world before the ninth month.
HEINRICH HEINE, *THOUGHTS AND FANCIES* (1869)

It is difficult, if not impossible, for most people to think otherwise than in the fashion of their own period.
GEORGE BERNARD SHAW, *SAINT JOAN* (1923)

Formalism is an effort to give structure. But when structure becomes not instrumental but a blind end in and of itself, it becomes a parody and destroys insight and imagination. That is the point of the long-run popularity of Molière's *Les Précieuses Ridicules* and any number of modern TV sitcoms.   ANONYMOUS

Introduction and Recapitulation   I

Now we will attempt to come full circle and are prepared to assess the entire endeavor (up to this point). In the opening chapter we identified three magisterial interpretations of economics, those of Pribram, Schumpeter, and Mitchell. We added (cautiously) that, in our treatment, we desired to both build on and complement these syntheses. Thus here we return to the foundations of these interpretations to see the way in which an understanding of the role of patristic legacies can affect the study of economics. Our own interpretation thus incorporates an expanded consciousness of the role of the patristic legacies which underlie and shape our thinking about economics.

The first of our tasks in this concluding chapter is to identify some of the conflicts found in the underlying patristic traditions and discuss the ways in which economists, over time, have employed them. Having done so, we then turn to another, but related, topic—the reason we believe, counter to the current graduate-training trend, that the study of the history of economic thought must be an integral part of any understanding of the subject. In a nutshell, this chapter serves in a sense as an Apologia.

2 Patristic Legacy Contradictions and How They Created a Literature

We have already defined the notion of a "patristic legacy" and have noted the manner in which these legacies shape our perceptions of science and art and, indeed, virtually everything we identify with learning. Frequently, these perceptions are clearly identifiable, as in the case of portraying physics as the prototypical science.[1]

Another quality of patristic legacies is their ability to remain seemingly dormant for long periods of time. An example will help make this point. We mentioned early in this study Maimonides' twelfth-century "perception" of the economic notion of uncertainty. Having lain dormant for several centuries, the concept surfaced again in the work of Cantillon. It then went through another period of dormancy, after which it seems to have been discovered "finally" (meaning that it did not disappear again) by Thünen, whose grasp of it was frail when compared to that of the "revisionists" Frank H. Knight and John Maynard Keynes (especially as seen in the latter's *Treatise on Probability*).

While other examples could be cited, the point is that our fascination with identifying and discussing patristic legacies derives from the belief that they are a tool useful in making sense of, and even giving structure to, an amorphous mass of sometimes contradictory conclusions. The magisterial interpretations which serve to give form to these legacies are essentially "modern" interpretive frameworks into which one fits the substance of past doctrines and dogma. These frameworks themselves then serve to shape perceptions further.

Among the educated, inherited patristic legacies are frequently believed to be more complex than those underlying the thought of the majority. While they may descend from different sources—sometimes shaped by personal idiosyncrasy, religious teaching, or the interpretation of personal experience—most of them can be seen as derivative from the same body of knowledge which is our general cultural heritage. Various legacies (important, since one legacy may reinforce another) can and oftentimes do mesh

---

1. The great physicist Isaac Newton not only was concerned with mechanics, but was one of the two inventors of the calculus (he called it *fluxions*). Newtonian physics predicated stability in terms of an equilibrium of forces. Economists, either interested in aping physicists or exploiting the calculus in its own right, came to point their economic investigations at the determination of equilibrium conditions. Had they sought to emulate biologists instead, they would not have sought after equilibrium, but rather after conditions encouraging mutations of one sort of another. The joke is that Newtonian physics was outmoded at least half a century ago, at the time Hubbell suggested (and others seem to have proven) that the universe was not in equilibrium, but rather is still expanding. Accordingly, modern physicists at their frontier have themselves gone beyond focusing solely on equilibrium conditions. Yet for the majority of economists, the patristic legacy of Newtonian physics, with its emphasis on equilibrium, remains dominant; it explains what they are looking for and perhaps what they choose to see.

to form a new *Gestalt*. Yet the reverse may also be true: at times these formative legacies seem to be in total conflict, or at least in conflict within certain bounds, and we may momentarily (if not longer) seem to make our own, often hodgepodge, choices. Isaiah Berlin, whose philosophical influence is much greater in Britain than elsewhere (and that fact, itself, can be explained in nationalistic patristic terms), accepts enthusiastically an essential disorganization in his own intellectual inheritance. This disorder is not so great as that experienced by Descartes—whose logical and precise mind despised intellectual "messiness"—because in essence for Berlin ideas are a tool (a means) in the process of man's self-realization, while for Descartes ideas were ends in themselves, approaching and even achieving the status of full truth. The difference is telling also with respect to the character of the cultures into which we are born and in which we flourish. Were one boldly to paint with a broom, one may hold that the charm of the British culture has been its reliance upon tests of practical success (some might call it a "pragmatic" quality), while part of the charm of the French culture (in Descartes's time and now) is its overwhelming devotion to tests of immanent symmetric strength. For a Berlin-type pluralist, the inconsistency between legacies is more of a *curiosum* than a conflict where one must take sides. On the other hand, Berlin's intellectual pluralism can drive logicians to the point of madness.

Some Patristic Traditions Affecting Economics   3

The Legacies of Communitarianism and Individualism   3.1

For our purposes it suffices to commence, as we did in the beginning of this study, with the views of Hobbes, Locke, and Rousseau. Each was as we have seen interested in the nature of successful community organization. Hobbes, persuaded that man was essentially too selfish or brutish to live communally if left to his own devices, believed that social communities had to of necessity be established by a superior force, to be modified later, as the need arose, by some general rationalizations (the social and government contracts). Rousseau, writing in the Cartesian tradition, held that if man's natural goodness were allowed expression (his version of the social contract), pure reason would eventually reign, and communities would take on a utopian grace.

Locke's criticism of Hobbes was both profound and reactive. Locke's view of social organization was predicated, first, on a Christian patristic legacy of individualism and, later, on a denial of full-spectrum communitarian power. While Hobbes and Rousseau were proceeding in opposite directions yet on the same track—both dealt principally with communitarianism as the ideal social form of organization, with Hobbes seeing it as the necessary product of man's need to protect himself from the vileness of others, and Rousseau perceiving it as a natural consequence of the expression of man's undeniable goodness—Locke and Rousseau were clearly at cross purposes, in that each denied the premises of the other. Locke began with the individual's God-given rights and a reasonable willingness to allow the state to exercise specified and very limited powers, while Rousseau began with the community and the willingness of unsoiled men to aggregate and work cheerfully to the community's purpose. We see then that Rousseau eschewed both the Lockean perception of the centrality of individualism and the Lockean belief in limiting the powers of government.

Later writers simply built on these designs. Starting with Hobbes's assumption of society as a jungle, Mandeville, for example, emerged with an argument leading to Rousseau's outcome but, of course, totally denying Rousseau's premises. While if anything the physiocrats were communitarian-minded and in the Rousseauian mold (understandable given the French cultural reverence for Rousseau), the British utilitarians, primarily committed to the Lockean traditions of individualism and limited governmental powers, only occasionally slipped into communitarian thinking.[2] Smith himself embraced both traditions, very clearly influenced by the physiocrats' communitarianism.[3]

Later French writers such as Cournot and Walras dealt with individual choice, but that choice was understood as leading to a communitarian consequence. Cournot sought to show logically how individual monopolists could maximize their profits, but his purpose was simply to identify areas of possible communitarian taxation. So, too, Walras, whose works (if and when they are actually read) are permeated with communitarian concerns.

The German Romantic and Historical Schools likewise seem to have appropriated the very same approaches. Both commenced with Rousseauian communitarian assumptions, but were eventually driven to Hobbesian conclusions: Prussia emerged as the Leviathan, the force that gave order to society. The Austrians (particularly Carl Menger, Böhm-Bawerk, Mises, and Hayek), again by way of contrast, seem to have begun as did the German Romantic and Historical Schools, with a communitarian focus, but in their later embrace of Lockean individualism, they came not to a nationalistic but rather to a free trade (internationalistic) conclusion. The German Historical School differed from its alleged successor, the American Institutionalists (particularly Commons

---

2. Shortly before the Second World War, the Royal Economic Society commissioned William Stark, a communitarian leftist, to produce a compilation of Bentham's papers. He did so in three volumes. What was amazing was that he managed to unearth so many statements in Bentham which had a communitarian premise.

3. Even if the deathbed story of his approving Bentham's *Letters on Usury* is apocryphal (and that is likely), it appears as though Bentham's position would likely have been acceptable.

after 1900 and perhaps Mitchell—and only possibly at times Veblen) in that the latter held to, if anything, a Hobbesian communitarian focus while absorbing along the way a strong commitment to a Lockean outcome, that is, the inherent nature of limited governmental power and largely the individual's right of choice.

The Methodological Legacies of Descartes's Scientific Truth   3.2
and Bacon's Scientific Process: Rationality versus Reason

As believers in Natural Law, many of the seventeenth-century writers both in Britain and on the Continent were inclined to give credence to the proposition respecting the regularity of certain phenomena, if only because they could demonstrate it empirically. However, such credence varied between thinking along the path advocated by Plato (a view quite consistent with such Church Fathers as St. Augustine) and the path advocated by Aristotle (a view endorsed by St. Thomas Aquinas). (Readers will recall that Pribram based his magisterial interpretation of early economic [Scholastic] thought on the consistency over the ages of choices between one and the other.)

What Platonists found persuasive was the test of immanent criticism—whether the argument held together logically. The Aristotelians, while occasionally persuaded by that test, preferred an empirical test in observable matters. In many ways Descartes became the effective successor of Plato. Being a communicant Roman Catholic, he did not deny revelation (something which clearly did not pass a test of logical precision), but for matters associated with nonrevealed regularities (as the Natural Law) he preferred a version of Plato's method. Descartes's *science* thus involved at least two important aspects: (1) it was based on logic, and (2) it related to a wide variety of disciplines. In all, the linkage in most instances was the application of the mathematical method, a purely logical technique the symbolism of which made it useful as a common language.

While the "parentage" of Descartes is evident, it is less obvious that Francis Bacon in Britain was the successor of Aristotle. Although Bacon's vision (or spectrum of interests) was much narrower than Aristotle's, he was clearly devoted to basing conclusions on cognitive observations. Bacon's particular contribution to science generally (and economics tangentially) was a research program of systematic observation and intellectual consolidation—his scientific method. But insofar as anyone was the successor to Aristotle, one can argue Bacon's case as successfully as any other.

Hobbes himself served an apprenticeship with Bacon as his Latin amanuensis. Hobbes and systematic logic were, we must accept, hardly fellow travelers, and insofar as the opening chapters of Hobbes's *Leviathan* tout anything, they tout systematic observation. Yet we will not argue that Hobbes was a pure "Baconian," instead being content to observe only that his work was closer to Bacon's than it was to Descartes's sense of science. Hobbes included a great deal that was not the result of systematic observation so much as imaginative speculation.

Irrespective of its origin, it seems clear that British Utilitarianism was well in the Aristotelian tradition, one which involved empiricism as well as analysis. Its tenets did not appeal to Cartesian logic; if anything they were generated within the framework of Bacon's scientific method. Further, insofar as Utilitarianism dominated the thinking of economists, especially in nineteenth-century Britain, they were ipso facto operating within the shadow of Bacon's perception of science, Jevons admittedly so. While Jevons was, at times, an ardent advocate of the use of mathematical expression, we can conclude that, in his advocacy of the philosophy of Utilitarianism, he embraced both legacies, drawing from the one the powers of the maximization calculus and from the other a "common sense" (derived from Baconian observation) view of individuals' likely preferences. When Jevons and his "disciple," Wicksteed, turned to mathematics, they did so more in the spirit which Marshall was later to characterize as efficiently exemplative for those learning the subject, rather than vital. The mathematics they knew was not high-powered; their handling of logic was more so.

By way of stark contrast, both Walras and Pareto (insofar as his economics was concerned) frequently wrote within the confines of Cartesian logic. Such errors as Pareto corrected in Walras's work were logical flaws, not empirical corrections. Yet, Pareto's economics, particularly his Law of Income Distribution, was clearly empirical, derived in a way quite consistent with Bacon's, not Descartes's, perception of science.[4] Yet there is a strong paradoxical element to Pareto. His economics, as we have just noted, was mostly Cartesian, while his various "laws" were synthetic. The paradox arises when one considers his last major book, *Trattato di Sociologia Generale* (translated into English as *Mind and Society*), in which he delineated economics from sociology by the test of (Cartesian) rationality. Why this sharp break? Perhaps it was simply ideological: his road to this conclusion involved much ideological experimentation. He began his intellectual career as a free-trade liberal (his economics there were based on Cartesian rationality), then briefly examined Marxism with an eye to adopting its views, but it did not appeal to him. On the other hand, his stance may simply have been no more than an effort at clarifying and classifying his own intellectual adventures. By 1911 he had decided that he was no longer interested in teaching economics (preferring something less restrictive) and sought permission to retire. From

---

4. Pareto also observed, based on his experience as a professional engineer, that in the typical production process a very small number of intermediate goods were accountable for a very large part of the costs. The inference was that cost control ought to start with those goods. J. Ignacio Lopes (of General Motors and Volkswagen fame) apparently utilized this law to the benefit of the corporate bottom line.

there he shifted to writing his major treatise on sociology.[5] His attitude during the development of his cynical disillusionment became effectively Hobbesian—men were cynical, ungenerous, and rarely guided by rational considerations.

The Patristic Legacy of the Right to Private Property   3.3

Aristotle believed that private ownership of property would lead to its being better maintained, an observation based on a consequentalist understanding of human actions. Locke's view, however, was predicated on another assumption: God, as viewed by the Christians, gave man the right to his own labor, and so what he produced was his personal estate (property). From the standpoint of modern economics, particularly as seen now in America and Europe, it was in Locke's assertion of the individual's rights to life, liberty, and property that we find the strongest statement of the principle, one that became the bedrock of the idea of a free market.

If individual ownership of land (realty) was originally the *exemplar*, ownership of chattels soon followed. In recent times efforts have been made, often successfully, to make the job-right a form of property right. Lately, the notion of intellectual rights as property rights has become a major focus, often the basis of discussion of American trade and foreign policy. Yet in the Rousseau-influenced sphere, individual property rights have not played so key a role. Here the focus is more on community needs than individual rights, so the centrality of property rights is not overwhelmingly apparent. We must stress, however, that this is not to assert that in all communitarian systems property rights do not exist, for even in Lenin's Soviet Union consumption goods were privately owned (it was producer goods which effectively belonged to the community—in name the workers, in effect the party or the state). The point reflects merely the degree of importance placed on the right of ownership and the place of the individual in the social sphere.

The Centrality of Work: The Labor Factor   3.4
versus Marginal Analysis

The theme of the status of work in society comes not from the Greek legacy but from an earlier Biblical source. If for the Greeks work was the role assigned to lesser types (not for the thinkers or the fighters), for the Jews and later the Christians work was both the result of Man's

---

5. This shift can be explained as a highly idiosyncratic episode: in the last thoroughly disillusioned years of his life he was honored by Mussolini (who sought to get points by honoring Pareto's brilliance), but totally ignored the honor (thus indicating a less than reciprocal opinion of *il Duce*).

Disobedience and yet (surely in the Jewish view) the source of his own physical independence.

Locke, an ardent Protestant, was Bible-oriented and so paid far more attention to the teachings of the Old Testament than did those steeped in the Roman Catholic and High-Church Anglican traditions. While Locke tutored in the Greek classics, it was that Biblical legacy which governed his judgments. Smith accepted the Lockean system as a given, and while he explicitly doubted that workers really could take care of themselves in market competition, he did express for them his overwhelming sympathy and moral endorsement; labor became critical to his theory of economic value. Ricardo also made labor the keystone of his theory of value, a position which after his time came really to define who is and who is not a classical economist.

Marx took Ricardo and extended him far beyond his own set bounds. Labor was redefined as labor power and endowed with the historical and moral authority for ownership. True, Marx's moral authority shifted the focus from individualism to communitarianism; but it was labor that compelled the radical reorientation.

3.5   The Preferred Way of Economic Life

Marx argued that each technological economic system (the foundation) created its own moral code (the superstructure). Thus the preferred way of life was essentially a technology spin-off. Some, particularly the ecclesiastics and Kant, argued that, irrespective of changes in the ways in which people produce and consume, there exist certain timeless moral absolutes. Irrespective of whether one accepts the Marxian general explanation for changes in the ways of life or one accepts that there are patristic legacies that stress immutabilities, it is certainly clear that, over recorded historical time, the roles of different economic activities have involved different divisions of the labor force.

It is a common exercise in conjectural history (*histoire raisonnée*) to argue that civilizations began with hunting and fishing, followed by the herding and domestication of animals for consumption. The next phase was agronomic, combining all the previous phases with the planting and tilling of crops. There presumably was always some trading, but the forms of trade evolved from straight barter to the use of a monetary (or some such) medium and ultimately to the development of several kinds of credit.

Modern economics is usually considered to have begun with the last phase, when most of the population lived in an agricultural economy, but where a transition to industrial production was just commencing. There are at least two patristic influences which are then apparent: the first deals with a conviction that the real economy was basically agricultural, and the second concerns interpersonal relations.

Obviously the physiocrats perceived the social order as bound by agriculture. Smith seemed to have assumed the same form of order. Both Ricardo and Malthus, while aware of the growth of the manufacturing sector, still believed that, in the end, the residual legatee was invariably the owner of land. Yet, the problems of factory labor were beginning to emerge at this time. Malthus was particularly frightened by the impending (and inevitable, he thought) industrial labor unrest, and Ricardo, perhaps influenced by Henry Thornton, came to realize that the substitution of machinery for labor aggravated the situation.

In terms of interpersonal relations and the social ethos, there was a difference between Smith and Malthus (on the one hand) and Ricardo (on the other). Smith and Malthus came from the gentry, Ricardo from a minority group involved in trading. Smith and Malthus favored the traditional agricultural society principles of status;[6] whatever Ricardo personally favored, his economics was predicated on contract.

The generation of Nassau Senior and John Stuart Mill came to face the fact that a growing proportion of the population worked and lived in an industrial manufacturing society, and that such a society was associated with great evils—what seemed to them the inhumane treatment of children, women, and, in the case of Mill particularly, working men. Both were interested in protective labor legislation, enactments which applied not to agricultural but to manufacturing employment.[7] It goes without any comment that the world of Owen, Hodgskin, and Marx was entirely focused on manufacturing employment.

Until recently (as we will note in the companion volume) "labor problems" were at the heart of labor economics. The old principle of status gave way; the foundation of manufacturing economics was the contract. Contracts were perceived in many different ways. The point of Commons's Institutional Economics, particularly as that point has more recently been picked up by such as Coase and Williamson, was that contracts have several faces and serve several quite different purposes. But the switch from status to contract was not the only change. Manufacturing led to widespread specialization, which in turn made every worker

6. In Shakespeare's *Merchant of Venice*, Antonio, a gentleman of the "old agricultural tradition," asks no questions about Bassano's ability to pay. Antonio boasts that their friendship was everything; the only trouble was that Antonio had no cash on hand. Shylock by contrast was a maximizer. One interpretation of Shakespeare's intent is that Shakespeare preferred the older values of fellowship, a world that clearly started to disappear with the emergence of Mercantilism. Ricardo's world was much more cynical. Of course we are not implying that Ricardo, himself, did not prefer the world of the gentry; indeed, his marriage and his style of life illustrates that he did.

7. Marx to the end of his life was obsessed with the inability of the agricultural proletariat to recognize their class identity.

in a manufacturing economy dependent on the market, both for his household income and for most of its consumption.[8]

4 The Role of Rhetoric

Here we come to a most troubling legacy, one which deals with the manner in which issues can be presented so that they conform as much as possible to (or conflict as little as possible with) the patristic legacies of the listener. Both Jevons and Marshall (among countless others) were alert to the problem. Their advice was to formulate ideas, insofar as possible, in logical (mathematical) terms, while at the same time expressing them in prose. The mathematical *rhetoric* is sufficient for expression, while the use of mathematical *equations* tends to obscure more than is revealed. The question one needs to face is more profound: How does one persuade? One answer is to choose the form of proof to which the auditor most easily responds—whether this be logic, evidence, or conformity to some of his patristic legacies.

But there is another, more difficult, answer, one which at times deals with the differences between generalization and abstraction, and in other instances is associated with analogy. It was not for nothing that Aesop wrote his fables, Jesus spoke his parables, and generations of young people were taught their value systems through the reading of history, and particularly biographies. Patristic legacies in the field of rhetoric are just too important to ignore. The quip "But that is anecdotal evidence" may serve to improve the scientific nature of a discourse; but anecdotal evidence is, nonetheless, persuasive to many who either do not know or are not impressed with scientific presentations. Insofar as economics employs epistemic assumptions, anecdotal evidence in the form of fables, parables, or stories from history plays a role. D. McCloskey has made a recent career of just this point. In *The Rhetoric of Economics* (1985) and *Knowledge and Persuasion in Economics* (1993), McCloskey maintained that economics should be viewed as a continuing conversation: the task of the economist is, after all, to *persuade*. In seeking to persuade, he must employ the tools that best allow the message to get across. The fact that empirical studies have thus far failed to resolve many of the differences among economists suggests that a more persuasive method of reasoning is needed. After all, to quote Marshall McLuhan, "the medium is the message." McCloskey of course did not invent the idea that the appropriate

---

8. Since 1970 there has been an emerging consciousness of new venues of change—the popular term is *postindustrialism*. This is not a topic within the purview of this volume, but we mention it simply to indicate that as technology has evolved other changes are occurring—not the least of which is a heightened awareness of the market importance of intellectual property.

rhetoric is important in attempting to persuade an audience, but she did succeed in showing how and when it can be employed.

This brings us to the next point: Why professional economists should know something about the history of their discipline.

Why Study the History of Economic Thought?   5

Some study history because it is there. After all, if "being there" is reason enough to climb mountains, it may be reason enough to study old books. Others eschew the study of the past as an intellectual luxury they simply cannot afford. Such was the view of Charles Snow in his famous Rede Lectures on "The Two Cultures." Snow's point was that the past was not only impoverished but that it was full of superstition and other errors. He thus advocated concentration on what he called the culture of science, by which he likely meant both the Baconian and the Cartesian types.

Doubtless there is much to be said for his opinion. Science has made great strides by ignoring previous "discoveries," employing instead replication of controlled experiments. However, we disagree with Snow's position. We have regularly asserted that economic thinking contains a great deal of epistemic material, and while much economic material can be observed as "hard" data, so long as there are epistemic foundations in economic literature it is critically important that economists come to grips with what shapes those elements. We study the past because that is where the data are. More importantly, not only are the data there, but much of the data can be best explained by putting them into historical and cultural context. For us, a major part of the cultural context is appreciating one's intellectual baggage, that is, one's patristic legacies.

There was until recently a general requirement that professional economists should know not only the history of their own discipline but also some of the cognate or parent disciplines. Under such conditions, graduate students were examined on what they knew of the discipline's past, and under pain of failure they often memorized titles, names, and dates. Such efforts—including formal language requirements that allow a more broad spectrum of economic ideas to be read—came to be seen as a waste of students' time. There was too much else, particularly mathematics and econometrics, to be mastered. As a result, the history of thought went the way of the language requirements.

While we are convinced that knowing the history of economics is important so that one can appreciate the critical significance of epistemic perceptions (and the influence they have even on hard data), we cannot think of a way to convince all others that we are right. It is not merely a matter of rhetorical choice. In the end it may come down to what type of economist one wants to be—a technocrat or an architect. Iphigenia Sulzberg, of the *New York Times* family, offers the parable of meeting several workmen. The first, when asked what he was doing, said that he was laying bricks; the second went beyond and said that he was building a wall. It was the third who understood what his life was spent doing; he said that he was building a cathedral. It is an elegant parable. Unfortunately not only do few economists have the architectural vision, but—what is even worse—a great many aspire to being no more than technocrats, that is, "bricklayers." And they generally get their wish, which may be the real punishment.

References

Albee, Ernest. 1902. *A History of English Utilitarianism.* London: Swan Sonnenschein and Co., Ltd.

Alchian, Armen A. 1987. "Property Rights." In John Eatwell, Murray Milgate, and Peter Newman, eds., *The New Palgrave: A Dictionary of Economics.* London: Macmillan.

Allen, Robert Loring. 1991. *Opening Doors: The Life and Work of Joseph Schumpeter.* 2 vols. New Brunswick, N.J.: Transaction Publishers.

Allen, William R. 1970. "Modern Defenders of Mercantilist Theory." *History of Political Economy,* vol. 2, no. 2 (fall), 381–97.

———. 1973. "Rearguard Response [to Coats, 1973]." *History of Political Economy,* vol. 5, no. 2 (fall), 496–98.

American Economic Association. 1887. "Report of the Organization of the American Economic Association." *Publications of the American Economic Association,* vol. I, 5–9; "Constitution of the American Economic Association," 35–37.

Aquinas, St. Thomas. *Summa Theologiæ.* Ed. and trans. Marcus Lefébure. London: Eyre and Spottiswoode; New York: McGraw-Hill.

Aristotle. *Politics.* Ed. Stephen Everson. Cambridge: Cambridge University Press.

Ashley, William. [1914] 1949. *The Economic Organization of England.* London: Longmans, Green and Co.

Aspromourgos, Tony. 1988. "The Life of William Petty in Relation to His Economics: A Tercentenary Interpretation." *History of Political Economy,* vol. 20, no. 3 (fall), 337–56.

Ayer, A. J. 1952. *Language, Truth, and Logic.* 2d ed. New York: Dover.

———. 1984. *Philosophy in the Twentieth Century.* New York: Vintage Books.

Backhaus, Jürgen G. 1995. "Introduction: Wilhelm Roscher (1817–1894)— A Centenary Reappraisal." *Journal of Economic Studies* (special issue: *Wilhelm Roscher and the "Historical Method,"* Jürgen G. Backhaus, ed.) vol. 22, nos. 3/4/5, 4–15.

Backhouse, Roger. 1985. *A History of Modern Economic Analysis.* New York: Basil Blackwell.

Bain, Alexander. 1882. *James Mill: A Biography.* London: Longmans, Green, and Co. (reprinted by Augustus M. Kelley, New York, 1967).

Barber, William J., ed. 1988. *Breaking the Academic Mould: Economists and American Higher Learning in the Nineteenth Century.* Middletown, Conn.: Wesleyan University Press.

Barbon, Nicholas. [1690] 1903. *A Discourse of Trade.* A Reprint of Economic Tracts, ed. Jacob Hollander. Baltimore: Johns Hopkins University Press.

Beccaria, Cesare. [1764] 1986. *On Crimes and Punishments.* Indianapolis: Hackett.

Beck, Herrmann. 1995. *The Origin of the Authoritarian Welfare State in Prussia.* Ann Arbor: University of Michigan Press.

Beer, Max. 1939. *An Inquiry into Physiocracy.* New York: George Allen and Unwin.

———. 1940. *A History of British Socialism.* 2 vols. London: George Allen and Unwin.

Bentham, Jeremy. [1787] 1952. *Defence of Usury.* In W. Stark, ed., *Jeremy Bentham's Economic Writings.* London: George Allen and Unwin Ltd.

———. [1789] 1948. *An Introduction to the Principles of Morals and Legislation.* New York: Hafner and Co.

———. [1802a] 1843. *Principles of the Civil Code.* In John Bowring, ed., *The Works of Jeremy Bentham.* Vol. I. Edinburgh: William Tait.

———. [1802b] 1931. *The Theory of Legislation.* Ed. C. K. Ogden. London: Kegan Paul, Trench, Trubner, and Co., Ltd.

———. 1952. *Jeremy Bentham's Economic Writings.* Edited by W. Stark. London: George Allen and Unwin Ltd.

Berle, Adolph A., and Gardner C. Means. 1932. *The Modern Corporation and Private Property.* New York: Macmillan.

Berlin, Isaiah. 1958. *Two Concepts of Liberty.* Oxford: Clarendon Press.

———. 1964. "Hobbes, Locke, and Professor Macpherson." *The Political Quarterly,* vol. 35, 444–68.

———. 1980. *Against the Current: Essays in the History of Ideas.* New York: Viking Press.

Bianchi, Marina. 1993. "How to Learn Sociality: True and False Solutions to Mandeville's Problem." *History of Political Economy,* vol. 25, no. 2 (summer), 209–40.

Black, R. D. Collison. 1972a. "Jevons, Marginalism, and Manchester." *The Manchester School,* vol. XL, no. 1 (March), 2–8.

———. 1972b. "W. S. Jevons and the Foundation of Modern Economics." *History of Political Economy,* vol. 4, no. 2 (fall), 364–78.

Blaug, Mark. 1972. "Was There a Marginal Revolution?" *History of Political Economy,* vol. 4, no. 2 (fall), 269–80.

———. 1985. *Economic Theory in Retrospect.* 4th ed. Cambridge: Cambridge University Press.

———. 1987. "Classical Economics." In John Eatwell, Murray Milgate, and Peter Newman, eds., *The New Palgrave: A Dictionary of Economics.* London: Macmillan.

Bodin, Jean. [1576] 1962. *Six livres de la republique.* (Translated in 1606 as *Six Books of the Commonwealth.*) Cambridge, Mass.: Harvard University Press.

Böhm-Bawerk, Eugen von. 1959. *Capital and Interest.* Vol. I: *History and Critique of Interest Theories;* Vol. II: *The Positive Theory of Capital;* Vol. III: *Further Essays on Capital and Interest.* Translated by Hans F. Sennholz. South Holland, Ill.: Libertarian Press.

Bonar, James. 1910. "Classical Economists." In R. H. Inglis Palgrave, ed., *Dictionary of Political Economy.* London: Macmillan (reprinted by Gale Research Co., Detroit, Mich., 1976).

Boorstin, Daniel J. 1983. *The Discoverers: A History of Man's Search to Know His World and Himself.* New York: Vintage.

Bowley, Marian. 1937. *Nassau Senior and Classical Economics*. London: Allen and Unwin.

——. 1972. "The Predecessors of Jevons—the Revolution that Wasn't." *The Manchester School*, vol. XL, no. 1 (March), 9–29.

Brentano, Ludwig Josef. 1888. *Die classische Nationalökonomie*. Leipzig.

Brewer, Anthony. 1988. "Cantillon and Mercantilism." *History of Political Economy*, vol. 20, no. 3 (fall), 447–60.

——. 1992. "Petty and Cantillon." *History of Political Economy*, vol. 24, no. 3 (fall), 711–28.

Buck, Philip W. 1942. *The Politics of Mercantilism*. New York: Henry Holt and Co.

Burns, Arthur F., and Wesley C. Mitchell. 1946. *Measuring Business Cycles*. New York: National Bureau of Economic Research.

Burns, Arthur R. 1936. *The Decline of Competition*. New York: McGraw-Hill.

Bury, J. E. 1932. *The Idea of Progress*. New York: Macmillan.

Cairnes, John E. [1888] 1965. *The Character and Logical Method of Political Economy*. 2d ed. New York: Augustus M. Kelley.

Caldwell, Bruce. 1982. *Beyond Positivism: Economic Methodology in the Twentieth Century*. London: George Allen and Unwin.

——. 1984. "Praxeology and Its Critics: An Appraisal." *History of Political Economy*, vol. 16, no. 3 (fall), 363–79.

——. 1986. "Towards a Broader Conception of Criticism." *History of Political Economy*, vol. 18, no. 4 (winter), 675–81.

Campbell, R. H., and A. S. Skinner. 1982. *The Origins and Nature of the Scottish Enlightenment*. Edinburgh: John Donald.

Cantillon, Richard. [1755] 1964. *Essai sur la Nature du Commerce en General*. Edited and translated by Henry Higgs. New York: Augustus M. Kelley.

Carabelli, Anna. 1988. *On Keynes's Method*. New York: St. Martin's Press.

Champernowne, D. G. 1959. "Arthur Cecil Pigou 1877–1959." *Journal of the Royal Statistical Society*, vol. CXXII, part II, 263–65.

Child, Sir Josiah. [1668] 1968. *Brief Observations Concerning Trade and Interest of Money*. Reprinted in *Sir Josiah Child: Selected Works, 1668–1697*. Farnborough, UK: Gregg Press.

——. 1690. *A New Discourse of Trade*. London: S. Crouch, T. Horn, and J. Hindmarsh.

Chitnis, Anand C. 1976. *The Scottish Enlightenment: A Social History*. London: Croom Helm.

Christ, Carl. 1952. *Economic Theory and Measurement: A Twenty Year Research Report, 1932–1952*. Cowles Commission for Research in Economics, University of Chicago.

Christensen, Paul P. 1989. "Hobbes and the Physiological Origins of Economic Science." *History of Political Economy*, vol. 21, no. 4 (winter), 689–709.

Cirillo, Renato. 1981. "The Influence of Auguste Walras on Léon Walras." *American Journal of Economics and Sociology*, vol. 40, no. 3 (July), 309–16.

——. 1983. "Was Vilfredo Pareto Really a 'Precursor' of Fascism?" *American Journal of Economics and Sociology*, vol. 42, no. 2 (April), 235–45.

——. 1984. "Léon Walras and Social Justice." *American Journal of Economics and Sociology*, vol. 43, no. 1 (January), 53–60.

Clark, John Bates. [1899] 1965. *The Distribution of Wealth: A Theory of Wages, Interest and Profits.* New York: Augustus M. Kelley.

———. 1914. *The Philosophy of Wealth: Economic Principles Newly Formulated.* Boston: Ginn and Company.

Clark, John Maurice. 1929. "Thorstein Bundy Veblen, 1857–1929." *The American Economic Review,* vol. XIX, no. 4 (December), 742–45.

———. 1968. "Clark, John Bates." In David L. Sills, ed., *International Encyclopedia of the Social Sciences.* New York: Macmillan and Free Press.

Clough, Shepard Bancroft, and Charles Woolsey Cole. 1952. *Economic History of Europe.* Boston: D. C. Heath.

Coase, Ronald H. 1972. "The Appointment of Pigou as Marshall's Successor." *Journal of Law and Economics,* vol. XV, no. 1 (April), 473–85.

———. 1984. "Alfred Marshall's Mother and Father." *History of Political Economy,* vol. 16, no. 4 (winter), 519–27.

Coats, A. W. 1967. "Alfred Marshall and the Early Development of the London School of Economics: Some Unpublished Letters." *Economica,* n.s., vol. XXXIV, no. 136 (November), 408–17.

———. 1973. "The Interpretation of Mercantilist Economics: Some Historiographical Problems." *History of Political Economy,* vol. 5, no. 2 (fall), 485–95.

Cole, Charles Woolsey. 1931. *French Mercantilist Doctrines Before Colbert.* New York: Smith.

———. 1939. *Colbert and a Century of French Mercantilism.* Two vols. New York: Columbia University Press.

———. 1943. *French Mercantilism, 1683–1700.* New York: Columbia University Press.

———. 1992. *On the History of Economic Thought.* London and New York: Routledge.

———. 1993. *The Sociology and Professionalization of Economics.* London and New York: Routledge.

Coleman, D. C. 1969. *Revisions in Mercantilism.* London: Methuen.

Coleman, William Oliver. 1995. *Rationalism and Anti-Rationalism in the Origins of Economics: The Philosophical Roots of Eighteenth Century Economic Thought.* Aldershot: Edward Elgar.

Commons, John Rogers. [1893] 1965. *The Distribution of Wealth.* New York: Augustus M. Kelley.

———. 1919. *Industrial Goodwill.* New York: McGraw Hill.

———. 1921. *Industrial Government.* New York: Macmillan.

———. [1924] 1974. *The Legal Foundations of Capitalism.* Clifton, N.J.: Augustus M. Kelley.

———. 1934. *Institutional Economics.* New York: Macmillan.

———. 1950. *The Economics of Collective Action.* New York: Macmillan.

Commons, John R., and Associates. 1919. *History of Labour in the United States.* 2 vols. New York: Macmillan.

Copleston, Frederick. 1963. *A History of Philosophy,* vol. VII: *Modern Philosophy.* Westminster, Md.: Newman Press.

Cournot, Augustin. [1838] 1963. *Researches into the Mathematical Principles of the Theory of Wealth.* Trans. by Nathaniel T. Bacon. Homewood, Ill.: Richard D. Irwin.

Creedy, John. 1980. "Some Recent Interpretations of *Mathematical Psychics.*" *History of Political Economy,* vol. 12, no. 2 (summer), 267–76.

Čuhel, Franz. [1907] 1995. "On the Theory of Needs." In Israel M. Kirzner, ed., *Classics in Austrian Economics: A Sampling in the History of a Tradition.* London: William Pickering.

Cunningham, W. [1907] 1968. *The Growth of English Industry and Commerce in Modern Times.* 4th ed. New York: Augustus M. Kelley.

———. [1910] 1968. *The Growth of English Industry and Commerce During the Early and Middle Ages.* 5th ed. New York: Augustus M. Kelley.

Dahrendorf, Ralf. 1995. *LSE: A History of the London School of Economics and Political Science, 1895–1995.* New York: Oxford University Press.

Daunton, Martin J. 1995. *Progress and Poverty: An Economic and Social History of Britain 1700–1850.* New York: Oxford University Press.

Davenant, Charles. 1695. *Essays upon the Ways and Means of Supplying the War.*

———. 1699. *An Essay upon the Probable Methods of Making a People Gainers in the Ballance of Trade.* London: James Knapton.

David, F. N. 1968. "Galton, Francis." In David L. Sills, ed., *International Encyclopedia of the Social Sciences.* New York: Macmillan and Free Press.

Deane, Phyllis M. 1978. *The Evolution of Economic Ideas.* Cambridge: Cambridge University Press.

———. 1987a. "King, Gregory." In John Eatwell, Murray Milgate, and Peter Newman, eds., *The New Palgrave: A Dictionary of Economics.* London: Macmillan.

———. 1987b. "Political Arithmetic." In John Eatwell, Murray Milgate, and Peter Newman, eds., *The New Palgrave. A Dictionary of Economics.* London: Macmillan.

Debreu, Gerard. 1959. *Theory of Value.* New Haven: Yale University Press.

———. 1992. "Random Walk and Life Philosophy." In Michael Szenberg, ed., *Eminent Economists.* Cambridge: Cambridge University Press.

Descartes, Réné. [1637] 1968. *Discourse on Method and the Meditations.* London: Penguin Books.

Dictionary of National Biography. Edited by Leslie Stephen and Stephen Lee. Oxford: Oxford University Press.

Dimand, Robert W. 1993. "Alfred Marshall and the Whewell Group of Mathematical Economists." *The Manchester School,* vol. LXI, no. 4 (December), 439–41.

Dopfer, Kurt. 1988. "How Historical Is Schmoller's Economic Theory?" *Journal of Institutional and Theoretical Economics,* vol. 144, no. 3 (June), 552–69.

Dorfman, Joseph. [1934] 1966. *Thorstein Veblen and His America.* New York: Augustus M. Kelley.

———. 1949. "Obituary: Wesley C. Mitchell (1874–1948)." *The Economic Journal,* vol. LIX, no. 235 (September), 448–58.

———. 1959. *The Economic Mind in American Civilization,* vols. III and IV. New York: Viking.

———. 1965. "The Foundations of Commons' Economics." Introductory essay to John R. Commons, *The Distribution of Wealth.* New York: Augustus M. Kelley.

Dugger, William M. 1995. "Veblenian Institutionalism: The Changing Concepts of Inquiry." *Journal of Economic Issues,* vol. XXIX, no. 4 (December), 1013–27.

Dupuit, Jules. [1844] 1952. "On the Measurement of the Utility of Public Works." Translated by R. H. Barback. *International Economic Papers,* no. 2. London and New York: Macmillan.

———. [1849] 1962. "On Tolls and Transport Charges." Trans. by Elizabeth Henderson. *International Economic Papers,* no. 11. London and New York: Macmillan.

Eagly, Robert V. 1974. *The Structure of Classical Economic Theory.* New York: Oxford University Press.

Edgeworth, F. Y. 1877. *New and Old Methods of Ethics.*

———. 1879. "The Hedonical Calculus." *Mind,* vol. IV, no. 15 (July), 394–408.

———. [1881] 1995. *Mathematical Psychics: An Essay on the Application of Mathematics to the Moral Sciences.* San Diego, Calif.: James and Gordon.

———. 1884. "The Philosophy of Chance." *Mind,* vol. 9, no. 34 (April), 223–35.

———. 1887. *Metretike, or the Method of Measuring Probability and Utility,* in Edgeworth (1994).

———. 1889a. Review of *The Alphabet of Economic Science,* by Philip Henry Wicksteed. *The Academy,* vol. 35, no. 874 (February 2), 71.

———. 1889b. Review of *Natural Inheritance,* by Francis Galton. *Nature,* vol. XXXIX, no. 1017 (April 25), 603–4.

———. 1889c. Opening Address to Section F of the British Association. *Nature,* vol. XL, no. 1038 (September 19), 496–509.

———. 1890a. Review of *Principles of Economics,* by Alfred Marshall. *Nature,* vol. 42, no. 1085 (August 14), 362–64.

———. 1890b. Review of *Principles of Economics,* by Alfred Marshall. *The Academy,* vol. XXXVIII, no. 956 (August 30), 165–66.

———. 1910. The following are from R. H. Inglis Palgrave, ed., *Dictionary of Political Economy.* London: Macmillan (reprinted by Gale Research Co., Detroit, Mich., 1976).

———. 1910a. "Cournot, Antoine Augustin," vol. I, 445–46.

———. 1910b. "Curves," vol. I, 473–74.

———. 1910c. "Demand Curves," vol. I, 542–44.

———. 1910d. "Dupuit, A. J. Étienne-Juvenal," vol. I, 654–55.

———. 1910e. "Utility," vol. III, 602.

———. 1912a. Review of *Laws of Wages: An Essay in Statistical Economics,* by Henry L. Moore, *The Economic Journal,* vol. XXII, no. 85 (March), 66–71.

———. 1912b. Response to H. L. Moore's Reply. *The Economic Journal,* vol. XXII, no. 86 (June), 317–23.

———. 1994. *Edgeworth on Chance, Economic Hazard, and Statistics.* Ed. by Philip Mirowski. Lanham, Md.: Rowman and Littlefield.

———. 1996. *F. Y. Edgeworth: Writings in Probability, Statistics and Economics.* Edited by C. R. McCann Jr. Cheltenham: Edward Elgar.

Egerton, Hugh E. 1910. "Hodgskin, Thomas." In R. H. Inglis Palgrave, ed., *Dictionary of Political Economy.* London: Macmillan (reprinted by Gale Research Co., Detroit, Mich., 1976).

Ekelund, Robert B., Jr. 1987. "Dupuit, Arsène-Jules-Emile Juvenal." In John

Eatwell, Murray Milgate, and Peter Newman, eds., *The New Palgrave: A Dictionary of Economics*. London: Macmillan.

Ekelund, Robert B., Jr., and Robert F. Hébert. 1973. "Public Economics at the Ecole des Ponts et Chaussées." *Journal of Public Economics*, vol. 2, 241–56.

Ekelund, Robert B., Jr., and Robert D. Tollison. 1981. *Mercantilism as a Rent-Seeking Society: Economic Regulation in Historical Perspective*. College Station: Texas A&M University Press.

Ely, Richard T. 1887. "Statement of Dr. Richard T. Ely." In Report of the Organization of the American Economic Association, *Publications of the American Economic Association*, vol. I, 14–20.

———. 1901. *An Introduction to Political Economy*. New York: Eaton and Mains.

Endres, A. M. 1985. "The Functions of Numerical Data in the Writings of Graunt, Petty, and Davenant." *History of Political Economy*, vol. 17, no. 2 (summer), 245–64.

———. 1987. "The King-Davenant 'Law' in Classical Economics." *History of Political Economy*, vol. 19, no. 4 (winter), 621–38.

Epstein, Roy J. 1987. *A History of Econometrics*. Amsterdam: North Holland.

Fechner, Gustav Theodor. [1860] 1966. *Elements of Psychophysics*. New York: Holt, Rinehart, Winston.

Finer, S. E. 1966. "Introduction." In *Vilfredo Pareto: Sociological Writings*, trans. by Derick Mirfin. New York: Praeger.

Finley, Moses I. 1973. *The Ancient Economy*. London: Chatto and Windus.

Fisher, Irving. [1897] 1963. "Cournot and Mathematical Economics." Introduction to the first English translation of A. A. Cournot, *Researches into the Mathematical Principles of the Theory of Wealth*, trans. by Nathaniel T. Bacon. Homewood, Ill.: Richard D. Irwin.

Fitzpatrick, Edward. 1944. *McCarthy of Wisconsin*. New York: Columbia University Press.

Fleetwood, Steve. 1995. *Hayek's Political Economy*. London: Routledge.

Foley, Vernard. 1973. "An Origin of the Tableau Économique." *History of Political Economy*, vol. 5, no. 1 (spring), 121–50.

Fox-Genovese, Elizabeth. 1976. *The Origins of Physiocracy: Economic Revolution and Social Order in Eighteenth-Century France*. Ithaca, N.Y.: Cornell University Press.

Foxwell, Herbert Somerton. 1899. Introduction to Anton Menger, *The Right to the Whole Produce of Labour*. London: Macmillan.

Friedman, David D. 1980. "In Defense of Thomas Aquinas and the Just Price." *History of Political Economy*, vol. 12, no. 2 (summer), 234–42.

Friedman, Milton. 1953. "The Methodology of Positive Economics." In *Essays in Positive Economics*. Chicago: University of Chicago Press.

———. 1987. "Laughlin, James Laurence." In John Eatwell, Murray Milgate, and Peter Newman, eds., *The New Palgrave: A Dictionary of Economics*. London: Macmillan.

Frisch, Ragnar. 1933. "Editorial." *Econometrica*, vol. 1, no. 1 (January), 1–4.

———. 1950. "Alfred Marshall's Theory of Value." *Quarterly Journal of Economics*, vol. LXIV, no. 4 (November), 495–524.

Funkhauser, H. Gray, and Helen M. Walker. 1935. "Playfair and His Charts." *Economic History*, vol. 3, no. 10 (February), 103–9.

Furniss, Edgar. [1918] 1965. *The Position of the Laborer in a System of Nationalism: A Study in the Labor Theories of the Later English Mercantilists.* New York: Augustus M. Kelley.

Galbraith, John Kenneth. 1967. *The New Industrial State.* Boston: Houghton Mifflin.

Galton, Francis. 1877. "Typical Laws of Heredity." *Nature,* vol. XV, no. 388 (April 5), 492–95; no. 389 (April 12), 512–14; no. 390 (April 19), 532–33.

Gide, Charles, and Charles Rist. 1947. *History of Economic Doctrines.* 7th ed. Boston: D. C. Heath.

Glass, D. V. 1963. "John Graunt and His *Natural and Political Observations.*" *Proceedings of the Royal Society of London* (series B), vol. 159, 1–32.

Gordon, Barry. 1987. "Biblical and Early Judeo-Christian Thought: Genesis to Augustine." In S. Todd Lowry, ed., *Pre-Classical Economic Thought.* Boston: Kluwer Academic Publishers.

———. 1989. *The Economic Problem in Biblical and Patristic Thought.* New York: E. J. Brill.

Gram, Harvey, and Vivian Walsh. 1983. "Joan Robinson's Economics in Retrospect." *Journal of Economic Literature,* vol. XXI, no. 2 (June), 518–50.

Gray, Alexander. 1931. *The Development of Economic Doctrine: An Introductory Survey.* New York: John Wiley and Sons, Inc.

———. 1946. *The Socialist Tradition: Moses to Lenin.* London: Longmans, Green and Co.

Gray, John. 1996. *Isaiah Berlin.* Princeton: Princeton University Press.

Groenewegen, Peter D. 1967. "Authorship of the *Natural and Political Observations Upon the Bills of Mortality.*" *Journal of the History of Ideas,* vol. 28, 601–2.

———. 1983. "Turgot's Place in the History of Economic Thought: A Bicentenary Estimate." *History of Political Economy,* vol. 15, no. 4 (winter), 585–616.

———. 1988. "Alfred Marshall and the Establishment of the Cambridge Economics Tripos." *History of Political Economy,* vol. 20, no. 4 (winter), 627–67.

———. 1995. *A Soaring Eagle: Alfred Marshall, 1842–1924.* Aldershot: Edward Elgar.

Gunning, J. Patrick. 1989. "Professor Caldwell on Ludwig von Mises' Methodology." In Murray N. Rothbard and Walter Block, eds., *The Review of Austrian Economics,* vol. 3, 163–76. Lexington, Mass.: Lexington Books.

Haberler, Gottfried von. 1946. *Prosperity and Depression: A Theoretical Analysis of Cyclical Movements.* 3d ed. Geneva: League of Nations. (1st edition 1937.)

Hacking, Ian. 1990. *The Taming of Chance.* Cambridge: Cambridge University Press.

Halévy, Elie. [1928] 1960. *The Growth of Philosophic Radicalism.* Translated by Mary Morris. Boston: Beacon Press.

Halmos, Paul R. 1957. "Nicolas Bourbaki." *Scientific American,* vol. 196, no. 5 (May), 88–99.

Hamilton, Alexander. 1961. *The Papers of Alexander Hamilton.* Edited by Harold C. Syrett. New York: Columbia University Press.

Hamilton, Walton. 1919. "The Institutional Approach to Economic Theory." *American Economic Review* Supplement 9 (March), 309–18.

Harcourt, G. C. 1993. "Joan Robinson 1903–1983." *The Economic Journal,* vol. 105, no. 432 (September), 1228–43.

Harris, Abram L. 1934. "Economic Evolution: Dialectical and Darwinian." *Journal of Political Economy,* vol. 42, no. 1 (February), 34–79.

Harrod, R. F. 1951. *The Life of John Maynard Keynes.* London: Macmillan.

Hayek, Friedrich A. von. 1935. *Collectivist Economic Planning: Critical Studies on the Possibilities of Socialism.* Chicago: University of Chicago Press.

———. 1944. *The Road to Serfdom.* Chicago: University of Chicago Press.

———. 1946. "The London School of Economics 1895–1945." *Economica,* n.s., vol. XIII, no. 49 (February), 1031.

———. 1948. *Individualism and Economic Order.* Chicago: University of Chicago Press.

———. 1952. *The Counter-Revolution of Science: Studies on the Abuse of Reason.* Glencoe, Ill.: The Free Press.

———. 1966. "Dr. Bernard Mandeville." *Proceedings of the British Academy.* London: Oxford University Press.

———. 1968. "Menger, Carl." In *International Encyclopedia of the Social Sciences,* vol. 10, 124–26. New York: Macmillan and Free Press.

———. 1975. "The Pretence of Knowledge." *The Swedish Journal of Economics,* vol. 77, no. 4 (December), 433–42.

Heckscher, Eli F. 1933. "Mercantilism." *Encyclopedia of the Social Sciences,* vol. 10. Edited by E. R. A. Seligman and Alvin Johnson. New York: Macmillan.

———. 1935. *Mercantilism.* Vols. I and II. Translated by Mendel Shapiro. London: George Allen and Unwin.

Heise, Paul A. 1994. "Adam Smith: The Man and His Reputation." Paper presented at the meeting of the History of Economics Society, Babson College, Babson Park, Mass., June 13.

Hennings, K. H. 1987. "Böhm-Bawerk, Eugen von." In John Eatwell, Murray Milgate, and Peter Newman, eds. *The New Palgrave: A Dictionary of Economics.* London: Macmillan.

Hicks, John R. 1937. "Mr. Keynes and the (Classics): A Suggested Interpretation." *Econometrica,* vol. 5, no. 2 (April), 147–59.

———. 1939. *Value and Capital: An Inquiry into Some Fundamental Principles of Economics.* Oxford: Oxford University Press.

———. 1974. *The Crisis in Keynesian Economics.* New York: Basic Books.

Higgs, Henry. 1897. *The Physiocrats: Six Lectures on the French Economistes of the Eighteenth Century.* London: Macmillan.

Hirsch, Abraham. 1986. "Caldwell on Praxeology and Its Critics: A Reappraisal." *History of Political Economy,* vol. 18, no. 4 (winter), 661–68.

Hobbes, Thomas. [1651] 1985. *Leviathan.* Edited with an Introduction by C. B. Macpherson. Harmondsworth, U.K.: Penguin Classics.

———. 1994. *The Correspondence of Thomas Hobbes.* Edited by Noel Malcolm. New York: Oxford University Press.

Hodgskin, Thomas. [1832] 1973. *The Natural and Artificial Right of Property Contrasted.* New York: Augustus M. Kelley.

Hodgson, Geoffrey M. 1994. "The Return of Institutional Economics." In Neil J. Smelser and Richard Swedberg, eds., *The Handbook of Economic Sociology.* Princeton: Princeton University Press.

Hollis, Martin. 1987. *The Cunning of Reason*. Cambridge: Cambridge University Press.

Hollis, Martin, and Edward J. Nell. 1975. *Rational Economic Man*. Cambridge: Cambridge University Press.

Holmes, Oliver Wendell, Jr. 1909. *The Common Law*. Boston: Little, Brown.

Homans, George C., and Charles P. Curtis Jr. 1934. *An Introduction to Pareto: His Sociology*. New York: Alfred A. Knopf.

Hont, Istvan, and Michael Ignatieff, eds. 1983. *Wealth and Virtue: The Shaping of Political Economy in the Scottish Enlightenment*. Cambridge: Cambridge University Press.

Hornich, Phillip W. von. 1684. *Oesterreich über alles wann es nur will*. Excerpted in Monroe (1924).

Horsefield, J. Keith. 1960. *British Monetary Experiments, 1650–1710*. Cambridge, Mass.: Harvard University Press.

Houghton, R. W. 1958. "A Note on the Early History of Consumer's Surplus." *Economica*, n.s., vol. XXV, no. 1 (February), 49–57.

Howey, Richard S. 1972. "The Origins of Marginalism." *History of Political Economy*, vol. 4, no. 2 (fall), 281–302.

Hull, Charles. [1899] 1986. Introduction to *The Economic Writings of Sir William Petty*, edited by Charles Hull. Fairfield, N.J.: Augustus M. Kelley.

Hume, David. [1739/40] 1984. *A Treatise of Human Nature*. Edited with an Introduction by Ernest C. Mossner. Harmondsworth: Penguin.

———. [1777] 1993. *An Enquiry Concerning Human Understanding: A Letter from a Gentleman to His Friend in Edinburgh*. Edited by Eric Steinberg. Indianapolis: Hackett.

———. 1955. *Writings on Economics*. Edited and with an Introduction by Eugene Rotwein. Madison: University of Wisconsin Press.

Hunt, E. K. 1977. "Value Theory in the Writings of the Classical Economists, Thomas Hodgskin, and Karl Marx." *History of Political Economy*, vol. 9, no. 3 (fall), 322–45.

———. 1979. "The Importance of Thorstein Veblen for Contemporary Marxism." *Journal of Economic Issues*, vol. XIII, no. 1 (March), 113–40.

Hutcheson, Francis. [1725] 1971. *An Inquiry into the Original of Our Ideas of Beauty and Virtue*. Volume I of the Collected Works of Francis Hutcheson. Hildesheim: Georg Olms Verlagsbuchhandlung.

Hutchison, Terence W. 1938. *The Significance and Basic Postulates of Economics*. London: Macmillan.

———. 1956. "Professor Machlup on Verification in Economics." *Southern Economic Journal*, vol. XXII, no. 4 (April), 476–83.

———. 1988. *Before Adam Smith: The Emergence of Political Economy, 1662–1776*. New York: Basil Blackwell.

Hyse, Richard. 1991. Translator's Introduction to Sismondi, *New Principles of Political Economy*. New Brunswick: Transaction.

Ingram, John Kells. 1879. Preface to T. E. Cliffe Leslie, *Essays in Political and Moral Philosophy*. London: Longmans, Green and Co.

Ingrao, Bruna, and Giorgio Israel. 1990. *The Invisible Hand: Economic Equilibrium in the History of Science*. Translated by Ian McGilvray. Cambridge, Mass.: MIT Press.

Jaffé, William. 1954. Translator's Introduction to Léon Walras, *Elements of Pure Economics*. Homewood, Ill.: Richard D. Irwin, Inc.

———. 1969. "A. N. Isnard, Progenitor of the Walrasian Grand Equilibrium Model." *History of Political Economy*, vol. 1, no. 1 (spring), 19–43.

———. 1972a. "Léon Walras's Role in the 'Marginal Revolution' of the 1870s." *History of Political Economy*, vol. 4, no. 2 (fall), 379–405.

———. 1972b. "Pareto Translated: A Review Article." *Journal of Economic Literature*, vol. 10, no. 4 (December), 1190–1201.

———. 1974. "Pareto's Three Manuals: Rebuttal." *Journal of Economic Literature*, vol. XII, no. 1 (March), 88–91.

———. 1977. "The Birth of Léon Walras's *Élements*." *History of Political Economy*, vol. 9, no. 2 (summer), 198–214.

———. 1983. *William Jaffé's Essays on Walras*. Edited by Donald A. Walker. Cambridge: Cambridge University Press.

Jalledeau, Joël. 1975. "The Methodological Conversion of John Bates Clark." *History of Political Economy*, vol. 7, no. 2 (summer), 209–26.

Jennings, Richard. [1855] 1969. *Natural Elements of Political Economy*. New York: Augustus M. Kelley.

Jevons, William Stanley. [1865] 1965. *The Coal Question: An Inquiry Concerning the Progress of the Nation, and the Probable Exhaustion of Our Coal-Mines*. Edited by A. W. Flux. New York: Augustus M. Kelley.

———. 1866. "Brief Account of a General Mathematical Theory of Political Economy." *Journal of the Statistical Society*, vol. XXIX, 235–53.

———. 1876. "The Future of Political Economy." *Fortnightly Review*, n.s., vol. XX, no. CXIX (November 1), 617–31.

———. 1881a. "Richard Cantillon and the Nationality of Political Economy." *The Contemporary Review*, vol. XXXIX (January), 61–80.

———. 1881b. Review of *Mathematical Psychics*, by F. Y. Edgeworth. *Mind*, vol. 6, no. 4 (October), 581–83.

———. 1882. *The State in Relation to Labour*. London: Macmillan.

———. [1883] 1965. *Methods of Social Reform*. New York: Augustus M. Kelley.

———. [1905] 1965. *The Principles of Economics*. Ed. by Henry Higgs. New York: Augustus M. Kelley.

———. [1911] 1958. *The Principles of Science: A Treatise on Logic and Scientific Method*. New York: Dover.

———. [1911] 1970. *The Theory of Political Economy*. 4th ed. Edited by R. D. C. Black. Harmondsworth: Penguin.

———. [1957] 1965. *The Theory of Political Economy*. Fifth edition. Edited by H. S. Jevons. New York: Augustus M. Kelley. (1st ed. 1871; 2d ed. 1879.)

Johnson, E. A. J. [1937] 1960. *Predecessors of Adam Smith: The Growth of British Economic Thought*. New York: Augustus M. Kelley.

Johnson, Elizabeth S., and Harry G. Johnson. 1974. "The Social and Intellectual Origins of *The General Theory*." *History of Political Economy*, vol. 6, no. 3 (fall), 261–77.

Johnson, Harry G. 1960. "Arthur Cecil Pigou, 1877–1959." *Canadian Journal of Economics and Political Science*, vol. XXVI, 150–55.

Kant, Immanuel. [1787] 1986. *Critique of Pure Reason*. Trans. by J. M. D. Meicklejohn. London: Everyman's Library.

Kennedy, Paul M. 1987. *The Rise and Fall of the Great Powers*. New York: Random House.

Keohane, Nannerl O. 1980. *Philosophy and the State in France: The Renaissance to the Enlightenment*. Princeton: Princeton University Press.

Keynes, John Maynard. [1921] 1971. *Treatise on Probability*. Volume VIII of *The Collected Writings of John Maynard Keynes*. London: Macmillan and St. Martin's Press for the Royal Economic Society.

———. [1923] 1971. *A Tract on Monetary Reform*. Volume IV of *The Collected Writings of John Maynard Keynes*. London: Macmillan and St. Martin's Press for the Royal Economic Society.

———. 1924. "Alfred Marshall, 1842–1924." *The Economic Journal*, vol. XXXIV, no. 135 (September), 311–72.

———. 1926. "The End of Laissez-Faire." *The New Republic*, vol. XLVIII, no. 612 (August 25), 13–15; no. 613 (September 1), 37–41.

———. [1930] 1971. *A Treatise on Money*. Volumes IV and V of *The Collected Writings of John Maynard Keynes*. London: Macmillan and St. Martin's Press for the Royal Economic Society.

———. 1932. "The Dilemma of Modern Socialism." *The Political Quarterly*, vol. 3, no. 2 (April/June), 155–61.

———. 1933. "National Self-Sufficiency." *The Yale Review*, vol. XXII, no. 4 (June), 755–69.

———. 1936a. *The General Theory of Employment, Interest, and Money*. New York: Harcourt, Brace, Jovanovich.

———. 1936b. "William Stanley Jevons, 1835–1882," *Journal of the Royal Statistical Society*, vol. XCIX, part III, 516–48.

———. [1938] 1949. "My Early Beliefs." In *Two Memoirs*. New York: Augustus M. Kelley.

———. 1940. "The Society's Jubilee 1890–1940." *The Economic Journal*, vol. L, no. 200 (December), 401–9.

———. 1973. *The Collected Writings of John Maynard Keynes*, vol. XIV: *The General Theory and After: Part II: Defence and Development*. London: Macmillan for the Royal Economic Society.

King, Gregory. 1696. *Natural and Politicall Observations and Conclusions upon the State and Condition of England*.

King, J. E. 1983. "Utopian or Scientific? A Reconsideration of the Ricardian Socialists." *History of Political Economy*, vol. 15, no. 3 (fall), 345–73.

Knight, Frank H. 1926. "Economics at Its Best." *American Economic Review*, vol. XVI, no. 1 (March), 51–58.

Koehn, Nancy F. 1994. *The Power of Commerce: Economy and Governance in the First British Empire*. Ithaca, N.Y.: Cornell University Press.

Koopmans, Tjalling. 1947. "Measurement without Theory." *Review of Economics and Statistics*, vol. 29, 161–72.

Koot, Gerard M. 1975. "T. E. Cliffe Leslie, Irish Social Reform, and the Origins of the English Historical School of Economics." *History of Political Economy*, vol. 7, no. 3 (fall), 312–36.

Kuczynski, Marguerite, and Ronald L. Meek. 1972. *Quesnay's Tableau Économique*. New York: Augustus M. Kelley.

Kuznets, Simon S. 1933. "National Income." *Encyclopedia of the Social Sciences*, vol. 11, 205–24. Edited by E. R. A. Seligman and Alvin Johnson. New York: Macmillan.

———. 1934. *National Income, 1929–1932.* Senate Document No. 124, 73d Congress, 2d Session, Washington: G.P.O.

———. 1937. *National Income and Capital Formation, 1919–1935.* New York: National Bureau of Economic Research.

———. 1938. *Commodity Flow and Capital Formation.* New York: National Bureau of Economic Research.

Langer, William. 1940. *An Encyclopedia of World History: Ancient, Medieval, and Modern, Chronologically Arranged.* Boston: Houghton Mifflin.

Langholm, Odd. 1987. "Scholastic Economics." In S. Todd Lowry, ed., *Pre-Classical Economic Thought.* Boston: Kluwer Academic Publishers.

Langlois, Richard N. 1985. "From the Knowledge of Economics to the Economics of Knowledge: Fritz Machlup on Methodology and on the 'Knowledge Society.' " In Warren J. Samuels, ed., *Research in the History of Economic Thought and Methodology,* vol. 3. Greenwich, Conn.: JAI Press.

Lavoie, Don. 1986. "Euclideanism versus Hermeneutics: A Reinterpretation of Misesian Apriorism." In Israel M. Kirzner, ed., *Subjectivism, Intelligibility and Economic Understanding.* New York: NYU Press.

Lawson, Tony. 1988. "Probability and Uncertainty in Economic Analysis." *Journal of Post Keynesian Economics,* vol. XI, no. 1 (fall), 38–65.

———. 1993. "Keynes and Conventions." *Review of Social Economy,* vol. LI, no. 2 (summer), 174–200.

Leavis, F. R. 1963. *Two Cultures? The Significance of C.P. Snow: With an Essay on Sir Charles Snow's Rede Lecture.* New York: Random House.

Leduc, Gaston. 1968. "Say, Jean Baptiste." *International Encyclopedia of the Social Sciences,* New York: Macmillan and Free Press.

Lerner, Abba P. 1944. *The Economics of Control: Principles of Welfare Economics.* New York: Macmillan.

Leslie, T. E. Cliffe. 1870. "The Political Economy of Adam Smith." *The Fortnightly Review,* n.s., vol. VIII, no. XLVII (November 1), 549–63.

———. 1875a. "Maine's Early History of Institutions." *The Fortnightly Review,* n.s., vol. XVII, no. XCIX (March 1), 305–20.

———. 1875b. "On the Philosophical Method of Political Economy." Dublin: Hodges, Foster, and Figgis.

Letwin, William. 1964. *The Origins of Scientific Economics: English Economic Thought, 1660–1776.* Garden City, N.J.: Doubleday.

Li, Ming Hsun. 1969. *The Great Recoinage of 1696–9.* London: Weidenfeld and Nicolson.

Lindahl, Erik. 1929. "Prisbildningsproblems uppläggning fran kapitalteoretisk synpunkt." *Ekonomisk Tidskrift,* vol. 31, no. 2, 31–81.

Lipson, Ephraim. 1931. *Economic History of England.* Vol. III: *The Age of Mercantilism.* London: A. and C. Black, Ltd.

List, Friedrich. 1827. *Outlines of American Political Economy, in a Series of Letters Addressed by Friedrich List to Charles J. Ingersoll.* Philadelphia: S. Parker.

———. [1885] 1991. *The National System of Political Economy.* Translated by Sampson S. Lloyd. New York: Augustus M. Kelley.

Locke, John. 1668. *Some of the Consequences That Are Likely to Follow upon Lessening of Interest to 4 Per Cent.* Unpublished.

———. [1690] 1980. *Second Treatise of Government.* Edited by C. B. Macpherson. Indianapolis, Ind.: Hackett Publishing Co., Inc.

———. [1691] 1968. *Some Considerations of the Consequences of the Lowering of Interest, and Raising the Value of Money,* in John Locke, *Several Papers Relating to Money, Interest and Trade, &c.* (1696). New York: Augustus M. Kelley.

———. [1695] 1968. *Further Considerations Concerning Raising the Value of Money,* in John Locke, *Several Papers Relating to Money, Interest and Trade, &c.* (1696). New York: Augustus M. Kelley.

Longfield, Mountifort. [1834] 1931. *Lectures on Political Economy.* London: London School of Economics and Political Science.

Lowenthal, Esther. [1911] 1972. *The Ricardian Socialists.* Clifton, N.J.: Augustus M. Kelley.

Lowndes, William. 1695. *An Essay for the Amendment of the Silver Coin.*

Lowry, S. Todd. 1979. "Recent Literature on Ancient Greek Economic Thought." *Journal of Economic Literature,* vol. XVII, no. 1 (March), 65–86.

———. 1987. "The Greek Heritage in Economic Thought." In S. Todd Lowry, ed., *Pre-Classical Economic Thought.* Boston: Kluwer Academic Publishers.

Lyons, David. 1965. *Forms and Limits of Utilitarianism.* London: Oxford University Press.

Macfie, A. L. 1959. "Adam Smith's *Moral Sentiments* as Foundation for his *Wealth of Nations.*" *Oxford Economic Papers,* n.s., vol. 11, no. 3 (October), 209–28.

Machiavelli, Niccolò. [1531] 1952. *The Prince.* New York: New American Library.

Machlup, Fritz. 1955. "The Problem of Verification in Economics." *Southern Economic Journal,* vol. XXII, no. 1 (July), 1–21.

———. 1956. "Rejoinder to a Reluctant Ultra-Empiricist." *Southern Economic Journal,* vol. XXII, no. 4 (April), 483–93.

———. 1974. "Friedrich von Hayek's Contribution to Economics." *The Swedish Journal of Economics,* vol. 76, no. 4 (December), 498–531.

MacLennan, Barbara. 1972. "Jevons's Philosophy of Science." *The Manchester School,* vol. XL, no. 1 (March), 53–71.

Macpherson, C. B. 1962. *The Political Theory of Possessive Individualism: Hobbes to Locke.* Oxford: Clarendon Press.

Magnusson, Lars. 1987. "Mercantilism and 'Reform' Mercantilism: The Rise of Economic Discourse in Sweden During the Eighteenth Century." *History of Political Economy,* vol. 19, no. 3 (fall), 415–33.

———. 1994. *Mercantilism.* London: Routledge.

Maine, Henry. 1873. *Ancient Law.* 5th ed. New York: Henry Holt and Co.

———. 1889. *Village-Communities in the East and West.* New York: Henry Holt and Co.

Malthus, Thomas Robert. [1798] 1965. *An Essay on the Principle of Population, as it Affects the Future Improvement of Society, with Remarks on the Speculations of Mr. Godwin, M. Condorcet, and Other Writers.* New York: Augustus M. Kelley.

———. [1820] 1974. *Principles of Political Economy*. 2d ed. Clifton, N.J.: Augustus M. Kelley.

———. 1827. *Definitions in Political Economy, Preceded by an Inquiry into the Rules Which Ought to Guide Political Economists in the Definition and Use of their Terms, with Remarks on the Deviation from these Rules in Their Writings*. London: J. Murray.

———. [1872] 1914. *An Essay on Population*. 2 vols. Edited by W. T. Layton. London: J. M. Dent.

Malynes, Gerard de. 1601a. *St. George for England Allegorically Described*. London.

———. 1601b. *A Treatise of the Canker of England's Common Wealth*. London.

———. [1622a] 1981. *Consuetudo, vel, Lex Mercatoria: Or the Ancient-Law Merchant*. Abington, England: Professional Books.

———. [1622b] 1971. *The Maintenance of Free Trade*. New York: Augustus M. Kelley.

Marshall, Alfred. 1872. Review of *The Theory of Political Economy*, by W. Stanley Jevons, *The Academy*, vol. III, no. 45 (1 April), 130–32.

———. 1873. "The Future of the Working Classes." *The Eagle*, vol. 9, 1023.

———. 1876. "On Mr. Mill's Theory of Value." *Fortnightly Review*, n.s., vol. XIX, no. CXII (April 1), 591–602.

———. 1881. Review of *Mathematical Psychics*, by F. Y. Edgeworth. *The Academy*, vol. 19, no. 476 (June 18), 457.

———. 1885. "On the Graphic Method of Statistics." *Journal of the Royal Statistical Society* (Jubilee volume), June 22–24.

———. 1897. "The Old Generation of Economists and the New." *Quarterly Journal of Economics*, vol. XI, no. 2 (January), 115–35.

———. 1907. "The Social Possibilities of Economic Chivalry." *The Economic Journal*, vol. XVII, no. 65 (March), 7–29.

———. 1920. *Principles of Economics*. 8th ed. London: Macmillan. (1st ed. 1890.)

———. [1923a] 1970. *Industry and Trade*. 4th ed. New York: Augustus M. Kelley.

———. [1923b]. *Money, Credit and Commerce*. London: Macmillan.

———. 1925. *Memorials of Alfred Marshall*. Edited by A. C. Pigou. London: Macmillan.

———. 1933. "Alfred Marshall, the Mathematician, as Seen by Himself." *Econometrica*, vol. 1, no. 2 (April), 221–22.

Marshall, Alfred, and Mary Paley Marshall. 1879. *The Economics of Industry*. London: Macmillan.

Marx, Karl. [1844] 1964. *Economic and Philosophic Manuscripts of 1844*. New York: International Publishers.

———. [1890] 1977. *Capital*, vol. I. 4th ed. Translated by Ben Fowkes. New York: Vintage.

———. 1904. *A Contribution to the Critique of Political Economy*. Translation of the 2d German edition of 1897. Translated by N. I. Stone. Chicago: Charles H. Kerr.

———. 1952. *A History of Economic Theories: From the Physiocrats to Adam Smith*. Ed. by Karl Kautsky. Trans. by Terence McCarthy. New York: The Langland Press.

———. 1975. *Karl Marx: Early Writings.* Translated by Rodney Livingstone and Gregor Benton. New York: Vintage Books.

Marx, Karl, and Friedrich Engels. 1959. *Karl Marx and Friedrich Engels: Basic Writings on Politics and Philosophy.* Ed. by Lewis S. Feuer. Garden City, N.J.: Anchor Books.

Mautner, Thomas (ed.). 1993. *Francis Hutcheson: Two Texts on Human Nature.* Cambridge: Cambridge University Press.

McCann, Charles R., Jr. 1994. *Probability Foundations of Economic Theory.* London: Routledge.

McCloskey, D. N. 1985. *The Rhetoric of Economics.* Madison: University of Wisconsin Press.

———. 1993. *Knowledge and Persuasion in Economics.* Cambridge: Cambridge University Press.

McCulloch, John Ramsay. 1837. *A Statistical Account of the British Empire: Exhibiting Its Extent, Physical Capacities, Population, Industry, and Civil and Religious Institutions.* 2d ed. London: Charles Knight and Co.

———. [1864] 1965. *The Principles of Political Economy.* 5th ed. New York: Augustus M. Kelley.

McLain, James J. 1977. *The Economic Writings of Du Pont de Nemours.* Newark: University of Delaware Press.

McWilliams-Tullberg, Rita. 1975. "Marshall's 'Tendency to Socialism.' " *History of Political Economy,* vol. 7, no. 1 (spring), 75–111.

———. 1992. "Alfred Marshall's Attitude Toward the *Economics of Industry.*" *Journal of the History of Economic Thought,* vol. 14, no. 2 (fall), 257–70.

Meek, Ronald L. 1962. *The Economics of Physiocracy: Essays and Translations.* London: Allen and Unwin.

Meikle, Scott. 1995. *Aristotle's Economic Thought.* Oxford: Clarendon Press.

Menger, Anton. 1899. *The Right to the Whole Produce of Labour; the Origin and Development of the Theory of Labour's Claim to the Whole Product of Industry.* Translated by M. E. Tanner; Introduction by H. S. Foxwell. London: Macmillan.

Menger, Carl. [1871] 1976. *Principles of Economics* (English translation of *Grundsätze der Volkswirtschaftslehre*). Translated by James Dingwall and Bert F. Hoselitz. New York: New York University Press.

———. [1883] 1963. *Problems of Economics and Sociology.* Trans. by Francis J. Nock. Urbana: University of Illinois Press.

Menger, Karl. 1973. "Austrian Marginal and Mathematical Economics." In J. R. Hicks and W. Weber, eds., *Carl Menger and the Austrian School of Economics.* Oxford: Clarendon Press, 38–60.

Milford, Karl. 1995. "Roscher's Epistemological and Methodological Position: Its Importance for the *Methodenstreit.*" *Journal of Economic Studies* (special issue: *Wilhelm Roscher and the "Historical Method,"* Jürgen G. Backhaus, ed.) vol. 22, nos. 3/4/5, 26–52.

Mill, James. [1825] 1967. *Essays on Government, Jurisprudence, Liberty of the Press, and Law of Nations.* New York: Augustus M. Kelley.

———. [1844] 1963. *Elements of Political Economy.* 3d ed. New York: Augustus M. Kelley.

———. 1966. *James Mill: Selected Economic Writings.* Ed. by Donald Winch. Edinburgh: Oliver and Boyd for the Scottish Economic Society.

Mill, John Stuart. [1838] 1987. "Bentham." In *Utilitarianism and Other Essays,* edited by Alan Ryan. Harmondsworth: Penguin.

———. [1859] 1956. *On Liberty.* New York: Liberal Arts Press.

———. 1861. "Utilitarianism." *Fraser's Magazine of Town and Country,* vol. LXIV, no. CCCLXXXII (October), 391–406; no. CCCLXXXIII (November), 525–34; no. CCCLXXXIV (December), 659–73.

———. [1871] 1987. *Principles of Political Economy.* Ed. by W. J. Ashley. Fairfield, N.J.: Augustus M. Kelley.

———. [1872] 1988. *The Logic of the Moral Sciences.* LaSalle, Ill.: Open Court Press.

———. [1873] 1957. *Autobiography.* Indianapolis: Bobbs-Merrill.

———. 1879. "Chapters on Socialism." *Fortnightly Review,* vol. XXV, n.s., Part I: no. CXLVI (February 1), 217–37; Part II: no. CXLVII (March 1), 373–82; Part III: no. CXLVIII (April 1), 515–303.

Mises, Ludwig von. [1933] 1960. *Epistemological Problems of Economics.* Trans. by George Reisman. Princeton: D. Van Nostrand Co.

———. 1947. *Planned Chaos.* New York: The Foundation for Economic Education.

———. 1966. *Human Action.* 3d ed. Chicago: Henry Regnery Co.

Misselden, Edward. [1622] 1971. *Free Trade, or the Meanes to Make Trade Florish.* New York: Augustus M. Kelley.

———. [1623] 1971. *The Circle of Commerce or the Balance of Trade.* New York: Augustus M. Kelley.

Mitchell, Lucy Sprague. 1953. *Two Lives: The Story of Wesley Clair Mitchell and Myself.* New York: Simon and Schuster.

Mitchell, Wesley Clair. 1903. *A History of the Greenbacks, with Special Reference to the Economic Consequences of Their Issue: 1862–65.* Chicago: University of Chicago Press.

———. [1908] 1966. *Gold, Prices and Wages Under the Greenback Standard.* New York: Augustus M. Kelley.

———. 1917. "Wieser's Theory of Social Economics." *Political Science Quarterly,* vol. XXXII, no. 1 (March), 95–118.

———. 1918. "Bentham's Felicific Calculus." *Political Science Quarterly,* vol. XXXIII, no. 2 (June), 161–83.

———. 1925. "Quantitative Analysis in Economic Theory." *American Economic Review,* vol. XV, no. 1 (March), 1–12.

———. 1927. *Business Cycles: The Problem and Its Setting.* New York, National Bureau of Economic Research.

———. 1929a. "Sombart's Hochkapitalismus." *Quarterly Journal of Economics,* vol. XLIII, no. 1 (February), 303–23.

———. 1929b. "Obituary: Thorstein Veblen: 1857–1929." *The Economic Journal,* vol. XXXIX, no. 156 (December), 646–50.

———. 1933. "Alfred Marshall." *Encyclopedia of the Social Sciences.* Edited by E. R. A. Seligman and Alvin Johnson. New York: Macmillan.

———. [1937] 1950. *The Backward Art of Spending Money and Other Essays.* New York: Augustus M. Kelley.

———. [1941] 1989. *Business Cycles and their Causes.* Philadelphia: Porcupine Press.

———. 1967; 1969. *Types of Economic Theory: From Mercantilism to Institu-*

tionalism. Vols. I and II. Ed. with an introduction by Joseph Dorfman. New York: Augustus M. Kelley.

Moggridge, Donald E. 1992. *Maynard Keynes: An Economist's Biography*. London: Routledge.

Monroe, A. E. 1924. *Early Economic Thought*. Cambridge, Mass.: Harvard University Press.

Montague, F. C. 1910. "Property." In R. H. Inglis Palgrave, ed., *Dictionary of Political Economy*. London: Macmillan (reprinted by Gale Research Co., Detroit, Mich., 1976).

Montchrétien, Antoine de. 1615. *Traité d'économie politique*. Rouen.

Montesquieu, Charles Louis. [1721] 1873. *Lettres Persanes*. Paris: Alfonse Lemerre.

———. [1734] 1965. *Considerations sur les causes de la grandeur des Romains et de leur decadence* (*Considerations on the Causes of the Greatness of the Romans and Their Decline*). Trans. by David Lowenthal. New York: Free Press.

———. [1748] 1927. *L'esprit des lois*. Paris: Garnier frères.

Moore, George Edward. 1903. *Principia Ethica*. Cambridge: Cambridge University Press.

Moore, Gregory C. G. 1995. "T. E. Cliffe Leslie and the English *Methodenstreit*." *Journal of the History of Economic Thought*, vol. 17, no. 1 (spring), 57–77.

Moore, Henry Ludwell. 1905. "The Personality of Antoine Augustin Cournot." *Quarterly Journal of Economics*, vol. XIX (May), 370–99.

———. [1911] 1967. *Laws of Wages: An Essay in Statistical Economics*. New York: Augustus M. Kelley.

———. 1912. "A Reply to Professor Edgeworth's Review of Professor Moore's *Laws of Wages*." *The Economic Journal*, vol. XXII, no. 86 (June), 314–17.

Morgenstern, Oskar. 1976. "The Collaboration Between Oskar Morgenstern and John von Neumann on the Theory of Games." *Journal of Economic Literature*, vol. XIV, no. 3 (September), 805–16.

Morris, Cynthia Taft. 1957. "Some Neglected Aspects of Sixteenth-Century Economic Thought." *Explorations in Entrepreneurial History*, vol. IX, no. 3 (February), 160–71.

Muchmore, Lynn. 1969. "Gerrard de Malynes and Mercantile Economics." *History of Political Economy*, vol. 1, no. 2 (fall), 336–58.

Müller, Adam. 1809. *Die Elemente der Staatskunst*. Wien: Wiener literarische Anstalt.

Mun, Thomas. [1664] 1986. *England's Treasure by Forraign Trade, or the Ballance of our Forraign Trade is the Rule of our Treasure*. Fairfield, N.J.: Augustus M. Kelley.

Murphy, Antoin E. 1986. *Richard Cantillon: Entrepreneur and Economist*. Oxford: Clarendon Press.

Myrdal, Gunnar. 1953. *The Political Element in the Development of Economic Theory*. London: Routledge, Kegan Paul.

Newman, Peter. 1987. "Edgeworth, Francis Ysidro." In John Eatwell, Murray Milgate, and Peter Newman, eds., *The New Palgrave: A Dictionary of Economics*. London: Macmillan.

Newmarch, William. 1861. "The Progress of Economic Science During the Last

Thirty Years: An Opening Address [before Section F]." *Journal of the Statistical Society*, vol. XXIV, Part IV (December), 451–67.

North, Douglass C. 1990. *Institutions, Institutional Change and Economic Performance*. New York: Cambridge University Press.

———. 1991. "Institutions." *Journal of Economic Perspectives*, vol. 5, no. 1, 97–112.

O'Brien, D. P. 1975. *The Classical Economists*. Oxford: Clarendon Press.

———. 1987. "McCulloch, John Ramsay." In John Eatwell, Murray Milgate, and Peter Newman, eds., *The New Palgrave: A Dictionary of Economics*. London: Macmillan.

———. 1988. *Lionel Robbins*. New York: St. Martin's Press.

O'Donnell, Margaret G. 1979. "Pigou: An Extension of Sidgwickian Thought." *History of Political Economy*, vol. 11, no. 4 (winter), 588–605.

O'Donnell, R. M. 1989. *Keynes: Philosophy, Economics, and Politics*. Cambridge: Cambridge University Press.

Owen, Robert. 1813–16. *A New View of Society, or, Essays on the Principle of the Formation of the Human Character, and the Application of the Principle to Practice*. In Owen, 1991.

———. 1820. *Report to the County of Lanark*. In Owen, 1991.

———. 1991. *A New View of Society, and Other Writings*. London: Penguin Books.

Pareto, Vilfredo. [1927] 1971. *Manual of Political Economy*. Trans. by Ann S. Schwier. New York: Augustus M. Kelley.

———. [1935] 1963. *The Mind and Society: A Treatise on General Sociology*. Edited by Arthur Livingston; translated by Andrew Bongiorno and Arthur Livingston. New York: Dover.

———. 1966. *Vilfredo Pareto: Sociological Writings*. Edited by S. E. Finer; translated by Derick Mirfin. New York: Praeger.

Pearson, Karl. 1914–30. *The Life, Letters and Labours of Francis Galton*. 3 vols. Cambridge: Cambridge University Press.

Perlman, Mark. 1958. *Labor Union Theories in America: Background and Development*. Evanston, Ill.: Row, Peterson.

———. 1976. Review of Charles Webster, *The Great Instauration: Science, Medicine, and Reform. Journal of Economic Literature*, vol. 14, 1289–91.

———. 1977. "Orthodoxy and Heterodoxy in Economics: A Retrospective View of Experiences in Britain and the U.S.A." *Zeitschrift für Nationalökonomie*, vol. 37, 151–64.

———. 1981. "*Population and Economic Change in Developing Countries*: A Review Article." *Journal of Economic Literature*, vol. XIX, no. 1 (March), 74–82.

———. 1986. "Perceptions of Our Discipline: Three Magisterial Treatments of the Evolution of Economic Thought." History of Economic Society Meetings, May 1985, George Mason University, Fairfax, Va. *Bulletin* [of the History of Economics Society] (winter), 9–28.

———. 1987. "Political Purpose and the National Accounts." In William A. Alonso and Paul Starr. *The Politics of Numbers*. New York City: Russell Sage for the National Committee for Research on the 1980 Census.

———. 1990. Review of William J. Barber, ed., *Breaking the Academic Mould:*

Economists and American Higher Learning in the Nineteenth Century.
    History of Political Economy (summer), 22, 406–8.

———. 1991. " 'Early' Capital Theory in the Economics Journals: A Study of
    Imputed Induced Demand." *Economic Notes,* vol. 20, no. 1, 58–88.

———. 1996. *"The Fable of the Bees,* Considered Anew." In Mark Perlman, *The
    Character of Economic Thought, Economic Characters, and Economic
    Institutions.* Ann Arbor: University of Michigan Press.

Perlman, Selig. 1928. *A Theory of the Labor Movement.* New York: Macmillan.

Perlman, Selig, and Philip Taft. 1935. *History of Labor in the United States,
    1896–1932.* Vol. 4. New York: Macmillan.

Petrella, Frank. 1970. "Individual, Group, or Government? Smith, Mill, and
    Sidgwick." *History of Political Economy,* vol. 2, no. 1 (spring), 152–76.

Petty, Sir William. [1899] 1986. *The Economic Writings of Sir William Petty.*
    Edited by Charles Hull. Fairfield, N.J.: Augustus M. Kelley.

Pigou, Arthur Cecil. 1914. *Unemployment.* New York: H. Holt.

———. 1932. *The Economics of Welfare.* 4th ed. London: Macmillan. (1st ed.
    1920)

———. [1929] 1967. *Industrial Fluctuations.* 2d ed. New York: Augustus M.
    Kelley.

———. 1933. *The Theory of Unemployment.* London: Macmillan.

———. 1939. "State Action and Laissez-Faire." In *Economics in Practice.* Lon-
    don: Macmillan.

———. 1951. "Some Aspects of Welfare Economics." *American Economic Re-
    view,* vol. XLI, no. 3 (June), 287–302.

Pivetti, Massimo. 1987. "Tooke, Thomas." In John Eatwell, Murray Milgate, and
    Peter Newman, eds., *The New Palgrave: A Dictionary of Economics.* Lon-
    don: Macmillan.

Plato. 1987. *Republic.* Translated by Desmond Lee. London: Penguin Books.

Polyani, Karl. 1944. *The Great Transformation.* New York: Farrar and Rinehart.

Popper, Karl. 1965. *Conjectures and Refutations: The Growth of Scientific
    Knowledge.* 2d ed. New York: Harper Torchbooks.

Pribram, Karl. 1983. *A History of Economic Reasoning.* Baltimore: Johns Hop-
    kins University Press.

Priestley, Joseph. 1768. *An Essay on the First Principles of Government; and on
    the Nature of Political, Civil, and Religious Liberty.* London: J. Dodsley.

Quesnay, François. 1972. *Quesnay's Tableau Economique.* Edited and translated
    by Marguerite Kuczynski and Ronald L. Meek. London: Macmillan, and
    New York: Augustus M. Kelley, for the Royal Economic Society and the
    American Economic Association.

Quetelet, Adolphe. [1842] 1969. *A Treatise on Man and the Development of His
    Faculties.* (Translation of *Sur l'homme et le développement de ses facultés*).
    Gainsville, Fla.: Scholars' Facsimiles and Reprints.

Ramstad, Yngve. 1987. "Institutional Existentialism: More on Why John R.
    Commons Has So Few Followers." *Journal of Economic Issues,* vol. XXI,
    no. 2 (June), 661–71.

———. 1995. "John R. Commons's Puzzling Inconsequentialism as an Eco-
    nomic Theorist." *Journal of Economic Issues,* vol. XXIX, no. 4 (Decem-
    ber), 991–1012.

Rawls, John. 1971. *A Theory of Justice*. Cambridge, Mass.: Belknap/Harvard.

Rhodes, George F., Jr. 1978. "A Note Interpreting Cournot's Economics by His General Epistemology." *History of Political Economy*, vol. 10, no. 2 (summer), 315–21.

Ricardo, David. 1816. *Proposals for an Economical and Secure Currency; with Observations on the Profits of the Bank of England, as They Regard the Public and the Proprietors of Bank Stock*. London: John Murray.

———. [1821] 1973. *The Principles of Political Economy and Taxation*. 3d ed. Introduction by Donald Winch. London: J. Dent.

Robbins, Lionel. 1938. "Interpersonal Comparisons of Utility: A Comment." *The Economic Journal*, vol. XLVIII, no. 192 (December), 635–41.

———. 1963. *Politics and Economics*. New York: St. Martin's Press.

———. 1965. *Bentham in the Twentieth Century*. London: Athlone Press.

———. 1970. *The Evolution of Modern Economic Theory, and Other Papers on the History of Economic Thought*. Chicago: Aldine.

———. 1971. *Autobiography of an Economist*. New York: St. Martin's Press.

———. 1984. *An Essay on the Nature and Significance of Economic Science*. 3d ed. London: Macmillan.

Roberts, Hazel van Dyke. 1935. *Boisguilbert: Economist of the Reign of Louis XIV*. New York: Columbia University Press.

Robertson, John. 1987. "Scottish Enlightenment." In John Eatwell, Murray Milgate, and Peter Newman, eds., *The New Palgrave: A Dictionary of Economics*. London: Macmillan.

Robinson, E. A. G. 1968. "Pigou, Arthur Cecil." In David L. Sills, ed., *International Encyclopedia of the Social Sciences*. New York: Macmillan and Free Press.

Robinson, Joan. 1933. *The Economics of Imperfect Competition*. London: Macmillan.

———. 1951– . *The Collected Papers of Joan Robinson*. 5 vols. Oxford: Basil Blackwell.

Roll, Eric. 1974. *A History of Economic Thought*. 4th ed. Homewood, Ill.: Richard D. Irwin.

Romanell, Patrick. 1984. *John Locke and Medicine: A New Key to Locke*. New York: Prometheus.

Roover, Raymond de. 1958. "The Concept of the Just Price: Theory and Economic Policy." *Journal of Economic History*, vol. 18, no. 4, 418–34.

Roscher, Wilhelm. 1878. *Principles of Political Economy*. 2 vols. Translated from the 13th German edition by John J. Lalor. Chicago: Callaghan and Co.

Rosenberg, Alexander. 1976. *Microeconomic Laws: A Philosophical Analysis*. Pittsburgh: University of Pittsburgh Press.

Rosenblum, Nancy L. 1978. *Bentham's Theory of the Modern State*. Cambridge, Mass.: Harvard University Press.

Rostow, Walt W. 1990. *Theorists of Economic Growth from David Hume to the Present*. New York: Oxford University Press.

Rothbard, Murray. 1957. "In Defense of 'Extreme Apriorism.' " *Southern Economic Journal*, vol. XXIII, no. 3 (January), 314–20.

———. 1976. "Praxeology: The Methodology of Austrian Economics." In Edwin G. Dolan, ed., *The Foundations of Modern Austrian Economics*. Kansas City: Sheed and Ward, Inc.

———. 1995. *An Austrian Perspective on the History of Economic Thought.* Volume I: *Economic Thought Before Adam Smith;* Volume II: *Classical Economics.* Aldershot, UK: Edward Elgar.

Rotwein, Eugene. 1986. "Flirting with Apriorism: Caldwell on Mises." *History of Political Economy,* vol. 18, no. 4 (winter), 669–73.

Rowse, A. L. 1932. "Mr. Keynes on Socialism, a Reply." *The Political Quarterly,* vol. 3, no. 3 (July/September), 409–15.

Runde, Jochen. 1990. "Keynesian Uncertainty and the Weight of Arguments." *Economics and Philosophy,* vol. 6, no. 2 (October), 275–92.

———. 1991. "Keynesian Uncertainty and the Instability of Beliefs." *Review of Political Economy,* vol. 3, no. 2 (April), 125–45.

Russell, Bertrand. 1903. *Principles of Mathematics.* London: George Allen and Unwin.

———. 1945. *A History of Western Philosophy.* New York: Simon and Schuster.

Rutherford, Malcolm. 1980. "Veblen on Owners, Managers, and the Control of Industry." *History of Political Economy,* vol. 12, no. 3 (fall), 434–40.

Ryan, Alan. 1987. "Property." In John Eatwell, Murray Milgate, and Peter Newman, eds., *The New Palgrave: A Dictionary of Economics.* London: Macmillan.

Samuels, Warren J. 1987a. "Ayers, Clarence Edwin." In John Eatwell, Murray Milgate, and Peter Newman, eds., *The New Palgrave: A Dictionary of Economics.* London: Macmillan.

———. 1987b. "Commons, John Rogers." In John Eatwell, Murray Milgate, and Peter Newman, eds., *The New Palgrave: A Dictionary of Economics.* London: Macmillan.

———. 1987c. "Institutional Economics." In John Eatwell, Murray Milgate, and Peter Newman, eds., *The New Palgrave: A Dictionary of Economics.* London: Macmillan.

Savage, Leonard J. 1972. *The Foundations of Statistics.* 2d ed. New York: Dover.

Say, Jean-Baptiste. [1880] 1964. *A Treatise on Political Economy, or the Production, Distribution and Consumption of Wealth.* American (6th) ed. Translated by C. R. Prinsep, with notes by Clement C. Biddle. New York: Augustus M. Kelley.

Schabas, Margaret. 1990. *A World Ruled by Number: William Stanley Jevons and the Rise of Mathematical Economics.* Princeton: Princeton University Press.

Schlick, Moritz. [1925] 1974. *General Theory of Knowledge.* 2d ed. Trans. by Albert E. Blumberg. New York: Springer-Verlag.

Schmoller, Gustav. [1884] 1989. *The Mercantile System and Its Historical Significance.* New York: Augustus M. Kelley.

Schumpeter, Joseph A. [1912] 1954. *Economic Doctrine and Method.* Translated by R. Aris. New York: Oxford University Press.

———. 1933. "The Common Sense of Econometrics." *Econometrica,* vol. 1, no. 1 (January), 5–12.

———. [1934] 1961. *The Theory of Economic Development.* (English edition). Translated by Redvers Opie. New York: Oxford University Press.

———. 1950. *Capitalism, Socialism, and Democracy.* New York: Harper and Row.

———. 1951. *Ten Great Economists, From Marx to Keynes.*

———. 1954. *History of Economic Analysis.* New York: Oxford University Press.

Schwier, Ann S., and J. F. Schwier. 1974. "Pareto's Three Manuals." *Journal of Economic Literature,* vol. XII, no. 1 (March), 78–87.

Scott, William Robert. [1900] 1966. *Francis Hutcheson.* New York: Augustus M. Kelley.

Senior, Nassau W. [1836] 1965. *An Outline of the Science of Political Economy.* New York: Augustus M. Kelley.

Shackle, G. L. S. 1967. *The Years of High Theory.* Cambridge: Cambridge University Press.

Shapin, Steven, and Simon Schaffer. 1985. *Leviathan and the Air Pump: Hobbes, Boyle and the Experimental Life.* Princeton: Princeton University Press.

Shionoya, Yuichi. 1991. "Sidgwick, Moore and Keynes: A Philosophical Analysis of Keynes's 'My Early Beliefs.' " In Bradley W. Bateman and John B. Davis, eds., *Keynes and Philosophy: Essays on the Origin of Keynes's Thought.* Aldershot: Edward Elgar.

Sidgwick, A., and E. M. Sidgwick. 1906. *Henry Sidgwick: A Memoir.* London: Macmillan.

Sidgwick, Henry. 1874. *Methods of Ethics.* London: Macmillan.

———. 1901. *Principles of Political Economy.* London: Macmillan.

Simich, J. L., and Rick Tilman. 1982. "Thorstein Veblen and His Marxist Critics: An Interpretive Review." *History of Political Economy,* vol. 14, no. 3 (fall), 323–41.

Sismondi, Jean Charles Leonard Simonde de. [1815] 1991. *Political Economy.* Fairfield, N.J.: Augustus M. Kelley.

———. [1827] 1991. *New Principles of Political Economy.* 2d ed. Translated by Richard Hyse. New Brunswick: Transaction.

Skidelsky, Robert. 1983. *John Maynard Keynes: Hopes Betrayed, 1883–1920.* London: Macmillan.

———. 1994. *John Maynard Keynes: The Economist as Savior, 1920–1937.* London: Macmillan.

Skinner, Andrew. 1966a. "Biographical Sketch: The Life of Sir James Steuart-Denham, 1713–1780." In Steuart, Sir James [1767] 1966, xxi–lvii.

———. 1966b. "Analytical Introduction." In Steuart, Sir James [1767] 1966, lviii–lxxxiv.

Small, Albion W. 1909. *The Cameralists: The Pioneers of German Social Polity.* Chicago: The University of Chicago Press; New York: Burt Franklin.

Smith, Adam. [1789] 1937. *An Inquiry into the Nature and Causes of the Wealth of Nations.* Ed. by Edwin Cannan. New York: Modern Library.

———. [1790] 1982. *The Theory of Moral Sentiments.* 6th ed. Edited by D. D. Raphael and A. L. Macfie. Indianapolis, Ind.: Liberty Press.

Smith, Barry. 1986. "Austrian Economics and Austrian Philosophy." In Wolfgang Grassl and Barry Smith, eds., *Austrian Economics: Historical and Philosophical Background.* London: Croom Helm.

Smithies, Arthur. 1950. "Memorial: Joseph Alois Schumpeter, 1883–1950." *The American Economic Review,* vol. XL, no. 4 (September), 628–45.

Snow, C. P. [1959] 1976. *The Two Cultures: And a Second Look. An Expanded Version of the 1959 'Two Cultures and the Scientific Revolution.'* Cambridge: Cambridge University Press.

Sotiroff, Georges. 1968. "Simonde de Sismondi, J. C. L." *International Encyclopedia of the Social Sciences.* New York: Macmillan and Free Press.

Sowell, Thomas. 1974. *Classical Economics Reconsidered.* Princeton: Princeton University Press.

———. 1987a. "Say, Jean-Baptiste." In John Eatwell, Murray Milgate, and Peter Newman, eds., *The New Palgrave: A Dictionary of Economics.* London: Macmillan.

———. 1987b. "Say's Law." In John Eatwell, Murray Milgate, and Peter Newman, eds., *The New Palgrave: A Dictionary of Economics.* London: Macmillan.

———. 1987c. "Sismondi, Jean Charles Leonard Simonde de." In John Eatwell, Murray Milgate, and Peter Newman, eds., *The New Palgrave: A Dictionary of Economics.* London: Macmillan.

———. 1987d. "Veblen, Thorstein." In John Eatwell, Murray Milgate, and Peter Newman, eds., *The New Palgrave: A Dictionary of Economics.* London: Macmillan.

Spengler, Joseph J. 1984. "Boisguilbert's economic views vis-à-vis those of contemporary réformateurs." *History of Political Economy,* vol. 16, no. 1 (Spring), 69–88.

———. 1986. "Boisguilbert's Economic Views vis-à-vis Those of Contemporary Réformateurs." *History of Political Economy,* vol. 16, no. 1 (spring), 69–88.

Spiegel, Henry W. 1991. *The Growth of Economic Thought.* 3d. ed. Durham, N.C.: Duke University Press.

Steedman, Ian. 1992. Introduction to *An Essay on the Co-ordination of the Laws of Distribution,* by Philip Henry Wicksteed. Aldershot, England: Edward Elgar.

Stephen, Leslie. [1900] 1968. *The English Utilitarians.* 3 vols. New York: Augustus M. Kelley.

Steuart, Sir James. [1767] 1967. *An Inquiry into the Principles of Political Oeconomy: being an Essay on the Science of Domestic Policy in Free Nations. In which are particularly considered Population, Agriculture, Trade, Industry, Money, Coin, Interest, Circulation, Banks, Exchange, Public Credit, and Taxes.* In General Sir James Steuart, ed., *The Works Political, Metaphysical and Chronological of Sir James Steuart.* Vols. I–IV. New York: Augustus M. Kelley.

———. 1772. *The Principle of Money as Applied to the State of the Coin in Bengal.* In General Sir James Steuart, ed., *The Works Political, Metaphysical and Chronological of Sir James Steuart.* Vol. 5. New York: Augustus M. Kelley.

Stigler, George J. 1950. "The Development of Utility Theory." *Journal of Political Economy,* Part I: vol. LVIII, no. 4 (August), 307–27; Part II: vol. LVIII, no. 5 (October), 373–96.

———. 1955. "The Nature and Role of Originality in Scientific Progress." *Economica,* vol. 22, no. 88, 293–302.

———. 1962. "Henry L. Moore and Statistical Economics." *Econometrica,* vol. 30, no. 1 (January), 1–21.

———. 1972. "The Adoption of the Marginal Utility Theory." *History of Political Economy,* vol. 4, no. 2 (fall), 571–86.

———. 1983. "Nobel Lecture: The Process and Progress of Economics." *Journal of Political Economy,* vol. 91, no. 4, 529–45.

Stigler, Stephen M. 1978. "Francis Ysidro Edgeworth, Statistician." *Journal of the Royal Statistical Society,* series A, vol. 141, part 3, 287–322.

———. 1986. *The History of Statistics: The Measurement of Uncertainty Before 1900.* Cambridge, Mass.: Balknap.

Stolper, Wolfgang F. 1968. "Schumpeter, Joseph A." In David L. Sills, ed., *International Encyclopedia of the Social Sciences.* New York: Macmillan and Free Press.

———. 1994. *Joseph Alois Schumpeter.* Princeton: Princeton University Press.

Stone, Richard. 1988. "Some Seventeenth Century Econometrics: Consumers' Behaviour." *Revue européenne des sciences sociales,* vol. XXVI, no. 81, 19–41.

Streissler, Erich. 1987. "Wieser, Friedrich, Freihers von." In John Eatwell, Murray Milgate, and Peter Newman, eds., *The New Palgrave: A Dictionary of Economics.* London: Macmillan.

Studenski, Paul. 1958. *The Income of Nations: Theory, Measurement, and Analysis.* Part I. New York: NYU Press.

Swedberg, Richard. 1991. *Schumpeter: A Biography.* Princeton: Princeton University Press.

Swift, Jonathan. [1729] 1991. *A Modest Proposal.* In *Swift's Irish Pamphlets,* edited by Joseph McMinn. Gerrards Cross, Buckinghamshire: Colin Smythe.

Tarascio, Vincent J. 1972. "A Correction: On the Genealogy of the So-Called Edgeworth-Bowley Diagram." *Western Economic Journal,* vol. 10 (June), 193–97.

———. 1974. "Vilfredo Pareto and the Translation of His *Manuel.*" *Journal of Economic Literature,* vol. XII, no. 1 (March), 91–96.

———. 1980. "Some Recent Interpretations of *Mathematical Psychics:* Reply." *History of Political Economy,* vol. 12, no. 2 (summer), 277–81.

Taylor, Overton H. 1929. "Economics and the Idea of Natural Laws." *The Quarterly Journal of Economics,* vol. XLIV, no. 4 (November), 1–39.

Taylor, W. L. 1957. "A Short Life of Sir James Steuart: Political Economist." *South African Journal of Economics,* vol. 25 (December), 290–302.

———. 1965. *Francis Hutcheson and David Hume as Predecessors of Adam Smith.* Durham, N.C.: Duke University Press.

Thompson, N. W. 1987. "Hodgskin, Thomas." In John Eatwell, Murray Milgate, and Peter Newman, eds., *The New Palgrave: A Dictionary of Economics.* London: Macmillan.

Tinbergen, Jan. 1939. *Statistical Testing of Business-Cycle Theories.* Geneva: League of Nations.

Torrance, John. 1995. *Karl Marx's Theory of Ideas.* Cambridge: Cambridge University Press.

Tribe, Keith. 1988. *Governing Economy: The Reformation of German Economic Discourse 1750–1840.* Cambridge: Cambridge University Press.

Trilling, Lionel. 1962. "Science, Literature, and Culture." *Commentary,* vol. 33, 61–77.

Tsuru, Shigeto. 1956. "On Reproduction Schemes." Appendix A in Paul M.

Sweezy, *The Theory of Capitalist Development*. New York: Modern Reader.

Tucker, G. L. S. 1960. *Progress and Profits in British Economic Thought, 1650–1850*. Cambridge: Cambridge University Press.

Turgot, Anne Robert Jacques. [1770] 1971. *Reflections on the Formation and the Distribution of Riches*. New York: Augustus M. Kelley.

Unwin, George. 1966. *Studies in Economic History: The Collected Papers of George Unwin*. Edited by R. H. Tawney. New York: Augustus M. Kelley.

Vaggi, Gianni. 1987. *The Economics of François Quesnay*. Durham, N.C.: Duke University Press.

Vaughn, Karen. 1980. *John Locke, Economist and Social Scientist*. Chicago: University of Chicago Press.

———. 1987. "Locke, John." In John Eatwell, Murray Milgate, and Peter Newman, eds., *The New Palgrave: A Dictionary of Economics*. London: Macmillan.

Veblen, Thorstein. [1904] 1923. *The Theory of Business Enterprise*. New York: Charles Scribner's Sons.

———. [1912] 1934. *The Theory of the Leisure Class: An Economic Study of Institutions*. 2d ed. New York: Modern Library.

———. 1950. *Elimination of the Unfit*. Saugatuck, Conn.: The 5x8 Press.

Vickers, Douglas. 1959. *Studies in the Theory of Money, 1690–1776*. Philadelphia: Chilton.

Vickery, William S. 1968. "Dupuit, Jules." In *International Encyclopedia of the Social Sciences*. New York: Macmillan and Free Press, 435–43.

Viner, Jacob. 1937. *Studies in International Trade*. New York: Harper and Brothers.

———. 1968. "Economic Thought: Mercantilist Thought." *International Encyclopedia of the Social Sciences*. New York: Macmillan and Free Press, 435–43.

———. 1978a. "The Economic Doctrines of the Christian Fathers." *History of Political Economy*, vol. 10, no. 1 (spring), 9–45.

———. 1978b. "The Economic Doctrines of the Scholastics." *History of Political Economy*, vol. 10, no. 1 (spring), 46–113.

Walras, Léon. [1926] 1954. *Elements of Pure Economics*. 4th ed. (definitive). Translated by William Jaffé. Homewood, Ill.: Richard D. Irwin, Inc.

Webster, Charles. 1976. *The Great Instauration: Science, Medicine, and Reform*. New York: Holmes and Meier.

Welch, C. 1987. "Utilitarianism." In John Eatwell, Murray Milgate, and Peter Newman, eds., *The New Palgrave: A Dictionary of Economics*. London: Macmillan.

Whitaker, John K. 1977. "Some Neglected Aspects of Alfred Marshall's Economic and Social Thought." *History of Political Economy*, vol. 9, no. 2 (summer), 161–97.

———. 1987. "Marshall, Alfred." In John Eatwell, Murray Milgate, and Peter Newman, eds., *The New Palgrave: A Dictionary of Economics*. London: Macmillan.

Wicksteed, Philip Henry. [1888] 1970. *The Alphabet of Economic Science*. New York: Augustus M. Kelley.

———. 1889. "On Certain Passages in Jevons' 'Theory of Political Economy'." *Quarterly Journal of Economics*, vol. 3 (April), 293–314.

———. [1894] 1992. *An Essay on the Co-ordination of the Laws of Distribution.* Aldershot, England: Edward Elgar.

———. 1910a. "Jevons, William Stanley." In R. H. Inglis Palgrave, ed. *Dictionary of Political Economy.* London: Macmillan (reprinted by Gale Research Co., Detroit, Mich., 1976), vol. II, 474–78.

———. [1910b] 1950. *The Common Sense of Political Economy.* New York: Augustus M. Kelley.

Wieser, Friedrich von. [1893] 1956. *Natural Value.* New York: Kelley and Millman.

———. [1927] 1967. *Social Economics.* Translated by A. Ford Hinrichs. New York: Augustus M. Kelley

Willey, Basil. 1953. *The Seventeenth Century Background.* New York: Doubleday.

Williamson, Oliver E. 1975. *Markets and Hierarchies: Analysis and Antitrust Implications.* New York: Free Press.

Wilson, George W. 1975. "The Economics of the Just Price." *History of Political Economy,* vol. 7, no. 1 (spring), 56–74.

Wittgenstein, Ludwig. [1921] 1963. *Tractatus Logico-Philosophicus.* Trans. by D. F. Pears and B. F. McGuinness. London: Routledge and Kegan Paul.

Zarnowitz, Victor. 1968. "Mitchell, Wesley C." In David L. Sills, ed., *International Encyclopedia of the Social Sciences.* New York: Macmillan and Free Press.

Index of Names

Subject Index